MCSD
IN A NUTSHELL

The Visual Basic Exams

MCSD
IN A NUTSHELL

The Visual Basic Exams

James Foxall

O'REILLY®

Beijing • Cambridge • Farnham • Köln • Paris • Sebastopol • Taipei • Tokyo

MCSD in a Nutshell: The Visual Basic Exams

by James Foxall

Published by O'Reilly & Associates, Inc., 101 Morris Street, Sebastopol, CA 95472.

Editor: Ron Petrusha

Production Editor: Jeffrey Holcomb

Cover Designer: Edie Freedman

Printing History:

      October 2000:   First Edition.

Library of Congress Cataloging-in-Publication Data

Foxall, James D.
   MCSD in a nutshell : the Visual Basic exams / James Foxall.
      p. cm.
   ISBN 1-56592-752-4
   1. Electronic data processing personnel--Certification. 2. Microsoft software--
      Examinations--Study guides. 3. Microsoft Visual BASIC. I. Title.

QA76.3.f69 2000
005.26'8--dc21   00-062361

ISBN: 1-56592-752-4
[M]

Table of Contents

Preface .... *xi*

Chapter 1—Introduction *1*

Chapter 2—Visual Basic Overview 7

   Forms 7
   Menus 9
   Controls 10
   Passing Parameters by Reference or by Value 20
   Naming Conventions 20

Chapter 3—Understanding COM *22*

   The Technologies and the Exams 22
   COM and ActiveX: A VB Programmer's Perspective 23
   Understanding COM 25
   Putting ActiveX Objects to Work 29
   Creating ActiveX Objects 31
   Using the Object Browser 46
   In-Process Versus Out-of-Process Servers 47
   Creating Three-Tiered Client/Server Applications 49
   Key Facts 52
   Applying What You've Learned 54
   Highlighter's Index 60

Chapter 4—Creating and Testing ActiveX Code Components 62

The Technologies and the Exams 63
Creating ActiveX Code Components in Visual Basic 63
Calling Object Servers Asynchronously Using Callbacks 88
Creating System Callbacks Using AddressOf 90
Creating Remote Servers 94
Creating Multithreaded Components 94
Testing and Debugging ActiveX Code Components 99
Key Facts 107
Applying What You've Learned 109
Highlighter's Index 120

Chapter 5—Creating ActiveX Controls 121

The Technologies and the Exams 121
Understanding ActiveX Controls 122
Creating a Control's User Interface 126
Creating a Control's Developer Interface 136
Integrating a Control with Its Container 166
Setting Procedure Attributes 175
Testing and Debugging ActiveX Controls 188
Key Facts 190
Applying What You've Learned 195
Highlighter's Index 214

Chapter 6—Creating and Using ActiveX Documents 216

The Technologies and the Exams 216
Understanding ActiveX Documents 216
Working with ActiveX Document Projects 220
Effectively Using UserDocument Events 223
Integrating an ActiveX Document with Its Container 224
Creating Multiple Document Projects 235
Asynchronously Receiving Data 238
Testing and Debugging ActiveX Documents 241
Key Facts 244
Applying What You've Learned 246
Highlighter's Index 256

Chapter 7—Working with Data 258

The Technologies and the Exams 258
Universal Data Access 259
Manipulating Data Using ActiveX Data Objects 260
Using the ADO Data Control 280
The Data Environment Designer 281
Key Facts 285
Applying What You've Learned 288
Highlighter's Index 299

Chapter 8—Creating Internet-Aware Applications 301

The Technologies and the Exams 302
Adding Browser Capabilities to a Program
Using the WebBrowser Control 302
Using Automation with Internet Explorer 313
Using the Internet Transfer Control 316
Using the Winsock Control 327
Creating Dynamic Web Pages Using DHTML 336
Key Facts 348
Applying What You've Learned 352
Highlighter's Index 373

Chapter 9—Testing and Debugging 375

The Technologies and the Exams 376
Implementing Error Handling 376
Using Visual Basic's Debugging Tools 385
Using Conditional Compilation 396
Key Facts 400
Applying What You've Learned 402
Highlighter's Index 418

Chapter 10—Implementing Help 420

The Technologies and the Exams 420
A Brief History of Help 421
Assigning a Help File to a Project 422
Understanding Help Context IDs 423
Linking Help Topics to Objects 424
Adding What's This Help to a Form 425

Displaying Help Using the Common Dialog Control 428
Distributing Help with Your Application 433
Key Facts 434
Applying What You've Learned 436
Highlighter's Index 448

Chapter 11—Optimizing an Application
for Distribution *450*

The Technologies and the Exams 450
Setting Compiler Optimizations 450
Key Facts 458
Applying What You've Learned 460
Highlighter's Index 462

Chapter 12—Creating Microsoft Transaction
Server Components *463*

The Technologies and the Exams 463
What Is MTS? 463
Installing MTS 470
Configuring MTS 471
Creating Packages 474
Creating MTS Components Using Visual Basic 477
Key Facts 480
Applying What You've Learned 483
Highlighter's Index 487

Chapter 13—Packaging and Deploying an Application ... *489*

The Technologies and the Exams 489
Making Components Backward Compatible
(or Not Breaking What Works) 490
Understanding File Dependencies 495
Creating a Setup Program Using the Package
and Deployment Wizard 502
Deploying a Package Using the Package
and Deployment Wizard 514
Managing Packaging Scripts 519
Creating and Deploying Packages in Silent Mode 519
Creating an AutoRun CD-ROM 520
Using License Keys for ActiveX Controls 520

Distributing a Component over the Internet 524
Distributing DCOM Servers 533
Managing the Windows System Registry 540
Key Facts 543
Applying What You've Learned 547
Highlighter's Index 552

Chapter 14—Visual SourceSafe and the Visual Component Manager *555*

The Technologies and the Exams 555
Microsoft Visual SourceSafe 555
The Visual Component Manager 571
Key Facts 579
Applying What You've Learned 581
Highlighter's Index 585

Index *587*

Preface

If you're an experienced Visual Basic programmer who is now taking the MCSD exams (or even if you're an experienced Visual Basic programmer who isn't taking the exams but who wants to get up to speed on a wide range of Visual Basic–related development technologies), this book is for you. Indeed, this book assumes you use Visual Basic as one of your primary development tools. If, on the other hand, you're a person with limited experience using Visual Basic and you're looking for a quick solution for passing the exams, then this isn't the book for you. You're not going to read pages and pages of basic information on how to program or use the elementary tools like the Menu Editor, and you won't receive a lot of hand-holding. In the O'Reilly tradition, this is a high-end book, and it would be a disservice to the professional developer to spend time on well-hashed or commonly known material. What you will find in this book, however, is a lot of *very* useful information on the technologies and techniques that receive heavy coverage on the exams.

As of Version 6, Visual Basic certification comprises two exams instead of one. Exam 70-176, *Designing and Implementing Desktop Applications with Microsoft Visual Basic 6.0*, measures your ability to design and implement Win32 desktop application solutions using Visual Basic. This exam covers topics related to developing applications run by a single user on a single computer, with the application residing on the hard drive of the user's computer and using local component object model (COM) components. Exam 70-175, *Designing and Implementing Distributed Applications with Microsoft Visual Basic 6.0*, measures your ability to design and implement distributed application solutions using Visual Basic. This exam covers topics related to client/server development using a network in a multitier environment, and distributing presentation services, business logic, and data services. This exam tests your ability to create applications that use different data services. The COM components used by the application may participate in transactions, and they can be shared by multiple users and multiple applications.

Although each exam covers some topics that aren't covered by the other exam, in truth, there is a lot of overlap. For instance, packaging and deploying an application receives considerable coverage on both exams (and correspondingly in this book as well). If you've ever read a set of Visual Basic study guides for both exams from the same publisher, you've undoubtedly noticed that there is a substantial amount of material reuse, but the books usually aren't discounted to compensate for this fact.

How This Book Is Unique

Rather than writing two separate books with a great amount of duplicate material, I've written this book to cover topics for both exams. If you're not going to take both exams, it should be easy for you to pick out the parts of this book that are important to you based on the published requirements for the exam you wish to take, and at the beginning of each chapter, I even state the exam for which the material is most suited.

This book is unique not only in that it presents the material for both exams in one text, but also in the way the material is presented. Most certification study guides fall into one of two categories: the "cram"-type books and the monstrous tomes. The cram-type books are designed to tell you (not necessarily teach you) what you need to know to pass an exam; such books are of little value once you've passed the exam. The monstrous tomes are the behemoths that attempt to cover every single item that might possibly appear on an exam (and a good deal more besides). Often, so much material is presented that the coverage of most topics is superficial at best. The unfortunate result is that important material receives the same terse coverage as superfluous material. This type of book may be slightly useful as a reference book after the exam, but most likely will get placed on a shelf somewhere and never looked at again.

Because this book is targeted at those intending to take the exams, many others who would benefit from this book may not give it a second glance. The truth is, this book has so much advanced and practical material that it is money well spent even if you have no intention of taking either of the exams. The advanced capabilities of Visual Basic are covered here in generous detail, complete with real-world advice culled from experience. If you currently use or intend to use any of the advanced technologies of Visual Basic, you'll find the material in this book invaluable in your work.

Who This Book Is For

I've taken the approach of creating a book for professional Visual Basic programmers who want to actually learn the material covered on the exams. Being certified certainly has its advantages, but it will get you only so far if you don't have the skills to back it up. This book does not cover topics you would know if you've spent any time with Visual Basic. For instance, you should already be familiar with how to add controls to a form and working with events. If you aren't, you should consider getting some hands-on experience with Visual Basic before attempting to pass the exams.

Visual Basic is so complex and so rich in its feature set and the diverse array of technologies that it embraces that it's highly unlikely that you use every aspect of it in your development. For instance, you may be an ADO guru, yet have never created an ActiveX control. Although it's unrealistic to expect a developer to use every feature and create every type of component supported by Visual Basic, that's exactly what the exams do. Although I won't cover the basics, I will cover the advanced concepts in great detail, so, for instance, no prior knowledge of creating ActiveX controls is necessary.

How This Book Is Organized

Since the Visual Basic exams focus heavily on Microsoft technologies, this book is mostly about understanding and using such technologies. As I said earlier, it's almost impossible to be an expert in all aspects of Visual Basic. Most professional programmers tend to specialize in some aspect of development, such as designing user interfaces or creating middle-tier components. While you focus on some areas, you also neglect others. This book will help you fill in the gaps in your expertise.

The book consists of the following 14 chapters:

Chapter 1, *Introduction*, discusses the two Visual Basic exams and how they relate to the material presented in *MCSD in a Nutshell*.

Chapter 2, *Visual Basic Overview*, gives you a brief synopsis of some of the basic material covered on the exam. This includes a discussion of the common ActiveX controls and the Forms collection. If you find any of this material challenging, you're going to have a very tough time getting through the harder material later.

Chapter 3, *Understanding COM*, teaches you Microsoft's underlying object technology known as the component object model, or COM. If you're familiar with ActiveX, then you're already familiar with COM to some extent. COM is important because it's the foundation upon which ActiveX technology is built. Programming COM in Visual Basic is very different from programming COM in C++. In Chapter 3, you'll receive thorough information about COM from a Visual Basic programmer's perspective. Even if you're creating COM objects now, there's a good chance that something in Chapter 3 will be new to you.

Chapter 4, *Creating and Testing ActiveX Code Components*, teaches you how to use COM and ActiveX to build ActiveX servers. You'll learn how to create in-process components in the form of ActiveX DLLs and out-of-process components in the form of ActiveX EXEs. You'll learn how to build components for different types of instancing, and you'll learn about interfacing clients and servers, including how to raise errors in a client application from within a server component. Chapter 4 also teaches you about Visual Basic's threading capabilities, and how to create multithreaded components. The Visual Basic exams have a bias toward testing components, and this chapter teaches you what you need to know to fully test both in-process and out-of-process components.

Chapter 5, *Creating ActiveX Controls*, teaches you how to take advantage of one of Visual Basic's most exciting innovations: the ability to create ActiveX controls. You'll learn how to create the user interface as well as the developer interface of a control, and you'll learn the differences between a control in user mode and a control in developer mode. This is a large chapter with a lot of useful information in it, and you may find it useful in the future as a reference for creating fully featured ActiveX controls.

Chapter 6, *Creating and Using ActiveX Documents*, teaches you this often misunderstood technology. Although ActiveX documents have been described as a solution looking for a problem, they allow for the creation of some pretty flexible web solutions. You may not use ActiveX documents in your development (most people don't), but they receive extensive coverage on the exams. This chapter will teach you what you need to know to pass the exams, as well as what you need to know to create functional ActiveX documents in a production environment.

Chapter 7, *Working with Data*, teaches you about OLE DB, the low-level interface that introduces Microsoft's Universal Data Access (UDA) strategy. OLE DB is not restricted to accessing Jet or ISAM databases, nor is it even restricted to accessing relational databases. Instead, OLE DB is capable of accessing data that resides in virtually any data source, including text files, mail servers, spreadsheets, and non-relational data, in addition to the standard relational database formats. This is all made possible by way of OLE DB providers, and Chapter 7 will teach you how OLE DB and OLE DB providers work together to access data. You'll also learn about Active Data Objects (ADO), Microsoft's newest data access object model. Despite what Microsoft might lead you to believe, ADO isn't the perfect replacement for DAO and RDO. In addition, you'll learn how ADO and OLE DB are critically linked technologies, and how to take advantage of them in your development. You'll learn about the similarities and differences between ADO and its predecessors. It's important to understand ADO not only to pass the exams but also to create highly functional production database applications.

Chapter 8, *Creating Internet-Aware Applications*, teaches you how to use Microsoft's Internet development technologies to create web-enabled applications. Web-enabled applications receive a lot of attention on the exams, yet you may not need to use many of the Internet development tools available within Visual Basic. By the time you're done with Chapter 8, you'll know all about these tools and how to use them. You'll learn how to control Internet Explorer through Automation and how to create web browsing capabilities within an application. This chapter also teaches you how to download files from sites that support HTTP or FTP protocols using the Internet Transfer control, and how to create multiple applications that can communicate over the Internet or an intranet by using the Winsock control. Finally, you'll learn how to create dynamic web pages using DHTML.

Chapter 9, *Testing and Debugging*, shows you how to use Visual Basic's comprehensive array of tools to track down and eliminate errors in your code. You'll learn about the different types of error handlers and how to choose an error handler, as well as how unhandled errors are affected by the call stack. Microsoft has put an emphasis on using Visual Basic's debugging tools on the Visual Basic exams, so you'll want to understand all of the nuances when you sit down to take a test.

Chapter 10, *Implementing Help*, discusses the different types of Help, and how Help files are compiled. You'll learn how to link Help files to a program, how to link specific Help topics to forms and controls, and how to implement the relatively new Help feature, "What's This?," in your programs. Chapter 10 also teaches you how to add advanced Help functionality to an application, using the Common Dialog control.

Chapter 11, *Optimizing an Application for Distribution*, shows you how to use Visual Basic's Compiler options to create the most efficient compiled components possible. You'll learn the differences between p-code and native code, and you'll receive guidelines on choosing the best compilation method for a given situation. When compiling to native code, Visual Basic's compiler offers you myriad optimization possibilities, but things aren't always as they seem. Chapter 11 explains each and every compilation option so you'll be better prepared to determine which options are best for any given situation.

Chapter 12, *Creating Microsoft Transaction Server Components*, demystifies Microsoft Transaction Server (MTS) and teaches you what you need to know to install and configure MTS and to create components and packages. Unless you use MTS, you may not even know exactly what MTS does. MTS is a promising technology, but it's not the easiest to grasp. When you're finished with Chapter 12, you'll understand MTS and be able to take advantage of the functionality available by creating MTS components.

Chapter 13, *Packaging and Deploying an Application*, teaches you how to create and distribute packages for your applications via custom setup programs. In this chapter you'll learn how to deploy to media such as floppy disks or CD-ROMs, as well as how to publish to the Internet. The Package and Deployment Wizard, Microsoft's replacement for the venerable Setup Wizard, can be used to create complex installations—if you know how to use it properly. This chapter also teaches you how to edit the script files used and created by the wizard to build even better custom setup programs. Distributing licensed components, such as ActiveX controls, adds complexity to the process, particularly when distributing to the Internet, but this chapter details the procedures of distributing components that require licensing keys. You'll even learn how to ensure COM component backward compatibility so that your setup programs don't break existing software installations.

Chapter 14, *Visual SourceSafe and the Visual Component Manager*, teaches you how to increase efficiency and reduce errors in a multi-developer environment. You'll learn how to set up and use Visual SourceSafe (which is not the most intuitive process) to manage source code in complex projects that are accessed by many people. This chapter also teaches you how to use the Visual Component Manager to publish and share components with other developers and across projects. "Components" doesn't just mean ActiveX components; many types of files and groups of files can be published as components, and Chapter 14 explains the process. You may not be using these tools in your day-to-day work; nevertheless, you will be expected to demonstrate an understanding of these tools on the exams.

This book includes a number of elements to help you better prepare for the exams. First, the chapters are written in a textbook format, and therefore they don't require that you be sitting at a computer in order to benefit from reading them. I know from personal experience that you're rarely sitting in front of your computer when you're trying to study, and this book has been written accordingly.

When you are ready to sit at a computer and experiment with the concepts, you'll want to take a look at the hands-on exercise. Each exercise consists of step-by-step instructions and incorporates one or more key concepts from the chapter it closes. These hands-on exercises are concise, and none of them should take you long to complete. However, completing the exercises is a great way to drive home the topics in a chapter

Since this book is written to teach you the topics necessary to pass the Visual Basic exams, it does, of course, include sample questions in each chapter. These questions appear at the end of each chapter in a section titled "Skills Assessment," and they are similar to questions that you may encounter on an exam. It's very difficult to create questions *exactly* like those on the exam, and it is this fact that makes this book so useful. If you study using only a cram-type preparatory guide, you may have trouble when the questions on the text differ, even slightly, from those you've studied. If you actually understand the material, as you should when you complete this book, you'll be able to answer questions regardless of the format in which they appear.

To make it easier to study, this book includes a "Key Facts" section at the end of each chapter. These sections contain bulleted key facts from each chapter and are designed to be used as a quick refresher just before you take an exam. I recommend that you arrive at the test facility 15 to 30 minutes early and spend your time reviewing the key facts. If a key fact isn't clear to you, refer back to the chapter for more information. If you have the time, consider reviewing the skills assessment questions as well. When time is limited, pick some questions from each chapter at random, or choose from chapters with which you are having particular difficulty. Once again, refer to the chapter text when something isn't clear.

Once you've completed the exams you wish to take, you'll be able to put this book on your shelf and use it as a comprehensive reference. It is especially useful if you need to use areas of Visual Basic that you don't ordinarily use. I hope you find this book to be a valuable tool for some time to come.

Conventions Used in This Book

Throughout this book, we've used the following typographic conventions:

`Constant width`
> Constant width in body text indicates a language construct, such as a VBA statement (like `For` or `Set`), an intrinsic or user-defined constant, a user-defined type, or an expression (like `colForms.Count - 1`). Code fragments and code examples appear exclusively in constant width text. In syntax statements and prototypes, text in constant width indicates such language elements as the function, procedure, or method's name and any other invariable elements required by the syntax.

`Constant width italic`
> Constant width italic in body text indicates argument and variable names. In syntax statements or prototypes, it indicates replaceable parameters.

Constant width bold

Constant width bold in body text indicates user input (i.e., a term that should be typed in by the user).

Italic

Italicized words in the text indicate intrinsic or user-defined functions, and procedure names. Many system elements like paths and filenames are also italicized, as are new items.

UPPERCASE

File extensions, such as EXE or DLL, are formatted in uppercase, roman font and do not begin with a leading period.

Obtaining the Chapter Exercises

All of the example exercises developed in *MCSD in a Nutshell* to give you hands-on experience in order to better prepare you for the test are available online. They are freely downloadable from the O'Reilly & Associates web site at *http://vb.oreilly.com*.

Request for Comments

The information in this book has been tested and verified, but you may find that features have changed (or even find mistakes!). You can send any errors you find, as well as suggestions for future editions, to:

O'Reilly & Associates
101 Morris Street
Sebastopol, CA 95472
(800) 998-9938 (in the U.S. or Canada)
(707) 829-0515 (international/local)
(707) 829-0104 (fax)

You can also send messages electronically. To be put on our mailing list or to request a catalog, send email to:

info@oreilly.com

To ask technical questions or comment on the book, send email to:

bookquestions@oreilly.com

There is a web site for the book, where examples, errata, and any plans for future editions are listed. The site also includes a link to a forum where you can discuss the book with the author and other readers. You can access this site at:

http://www.oreilly.com/catalog/mcsdnut

For more information about this book and others, see the O'Reilly web site:

http://www.oreilly.com

For technical information on Visual Basic programming, to participate in VB discussion forums, or to acquaint yourself with O'Reilly's line of Visual Basic books, you can access the O'Reilly Visual Basic web site at:

http://vb.oreilly.com

Acknowledgments

First of all, I would like to thank Ron Petrusha for his great input and for guiding me in writing the book I wanted to make.

Thanks as well to Matt Wagner, for reasons too numerous to mention, and of course, a hearty thanks to Cary Prague for getting me started in this business!

Also, special thanks to Mike Hartman, Linda Foxall, Dave Foxall, Chris Wright, and Ed Spence. Oh yeah, let's not forget the crazy Lingelbachs (hey Doctor John, where's my WD-40?).

CHAPTER 1

Introduction

Read this book, and you're going to become a master of all things Visual Basic. Convinced? You'd better be, because by making the decision to pursue Visual Basic certification, you've committed yourself to learning the ins and outs of the entire family of Microsoft technologies touched by Visual Basic—many of which you've probably never used. This is not a trivial task, and even though many other books treat it as such, I take it very seriously in *MCSD in a Nutshell*. If you've read other MCSD study guides, you've undoubtedly noticed the superfluous rehash of basic information and documentation-like explanations. However, if the documentation were thorough enough (and it isn't), you wouldn't be turning to a different source for information. I've read a lot of study guides, and I've been disappointed by all of them in some way. As a result, I've written this book to be the book I wish I had read before taking the exams.

Having been where you are now, I fully appreciate the time and effort that it takes to become a Microsoft Certified Professional, and for those truly ambitious, a Microsoft Certified Solution Developer. You'll find that this book is written to help you pass the exams, by someone who's been there. I want you to succeed.

Surprisingly, some of the authors of certification books aren't even certified. How they can possibly feel that they're in a position to help a reader is beyond me. I'm an MCSD, and I've taken and passed both Visual Basic 6 exams. It is my sincerest desire to help you pass the Visual Basic exams, and hopefully my personal experience and long hours will be of benefit to you.

The *Preface* includes some very important information on the structure and uniqueness of this book. If you haven't already, I strongly encourage you to read the *Preface* before proceeding.

Visual Basic is a complex language, and even the most die-hard Visual Basic developer doesn't use all of its available features. Nevertheless, the exams will test you on just about every aspect of Visual Basic, and therefore some sort of study material is necessary. It used to be that the Visual Basic exam (there was only one exam per release prior to Visual Basic 6) focused on assessing your programming skills: could you write a For...Next loop? Did you understand how a certain looping construct worked? Could you choose appropriate datatypes? *Those days are gone.* Now, you have a set of exams designed primarily to test your knowledge of Microsoft technologies. To pass the exams, you have to know the technologies and how they fit together.

There are two Visual Basic exams: *70-176 Designing and Implementing Desktop Applications with Microsoft Visual Basic*, and *70-175 Designing and Implementing Distributed Applications with Microsoft Visual Basic*. Of the two, exam 70-175 (Distributing) is generally considered the more difficult, and therefore it's recommended that you take 70-176 (Desktop) first.

The first exam I took was the Desktop exam, and I was surprised (not pleasantly so) at how many questions I encountered about packaging and deploying an application. It would seem that this is a topic for the Distributing exam, but it receives heavy coverage on *both* exams. As a matter of fact, there is a lot of overlap in subject matter between the two exams.

In Table 1-1, I've taken the official skills that each exam attempts to measure and placed them so that you can compare their differences and similarities. Whenever skills from the exams differ slightly, I've italicized the differences. Note that often a word or two is all that's different; usually the word "desktop" is replaced with the word "distributed." In some ways, the Distributing exam (70-175) is an extension of the Desktop exam (70-176). Make no mistake, *you will encounter similar material on both exams*. However, in order to pass the Distributed exam, you will have to demonstrate knowledge above and beyond that necessary to pass the Desktop exam.

Note that in Table 1-1, three topic areas that are indicated with an "NA" in the Chapters column are not covered. Because these topics are central to most or all Visual Basic development, this book assumes that, as an advanced developer, you're already thoroughly familiar with this material.

Table 1-1: Skills Measured on the Visual Basic Exams

70-176 (Desktop)	70-175 (Distributing)	Chapters
Access the potential impact of the logical design on performance, maintainability, extensibility, and availability.	Assess the potential impact of the logical design on performance, maintainability, extensibility, *scalability*, availability, and *security*.	3, 4, 7, 12
Design Visual Basic components to access data from a database.	Design Visual Basic components to access data from a database *in a multitier application*.	7, 12
Design the properties, methods, and events of components.	Design the properties, methods, and events of components.	3, 4, 5, 6
Establish the environment for source code version control.	Establish the environment for source code version control.	14

Table 1-1: Skills Measured on the Visual Basic Exams (continued)

70-176 (Desktop)	70-175 (Distributing)	Chapters
Install and configure Visual Basic for developing *desktop* applications.	Install and configure Visual Basic for developing *distributed* applications.	NA
Implement navigational design.	Implement navigational design.	NA
Create data input forms and dialog boxes.	Create data input forms and dialog boxes.	NA
Write code that validates user input.	Write code that validates user input.	8
Add an ActiveX control to the toolbox.	Add an ActiveX control to the toolbox.	5
Create a web page by using the DHTML Page Designer to dynamically change attributes of elements, change content, change styles, and position elements.	Create a web page by using the DHTML Page Designer to dynamically change attributes of elements, change content, change styles, and position elements.	8
Use data binding to display and manipulate data from a data source.	Use data binding to display and manipulate data from a data source.	7
Instantiate and invoke a COM component.	Instantiate and invoke a COM component.	4
Create callback procedures to enable asynchronous processing between COM components and Visual Basic client applications.	Create callback procedures to enable asynchronous processing between COM components and Visual Basic client applications.	4
Implement online user assistance in a *desktop* application.	Implement online user assistance in a *distributed* application.	10
Implement error handling for the user interface in *desktop* applications.	Implement error handling for the user interface in *distributed* applications.	9
Create a COM component that implements business rules or logic. Components include DLLs, ActiveX controls, and active documents.	Create a COM component that implements business rules or logic. Components include DLLs, ActiveX controls, and active documents.	4, 5, 6
Create ActiveX controls.	Create ActiveX controls.	4
Create an active document.	Create an active document.	6
Debug a COM client written in Visual Basic.	Debug Visual Basic code that uses objects from a COM component.	4, 9
Compile a project with class modules into a COM component.	Compile a project with class modules into a COM component.	4
Use Visual Component Manager to manage components.	Use Visual Component Manager to manage components.	14
Register and unregister a COM component.	Register and unregister a COM component.	4, 13
Access and manipulate a data source by using ADO and the ADO Data control.	Access and manipulate a data source by using ADO and the ADO Data control.	7
	Access and manipulate data by using the Execute Direct model.	7
	Access and manipulate data by using the Prepare/Execute model.	7
	Access and manipulate data by using the Stored Procedures model.	7

Table 1-1: Skills Measured on the Visual Basic Exams (continued)

70-176 (Desktop)	70-175 (Distributing)	Chapters
	Retrieve and manipulate data by using different cursor locations. Cursor locations include client-side and server-side.	7
	Retrieve and manipulate data by using different cursor types. Cursor types include forward-only, static, dynamic, and keyset.	7
	Use the ADO Errors collection to handle database errors.	7
	Manage database transactions to ensure data consistency and recoverability.	7
	Write SQL statements that retrieve and modify data.	7
	Write SQL statements that use joins to combine data from multiple tables.	7
	Use appropriate locking strategies to ensure data integrity. Locking strategies include read-only, pessimistic, optimistic, and batch optimistic.	7
Given a scenario, select the appropriate compiler options.	Given a scenario, select the appropriate compiler options.	11
Control an application by using conditional compilation.	Control an application by using conditional compilation.	13
Set watch expressions during program execution.	Set watch expressions during program execution.	9
Monitor the values of expressions and variables by using the Immediate window.	Monitor the values of expressions and variables by using the Immediate window.	9
Implement project groups to support the development and debugging processes.	Implement project groups to support the development and debugging processes.	4, 5
Given a scenario, define the scope of a watch variable.	Given a scenario, define the scope of a watch variable.	9
Use the Package and Deployment Wizard to create a setup program that installs a *desktop* application, registers the COM components, and allows for uninstall.	Use the Package and Deployment Wizard to create a setup program that installs a *distributed* application, registers the COM components, and allows for uninstall.	13
Plan and implement floppy disk–based deployment or compact disc–based deployment for a *desktop* application.	Plan and implement floppy disk–based deployment or compact disc–based deployment for a *distributed* application.	13
	Register a component that implements DCOM.	13
	Configure DCOM on a client computer and on a server computer.	13
Plan and implement web-based deployment for a *desktop* application.	Plan and implement web-based deployment for a *distributed* application.	13

Table 1-1: Skills Measured on the Visual Basic Exams (continued)

70-176 (Desktop)	70-175 (Distributing)	Chapters
Plan and implement network-based deployment for a *desktop* application.	Plan and implement network-based deployment for a *distributed* application.	13
Fix errors, and take measures to prevent future errors.	Fix errors, and take measures to prevent future errors.	9
Deploy application updates for *desktop* applications.	Deploy application updates for *distributed* applications.	13
	Implement load balancing.	3, 12
	Choose the appropriate threading model for a COM component.	4
	Design and create components that will be used with MTS.	12
	Create a package by using the MTS Explorer.	12
	Add components to an MTS package.	12
	Use role-based security to limit use of an MTS package to specific users.	12
	Use an active document to present information within a web browser.	6
	Configure a server computer to run MTS.	12
	Configure a client computer to use an MTS component.	12
Write code that processes data entered on a form.	Write code that processes data entered on a form.	7

 In each chapter, I'll outline which skills are addressed and tell you the exam to which the material is most applicable.

Both exams are timed, meaning that you have a limited amount of time to complete them. You can't take any materials into the testing room with you, so forget crib sheets or reference books. The exams have multiple-choice questions, many requiring only a single answer. Some questions require multiple answers, however. The exam will let you know when multiple answers are required, and will often tell you how many answers to select.

Many, many people fail an exam the first time they take it. Just because you use Visual Basic every day does not ensure that you will pass an exam the first time *if you don't prepare*! Questions on the exams are deliberately designed to trip you up. Often, a question's sly phrasing will cause you to give an incorrect answer when you really do know the right answer. If you're reading through the answers for a question and you come to an answer that looks like the right one, *keep reading*! Often a slight alteration of words makes a later answer the better one. Also, if you encounter two answers that are total opposites, *reread the question*. A single word in the question may mean the difference between which of the opposing answers is correct.

I recommend that you work through an exam from beginning to end, answering each question as best you can. If you encounter a question whose answer you are unsure of, or a question that you believe will take you some time to answer, use the exam software's Marking feature to mark a question and return to it later. To mark a question, select the Mark checkbox. After you've made a pass through all questions, you'll see a list of all question numbers. Those that you marked appear highlighted, so you can return to them easily. After you make your first pass through the questions, go back and address each question that you marked. If you feel you have chosen the correct answer on the second pass, unmark the question. Once you've gone through all marked questions, make another pass through the questions you still have marked. If you are able to get through all questions and unmark them, use the time to go through the questions sequentially, starting at the beginning; sometimes answering a later question triggers your memory to an earlier question whose answer you need to change.

 If you have never taken a Microsoft exam, be sure to take the practice exam that is available when you first sign in. It will teach you how to use the exam's features, such as the Marking feature, and the time spent on a practice exam doesn't count against the time allotted you for the real thing.

It's a good idea to study the night before you take an exam, as well as the day of the exam. You should get a good night's sleep and eat a decent breakfast (remember those study habits that you were *supposed* to practice in school?). Also, make sure to arrive at the test facility early. If you have time, review the key fact summaries at the end of each chapter *just before entering the testing facility*. (Start with the chapters you feel the least comfortable with.)

If you expect the exams to be extremely difficult, and you study accordingly, you should find the exams relatively easier when you finally take one. If you enter an exam believing it will be a breeze, you may be unpleasantly surprised. Therefore, don't be in a rush to take an exam. If you can, schedule an exam for a few weeks in the future and create a study schedule leading up to the exam. Be diligent, and soon you'll have that certification. And believe me, it's a very cool feeling when, at the end of the exam, a screen pops up to tell you you've passed!

Good luck!

CHAPTER 2

Visual Basic Overview

I must reiterate that this book is not intended to teach you everything about Visual Basic, nor is it intended to cover *everything* on the exams. As you can tell from the *Preface*, this book covers many different topics in depth. Still, there are a number of questions on the exams related to material that doesn't appear in this book. If you use Visual Basic regularly, chances are you're already familiar with much of this material. For instance, you should be able to add a menu to a form, add an ActiveX control to a project, and create a Do loop.

Microsoft is famous for meticulously choosing and wording questions to trip you up, and you'll need a little prepping on some common topics before taking the exams. Although you might encounter a question about something you do frequently, the question may come from an angle that you're not expecting. For instance, can you (off the top of your head) write the code necessary to switch from one tab to another using the TabStrip control? Or add a node to a TreeView control? Sure, you could probably sit down and write this code—taking advantage of the IntelliSense dropdowns. If you're like me, you probably have an extensive library of routines and often cut and paste such code. However, you don't get these little luxuries when taking the exams.

The following sections highlight specific aspects of topics with which you should be familiar. If any of these topics is new to you, I encourage you to experiment with them on your own and consult the online help. Because of my commitment to providing in-depth information on advanced capabilities, the material in this chapter discusses the fundamentals that are likely to be on the exams but whose details even the experienced VB programmer may have forgotten.

Forms

If you've worked with Visual Basic to any degree, you're probably comfortable working with forms and controls. However, it's not uncommon to encounter a not-so-obvious question on a fairly straightforward subject. For instance, you might encounter the question: "What is the order in which the following events occur when a form is loaded? Load, Initialize, Resize, GotFocus, and Activate?" The correct order is: Initialize, Load, Resize, Activate, and finally, GotFocus. If you're unfamiliar with any of these events, you should get familiar with them before taking the exams.

You probably use the Forms collection in most projects you create. Here's a quick rundown of facts about the Forms collection that might come in handy when taking the exams:

- To load a form, use the Load statement like this:

```
Load frmMain
```

  Loading a form using the Load statement doesn't display the form.

- To load a form *and* display it, use the Show method, like this:

```
frmMain.Show
```

- To unload a form, use the Unload statement, like this:

```
Unload frmMain
```

Now, here's a fact that most experienced programmers have probably learned the hard way:

- Unloading a form using the Unload statement only unloads the user interface portion of the form, not the code portion. This means that module level-data persists, and the next time you use the form you may get unexpected results. The only way to fully unload both the user interface and the code component of a form is to set the form equal to Nothing after unloading the form, like this:

```
Unload frmMain
Set frmMain = Nothing
```

- Another important fact about the Forms collection is that referencing a form that isn't loaded causes the form to be loaded. For example, new developers often think that to test whether or not a form is loaded, you could reference a property of the form and check for a runtime error. Under this assumption, you might write the following code:

```
' Trap a possible run-time error.
On Error Resume Next
'* We're just going to set the Visible property of the form to
'* whatever value it has already. If the form is loaded, this will have
'* no effect on the form. If it is not loaded, it raises an
'* error.
frmMain.Visible = frmMain.Visible

If Err.Number <> 0 Then
    ' The form isn't loaded.
Else
    ' The form is loaded.
End If
```

In reality, this code never generates an error. Referencing a form that isn't already loaded causes the form to load automatically. Therefore, no error ever occurs. The proper way to determine if a form is loaded is to take advantage of the fact that only loaded forms appear in the Forms collection, and to look through the Forms collection as shown in the following (simplified) procedure:

```
Public Function IsFormLoaded(strFormName As String) As Boolean

    Dim lngCount As Long

    For lngCount = 0 To Forms.Count - 1
        If Forms(lngCount).Name = strFormName Then
            IsFormLoaded = True
            Exit Function
        End If
    Next lngCount

    IsFormLoaded = False

End Function
```

Menus

Visual Basic includes a tool you can use to build menus for your forms: the Menu Editor. You need to know some fundamentals about using Visual Basic–provided menus in your programs.

A couple of items that are frequently asked on the exams are:

1. How do you dynamically create a menu item at runtime?

2. How do you display a pop-up menu at runtime?

To dynamically create menus at runtime, you have to create a menu array at design time—much like you'd create a control array. To create a menu array, create a menu item using the Menu Editor and assign the menu item an Index. (Typically, you'd also hide the menu item by setting its Visible property to False, which corresponds to unchecking the Visible box for that item in the Menu Editor.) Then use the Load statement to load a new menu item and change its properties as desired. When you use the Load statement, you must specify an index value not currently being used. For example, the following code creates a new menu item using a menu array:

```
'* The menu item mnuTemplate has an index
'* of 0, and is therefore the first menu item
'* of a control array. Create a new menu item
'* by adding to this array.

Load mnuTemplate(1)

'* Customize the menu item.
With mnuTemplate(1)
    .Caption = "New Menu Item"
    .Visible = True
    .Enabled = False
End With
```

Shortcut (or pop-up) menus are used throughout Windows, and you can display any dropdown menu created with the Menu Editor as a Shortcut menu. Creating a dropdown menu is exactly like creating a regular menu; it's the way you display it that makes it a Shortcut menu. Usually, you'll use the Menu Editor to make the menu invisible (by setting the Visible property of the top menu item to **False**) so that the menu doesn't appear on the menu bar. To display the menu as a Shortcut menu, use the PopupMenu method of the form, passing the method a reference to the top menu item. For instance, say you have defined the menu shown in Figure 2-1.

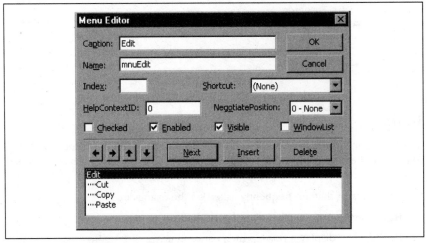

Figure 2-1: Shortcut menus are created using the Menu Editor

To display the Edit menu shown in Figure 2-1 as a Shortcut menu when the user right-clicks the form, you could use the following code:

```
If Button = vbRightButton Then
    PopupMenu mnuEdit
End If
```

Most applications display Shortcut menus on the MouseUp event, not the MouseDown event. Both events are passed the same parameters when they're fired: *Button*, indicating the mouse button pressed; *Shift*, indicating the state of the Shift, Alt, and Ctrl keys; and *X* and *Y*, indicating the horizontal and vertical mouse coordinates when the button was pressed.

Controls

Another area where you may miss questions on a familiar topic is ActiveX controls. If you're like me, you probably have lots of routines for working with the list view, tree view, and other such ActiveX controls, and you probably cut and paste a lot. Although this speeds up development, it sometimes means that you don't have certain techniques committed to memory. You could write the necessary code if you sat down at a computer, but you might not remember syntax off the top of your head. The following is a summary of the ActiveX controls on which you may be tested, along with some facts that you should commit to memory.

 Surprisingly, a number of Visual Basic developers have little or no experience working with the advanced controls such as the Tree-View and the ListView controls. For instance, you may be a middle-tier developer who never creates interfaces, or you may be getting by with the standard control set. If you aren't comfortable using the controls discussed here, crack open the Visual Basic docs or consult *Visual Basic Controls in a Nutshell*, published by O'Reilly & Associates, and spend a little time playing with the controls. It's just not feasible to teach you how to use these controls here, but you need to know how nonetheless.

The TreeView ActiveX Control

The TreeView control is used to display hierarchical lists. The most common example of the TreeView control is the one that appears in the left side of Explorer, which is used to navigate the folders and drives on a computer. A few key items to remember for the exams is how nodes are added to a tree view, how to detect when a node is clicked, and how to determine which node exists under any given coordinate.

Nodes are added to a TreeView control by first declaring a variable as a Node, then setting the variable to a new Node object by calling the Add method of the TreeView control's Nodes collection. The following code adds a single node to a TreeView control:

```
Dim nodExample As Node

Set nodExample = TreeView1.Nodes.Add
nodExample.Text = "New Node"
```

When adding nodes to a TreeView control, you can add the node anywhere in the list by specifying the *Relative* argument (the index or key of the existing node at which the new node will be placed) and the *Relationship* argument (a constant defining the location in relation to the *Relative* node at which the node will be added). The possible values for *Relationship* are shown in Table 2-1.

Table 2-1: Possible Values for the Nodes.Add Method's Relationship Argument

Value	Description
tvwFirst	The Node is placed before all other nodes at the same level of the node named in *relative*.
tvwLast	The Node is placed after all other nodes at the same level of the node named in *relative*.

Table 2-1: Possible Values for the Nodes.Add Method's Relationship Argument (continued)

Value	Description
tvwNext	The Node is placed after the node named in *relative*.
tvwPrevious	The Node is placed before the node named in *relative*.
tvwChild	The Node becomes the child node of the node named in *relative*.

Microsoft has been inconsistent in making some collections 1-based and others 0-based. For instance, the Forms collection is 0-based. However, the Nodes collection of a TreeView control (like most collections in the Windows Common controls) is 1-based.

The following code adds a new node to a TreeView control, then adds a second node as a child of the first (the result is shown in Figure 2-2):

```
Dim nodExample As Node
Dim lngIndex   As Long

' Create a top level node.
Set nodExample = TreeView1.Nodes.Add
nodExample.Text = "Parent"
lngIndex = nodExample.Index

' Create a child node.
Set nodExample = TreeView1.Nodes.Add(lngIndex, _tvwChild)
nodExample.Text = "Child"
```

You must have the LineStyle property of the TreeView control set to show root lines (i.e., set to **tvwRootLines**) or you won't see the child added in this example.

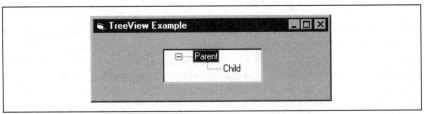

Figure 2-2: The TreeView control is used to create hierarchical lists

You use the NodeClick event to tell when a given node is clicked. The NodeClick event passes a reference to the Node object that is clicked as a parameter. To display the text of a clicked node, for example, you could use code like this:

```
Private Sub TreeView1_NodeClick(ByVal Node As MSComctlLib.Node)

    MsgBox Node.Text, vbInformation Or vbOKOnly

End Sub
```

At times, you may need to determine which node lies at a particular set of X and Y coordinates. The TreeView control includes a method called HitTest, which takes *X* and *Y* values and returns a Node object. If no node exists at the location specified by *X* and *Y*, the node variable will be empty; therefore, it's best to always test this condition. The following example shows how you can place the text of the node under the mouse in a Label control:

```
Private Sub TreeView1_MouseMove(Button As Integer, Shift As Integer, _
                                x As Single, y As Single)

    Dim nodMove As Node

    Set nodMove = TreeView1.HitTest(x, y)

    If Not (nodMove Is Nothing) Then
        lblnode.Caption = nodMove.Text
    End If

End Sub
```

The ListView ActiveX Control

The ListView control allows you to create columnar lists. Although more programming is required to build a list view than is necessary to fill a list box, the additional work is usually well worth the trouble. For the exam, you should know how to add an item to the list and how to reference columns of an item.

Adding items to a ListView control is similar to adding items to a TreeView control in that you use the Add method of a collection. Where a TreeView control consists of Nodes, a ListView control consists of ListItems. The following code uses the List-Items collection to add a new item to a list view control:

```
Dim litmExample As ListItem

' Add a new item to the list.
Set litmExample = ListView1.ListItems.Add()
litmExample.Text = "Sample Item"
```

Unlike the traditional ListBox control, the ListView control can display columns of data. Columns can be defined using the property pages of the ListView control, or they can be added at runtime by using the Add method of the ColumnHeaders collection. To get or set the text displayed in the first column, you reference the Text property of the list item. To access the values of secondary columns, you use the SubItems collection of the list item. Each column after the first is considered a sub item, and sub items are 1-based. For example, the following code populates three columns of data (the result is shown in Figure 2-3):

```
Dim litmExample     As ListItem
Dim objColumnHeader As ColumnHeader
```

```
'* Columns only appear when the list view is in Report view.
ListView1.View = lvwReport

'* If the column headers aren't defined at design time,
'* they must be created at runtime as done here.
Set objColumnHeader = ListView1.ColumnHeaders.Add(1)
Set objColumnHeader = ListView1.ColumnHeaders.Add(2)
Set objColumnHeader = ListView1.ColumnHeaders.Add(3)

' Add a new item to the list.
Set litmExample = ListView1.ListItems.Add()
litmExample.Text = "Sample Item"

litmExample.SubItems(1) = "Data #2"
litmExample.SubItems(2) = "Data #3"
```

 In order for columns to appear, the ListView control's View property must be set to `lvwReport`.

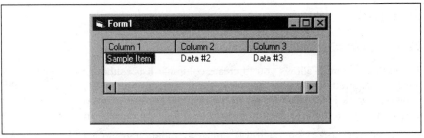

Figure 2-3: Use the SubItems collection to reference secondary columns in a list view

The ImageList ActiveX Control

The ImageList control acts as a repository for images that can be used with other controls. All images placed in the ImageList are part of the ListImages collection, and each image can be referenced by an index or key. Adding pictures to an ImageList control is usually done using the Properties dialog box at design time (see Figure 2-4), but it can also be performed at runtime using code. The main items to note before going into the exams is how to associate an ImageList control with another control, such as a TreeView or ListView control, and how to assign pictures in the ImageList control to items in the associated control.

Controls that can be linked to an ImageList control usually have an ImageList property. This property doesn't appear in the Properties window, and therefore it must be set through code or by using the property pages of the control. To associate an ImageList control with a TreeView control, for instance, you could use a statement such as this:

```
TreeView1.ImageList = ImageList1
```

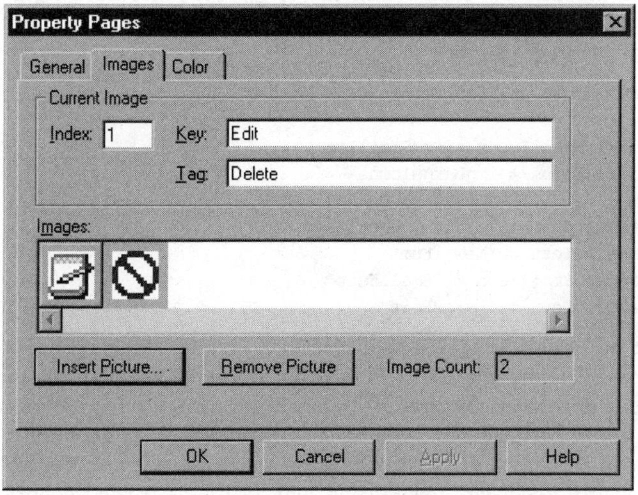

Figure 2-4: To add images to an ImageList control, use the property pages

ListView controls have two modes—one that displays small icons and one that displays large icons. Usually, the large images are actual 32×32–pixel icons, whereas the small images are 16×16–pixel bitmaps. A single ImageList control can only store images of the same size. When images are displayed by using the Picture object of the ImageList control, they are always displayed at the same size in which they are stored. Usually, a ListView control needs to be associated with two ImageList controls in order to display large and small images. Therefore, the ListView control actually has two properties for associated ImageList controls: one for large images (the Icons property), and one for small images (the SmallIcons property). The following code shows how you might associate ImageList controls with these two properties of the ListView control:

```
Set ListView1.SmallIcons = imgSmall
Set ListView1.Icons = imgIcons
```

Once an image list is associated with another control, you can reference an image by its key. Exactly how you do this depends on which control you are populating. When using the TreeView control, you set the Image property of a given node like this:

```
Dim nodExample As Node

TreeView1.ImageList = ImageList1

Set nodExample = TreeView1.Nodes.Add
nodExample.Text = "New Node"
nodExample.Image = "Edit"
```

where "Edit" is the key assigned to an image in the ImageList control named ImageList1.

When using the ListView control, you can assign large and small icons separately using two different properties (LargeIcons and SmallIcons). The following code shows how you might do this:

```
Dim ltmExample As ListItem

ListView1.SmallIcons = imgSmallIcons
ListView1.Icons = imgLargeIcons

Set ltmExample = ListView1.ListItems.Add
ltmExample.Text = "New item"
ltmExample.SmallIcon = "SmallEdit"
ltmExample.Icon = "LargeEdit"
```

Remember, to use an ImageList control with a TreeView or ListView control, you must first associate the image list with the other control. How you do this depends on whether the control with which you are working is a tree view or a list view. And if the control is a list view, you must assign the ImageList control to either the SmallIcons or the Icons property. Once an image list is associated with another control, you can assign an image to an item of the associated control using the image's key. In addition, images can be assigned to more than one item, and ImageList controls can be associated with more than one other control.

The Toolbar ActiveX Control

Toolbars usually appear at the top of a window and consist of buttons, which often correspond to menu items, providing a graphical, one-click way to access the common functionality of an application. The Toolbar control allows you to build toolbars by adding buttons to a Buttons collection. Buttons may contain text, images, or both. Like controls such as the TreeView control, images on the Toolbar control are provided by an associated ImageList control. A button can be a traditional button, a toggle button, part of a toggle group (similar to an option group), a separator, a placeholder, or a dropdown. A button's type is determined by its Style property. When a button is made a placeholder, you can put any other type of control (such as a text box) on top of the separator.

An image list can be associated with a toolbar at design time (using the property pages), or at runtime (using code). To assign an image to a button at design time, enter the image's key in the Image field on the toolbar's property pages (see Figure 2-5).

Everything you can do in the property pages you can do in code. For example, the following code associates an image list with the Toolbar control, creates a new button with a key of New as a default (normal) button, and assigns the image with the key of NewImage in the Image List control as the button's image:

```
Dim btnNew As Button

Set Toolbar1.ImageList = ImageList1

Set btnNew = Toolbar1.Buttons.Add(, "New", , tbrDefault, "NewImage")
btnNew.ToolTipText = "New"
btnNew.Description = btnNew.ToolTipText
```

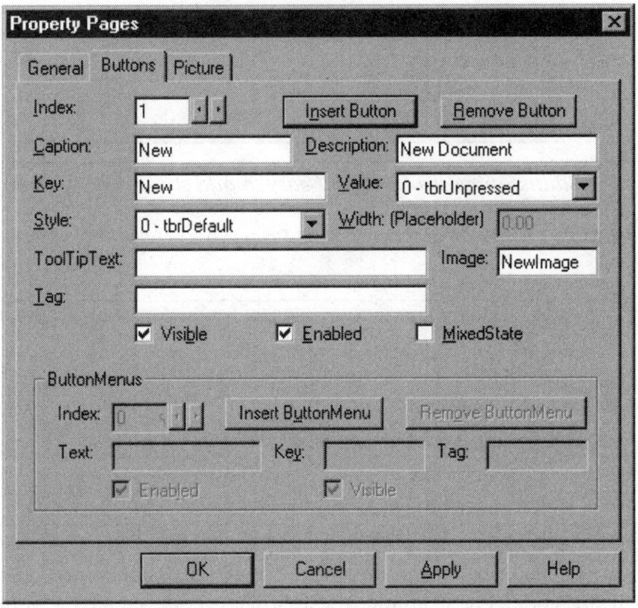

Figure 2-5: Using the property pages is the easiest way to create buttons

Use the ButtonClick event (not the Click event) to determine which button was clicked and to act accordingly. The ButtonClick event passes a reference to the clicked button. The following code illustrates how you might use this event:

```
Private Sub Toolbar1_ButtonClick(ByVal Button As MSComctlLib.Button)

Select Case Button.Key
    Case Is = "New"
        ' Save the file.
    Case Is = "Open"
        ' Open a file.
    Case Is = "Exit"
        ' Call the exit function.
End Select

End Sub
```

The StatusBar ActiveX Control

The StatusBar control allows you to easily add a status bar to the edge of a window. Status bars can contain many types of data (see Figure 2-6). The StatusBar control is made up of Panel objects, each of which can contain text, a picture, or both. You can specify text or an image (by using an ImageList control), or you can set a Panel's Style property to one of the values in Table 2-2 to automatically display common data.

Figure 2-6: The StatusBar control makes it easy to add status bars to your programs

Table 2-2: Possible Values for a Panel's Style Property

Value	Description
sbrText	(Default) Displays text and/or a bitmap. Set the text with the Text property.
sbrCaps	Displays the status of the Caps Lock key.
sbrNum	Displays the status of the Number lock key.
sbrIns	Displays the status of the Insert key.
sbrScrl	Displays the status of the Scroll Lock key.
sbrTime	Displays the current time in the system format.
sbrDate	Displays the current date in the system format.

You can use the status bar's property pages to define panels, or you can define the panels using code. For example, the following code creates a status bar that looks like the one shown in Figure 2-6:

```
Dim pnlNew As Panel

' Place text in the first panel.
StatusBar1.Panels(1).Text = "Simple text"

' Remove the sunken appearance of the first panel.
StatusBar1.Panels(1).Bevel = sbrNoBevel

' Add a new panel and make it display the time.
Set pnlNew = StatusBar1.Panels.Add(, , , sbrTime)

' Add an image next to the time.
Set pnlNew.Picture = ImageList1.ListImages("Clock").Picture

' Add a new panel and make it display the status of
' insert mode.
Set pnlNew = StatusBar1.Panels.Add(, , , sbrIns)

' Reduce the width of this panel.
pnlNew.Width = 500
```

The TabStrip ActiveX Control

The TabStrip control is used to build tabular interfaces (see Figure 2-7). Tabbed dialogs boxes are so common right now that it would be difficult to find an application that doesn't use at least one. The TabStrip control is composed of a Tabs collection. You can create tabs at design time using the property pages, or you can create tabs at runtime using code.

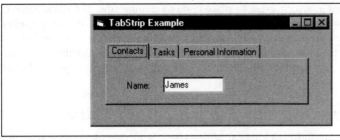

Figure 2-7: The TabStrip control is used to build the dynamic tabular interfaces that are so common in Windows

Using the TabStrip control isn't as straightforward as using some of the other Windows Common Controls. Unlike some third-party tab controls that let you place controls directly on their tabs, you must create a container control for each tab, and then hide and show the containers as necessary. The easiest way to do this is to create a control array of container controls without a border (frames work well), size them to fit within the tab strip's outline, and layer them one on top of another. You can then hide and show the containers by using code such as the following:

```
Private Sub TabStrip1_Click()

    Static m_intCurrentFrame As Integer

    ' REMEMBER: Tab indexes are 1 based, but the control array
    ' used here is 0 based.
    If TabStrip1.SelectedItem.Index - 1 = m_intCurrentFrame Then
        ' The proper frame is visible, get out.
        Exit Sub
    End If

    ' Show the new frame.
    Frame1(TabStrip1.SelectedItem.Index - 1).Visible = True

    ' Hide the old frame.
    Frame1(m_intCurrentFrame).Visible = False

    ' Store the current frame.
    m_intCurrentFrame = TabStrip1.SelectedItem.Index - 1

End Sub
```

 Tabs in most Windows applications respond to the MouseDown event. However, placing this code in the MouseDown event causes it to fail because the SelectedItem property doesn't reference the newly clicked tab yet. Therefore, place this code in the Click or MouseUp events.

You may be asked in which event to place code to change tabs. The Click event is probably the best place, but if Click is not an option, then select MouseUp (never MouseDown). Another thing to note is that you should always hide and show container controls; don't attempt to get the same results by fiddling with the ZOrder. If you do, controls on invisible tabs will still respond to keyboard shortcuts.

Passing Parameters by Reference or by Value

Visual Basic allows you to pass data as arguments to a procedure by reference (the default) or by value. When a variable is passed by reference to a parameter of a procedure, the procedure receives a pointer to the original variable. Any subsequent changes made to the parameter are made to the original variable. To pass data by value so that changes made to the parameter are not propagated to the original data, explicitly use ByVal when declaring the parameter, as in this function declaration:

```
Public Function CalculateAge(ByVal varBirthDate As Date)
```

Naming Conventions

Throughout this book, I have attempted to strictly adhere to a naming convention for all variable and control references shown in code. If you're not currently using a naming convention, you should be. Essentially, a naming convention consists of prefixing all variable or object references using an accepted prefix. Although I can't outline all of the conventions used throughout the book, here is a short listing of the prefixes for common datatypes:

Datatype	Prefix	Example
Boolean	bln	blnLoggedIn
Currency	cur	curSalary
Control	ctl	ctlLastControl
Double	dbl	dblMiles
ErrObject	err	errLastError
Handle	hwnd	hwndPicture
Integer	int	intAge
Long	lng	lngOnHand
Object	obj	objUserTable
Single	sng	sngYears
String	str	strName
User-defined type	udt	udtEmployee
Variant (including Dates)	vnt	vntDateHired

For complete information on implementing a naming convention (including the prefixes for standard and ActiveX controls), I recommend you read my book, *Practical Standards for Microsoft Visual Basic*, published by Microsoft Press.

This chapter is simply a refresher to get your feet damp (not even wet) before digging into the real technical material. If you find any of the subjects discussed here challenging, you'll probably have a difficult time with the rest of the book. If this is the case, you might want to review the material in *VB/VBA in a Nutshell* and *Visual Basic Controls in a Nutshell*, both published by O'Reilly. For the rest of you, get comfortable, because the rest of the chapters are going to dive into some really technical topics (and dive deep) to prepare you for the Microsoft Visual Basic certifications exams. Good luck!

*Visual Basic
Overview*

CHAPTER 3

Understanding COM

COM is the foundation of ActiveX, and thus of Visual Basic itself. Understanding COM is crucial to passing either of the exams. As you can see from Table 3-1, only the information on creating n-tier solutions is exam-specific.

Table 3-1: Coverage of COM-Related Topics on the Exams

Topic	Covered on Exam
Understanding COM and its relationship to ActiveX	Both
Understanding the types of COM components	Both
COM interfaces	Both
Instantiating COM objects	Both
Early versus late binding	Both
COM object lifetime	Both
Object browser	Both
In-process versus out-of-process	Both
Creating n-tier solutions	Distributed

The Technologies and the Exams

In this chapter, you'll learn the information necessary to pass COM-related questions on both exams. Although each exam covers COM in a slightly different way, you need to understand this in order to pass either of the exams; this should be considered core information for both exams. You'll encounter some questions on COM directly, as well as a lot of questions about technologies—such as ActiveX controls—that are built on COM.

COM and ActiveX: A VB Programmer's Perspective

Many Visual Basic programmers are unfamiliar with Microsoft's underlying object technology, known as the Component Object Model, or COM. ActiveX, on the other hand, has become such a buzzword/Microsoft mantra that anyone developing for Windows who hasn't heard the term has probably been programming in a closet. COM is important because it's the foundation upon which ActiveX technology exists, and ActiveX is quickly becoming the basis upon which most new technologies are established.

Because Visual Basic hides so much of the underlying technology of COM and of ActiveX, it's very understandable that so many Visual Basic programmers are ignorant of the details of COM. You don't need to be an expert on COM to pass an exam, but you need to have a solid understanding of the principles of COM. More importantly, understanding the basics of COM will make you a better programmer.

This chapter explains COM from the perspective of a Visual Basic programmer—it's not meant to serve as a complete dissertation on this important technology. There are many books devoted entirely to COM, and you're encouraged to read them to better your development skills. However, the material in this chapter will give you sufficient knowledge to pass the Visual Basic exam.

OLE by Any Other Name Is ActiveX!

Not long ago, Microsoft's big technical buzz word was OLE (Object Linking and Embedding). Now, the term OLE is rarely spoken, but you can't read a technical publication or talk to a programmer without hearing the term ActiveX. Not surprisingly, this has left many new programmers and veterans alike asking "What happened to OLE?" Did ActiveX replace OLE? Not exactly. The truth is, ActiveX is OLE. Specifically, ActiveX is OLE 2.0, the second iteration of OLE technology.

Changing the name OLE to ActiveX was more of a marketing and public relations decision than anything else, driven primarily by the need for Microsoft to have an Internet technology presence. Now, the term ActiveX is often associated with the Internet, but the Internet is really secondary. You can do some great things with ActiveX technology and the Internet, but most ActiveX applications don't have anything to do with the Internet at all.

ActiveX technology manifests itself in the form of objects. You'll learn specifically what an object is and how it is used in the following section. For now, it's important only that you understand that there are essentially three types of ActiveX objects. These are:

- ActiveX Code Components (DLLs or EXEs)
- ActiveX Controls (OCXs)
- ActiveX documents (DLLs or EXEs)

ActiveX clients are not a type of ActiveX object. Rather, they are applications that use the ActiveX objects of another application. Each of the three types of ActiveX objects—code components, controls, and documents—is a unique beast in its own right, and you'll have to show a thorough understanding of all three in order to pass the Visual Basic exams. Before you can truly understand any of these objects/applications, however, you must first have a solid grasp of COM.

In this chapter, you'll learn about COM and COM interfaces. Visual Basic shields the developer from a lot of the "guts" of COM, but you are still expected to demonstrate an understanding of these technical details on the exams. This chapter discusses the technical details of COM, including the IDispatch and IUnknown interfaces, as well as the technical aspects that you will encounter when creating COM objects using Visual Basic.

 Most of the topics covered in this chapter are discussed in additional detail in later chapters. After reading all of the chapters, you should have a very solid understanding of COM and ActiveX.

Building on Class Modules

Visual Basic 4 was the first version of Visual Basic to include the ability to create class modules. These class modules allowed you to build code objects that could easily be maintained and shared among applications. ActiveX COM objects are, in some ways, an extension of these standard class modules. In other respects, they add a whole new dimension to working with classes.

ActiveX code components are created in much the same way as class modules were created in Visual Basic 4. ActiveX controls and documents, on the other hand, are built upon entirely new class types, which you will learn more about in Chapter 4, *Creating and Testing ActiveX Code Components*; Chapter 5, *Creating ActiveX Controls*; and Chapter 6, *Creating and Using ActiveX Documents*.

On the Exams

If you haven't created classes using Visual Basic's class modules before, you're depriving yourself of their great benefits (reusability, maintainability, etc.), and you're going to find the Visual Basic exam difficult. Chapter 4 is devoted to working with class modules, and you'll continue to be exposed to building classes throughout this book. This material is covered very extensively in this book because of the large proportion of questions on the exam pertaining to the subject matter. If you don't thoroughly understand classes, you won't understand the complexities of creating ActiveX components, and you probably won't pass the exams.

Even though classes receive respectable coverage in this book, you should have some hands-on experience with classes to fully understand the complexities and benefits of classes. Start considering ways to use classes in your own applications if you haven't already.

Understanding COM

ActiveX technology is built on a foundation of objects. This foundation is known as the Component Object Model, or COM. Don't confuse COM objects with object oriented programming—they are two different things. (COM is a standard for compiled, reusable objects, while object-oriented programming is a methodology of writing applications.) For the COM foundation to be successful, it requires that a COM object adhere to a number of core requirements. These requirements are the basis, or framework, of all COM (ActiveX) objects. COM is an object-oriented architecture for building applications. COM is all about creating, servicing, and releasing objects, and it is the foundation on which all ActiveX components are built. These objects, known as COM objects, share a number of characteristics. These characteristics essentially fall into one of two categories: providing a model for an object definition, or providing services for the creation of objects and the communication between client and server.

Common characteristics of COM objects are:

- COM objects provide for encapsulation of data and code.
- COM objects employ a mechanism for referencing and releasing objects.
- COM objects are created from classes.
- COM objects expose standard interfaces.

Encapsulation of Data and Code

COM objects are an *encapsulation* of data and code; that is, the objects are comprised both of their code and all of the data they use. For example, say you need to keep track of employees in an organization, and that you need to store a number of pieces of information for each employee such as Name, Date Hired, and Position. In addition, suppose you need methods for adding and removing employees, and you want all of this information and functionality available to a number of different applications in different departments within your organiza-tion. You could write the necessary code to do all of this in each application throughout your organization, but that would be highly inefficient to implement and a nightmare to maintain. A better approach is to take advantage of COM and encapsulate all of the employee data and functionality (adding and deleting routines, etc.) into a single, re-usable object. Then, all of your different applica-tions could work with the employee data through a consistent interface—the employee object's interface.

The encapsulation of data and code is a key point to understand here. By encap-sulating the data *and* the routines that manipulate the data into a single object, you free the end-user applications from the intricacies of data maintenance. For example, suppose company policy changed such that when a new employee is added to the system, a special tax form needs to be printed. If the data and code routines weren't encapsulated in a common object, you would need to modify each and every application that contained code to create a new employee record. By using a COM object, you need to change only the code in one location (within the object), and as long as you don't modify the interface of the object (discussed in detail in the next section), all of the applications that use the object to create a new employee will instantly have the policy change in effect.

A key benefit of COM objects is: COM objects provide encapsulation of data and code, thereby increasing maintainability.

Exposing a Standard Interface

In order for an application to use a COM object, the COM object must expose an *interface*. An interface is a set of exposed functionality (essentially code procedures), that can be called from client applications. Interfaces are the means by which client applications communicate with objects. Some COM components expose a limited interface, while some expose complex interfaces. The content of your component's interface is up to you. However, the interface must be defined in a standard way so that client applications can use it.

The term Interface actually has two meanings when working with ActiveX components. On one hand, you create an interface for a component, as discussed next; we'll refer to it as a *component interface*. At the same time, however, COM has a strict definition of a *COM interface* (that which makes a COM object a COM object), which you have no control over. Visual Basic handles the details of the COM interface; you'll learn about this later in this chapter.

The component interface you create for an object will consist of one or more of the following:

- Properties
- Methods
- Events

Say for instance that you are creating an Employee object. You must first decide how you want client applications to interact with your object. You might want them to be able to retrieve the name of an employee, as well as other information such as sex, age, and the date the employee was hired. In order for a client to get these values from the object, you must expose an interface member for each of the items. Since these interface members expose attribute values, not functions, they are called *properties*. In addition to attributes, or properties, you can also expose functions. Publicly exposed functions, such as a Delete function, are called *methods*. You have complete control over what a method does. For instance, the Delete function for the employee object in this discussion would need to perform all of the necessary actions to delete the employee, including such things as removing them from their assigned department, notifying accounting to remove the employee from the payroll, etc.

Properties and methods allow a client application to communicate with an object in one direction: the client can call in to the object to invoke some functionality or to retrieve or set a property value. But communication in the other direction is also possible. Objects can be designed to initiate communications with a client by way of *events*. You can use events to notify a client when a condition is met, such as when another user changes the department of an active employee object.

Together, properties, methods, and events make up an object's programming (or component) interface. This interface acts as a contract between the client application and the object. Any and all communication between the client and the object must transpire through this interface (see Figure 3-1).

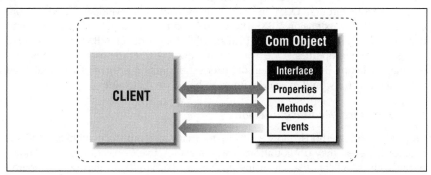

Figure 3-1: An object's interface is the mechanism that allows it to interact with its clients

Visual Basic handles the technical implementation of how clients use COM objects. Your responsibility is to define the properties, methods, and events of the object so that its interface is logical, consistent, and exposes all of the functionality a client needs to use the object.

You can create as many properties, methods, and events for an object as you deem necessary. However, it is extremely important that you understand how to choose the best interface type for any given functionality or data that you want to expose. The following sections give an explanation of each of interface type (also called member type): Property, Method, and Event.

Exposing object attributes as properties

You are probably familiar with object properties. Each and every control you place on a form has at least one property: the Name property. Most controls have considerably more, such as Left, Top, Alignable, and BackColor. Properties are attributes that define an object. When used in code, properties are almost always referred to using an equal (=) sign. When setting a property, the property reference is placed on the left of the equal sign, while the value you want to assign to it is placed on the right. When obtaining the value of a property, the property reference is placed on the right side of the equal sign.

The following statement sets the Text property of a text box control, which is an object:

```
Text1.Text = "Visual Basic"
```

This next statement retrieves the value of the Text property and prints it to the Immediate window:

```
Debug.Print Text1.Text
```

Exposing object functionality as methods

Methods are exposed code routines. When a method or property is exposed to client applications, it is called a public method or public property, respectively. The standard ListBox control has a number of public methods such as AddItem, RemoveItem, and Clear. Methods may or may not return a value, but they never appear in the Properties window. Methods are new to ActiveX controls and are made possible through COM. Before ActiveX controls, developers used custom controls with the extension VBX. These VBX controls were not COM objects, and they did not support methods. Instead, the functions of VBX controls were exposed using properties. One way many VBX controls exposed functions was through an Action property. When the user set the Action property to a predefined value, the control would execute a function based on that value.

Exposing object feedback as events

Properties and methods allow a client to easily communicate with an ActiveX object. However, they do not afford a way for an ActiveX object to easily communicate with the clients that are using it. One workaround is to expose a property, such as a Status property, that the client could continually evaluate. When the property returned an anticipated value, the client could perform any necessary functions. But this is a hack at best. It makes code difficult to follow, and forces clients to either check the property within a loop, or start a timer to check the property at regular intervals. This in turn can cause an enormous drag on performance.

COM objects allow you to expose *events*, just as Visual Basic objects, such as controls and forms, expose events. By raising an event, the object alleviates the need for the client to implement odd hacks, such as checking property values in loops, to determine when a condition is met within the object. When you define objects, you have full control over what events are exposed (if any), the parameters included with each event, and the conditions under which any given event is raised.

 In addition to creating object events, ActiveX clients can communicate with ActiveX servers (objects) using *OLE callbacks*. OLE callbacks are discussed in Chapter 4.

Standard COM Interface

In order for a COM object to be used, it needs to be *instantiated*. Instantiation is the process that creates a new object instance in memory, as well as a *reference* that can be given to client applications to access the object. There are two levels of instantiating and referencing objects. First, there is the code that you write in Visual Basic. The second level is where COM itself actually creates objects and provides references. Mercifully, Visual Basic shields you from the second level, making it very easy to instantiate and reference COM objects from within Visual Basic.

On the Exams

Although the focus of this and the proceeding chapters is on creating custom component interfaces, COM objects have a number of standard interfaces (called COM interfaces) that, as a Visual Basic programmer, you'll never directly use. These standard interfaces implement the core functionality of COM objects and are hidden from you by Visual Basic. Ordinarily, *you will never call the functions of these interfaces directly.* Even though you don't directly work with them in Visual Basic, you are still likely to encounter one or more questions regarding these standard interfaces on the exams.

The IUnknown interface, the base interface from which all COM interfaces are inherited, is involved with returning references to an object's other interfaces, counting object references, and deleting objects that are no longer used. The IUnknown interface has the following three functions:

- AddRef
- Release
- QueryInterface

Every COM object has an internal counter that keeps track of the number of clients referencing the object. When you create an object reference in Visual Basic using the techniques discussed in this chapter, the AddRef function of the IUnknown interface for that object is invoked and its internal object reference counter is incremented. Once again, it's important to note that this is handled by Visual Basic and COM; you never directly call the AddRef function. When you destroy an object reference, the Release function of the IUnknown interface is invoked. The Release function decrements the internal reference counter. When the internal reference counter reaches 0, COM destroys the object, freeing the system resources used by the object.

While you don't have to understand all of the internal COM interfaces, it is critical that you understand the COM interfaces used to create and release object references. In the sections "Creating ActiveX Objects," and "Releasing ActiveX Objects," later in this chapter, you will learn how to create and destroy object references in Visual Basic.

Putting ActiveX Objects to Work

ActiveX objects generally fall into one of two categories: objects that are referenced only through code (ActiveX code components known as ActiveX DLLs), and objects that can be embedded on a parent object (such as an ActiveX control, which can be embedded on a form or web page). Within these two categories, there are many "flavors" of ActiveX objects. You need to be able to determine which type of object is best for a given situation. Each type of ActiveX component is discussed in this section. However, you will need to read all of the chapters that focus on one type of component to fully understand the strengths, weaknesses, and purposes of each.

Sharing Code Functionality Through Automation

Automation is the process of using objects in one application (the server) from another application (the client). Word, for example, exposes almost all of its functionality through ActiveX objects. By creating a reference to Word's objects and then manipulating the properties and methods of those objects, you can control Word. This is Automation, and it allows you to easily reuse components. For instance, you can use Automation with Excel to perform complex mathematical functions using the code that's been written and tested within Excel, rather than having to write and debug the complex code yourself. Applications that expose objects for Automation are called ActiveX *servers*. Often, solutions involve Automation with multiple servers, such as reading data from an Access database and sending the data to a Word document. You'll learn how to create ActiveX servers in Chapter 4.

Speeding Development Using ActiveX Controls

ActiveX controls are probably the best understood of the various ActiveX objects—at least from a user's perspective. ActiveX controls let you incorporate complex functionality into an application with minimal effort. ActiveX controls are quite common, and Visual Basic ships with a number of them. The Common Dialog control, which allows developers to quickly and easily add file system browsing operations to their Visual Basic applications, is an ActiveX control. Not too long ago, ActiveX controls had to be developed in C. As of Visual Basic 5, you can create these reusable objects using Visual Basic. Creating ActiveX controls using Visual Basic is discussed in Chapter 4.

Creating Reusable Forms Using ActiveX Documents

ActiveX documents are the newest type of ActiveX object, and probably the least understood. Think of an ActiveX document as a form that behaves like an ActiveX control or embedded object. This "form" can be opened in any container that supports ActiveX documents. Currently, Microsoft Explorer and Binder are the only applications that act as a container of ActiveX documents, but this may change in the near future. Some say that ActiveX documents were a solution looking for a problem, and that there are now better alternatives to ActiveX documents, such as DHTML. Even though ActiveX documents haven't been widely accepted in the real world, and chances are good you've never used one, you are still required to demonstrate a proficiency of them on the exams. Creating ActiveX documents is discussed in detail in Chapter 6.

Using the OLE Control to Expose Objects

The OLE control, which has been around for quite a while now, lets you expose documents created in ActiveX servers by embedding them in a Visual Basic form. The truly nice feature of the OLE control is that it not only allows you to expose a document, such as a Word document, it also lets you expose the parent application's interface right on your own forms. This functionality is called *in-place activation*, and is usually initiated by the user double-clicking the document contained in an OLE control. Once the document is activated, the interface elements of the document's parent, such as its toolbars and menus, become visible and usable within your application.

Creating ActiveX Objects

ActiveX objects are used in client applications by way of an *object reference*. An object reference can exist only once an object has been created, or instantiated. The process of obtaining a reference to an object is known as *binding*. Once an object is instantiated and a valid reference to the object is obtained, the client application can manipulate the object's properties and methods and respond to its events by using the object variable that is bound to the object. There are two methods used to bind an object to a variable: *early binding* and *late binding*. Regardless of the method of binding you choose, you'll use the Set statement to create an object reference.

On the Exams

Understanding the difference between early and late binding is critical to your success in using ActiveX servers, as well as in passing the exams. Be prepared—you will be asked questions about early binding versus late binding.

Creating an Object Reference Using the Set Statement

Before diving into early versus late binding, you must first understand how objects are manipulated using object variables. Once you obtain a reference to an object and assign it to a variable, you can manipulate the object using the variable. To assign an object reference to a variable, you use the Set statement.

The following code creates an object variable, and then assigns a reference to an existing text box control to the variable. Finally, the text contained in the control is printed:

```
Dim obj As Object
Set obj = Text1
Debug.Print obj.Text
```

A text box is a COM object (as are all of Visual Basic's controls). As a COM object, the text box has properties, methods, and events, all of which can be utilized via an object variable. Notice the Set statement on the second line. Whenever you assign an object to a variable, you *must* use the Set statement, as opposed to using only an equal sign. If you don't use the Set statement, your code will fail. Although this error is relatively easy to catch while debugging when the variable involved is dimensioned as type Object or as a specific object type, it's difficult to catch these errors if the variable is a Variant. This is just one of the many reasons to avoid using Variant variables.

Consider the following code:

```
Dim obj As Variant
obj = Text1
Debug.Print obj.Text
```

Executing this code causes the following error on the third line:

```
Run-time error '424'
Object Required
```

The cause of this error may not be immediately apparent to you. The following steps explain, in order, exactly what is happening:

1. A new variable of type Variant is created. This variable is called *obj*. Remember, variants can contain any type of data, including integers, strings, and even objects. You are often at the mercy of Visual Basic to determine what type of data it stores.

2. The variable *obj* is set to Text1. Because there is no Set statement on this line, Visual Basic assumes, as it must, that you are not assigning an object. Therefore, since there is no explicit property of Text1 referenced, it uses the text box's default property, Text. So, the contents of Text1's Text property is assigned to the *obj* variable, and the *obj* variable contains string data, not an object reference.

3. The last line of code attempts to print the Text property of the *obj* variable. However, the *obj* variable does not contain an object, it contains a string, and the error occurs.

On the Exams

You will be asked to demonstrate your understanding of how to place an object reference in an object variable. Remember, you must use the Set statement.

Calling an Object's Members Using Dispatch IDs

In order to fully understand binding, you must understand how COM handles interface calls made by clients. Each interface element (property, method, or event) of a COM object has a unique associated *Dispatch ID*. These Dispatch IDs are what are actually used by COM to reference an interface member. The member's name, although used in code, is not what is used by COM to access an interface member. For the most part, Visual Basic automatically assigns Dispatch IDs when you compile an ActiveX component. In an effort to promote consistency and standardization, Microsoft has defined a number of standard Dispatch IDs. For example, the Dispatch ID of 0 is always assigned to the default property of an object. As you'll see in Chapter 5, you can assign standard Dispatch IDs to custom members of your ActiveX objects. Other than these standard Dispatch IDs, you cannot control the assignment of Dispatch IDs.

You never actually use a Dispatch ID to call a member of an object; you reference a member's name instead. The calls you make to a member using its name must, however, be cross-referenced to the proper Dispatch ID. Early binding and late binding are two different processes for retrieving the correct Dispatch IDs for member calls.

COM supports a number of standard interfaces that you, as a Visual Basic programmer, never see. Earlier, you learned how the IUnknown interface manages reference counts. In addition to the IUnknown interface, COM exposes an interface called IDispatch. The IDispatch interface contains the functions shown in Table 3-2 for invoking members of an object.

Table 3-2: IDispatch Interface Members

Function	Purpose
GetTypeInfoCount	Determines if type information is available for this interface
GetTypeInfo	Retrieves type information for the interface
GetIDsOfNames	Finds the Dispatch ID for a method or property
Invoke	Executes a method or set or retrieves a property value

---

On the Exams

Like the IUnknown interface, you will never directly call the functions of the IDispatch interface. However, these functions are used when binding to an object, and you will have to demonstrate an understanding of them on the exams.

Binding an Object Reference to a Variable

As discussed earlier, objects can contain any number of properties, methods, and events; every object is different. When you write code to manipulate an object, Visual Basic must understand the interface of the object or your code won't work. Resolving the interface members occurs when your object variable is *bound* to an object. There are two forms of binding: *early binding* and *late binding*, and binding can occur at runtime or at compile time. There are benefits to both types of binding, but in general, early binding is superior because code that uses late-bound objects requires at least 50% more work by Visual Basic than code that uses early-bound objects, and therefore early binding objects results in significantly better performance under most conditions.

Late binding

When you dimension a variable as type Object, as shown in the following code, you are late binding to the object:

```
Dim x As Object

Set x = New MyObject
```

When you late bind an object, the binding occurs at runtime when the `Set` statement is executed. When you reference an interface member in code, such as by setting a property, Visual Basic must obtain the Dispatch ID of the member in order to successfully call the member. The following is what occurs when you reference a member of a late-bound object:

1. A call is made to the `GetIDsOfNames` function of the `IDispatch` interface to find the Dispatch ID of the property or method you specify.

2. An array of variants containing the parameters of the member is created.

3. The Invoke function of the `IDispatch` interface is called to execute the method or set the property.

These steps require a great deal of overhead and adversely effect the performance of an application. Remember, late binding is *not* the preferred method of binding. There are, however, some occasions where late binding is desirable. You might want to use late binding when:

* You want to write code that can work with many different types of objects.

* A type library is not available (see next section).

Early binding

If Visual Basic can determine a Dispatch ID for a member at compile time, there is no need to call the `GetIDsOfNames` function in the `IDispatch` interface. Instead, the Dispatch ID can be saved within the compiled program file, resulting in considerably faster calls to object members. When an object variable is declared so that the Dispatch IDs of the object can be resolved at design time, the object variable is said to be *early bound*.

The following are important reasons to use early binding:

* Speed.
* Speed.
* More speed.
* Objects, their properties, and their methods appear in the IntelliSense dropdown lists. (The IntelliSense dropdown lists are the lists that appear when you press a period (.) after typing an object's name.)
* The compiler can check for syntax and reference errors in your code. This is because Visual Basic can validate that a given member exists and that you have supplied the proper number and type of parameters at design time.

The following must occur to perform early binding:

1. The type library of the object must be referenced.
2. An object variable must be declared as a specific object type (i.e., not As Object).

Type libraries are resources that contain detailed Automation descriptions of objects. Clients fetch information about objects from an Automation server by inspecting the server component's type library, which provides information about the interfaces supported by the object, including:

- Descriptions of the properties, methods, and events provided by the object
- The return types and parameters of the object's methods and events
- The Dispatch IDs of the methods and properties
- The name of the help file and help topics to be displayed for the object and its methods and properties

Type library information can be included in an EXE or DLL file, or distributed as standalone type library files with the extension TLB, or sometimesO OLB (Object Library). When you create an ActiveX component with Visual Basic, the type library information is compiled directly into the component file. One of the benefits of external type library files is that they can be distributed to developers who can use them to write applications that early bind to objects—without the developers needing to have the actual applications containing the objects.

To create a reference to a type library:

1. Choose References from the Project menu to display the References dialog box.
2. Locate the ActiveX Automation server type library whose object(s) you want to work with, and select its checkbox.
3. Click OK to accept your selections and close the References dialog box. You won't notice anything different until you attempt to declare a variable. At that time, the newly referenced server appears in the dropdown list of valid datatypes.
4. Dimension a variable in code as a specific object type belonging to the type library you referenced.

The order in which selected objects appear within the References dialog box determines their *priority*. In Chapter 4, you'll learn how to create global ActiveX components whose functions appear to be part of Visual Basic and require no explicit object variable reference. When Visual Basic encounters such a function call, it must look at the referenced servers to determine which global server contains the function. The priority of the servers in the Reference dialog box determines the order in which the servers are looked at by Visual Basic. Once a global server is found that contains the function, Visual Basic stops looking and calls the function in the server.

Once you create a reference to a type library, the objects of the newly referenced Automation server become available just as though they are internal Visual Basic objects. The easiest way to see this is by typing a Dim statement in a module. After typing the keyword **As** (as in **Dim MyVariable As...**) and pressing the spacebar, the IntelliSense dropdown list displays the available datatypes. In addition to the standard datatypes such as String and Integer and Visual Basic's object types, you'll also see the Automation server you referenced.

Figure 3-2 shows the IntelliSense dropdown list displaying the Word Automation server in a project in which the Microsoft Word 8 object library has been referenced.

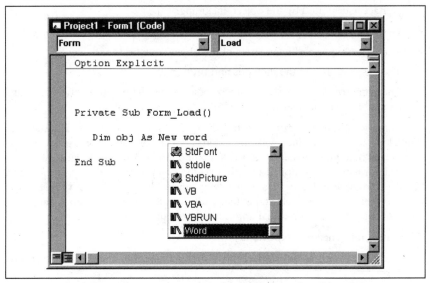

Figure 3-2: Early-bound servers appear in the IntelliSense dropdown list

Once you select an Automation server and type a period (.), the dropdown list displays the objects available from the server. Figure 3-3 shows the IntelliSense dropdown list displaying Word's objects.

When you declare a variable as a specific type of object, you are always early binding to the object. Nevertheless, you have two ways to actually create an early-bound object. Consider this code example, which creates a reference to a fictitious Employee object:

```
Dim x as Employee
Set x = New Employee
```

This code dimensions a variable as an Employee object. It then instantiates a new Employee object and assigns it to the variable. In addition to the **Set** statement, you can use the keyword **New** in a **Dim** statement to create a variable, like this:

```
Dim x as New Employee
```

There are a few issues you need to understand when using the **New** keyword. First, using **New** on a **Dim** statement doesn't actually instantiate an object like the **Set** statement does. Instead, it creates an object variable that is "ready to go." What this means is that as soon as you use the object variable in any way, such as

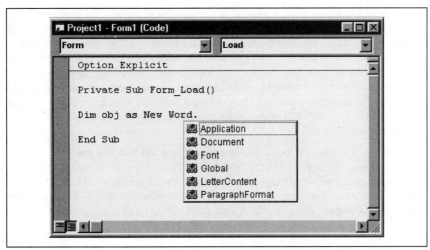

Figure 3-3: Early-bound objects are available as though they are internal Visual Basic objects

by referencing a property of the object held within the variable, Visual Basic will create a new object. This means that an object variable declared with the keyword New may have an object in it when you think it doesn't.

Consider the following code, which references Word's Application object:

```
Dim objWord As New Word.Application

objWord.Activate

Set objWord = Nothing

objWord.Activate
```

Setting an object variable to Nothing releases the object reference (you'll learn a lot about Nothing later in this chapter). You might think the fourth line would generate an error 91—*Object Variable or With Variable Not Set*. Actually, you would get this error if the variable was declared without using the keyword New. However, variables declared with the keyword New are always "ready to go." The third line does indeed release the object reference and causes the object to be destroyed. However, when you reference the object variable on the fourth line, Visual Basic automatically instantiates a new object and assigns it to the object variable. How many objects are instantiated after the first line of code executes? None. How many after the fourth executes? One.

 Early binding is *considerably* faster than late binding.

Early binding has two approaches. This section has discussed the first approach, using Dispatch IDs. Visual Basic supports a second approach, called *vtable binding*. With vtable binding, Visual Basic can obtain an offset into a virtual function table (called a *vtable*), and can use the offset to call a function directly, without having to call the Invoke method of the IDispatch interface. Using vtable binding to call a method of an in-process component created with Visual Basic requires no more overhead than calling a function within the client application itself. Hence, vtable binding is faster than binding to Dispatch IDs (called DispID binding).

Applications that support both vtable and IDispatch binding are said to have *dual interfaces*. All objects created with Visual Basic support IDispatch binding (both early and late) *and* vtable binding, and therefore all Visual Basic objects expose dual interfaces. You do not have to specify a method of binding when using objects within Visual Basic; Visual Basic determines the optimum method available and uses it.

Referencing object servers that expose events

Many types of ActiveX objects can have events. An event is essentially an outgoing interface of a component; it is almost the inverse of a method. In fact, an event acts very much as if a server is calling a method within its client. An object that has events is called an *event source*.

Using events of ActiveX controls is fairly straightforward. First, you place the ActiveX control on a form, then you double-click the control to access the code window and the control's events. Although not as obvious, it is also possible to use events from an Automation server even though the server has no user interface and isn't placed upon a form. In order to use a server that has events, you *must* early bind to the server's objects. In this section you'll learn about the general concepts behind using a server's events, including how to bind to servers that expose events. In Chapter 4, you'll learn how to create events for your ActiveX objects.

To use an Automation server that exposes events, you need to let Visual Basic know that the server is an event source by adding the WithEvents keyword to the Dim statement used to create an object variable. The following Dim statement creates a new fictitious Employee object that has events:

```
Dim WithEvents objMyVariable As Employee
```

On the Exams

You will be asked to demonstrate the proper way to use the WithEvents keyword to declare an object. Remember that the WithEvents keyword appears after the Dim statement. Also, be sure to read and memorize the limitations of using WithEvents, which are discussed later in this section.

A Dim statement that contains WithEvents *must* be declared in a class-based module such as a class module or a form module; you can't declare a variable using WithEvents in a standard code module. In addition, the object must have module-level scope, which means it must be declared in the Declarations section of the module, not within a specific procedure. Figure 3-4 shows a simple declaration of the object outlined in Table 3-3.

Table 3-3: Members of the clsMyObject Class

Property	Setting
Object Name	clsMyObject
Properties	none
Methods	none
Events	TestEvent

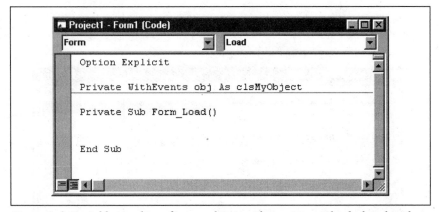

Figure 3-4: Variables used to reference objects with events must be declared in the declarations section of a class-based module

Once you've properly declared an object variable using WithEvents, the object appears in the object list of the module's code window as shown in Figure 3-5.

After selecting the object from the object list, you can access the events of the object just as you would those of a control on a form (see Figure 3-6).

Dimensioning an object using WithEvents has the following limitations:

- The object variable must be declared as a specific type of object, not as a generic Object. For instance, this statement would not work:

  ```
  Dim WithEvents obj as Object     ' Incorrect
  ```

  Because you cannot dimension a variable as Object if you want to support its events, objects dimensioned using WithEvents are always early bound.

- You cannot use the keyword New when declaring a variable using WithEvents. You must first declare the object, then use the Set statement to instantiate the object.

- You cannot dimension a variable using WithEvents in a standard module.

- You cannot create a variable array using WithEvents.

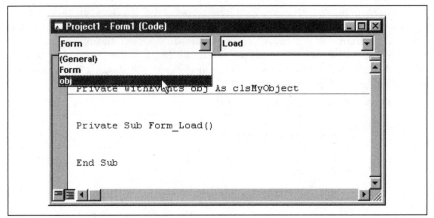

Figure 3-5: Object variables declared using WithEvents appear in the object dropdown list of the code window

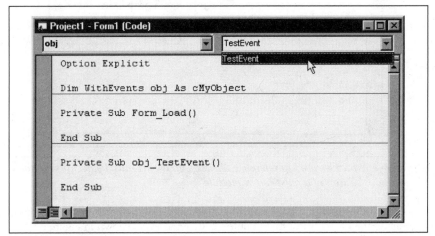

Figure 3-6: The events of the object variable appear in the Events dropdown list of the code window

 Be sure to follow the examples throughout Chapter 4 to better understand working with a server's events.

Although using New (with Set or with Dim) is the preferred way to create object references, it is not the only way. In the next section, you'll learn how to create and obtain object references using the *CreateObject* and *GetObject* functions.

Using CreateObject and GetObject

In addition to creating new instances of an object using the keyword New, you can also create objects using the *CreateObject* function. (To retrieve a reference to an existing object, you can use the *GetObject* function.)

The *CreateObject* function has the following syntax:

```
CreateObject(class, [servername])
```

The **class** argument is the application or library name and the name of the class to create. The **servername** parameter is used to designate a server when creating objects on other computers.

Creating an object using the *CreateObject* function is usually performed when late binding an object.

Consider the following code:

```
Dim obj As Object

Set obj = CreateObject("word.application")
```

This code creates a new Microsoft Word Application object using late binding. The parameter for the *CreateObject* function is the class you want to create (prefixed by its server name). This is the same string you would use if you were early binding. For example, the next two code samples create a new Word object, just as the preceding code example does, but both examples use early binding:

```
Dim obj As New Word.Application
```

or

```
Dim obj as Word.Application
Set obj = New Word.Application
```

 The samples that follow assume that a reference to the Word object library has been added in the References dialog box.

You should use *CreateObject* when there is no current instance of the object and early binding is not an option. The advantage to using *CreateObject* to late bind an object is that you can create any type of object you want in an object variable. When you define an object variable for early binding, the object can only hold a reference to an object of the declared type.

 You can also use *CreateObject* when early binding; however, a better option is to dimension the object variable as a specific type and instantiate the object using the New keyword.

CreateObject creates a new instance of the object, even if the specified object is already instantiated. To retrieve a reference to an already instantiated object, or to start the object's application and have it load a file, use the *GetObject* function.

 If an object has registered itself as a single-instance object (such as in Word 6.0), only one instance of the object is ever created, no matter how many times *CreateObject* is called.

The *GetObject* function has the following syntax:

```
GetObject([pathname] [, class])
```

pathname is the full path and filename of the file you want the server to load, and the *class* parameter is the full class identifier, just like the one used in the *CreateObject* function. If you pass a zero-length string to *pathname*, a new object of the specified class type is created. For example, the following code creates a new Word document:

```
Dim obj as Object
Set obj = GetObject("", "word.document")
```

This next piece of code opens an existing Word document called *test.doc*:

```
Dim obj as Object
Set obj = GetObject("c:\test.doc", "word.document")
```

 If no current instance of the desired object is found when you call *GetObject*, no object is created and an error is returned.

You can omit the class name if you supply a valid filename. If you omit the class name, Visual Basic will attempt to determine the Automation server by looking in the registry, just as it does when you double-click a file in Explorer. Be warned, however, that it is possible for a user to have a different server configured for a file extension than the one you expect.

For example, the following sample code will use an existing instance of Word and open the *test.doc* document *if* Word is currently running *and* files with the extension *.doc* are registered for Word:

```
Dim obj as Object
Set obj = GetObject("c:\test.doc")
```

Visual Basic puts you in full control of instantiating objects. However, destroying unused objects is handled by COM itself. If you don't understand how COM destroys objects, you may create applications that take up more resources than necessary and that may not perform as intended. The next section explains the lifetime of an ActiveX object, and how to use this knowledge to make your applications clean up after themselves.

Understanding the Lifetime of an ActiveX Object

An object exists as long as an application has a reference to it. Fortunately, COM itself handles the details of keeping track of the references to a given object; you don't have to worry about this when creating or using objects. Even though COM keeps track of the number of references that exist for an object and destroys the object when that count reaches zero, this does not eliminate all responsibility on your part. You still need to know the following key points of an object's lifetime, and what they mean to your application:

- An object is created (and hence referenced) when an object variable is declared with **As New** and a member of the object is referenced.

- An object is created (and hence referenced) when an object variable is assigned an object using **Set** with **New**.

- An object is referenced when an object variable is assigned an existing object using the **Set** statement.

- An object reference is released when an object variable is set to **Nothing** (see the following section "Releasing ActiveX Objects").

- An object is destroyed when the last reference to it is released.

The way to tell whether or not an object variable contains an object while debugging is to use the Locals window or the Watches window. *You will be asked this on the exams.* These windows are discussed in detail in Chapter 9, *Testing and Debugging.*

In order to better understand the lifetime of an ActiveX object, it's best to create a simple project. Follow these instructions to create a small test project in Visual Basic:

1. Create a new Visual Basic Standard EXE project

2. Add a new class to the project and call it **clsMyObject**.

3. Add the following code to the default form's Load event:

```
Dim obj As clsMyObject

Stop      ' First locals check

Set obj = New clsMyObject

Stop      ' Second locals check
```

4. Run the project by pressing F5.

When code execution halts at the first Stop statement, display the Locals window by choosing Locals Window from the View menu. The Locals window will look like the one in Figure 3-7.

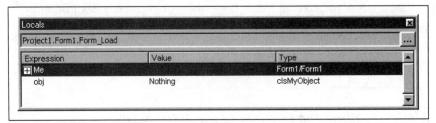

Figure 3-7: An object variable that does not contain a reference to an object displays Nothing as its value in the Locals window

As you can see, the *obj* object variable contains Nothing; that is, there is no instantiated object assigned to it. Continue code execution by pressing F5 once again. When code execution pauses at the second Stop statement, look again at the Locals window. This time, there is no Value column (see Figure 3-8). Having no value is quite different than having a value of Nothing, just as a Null is not the same as a zero-length string. Also note that the Type column of the variable now contains the name of the class twice, denoting the type of variable and the class instance that it references.

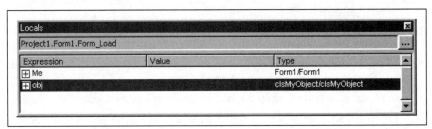

Figure 3-8: An object variable that contains a reference to an object does not have a value in the Locals Window

---

On the Exams

You will be asked how to determine the contents of an object variable. Remember, the Locals window and the Watches window are the proper tools.

Understanding the lifetime of ActiveX objects is very important. You've now seen how and when object references are created, but you also need to know how to explicitly release an object reference. Only when all references to an ActiveX object are released can the object be destroyed and the resources it uses reclaimed. The next section explains how to release ActiveX object references.

Releasing ActiveX Objects

When you no longer need an object, the object should be destroyed. Destroying an object frees up all of the resources used by the object. Objects are destroyed automatically when the last reference to the object is released, so your job consists of releasing object references when they are no longer needed. Once you release the last reference, COM destroys the object for you. There is only one correct way to release the object reference, and you will be asked how to do this on the exams.

You can never be assured that an object is fully released *and* all the memory being used by an object is freed by letting an object's variable go out of scope. This is *not* the preferred way of releasing an object, and it is *not* recommended.

To release an object, set the object variable equal to `Nothing`, as shown in the following line of code:

```
Set obj = Nothing
```

Once again, notice the `Set` statement. Just as when assigning an object reference, you must use the `Set` statement when setting the object to `Nothing`. When you set an object variable equal to `Nothing`, you can be assured that the object reference is fully released. If any other variables are referencing the object, however, the object will not be destroyed. After the last reference is released, COM destroys the object.

On the Exams

You will probably be asked how to release an object reference. Remember, setting the object variable to `Nothing` is the only way to ensure the object reference is fully released.

Remember, if you reference a property or method of an object variable declared with `As New` and the variable currently contains `Nothing`, a new instance of the object is automatically instantiated.

If you don't correctly release object references, your application may become sluggish and consume more resources than it should. Also, you may inadvertently make references to incorrect objects (for example, if you think that an object reference points to an object that it does not actually point to or that a variable contains `Nothing` when it actually points to an object).

Using the Object Browser

Applications can and often do contain numerous objects, and each object may have dozens of members. Because it can be difficult to remember all of the objects and members of an application, Visual Basic includes the Object Browser (see Figure 3-9). The Object Browser lets you view all of the objects referenced in a project, as well as all of the members of those objects. To use the Object Browser, choose Object Browser from the View menu or press the F2 key. Once the Object Browser is loaded, you can select from any of the object libraries referenced in the current project using the top dropdown list. Once you've selected an object library, all objects within the library are displayed in the Classes list box. Selecting an object from the Classes list box displays all of the properties and methods of the class/object.

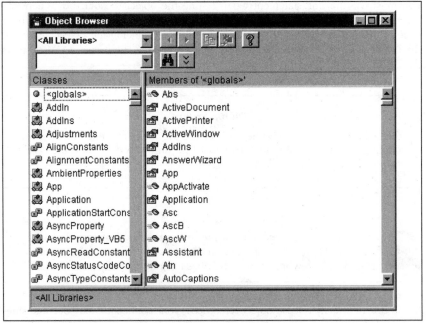

Figure 3-9: The Object Browser is the best tool for exploring an object's properties and methods

The second dropdown list on the Object Browser is used for searching. To search for a string, simply type the string in the second dropdown list and click Search.

Only the object library or libraries specified in the first dropdown list are searched. In addition to searching, you can use the Object Browser to quickly move to the code of a class, module, or procedure in your project by double-clicking the member in question in the Members list box.

The Object Browser is an indispensable tool for working with objects, and you should get accustomed to using it. So far, this chapter has taught you about what constitutes the interface of an object, how to create and release object references, and how to use the Object Browser to view objects and their members. Next, you'll learn about the different types of programs (servers) that expose objects.

In-Process Versus Out-of-Process Servers

All 32-bit Windows applications run in their own process space, and Windows can run many different processes at once because Windows is a multitasking environment, able to switch from one process to another at an incredibly fast rate.

COM

On the Exams

It is extremely important both for passing the Visual Basic exam and for developing efficient applications that you understand how processes are handled when using ActiveX components. Specifically, you need to understand the difference between an in-process and an out-of-process server.

In-process servers are ActiveX components that run in the same process space as the client application using them. In-process ActiveX code components are compiled as ActiveX DLLs. *Out-of-process servers* are ActiveX components that run in their own process space, and therefore can be shared by many clients at one time. Out-of-process servers are compiled as ActiveX EXE files. When a client makes a property or method call to an in-process server or an out-of-process server, code execution in the client halts until the server is finished executing its code (see Figure 3-10). There are benefits and drawbacks to both types of servers. What constitutes a benefit versus a drawback, however, depends on the situation.

Table 3-4 lists the different types of ActiveX applications (objects) you can create with Visual Basic and whether they are in-process or out-of-process components.

Table 3-4: In-Process and Out-of-Process ActiveX Components

Project Type	Component	Server Type
ActiveX EXE	ActiveX-enabled application	Out-of-process
ActiveX DLL	ActiveX code component	In-process
ActiveX Control	ActiveX control	In-process
ActiveX Document DLL	ActiveX document	In-process
ActiveX Document EXE	ActiveX document	Out-of-process

As you can see, ActiveX applications with an EXE extension are out-of-process servers, whereas those with the DLL extension are in-process servers.

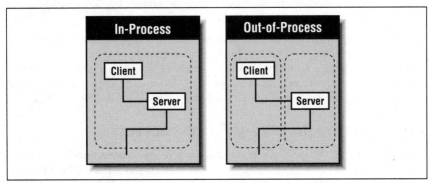

Figure 3-10: In-process servers run in the same process space as their clients, while out-of-process servers always run in their own process

In-process servers are considerably faster than out-of-process servers. When you attempt to bind an out-of-process server to a client, ActiveX creates a proxy object that has the same interface as the out-of-process server. When you make a call to a property or method of the bound server, you actually make a call to the proxy server. Windows then copies the parameters you passed to the property or method to the process in which the out-of-process server is running (see Figure 3-11). This operation is called *marshaling*. Marshaling takes system resources—both in time and memory. Therefore, out-of-process servers are slower and use more resources than in-process servers.

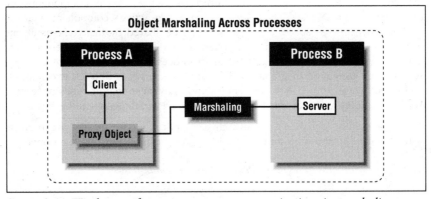

Figure 3-11: Windows performs cross-process communication via marshaling

If a client makes a call to an out-of-process server that is currently executing code for another process, the request is queued and is effectively blocked until the server is finished with what it is doing. (This is not the case with in-process servers, as you'll see in Chapter 4.) The client application is in a halted state, waiting for the out-of-process server to return execution back to the client. To prevent blocking, you could instantiate a separate instance of the server for each client, but then you incur the overhead of running multiple applications, each being marshaled by the operating system. With an in-process server, each client is running its own server so there is no queuing involved.

ActiveX is an awesome, and somewhat daunting, technology. To fully leverage your skills as a developer you need to understand COM, and properly implement COM functionality in your applications where appropriate. The Microsoft Visual Basic exams stress these skills; expect numerous questions on COM.

Creating Three-Tiered Client/Server Applications

You've probably heard the term three-tiered client/server, but you may not have been involved with an actual implementation of such a solution. Three-tiered applications are the current "holy-grail" of software development. In truth, creating large three-tiered applications is a lot of work and requires extensive technical knowledge and patience. Even though you may not yet be creating three-tiered applications, you will nevertheless encounter questions about this on the exams.

In Chapter 12, *Creating Microsoft Transaction Server Components*, you'll learn about Microsoft Transaction Server (MTS) and how it aids in the implementation of three-tiered applications. This chapter explains what three-tiered applications are and why you might use them. In addition, you'll learn about a few of the problems associated with creating applications using the three-tiered architecture.

Three-tiered applications are designed around COM and the benefits of COM, and they are primarily database-driven applications. Traditional database application architecture is usually composed of two tiers: the application and the database (see Figure 3-12). The application itself contains the user-interface, the business rules, and the code to access the database. Two-tiered applications work well on a small scale, and they are the most common form of network-based application in use today.

Including the business rules within the application causes a number of problems when it comes time to distribute new business rules. For instance, if there is a change in the way taxes must be handled within your application, every user that performs tax calculations *must* obtain the latest version of the application. If only some users obtain the update, there's a tremendous risk of generating inaccurate data. Ensuring a complete distribution of such a critical update to the entire user population in a large company can be difficult.

The performance of two-tiered applications is also an issue. Because two-tiered applications consist of all of their code, business rules, and data access routines,

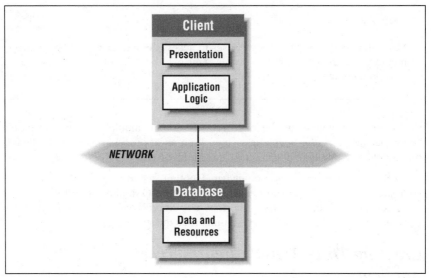

Figure 3-12: Two-tiered applications contain all of their code, business rules, and database access routines in a single application file

and because they run on the client machine, the client machine incurs all of the resource costs associated with the application. This isn't the case with three-tiered applications. Also, two-tier applications use a file server data provider such as Jet rather than a client/server data provider such as SQL Server. With two-tiered file server databases, the client performs all of the data manipulation. If a client needs to query 500,000 records and return a result set of 5 customers, the client machine must perform all of the data access via the network connection. This can take an anguishing amount of time. Finally, the database must maintain connections to each active client. This once again consumes resources, and reduces performance as more clients access the database.

In addition to performance being an issue with the database in a two-tiered system, so are locking contentions. When a client requests a row of data to edit from the database, a row lock or page lock is placed on the table. While the data is locked, other clients are prevented from manipulating the data, and must wait until the locks are freed to proceed.

Database security is also a concern in a two-tiered environment. In two-tiered situations, permission must be given to users at the table level. Users with permission to access a table are free to perform any actions within the constraints of their permissions. The user must also be given full read and modify rights to the folder containing the database, which exposes a number of other security challenges.

With three-tiered applications, the application logic (business rules), data components, and client interface (presentation) exist as separate components, as shown in Figure 3-13. The middle-tier is composed of COM objects that encapsulate the application logic and database access routines. The client applications use the objects of the middle-tier servers to add, modify, delete, and search the database, in addition to call application logic routines.

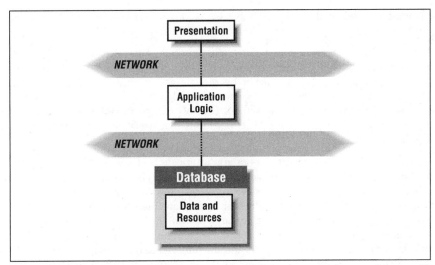

Figure 3-13: Three-tiered applications separate presentation, application logic, and data access into distinct components

The three-tiered approach has a number of benefits. First is the issue of maintainability and ease of deployment. The middle-tier servers run on dedicated servers rather than on the client machine. The middle-tier objects can and do serve many different clients. These clients may be a variety of applications running on different platforms. As long as they can access COM objects, they can use middle-tier objects and access the back-end database. Because the COM objects are isolated on one or more servers, updating the objects requires updating only those servers. When a change in the way data is accessed or the way business rules are applied causes the need for a new object to be written, it can be deployed to a few machines rather than to hundreds or thousands. Because all database access is performed through the middle-tier objects, anyone accessing the database is using the most current objects with the most current business rules.

Performance is another benefit gained by using middle-tier objects running on dedicated machines. The client applications aren't accessing the database directly, and therefore network bandwidth use is kept at a minimum. Most often, the machines running the middle-tier objects are very fast computers loaded with memory. The objects often have to serve a large number of clients, so fast and reliable hardware is a must. Another performance benefit is that middle-tier components can share database connections. The lower the number of active connections to the database, the faster the performance of database access.

Because all of the database access for the client applications are handled by the COM objects, the COM objects can actually manipulate multiple databases from different data sources transparently. The client application doesn't have to know the details of the databases involved. The ability to access multiple data sources is very important in large corporate environments where many different types of legacy data exist. In addition, since all database access is handled through the COM objects, developers can phase out one data source in favor of another by changing the code within the COM objects. As long as the interfaces of the objects don't change, clients will continue to work with the new COM objects.

The client application (the first tier) only presents data; it runs on the client machine and exposes the user interface. It works with the database by manipulating the middle-tier objects—never by directly accessing the database directly. The front-end client application is often composed of ActiveX controls that further encapsulate functionality. These ActiveX controls can be incorporated into many different types of clients, giving all applications that use them a consistent interface to the middle-tier objects.

Designing and implementing three-tier applications is a challenging task, and it's a methodology that's gaining huge acceptance. You will encounter questions on the exams related to three-tiered applications. You might be asked to specify on which tier an ActiveX control might best be implemented (the client application). You may also be given the parts of an application (such as user interface or accounting logic) and be asked to isolate the components into one of the tiers. Be sure to have a good grasp of COM and an understanding of the material in this section; then read about COM components in Chapter 4, DCOM in Chapter 13, and Microsoft Transaction Server in Chapter 12. All of these concepts are related, and you'll need to grasp them all to pass the exams.

Key Facts

This chapter has discussed COM, the basic foundation of ActiveX. The following are key points to understand in order to answer COM-related questions correctly on the Visual Basic exams:

- OLE is now ActiveX.

- There are three types of ActiveX objects: code components (DLLs), controls, and documents.

- ActiveX technology is built on a foundation of objects, known as the component object model (COM).

- COM objects encapsulate data and code, shielding the client from the intricacies of managing the data.

- COM objects employ a standard mechanism for referencing and releasing objects.

- COM objects are created from classes.

- COM objects expose a standard interface.

- Automation is the process of using objects that belong to another application to control that application and/or use its functionality.

- Late binding occurs when object variables are declared **As Object**. All property, method, and event calls are resolved at runtime.

- Early binding is the process of creating a reference to a type library, and declaring object variables as specific object types. All property, method, and event calls are resolved at compile time.

- Early binding, which is faster than late binding, is the preferred method of binding objects.

- The Set statement is used to create a reference between an object and an object variable.

- The New keyword allows you to instantiate an object without using Set.

- To view the contents of an object variable, use the Locals or Watches windows.

- To dimension an object that has events, use the WithEvents keyword.

- To create a reference to a late-bound object when there is no current instance of the object, use the *CreateObject* function.

- To use the current instance of an instantiated object, or to start the object's application and have it load a file, use the *GetObject* function.

- An object is created (and hence referenced) when an object variable is declared with As New and then has one of its members referenced.

- An object is created (and hence referenced) when an object variable is assigned an object using Set with As New.

- An object is referenced when an object variable is assigned an existing object reference using the Set statement.

- An object reference is released when an object variable is set to Nothing.

- An object reference is released when an object variable goes out of scope and the variable is destroyed.

- An object is destroyed when the last reference to it is released.

- To view detailed information about an object or class, use the Object Browser.

- In-process servers are ActiveX components that run in the same process space as the client application that is using the servers.

- Out-of-process servers are ActiveX components that run in a process space separate from their clients. Multiple clients may share a single out-of-process server.

- Marshaling is the operating system procedure that allows an ActiveX client to access the interface (and hence the memory) of an out-of-process server.

- Two-tiered applications are suitable for department-size deployments.

- In two-tiered applications, the presentation, application logic (business rules), and data access are incorporated into one application, accessing a file server database.

- Three-tiered applications have better security, faster performance, and more scalability than two-tiered applications.

- Microsoft Transaction Server is designed to manage the middle-tier in three-tiered applications.

Applying What You've Learned

It's now time to apply what you've learned about COM. First, answer all of the questions in the Skills Assessment. By correctly answering all of these questions, you'll be demonstrating a solid understanding of COM. After you've answered the assessment questions, work through the hands-on exercises.

Skills Assessment

1. Which routines show early binding?

   a. `Dim x as Object`

      `Set x = New Employee`

   b. `Dim x as New Employee`

   c. `Dim x as Object`

      `Set x = CreateObject("Business.Employee")`

   d. `Dim x as Employee`

      `Set x = New Employee`

2. How many instances of *clsMyClass* exist at the `Stop` statement?

   ```
   Dim obj As New clsMyClass
   Dim obj2 As clsMyClass
   Stop
   ```

   a. 1

   b. 2

3. Which of the following are in-process servers?

   a. ActiveX DLL

   b. ActiveX control

   c. ActiveX EXE

4. Which of the following are true statements?

   a. COM objects provide encapsulation of data and code.

   b. COM objects employ a standard mechanism for referencing and releasing objects.

   c. To use COM objects, a type library must be available.

   d. COM objects are created from classes.

5. What is the process of using objects that belong to another application to control that application?

   a. Dynamic Data Exchange (DDE)

   b. Automation

6. Which form of binding produces faster applications?

   a. Early binding

   b. Late binding

7. Which is the proper way to declare an object variable for an Employee object that has events?

    a. `Dim objEmployee WithEvents As New clsEmployee`

    b. `Dim WithEvents objEmployee As clsEmployee`

    c. `Dim WithEvents objEmployee as New clsEmployee`

    d. `Dim objEmployee WithEvents As clsEmployee`

8. Given the code below that uses an object based on a clsEmployee class that has a single property called Name, how many Employee objects are instantiated at the Stop statement?

```
Dim obj As New Employee
Set obj = Nothing
obj.Name = "John Doe"
Stop
```

    a. 0

    b. 1

    c. 2

9. What two tools can you use to determine the contents of an object variable?

    a. Object Browser

    b. Locals window

    c. Immediate window

    d. Watches window

10. In which two situations should you use the *CreateObject* function?

    a. Creating a reference to an object when there is no current instance of the object.

    b. You want to assign many different types of objects to an object variable.

    c. You want to pass the object to functions that can handle many different types of objects.

    d. You want to create an instance of an existing object.

11. The actual process the Windows operating system uses to allow an ActiveX process to access the interface (and hence the memory) of an out-of-process server is called:

    a. Multitasking

    b. Marshaling

    c. COM

12. Which part of a three-tiered application might best be implemented as an ActiveX control?

    a. Database access

    b. Business rules (middle-tier)

    c. Presentation

13. Which tier in a three-tiered application would be most suitable for implementing tax calculation routines in a personal finance application?

    a. Presentation

    b. Business rules (middle-tier)

    c. Data components

14. What are two advantages that three-tiered applications have over two-tiered applications?

    a. Easier to develop

    b. Better security

    c. Serve larger clients

    d. Require less hardware

Answers to Skills Assessment

1. b, d	4. a, b, d	7. b	10. a, b	13. b
2. a	5. b	8. b	11. b	14. b, c
3. a, b	6. a	9. b, d	12. c	

Hands-on Exercises

Now that you have a thorough background of COM and ActiveX objects, you're going to put the knowledge to use to create an ActiveX client. Remember, an ActiveX client is not a form of ActiveX object, but rather an application that makes use of other ActiveX objects. In Exercise 3-1, you are going to create a client that uses Automation to access functions and features of Microsoft Excel.

Exercise 3-1: Creating an Excel client in Visual Basic

In this exercise, you'll apply several of the skills covered in this chapter to create an ActiveX client that manipulates Excel through Automation. This exercise was written to work with Excel 97 or later. You need to have Excel installed on your computer in order to complete this exercise.

 This exercise references a number of objects and properties of Excel. It is beyond the scope of this text to teach Excel's object model. For more information on the details of the objects and properties discussed here, refer to Excel's documentation or to the book *Writing Excel Macros*, by Steve Roman, also available from O'Reilly.

Section 1. Creating a reference to Excel's type library. In this section, you'll create a new Visual Basic project and add a reference to Excel's type library. This will allow you to create an instance of Excel's Application object using early binding. The steps are:

1. Start Visual Basic and create a new Standard EXE project.

2. Choose References from the Project menu to display the References dialog box.

3. Locate the type library titled Microsoft Excel 8.0 Object Library (if you have a different version of Excel, the name of the type library may differ) and select its checkbox.

4. Click OK to close the References dialog box.

Section 2. Getting an instance of Excel's Application object. Now that you've created the reference to Excel's type library, you need to write code to get an instance of Excel's main object, the Application object.

5. Create a form-level object variable to contain the reference to Excel's Application object by adding the following line of code to the default form's Declarations section:

```
Dim objExcel as Excel.Application
```

6. Add a new command button to the form, name it cmdUseExcel, and set its Caption property to "Use Excel."

7. Make the command button obtain an instance of a new Excel Application object using the *CreateObject* function, by adding the following code to the command button's Click event:

```
Set objExcel = CreateObject("Excel.Application")
```

 Although *CreateObject* is used here for illustrative purposes, you could (and probably should) use the statement Set objExcel = New Excel.Application. You could also avoid having to use a Set statement altogether by dimensioning the variable using the New keyword. This is not always the best solution, however, as explained earlier in this chapter.

Section 3. Displaying Excel and creating a new workbook. Now the fun begins. Once you have a reference to the Excel Application object, you can fully manipulate the object. In this section, you are going to force Excel to show itself, then you are going to create a new workbook and a new worksheet within the workbook. All of the code in this section needs to be entered in the cmdUseExcel command button's Click event, *after* the Set statement you entered in the previous part.

8. When the Excel Application object is first instantiated with the Set statement, Excel isn't visible. Force Excel to display itself using the Visible property of its Application object. Enter this line of code after the Set statement discussed in the previous section:

```
objExcel.Visible = True
```

9. Next, create a new workbook by using the Workbooks collection of the Application object. Enter this line of code:

```
objExcel.Workbooks.Add
```

Section 4. Manipulating data on the worksheet. Now that you have a new workbook, you're going to add some data to its first worksheet. Then you're going to select the data and have Excel total the selected cells. Once the data is totaled, you'll have Excel bold the text in all of the data cells, including the Sum cell.

10. You manipulate cells in a worksheet by manipulating the ActiveCell object. The ActiveCell object is a property of the Application object, so you use the Application reference when manipulating cells. Entering data in a cell involves first selecting the cell, then passing data to the selected cell. To select a cell, use the Select method of the Range object (also an object property of the Application object). The Range object accepts a starting column and row and an ending column and row. Since you're selecting only one cell at a time, you can omit the ending column and row. Once the range is set, use the FormulaR1C1 property to place data in the cell. Add the following code statements to place data in the first 4 cells:

```
objExcel.Range("A1").Select
objExcel.ActiveCell.FormulaR1C1 = "100"
objExcel.Range("B1").Select
objExcel.ActiveCell.FormulaR1C1 = "150"
objExcel.Range("C1").Select
objExcel.ActiveCell.FormulaR1C1 = "200"
objExcel.Range("D1").Select
objExcel.ActiveCell.FormulaR1C1 = "250"
```

11. Next, use the Range object again to select a range of cells. Enter this line of code to select the 4 cells in which you have placed data:

```
objExcel.Range("A1:D1").Select
```

12. Now that you have the range of cells selected, you'll once again use the FormulaR1C1 method to add data to a cell. This time, however, you're going to enter an actual formula, rather than a constant as you did in the code in step 1 of this section. Enter this line of code:

```
objExcel.ActiveCell.FormulaR1C1 = "=SUM(RC[-4]:RC[-1])"
```

13. Next, use the Range object again to select not only the first 4 cells, but also the new cell that holds the summation formula. Enter this line of code to select all 5 cells:

```
objExcel.Range("A1:E1").Select
```

14. To show a sum of all four selected cells, you must activate a cell in which to place the summation. Once again, use the Range object, but this time use the Activate method instead of the Select method. If you used the Select method, the range would be deselected. Add this line of code now:

```
objExcel.Range("E1").Activate
```

15. Finally, apply a bold format to all of the selected cells using the Selection object by adding this next line of code:

```
objExcel.Selection.Font.Bold = True
```

Here is a complete listing of the cmdUseExcel command button's Click event:

```
Set objExcel = CreateObject("Excel.Application")

objExcel.Visible = True

objExcel.Workbooks.Add

objExcel.Range("A1").Select
objExcel.ActiveCell.FormulaR1C1 = "100"
objExcel.Range("B1").Select
objExcel.ActiveCell.FormulaR1C1 = "150"
objExcel.Range("C1").Select
objExcel.ActiveCell.FormulaR1C1 = "200"
objExcel.Range("D1").Select
objExcel.ActiveCell.FormulaR1C1 = "250"

objExcel.Range("A1:D1").Select

objExcel.Range("E1").Activate

objExcel.ActiveCell.FormulaR1C1 = "=SUM(RC[-4]:RC[-1])"

objExcel.Range("A1:E1").Select

objExcel.Selection.Font.Bold = True
```

Section 5. Releasing the Excel object. Once your application has finished using the Excel object, it needs to release the reference to it. To release an object variable's reference to an object, you set the object variable to Nothing. Note: when you set the object variable to Nothing, the object is released, but Excel does not close down; it remains running. This is just a peculiar feature of Excel itself. In this part, you're going to create a button that closes the workbook you created and fully releases the object variable.

16. Add a new command button to the form and name it cmdCloseWorkbook. Change the Caption property of the new command button to "Close Work- book."

17. Make the command button close the active workbook by using the Close method of the ActiveWorkbook object. The parameter is used to tell Excel whether or not to save changes. Add this code to the new command button's Click event:

```
objExcel.ActiveWorkbook.Close False
```

18. Finally, release the object reference by setting the object variable to Nothing with this line of code:

```
Set objExcel = Nothing
```

Section 6. Running the Excel client. Your project is now complete and you're ready to test it. Run the project and click the Use Excel command button. Excel loads, and your client adds data to the first 4 cells, sums them in the fifth cell, and then bolds all of the cells (see Figure 3-14). When you're satisfied that all of this has completed successfully, click the Close Workbook command button to close the active workbook and release the object variable reference.

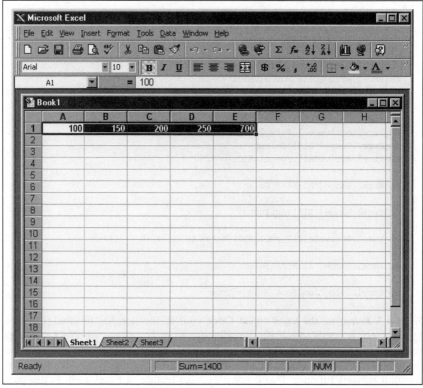

Figure 3-14: Controlling Excel through Automation is easy using a Visual Basic client

Highlighter's Index

COM

Microsoft's underlying object technology
OLE is now ActiveX

COM Components

Built on class modules
Encapsulate data and code
Have standard and custom interfaces
Variety of types of COM components
Objects are instantiated using object variables
COM objects have a lifetime

Binding

DispatchIDs
Early binding is faster than late binding
vTable binding

In-Process Versus Out-of-Process

In-process is faster than out-of-process
ActiveX DLLs run in-process
ActiveX EXEs run out-of-process

COM

CHAPTER 4

Creating and Testing ActiveX
Code Components

Chapter 3, *Understanding COM*, covered COM, the foundation of ActiveX, and taught you how to create an Excel client application. You are able to create an Excel client because Excel is an out-of-process ActiveX server. ActiveX servers expose objects that can be created and controlled by other applications (clients). This chapter will teach you how to create your own in-process (DLL) and out-of-process (EXE) servers (collectively referred to as ActiveX code components).

In this chapter you'll learn how to create ActiveX code components and enable them for different types of instancing, and you'll learn all about interfacing between clients and servers, including raising errors within client applications. In addition, you'll learn about creating multithreaded objects with Visual Basic—a topic of growing importance. Finally, you'll learn the proper techniques for testing both in-process and out-of-process components.

Most of the techniques discussed in this chapter apply equally to creating class modules that are not exposed to clients, but rather that are only used within the application. Such classes are used just like the server classes discussed in this chapter, so there is no need to devote a section or chapter solely to these classes. In a Standard EXE project, all classes are private to the application. In an ActiveX type of project, the Instancing property of a class (discussed later in this chapter) determines whether or not the class is visible to client applications. For more information on how objects are derived from classes, refer to Chapter 3, *Understanding COM*.

The Technologies and the Exams

Both exams ask questions related to ActiveX servers. In particular, you'll probably be asked questions on how to debug ActiveX components on both exams, and therefore this topic receives extensive coverage in the text and is also covered in the hands-on exercises. The Distributing exam (70-175) will ask questions related to creating ActiveX components for use with Microsoft Transaction Server (MTS). MTS components are always ActiveX DLLs, so you'll want to fully understand how to create ActiveX DLLs in addition to learning the MTS-specific information in Chapter 12, *Creating Microsoft Transaction Server Components*. Also covered on the Distributed exam is Visual Basic's threading model and how to create multithreaded components. If you've never created a multithreaded component, you'll want to read this section carefully; you won't be able to fake it on the exams. Although neither exam specification mentions `AddressOf`, you may encounter questions about `AddressOf` on either exam. In short, all of this material (as delineated in Table 4-1) is very important for both exams, and you should fully understand all that is discussed here before taking either exam.

Table 4-1: Coverage of ActiveX Components on the Exams

Topic	Covered on Exam
Creating ActiveX code components	Both
Implementing an interface	Both
Using implements	Both
Raising errors in a client application	Both
Creating asynchronous callbacks	Both
Creating system callbacks using `AddressOf`	Both
Creating remote servers	Both
Creating multithreaded components	Distributed
Testing and debugging ActiveX code components	Both

Creating ActiveX Code Components in Visual Basic

In order to create efficient ActiveX servers, you must first decide what type of ActiveX code component you will be building. The New Project dialog box shown in Figure 4-1 lets you select the type of project to create: an in-process ActiveX DLL or an out-of-process ActiveX EXE.

 You can change an existing project to a different project type using the Project Properties window (discussed later in this chapter), but if objects in your project are not compatible with the newly selected format, they will be forced to fit (for example, Standard EXEs require a startup object while some other project types don't), and you may have to make changes to the project to get it to work correctly.

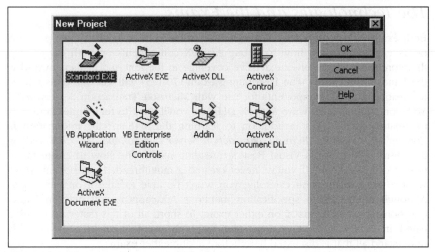

Figure 4-1: Project types are specified when creating new projects

Setting an Object's Instancing Property

Every class that you expose to Automation as an object, whether in an in-process or out-of-process server, has an *Instancing* property. The Instancing property determines how and when an object can be created. To set the Instancing property of an object, set the Instancing property of the class module from which the object is derived. (To change properties of a class module, display the class module in a code module window. When the class module's Code window is active, the Properties window displays the properties for the class.)

Your objects can have any of the following Instancing settings:

1-Private

 When you set a class's Instancing property to 1-Private, other applications (clients) aren't allowed access to type library information about the class (the class cannot be viewed in the Object Browser), and clients cannot create instances of the class.

 You should mark classes as 1-Private when they are for use only within your ActiveX code component.

2-PublicNotCreatable

 Clients can use objects marked as 2-PublicNotCreatable only if the object was instantiated within your application; clients cannot instantiate new objects from the class. Therefore, clients cannot use the *CreateObject* function or the New operator to create objects from the class. Use this setting to create objects that can be used by clients, but that must be instantiated by your application. Typically, such objects are instantiated as a child of a creatable class when you don't want the client to be able to create new instances but you do want it to be able to manipulate existing instances.

3-SingleUse

When you set a class's Instancing property to 3-SingleUse, every object instantiated from the class starts a new instance of the *server application*; each server manages only one instance of the object. This setting cannot be used with ActiveX DLLs, only ActiveX EXEs. You may choose to create single-instance ActiveX EXEs when creating a single-threaded component and sharing global data among clients is a concern.

4-GlobalSingleUse

Classes set to GlobalSingleUse are similar to SingleUse classes in that only one client can use an instance of the object at any point in time, and that each time a client instantiates an object from the class, a new instance of the server application is started. However, when an object is GlobalSingleUse, the methods and properties of the object appear as though they are intrinsic Visual Basic methods and properties.

For example, consider this code:

```
' This code goes in a standard module.
' Declare a global variable to contain the instance of
' of the class.
Public objUtility As New clsUtilities

' This code goes in a form that uses a property of the
' Utilities object.
Private Sub cmd_Click()

    txtTextTaxRate.Text = objUtility.LocalTaxRate

End Sub
```

This procedure retrieves the LocalTaxRate of the Utilities object. If the Utilities object is set as a GlobalSingleUse object, you don't have to explicitly reference the object variable as shown above; the methods and properties of the object are available as though they are built-in Visual Basic functions. With the clsUtilities class set to GlobalSingleUse, you could use the following code instead of the previous procedure:

```
' Declare a global variable to contain the instance of
' of the class.
Public objUtility As New clsUtilities

' This code goes in a form that uses a property of the
' Utilities object.
Private Sub cmd_Click()

    txtTextTaxRate.Text = LocalTaxRate

End Sub
```

As with SingleUse objects, GlobalSingleUse objects are not applicable to ActiveX DLLs.

5-MultiUse

A class marked as 5-MultiUse will allow any number of objects to be instantiated from it; one instance of the server application can provide any number of objects derived from the class. This is the default Instancing property of an ActiveX DLL class. Often, multiuse classes are created to encapsulate a record in a database. For instance, in a contact management application, you probably don't care how many contacts are created or edited, so you could create a multiuse clsContact class.

6-GlobalMultiUse

GlobalMultiUse is similar to MultiUse. However, when an object's Instancing property is set to GlobalMultiUse, the methods and properties of the object appear as if they are intrinsic Visual Basic methods and properties (see the text on GlobalSingleUse).

Table 4-2 shows the allowable settings for Instancing based on project type (ActiveX EXE, ActiveX DLL, ActiveX Control, or Standard EXE).

Table 4-2: Instancing Properties for Different Project Types

Setting	ActiveX EXE	ActiveX DLL	ActiveX Control	Std. EXE
Private	✗	✗	✗	✗
PublicNotCreatable	✗	✗	✗	
SingleUse	✗			
GlobalSingleUse	✗			
MultiUse	✗	✗		
GlobalMultiUse	✗	✗		

Once you understand instancing, you're ready to start creating in-process and out-of-process ActiveX servers.

On the Exams

Be sure you understand object instancing; you will be expected to demonstrate your understanding on the exams.

Deciding on a Project Type: ActiveX EXE or DLL

Both ActiveX EXEs and ActiveX DLLs are Automation servers; clients can manipulate the public objects of the servers. When creating Automation servers, you must decide which type of server best suits the needs of a given situation. Remember, ActiveX EXEs run out-of-process, while ActiveX DLLs run in-process. There are benefits to both, and the following are general guidelines for determining the type of server to create:

- If the server is ever to be run as a standalone application, it *must* be an ActiveX EXE.

- If you want the server to run in the same process space as the client (giving better performance), make the ActiveX server a DLL.

- If you want the server to run in a separate process space (or even on a separate machine) from the client, allowing both client and server to execute functions concurrently, make the ActiveX server an EXE.

- If you want one server to serve many clients, sharing global variables, make the server an EXE.

 For a complete explanation of the behavior and benefits of in-process versus out-of-process components, refer to Chapter 3.

ActiveX objects are created from class modules; you can't have an ActiveX component without having some sort of class module. So whether you create an ActiveX EXE or an ActiveX DLL, all new projects will have at least one object: a class module. Therefore, you will always have to determine the instancing of at least one class in an ActiveX EXE or ActiveX DLL project.

Setting Project Properties for ActiveX Code Components

After creating a new ActiveX project, you should immediately change some of the project's properties to tailor the behavior of the ActiveX server. To access the Project Properties dialog box shown in Figure 4-2, choose Project Properties from the Tools menu.

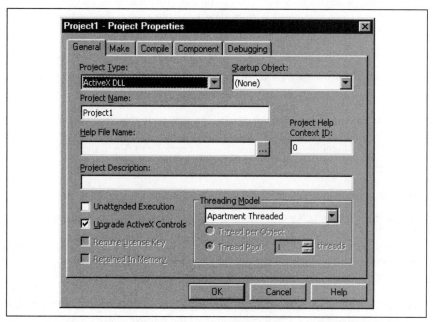

Figure 4-2: Use the Project Properties dialog box to tailor your ActiveX applications

The Project Type property is set for you when you create a project, but you can change it if needed. The fields you most need to be concerned with, and that relate specifically to ActiveX projects, are Startup Object, Project Name, Project Description, and Unattended Execution.

You will see the terms "ActiveX servers" and "ActiveX code components" used interchangeably throughout this chapter. They are the same thing.

Selecting a startup object

With both types of ActiveX servers, you have the option of designating Sub Main as a startup object, or you may select None. If you select Sub Main, you *must* have a standard module in your project with a subroutine called *Main*. This subroutine is the first code executed when your component starts. (Note that this behavior is the same as it is for Standard EXE projects.) Sub Main is the perfect place to put initialization code for the entire component (as opposed to initialization code for an individual class.)

You cannot designate a form as a startup object of an ActiveX code component. You must select Sub Main or None. If you want to display a startup form for your server, designate Sub Main as your startup object and create a Sub Main subroutine in a standard module that loads and displays your startup form.

If you don't specify a startup object (i.e., if you select None), the first code that is executed when your server starts is the code of the first object instantiated. For example, if you had an object called Employee, and a client application instantiated an instance of the Employee object, the first code that would execute in the ActiveX server application is the code from the Initialize event of the Employee class. After the Initialize event is fired, events continue to fire in their normal order of execution.

Naming your project

The project's Name property is extremely important. The text you enter in the project's Name property is displayed in the Object Browser; the text becomes the component's library name in the type library. In addition, the project name is required to instantiate new objects. As you'll recall from Chapter 3, you can use the *CreateObject* function to create a new instance of an object. The *CreateObject* function requires you to pass to it two values: the project name and the class name. For example, when you used *CreateObject* to create a new instance of Excel's Application object in Hands-on Exercise 3-1, you used the following statement:

```
Set objExcel = CreateObject("Excel.Application")
```

The first substring of *CreateObject*'s parameter is the Project Name, in this case Excel, while the second substring is the name of the class to instantiate. These two values are always separated by a period. If you were to expose a public class called Employee in a project with its Project Name set to Sales, clients could instantiate a new Employee object using either of the following statements:

```
Set objEmployee = CreateObject("Sales.Employee")
```

or:

```
Dim objEmployee As New Sales.Employee
```

 The Project Name property cannot include spaces.

Giving your project a description

The project description text is what the Object Browser displays to describe the type library of the component, and it's the text that appears in the list on the References dialog box. If you don't supply a project description, the project name property is displayed instead; however, you should always enter a project description.

 Most ActiveX developers prefix their project descriptions with their company name. For example, a spin control written by Odin Technologies may have a project description of Odin Technologies—Spin Button control. It's considered *very* bad form to prefix your project description with a nonalphabetic character just to have it appear at the top of the list. The component list is not a popularity or voting contest; users will locate your server in the list if they need it.

Marking your project for unattended execution

The Unattended Execution property is used to suppress the display of user-interface elements in multithreaded components. Creating multithreaded components is discussed in detail later in this chapter.

Component tab settings

In addition to the settings on the General tab, there are some settings on the Component tab (see Figure 4-3) that affect the behavior of an ActiveX server as well. The names and definitions of these settings are:

Start Mode
> Determines whether or not your ActiveX EXE server starts as a standalone program or as an ActiveX component. Start Mode is discussed in more detail later in this chapter.

Remote Server

Lets you create remote automation servers designed to be run across networks. Remote Servers are discussed later in this chapter.

Version Compatibility

Allows you to create updated components that don't break clients designed to use an older version of the component. The Version Compatibility option is discussed in detail in Chapter 11, *Optimizing an Application for Distribution*.

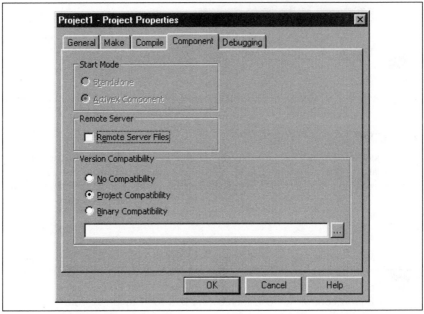

Figure 4-3: The Component tab contains settings that affect the behavior and interoperability of a component

Implementing an Interface

Once you've created a new ActiveX EXE or DLL and set the appropriate project properties, all you have is the shell of a component. A client can instantiate a public object of the server, but it can't actually interact with the server. To allow client applications to interact with your ActiveX code component, you must expose an interface. The interface of your component consists of the public objects available in the component, as well as properties, methods, and events of those objects.

Creating properties using property procedures

Properties are the attributes of objects. Think for a moment in terms of a Combo-Box control. The combo box has a number of properties, such as Height and Width. Some properties are read-only (such as Height), while others can be changed in addition to having their values read.

There are two ways to add properties to a class. The first (and least desirable) is to declare public variables. Any variable declared as Public instantly becomes a property of the class. For example, say you have the following statement in the Declarations section of a class module named ObjectVariable:

```
Public Quantity as Long
```

Clients could read the property and write to the property using code such as this:

```
ObjectVariable.Quantity = ObjectVariable.Quantity + 1
```

This works, but there are severe limitations that make this approach *very* undesirable. What if you need to execute code whenever the value of the property is changed? Since the client application can access the variable directly, you have no way of knowing when the value of the variable changes. What if you want the client to be able to read the property but not write to it? Once again, you have no control over this. Now, perhaps the most important problem: how do you control data validation? For instance, how could you ensure that quantity was never set to a negative value? Don't spend too much time trying to work this one out—you can't do it with a public variable. Instead of exposing public variables, you should create properties for a class using *property procedures.*

Property procedures let you execute code when a property is changed, validate property values, and expose properties as read-only, write-only, or both read and write.

The three types of property procedures are:

Property Get
    Returns the value of a property

Property Let
    Sets the value of a property

Property Set
    Sets the value of a property that contains an object

Defining Property Get procedures. To make a property that can have its value read as well as changed by clients (a read-write property), you must define two property procedures: a Property Get procedure and a Property Let/Set procedure. To make a property read-only, you only create a Property Get procedure. In the event you want to make a property write-only (something you probably won't ever have to do), create a Property Let (or Set) procedure but no Property Get procedure.

Declaring a property procedure is similar to declaring a standard Function or Sub procedure. Property Get statements are similar to Function procedures in that they return a value: the value of the property. Property Let statements, on the other hand, are more like Sub procedures; they require at least one argument (the value to be assigned to the property), but don't return a value. The following is an example of a Property Get procedure:

```
Private m_lngHeight As Long

Public Property Get Height() as Long
```

```
    Height = m_lngHeight

End Property
```

 When creating property procedures, Visual Basic creates a shell that defines the property's value as a variant. Instead, use the most explicit (strongest) datatype possible for all arguments and return values. This helps further eliminate the possibility that a bad value will be used as a property value.

The first part of the declaration simply designates whether the property is public or private. If you want client applications to have access to the property, you must create a public property procedure. Following the keyword Public or Private is Property Get, then the property name, then the datatype returned by the property. Instead of using End Sub or End Function as you do with ordinary procedures, you use End Property for all three types of property procedures.

In the preceding code example, m_lngHeight is a private variable declared in the Declarations section of the class module. Although the value of the Height property is stored in this variable, the client application never accesses the variable directly; the Property Get procedure passes the value of the height variable to the client when it queries the Height property.

Defining Property Let procedures. Property Let procedures are similar to Sub procedures in that they don't return a value. Look at the following example of a Property Let procedure:

```
Private m_lngHeight As Long

Public Property Let Height(ByVal New_Height As Long)

    m_lngHeight = New_Height

End Property
```

The procedure above lets the client pass in a new value for Height in the *New_Height* argument. The procedure then stores the value in the private variable m_lngHeight.

So far, the Property Let and Property Get procedures shown previously don't do anything different than if you were to simply declare a public variable. But look at this variation of the previous Property Let procedure:

```
Public Property Let Height(ByVal New_Height As Long)

    ' Don't allow values less than 10.
    If New_Height < 10 Then Exit Property

    ' Store the new value.
    m_lngHeight = New_Height

End Property
```

This Property Let procedure allows the client application to set the Height property to any value greater than or equal to 10. If a value less than 10 is passed to the property, the property procedure is exited without the variable m_lngHeight ever being changed. In addition to data validation, you could add other code, and even call other procedures.

Matching Property Get and Let parameters. If you make a property whose value can be both retrieved and set by a client, the parameters of the Property Get and Property Let procedures must match. Consider these two procedures:

```
Public Property Get Color() as OLE_COLOR
   ...
End Property

Public Property Let Color(ByVal New_Color As OLE_COLOR)
   ...
End Property
```

The datatype returned by the Property Get procedure is the same as the datatype of the value accepted by the Property Let procedure. If you attempt to create a Property Let and a Property Get procedure for the same property and you specify different datatypes for each, you'll get a compile error and your code won't compile.

Creating properties with multiple parameters. Although it's not intuitive, you can create properties with multiple parameters. The reason it's not intuitive is it doesn't make much sense to have a property such as Height accept two values. However, you can use multiple parameters to create an array for a property. For example, look at these two property procedures:

```
' Dimension array in Declarations section
Dim m_alngMyArray(255,255) As Long


Public Property Get Value(ByVal X As Byte, _
                          ByVal Y As Byte) as Long
   Value = m_alngMyArray(X,Y)

End Property


Public Property Let Value(ByVal X As Byte, _
                          ByVal Y As Byte, New_Value as Long)
   m_alngMyArray(X,Y) = New_Value

End Property
```

The final parameter in any Property Let procedure (whether single parameter or multiple parameter) is always the value to assign to the property.

The two property procedures listed above create a property array. To set the value of a particular array element, the Property Let procedure is called and passed the *X* and *Y* arguments and the new value to place in the array cell, like this:

```
obj.Value(0,5) = 7
```

To retrieve the value of a cell, the Property Get procedure is called with the *X* and *Y* parameters of the array cell whose value is to be returned, like this:

```
Debug.Print obj.Value(0,5)
```

As with single-parameter properties, the datatypes of multiple-parameter properties procedures must be consistent between Property Let and Property Get procedures.

Using Property Set procedures. Just as you can't set an object reference in code using only an equals sign, you can't pass object references to a Property Let procedure. Instead, you use Property Set procedures. Look at the following Property Get procedure:

```
Public Property Get MyObject() As Object
    ...
End Property
```

You might think that a **Property Let** declaration with an Object parameter would allow you to create a writable version of the MyObject property. However, from what you learned in Chapter 3, would the following code work?

```
Dim obj As Object
obj = New MyObject
```

No, this code won't work because **Set** is required when assigning object references. In order for this to work, you'd have to use a **Set** statement like this:

```
Dim obj As Object
Set obj = New MyObject
```

Property Set statements look like **Property Let** statements. For instance, the following property procedure would let you set the value of the MyObject property discussed previously to an object reference:

```
Public Property Set MyObject(New_MyObject As Object)
    ...
End Property
```

 While you have to use **Property Set** statements to create a writable object property, there is no special form of **Property Get**; **Property Get** returns object references without a problem.

You'll learn more about passing objects to property procedures later in this chapter in the section "Calling Object Servers Asynchronously Using Callbacks."

Exposing functions as methods

Unlike a property, which acts as an object attribute, methods are publicly exposed functions. Methods are easier to create than properties because they are defined just like ordinary Sub and Function procedures. To create a method within a class, simply create a public Sub or Function procedure like this:

```
Public Function AddTwoNumbers(Num1 As Integer, _
                             Num2 As Integer) As Long

    AddTwoNumbers = Num1 + Num2

End Function
```

A client could call the method like this:

```
Dim lngResult As Long
lngResult = object.AddTwoNumbers(100,47)
```

Just as with normal Sub and Function procedures, methods created with the keyword **Function** return values, while methods created with **Sub** do not.

Creating Friend procedures

Often, you'll want to expose properties and methods for a class so that they can be called from other modules within your application, but you don't want those properties and methods exposed to clients using the server. If you make a procedure private, however, only procedures within the module in which the procedure exists can use the private procedure. This creates the dilemma that the **Friend** keyword is designed to solve.

The **Friend** keyword (used in place of **Public** or **Private**) denotes a property or method as being *private to the program containing the object.* The following shows a property declared as **Friend**:

```
Friend Property Get HiddenProperty() As String
    ...
End Property
```

Friend methods are created much like public methods; simply substitute **Public** with **Friend**, like this:

```
Friend Sub DoSomethingPrivate()
    ...
End Sub
```

When a property or method is declared as **Friend**, all form and code modules in your project can call the method or reference the property, but the method or property is not actually part of the class's interface. The Friend procedure does not appear in the Object Browser because it's not included in the type library or the public interface of the application, and therefore client applications cannot access the method or property.

To use a Friend procedure within an application, you *must* early bind the object variable derived from the class that contains the Friend procedure. That is, you must declare the object variable whose Friend procedure you wish to call as a specific class type, not as an object; you cannot access Friend procedures using an object variable declared As Object (late bound) because the procedure doesn't exist in the public interface of the class, which is used when an object is late bound.

Communicating with clients by exposing events

Anyone who has ever programmed in Visual Basic, regardless of version, has used events. Visual Basic is an event-driven language; you can't write Visual Basic code without using events. Relatively new to Visual Basic is the ability to create events for your own objects.

To create an event within a class, you must:

1. Declare the event in the Declarations section of the class module.

2. Write code to raise the event where appropriate.

To use events of an ActiveX code component within a client you must:

1. Dimension an object variable using the WithEvents keyword.

2. Add code to the event.

Creating custom events within an ActiveX code component. The ability to create custom events is very cool. Your servers can use events to notify clients whenever and however you deem necessary without the need for creating OLE callbacks (discussed later in this chapter). The uses for custom events are almost infinite, but some common implementations are to notify a client when:

- An out-of-process server has completed a task.

- There is user input to the server's interface.

- A certain condition has been met.

When a server has a user interface, it's often necessary to notify a client when the user selects items or otherwise interacts with the interface. For example, you could create an ActiveX DLL that displays a Custom Color Selection form. When the user selects a color, you could raise an event to notify the client that the selected color has changed and tell it which color was selected. The client is then free to perform whatever actions are appropriate, such as changing the background of a form to reflect the current selection.

A custom event is often the best way to notify a client when a certain condition has been met. Say you had an object called EggCarton, with a property called EggCount and a method called AddOneEgg. When the EggCarton object is instantiated, the EggCount property contains 0 eggs, and at any given time the EggCarton can hold only 12 eggs. Each time the AddOneEgg method is called, the EggCount property is increased by 1. You could create a custom event called CartonAlmostFull that would fire when the EggCount property reached 11, notifying the client that the carton has almost reached capacity. You could even create a property called EggCountWarning to contain the number of eggs the carton must contain before the CartonAlmostFull event is fired. There are probably more efficient ways to handle this particular scenario, but it serves to illustrate the use of events to notify a client of a specified condition.

Custom events are declared in the Declarations section of a class module. The declaration for a custom event has the following syntax:

Event *EventName*([*argumentlist*])

argumentlist is a list of parameters that the server will pass to the event handler. Arguments are completely optional, and an event doesn't have to expose any arguments. To better understand how to declare an event and how to specify arguments, it helps to look at a standard event in Visual Basic and compare it with an equivalent event declaration. The following is the form class's MouseDown procedure:

```
Private Sub Form1_MouseDown(Button As Integer, Shift As Integer, _
                  X As Single, Y As Single)

End Sub
```

When you declare an event, you don't specify whether the event is `Public` or `Private`; all declared events in a public object are public to any applications using the object. When a custom event procedure is created within the client application, it is created as `Private` by default, but you can change it just as you can for standard Visual Basic events.

You could declare an equivalent event for the MouseDown event with the following statement:

```
Event MouseDown(Button As Integer, Shift As Integer, _
                  X As Single, Y As Single)
```

As you can see, the argument list in the Declarations section appears just as it would in the event procedure within the client.

You can use type-definition characters within the declarations statement, but they will appear in "long hand" in the event procedure, as shown in the previous code. If you're still using type-definition characters, you should start using a good naming convention instead.

argumentlist has the following format:

    [ByVal | ByRef] *varname*[( )] [As *type*]

The format of an event declaration's argument list is similar to the declaration of a Sub or Function procedure's argument list, except that events cannot have Optional or ParamArray arguments and named arguments cannot be used in the event procedures.

Just as with standard procedures, all arguments are passed by reference (ByRef) by default. To pass an argument by value (ByVal), you must supply the ByVal keyword. While an event's argument list is similar to a Sub or Function procedure, it cannot return a value as functions do.

Once you have an event declared within a class module, you must *raise* the event at the appropriate time. When the event is raised, the corresponding event procedure within the client is executed. To raise an event, use the RaiseEvent statement.

The RaiseEvent statement has the following format:

RaiseEvent *EventName*([*argumentlist*])

Once again, *argumentlist* is an optional list of parameters to pass to the corresponding event procedure. The argument list of a RaiseEvent statement is a comma-separated list of variables, arrays, or expressions. Each element of the argument list must correspond to an element of the argument list in the event declaration statement. (Remember, you cannot use named arguments.) If there are no arguments for the event, omit the parentheses.

You can use RaiseEvent only to raise events that you *specifically declare* within the class module. This is most restrictive to form modules; you can't raise a form's event (such as Load) using RaiseEvent. If an argument is declared ByRef (the default), you must supply a variable in the RaiseEvent statement. If an argument is declared ByVal, however, you may supply either a constant or an expression as the argument in the RaiseEvent statement.

A common argument of custom events is the *Cancel* argument. Consider the following custom event:

    Event BeforeUpdate(NewValue as String, Cancel as Boolean)

This event could be used in a class that performs data input and output. In such a case, the event would be fired before an update occurred to a record. The *NewValue* parameter would pass the data that is to be written to the record, while the *Cancel* parameter is used as a mechanism for the client to cancel the update. Look at the following procedure, which raises the BeforeUpdate event:

```
Public Sub SaveNewValue(NewValue As String)
    Dim blnCancel As Boolean

    blnCancel = False
    RaiseEvent BeforeUpdate(NewValue, blnCancel)

    If Not (blnCancel) Then
        ' Save code goes here
    End If

End Sub
```

This procedure is a method in the class that accepts a string as the new value to be saved in a database. The BeforeUpdate event is raised prior to the actual code that makes changes to the database. The BeforeUpdate event passes to its event procedure both the string that is to be written to the database and a reference to the *blnCancel* variable that has been initialized to **False**. If the *Cancel* parameter in the event procedure (the reference to *blnCancel* in the procedure just shown) isn't modified, *blnCancel* will remain **False**. However, users who decide not to save the value can set the *Cancel* parameter to **True** in the event procedure, and the save code won't execute. The next section will show you what custom event procedures look like within a client.

In the previous example, because *NewValue* is passed **ByRef**, it can be changed within the event procedure. If you didn't want this behavior, you could add **ByVal** to the argument in the event declaration.

Using custom events within a client application. An object that exposes events is known as an *event source*. To handle an event source's events within a client application, you need to declare an object variable using the **WithEvents** keyword. The following is the format of a **Dim** statement using **WithEvents**:

```
Dim WithEvents obj As ObjectClass
```

ObjectClass refers to an actual object type; you can't declare an object variable **As Object** when using **WithEvents**.

Dimensioning an object using **WithEvents** has the following limitations:

* Object variables declared **WithEvents** *must* be declared in a class-based module (e.g., class or form); you can't declare them in a standard module.

* The object variable must be declared as a specific type of object, not as a generic object. For instance, this statement would not work:

```
Dim WithEvents obj as Object        ' Incorrect
```

This limitation means that an object declared **WithEvents** is always early bound.

- You cannot use the New keyword when declaring a variable using WithEvents. You must first declare the object, and then use the Set statement to instantiate the object.

- You cannot create a variable array using WithEvents.

Consider the following object definition:

Propert	Setting
Object name	cMyObject
Properties	none
Methods	none
Events	BeforeUpdate

Figure 4-4 shows a declaration of an object variable that supports this object's event.

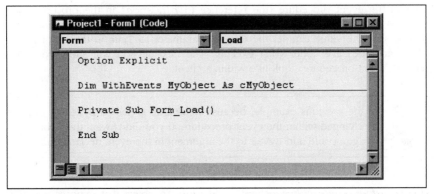

Figure 4-4: Object variables supporting events must be declared in the declarations section of a class-based module

Once you've properly declared an object variable using WithEvents, the object appears in the Object list of the module's Code window, as shown in Figure 4-5. After selecting the object from the Object list, you can access the events of the object just as you would a control on a form (see Figure 4-6).

 Be sure to perform the exercises at the end of this chapter to fully understand creating and using custom events.

Implementing Implements (sharing common interfaces)

Creating ActiveX objects is all about code reuse. You write ActiveX components (ActiveX servers, controls, or documents), and then reuse them as often as necessary. Another method of code reuse is using the Implements statement to enable one class to implement the interface of another class. Implements makes it easy to

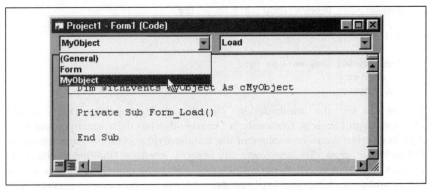

Figure 4-5: Object variables declared using WithEvents appear in the Object dropdown list of the Code window

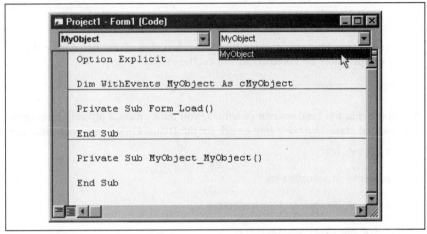

Figure 4-6: The events of an object variable appear in the Events dropdown of the Code window, just as events of controls do

create many different, yet similar, objects. At first glance, `Implements` appears to act simply as an interface template for the outer object (the object that implements the interface of another object). These inner interfaces are called *abstract classes*.

For example, suppose you have a DeluxeFridge class and a StandardFridge class, both of which return information about a particular refrigerator. Since a deluxe refrigerator is a modified version of a standard refrigerator, it makes sense to reuse part of the implementation of the StandardFridge class within the DeluxeFridge class.

Here is the definition of the StandardFridge class:

```
Option Explicit

Property Get Doors() As Byte
    Doors = 2
End Property
```

```
Property Get DoorsOrientation() As String
    DoorsOrientation = "Vertical"
End Property

Property Get Shelves() As Byte
    Shelves = 4
End Property
```

As you can see, the StandardFridge class has three properties: Doors, Doors-Orientation, and Shelves. Obviously, a DeluxeFridge has these same properties, so it makes perfect sense to implement the StandardFridge class interface within the DeluxeFridge class. To implement an object's interface (the inner object, or abstract class) within the interface of another object (the outer object), you use the Implements statement. The Implements statement has the following syntax:

```
Implements classname
```

On the Exams

An object can implement more than one class's interface. Remember this; you will probably be asked about this on the exams.

After specifying the Implements statement, you must create a private object of the implemented class. The basic framework for the DeluxeFridge class looks like this:

```
Option Explicit

Implements StandardFridge

Private objSFridge As StandardFridge

Private Sub Class_Initialize()
    Set objSFridge = New StandardFridge
End Sub
```

This is where it gets somewhat confusing. In order for your class module to compile, you must implement *all* of the interface elements of the inner object. To do this, open the Object dropdown list in the class module and select the class object that you specified using Implements, and then select each and every inter-face element of the class from the Procedures → Events dropdown list on the right. You won't actually place code in these private procedures, but *they must be there or the code will not compile*. The DeluxeFridge object now looks like this:

```
Option Explicit

Implements StandardFridge

Private objSFridge As StandardFridge
```

```
Private Sub Class_Initialize()
    Set objSFridge = New StandardFridge
End Sub

Private Property Get StandardFridge_Doors() As Byte
    '* Empty. This is delegated to the inner class.
End Property

Private Property Get StandardFridge_DoorsOrientation() _
    As String
    '* Empty. This is delegated to the inner class.
End Property

Private Property Get StandardFridge_Shelves() As Byte
    '* Empty. This is delegated to the inner class.
End Property
```

The last step is to add the equivalent interface elements to the DeluxeFridge class. Since the inner object StandardFridge contains three properties, you must declare the same three properties for the DeluxeFridge class. When a property or method of the outer object uses the equivalent property or method of the inner object, it's called *delegating*. The DeluxeFridge class delegates its Doors and DoorsOrientation properties to the StandardFridge class because the values are the same, so you would create the following properties within the DeluxeFridge class:

```
Public Property Get Doors() As Byte
    Doors = objSFridge.Doors
End Property

Public Property Get DoorsOrientation() As String
    DoorsOrientation = objSFridge.DoorsOrientation
End Property
```

As you can see, the DeluxeFridge class simply passes the appropriate property value from the implemented class back to the client referencing the property. Using **Implements** lets you not only delegate to the implemented object but also supply your own code instead of using delegation. The DeluxeFridge in this example has six shelves, as opposed to the four shelves of the StandardFridge class. So, instead of delegating to the implemented StandardFridge class, you would supply your own code for the Shelves property, like this:

```
Public Property Get Shelves() As Integer
    Shelves = 6
End Property
```

 If you don't want to implement a specific member of an inner class, you must still provide the procedure in code. However, you can (and should) raise an error (Const **E_NOTIMPL** = &H80004001) when a client calls the nonimplemented procedure. Raising errors is discussed in the next section of this chapter.

Creating an Application object

In Hands-on Exercise 3-1, you manipulated the Application object of the Excel server. Most ActiveX EXE servers have an object that acts as the primary object, or as the top-level object in the object model. More often than not, this object is called the Application object. The Application object contains the properties and methods of the application itself, such as the window state of a single-document interface application.

The name of an object is determined by the name of the class module from which it is derived, so to make a class module an Application object, change the name of the class module to Application.

In addition to correctly naming the class module, it is important that you correctly set the Instancing property of the class module. An Application object must always be available to its clients, so it should have its Instancing property set to a value that permits object creation by clients.

Hands-on Exercise 4-2 shows you how to create and use an Application object.

Raising Errors in a Client Application

It is extremely important that ActiveX objects correctly handle runtime errors. When an error is encountered within a standard application, a message box usually tells the user about the error. This won't do for ActiveX servers. Often, a user doesn't even realize an ActiveX server is in use. For example, suppose you have a loan calculation ActiveX DLL is called by numerous financial applications. If the loan calculation routine encounters an error and displays a message box, the user might get confused. Message boxes often contain the name of the application, and the name of the loan calculation server would not be the same as the name of the client application using the server. In addition, the client application making the call to the DLL would have no way of knowing that an error occurred, let alone which error occurred.

Before you can understand how to best handle errors within an ActiveX component, you need to understand what happens when an error is encountered within a component. When an unhandled error is encountered within an ActiveX component, the error is immediately raised *within the client application*. For example, consider the following procedure of a fictitious ActiveX DLL:

```
Public Function Divide(Numerator as Integer, _
                       Denominator as Integer) As Integer

    Divide = Numerator / Denominator

End Function
```

This function doesn't include an error handler (On Error Goto . . .). So what happens when a client calls this method using the following statement?

```
MsgBox obj.divide(6, 0)
```

You can't divide a number by 0, so a "division by 0" error occurs. Does the error get raised within the DLL? No, the error is raised *within the client at the statement that called the method.*

Now, consider this procedure:

```
Public Function Divide(Numerator as Integer, _
                        Denominator as Integer) As Integer

    On Error Resume Next

    Divide = Numerator / Denominator

End Function
```

Where is the error raised this time? Nowhere. Since the error is trapped, no error is raised. Because the procedure *Divide* is declared as Integer, the return value of *Divide* is not actually set because of the trapped error, and variables declared as Integer are initialized to 0, the calling procedure gets a return value of 0.

Although you can let errors within your component be automatically raised within the client application by omitting an error handler, this is not good practice. Client applications don't want to be concerned with exactly what errors occur within your code, but rather only in how those errors matter to them. In the previous example, wouldn't it make more sense to return an error such as "Denominator Out of Range," or "Denominator Cannot be Zero?" To control when and what errors are raised within a client, use the Raise method of the Err object. The Raise method has the following syntax:

```
object.Raise number, [source], [description], [helpfile], [helpcontext]
```

All parameters except *number* are optional. The Raise method of the Err object actually generates a runtime error just as though the error was encountered and not trapped in an error handler. By adding error trapping to your procedures and using Err.Raise to raise errors, you control how and when an error is passed to the client application.

The following are explanations of the Err.Raise parameters as defined by Visual Basic's Help:

Number
>Required. Long integer that identifies the nature of the error. Visual Basic errors (both Visual Basic–defined and user-defined errors) are in the range 0 to 65535. When setting the Number property to your own error code in a class module, you add your error code number to the **vbObjectError** constant. For example, to generate the error number 1050, use **vbObjectError** + 1050 as the *Number* argument.

Source
>Optional. String expression naming the object or application that generated the error. When setting this property for an object, use the format *project.class*. If source is not specified, the programmatic identifier (ID) of the current Visual Basic project is used. The programmatic ID is assigned to your project at compile time, and it is used (most often in the registry) to identify your component.

Description

Optional. String expression describing the error. If unspecified, the value in *Number* is examined. If it can be mapped to a Visual Basic runtime error code, the string returned by the *Error* function is used as *Description*. If there is no Visual Basic error corresponding to *Number*, the text "Application-defined or object-defined error" is used.

Helpfile

Optional. The fully qualified path to the Microsoft Windows Help file in which help on this error can be found. If unspecified, Visual Basic uses the fully qualified drive, path, and filename of the Visual Basic Help file.

Helpcontext

Optional. The context identifier (ID) of a topic within Help file that provides help for the error. If omitted, the Visual Basic Help file context ID for the error corresponding to the *Number* argument is used, if it exists.

You can raise either a standard or a custom error. The following shows how you might use Err.Raise to raise an error in the procedure discussed previously:

```
Public Function Divide(Numerator As Integer, _
                       Denominator As Integer) As Integer

    On Error Resume Next
    Dim lngErrorNumber As Long

    Divide = Numerator / Denominator

    lngErrorNumber = Err.Number

    If lngErrorNumber > 0 Then
        ' Turn off error handling so the Raise
        '* method raises the error in the client.
        On Error GoTo 0
        Err.Raise lngErrorNumber
        On Error Resume Next
    End If

End Function
```

 One critical element of raising errors is often overlooked: you must turn off the error handler of the procedure if the error is to be raised in the client! If the procedure raising the error has an active error handler, the error handler will handle the error generated by the Err.Raise method. Don't forget to turn the error handler back on after raising the error with the client.

Of course, this example behaves just as if there were no error handling because the same message is returned to the client. Note how the error number is retrieved prior to turning off the error handler. When you turn off the error handler, Err.Number may be reset to 0. If you try to raise error number 0, an error occurs.

Different types of error messages are stored in different value ranges. Visual Basic error messages fall within 0 to 65536, with Visual Basic using the first 512 (0 through 511). Although errors can be raised within the range of 0 to 65536, this range does not correspond to the actual value of the error number. Instead, Visual Basic error messages are offset within the error number. Visual Basic includes a constant called vbObjectError that is used to specify error numbers in the correct range for Visual Basic applications using the offset. To specify a custom error number, add your error number to the vbObjectError offset constant.

 Because Visual Basic itself uses the vbObjectError constant, you need to specify errors in the range vbObjectError + 512 to vbObjectError + 65536.

The following procedure raises a custom error:

```
Public Function Divide(Numerator As Integer, _
    Denominator As Integer) As Integer

If Denominator = 0 Then
    Err.Raise vbObjectError + 512, , _
        "Denominator Out of Range"
    Exit Function
End If

Divide = Numerator / Denominator

End Function
```

This procedure evaluates *Denominator*. If *Denominator* is zero, the custom error message presented in Figure 4-7 might be shown by the client.

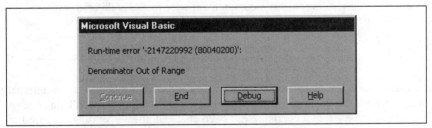

Figure 4-7: Custom errors are displayed just like standard errors

Note the very strange runtime error number. In order for the client to know the actual error number within the server application, it must subtract the vbObjectError constant from the returned error number. Hence:

```
-2147220992  - vbObjectError = 512
```

Important issues to remember about raising errors in an ActiveX server:

- Unhandled errors in a server are raised immediately within the client.

- Trapped errors in a server are not raised within the client.

- To explicitly generate a runtime error, use Err.Raise.

- You must turn off any active error handlers before using Err.Raise or the error handler will handle the error and not pass it to the client.

- If you need the number of a generated error, retrieve it prior to turning off the error handler.

- You may create custom error messages in the range 512 + vbObjectError to 65536 + vbObjectError.

Calling Object Servers Asynchronously Using Callbacks

It's often necessary for a server to notify a client. For instance, a server may need to let a client know when a timer event has occurred, or when a user has performed a certain task with the server's interface. Visual Basic now allows you to create events for ActiveX servers, but sometimes it is still necessary to notify clients the "old-fashioned way," using OLE callbacks.

The ability to create custom events within an ActiveX component is relatively new to Visual Basic. Previously, for an ActiveX DLL or EXE to communicate with a client, an OLE callback had to be performed. One of the most compelling reasons for using an OLE callback occurs when early binding to an object is not possible. Earlier in this chapter, it was stated that to dimension a variable using WithEvents, which is required in order to take advantage of custom events, you must early bind the object. Obviously, if early binding is not possible, you will have to use an OLE callback to enable communication between server and client.

On the Exams

Although custom events are most often superior to OLE callbacks, callbacks are still used and you will most likely encounter questions related to OLE callbacks on the exams.

To create an OLE callback, the client application passes a reference to an internal object to the ActiveX server. At the appropriate time, such as when a long process has been completed or a condition has been changed, the server calls a method of the object that has been passed to it. Figure 4-8 illustrates an OLE callback.

Examine this code from an ActiveX server:

```
'* This statement goes in the declarations section.
Private m_objClient As Object

Public Property Set CallBackObject(obj as Object)

    Set m_objClient = obj

    Call PerformSomeAction()
```

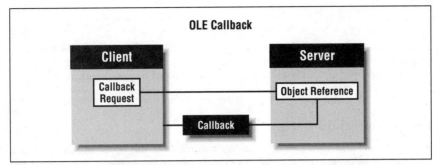

Figure 4-8: OLE callbacks provide two-way communication between servers and clients

```
End Property

Private Sub NotifyClients()

    m_objclient.ProcessComplete

End Sub
```

This code accomplishes three things. First, a module-level object variable is defined to hold the callback object. The Property Set procedure is used by a client to pass a callback object to the server. When the server receives a callback object, it performs an action. This action may trigger a timer, or display a form from which a user can make selections—in short, it can do anything you want. When the process is finished and the NotifyClients procedure is called, the client is notified by the server, triggering the ProcessComplete method of the callback object (this is truly late binding at work). Obviously, this method must exist and must be a public method of the client's callback object.

The following shows what the code of a client might look like:

```
Option Explicit
Dim objCallBack As New CallBackExample.clsCallBack

Private Sub Command1_Click()

Set objCallBack.CallBackObject = Me

End Sub

Public Sub ProcessComplete()

    MsgBox "The server has completed its process!"

End Sub
```

This code creates a new instance of an object (the clsCallBack class in project Call-BackExample) in the Declarations section of a form module. The Click event of a command button calls the CallBackObject method and passes a reference to its parent form. The parent form in turn has a public method called ProcessComplete that, when called, displays a message box. Although this example uses a form module, this would also work with a class module.

Key points to understand about OLE callbacks:

- An object that raises events has no control over the order in which clients receive its events. By contrast, a component making callbacks can control the order in which clients are called back. It might give some clients higher priority, for example.

- When an object raises an event, all of its clients handle the event before the object that raised the event gets control again. However, a component making callbacks gets control back after each call it makes to a client.

- If an event contains a `ByRef` argument, that argument can be altered by any client that uses the event procedure. If multiple objects change the value, only the last client's changes are visible to the object that raised the event, because the object that raised the event doesn't get control again until all of its clients have handled the event. However, a component making callbacks can examine changes to `ByRef` arguments after every call to a client, and can pass the next client fresh values for those arguments.

- A server making callbacks will receive errors that occur within the callback method of the client, and it must be prepared to handle them.

- OLE callbacks on early-bound objects are faster than events because they can be vtable-bound.

Creating System Callbacks Using AddressOf

In C programming, many functions are executed using *pointers*. A pointer is a memory address; if you know the memory address of a function, you can call that function using its pointer. Visual Basic itself does not let you call functions using pointers as you can with C. Officially, Visual Basic shields developers from using pointers because it's very easy to create applications that crash or otherwise exhibit erratic and unpredictable behavior by incorrectly using pointers.

The Windows API, on the other hand, is a set of C libraries. In order to use some of the capabilities of the Windows API, it's necessary to use pointers because some Windows functions need to call a function within the application accessing the API. This behavior is similar to an OLE callback, but OLE is not involved. Since API functions are system functions, this technique is commonly called a *system callback*. Visual Basic includes an operator that allows you to retrieve the pointer to a procedure in your Visual Basic code: `AddressOf`. `AddressOf` has the following syntax:

```
AddressOf procedure_name
```

It's important to note the format of `AddressOf` because you will most likely have to demonstrate the proper way to use it. To obtain the pointer to a procedure called *MyProc*, for instance, you would use a statement such as this:

```
AddressOf MyProc
```

Notice that the procedure name is not surrounded by quotes, brackets, or any other type of character.

You cannot use the result of `AddressOf` within Visual Basic to execute a function within your project, but you can use `AddressOf` to pass a procedure's pointer to an API function. The API function can then use the address (pointer) to call the function in your Visual Basic project.

There are many Windows API calls that make use of function pointers. For example, the *SetTimer* API can be used to create a timer using pure Visual Basic code, without using controls. Timers created using the *SetTimer* API function are more accurate than timers created using the Visual Basic Timer control. In order to create a timer using code, however, the Windows API needs to have a pointer to a function within your project to call when a time interval elapses.

This following procedure creates and kills a code-only timer. When the *StartTimer* procedure is called, it creates a code timer for a specified number of milliseconds using the *SetTimer* API function. Note that `AddressOf` is used to pass a function pointer as the fourth argument of *SetTimer*. When the designated time has elapsed, the *SetTimer* API uses the function pointer to call the *TimerOccurred* procedure. The first thing that the *TimerOccurred* event does is kill the timer. If you don't kill the timer, it is possible that *SetTimer* will call the procedure again before the message box is displayed.

 Anytime you use `AddressOf`, you risk causing a general protection fault (GPF) or worse. For instance, I called *SetTimer* using code in a command button, and before the timer event fired, I stopped the project. As I sit here, the project is stopped, Visual Basic is locked up, and a steady stream of message boxes are appearing. Soon I'll run out of memory or stack space—no fun. The "three-fingered salute" is the only solution to my problem.

```
Option Explicit

Private m_lngTimerID As Long

Declare Function SetTimer Lib "user32" (ByVal hwnd As Long, _
            ByVal nIDEvent As Long, ByVal uElapse As Long, _
            ByVal lpTimerFunc As Long) As Long

Declare Function KillTimer Lib "user32" (ByVal hwnd As Long, _
            ByVal nIDEvent As Long) As Long


Public Sub TimerOccurred(ByVal hwnd As Long, ByVal uMsg As Long, _
            ByVal idEvent As Long, ByVal dwTime As Long)
```

```
'* Stop the timer.
Call StopTimer

MsgBox "Customer timer event occurred!", vbInformation Or vbOKOnly

End Sub


Public Sub StartTimer(lngMilliseconds As Long)

    '* If a timer is already started, don't attempt to
    '* subclass again - the program will probably GPF.
    If m_lngTimerID <> 0 Then GoTo PROC_EXIT

    '* Start the timer, passing the address of a procedure in this
    '* project. When the timer is complete, it will call the procedure.
    m_lngTimerID = SetTimer(0, 0, lngMilliseconds, AddressOf _
        TimerOccurred)

    '* See if SetTimer failed.
    If m_lngTimerID = 0 Then
        MsgBox "The timer was not created successfully!", vbExclamation _
                Or vbOKOnly
        GoTo PROC_EXIT
    End If

PROC_EXIT:
    Exit Sub

End Sub


Public Sub StopTimer()

    Dim lngResult As Long

    '* Get out if no timer is active.
    If m_lngTimerID = 0 Then GoTo PROC_EXIT

    '* Kill the active timer.
    lngResult = KillTimer(0, m_lngTimerID)

    '* See if timer was killed successfully.
    If lngResult = 0 Then
        MsgBox "Unable to stop the timer.", vbExclamation Or vbOKOnly
        GoTo PROC_EXIT
    End If

    m_lngTimerID = 0

PROC_EXIT:
    Exit Sub

End Sub
```

The **AddressOf** keyword has the following restrictions:

- The sub, function, or property procedure you call with **AddressOf** must be in the same project as the related declarations and procedures.

- You can only use **AddressOf** with user-defined procedures (subs, functions, or properties). You cannot use **AddressOf** with external functions declared with the **Declare** statement or with functions referenced from type libraries.

- You can pass an address pointer to an argument that is typed **As Any** or **As Long** in a declared Sub, Function, or user-defined type definition.

- You cannot use **AddressOf** to obtain a pointer to a procedure in a class-based module, only in ordinary modules.

AddressOf is often used to *subclass* an existing form or control in a project. Visual Basic exposes a number of events for different types of objects such as forms and text boxes. However, Visual Basic does not expose all of the possible events for most of these objects. Since Windows knows about these events, your application should be able to know about them as well. In order to accomplish this, subclass the window of a form or control, intercepting all of its events. Subclassing presents a number of problems, not the least of which is the potential for creating a very unstable application. Although fully implementing subclassing is beyond the scope of this book, here is the general principle:

1. Use **AddressOf** to pass a function pointer to the Windows API, along with the handle of the window you are subclassing, creating a Windows "hook."

2. The procedure designated by **AddressOf** will fire for each event that occurs for the subclassed window. This can be a *lot* of events!

3. Look for specific events by comparing a value returned to your procedure by the API to a constant for the message you are trying to intercept.

4. Act on the messages you are looking for, and pass the remaining messages back to the messaging queue to be used by other processes.

 Subclassing windows by using Visual Basic code is error-prone; you'll find yourself rebooting, or at least restarting Visual Basic, repeatedly. Using a third-party subclassing ActiveX control, however, usually doesn't pose such problems during debugging.

Visual Basic Help lists the following limitations and risks of using function pointers obtained with **AddressOf**:

- If your application fires a callback function while in break mode, the code will be executed, but any breaks or steps will be ignored. If the callback function generates an exception, you can catch it and return the current value. Resets are prohibited in break mode when a callback function is on the stack.

- *Thunking* is the way that Windows enables relocatable code. If you delete a callback function in break mode, its thunk is modified to return 0. This value will be correct most of the time—but not all of the time. If you delete a callback function in break mode and then type it again, it's possible that some callees will not know about the new address. Thunks aren't used in the EXE—the pointer is passed directly to the entry point.

- If you pass a callback function that takes a different number of arguments than the caller expects, or that mistakenly calls an argument with ByRef or ByVal, your application may fail. Be careful to pass a function with the correct signature.

- When subclassing a window, you pass a function pointer to Windows as the Windows procedure (WindowProc). When running your application in the IDE, however, it's possible that the WindowProc will be called after the underlying function has already been destroyed. This will likely cause a GPF and may bring down the Visual Basic development environment.

- Pointers to Visual Basic functions cannot be passed within Visual Basic itself. Currently, only pointers from Visual Basic to a DLL function (not an ActiveX DLL) are supported.

- Errors within a callback procedure must not be propagated back to the external procedure that initially called it. You can accomplish this by placing the On Error Resume Next statement at the beginning of the callback procedure or by using more robust error-handling techniques.

Creating Remote Servers

Remote servers are ActiveX servers that run on other computers or network servers across a LAN. There is nothing unique about creating remote servers; however, the way they are deployed is different. Deploying ActiveX remote servers is discussed in Chapter 13, *Packaging and Deploying an Application*.

Creating Multithreaded Components

Have you ever wondered how Internet Explorer is able to retrieve text, display pictures, *and* respond to your input—apparently all at the same time? It can do this because it's a multithreaded application (see Figure 4-9). Visual Basic does not allow you to create multithreaded clients; however, it does allow you to create multithreaded servers. This becomes increasingly important as more and more ActiveX clients are becoming multithreaded.

In the discussion of in-process versus out-of-process servers in Chapter 3, we saw that in a multitasking operating system like Windows 98, the processor rapidly switches between processes so that both processes appear to be executing at the same time. This is not entirely true. Actually, the processor is switching between *threads of execution*, not processes. A thread is like a process within a process; it's the sequence of operations that take place within a process. Each process has at least one thread of execution.

Serialization

A single-threaded ActiveX server can process only one request (property or method call) at a time. As requests are made to the server by different clients, they

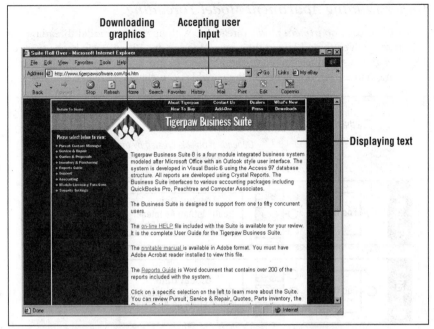

Figure 4-9: Multithreaded applications can perform many tasks, seemingly simultaneously

are placed in a queue and executed in the order in which they are made. This method of queuing requests is known as *serialization*. When a multithreaded client accesses a single-thread server, serialization occurs and only one thread of the client application can be served at a time.

How a Process Can Yield Control of the Processor

Because Windows is a multithreaded, multitasking operating system, processes can temporarily yield control of the processor so that the processor is free to execute other requests. When not anticipated, this can cause unexpected results—which is why you're often cautioned against calling statements like DoEvents in your code. Control of the processor can be yielded in the following ways:

- Calling DoEvents
- Invoking the properties or methods of an object on another thread or in another process
- Raising an event that's handled by an object on another thread or in another process
- Invoking a cross-thread or cross-process method from within a method
- Showing a form

Understanding Apartment Model Threading

Visual Basic uses *apartment model* threading. With apartment model threading, all objects on a given thread live in their own "apartment;" Visual Basic keeps track of separate global variables for each thread (see Figure 4-10). The variables retain their same names, but the values of the variables can change between threads.

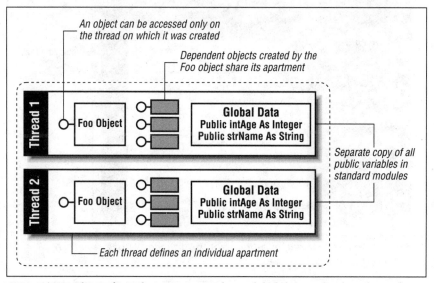

Figure 4-10: Objects from the same server share global data with other objects from the same server if they're on the same thread

In addition to maintaining a separate copy of global data (public variables of standard modules), a Sub Main procedure is executed for each new thread on which an object is created. If this didn't occur, the global data for the thread couldn't be initialized.

 All Visual Basic applications use apartment model threading. However, single-threaded objects have only one "apartment." This makes all single-threaded DLLs created with Visual Basic safe to use with multithreaded clients. Since only one thread is used, however, there is a performance penalty because calls to the server from other threads require cross-thread marshaling.

Although Visual Basic 5 could handle maintaining separate global variables between threads, it couldn't handle other shared resources such as forms, controls, and user documents. In order to create multithreaded components in Visual Basic 5, you had to remove all user-interface elements and set the component to run with "Unattended Execution." With Visual Basic 6, Forms, User-Controls, UserDocuments, and ActiveX designers are all thread-safe. Message boxes are not thread-safe interface elements, however, so you must remove all code statements that display a message box.

 The only way objects in different threads ("apartments") can communicate with objects in other threads is by having a client pass them a reference to the other thread (use an OLE callback). When this happens, Windows uses cross-thread marshaling to provide synchronization, much as it does to marshal between processes. Also like marshaling between processes, cross-thread marshaling is slow.

Controlling Thread Use in an ActiveX EXE

Since ActiveX EXEs run in their own process space, they can create threads. The type of threading a server uses depends on its settings in the Project Properties dialog box. When compiled with the "Thread per Object" option, the server creates a new thread for every new object instantiated *externally* (by a client); each externally created object runs in its own thread. A new thread is not created for objects instantiated internally by the server itself. If the Thread Pool option is selected, the server is limited to creating only the specified number of threads. The threads are used in a round-robin approach, with each new object being created on the next thread (see Figure 4-11).

ActiveX Code
Components

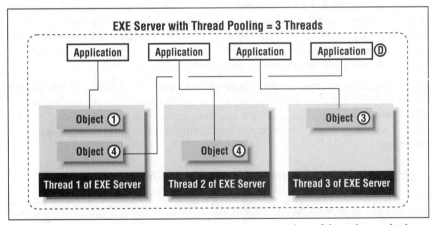

Figure 4-11: Thread pooling controls the maximum number of threads on which an EXE server can create objects

No matter how many objects the server creates, no more than the specified number of threads are ever created. This raises some very important issues. First, since objects are created on threads in a round-robin approach rather than based on client requests, objects from different clients may share the same thread. Remember, objects on a thread share global variables and resources, and requests to objects on the thread may be blocked and queued if the thread is busy executing a request on a different object.

If you change the threading model of an existing project that uses single-thread ActiveX controls, an error will occur. Visual Basic will not allow single-threaded controls in a multithreaded (apartment-threaded) project.

Not only can you *not* depend on a thread serving only one client, you cannot depend on threads sharing equal work. For example, suppose you have four threads, each handling five objects. If the server's clients, by coincidence, destroy all five objects on thread two, will the next five instantiated objects be created on thread two? Unfortunately, no. No matter how unbalanced the threads become, objects will continue to be created in a round-robin approach. Obviously, the more objects a thread supports, the more performance is affected.

By allowing you to control the number of threads created, Visual Basic lets you control, to some extent, the amount of system resources used by your component. However, the drawbacks tend to outweigh the advantages. Consequently, it's usually best not to use thread pooling. Instead, consider creating a single-threaded server by setting Thread Pool = 1, or create a multithreaded server with one thread per object.

Controlling Thread Use in an ActiveX DLL

ActiveX DLLs run in the process space of their clients and therefore cannot create threads themselves. If a multithreaded client creates objects in a single-thread DLL, all objects from the DLL are created on the *same thread that instantiated the original DLL object.* Cross-thread marshaling is used for all other threads to work with objects of the DLL, possibly having a huge impact on performance. So, a multithreaded client is best served with a multithreaded DLL.

Since no threads are created by an ActiveX DLL, the Thread Pool and Thread per Object properties are not available. However, you do have the option of creating a single-threaded or apartment-threaded server. Remember, single-threaded servers created in Visual Basic are actually apartment-threaded servers with only one apartment.

Limitations of Apartment Model Threading

Although apartment model threading has a number of benefits, it has a number of limitations as well. To correctly implement multithreaded components using apartment model threading, you must fully understand the ramifications of the threading options. The limitations of apartment model threading include:

- You cannot debug multithreaded projects in the Visual Basic design environment (see the next section for more information).

- MDI forms are not allowed in apartment-threaded projects because of the mechanisms they use to communicate with child forms.

- Single-threaded controls (such as the MSChart control included with the Professional and Enterprise editions of Visual Basic, for example) perform poorly and may cause problems when used in multithreaded clients.

- Friend properties and methods are treated similarly to local data in that they can be called only by objects on the same thread because they are not exposed in the object's interface.

- ActiveX documents in ActiveX EXE projects are not apartment-model thread-safe unless the threading option used is Thread per Object or Thread Pool with a pool size greater than one.

- Forms shown as `vbModal` are modal only to code and forms on the same thread. This means only code within the thread will be blocked and forms in other threads remain active.

- Dragging and dropping between forms only works if the forms are on the same thread. OLE drag and drop will work with forms across threads (or processes).

- DDE between forms will only work for forms on the same thread.

- Components instantiated as application-level objects in the Contents collection of the ASP Application object cannot be apartment threaded.

Testing and Debugging ActiveX Code Components

Testing and debugging ActiveX components can be quite a challenge, and each type of component must be tested and debugged in its own way. In this section you'll learn the techniques related specifically to debugging ActiveX components. This section will not teach you how to use Visual Basic's debugging tools, such as the Immediate or Watches windows; these are covered in detail in Chapter 9, *Testing and Debugging*.

All of the various testing procedures require that you create a client project to use your component. Unless you're using OLE callbacks, a standard EXE works fine as a client. However, if you use OLE callbacks, the client project will need to be an ActiveX EXE so that it can expose public objects to pass to the callback mechanism of the server.

Testing and Debugging ActiveX DLLs

Visual Basic 6 greatly simplifies testing and debugging ActiveX DLLs by allowing you to work with multiple projects in one instance of the Visual Basic IDE. To add a project to a currently opened project, choose Add Project from the File menu. The Project Explorer window shows you all open projects and lets you easily select objects from any of them (see Figure 4-12).

To debug an ActiveX DLL, follow these steps:

1. Create a project group (using the Add Project dialog box) containing the ActiveX DLL project and a client (testing) project. This testing project can be an ActiveX EXE or standard EXE.

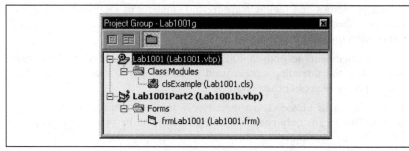

Figure 4-12: The Project Explorer is an indispensable tool for debugging ActiveX components

2. Make the client (testing) project the startup project by right-clicking on it in the Project Explorer and selecting Set as Startup. The name of the project designated as the startup project appears in bold in the Project Explorer window.

3. Select any object in the test project in the Project Explorer window to make it the active project.

4. Choose References from the Project menu to display the References dialog box.

5. Locate the server to be tested in the list of references and select its checkbox. Remember, a component's project name determines how it appears in the list; if you create an ActiveX component but don't change its name, it will appear as Project1, Project2, and so on. Once the server is selected, click OK. The server is now early bound.

6. Create object variables within the test project, as discussed throughout this chapter.

At least one class of your ActiveX component must have its Instancing property set to a value other than Private or PublicNotCreatable. If your project doesn't expose any public objects, it will not appear in the References dialog box.

When you debug a component by running it and a client in the same instance of Visual Basic, you can switch among any of the objects (forms, modules, etc.) of either project at any time, just as if they existed in a single project. The rules of accessing objects in a single project—for example, being unable to access a form in design view while the projects are running—still apply, however. Breakpoints and other debugging tools also work (see Chapter 9 for information on debugging tools and techniques).

To test an ActiveX DLL, create a project group containing the ActiveX DLL project and a client project.

Testing and Debugging ActiveX EXEs

Testing out-of-process EXEs is different than testing in-process DLLs. Just as EXEs are designed to run in their own process, they must be tested in their own process. To do this, you test the EXE in a separate instance of Visual Basic from the test client. Testing EXEs using separate instances of Visual Basic is not difficult, but the testing procedure needs to be set up correctly.

The first step in debugging an ActiveX EXE project is opening the project in an instance of Visual Basic and setting the Start Mode of the project. ActiveX EXEs can run as standalone applications or as out-of-process servers, and often the behavior of an ActiveX EXE depends on whether it was started as a standalone application or as a server. For instance, you wouldn't want a user to be able to shut down an application that was started as, and is being used as, a server. This would destroy all active objects being used by clients. Because of this need to test an EXE under both conditions, Visual Basic lets you run your EXE as though it was started as a standalone application or as a server. The behavior of the EXE is determined by the StartMode property on the Project Properties dialog box (see Figure 4-13). To change the Start Mode of an EXE, choose Project Properties from the Project menu and select the Component tab.

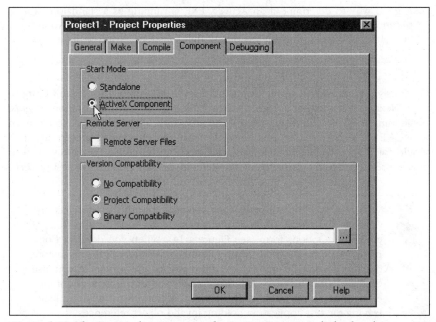

Figure 4-13: The StartMode property on the Project Properties dialog box lets you test your EXE as a standalone application or as an out-of-process server

Changing the StartMode property of an ActiveX EXE affects only how the server is started while running in the Visual Basic design environment; it has nothing to do with how the EXE is started as a compiled program. However, StartMode is a property of the Application object, so you can check it at runtime to determine how the component was started. When queried at runtime, the StartMode property returns one of the two values described in Table 4-3.

Table 4-3: Values of the StartMode Property

Value	Constant	Description
0	vbSModeStandalone	Application started as a standalone project
1	VbSModeAutomation	Application started as an ActiveX component

Using the StartMode property is simple. For example, you could use code like this if a user tries to close your component:

```
If App.StartMode = vbSModeStandalone Then
    ' Allow them to close it.
Else
    ' Don't allow them to close it.
End If
```

On the Exams

A good way to determine if an ActiveX EXE is running as a standalone application or as a server is to check the StartMode property of the Application object. You will probably encounter this question on one of the exams.

Obviously, to test an EXE server, you should set the Start Mode to ActiveX Component. Next, put the project in run mode by pressing F5. The EXE component *must* be in run mode or you won't be able to test and debug it! When you run an ActiveX EXE, Visual Basic creates a registry entry for the running project, just as it would for a compiled component, as discussed in Chapter 3. This allows you to create a reference to the server using the References dialog box in the test project.

 When debugging out-of-process servers, you should deselect the Compile On Demand checkbox, which is available on the General tab of the Options form (see Figure 4-14). When you deselect Compile On Demand, you'll know about compilation problems before the test project begins to use objects from the server. If you use Compile On Demand and the component encounters a compile error at any time while it is running, the component will terminate, leaving the test application holding invalid object references.

The next step is to start another instance of Visual Basic and create a test project. Generally, standard EXE projects work fine unless your component uses callbacks. If your component uses callbacks, you'll need to create an ActiveX EXE with public objects as the test project.

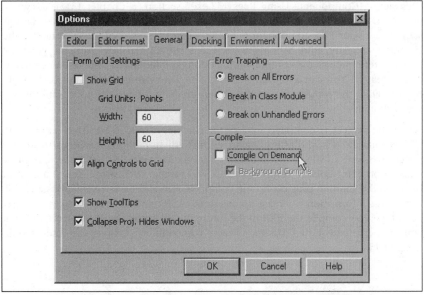

Figure 4-14: Deselecting Compile On Demand prevents compilation errors from occurring at inappropriate times

When Visual Basic contains the test project, choose References from the Project menu to access the References dialog box. Locate the ActiveX EXE component in the list and select its checkbox. Remember, the component's project name is what appears in the list.

 You cannot add a reference to the EXE component if its project name is the same as that of the test project. This can occur, for instance, if you leave both projects with the default name Project1.

If your component project is running but does not appear in the References dialog box of your test project, you probably haven't exposed any public classes. Stop the EXE component and make sure that at least one of its class modules has its Instancing property set to a value *other than* private or PublicNotCreatable.

Once you've set a project reference, you can declare and use ActiveX EXE objects. What's great about this is that you have all of Visual Basic's debugging tools at your disposal even while running both projects simultaneously. For example, if you place a breakpoint (discussed in Chapter 9) on a statement in the test project that calls a method of the server, and then single-step through the code (also discussed in Chapter 9), you'll actually step from the client code into the server code, as though you were debugging one application!

Every time you start Visual Basic, load your EXE component, and run the project, Visual Basic creates a temporary registry entry so that the component appears in the References dialog box. When ActiveX components are registered (see the

"Registering Components Using Regsvr32.exe" section in Chapter 13), it assigns a unique ID to each component called a Class ID (CLSID). Each time Visual Basic is started and your EXE component is loaded anew, a new CLSID is assigned to the temporary registry entry when the project is run. When this happens, your test project's reference to the component is no longer valid and a new reference needs to be created. You can avoid having to create a new reference to the component by compiling the project into an EXE *before* creating a reference to it from the test application.

When the project is compiled into an executable, a unique CLSID is assigned to the executable. Visual Basic is smart enough to use this information to always assign the same CLSID to the temporary registration entry. Actually, the temporary registration entry doesn't get the *exact* CLSID, because this would create a conflict between the running project and the compiled component, but Visual Basic is able to use this information to create a consistent CLSID that your test project can use. Each time you compile the EXE in the future, it will always have the same CLSID if you properly use Visual Basic's version compatibility options, as discussed in Chapter 13.

On the Exams

Make absolutely sure you read Chapter 13 and understand how to register and unregister ActiveX components. You will encounter numerous questions regarding registering components on the exams.

For review purposes, the steps to testing an out-of-process EXE are as follows:

1. Start an instance of Visual Basic and load the EXE component.

2. Create a compiled version of the component.

3. Run the component project in the Visual Basic environment.

4. Start a new instance of Visual Basic and load or create a test project.

5. Choose References from the Project menu to add a reference to the running component project.

6. Create and test objects of the component.

Testing and Debugging Multithreaded Components

When components are run in the Visual Basic environment, they always run as single-threaded components *even if they're designed as multithreaded components*. Because of this, you cannot test multithreaded components the way you test single-threaded components. The only way to test a multithreaded component *running multithreaded* is to compile the component into an EXE or DLL and use it with a test project. Since you can't debug the component "live," the component needs some way to communicate when errors occur.

When a server is set for unattended execution, all visual elements including forms, UserControls, UserDocuments, ActiveX designers, message boxes, and error messages are suppressed. While you had to mark servers for Unattended Execution to make them multithreaded in Visual Basic 5, you do not have to do so in Visual Basic 6. However, if you want to make an Unattended Execution server, you can still do so. First, remove all of the visual elements from the project, then choose Project Properties from the Project menu and select the Unattended Execution checkbox (see Figure 4-15).

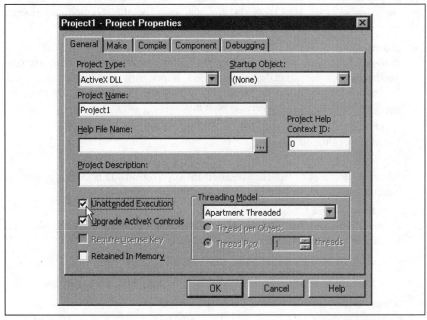

Figure 4-15: Check the Unattended Execution checkbox if you want to suppress all visual elements in the project

Although a component marked for unattended execution can't communicate by way of a user interface, there are other options. Most notably, you can log information to a log file, and Visual Basic has the built-in ability to generate log files. The behavior of event logging is controlled by two properties of the Application object:

- LogMode
- LogPath

LogPath is the full path and filename of the file to which you want information logged. If you don't specify a LogPath, then:

- On Windows NT, events are written to the Windows NT Application Event Log.
- On Windows 9x, events are written to a file called *vbevents.log*.

The odd part about these two properties is that they are read-only at runtime. To set these properties, you make a call to the StartLogging method of the Application object. The StartLogging method has the following syntax:

```
App.StartLogging logTarget, logMode
```

The *logTarget* parameter is the path and filename of the log file. You cannot omit this property, but you can set it to a zero-length string ("") to have the log written to the Windows NT Application Event Log or to the *vbevents.log* file. The second parameter, *logMode*, tells Visual Basic what method of logging to use. The four primary choices for *logMode* are members of the **LogModeConstants** enumeration, as follows:

vbLogAuto (0)
> Causes all logging to be sent to the specified file in the LogPath (the *logTarget* of the StartLogging method). If no path and file are specified, events are logged to the Windows NT Application Event Log or the *vbevents. log* file, depending on the version of Windows.

vbLogOff (1)
> Turns all logging off.

vbLogToFile (2)
> Forces all logging to the file specified in App.LogPath. If no file is specified, logging is ignored and the log mode is set to 1.

VbLogToNT (3)
> Forces logging to the NT event log. On Win9x, logging is ignored and LogMode is set to vbLogOff.

When logging is enabled, Visual Basic automatically logs:

- Text from the message boxes that your component attempts to display

- System errors, such as "Out of Stack Space"

In addition to these automatically logged items, you can log text to the log file at any time using the LogEvents method of the Application object. The LogEvents method has the following syntax:

```
object.LogEvent logText, EventType
```

logText is the text to write to the log file, while *EventType* can be one of the constants listed in the following table:

Constant	Value	Description
vbLogEventTypeError	1	Error
vbLogEventTypeWarning	2	Warning
vbLogEventTypeInformation	4	Information

For example, the following code starts logging events to a file called *Test.log*, writes a message to the log file, and then turns off logging:

```
App.StartLogging "c:\Test.log", 2
App.LogEvent "This is a test", vbLogEventTypeInformation
App.StartLogging "", 1
```

When running a component within the Visual Basic IDE, no logging occurs.

Key Facts

This chapter has discussed how to create and test ActiveX servers. The following are key points to understand in order to pass ActiveX code component–related questions on the Visual Basic exams:

- You can change the type of project at any time on the Project Properties dialog box.

- A class's Instancing property dictates how and when an object can be created.

- A server that needs to be run as a standalone application must be an ActiveX EXE.

- ActiveX DLLs run in the same process as their clients, giving better performance than ActiveX EXEs.

- ActiveX EXEs run in a separate process space than their clients.

- To create a server that is able to serve many clients, sharing global variables, make the server an EXE.

- ActiveX servers must expose at least one public class.

- Property Get procedures are used to create a readable property.

- Property Let procedures are used to create a writable property.

- Property Set procedures are used to create a writable property that accepts an object reference.

- It is possible to create properties that accept multiple parameters.

- Public Sub and Function procedures created in a class module become object methods.

- Friend procedures are visible within the project, but not to clients outside the project.

- An object can communicate with a client using an event or a callback.

- Callbacks are faster than events.

- Object variables declared WithEvents must be declared in a class-based module such as a class module or form module; you can't declare them in a standard module.

- An object variable declared WithEvents must be declared as a specific type of object, not as a generic Object.

- You cannot use the keyword New when declaring a variable using WithEvents; you must first declare the object, then use the Set statement to instantiate it.

- You cannot create a variable array using `WithEvents`.

- An object that raises events has no control over the order in which clients receive its events.

- A component making callbacks can control the order in which it calls clients back.

- When an object raises an event, all of its clients handle the event before the object that raised the event gets control again.

- A component making callbacks gets control back after each call it makes to a client.

- If an event contains a `ByRef` argument, that argument can be altered by any client that uses the event procedure.

- A server making callbacks will receive errors that occur within the Callback method, and it must be prepared to handle them.

- To pass a pointer of a procedure within your project to a DLL, use `AddressOf`.

- A class can "inherit" another class's interface by using the `Implements` statement.

- A class module may implement the interface of multiple classes.

- If you do not want to implement a specific member of an inner (implemented) class, you must still provide the procedure in code, but raise an error when the member is called.

- Most servers have a top-level object (usually called the Application object) that is used to manipulate the server.

- Unhandled errors within a server are raised in the client at the statement that called the server's procedure.

- You can raise an error in a client at any time by using the Raise method of the Err object.

- You must turn off any active error handlers prior to raising an error in a server, or the error handler will trap the error and the client will never receive it.

- You may create custom error messages in the range 512 + `vbObjectError` to 65536 + `vbObjectError`.

- Visual Basic lets you create apartment model multithreaded servers.

- Objects of a server on the same thread share global variables.

- To make a multithreaded component suppress all of its visual elements, select the Unattended Execution checkbox on the Project Properties dialog box.

- You can specify the maximum number of threads an EXE can create by using thread pooling.

- When thread pooling is used, objects from different clients may share the same thread.

- Each object created by a multithreaded DLL is created on the thread that creates the object.

- To test in-process components, create a project group that contains both the component project and a test project.

- Out-of-process components must be tested in a separate instance of Visual Basic.

- If your component uses callbacks, your test project needs to be an ActiveX EXE.

- The StartMode property on the Project Properties dialog box dictates the behavior of a component running in the IDE.

- Multithreaded components must be tested in a compiled state.

Applying What You've Learned

It's now time to apply what you've learned about creating ActiveX code components. First, answer all of the questions in the "Skills Assessment." If you can answer all of these questions correctly, you'll be demonstrating a solid understanding of creating ActiveX code components. After this has been accomplished, work through the "Hands-on Exercises."

Skills Assessment

1. An ActiveX component must have at least one class with its Instancing property set to something other than (pick two):

   a. Private

   b. MultiUse

   c. PublicNotCreatable

   d. SingleUse

2. What type of ActiveX component can serve more than one client, with the clients sharing global data?

   a. EXE

   b. DLL

3. Which type of ActiveX component generally gives better performance?

   a. Out-of-process

   b. In-process

4. Which of the following is a valid use of Property Let?

   a. `Public Property Let MyProperty(obj As Object)`
      `End Property`

   b. `Public Property Let MyProperty(x As Integer, _`
      `    Optional y As Integer)`
      `End Property`

   c. `Public Property Let MyProperty(bValue As Byte)`
      `End Property`

5. Which of the following creates a method in a class?

    a. `Private Sub MyMethod()`

       `End Sub`

    b. `Public Method MyMethod()`

       `End Method`

    c. `Public Function MyMethod() As Long`

       `End Function`

6. Which is *not* true of Friend procedures?

    a. They can be called from within the class that contains them.

    b. They cannot be called from other classes within the project that contains them.

    c. They can be called from standard modules within the project that contains them.

    d. They cannot be called from client applications.

7. Which of the following is a valid procedure declaration?

    a. Sub Friend MySub()

    b. Private Friend MySub()

    c. Friend Sub MySub()

8. Which of the following is a valid use of `WithEvents`?

    a. `Dim WithEvents obj As New Object`

    b. `Dim obj WithEvents As clsMyObject`

    c. `Dim obj WithEvents As New clsMyObject`

    d. `Dim WithEvents obj As clsMyObject`

9. Which are the two best methods to notify a client when a database connection has been lost?

    a. Expose an event.

    b. Use Err.Raise.

    c. Create a callback.

10. Which is the correct way to use the `AddressOf` operator?

    a. `AddressOf "MyProc"`

    b. `AddressOf MyProc`

    c. `AddressOf [MyProc]`

11. Which two statements are true about the `Implements` statement:

    a. `Implements` can be used only once per project.

    b. You must implement every public member of an implemented class.

    c. `Implements` cannot be used in a standard module.

    d. `Implements` can only be used once per class module.

12. What happens when an untrapped error is encountered in a server component?

    a. The component crashes.

    b. The error is displayed to the user.

    c. The error is raised in the client application.

    d. The error is raised in the server application.

13. Which of the following is true about using Err.Raise in a server component?

    a. If the procedure has error trapping, the client never receives the error.

    b. You can raise only standard errors.

14. To create a custom error, you must:

    a. Store the error message in a resource file.

    b. Give the error a number between range 512 + `vbObjectError` to 65536 + `vbObjectError`.

    c. Make a call to the Windows API.

15. Which is true about creating multithreaded components in Visual Basic?

    a. You can create multithreaded clients.

    b. Multithreaded objects work on network servers only.

    c. Visual Basic uses apartment model threading.

16. Which is true about thread pooling?

    a. Different clients may be served by the same thread.

    b. Thread pooling creates faster servers.

    c. ActiveX DLLs can use thread pooling.

17. What is the best approach for testing a ActiveX DLL?

    a. Create a project group.

    b. Add a reference to the compiled DLL.

    c. Run the DLL in a separate instance of VB.

18. What is the best approach for testing a single-thread ActiveX EXE?

    a. Create a project group.

    b. Run the EXE component in a separate instance of Visual Basic from the testing project.

19. How can a component determine if it was started as a server or a standalone application?

    a. Check the StartedAsServer property.

    b. Check the Client property and trap any resulting errors.

    c. Check the StartMode property.

Answers to Skills Assessment

1. a, c	5. c	9. a, c	13. a	17. a
2. a	6. b	10. b	14. b	18. b
3. b	7. c	11. b, c	15. c	19. c
4. c	8. d	12. c	16. a	

Hands-on Exercises

Now that you have a thorough background of creating ActiveX code components, you're going to put that knowledge to use. Complete all of these exercises to help solidify your understanding of ActiveX EXEs and DLLs.

Exercise 4-1. Creating an ActiveX DLL

In this exercise, you'll create an ActiveX DLL and a project for testing the DLL.

This exercise applies the following topics:

- Creating an ActiveX DLL
- Creating a public method
- Dimensioning an object variable using the New keyword
- Destroying an object reference by setting an Object variable to Nothing
- Testing an in-process server

Section 1. Creating the ActiveX DLL. The DLL you are going to create is a simple one, containing just one method. This method accepts a full path- and filename as its parameter and returns only the filename portion:

1. Start Visual Basic and create a new ActiveX DLL.

2. Change the name of the default class to **clsExample**.

3. Create a public method by adding the following procedure to the class:

```
Public Function GetFileName(szString As String) As String
    On Error Resume Next
    Dim intPosition As Integer

    For intPosition = Len(szString) To 1 Step -1
        If Mid$(szString, intPosition, 1) = "\" Then
            GetFileName = Mid$(szString, intPosition + 1)
            Exit Function
        End If
    Next intPosition

End Function
```

4. Click on the project in the Project Explorer window and change its name to **Exercise401**.

Section 2. Creating the test project. ActiveX DLLs are tested by creating a project group. In this section, you're going to add a new project to the Visual Basic environment and create a reference within the new project to the DLL project you've created. Then, you'll add a command button that creates a reference to the DLL, calls the method, and then destroys the reference to the DLL:

5. Add a new Standard EXE test project by choosing Add Project from the File menu.

6. Choose References from the Project menu to display the References dialog box.

7. Add a reference to the ActiveX DLL by selecting the Exercise401 checkbox (see Figure 4-16).

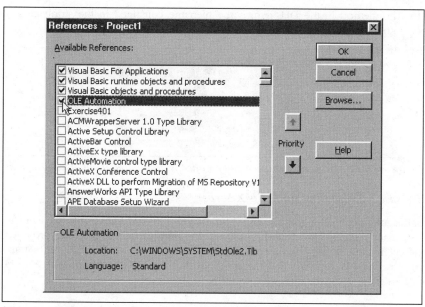

Figure 4-16: To test an in-process server, create a reference to it from within the test project using the References dialog box

8. Add a new command button to the form. Set its Name to **cmdUseDLL** and its Caption to **Use DLL**.

9. Add the following code to the command button:

```
Dim obj As New clsExample

MsgBox "FileName = " & obj.GetFileName("c:\mcsd\sample.txt")

Set obj = Nothing
```

10. Add a breakpoint to the line with the message box by placing the cursor on the line and pressing F9.

11. Change the name of the second project to **Exercise401Section2**.

Section 3. Testing the DLL. In this section, you're going to run the test project and see how it's possible to switch between the code of the test project and that of the DLL.

12. Make the second project the startup project by right-clicking its Project name in the Project Explorer window and selecting Set As Start Up.

13. Run the test project by pressing F5 and clicking the command button.

14. Code execution stops at the message box statement. Press F8 to see how the code steps right into the code of the DLL!

15. Press F5 to continue code execution.

16. The method in the DLL returns the filename contained in the string passed into it (see Figure 4-17).

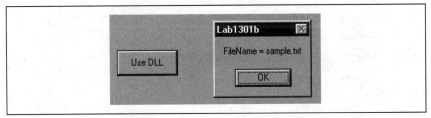

Figure 4-17: In-process servers work well for encapsulating frequently-used functions

Exercise 4-2. Creating an ActiveX Server

In this exercise, you're going to create an ActiveX EXE text file viewer. A client can instantiate a server object, and by calling one method and setting one property, the client can display the contents of a text file in a list box. The only error trapping involved is verifying that the specified file exists. If the file doesn't exist, a custom event is raised.

 This application could be optimized, but it demonstrates many techniques using a simple approach.

This exercise applies the following topics:

- Creating an ActiveX EXE
- Creating a method
- Creating a property procedure
- Creating a Friend procedure
- Creating and raising an event
- Testing an out-of-process component

Section 1. Creating the ActiveX EXE. In this section, you're going to create the ActiveX EXE with a number of interface members, including a property, methods, and an event:

1. Start Visual Basic and create a new ActiveX EXE.

2. Click on the project in the Project Explorer window and change its name to **Exercise402**.

3. Change the name of the default class module to **clsTextViewer**.

4. Open the References dialog box (Project → References) and add a reference to Microsoft Scripting Runtime to the project. This library includes the File System object model, which we'll use in this project.

5. Add a new form to the project and name it **frmTextViewer**.

6. Add a new text box to the form and name it **txtDisplay**.

7. Set the MultiLine property of the text box to True.

8. Set the Text property of the text box to " " (empty), and make the text box fill the form, as shown in Figure 4-18.

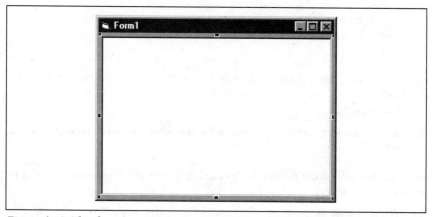

Figure 4-18: This form becomes a generic text file viewer

9. Add the following method to the class module (this method shows the text viewer form):

```
Public Sub ShowTextViewer()
    frmTextViewer.Show
End Sub
```

10. Add the following property procedure that allows the client to specify a file to display:

```
Public Property Let FileName(New_FileName As String)
    Dim strString     As String
    Dim objFileSys As New FileSystemObject
    Dim objTxtStream As TextStream

    If Not FileExists(New_FileName) Then
        RaiseEvent BadFile
```

```
        Exit Property
    End If

    Set objTxtStream = objFileSys.OpenTextFile(New_FileName, _
                        ForReading, False)
    frmTextViewer.txtDisplay.Text = objTxtStream.ReadAll()

    objTxtStream.Close
    Set objTxtStream = Nothing
    Set objFileSys = Nothing

End Property
```

11. Add the following Friend method, which determines whether the specified file exists (note: since this method is declared as **Friend**, it will be invisible outside of the project but can be called freely from within the project):

```
Friend Function FileExists(FileName As String) As Boolean

    If Dir$(FileName) <> "" Then
        FileExists = True
    Else
        FileExists = False
    End If

End Function
```

12. Add the following event declaration to the Declarations section of the class module:

```
Event BadFile()
```

13. Save the project, and then compile it by choosing the Make command on the File menu.

Section 2. Creating a test project. In this section, you're going to create a project to test the ActiveX server.

14. Set the StartMode property of the ActiveX EXE to ActiveX Component. You access the StartMode property by choosing Properties from the Project menu and clicking the Component tab.

15. Put the EXE component in run mode by pressing F5.

16. Start another instance of Visual Basic and create a Standard EXE.

17. Create a reference to the instance of Visual Basic running the EXE component by choosing References from the Project menu, locating Exercise402, and selecting its checkbox.

18. Add a command button to the default form and set its caption to "Show Text File."

19. Add the following **WithEvents** variable declaration to the Declarations section of the form:

```
Dim WithEvents obj As clsTextViewer
```

20. Add the following code to the command button's Click event. Note: this code assumes that the text file *test.txt* exists on your computer, yet it probably doesn't. You'll need to locate a valid text file on your computer (or create one using a text editor) for the viewer to display:

```
Set obj = New clsTextViewer

obj.ShowTextViewer
obj.filename = "C:\test.txt"

Set obj = Nothing
```

21. Open the Object dropdown list in the Code window and select *obj*.

22. Add the following statement to the BadFile event of the *obj* object:

```
MsgBox "The Filename is invalid!", vbOKOnly
```

Section 3. Testing the ActiveX EXE component. In this section, you're going to test the component.

23. Run the test project by pressing F5.

24. Click the Show Text File command button.

25. If you specified a valid text file, the file is displayed in the viewer form's text box. However, if you specified a file that doesn't exist, the viewer form will display (as a result of the ShowTextViewer method), but the text box will remain empty and a message box is displayed.

Exercise 4-3. Create an OLE callback and an event

In this exercise, you're going to create a project with two classes. One class is going to act as a parent class, while the other will act as a child of the parent. In addition to the two classes, the project is going to have a form with two buttons. Clicking the first button causes the parent class to trigger a callback in the child class. This callback simply invokes a method of the parent class and displays a message box. The second command button causes the parent class to trigger a method containing an Err.Raise statement in the child class. This will demonstrate how an error is raised at the calling statement in the parent class.

This exercise applies the following topics:

- Creating an OLE callback

- Raising an error in a class module

Section 1. Creating the child class. In this section, you're going to create the child class. This class will be instantiated by a parent class, and it will contain two methods. The first method, SetParent, accepts an object reference and performs a callback to the specified object (derived from the parent class). The second method, TriggerError, raises an error message at the statement that made the procedure call.

1. Start Visual Basic and create a new Standard EXE project.

2. Click on the project in the Project Explorer window and change the project's name to **Exercise403**.

3. Add a new class module to the project and name it **clsChild**.

4. Add the following code to the class:

```
Public Sub SetParent(objMyParent As clsParent)
    objMyParent.CallBackReceived
End Sub

Public Sub TriggerError()
    Err.Raise 1
End Sub
```

Section 2. Creating the parent class. In this section, you'll create the parent class. This class will be instantiated by the project's form, and it will contain three methods. The first method, TriggerCallback, passes a reference of itself to the child class. The child class uses this reference to make a callback to the second method, called CallBackReceived. The final method, TriggerChildError, calls the procedure in the child that raises an error. The error raised happens to be error #1, but this is completely arbitrary and only used for demonstration purposes.

5. Add a new class module to the project and name it **clsParent**.

6. Add the following statement to the Declarations section of the class module:

```
Private objChild As New clsChild
```

7. Add the following three procedures to the class module:

```
Public Sub TriggerCallback()
    objChild.SetParent Me
End Sub

Public Sub CallBackReceived()
    MsgBox "Callback received!", vbOKOnly
End Sub

Public Sub TriggerChildError()
    objChild.TriggerError
End Sub
```

Section 3. Finishing the form. In this section, you'll add two buttons and code to the form:

8. Change the Name of the default form to **frmExercise403** and the Caption to **Exercise403**.

9. Add the following statement to the Declarations section of the form module:

```
Private objParent As New clsParent
```

10. Add a new command button to the form. Set its Name to **cmdTriggerCallback** and its Caption to **Trigger Callback**.

11. Add the following statement to the command button's Click event:

```
objParent.TriggerCallback
```

12. Add another new command button to the form. Set its Name to **cmdTriggerError** and its Caption to **Trigger Error**.

13. Add the following statement to the Click event of the new command button:

```
objParent.TriggerChildError
```

Section 4. Testing the callback and raising the error. In this section, you'll test your project. In order for the error raised in the child class to be raised in the parent class, you must set Visual Basic's error trapping to Break on Unhandled Errors. This will make Visual Basic's error handling behave as though the project were running as a compiled application:

14. Choose Tools from the Options menu, click the General tab, and select the Break on Unhandled Errors radio button (see Figure 4-19).

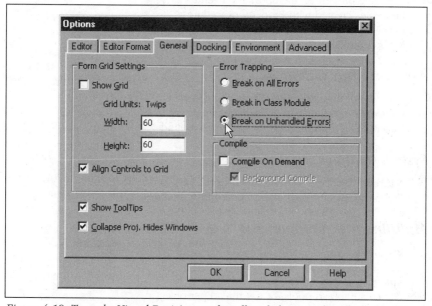

Figure 4-19: To make Visual Basic's error handling behave as though the project were running as a compiled application, select Break on Unhandled Errors

15. Run the project by pressing F5.

16. Click the Trigger Callback button and you'll see the message box displayed. Note how the message box is actually displayed in a procedure within the parent class. This method is called by the callback in the child class.

17. Click the Trigger Error button and Visual Basic displays an error message.

18. Click the Debug button on the error form, and note how the error is raised at the statement that called the method: not at the actual line in which the error occurs, even though there is no error handler in the procedure containing the error.

Highlighter's Index

ActiveX Components

Can be DLLs or EXEs
Have different types of instancing
Use Implements to implement the interface of another class
Can raise errors in client applications
System callbacks use `AddressOf`
Can have private, public, and friend members

ActiveX Component Interfaces

Can have properties, methods, and events
Properties created with Property procedures
Events raised with `RaiseEvent`
Methods are standard Sub and Function procedures

Asynchronous Callbacks

Can control the order that clients receive events
Control is kept between client notifications
Faster than events because they are early bound

System Callbacks with AddressOf

`AddressOf` obtains a pointer to a Visual Basic procedure
Can only be performed with standard BAS modules

Multithreaded Components

Visual Basic can create multithreaded servers but not clients
Queuing of requests is serialization
Apartment model threading
Can create thread pools, or use thread per object
Cannot debug multithreaded objects in Visual Basic
No MDI forms in multithreaded components

Testing and Debugging Components

To test DLLs, use a project group
To test EXEs, use two instances of Visual Basic

CHAPTER 5

Creating ActiveX Controls

The ability to create ActiveX custom controls is considered by many to be one of the most exciting innovations in Visual Basic. ActiveX controls truly embody Microsoft's component object model philosophy by allowing you to create reusable "black box" components that can be easily integrated into larger applications. The language used to write a client application hosting an ActiveX control is immaterial, as long as the language supports ActiveX technology.

In this chapter you'll learn all about ActiveX controls, including how to create their user interfaces and programming interfaces. You'll also learn about procedure attributes, as well as the proper way to test and debug ActiveX controls.

The Technologies and the Exams

Creating ActiveX controls is one of the most useful, advanced Visual Basic capabilities. Microsoft is proud of the fact that Visual Basic can create controls, so you can expect to encounter questions related to creating and testing ActiveX controls on both exams (see Table 5-1).

Table 5-1: Coverage of Active X Controls on the Exams

Topic	Covered on Exam
The UserControl object	Both
Creating aggregate controls	Both
Creating invisible-at-runtime controls	Both
Creating owner-draw controls	Both
Dynamically sizing constituent controls	Both
Regulating focus behavior of a UserControl	Both
Giving a control access keys	Both
Creating container controls	Both
Active at design time	Both
Creating a development interface	Both

Table 5-1: Coverage of Active X Controls on the Exams (continued)

Topic	Covered on Exam
Creating enumerations	Both
Property pages	Both
Property persistence	Both
Implementing custom events	Both
Ambient properties	Both
Extender object	Both
Procedure attributes	Both
Creating bound controls	Both
Testing and debugging ActiveX controls	Both

Understanding ActiveX Controls

For years, Visual Basic programmers have been using custom controls to extend the functionality of their applications. It started with VBX controls—16-bit custom controls written in C that let programmers plug in all sorts of functions, such as dropdown calendars, fancy grids, status bars, toolbars, and more. The underlying technology of VBX controls didn't lend itself to migrating to 32-bit, so when Visual Basic 4 came out (allowing the creation of both 16- and 32-bit applications), a new custom control standard emerged, based on OLE technology. These custom controls, commonly called OLE controls, came in both 16- and 32-bit flavors and had the extension OCX.

While Visual Basic 4 allowed you to create both 16- and 32-bit applications that could use OLE controls, it didn't allow you to create the controls themselves; you had to use a lower-level language like C. As you know from Chapter 3, *Understanding COM*, OLE has become ActiveX, and Visual Basic is loaded to the gills with ActiveX technology. As of Visual Basic 5, OLE controls (now called ActiveX controls) are no longer the domain of C programmers. However, creating quality ActiveX controls is quite a bit more involved than creating ordinary applications.

On the Exams

You can absolutely *count on* having to demonstrate your understanding of creating ActiveX Controls when you take either exam.

ActiveX Controls are similar to ActiveX code components in that they have properties, methods, and events, and they are based on COM. However, unlike ActiveX code components, ActiveX controls are embedded on forms or web pages. To add ActiveX controls to your project, you still have to create a reference to them, but you don't use the References dialog box as you do for ActiveX DLLs or EXEs. Instead, you use the Components dialog box (see Figure 5-1), accessed by choosing Components from the Project menu. Once you've selected a control on the Controls tab of the Components dialog box, that control will appear in the toolbox along with Visual Basic's standard set of controls.

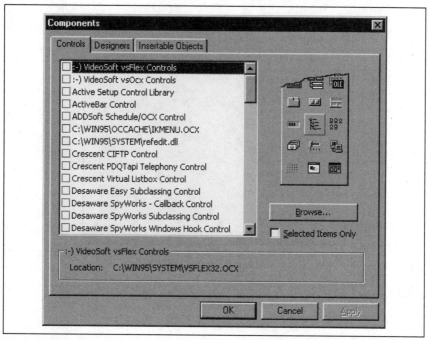

Figure 5-1: Use the Components dialog box to add ActiveX controls to a project

Laying the Foundation: The UserControl Object

ActiveX controls are built on UserControl objects; you cannot create an ActiveX control without using a UserControl object. UserControls are very similar to forms (you can embed other controls in them), and they have properties, methods, and events. However, although most of the properties, methods, and events of User-Controls are the same as those for forms, a number of notable differences exist, which are discussed throughout this chapter.

When you create a new ActiveX Control project, the project contains one default UserControl (see Figure 5-2). You can have multiple UserControls in a single project.

When you add a custom control to a project, each UserControl within the custom control OCX appears in the toolbox with its own icon. The icon displayed in the toolbox is the picture assigned to the ToolboxBitmap property of the UserControl. Toolbox bitmaps must be 16×15 pixels.

 The source code and property values for a UserControl object are stored in a text file with a CTL extension. A CTL file is equivalent to the Visual Basic FRM file used to store information about a form. Binary elements (such as bitmaps), which cannot be stored as text, are packaged in files with a CTX extension. A CTX file is equivalent to a Visual Basic FRX file used to store binary elements of a form.

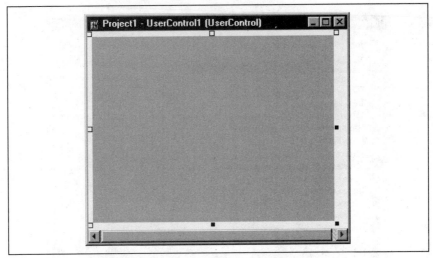

Figure 5-2: UserControls look and behave much like forms

Distinguishing Between the Four Types of Controls

There are essentially four types of ActiveX controls:

- Aggregate controls
- Owner-Draw controls
- Invisible controls
- Container controls

Regardless of which type of control you choose to create, you'll perform the following steps:

1. Create the user interface for the control.
2. Define the properties and methods of the control.
3. Create the events that will allow an application to respond to the control.
4. Add property pages to the control.
5. Test and debug the control.

Aggregate controls

Aggregate controls (sometimes called *subclassed* or *composite* controls) are ActiveX custom controls built around other controls, such as those of the standard text box or list box. The controls used within an aggregate control are called constituent controls. An aggregate control may contain only one constituent control, or it may be made up of many constituent controls, such as a complex grid control (see Figure 5-3).

Aggregate controls are the most common type of control, and they're most often used to extend the functionality of standard controls. For example, you could build an aggregate control that adds limit-to-list functionality to a standard combo box.

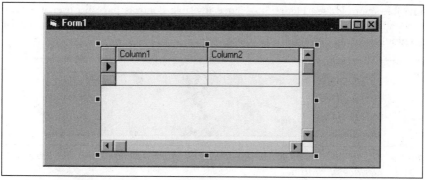

Figure 5-3: Aggregate controls can be quite complex

By encapsulating all of the functionality necessary to make a combo box accept only entries that exist in its list, you can easily add such combo boxes to all of your projects. Without encapsulating the functionality, you would need to add the special code to each and every combo box on each and every control in a project. In addition, since all of the projects would share a single control component (the ActiveX control), you can add enhancements and fix problems in one project (the ActiveX control project), recompile the project into a new ActiveX control (OCX), and all of the projects and programs that use the control automatically use the updated version.

Owner-draw controls

Owner-draw controls are similar to blank forms in that they have no controls on them. Their interface consists of whatever you draw on them using Visual Basic's drawing methods or API graphics function calls. Some examples of owner-draw controls are custom sliders (see Figure 5-4) and radio knobs—controls that you can't create by building on the functionality of standard controls.

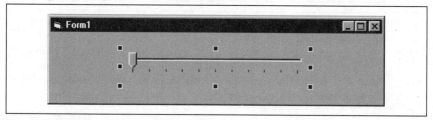

Figure 5-4: Owner-draw controls can have any appearance you can imagine; their interface is created from scratch

Owner-draw controls are often considerably more difficult to create than aggregate controls; however, owner-draw controls allow for substantially more flexibility.

Invisible controls

Invisible controls have a physical appearance at design time but aren't visible at runtime. Visual Basic's Timer control and MAPI controls are excellent examples of invisible controls (see Figure 5-5). Since invisible controls have no user interface, the end-user never interacts with an invisible control. Invisible controls can be manipulated only through Visual Basic code.

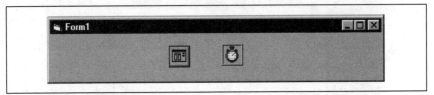

Figure 5-5: Invisible controls usually appear as icons in design time; they have no visible interface at runtime

Container controls

Container controls are ActiveX controls that allow a user to place other controls directly on them at design time. They are different from aggregate controls, which are compiled with other controls embedded in them. The most commonly used container controls are frames, tabbed dialog boxes, and picture boxes, and they are often used to group controls such as radio buttons (see Figure 5-6). Radio buttons are mutually exclusive *per container*; that is, only one radio button per container can be selected.

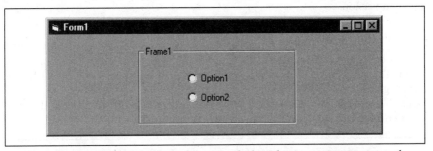

Figure 5-6: A developer can place other controls directly on a container control

Before you begin creating an ActiveX control, you should take time to adequately assess the requirements for the control and carefully choose the type of control to create. Once you decide the type of control to create, you can proceed with creating the user interface for the control.

Creating a Control's User Interface

For the most part, creating the user interface of an ActiveX control is much like creating the user interface of a form. If the ActiveX control is to be an aggregate control, you add controls to it. If it is to be an owner-draw control, you add the necessary code to give your control a physical appearance. You may decide to give your users some ability to define the appearance of your control by exposing appearance-related properties such as BackColor or Font. In this section, you'll learn the ins and outs of designing a user interface. The next section discusses the techniques involved in exposing interface elements as public properties.

Dynamically Sizing Constituent Controls

To give an ActiveX control a good user interface, you'll more than likely have to use the UserControl's Resize event. Most custom controls can be resized in the design environment, and each time the control is resized, it needs to update its appearance. Visual Basic and ActiveX handle all of the details of letting the user change the size of your control. However, changing the physical size of a control is like changing the size of a form; none of the interface elements of the User-Control adjust their size automatically.

For instance, suppose you wanted to create a custom text box control that displays text in red, whenever a negative number is entered into its Text property, and black otherwise. This control is most easily constructed by building on the functionality of the standard text box, thereby making the control an aggregate control. You would start such a project by adding a simple text box control to the User-Control, as shown in Figure 5-7. In Figure 5-7, the background of the UserControl is set to light yellow so that you can easily see its physical size throughout this example.

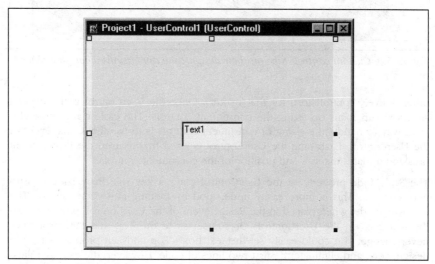

Figure 5-7: This simple aggregate control is built on the standard text box

When you add the ActiveX control to a form (which you'll learn how to do later in this chapter), the control is created with the same dimensions that the UserControl had at design time. Figure 5-8 shows the UserControl from Figure 5-7 as it appears when first placed on a form. As you can see, this is not the desired appearance. In order for the control to look like an ordinary text box, you should see no distinction between the UserControl background and the text box it contains. If you were to resize the user control, the text box's top and left corners would stay the same in relation to the top and left corners of the UserControl object, and the width and height of the text box would remain constant.

The first step in correcting this problem is to change the size of the UserControl to the size you want it to appear when first added to a form (or web page, or any

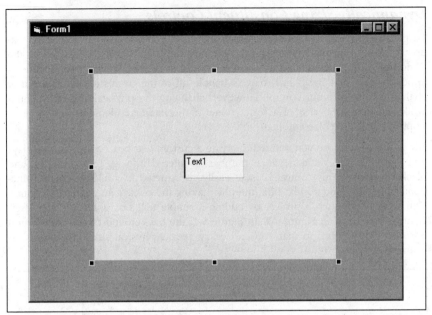

Figure 5-8: Custom controls take on their design-time dimensions when first placed on a form

other ActiveX control host, for that matter). Once the UserControl is the desired size, you can focus on sizing the constituent controls. The easiest and most effi-cient way to handle the sizing of constituent controls is to use the Resize event of the UserControl. Each time the UserControl is sized by the user, the Resize event fires and updates the size and position of the constituent controls.

The ScaleMode property of the UserControl plays a key role in resizing constit-uent controls. This is more easily understood by looking at a code sample. The following code, when placed in the Resize event of the UserControl, properly sizes the text box on the UserControl. Of course, since the Top and Left properties never change, you could easily set the text box's Top and Left properties to 0 in design view, and eliminate the first two lines of code. However, the example illus-trates that you have total control of the size and placement of the constituent control. (If you want to split hairs, you could reduce all four lines of code and use the Move method.)

```
Private Sub UserControl_Resize()

    Text1.Left = 0
    Text1.Top = 0
    Text1.Width = UserControl.ScaleWidth
    Text1.Height = UserControl.ScaleHeight

End Sub
```

When you set a Top, Left, Width, or Height property of a control, the coordinates used are in the ScaleMode of the container. The reason you use the ScaleWidth and ScaleHeight properties of the UserControl, rather than its Width or Height properties, is that the UserControl's Width and Height properties are always expressed in twips (there are 1,440 twips in an inch), regardless of the ScaleMode of the parent form. If the ScaleMode of the UserControl is ever changed from twips, either by your changing it before compiling it or by a user changing it through an exposed property, the Resize event would not correctly resize the constituent controls if you used the Width or Height of the control because the coordinates returned by the UserControl's Width and Height properties may be in an incorrect scale. Figure 5-9 shows the same UserControl as before, only this time the Resize event code was added before the UserControl was placed on the form.

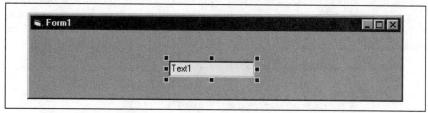

Figure 5-9: With a little bit of code, your custom controls can take on the appearance of a standard control

As you can see, the background of the UserControl is no longer visible because the constituent text box completely fills the UserControl's surface. The User-Control now looks like an ordinary text box, and it's ready for code to define its behavior (covered later in this chapter).

Using the Paint Event to Create Owner-Draw Controls

Unlike aggregate controls, owner-draw controls don't contain constituent controls. Therefore, you have to execute code to update the appearance of the control when its size is changed. The Paint event of the UserControl is the obvious place to put the code to draw the UserControl's interface. Like the Resize event, the Paint event is fired whenever the UserControl is resized. In addition, the Paint event is fired whenever a portion of the control that was obscured by another window is uncovered. If you don't place the code to draw the interface in the Paint event, your control will not repaint itself when uncovered, unless its Auto-Redraw property is set to True. When the AutoRedraw property is set to True, the UserControl retains a copy of its appearance in memory, which creates additional overhead and is generally not desirable.

Regulating the Focus Behavior of a UserControl

When a control is the active control at runtime, it is said to have the *focus*. A text box has the focus when the caret appears in it and the user can enter text. When a list box has the focus, the arrow keys can be used to move the selection rectangle within the list. Each type of control has its own focus behavior, and some controls, such as the label control, can't receive the focus at all. You dictate the focus behavior of your UserControls using two focus-related properties: CanGetFocus and ForwardFocus.

Using the CanGetFocus property of the UserControl

When CanGetFocus is set to True (the default), the control can receive the focus by the user clicking on it, tabbing into it, or pressing the UserControl's Access Key combination. If the UserControl contains a constituent control that can receive the focus (such as a text box), the constituent control *always* receives the focus; the UserControl itself cannot receive the focus. If there are no constituent controls on the UserControl, as is the case with owner-draw controls, the control itself gets the focus. When this is the case, you are responsible for writing whatever code is necessary to display the control with focus.

For example, suppose you have a basic owner-draw custom control that displays a yellow rectangle with a border, and that you wanted to draw a black rectangle within the borders of the control to show that the control has the focus (see Figure 5-10). You could use the following code procedures to accomplish this:

```
Private Sub UserControl_GotFocus()

    UserControl.Line (5, 5)-(UserControl.ScaleWidth - 5, _
        \ UserControl.ScaleHeight - 5), , B

End Sub


Private Sub UserControl_LostFocus()

    UserControl.Cls

End Sub
```

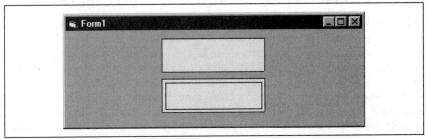

Figure 5-10: You must write code to add a focus effect to an owner-draw control

This code simply draws a rectangle when the control gets the focus, and clears the rectangle when the control loses the focus.

When a UserControl's CanGetFocus property is set to False, the control cannot receive the focus (this is the behavior of the standard Label control). Note, however, that you cannot set the CanGetFocus property of a UserControl to False as long as there is at least one constituent control on the UserControl that can receive the focus.

Using the ForwardFocus property of the UserControl

The ForwardFocus property of the UserControl allows you to give an ActiveX control the behavior of a label whose access key has been pressed. A label control, which cannot receive the focus, can pass the focus to the next control in the tab order when its access key is pressed. An access key is a key that, when pressed in conjunction with the Alt key, causes a control to receive the focus or trigger one of its events. (The next section will teach you how to add access keys to your controls.) Labels often have access keys so that a user can quickly give the focus to a text box related to the label.

Figure 5-11 shows a form with a label control and three text boxes. Notice that the T in the label has an underline. This underline indicates that the letter T is an access key, and that when pressed in conjunction with the Alt key, the next control in the tab order (in this case, Text1), will receive the focus.

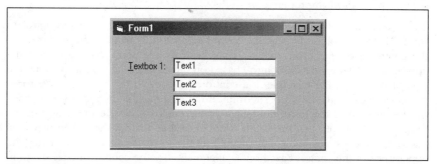

Figure 5-11: Label access keys, such as the T in this label, help provide efficient keyboard navigation

If the ForwardFocus property is set to `False`, the UserControl (or one of its constituent controls) will receive the focus when one of its access keys is pressed. The ForwardFocus property can be changed at the control's authoring time, but it cannot be changed once the control is compiled.

Giving a Control Access Keys

You can easily assign access keys to your custom controls by using the Access-Keys property and the AccessKeyPress event of the UserControl. To make a particular key an access key, simply add it to the string value of the AccessKeys property. For instance, to assign the F and the R keys as access keys, set the AccessKeys property to "fr." If the UserControl has constituent controls that have access keys assigned to them, they automatically become access keys of the User-Control, but they do not appear in the AccessKeys property.

When a user presses the Alt key in combination with one of your control's access keys, two things occur:

1. If the ForwardFocus property of the UserControl is set to `False`, the User-Control itself will get the focus. As stated earlier, if the UserControl contains a constituent control that can get the focus, the UserControl cannot receive

the focus and instead the constituent control receives the focus. If the ForwardFocus property is set to True, the next control in the tab order receives the focus.

2. The AccessKeyPress event of the UserControl fires. If you want to execute code based on the particular access key that is pressed, this is the place to put the code.

Designating a Control as Alignable

Alignable controls have an Align property that allows them to be automatically attached to the top, right, bottom, or left side of a form. Status bars and toolbars are common types of alignable controls. Status bars and toolbars have an Align property because they are often placed on MDI forms, and *only controls that are alignable or invisible at runtime can be placed on MDI forms*. Most container controls have an Align property.

To make a control alignable, set the Alignable property of the UserControl to True. The parent object hosting the control automatically handles the alignment of the control. However, you will probably need to add some code to adjust the appearance of your ActiveX control, based on the edge of the parent to which the control is aligned. For example, if a control is aligned to the bottom of the form, its width takes on the width of the form. If the alignment is then changed to dock on the left side of the form, the height of the control takes on the height of the form. Note, however, that the width is not altered and is still the current width of the form. At this point, the control would fill the form. If you want to change the appearance of the control based on its alignment, use the control's Resize event in conjunction with the Extender object discussed later in this chapter.

Creating a Container Control

Container controls allow a user to place other controls directly onto them. Commonly used container controls are the Picture Box control and the Frame control. When controls are placed on a container, they move with the container. This makes it easy to create control groupings that you can move around on a form. In addition, controls that employ mutual exclusivity, such as option buttons, are mutually exclusive *to the container on which they are placed*. For instance, if you wanted to create three unique sets of radio buttons, you would place each set on a different container (the form itself counts as a container). To make your ActiveX control a container control, all you have to do is set its ControlContainer property to True.

Conserving resources and improving performance

Container controls are known as *heavyweight* controls; because of the code necessary to keep track of the ContainedControls collection, an additional amount of overhead is incurred when using them. In addition, clipping needs to be implemented so that a contained control can properly repaint itself when controls have been placed on it, and clipping takes resources as well. You should set a UserControl's ControlContainer property to True only if it is appropriate for the control.

Support for the ControlContainer feature is provided by the object (parent) on which your control is placed, and some objects don't support container controls. If your container control is placed on an object that does not provide this feature, your control will work normally except for the fact that the user cannot place controls on your ActiveX control.

Using the ContainedControls collection

All of the controls placed by a developer on your container control are called *contained controls*. Just as you can use the Controls collection of a form to get a reference to the controls placed on the form, you can also get a reference to the contained controls on a container control. Unlike when working with forms, however, you do not use the Controls collection of the UserControl object. When you reference the Controls collection of the UserControl object, you're referencing any constituent controls placed on the UserControl at the UserControl's *authoring* time. To access the controls placed on a compiled UserControl by a user, use the ContainedControls collection.

The following code loops through all of the constituent controls placed on a User-Control at its authoring time:

```
Dim obj As Control

For Each obj In UserControl.Controls
    MsgBox "Control Name = " & obj.Name, vbOKOnly
Next
```

This next section of code loops through the controls placed on the container control by an end user (developer):

```
Dim obj As Control

For Each obj In UserControl.ContainedControls
    MsgBox "Control Name = " & obj.Name, vbOKOnly
Next
```

When a UserControl's Initialize event occurs, the control has not been fully sited. That is, the control is still being created on the container (later in this chapter, you'll learn how controls are recreated whenever the project they are in switches from run mode to design mode or vice versa). Therefore, you cannot reference the ContainedControls collection in the Initialize event. By the time the ReadProperties event is called, however, the control is fully sited and you can use the ContainedControls collection to get a reference to the contained controls. (The ReadProperties event is discussed later in this chapter.)

Not all containers support contained controls. Therefore, it's best to always use error handling on procedures that make references to the ContainedControls collection. For that matter, it's best to use error handling in every procedure.

Avoiding hair loss when creating container controls

When you set a UserControl's ControlContainer property to **True**, make sure that the BackStyle property of the UserControl is set to Opaque. If the BackStyle is set to Transparent, a user can place controls on the container control, but as soon as the user does, the controls disappear! The contained controls will still appear in the Object dropdown list of the Properties window, but they will not appear on the form or container control on which they were placed.

If you were not aware that the BackStyle property is the key, you could spend hours trying to find out why the controls disappear.

 Always check the BackStyle property and make sure it is set to Opaque when setting the ControlContainer property to **True**.

Allowing a Control to Become Active at Design Time

Some controls, like Microsoft's Data Bound Grid control, allow you to edit the control at design time. When edited at design time, a control is activated and behaves very much as it does at runtime. To enable a control to be edited at design time, set the EditAtDesignTime property of the UserControl to **True**. Once the EditAtDesignTime property is set to True, an Edit item appears on the control's Shortcut menu when a developer right-clicks the control in design view. The EditAtDesignTime property can be changed only at the control's authoring time; once the control is compiled, the property cannot be changed.

When the developer selects Edit from the context menu, the control is placed in run mode just as though the entire project were running. The only difference is that while the events of the control execute, they are not raised to the container application. For example, assume you have an ActiveX control that exposes the Click event of the UserControl. The code placed in the UserControl's Click event by a developer executes when the UserControl is clicked while the project is running. However, the Click event of the control is not raised if the control is being edited at design time. If Visual Basic encounters a RaiseEvent method while the control is activated, the RaiseEvent statement is ignored and no error occurs.

 The primary benefit of enabling editing at design time is to let the developer interactively set properties rather than having to enter them manually in the Properties window. For example, the Data Bound Grid control lets you interactively size columns at design time. Few controls support editing at design time.

Creating Invisible Controls

Although creating an interface for an ActiveX control is important, it's also important to know how to create a control that has no interface, that is, a control that is invisible at runtime, such as Visual Basic's Timer or MAPI controls (refer to Figure 5-5).

Instead of creating a control that is invisible at runtime, consider creating an ActiveX DLL instead. Controls require more resources than in-process ActiveX DLLs.

The way to make a control invisible at runtime is to set the UserControl's Invisible-AtRuntime property to **True**. Obviously, you could set the control's Visible property to **False** instead, but the Visible property of an ActiveX control is available to the container hosting the control. To ensure that a control stays invisible at runtime, you must set the InvisibleAtRuntime property to **True**.

As was discussed in the section on creating container controls, some container objects may not support all features made available to Visual Basic ActiveX controls. The InvisibleAtRuntime property is one of these features. If you place a control with its InvisibleAtRuntime property set to **True** on a container that does not support this property, the control will be visible at runtime.

ActiveX
Controls

Giving a UserControl a Toolbox Bitmap

One interface element of your custom control that you may overlook is its toolbox bitmap. This is the picture displayed in the toolbox of a project once your ActiveX control has been added, using the Components dialog box(see Figure 5-12).

Adding a custom toolbox bitmap to your controls is simple. The only real work involved is designing an intuitive bitmap using your favorite graphics program. (Windows Paint works just fine). The bitmap needs to be 16 pixels wide by 15 pixels high. Once you've created the bitmap, simply assign it to the UserControl's ToolboxBitmap property.

Creating an intuitive, attractive, and functional interface for all of your controls should be an important goal. If you're not comfortable creating interfaces, solicit input from users whose opinions you trust. Often, someone who has used controls similar to what you're trying to create can offer valuable advice on what an interface should, and should not, look like.

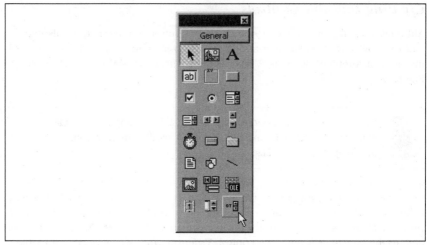

Figure 5-12: All of your ActiveX controls should have a unique, identifying toolbox bitmap like this Spin Button control

Creating a Control's Developer Interface

The usability and functionality of a control's user interface, although extremely important, is often only a small part of a control's entire interface. In addition to the need for a control to interact with an end user, the control needs to expose a development interface that programmers can use to change the control's appearance, invoke control functions, and retrieve control notifications. These three development requirements are fulfilled by the creation of control properties, methods, and events, respectively.

Exposing Control Attributes as Properties

Adding properties to an ActiveX control is performed almost exactly like adding a property to an ActiveX code component—by creating property procedures. Since much of the information on adding properties to a control duplicates the material presented in Chapter 4, *Creating and Testing ActiveX Code Components*, these topics will receive only cursory coverage here. However, the concepts specifically related to ActiveX custom controls that have not been discussed previously are discussed in more detail here.

Creating property procedures

As discussed in Chapter 4, the three types of property procedures are:

Property Get
Used to return the value of a property

Property Let
Used to set the value of a property

Property Set
Used to set the value of a property that contains an object

The next sections describe how to use these property procedures. For a more in-depth discussion, refer to Chapter 4.

Creating readable properties using Property Get procedures. Property Get procedures are similar to Function procedures in that they return values. Property Get procedures expose the values of a control's properties. A Property Get procedure has the following syntax:

```
[Public/Private] Property Get PropertyName() As DataType
```

In order for users to access the Property Get procedure, it must be declared as `Public`. You can use the `Private` or `Friend` keyword when declaring property procedures, just as you can for property procedures of ActiveX code components, but such procedures will not be included in the component's type library, and they won't be available to other applications.

On the Exams

Be sure to read the discussion in Chapter 4 on creating Friend procedures. You *will* be asked about using `Friend` on the exams.

Generally, a Property Get procedure returns the value of a *member* variable. A member variable is a private module-level variable used to store information needed internally by the User control. For example, suppose you have a control and you want to expose a property called DateFormat. To do this, you would first create a module-level member variable like this:

```
Private m_DateFormat As String
```

The module-level variable will hold the actual date format at all times. To expose the value in this variable, you create a property procedure such as this:

```
Public Property Get DateFormat() As String
    DateFormat = m_DateFormat
End Property
```

Property procedures don't always expose member variables. Often, they expose properties of constituent controls. To learn how to do this, see the section "Delegating properties to constituent controls" later in this chapter.

The benefits of using a property procedure to expose a value, rather than simply declaring a module variable as Public, are demonstrated in the next example.

Creating writable properties using Property Let procedures. While a Property Get procedure is used to view or retrieve the value of property, it cannot be used to change the value of a property. To allow a user to change the value of a property, you use a Property Let procedure. Property Let procedures are similar to Sub procedures in that they don't return a value, but they always accept at least one parameter. The format of a Property Let procedure is:

```
[Public/Private] Property Let PropertyName
    (ByVal NewValue As NewValueDataType)
```

Generally, you set the value of a member variable equal to the value passed to the property procedure. For example, to create a Property Let procedure that allows a user to change the property discussed in the previous section, you could use the following code:

```
Public Property Let DateFormat(New_DateFormat As String)
    m_DateFormat = New_DateFormat
End Property
```

The great thing about using Property Let procedures, as opposed to simply exposing a public variable, is that you have complete control over the property. For example, if you exposed a public string variable called *DateFormat* instead of using the property procedures discussed here, the user could set the value of *DateFormat* to any string. However, by using a Property Let procedure, you can add data validation such as this:

```
Public Property Let DateFormat(New_DateFormat As String)

    If New_DateFormat <> "m/d/yy" And New_DateFormat <> "mm/d/yy" Then
        Exit Property
    End If

    m_DateFormat = New_DateFormat

    PropertyChanged "DateFormat"

End Property
```

Property Let procedures allow you to validate proposed property values and call any code procedure or execute any code statement (such as raising a custom event) when the property is changed.

 If you paid close attention to the preceding code, you may have noticed the PropertyChanged statement. The PropertyChanged statement is discussed in the section "Implementing Property Persistence." It's shown here to illustrate that it's used with Property Let procedures and is important.

Matching Property Get and Property Let parameters. If you make a property both readable and writable using both a Property Get and a Property Let procedure, the parameters of the two procedures *must* match. In the following two property procedures, the word *type* is used in place of an actual datatype, to illustrate which datatypes must match:

```
Public Property Get Color() as type
   ...
End Property

Public Property Let Color(ByVal new_color As type)
   ...
End Property
```

The datatype returned by the Property Get procedure is the same as the datatype of the parameter accepted by the Property Let procedure. If you attempt to create a Property Let and a Property Get procedure for the same property name using different datatypes, you'll get an error when you attempt to compile.

 Properties can accept and return multiple values. Please refer to Chapter 4 on how to create Property Let and Property Get procedures that work with multiple parameters.

Property procedures that accept objects as parameters rather than a traditional datatype such as a string must be declared as Property Set procedures. Refer to Chapter 4 for specific information on creating and using Property Set procedures.

Delegating property procedures to the UserControl

Although the UserControl has a number of properties such as BackColor and Font, these properties aren't directly exposed to developers using the control. However, you can easily expose inherent UserControl properties by creating Property Let and Property Get statements that *delegate* to corresponding properties of the User-Control. For example, the following two procedures expose the BackColor property of the UserControl so that a developer can both retrieve and change the BackColor property of the UserControl:

```
Public Property Get BackColor() As OLE_COLOR

    BackColor = UserControl.BackColor

End Property

Public Property Let BackColor(New_BackColor As OLE_COLOR)

    UserControl.BackColor = New_BackColor

    PropertyChanged "BackColor"

End Property
```

OLE_COLOR is a standard datatype, and it's discussed in the section "Defining color properties," later in this chapter. The important concept here is that these property procedures delegate to a property of the UserControl, rather than to a member variable.

When you create a property procedure that has the same name as a property of the UserControl, code that you write within the UserControl project always refers to the property procedure, not the actual property of the UserControl. To make changes to a property of the UserControl that has corresponding property procedures, prefix the UserControl property reference with the UserControl object.

If you don't pay careful attention to this detail, you can create potential problems in your code. For example, using the following Property Let procedure in place of the one shown previously, would cause an "Out of Stack Space" error when a developer attempted to set the BackColor property:

```
Public Property Let BackColor(New_BackColor As OLE_COLOR)

    BackColor = New_BackColor          ' Incorrect
    PropertyChanged "BackColor"

End Property
```

The reason for an "Out of Stack Space" error is that in the statement BackColor = New_BackColor, the BackColor on the left of the = sign refers to the BackColor property procedure, not the actual property of the UserControl. This incorrect reference causes the BackColor Property Let procedure to be called recursively until the stack space has been exhausted. By prefixing the property reference with the UserControl object, as shown in the first Property Let procedure, the Back-Color property of the UserControl is referenced.

 You must keep in mind that your ActiveX control is *always* running when a developer is using it, regardless of whether or not the hosting program is a project in design view or a running compiled application. Because the control is always in run mode, you cannot expose design-time properties of the UserControl. Attempting to expose a design-time–only property of the UserControl causes a compile error to occur when you attempt to compile the control.

Delegating properties to constituent controls

When creating an aggregate control (an ActiveX control that contains constituent controls), it's common to delegate properties of the ActiveX control to one or more of its constituent controls. Suppose you're creating a custom control designed to behave like a standard text box, except that the ActiveX control will allow only numbers to be entered.

Exposing properties of the text box, such as BackColor, Font, or Text, is extremely easy to do using Property Get and Property Let procedures. For instance, to expose the Text property of the text box as a Text property of the custom control, you could use a Property Let procedure such as this (don't worry about the PropertyChanged statement—you'll learn about that shortly):

```
Public Property Let Text(New_Text As String)

    Text1.Text = New_Text

    PropertyChanged "Text"

End Property
```

Just as when using property procedures to set member variables, you can add validation code (or any other code for that matter) to the Property Let procedure that delegates to a constituent control. In this case, the text box needs to allow numeric-only input, and allowing a programmer to pass anything other than a number to the Text property of the control doesn't make any sense. It's easy to restrict the Text property to a number by modifying the Property Let procedure like this:

```
Public Property Let Text(New_Text As String)

    If Not IsNumeric(New_Text) Then Exit Property

    Text1.Text = New_Text

    PropertyChanged "Text"

End Property
```

Since the Text property can accept only numbers, the name of the property (Text) isn't really applicable. It would be more appropriate to give the control a Value property. The following code shows how you can delegate a property to a constituent control, even when the property names are different:

```
Public Property Let Value(New_Value As String)

    If Not IsNumeric(New_Value) Then Exit Property

    Text1.Text = New_Value

    PropertyChanged "Value"

End Property
```

Mapping a property to multiple constituent controls. Because you have complete control of code execution within a Property procedure, you aren't limited to delegating a property to a single constituent control. For instance, the following code sets the BackColor properties of two constituent controls, as well as a property of the UserControl, when a single BackColor Property Let procedure is called:

```
Public Property Let BackColor(New_BackColor As OLE_COLOR)

    UserControl.BackColor = New_BackColor
    Text1.BackColor = New_BackColor
    Combo1.BackColor = New_BackColor

End Property
```

Avoiding errors when delegating to constituent controls. It can't be emphasized enough that a custom control is always running when a developer is using it, even when its interface is not active and the control is on a container in the design environment. This means that all of the constituent controls are running as well. If you attempt to expose a design-time–only property of a constituent control through your custom control, a compile error occurs when you attempt to compile the control.

Maintaining authority of your constituent controls. Although it may appear easier to expose a constituent control as a property of the UserControl, rather than create property procedures and delegate them to properties of constituent controls, don't. At first, it may seem that you are doing the developer a favor, but you're not. For one thing, it's a good idea to expose properties through property procedures so that you can perform data validation. When you expose a control as an Object property, the developer has *direct access to each and every property and method* of the constituent control. In the previous example, the developer could set the Text property of the text box to whatever he desired—bypassing your validation code.

Earlier in this chapter you were shown how to synchronize the size of a constituent control with the size of the UserControl. If you were to let a developer change the Height, Width, Top, or Left properties of a constituent control directly, all of the wonderful appearance code you've written could be completely circumvented.

If losing authority over the appearance and data validation of your constituent controls isn't reason enough not to expose a constituent control as an Object property (yet it should be), consider performance.

You might expect to be able to expose a text box using the following Property Get statement:

```
Property Get Text1() As TextBox

    Set Text1 = Text1

End Property
```

This code actually fails when compiled because the TextBox control is an intrinsic Visual Basic datatype; it can't be exposed outside of Visual Basic and therefore cannot be the datatype of a public member of a UserControl. You could, instead, expose the constituent control using the following Property Get procedure:

```
Property Get Text1() As Object

    Set Text1 = Text1

End Property
```

Declaring an object variable **As Object**, however, causes the object to use late binding, causing performance to suffer considerably.

 Refer to Chapter 3 for more information on early and late binding.

Defining color properties

You're probably familiar with the way you can select a color for a property in the Properties window. When you click on a color property, such as BackColor, Visual Basic displays a dropdown arrow. Clicking the dropdown arrow displays a dropdown color palette from which you can select a system or a palette color (see Figure 5-13).

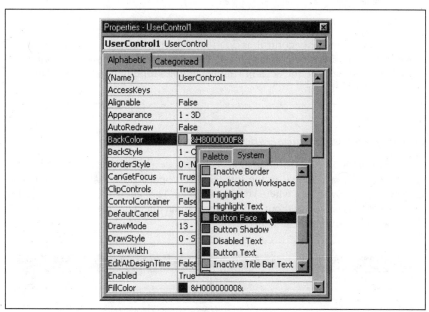

Figure 5-13: Visual Basic provides color palettes for easy color selection in the Properties window

You can have Visual Basic display such a color palette for your custom color properties by using the OLE_COLOR datatype. The OLE_COLOR datatype is a valid datatype, like Integer or Boolean, and OLE_COLOR actually stores its value as a Long. However, using OLE_COLOR instead of Long causes Visual Basic to treat the property in a unique way.

The following module code shows the OLE_COLOR datatype used in both a Property Get and a Property Let statement. In this example, a developer can select her favorite color from a dropdown color palette in the Properties window. The selected color is then stored (as a Long) in a member variable, and the BackColor of the UserControl is set to the selected color. The Property Get procedure returns the selected color by retrieving the value from the member variable:

```
Option Explicit
Dim m_FavoriteColor As OLE_COLOR

Public Property Let FavoriteColor(New_FavoriteColor As OLE_COLOR)

    m_FavoriteColor = New_FavoriteColor
    UserControl.BackColor = m_FavoriteColor
```

```
End Property


Public Property Get FavoriteColor() As OLE_COLOR

    FavoriteColor = m_FavoriteColor

End Property
```

 Each time the control is loaded, FavoriteColor is lost because m_FavoriteColor is reinitialized. To learn about saving and restoring properties, see the section "Implementing Property Persistence," later in this chapter.

Defining and using Enumerations (Enums)

Enumerations allow you to enumerate and expose named constants for a property's values. Enums appear in the IntelliSense dropdown lists (also called autolist members dropdown list) when you write code. This allows a developer to use your named constants without having to commit them to memory. Figure 5-14 shows a simple enumeration in action.

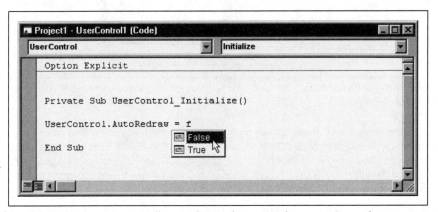

Figure 5-14: Enumerations alleviate the need to remember many named constants

While the enumeration shown here is a simple one, consisting of only **True** or **False**, enums can contain many values. An enumeration is really a collection of Long Integers, and named members of an enumeration must correspond to a valid Long value. Therefore, an enumeration is really just a collection of Long Integer constants that are saved in the object's type library and are accessible by name. Enumerations are declared in a manner similar to a function or property declaration. The following code shows the syntax of an enumeration procedure:

```
Public Enum [EnumName]
    EnumNamedConstant1 = [Long Integer]
```

```
    EnumNamedConstant2 = [Long Integer]
End Enum
```

For illustration, the `TrueFalse` enumeration shown in Figure 5-14 might be declared like this:

```
Public Enum TrueFalse
    False = 0
    True = -1
End Enum
```

Enums are not restricted to containing simple True/False constants. The following Enum allows a developer to choose from several different orientation settings:

```
Public Enum eOrientation
    eVertical = 0
    eHorizontal = 1
    eLeftDiagonal = 2
    eRightDiagonal = 3
End Enum
```

> Enumerations can contain whatever type of named constants you want to create, but each named constant must have a corresponding Long Integer value, and public Enums must be declared within the Declarations section of the class module in which they are used.

Just creating an enumeration does not expose it as a set of possible values to developers referencing a property. Once you've created an enumeration, you must use it as a datatype for all parameters within procedures for which you want to use its values. For instance, to expose the `eOrientation` enumeration shown previously, you could use it as a datatype for an Orientation property of an object by using the following Property Let and Property Get procedures:

```
Public Property Let Orientation (New_Orientation As eOrientation)
    . . .
End Property

Public Property Get Orientation() As eOrientation
    . . .
End Property
```

When the developer references a property declared as an enumeration, the enumeration values appear in the autolist members dropdown list, as shown in Figure 5-15.

> Using an enumeration as a property datatype does not restrict the allowable property values to those declared in the enumeration. For example, a developer could set the Orientation property discussed here to 7, even though there is no enumeration with the value of 7. Because of this behavior, you still need to add data validation to property procedures based on enumerations.

Active X
Controls

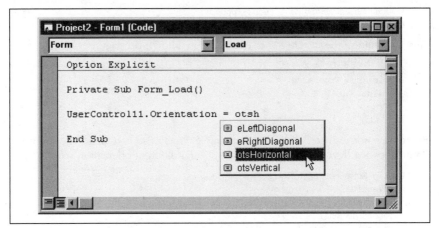

Figure 5-15: Custom enumerations make your controls easier to program

Your enumerations are available in the code window, and developers can select values from an enumeration in the Properties window (see Figure 5-16) and view the values using the Object Browser.

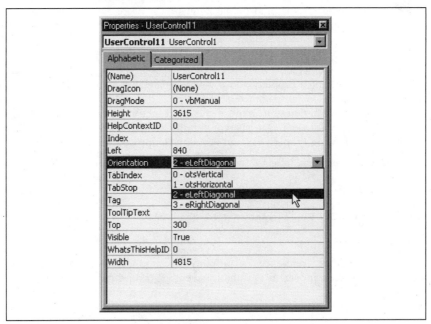

Figure 5-16: Public enumerations make it easy to set values in the Properties window

Providing property pages

Visual Basic's Properties window provides an easy way to set simple design-time properties. However, it falls short when you need to expose complex properties, such as allowing a developer to work with collections like the column headers of a grid control. Most grid controls let a developer create columns at design time. Since the developer controls how many columns the grid contains, you have no way of exposing column header information (other than a ColumnCount property perhaps) through the Properties window. To allow complete design-time property changes and to make it easier to set properties for complex controls, most commercial ActiveX controls provide *property pages*. Property pages are tabbed dialog boxes that offer unique interfaces for manipulating the properties of a control.

The easiest way to tell if a control exposes property pages is to look for a (Custom) property in the Properties window (see Figure 5-17). If the control contains a (Custom) property, double-clicking the property or clicking its build button displays its custom property pages. Figure 5-18 shows the custom property pages of Microsoft's Data Bound Grid control that comes with Visual Basic.

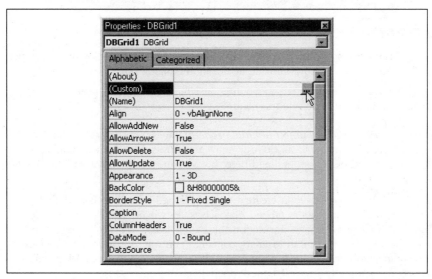

Figure 5-17: To access a control's custom property pages, use its (Custom) property

Property pages exhibit the following standard behaviors:

- Property pages always appear as tabbed dialog boxes, even when containing only one tab.
- Property pages always have OK, Cancel, and Apply buttons (property pages created in Visual Basic do not contain a Help button).
- When property pages are first displayed, they reflect the state of the currently selected ActiveX control(s).

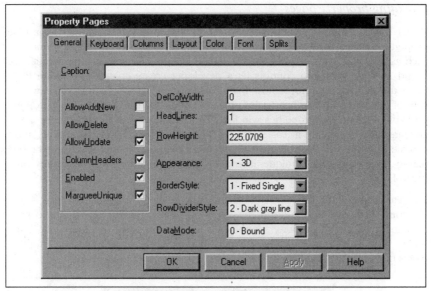

Figure 5-18: Property pages make setting design-time properties easier

- Clicking Apply instantly applies any property changes made by the developer to the selected control(s), without closing the dialog box.

- Switching from one tab to another instantly applies any property changes from the page to all selected controls.

Using the PropertyPage object to build property pages. You can (and should) add custom property pages to all of your ActiveX controls. Visual Basic handles some of the standard behaviors outlined here, but you must implement code to handle others.

First of all, you don't have to create a tabbed dialog box; Visual Basic handles the creation and display of the tabbed dialog box. However, you do have to design each tab that you want to appear on the dialog box. You don't use a standard form to do this, or even an ordinary container control, as you might when using third-party tab controls. Instead, Visual Basic contains an object used specifically for creating property page tabs: the PropertyPage object.

The steps involved in creating custom property pages are:

1. Add one or more PropertyPage objects to the project.

2. Set any appropriate properties of each property page.

3. Link a UserControl to its appropriate property pages.

4. Design the user interface of the property pages to reflect the public properties of the control.

5. Add code to set the property page interface to reflect the current state of the selected control(s).

6. Add code to apply changes made on each property page to the selected control(s).

Adding a property page to a project is easy: choose Add Property Page from the Project menu. Property pages look very much like forms or UserControls in design mode (see Figure 5-19).

 The dialog box shown in Figure 5-19 shows a single property page; each tab in a set of property pages is defined using a separate PropertyPage object.

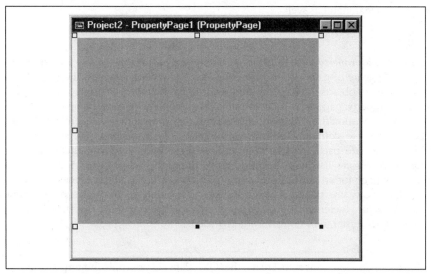

Figure 5-19: PropertyPage objects look similar to UserControls

Setting PropertyPage object properties. It's usually best avoid changing most of the PropertyPage object properties. Since your property pages are hosted on a standard tabbed dialog box provided by COM, any major changes to the appearance of a property page will show up glaringly to developers using your control. Although you should refrain from changing most appearance properties of the PropertyPage object, there is one property you should almost always change: the StandardSize property.

The StandardSize property lets you control the size of the property pages displayed for a control. The StandardSize property has a default value of *0 - Custom*. Whenever you manually change the size of the property page, its StandardSize property automatically changes to *0 - Custom*. The other two possible values for Standard-Size are *1 - Small*, and *2 - Large*. Because property pages are used to give developers a common method of changing ActiveX control properties, the general appearance of property pages of different controls should remain constant. This includes using system colors and common sizes. Although you can create custom-sized PropertyPage objects, it's discouraged for several reasons, including the fact that some ActiveX container applications are only able to display large property pages. Therefore, to make your properties pages more cross-application friendly, set the StandardSize property value to *2 - Large*. Even if you don't intend to have a control used outside of the Visual Basic environment, you should still consider using the values *1 - Small*, or *2 - Large*.

You should always change the Name property of a property page to something meaningful. In addition, the text placed in the Caption property becomes the text displayed on the tab in the property pages, so you should always set the Caption property to something meaningful as well.

Designing a property page interface. Property pages can be simple or complex. The complexity of a set of property pages generally depends upon the number of PropertyPage objects (tabs) supported by a control, as well as the layouts of each of the property page tabs. The layout of the property page is completely up to you, but you should try to group related properties onto the same property page. Text boxes are commonly used to reference text or numeric property values, checkboxes are used for true/false values, and option buttons, list boxes, and combo boxes are used for multiple choice property values. Figure 5-20 shows a property page for an ActiveX custom Spin Button control. On this property page, a developer can use the text boxes to enter the numeric properties of the Spin Button (Value, Increment, Min, and Max). To make selecting the orientation of the Spin control easier, radio buttons are provided.

You don't have to create the OK, Cancel, or Apply button; COM adds these to the dialog at runtime.

Try to make your property pages as clean and intuitive as possible. Linking prop-erties of a control to specific property pages is easy (as you'll see in the next two sections). Therefore, the ease of use and the intuitiveness of your property pages deserve the most attention.

Making a property page reflect current property values. Just adding controls to a property page object doesn't link the properties of your custom control to the corresponding controls on a property page. The linking of controls on a property page to the properties of an ActiveX control requires two steps. The first is to make the controls on the property page reflect the property values of the currently

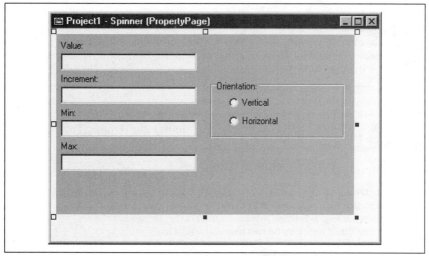

Figure 5-20: Property pages should allow for intuitively entering property values

selected custom control (or controls, as you'll see). Obviously, when your property pages are first displayed, they need to reflect immediately the current state of the selected control(s). The PropertyPage object includes a special event called SelectionChanged that can be used to do just this.

The SelectionChanged event fires when the selection of controls has changed (for instance, when the developer held down Ctrl while clicking an additional control), as well as the first time the property pages of one or more controls is displayed. You use this event in conjunction with the SelectedControls collection (discussed next) to ensure that the property pages always accurately reflect all selected controls.

The SelectionChanged event has the following format:

```
Private Sub PropertyPage_SelectionChanged()

End Sub
```

The SelectionChanged event is where you add code to update the controls on the property pages to reflect the currently selected controls' property values. Some containers allow you to select multiple controls and change all of their related properties at once. Since it is impossible to reference a single UserControl object and expect such a container to properly make property changes to other selected controls, you can't simply reference your UserControl object in code. Fortunately, this situation is easy to handle, using the SelectedControls collection.

The SelectedControls collection gives you the ability to reference properties of multiple controls. If a single control is selected, rather than a group of controls, or if the parent of the custom control doesn't support the selection of multiple controls, the SelectedControls collection contains only one control; you don't need to write special exception code.

The SelectedControls collection doesn't behave as you might expect. Instead of iterating every item in the collection, you reference only index 0 (the first element in the collection). Element 0 references *all* of the selected controls. No other index values are used at this time.

The SelectedControls collection is best understood by looking at code that uses it. The following procedure contains code to update the PropertyPage object in Figure 5-20:

```
Private Sub PropertyPage_SelectionChanged()

    txtMax.Text = SelectedControls(0).Max
    txtMin.Text = SelectedControls(0).Min
    txtIncrement.Text = SelectedControls(0).Increment
    txtValue.Text = SelectedControls(0).Value

    If SelectedControls(0).Orientation = 0 Then
      optOrientation(0).Value = True
    Else
      optOrientation(0).Value = False
    End If

End Sub
```

As you can see, you use `SelectedControls(0)` in place of a UserControl reference. The container hosting the control is responsible for interacting with all selected controls.

Applying property page changes to selected controls. Once you've created the interface of your PropertyPage objects and added code to reflect the property values of selected controls, you need to add code that applies changes made on the property pages to the selected control(s). This is a lot simpler than you might expect.

To ensure that changes to your property pages are correctly applied to the selected controls, do the following:

1. Set the Changed property of the PropertyPage object to **True** whenever a property value on the property page is changed.

2. Add code to the ApplyChanges event of the PropertyPage to update the properties of the SelectedControls collection.

Because the interface of a property page can be very complex, the PropertyPage object itself is not "smart;" it can't automatically determine when a developer has made changes to the values on the property page. If a property page doesn't know changes have been made to controls it contains, the Apply button will not be enabled, nor will changes be automatically applied when a developer switches tabs or closes the property pages using the OK button. You tell the PropertyPage object that one or more property values have changed by setting the Changed property of the property page to **True**. When you do this is entirely up to you, but the following are some common ways to notify a PropertyPage object when a change is made to a property value displayed on the property page:

For a text box:

```
Private Sub txtValue_Change()
    ...
    PropertyPage.Changed = True
End Sub
```

For an option button:

```
Private Sub optOrientation_Click(Index As Integer)
    ...
    PropertyPage.Changed = True
End Sub
```

For a checkbox:

```
Private Sub Check1_Click()
    ...
    PropertyPage.Changed = True
End Sub
```

As long as you set the Changed property of a PropertyPage object to True each time a developer makes a change to a property value, the ProperyPage object will know that changes have been made and can act accordingly. However, knowing changes have been made is not enough. Just as you had to write code to reflect a control's property values on a property page, you must also write code to apply changes made on the property page to the selected control(s). The PropertyPage object includes an ApplyChanges event for this purpose.

The ApplyChanges event is called whenever a developer does one of the following:

ActiveX Controls

- Clicks the Apply button on the property pages

- Switches from one property page to another

- Clicks the OK button on the property pages

 It is extremely important to remember that the ApplyChanges event fires only when one of the aforementioned occurs *and* if the Changed property of the current property page has been set to True.

The code that you add to the ApplyChanges event is pretty much the opposite of the code you place in the SelectionChanged event. Instead of retrieving values from the SelectedControls collection and updating the display on a property page, you retrieve the values of the properties on the property page and update the corresponding properties of the SelectedControls collection. The following procedure shows the ApplyChanges event that corresponds with the SelectionChanged event shown earlier:

```
Private Sub PropertyPage_ApplyChanges()

    SelectedControls(0).Max = txtMax.Text
    SelectedControls(0).Min = txtMin.Text
```

```
SelectedControls(0).Increment = txtIncrement.Text
SelectedControls(0).Value = txtValue.Text

If optOrientation(0).Value = True Then
   SelectedControls(0).Orientation = 0
Else
   SelectedControls(0).Orientation = 1
End If

   End Sub
```

A wonderful feature of PropertyPage objects is that you don't have to write validation code for the controls on the property page; data validation is handled in your Property Let procedures. This is just one more reason why you should always use Property Let procedures rather than declaring public variables or exposing constituent controls as object properties.

Assigning property pages to a control. Once property pages are created for a control, they need to be assigned to the control. You can assign any of the custom property pages that you've created, and you can assign one or more of the standard property pages made available by Visual Basic. In addition, you also specify the order in which the property pages appear as tabs. To assign property pages to a control, select the UserControl object to display its properties in the Properties window, click once on the PropertyPages property in the Properties window to display the ellipses button, then click the ellipses button to display the Connect Property Pages dialog box shown in Figure 5-21.

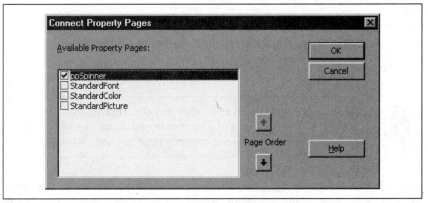

Figure 5-21: The Connect Property Pages dialog box is used to assign property pages to a UserControl

The StandardFont, StandardPicture, and StandardColor property pages are standard property pages provided by Visual Basic. These allow you to add Font, Picture, and Color property pages without having to create them from scratch. To assign a property page to the control, simply select its checkbox. The order in which the property pages appear in the list is the order that their corresponding tabs appear on the Property Page dialog box for the control. To adjust the order of the property pages, use the up and down arrow buttons.

Implementing Property Persistence

The last, and maybe the most important, issue that needs to be discussed concerning ActiveX control properties is *property persistence*, which allows a control to remember, or persist, its property values between sessions. This allows the values of a control's property to be restored to the state they were in when the project was last saved. To understand property persistence, you must first understand the lifetime of an ActiveX control.

Understanding an ActiveX control's lifetime

When you first add a custom control to a form, a new instance of the control is created. You might think that this is the only new instance of the control that will be created while the project is loaded. However, this is a common misconception that can cause serious problems for a control developer.

Whenever an ActiveX control switches between run and design mode, the control is destroyed and recreated. So, each time the developer presses F5 to run a Visual Basic project containing an ActiveX control, the current instance of the control in design mode is destroyed, and another is created on the form in run mode. Then, when the developer stops running the project, the current instance of the control is destroyed and another new instance is created on the container (usually a form) in design mode. Without a mechanism to persist property values, an ActiveX control would have all of its properties initialized to their default values each time it was created. Obviously, this won't do. An ActiveX control needs to be able to store property settings between instances, or it's useless. What's the point of letting a developer set public properties of a control if the control always reverts to its default property values? Visual Basic includes built-in functionality to make implementing property persistence relatively easy—if you understand the intricacies of how it works.

Four key events occur as a control instance is created and destroyed. These are:

- Initialize
- InitProperties
- ReadProperties
- WriteProperties

The Initialize event is *always* the first event fired when a new instance of a control is created. You might be tempted to place property initialization code (setting property defaults) in the Initialize event, but this is the wrong place for such code. The Initialize event fires *every* time a new instance is created, not just the first time a new instance of the control is created, as it is placed on a form or other container. Therefore, if you used the Initialize event to initialize properties for a control, the control's properties would revert back to the defaults each time the control is destroyed and recreated. This gives the same effect as not implementing property persistence at all.

The InitProperties event fires only once—the *first time* an instance of a control is created. This occurs when a control is first placed on a form or other container, but not when the control is created when switching between design and run mode in a project. The InitProperties event is where you place the code to initialize default property values for a new control. Once a control is placed on a form, the InitProperties event is never called again.

The ReadProperties event fires every time a new instance of the control is created, *except for the first time*. The ReadProperties event is where you place code to read previously saved property values and apply them to the control. Because this event fires whenever a new instance of the control is created, it is executed each time the project containing the control is switched between run and design mode, and it occurs when the control is created by loading the form on which the control resides in Visual Basic's design view.

The WriteProperties event fires whenever *a design-time instance* of the control is destroyed. This occurs when the developer switches a project from design mode to run mode, and any time the developer saves the form on which the control is placed. The WriteProperties event is where you place code to save the current property values of the control so that they can be retrieved later in the Read-Properties event.

The order of ActiveX control events is:

1. Initialize event (occurs each time an instance of the control is created)

2. InitProperties event (occurs only the first time an instance of the control is created)

3. ReadProperties event (occurs each subsequent time an instance of the control is created)

4. Resize event (occurs each time a new instance of the control is created or the control is resized)

5. Paint event (occurs each time the control needs to paint all or part of itself)

6. WriteProperties event (occurs whenever a design-time instance of the control is destroyed)

7. Terminate event (occurs whenever an instance of the control is about to be destroyed)

 Do not put any code in the Initialize event that relies on the accuracy of property values read during the ReadProperties event, because the ReadProperties event fires after the Initialize event.

Using the PropertyBag to maintain property persistence

ActiveX controls store their property values using a *PropertyBag* object. The PropertyBag object includes two methods for reading and writing property values: the ReadProperty method and the WriteProperty method. The location in which property data is saved depends on the type of data being stored, and whether the control is in run mode, design mode, or in a compiled executable.

There are essentially three types of property data you can store:

- Single-value text information, such as a control's BackColor or Text property
- Single-value binary information, such as bitmaps and fonts
- Complex properties, such as arrays

Single-value text information is stored in the Visual Basic source file that defines the host of the control (FRM files for forms, CTL files for UserControls, DOB files for UserDocuments, and PAG files for property pages). While source files are an excellent place to store text information, they can't be used to store binary information because they are simple text files. Binary property information is stored in a file having the same name as the host container's main filename, with a different extension. The following lists the extensions used to store binary information:

- FRX for forms
- CTX for ActiveX UserControls
- DOX for UserDocuments
- PGX for property pages

Although text and binary information are stored in different locations, they are saved and retrieved in code in a similar manner.

 Changes made to properties while the control's host project is in run mode, or when it is running as a compiled program, are not saved at all. If you change the BackColor property of a TextBox control at runtime, for example, the property change is not saved and the control reverts back to its previously saved properties the next time the program is started or the control is put in design mode.

ActiveX Controls

Saving text information using the PropertyBag. Visual Basic doesn't keep track internally of all of the public properties of your control; you have to explicitly save each property value that will need to be retrieved at a later time. Both text and binary data are saved using the WriteProperty method of the PropertyBag object. The WriteProperty method has the following syntax:

```
PropBag.WriteProperty(DataName, Value[, DefaultValue])
```

The *DataName* parameter specifies the name of the property whose value is being saved. The *Value* parameter is the actual data to store for the property.

Each time the WriteProperties event of a UserControl occurs, Visual Basic erases all previously saved property values. If you specify a value for *DefaultValue* that is equal to the value of the *Value* parameter, Visual Basic won't save the property value in the container's source file. This works in conjunction with the ReadProperty function that retrieves stored values. If no stored value exists, the default property is used. This helps to greatly reduce the amount of space needed to store property values. You should always specify a *DefaultValue* for each property saved to the PropertyBag. You must also supply a *DefaultValue* for the ReadProperty method, discussed in the next section.

Figure 5-22 shows a WriteProperties event that uses the WriteProperty method of the PropertyBag object to store property values. The `Call` statement is necessary, and you'll get a compile error if you omit it.

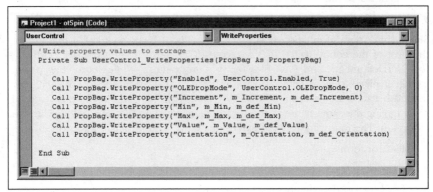

```
Project1 - otSpin (Code)

UserControl                                    WriteProperties

    'Write property values to storage
    Private Sub UserControl_WriteProperties(PropBag As PropertyBag)

        Call PropBag.WriteProperty("Enabled", UserControl.Enabled, True)
        Call PropBag.WriteProperty("OLEDropMode", UserControl.OLEDropMode, 0)
        Call PropBag.WriteProperty("Increment", m_Increment, m_def_Increment)
        Call PropBag.WriteProperty("Min", m_Min, m_def_Min)
        Call PropBag.WriteProperty("Max", m_Max, m_def_Max)
        Call PropBag.WriteProperty("Value", m_Value, m_def_Value)
        Call PropBag.WriteProperty("Orientation", m_Orientation, m_def_Orientation)

    End Sub
```

Figure 5-22: Property values are saved using the WriteProperties event of the UserControls with the WriteProperty method of the PropertyBag object

As you can see, all of the property values being stored in Figure 5-22 have a default value specified. Some of these properties store UserControl properties such as Enabled and OLEDropMode, while others store the values of member variables. You could store property values of constituent controls in the same way.

Reading text information using the PropertyBag. Property values are read from the PropertyBag in much the same way they are saved. Property values are saved using the WriteProperty method of the PropertyBag but retrieved using the ReadProperty method.

The ReadProperty method has the following syntax:

```
PropBag.ReadProperty(DataName[, DefaultValue])
```

The *DataName* parameter must correlate exactly with the *DataName* specified when the property value was saved with the WriteProperties event. If the *DataName* parameters are different, Visual Basic believes they are different properties. When you specify a *DefaultValue*, Visual Basic uses it when a saved value of the specified property isn't found. Remember from the previous section that when the value of a property is the same as the default value specified in the WriteProperty method call, no information is stored in the source file, keeping the file size to a minimum. Figure 5-23 shows the ReadProperties event used to retrieve the property values stored in the WriteProperties event shown in Figure 5-22.

Notice that there is a ReadProperty method for each WriteProperty method shown in Figure 5-22. Also, notice how the values returned from the PropertyBag are placed in internal member variables rather than passed to their specific property procedure. For example, the statement:

```
m_Min = PropBag.ReadProperty("Min", m_def_Min)
```

```
Project1 - otSpin (Code)
UserControl                              ReadProperties
'Load property values from storage
Private Sub UserControl_ReadProperties(PropBag As PropertyBag)

    UserControl.Enabled = PropBag.ReadProperty("Enabled", True)
    UserControl.OLEDropMode = PropBag.ReadProperty("OLEDropMode", 0)
    m_Increment = PropBag.ReadProperty("Increment", m_def_Increment)
    m_Min = PropBag.ReadProperty("Min", m_def_Min)
    m_Max = PropBag.ReadProperty("Max", m_def_Max)
    m_Value = PropBag.ReadProperty("Value", m_def_Value)
    m_Orientation = PropBag.ReadProperty("Orientation", m_def_Orientation)

End Sub
```

Figure 5-23: Use the ReadProperty method of the PropertyBag object to retrieve
property values saved with the WriteProperty method of the PropertyBag object

---

On the Exams

You do not use a `Call` statement to invoke the ReadProperty method, but
`Call` is required when using the WriteProperty method. You may be asked
to demonstrate this understanding on the exams.

---

is used to retrieve the custom property Min of the UserControl. This value could
be retrieved and sent directly to the Property Let procedure of the Min property
like this:

```
Min = PropBag.ReadProperty("Min", m_def_Min)
```

This statement sets the Min property just as if a developer changed the property
in the Properties window. However, it is often desirable to read many different
properties that affect the appearance of a control prior to updating the actual
display of the control. For example, suppose you're retrieving four properties
from the PropertyBag, and all of those properties relate to the appearance of the
control. Most likely, each Property Let statement of the appearance-related properties calls code to update the appearance of the control. That way, the appearance
is updated each time a developer makes a change to an appearance related property. If you passed the values returned by ReadProperty directly to the Property
Let procedures, the appearance of the control would be updated four times. By
setting the internal member variables and then calling the code that changes the
control's appearance only once, you have increased the speed at which the
control initializes and possibly reduced display flicker caused by continually
changing the appearance of the control on its form.

Notifying Visual Basic when a property changes. To increase the performance of
ActiveX controls, Visual Basic invokes the WriteProperties event of the User-
Control only when a property has been changed. Obviously, if no property values
have been changed, there is no need to incur the overhead of saving property

---

values. Visual Basic needs to know when a property value has changed so that it can trigger the WriteProperties event and display new values in the Properties window. You dictate when a property value is officially changed by using the PropertyChanged method of the UserControl object. The PropertyChanged method has the following syntax:

```
UserControl.PropertyChanged PropertyName
```

Look at the following Property Let procedure from earlier in this chapter:

```
Public Property Let Value(New_Value As String)

    If Not IsNumeric(New_Value) Then Exit Property

    Text1.Text = New_Value

    PropertyChanged "Value"

End Property
```

This statement could be entered as `UserControl.PropertyChanged = "Value"`, but the reference to UserControl isn't necessary.

By calling the PropertyChanged method, you tell Visual Basic that the named property's value has changed. Visual Basic then updates the Properties window to display the new value, and it knows internally to invoke the WriteProperties event of the UserControl at the appropriate time.

Note how the PropertyChanged method is the last statement in the procedure. If you were to place it as the first statement in the procedure, the PropertyChanged method would be called even if an incorrect value (in this case any non-numeric information) was passed to the property procedure. Call the PropertyChanged method only if the property was actually changed.

Saving and retrieving binary properties using the PropertyBag. You know from the previous section that text property information is stored in the container's source file, while binary information is stored in a file of the same name as the source file but with a different extension. Although the two types of data are stored in different places, they are both stored using the methods of the Property-Bag object.

Recall from Chapter 3 that when assigning an object reference to an object variable, you must use the Set statement. When saving and retrieving binary information, such as bitmaps, to and from the PropertyBag, you apply similar principles. Suppose you want to store a picture contained in the Picture property of the UserControl. To save the Picture property to the PropertyBag as binary information, you would use a statement such this:

```
Call PropBag.WriteProperty("Picture", UserControl.Picture, Nothing)
```

Notice the keyword Nothing is used as the default value. When a binary property has its value set to Nothing, the text (None) appears in the Properties window. Other than the use of the Nothing keyword, the WriteProperty for binary data is the same as for text data. However, when reading the value from the PropertyBag you must use a Set statement like this:

```
Set UserControl.Picture = PropBag.ReadProperty("Picture", Nothing)
```

That's all there is to saving binary information to the PropertyBag. Fortunately, Visual Basic handles all of the details of reading and writing the information; you simply have to make the appropriate method calls.

Saving arrays to the PropertyBag. Often, you'll need to store complex property information, such as an array, using the PropertyBag object. Although not readily apparent, this is rather easy to do. The key point to remember is that Visual Basic *doesn't know* what properties to save in the PropertyBag, which is why you must specify a name when writing or reading a property using the PropertyBag object. Since Visual Basic doesn't know about your properties, and you get to specify any property names you want, you're not limited to the names of the public properties of your control; you can save as many property values as you want to the PropertyBag.

An array is simply a defined number of data elements. It stands to reason, then, that you can store each element of the array using the PropertyBag by saving each element as a uniquely named property.

All you need to do to read and write arrays of information using the PropertyBag is to save the total number of array elements, and then use a loop and some string concatenation to store and retrieve the values (see Figure 5-24).

Figure 5-24 shows how you can store data within an array that has an unknown number of elements. The For...Next loop shown here creates a single property for each array element. By concatenating the text Array with the element number, you end up creating the following 10 unique property values:

```
Array0
Array1
Array2
Array3
Array4
Array5
Array6
Array7
Array8
Array9
```

Note that if the number of array elements remains constant, you don't need to write or read the total number of array elements, nor do you need to ReDim the array.

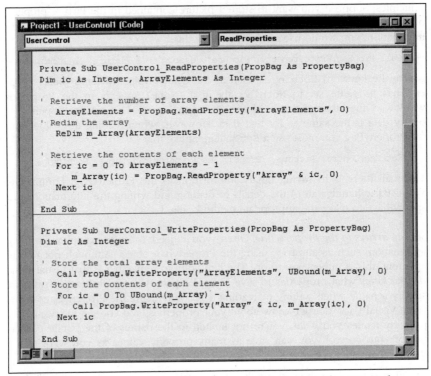

```
Project1 - UserControl1 [Code]                              _ □ x
UserControl                    ▼  ReadProperties                ▼

Private Sub UserControl_ReadProperties(PropBag As PropertyBag)
Dim ic As Integer, ArrayElements As Integer

  ' Retrieve the number of array elements
    ArrayElements = PropBag.ReadProperty("ArrayElements", 0)
  ' Redim the array
    ReDim m_Array(ArrayElements)

  ' Retrieve the contents of each element
    For ic = 0 To ArrayElements - 1
        m_Array(ic) = PropBag.ReadProperty("Array" & ic, 0)
    Next ic

End Sub

Private Sub UserControl_WriteProperties(PropBag As PropertyBag)
Dim ic As Integer

  ' Store the total array elements
    Call PropBag.WriteProperty("ArrayElements", UBound(m_Array), 0)
  ' Store the contents of each element
    For ic = 0 To UBound(m_Array) - 1
        Call PropBag.WriteProperty("Array" & ic, m_Array(ic), 0)
    Next ic

End Sub
```

Figure 5-24: Use looping techniques to store and retrieve array elements in the PropertyBag

One particularly nice feature of the PropertyBag is that each time properties are saved, all previously saved properties are first erased. So, if you are saving data of a variable size array, and the array has been made smaller since the last time the elements were saved, you don't need to worry about deleting the unused values from the PropertyBag.

 Use a similar For...Next loop in the ReadProperties event to retrieve the array values from the PropertyBag.

Adding Methods to ActiveX Controls

Creating methods for an ActiveX control is the same as creating a method for an ActiveX code component: declare a Public Sub or a Public Function procedure. Methods declared as Sub do not return values, but those declared as Function do.

Refer to Chapter 4 for more information on creating methods.

Creating Friend Procedures

Creating Friend procedures is the same whether you are creating ActiveX controls or ActiveX code components. And although Friend procedures are discussed in Chapter 4, this information bears repeating because you will have to demonstrate an understanding of Friend procedures on the exams.

Friend procedures are methods or properties that are available to all modules within an ActiveX control project but not to clients using the control. When you expose a method or property as `Public`, all clients that use the control have access to the method or property. If you declare the method or property as `Private`, clients cannot access the method or property, but neither can other modules or forms within the control project. The `Friend` keyword, when used in place of the `Public` or `Private` keywords, allows code within the project to reference the method or property as though it were declared as `Public`, but clients can neither see nor reference the method or property.

The following shows a property declared as `Friend`:

```
Friend Property Get HiddenProperty() As String
    ...
End Property
```

ActiveX Controls

When a property or method is declared as `Friend`, all modules (both form and code) in the project can call the method or reference the property like normal, but the method or property is not actually part of the class's interface and it is not included in the type library. Therefore, Friend procedures do not appear in the Object Browser, and client applications cannot access them.

Creating and Raising Custom Events

Like methods and properties, creating custom events for an ActiveX control is very much the same as creating events for ActiveX code components.

 Chapter 4 discusses custom events in detail. However, because you will have to demonstrate an understanding of creating and raising events in an ActiveX control, the topic is covered here again. Be sure to study the text in Chapter 4 on creating and using custom events.

Creating and raising custom events within an ActiveX Control

When creating ActiveX controls, it's often necessary to notify a client when the user selects items or otherwise interacts with the interface of the control. Also, a control often needs a way to notify a client when a certain condition has been met. Events allow controls to notify their clients whenever and however you deem necessary without the need of OLE callbacks.

The declaration for a custom event has the following format:

Event EventName([*argumentlist*])

argumentlist is an optional list of parameters to be passed to the client receiving an event.

When you declare an event, don't specify whether the event is public or private; custom events are always public to their hosts. The event procedure created within the client application for the control is private by default, but the user can change the event from private to public, just as you can change this for standard Visual Basic events. After public or private, the name of the object as given at design time by the developer using the control is displayed; for instance, `Private cmdCancel_Click()`. Once you get past the object name, you're dealing with elements defined by the event declaration procedure. You could declare a custom event for the MouseDown event shown previously using the following statement:

```
Event MouseDown(Button As Integer, Shift As Integer, X As Single, _
          Y As Single)
```

As you can see, the argument list in the declarations section appears just as it would appear within the event procedure of the client.

You can use type declaration characters within the declarations statement, but they will appear in "long hand," as shown earlier.

The *argumentlist* has the following format:

```
[ByVal | ByRef] varname[( )] [As type]
```

The format of an event declaration's argument list is similar to that of a Sub or Function procedure declaration argument list, except events cannot have `Optional` or `ParamArray` arguments. In addition, events cannot return a value as functions do.

Just as with standard procedures, all arguments are passed by reference (`ByRef`) by default. To pass an argument by value (`ByVal`), you must supply the `ByVal` keyword.

Once you have an event declared within a UserControl module, you must *raise* the event at appropriate times. When the event is raised, the corresponding event procedure within the client is executed. To raise an event, you use the `RaiseEvent` statement, which has the following syntax:

RaiseEvent *EventName*([*argumentlist*])

Once again, *argumentlist* is an optional list of parameters to pass to the corresponding event procedure. The argument list of a `RaiseEvent` statement is a comma-separated list of variables, arrays, or expressions; each element of the argument list must correspond to an element of the argument list in the event declaration statement. If there are no arguments for the event, omit the parentheses.

If an argument is declared `ByRef` (the default), you must supply a variable in the `RaiseEvent` statement. However, if an argument is declared `ByVal`, you can supply a constant or an expression to the argument in the `RaiseEvent` statement.

Cancel is a common argument of custom events. Consider the following custom event:

```
Event BeforeUpdate(NewValue As String, Cancel As Boolean)
```

This event could be used in a custom control that performs data input and output. In this case, the event could be fired before an update to a record occurred. The *NewValue* parameter passes the data that is to be written to the record, while the *Cancel* parameter is used as a mechanism for the client to cancel the update. Look at the following procedure, which raises this sample BeforeUpdate event:

```
Public Sub SaveNewValue(NewValue As String)

    Dim blnCancel As Boolean

    blnCancel = False
    RaiseEvent BeforeUpdate(NewValue, blnCancel)

    If Not blnCancel Then
        ' Save code goes here
    End If

End Sub
```

This public procedure is a method of the UserControl class. It accepts a string as the value to be saved in a database. The BeforeUpdate event is raised prior to the actual code that makes changes to the database. The event passes both the string that is to be written and a reference to the *blnCancel* Boolean variable, which defaults to `False`.

If the *Cancel* parameter in the event procedure (the reference to *blnCancel* in the previous procedure) is not modified, *blnCancel* remains `False`. However, if it is determined within the event procedure to not save the value, the *Cancel* parameter can be set to `True` and the save code won't execute. The next section shows you what custom event procedures look like in a client.

In the previous example, *NewValue* is passed `ByRef`, so it can be changed within the event procedure. If you didn't want this behavior, you could add `ByVal` to the argument in the event declaration.

Determining when events are frozen

A container in design view cannot receive events from a control. There are other times, in addition to design time, that a container is unable to receive events from controls placed upon it. An example of this is when a message box is displayed using the *MsgBox* function. Visual Basic provides a mechanism for determining whether or not events are frozen, but it doesn't notify a control when the frozen status of events changes.

To determine if a control's container has its events frozen, use the EventsFrozen property of the UserControl object, like this:

```
If UserControl.EventsFrozen Then
    ...
End If
```

The proper implementation of properties, methods, and events allows controls to be flexible with respect to developers using the controls and end users interacting with the controls. In the next section, you'll learn how to make controls that are flexible with respect to their containers.

Integrating a Control with Its Container

Properties, methods, and events all allow a developer to write code to communicate with a control. While these mechanisms help a control integrate with its container or parent, they don't allow the full integration found in commercial controls. Seamless integration of a control with its parent is achieved by using additional objects and collections exposed by ActiveX: the AmbientProperties object, Extender object, and ParentControls collection.

Adjusting a Control's Appearance to Complement Its Container

A control should integrate its appearance as closely as possible to the appearance of its container. For instance, the BackColor of your control should usually adjust to match the BackColor of the form on which it is placed. ActiveX controls include two features to aid you in integrating a control's appearance with that of its container: the Ambient property and the AmbientChanged event.

Tailoring appearance using the Ambient property

All ActiveX containers expose a set of ambient properties available through the Ambient property of the UserControl. Ambient properties are properties intended to be used by ActiveX custom controls to better integrate their appearance and behavior with their containers.

The Ambient property returns a reference to an AmbientProperties object. The AmbientProperties object, in turn, exposes a number of standard properties for use by a control. Table 5-2 shows the standard ambient properties and their uses.

Table 5-2: Standard Ambient Properties and Their Uses

Property	Purpose
BackColor	A Color property that contains the suggested interior color of the contained control. If the container does not support this property, the default used is 0x80000005—the system color for a window background.
DisplayAsDefault	A Boolean value that specifies whether or not the control is the default control. If the container does not support this property, the value returned is **False**. Some controls, such as command buttons, can be made default controls. A default control responds to the Enter key, regardless of the current control that has the focus. A control designated as the default control usually alters its display to signify this. This visual indicator is often a heavier border, but it could be anything you design.
DisplayName	A String value containing the name that the control should display for itself. If the container does not support this property, the value is an empty string (**""**). Otherwise, this property returns the name the developer has given the control. Some controls, such as the standard ComboBox, display their name in design view.
Font	A Font object that contains the suggested font information of the contained control. If the container does not support this property, the Font object contained is MS Sans Serif 8.
ForeColor	A Color property that contains the suggested foreground color of the contained control. If the container does not support this property, the value returned is 0x80000008—the system color for window text.
LocaleID	A Long value specifying the language and country of the user. If the container does not support this property, the value returned is the current system locale ID.
MessageReflect	A Boolean value that specifies whether or not the container supports message reflection. If the container does not support this property, the value **False** is returned.
Palette	A Picture object whose palette specifies the suggested palette for the contained control.
RightToLeft	A Boolean value that indicates whether or not text is displayed from right to left on a bi-directional system. If the container does not support this property, the value returned is **False**.
ScaleUnits	A String value containing the name of the coordinate units being used by the container. If the container does not support this property, the value returned is an empty string, (**""**).
ShowGrabHandles	A Boolean value that specifies whether or not the container manages the display of grab handles. If the container does not support this property, the value returned is **True**.
ShowHatching	A Boolean value that indicates whether the container manages the display of hatching. If the container does not support this property, the value returned is **True**.
SupportsMnemonics	A Boolean value that specifies whether or not the container can handle access keys for the control. If the container does not support this property, the value returned is **False**.
TextAlign	An enumeration that specifies how text is to be aligned. If the container does not support this property, the value returned is 0—General Align.
UserMode	A Boolean value that specifies whether or not the environment is in design mode or end-user (runtime) mode. If the container does not support this property or if Visual Basic is in Run Mode, the value returned is **True**.

Table 5-2: Standard Ambient Properties and Their Uses (continued)

Property	Purpose
UIDead	A Boolean value that indicates whether the user interface is nonresponsive. If the container does not support this property, the value returned is `False`.

 Visual Basic handles the implementation of MessageReflect, Show-GrabHandles, ShowHatching, SupportsMnemonics, and UIDead; you shouldn't need to use these properties when designing controls for the Visual Basic environment.

Not all properties are exposed by every type of container. If a container doesn't expose one of the standard properties, a default value is returned and no error is raised when you reference the property. However, if you design your control to work with nonstandard properties, your control becomes container-specific. A control does not have to apply any of the suggested ambient settings, but controls that do implement them have a better integrated appearance with the rest of the project in which they are placed.

Using the AmbientChanged event

The AmbientProperties object is powerful, but for a control to truly integrate its appearance with that of its container, it must not only initialize its appearance to match its container, it must also adjust its appearance when appropriate. For instance, if a developer changes the BackColor of a form containing an ActiveX control, the control should adjust its BackColor to match. To enable your control to respond to changes in the AmbientProperties object, ActiveX controls have an AmbientChanged event.

The AmbientChanged event has the following format:

```
Private Sub UserControl_AmbientChanged(PropertyName As String)

End Sub
```

The AmbientChanged event supplies the name of the property changed, but not the new value of the property. To retrieve the new value, you have to use the AmbientProperties object. For example, you could use an `If...Then` statement or a `Select Case` construct like this:

```
Private Sub UserControl_AmbientChanged(PropertyName As String)

Select Case PropertyName
    Case Is = "BackColor"

    Case Is = "Font"

End Select

End Sub
```

The AmbientChanged event doesn't fire when an instance of an ActiveX control is first placed on a container. To initiate your control's appearance using the Ambient-Properties object, you'll need to execute such code elsewhere. The most obvious place to put code for this is in the control's Initialize event. However, the Ambient-Properties object is not available in the Initialize event because the control is not officially attached to its container (sited) at the time the Initialize event occurs. The best place to put such code is actually within the InitProperties or the ReadProperties events. When the InitProperties and the ReadProperties events are fired, the control is fully cited and the AmbientProperties object is available.

 The AmbientChanged event is not raised when the control is placed on a Visual Basic form and the FontTransparent property of the form is changed.

The following sections provide examples of the more commonly used Ambient properties.

Adjusting a control's BackColor to match its container. Making a control adjust its BackColor to that of its container actually requires adjustments to the control's BackColor in three places:

1. In the InitProperties event, so that the control displays the proper BackColor when first placed on a container.

2. In the ReadProperties event, so that the control displays the proper Back-Color when the control is created in run mode.

3. In the AmbientChanged event, so that the control changes its BackColor accordingly when the developer changes the BackColor of the container.

To accomplish these three tasks, you could use procedures like the following:

```
Private Sub UserControl_InitProperties()

    UserControl.BackColor = Ambient.BackColor

End Sub

Private Sub UserControl_ReadProperties(PropBag As PropertyBag)

    UserControl.BackColor = Ambient.BackColor

End Sub

Private Sub UserControl_AmbientChanged(PropertyName As String)

    If PropertyName = "BackColor" Then
        UserControl.BackColor = Ambient.BackColor
    End If

End Sub
```

Changing design time and runtime appearances with the UserMode property. The UserMode property is one of the most commonly used and perhaps the most powerful Ambient property. It's often desirable to give a control a different appearance in design time than it has at runtime. A classic example of this is the standard Visual Basic combo box. At design time, the combo box contains the name given to it by the developer. However, at runtime the name is gone. This functionality is easy to implement using the UserMode property, the AmbientProperties object, and the AmbientChanged event.

On the Exams

You will encounter questions related to the UserMode property on the exams.

The first step to implementing this behavior is to add code to the InitProperties event, like this:

```
Private Sub UserControl_InitProperties()

    Text1.Text = Ambient.DisplayName

End Sub
```

Notice how UserMode is not tested in this procedure. The InitProperties event fires only the first time an instance of a control is added to a container, and this occurs only at design time. However, you'll need to account for when the control is recreated when switching from runtime to design time. The ReadProperties event fires every time an instance of the control is created *after* the initial instance. This means that the event fires at both design time and runtime, so you need to check the UserMode property to determine the mode and then display the name of the control if the control is at design time. This is done with code like this:

```
Private Sub UserControl_ReadProperties(PropBag As PropertyBag)

    If Not (Ambient.UserMode) Then
        Text1.Text = Ambient.DisplayName
    End If

End Sub
```

The UserMode property returns **True** if the control is currently being used by a *user* as opposed to a developer. Therefore, UserMode returns **True** at runtime and **False** at design time. The preceding code simply tests the UserMode and displays the control's name in the text box if the control is at design time.

Since the user can change the name of the control at any time, you'll have to ensure that the name displayed at design time is always the current name. This is where the AmbientChanged event comes. The code for the AmbientChanged event is essentially the same as that for the ReadProperties event, with the minor addition of only changing the name when the name of the control has been changed, not when other Ambient properties are modified:

```
' This code goes in the ReadProperties event.
If PropertyName = "DisplayName" Then

    If Not (Ambient.UserMode) Then
        Text1.Text = Ambient.DisplayName
    End If

End If
```

Figure 5-25 and Figure 5-26 show the design-time and runtime appearance of a control that implements the behavior discussed in this section. You'll create such a control in the Hands-on Exercise 5-1 at the end of this chapter.

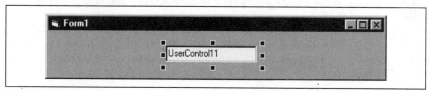

Figure 5-25: At design time, this control displays its name, which is retrieved using the DisplayName property of the AmbientProperties object

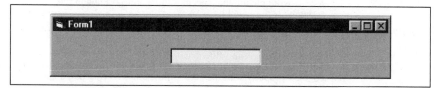

Figure 5-26: The control changes its appearance at runtime by using the RunMode property to determine if the control is at runtime or design time

Accessing Properties of the Extender Object

Although the AmbientProperties object is powerful and allows you to create controls that exhibit flexibility in maintaining a consistent appearance with their containers, it doesn't give you access to the properties of a control maintained by the control's container. Such properties—which include Left, Top, Width, Height, Visible and Enabled—are called *extender properties*. Extender properties are accessed using the Extender object. Like the AmbientProperties object, the Extender object is not available in the Initialize event, but it is available in the InitProperties and ReadProperties events. Table 5-3 lists the standard extender properties.

Table 5-3: Standard Extender Properties

Property	Description
Name	A read-only String containing the user-defined name of the control
Visible	A read/write Boolean value that indicates whether the control is visible or not
Parent	A read-only object that represents the container of the control, such as a form in Visual Basic
Cancel	A read-only Boolean value that indicates whether or not the control is the Cancel button for the container
Default	A read-only Boolean value that indicates whether or not the control is the default button for the container

Using additional properties and methods of the Extender object

Visual Basic provides many properties in addition to the standard extender properties. However, not all containers do so. Before using a nonstandard extender property, check the documentation of each of the different containers to which you intend to deploy your control to verify that a given property is supported. Table 5-4 lists and defines additional extender properties supported by Visual Basic.

 An easy way to determine if a property is supported in a container is to look at the Properties window of the container and note the properties listed.

Table 5-4: Additional Extender Properties Supported by Visual Basic

Property	Description
Container	A read-only object that represents the visual container of the control.
DragIcon	A read/write picture that specifies the icon to use when the control is dragged.
DragMode	A read/write integer that specifies if the control will automatically drag, or if the user of the control must call the Drag method.
Enabled	A read-only Boolean value that specifies if the control is enabled. This extender property is not present unless the control also has an Enabled property with the correct procedure ID (discussed later in this chapter).
Height	A read/write Integer that specifies the height of the control in the container's scale units.
HelpContextID	A read/write Integer that specifies the context ID to use when the F1 key is pressed when the control has the focus.
Index	A read-only Integer that specifies the position in a control array this instance of the control occupies.
Left	A read/write Integer that specifies the position of the left edge of the control to the left edge of the container in the container's scale units.
TabIndex	A read/write Integer that specifies the position of the control in the tab order of the controls in the container.
TabStop	A read/write Boolean value that specifies if Tab will stop on the control.
Tag	A read/write String that contains a user-defined value.
ToolTipText	A read/write String that contains the text to be displayed when the cursor hovers over the control for more than a second.
Top	A read/write Integer that specifies the position of the top edge of the control to the top edge of the container in the container's scale units.
WhatThisHelpID	A read/write Integer that specifies the context ID to use when the What's This pop up is used on the control.
Width	A read/write Integer that specifies the width of the control in the container's scale units.

Visual Basic, and possibly other containers, support additional methods of the Extender object. These methods are listed in Table 5-5.

Table 5-5: Additional Extender Methods Supported by Visual Basic

Methods	Description
Drag	Begins, ends, or cancels a drag operation of the control
Move	Moves the position of the control
SetFocus	Sets the focus to the control
ShowWhatsThis	Displays a selected topic in a Help file using the What's This pop up provided by Help
Zorder	Places the control at the front or back of the z-order within its graphical level

Additional properties and methods aren't all you get from Visual Basic. Visual Basic provides the additional Extender events listed in Table 5-6 as well.

Table 5-6: Additional Extender Events Supported by Visual Basic

Event	Description
DragDrop	Raised when another control on the form is dropped on this control
DragOver	Raised when another control on the form is dragged over this control
GotFocus	Raised when this control gets the focus
LostFocus	Raised when this control loses the focus

You generally don't have much need to use the Extender object; ActiveX containers are nice enough to handle the details of the Extender object for controls. However, it's important to understand what is available using the Extender object so that you can take advantage of this functionality when the need arises.

The Extender object is accessed in much the same way as the AmbientProperties object. For instance, you can set the Text property of a constituent control to the developer-given name of the custom control when the control is first created, using code like this:

```
Private Sub UserControl_InitProperties()

    Text1.Text = Extender.Name

End Sub
```

 Although the name given to a control by a developer is supplied by both the AmbientProperties object and the Extender object, it's important to understand that there is no event for Extender property changes. With Ambient properties, you can use the Ambient-Changed event to respond to changes of Ambient property values; you cannot implement the same behavior using the Extender object.

When using the Extender object, remember these key points:

- Use the Extender object as little as possible. The properties, methods, and events of the Extender object are primarily intended for developers using your control, not for use by the control itself.

- Not all properties, methods, or events are provided by all containers. Always implement error trapping when accessing the Extender object. For that matter, you should always implement error handling.

- Avoid using the Visible property of the Extender object. If you want your control to be invisible at runtime, set its InvisibleAtRuntime property to True.

- Extender object properties are always late bound because Visual Basic has no way of knowing what sort of container the control may be placed on.

Avoiding property collisions

You should avoid creating custom properties that have the same name as Extender properties; extender properties take precedence over internal properties of the same name. When developers change such a property in code or by using the Properties window, they'll always change the Extender property, not your custom property. It's interesting to note, however, that a developer can always programmatically access your custom properties, bypassing the extender properties, by using the built-in Object property of a control like this:

```
ControlName.Object.PropertyName = New_Value
```

If at all possible, refrain from creating custom properties with the same name as an Extender property. The one exception is the Enabled property, which requires special consideration. You'll learn how to create an Enabled property later in this chapter.

Using the Parent Object and ParentControls Collection

In addition to accessing the AmbientProperties and Extender objects, you can directly access the parent of the control, as well as the other controls placed on the parent.

Accessing the parent of an ActiveX control

You can obtain a direct object reference to the container (parent) of an ActiveX control using the Parent property of the UserControl object. For instance, to display the BackColor property value of a control's parent, you could use a simple statement such as this:

```
MsgBox UserControl.Parent.BackColor, vbOKOnly
```

 The explicit reference to the UserControl object is not needed if the code resides in the UserControl's module. The statement could have also been written as MsgBox Parent.BackColor, vbOKOnly.

Accessing the other controls on an ActiveX control's parent

To further extend the ability of an ActiveX control to integrate with its parent (usually a form), the Controls collection of the parent is exposed to the ActiveX control in the form of the ParentControls collection. The ParentControls collection is a property of the UserControl object. For instance, to reference a count of the number of controls on the parent, you could use code such as this:

```
UserControl.ParentControls.Count
```

or:

```
ParentControls.Count
```

Using the ParentControls collection, you can get a count of the number of controls on the parent, and you can get a direct reference to any of those controls. Unlike referencing the Controls collection of a form, the ParentControls collection returns the parent itself. Therefore, the Count property of the ParentControls collection will always be one higher than the actual number of controls on the parent.

 You cannot add or remove controls using the ParentControls collection.

To manipulate a specific control of the parent's contained controls, use the Item property of the ParentControls collection in conjunction with the index of the control. For example, the following code iterates through all of the controls in the ParentControls collection (including the Parent object itself), and prints the Name and Left properties of each control:

```
Dim intControlIndex As Integer

For intControlIndex = 0 To ParentControls.Count - 1
    Debug.Print ParentControls.Item(intControlIndex).Name
    Debug.Print ParentControls.Item(intControlIndex).Left
Next intControlIndex
```

Throughout this chapter, you've been exposed to the most common and obvious elements of creating ActiveX controls. You're now going to learn about the aspects of control creation that are often overlooked, ignored, or incorrectly implemented.

Setting Procedure Attributes

The proper implementation of properties, methods, and events extends beyond simply adding the appropriate procedures to a control's module. For instance, a property value entered in the Properties window by a developer does not trigger the Property Let procedure until the entire value is committed (by pressing the Tab key or otherwise moving off the property). However, text boxes and labels implement a behavior for their Text and Caption properties, respectively, that allow them to immediately update the text displayed in the control to match, character for character, the text entered into those properties *as they are typed.*

In addition, you may have noticed how every standard Visual Basic control has a default property. The default property is the property used when the control is referenced in code without an explicit property referenced. Also, every standard control has a default event whose event procedure is shown when you double-click a control that has no defined event procedures. You can implement all of these behaviors and more by setting *procedure attributes*.

Procedure attributes are set by selecting the control whose procedure attributes you want to define, and choosing Procedure Attributes from the Tools menu (see Figure 5-27).

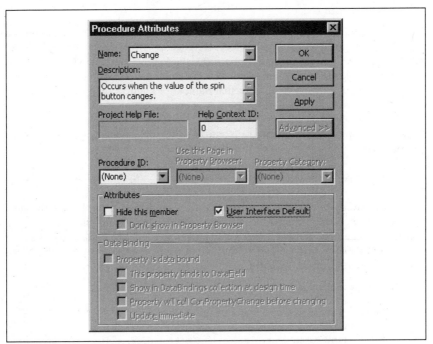

Figure 5-27: The Procedure Attributes dialog box lets you refine a control's procedures

Giving Procedures Descriptions

The Object Browser discussed in Chapter 3 is the easiest tool users can use to browse the various properties and methods of your controls. If you've used the Object Browser, you've undoubtedly noticed that selecting a property, method, or event in the Object Browser displays a description of the item. Additionally, you can view property descriptions by right-clicking the Properties window, selecting Description, and then clicking the property whose description you want to view. The actual description appears below the Properties window.

Adding descriptions to the properties of your controls is simple. Select the property, method, or event in the Name dropdown list of the Procedure Attributes dialog box, and enter a description in the Description field. Procedure descriptions entered on the Procedure Attributes dialog box are visible to users browsing your objects using the Object Browser (because the descriptions are stored in the type library), as well as when viewing descriptions in the Properties window.

 You can access the Procedure Attributes dialog box from the Object Browser by opening a project, choosing Object Browser from the View menu, right-clicking any custom procedure, and selecting Properties.

Linking a Procedure to a Help File

Most objects provide context-sensitive help for their members. When an object provides such help, a user can select a procedure in the Object Browser and press F1 to view help text on the specific procedure.

To link procedures of your controls to specific help topics, follow these steps:

1. Choose Project Properties from the Projects menu to display the Project Properties dialog box and specify a valid help file in the Help File Name field.

2. Display the Procedure Attributes dialog box by choosing Procedure Attributes from the Tools menu.

3. Select a procedure you want to link to a help topic in the Name field, and type the corresponding Help Context ID in the field provided.

Hiding Procedures

There may be times when you want to expose procedures to outside applications but you don't want just anybody to access them. One of the major reasons for hiding a member is to maintain backward compatibility. Once you've distributed a component, the component's interface is considered a contract between the client and the component, and should not be broken (see Chapter 3 and Chapter 13, *Packaging and Deploying an Application*). If you want to discontinue an older interface, you can hide it rather than remove it. That way, old components will work because the interface is still available to them, but new developers won't even know the old interface exists. Another reason to create a hidden member is to add a "backdoor" to a security control to ensure you never get left out in the cold by an irresponsible user.

You can hide publicly exposed procedures from the outside world at one of two levels:

• You can prevent a property from appearing in the Properties window only by selecting the property procedure and selecting its "Don't Show in Property Browser" checkbox in the Procedure Attributes dialog box. The property will appear in the Object Browser, however, and you can write code to access it, but it will not appear in the Properties window.

• You can prevent a property or method from appearing in either the Properties window or the Object Browser by selecting the property or procedure in the Name field of the Procedure Attributes dialog box and selecting its "Hide this member" checkbox (refer to Figure 5-27). When you hide a procedure in this manner, anyone can still write code to access the procedure—if they know it exists. This affords a certain level of security because the procedure will not appear in the Properties window or the Object Browser.

Linking a Property Page to a Property

Earlier in this chapter you learned all about creating PropertyPage objects. Property pages are great for creating an interface for complex properties that cannot be defined using a single value, such as defining columns in a grid. You know that a developer can access a control's custom property pages by selecting the Custom property of the control in the Properties window. However, this is not the only way. You can make a specific property access a specific property page using the Procedure Attributes dialog box. When a property is linked to a property page in this fashion, the developer cannot enter values directly into the property on the Properties window. Instead, selecting the property displays a button with an ellipsis, like the standard Picture property of a form (see Figure 5-28). Clicking the button displays the linked property page.

Figure 5-28: A property linked to a property page displays an ellipsis button when selected

 You don't need to link properties declared as type Font, OLE_COLOR, or Picture to property pages. Visual Basic automatically associates these types of properties with the corresponding type of property page.

To link a property to a property page, select the control whose properties you want to set, choose Procedure Attributes from the Tools menu to display the Procedure Attributes dialog box, click Advanced to access the advanced settings, select a property procedure, and select the property page to link to the property from the "Use this Page in Property Browser" dropdown list.

You can link more than one property to the same property page. Although this is a natural if you have two properties that share an identical property page layout, this also works well when you have a property that shares *part* of another property's property page layout. In order for properties to share only parts of a property page layout, you need a way to determine what property is selected when the property page is shown so that you can make any necessary changes to the appearance of the page. This is precisely the purpose of the EditProperty event of the PropertyPage object.

The EditProperty event has the following format:

```
Private Sub PropertyPage_EditProperty(PropertyName As String)

End Sub
```

When the developer clicks the ellipsis button of a property associated with a property page, the page triggers its EditProperty event in addition to its other events. The *PropertyName* parameter contains the name of the property used to display the property page. It's here that you place code necessary to alter the appearance or behavior of the property page based on the selected property. For instance, you may want to set the focus to a specific control on the page, hide or show controls, or enable or disable controls on the page, depending on the property used to access the page.

Categorizing Property Procedures

You can assign properties of your controls to categories just as the standard Visual Basic controls have categorized properties. If you categorize your properties, a user can easily browse the different categories in the Properties window by selecting the Categorized tab.

To assign a property to a category, select the control whose properties you want to set, choose Procedure Attributes from the Tools menu to display the Procedure Attributes dialog box, click Advanced to access the advanced settings, select a property procedure, and select the desired category from the Product Category dropdown list. To use a category name that is not defined, simply enter the category name in the text box portion of the Product Category dropdown list.

Creating Member Defaults

Each ActiveX control you can add to a project has a default event and property. The default event is the event procedure created when you double-click a control that has no defined events. The default property is the property that's automatically selected in the property sheet when you select a control, and it's the property used when you reference the control in code without explicitly providing a property identifier. Actually, when you select a control, Visual Basic attempts to select a property of the same name as the last selected property of the previously selected control. If the newly selected control does not have the property, the default property is used.

For example, the Text property is the default property of the text box, and you can access the Text property like this:

```
Text1.Text = "New Text"
```

or like this:

```
Text1 = "New Text"
```

Making an event or property procedure a default is easy; deciding which event and property to make defaults requires a little more thought. You should always attempt to make the default event and property of a control the most commonly used event and property.

To make an event or property procedure the default event or property of a control, select the control whose properties you want to set, choose Procedure Attributes from the Tools menu to display the Procedure Attributes dialog box, click Advanced to access the advanced settings, select a property procedure, and select the User Interface Default checkbox.

 You can make only one event and one property procedure the default of their respective type. If you attempt to assign a procedure as the interface default when one is already assigned as the default for that type, Visual Basic displays a warning.

Assigning a Standard Procedure ID

Every property and method in the type library of a control has an identification number, called a procedure ID (also known as a DispatchID or DISPID). When a container uses a control, it can access a property or a method by its name using late binding or by its DISPID using early binding (see Chapter 3 for more information on binding and DISPIDs). Although every method and property you expose will have a unique DISPID, there are a number of reserved values for important procedure DISPIDs.

By assigning these specific DISPIDs to properties and methods of your controls, you can extend their functionality. This is most evident in three particular cases:

- Allowing a control to be enabled and disabled
- Giving a control an About box
- Creating a Caption or Text property

Allowing a control to be enabled and disabled

Almost every control, regardless of its runtime visibility or its interface method (aggregate or owner-draw), has an Enabled property. The Enabled property is a property of the Extender object, but it requires special consideration to implement correctly. First, although the Enabled property is a property of the Extender object, you must still create a Property Let and Property Get procedure. This procedure must then delegate to the Enabled property of the UserControl. For example:

```
Public Property Get Enabled() As Boolean

    Enabled = UserControl.Enabled

End Property
```

```
Public Property Let Enabled(ByVal NewValue As Boolean)

    UserControl.Enabled = NewValue
    PropertyChanged "Enabled"

End Property
```

Simply creating a custom Enabled property with Property Let and Property Get statements is not sufficient, though it may appear to be at first. A container such as a form is supposed to govern the Enabled properties of the controls placed on it to ensure consistent behavior. For instance, when you set the Enabled property of a form to False, all of the controls on the form are disabled. However, their appearance is that of their Enabled state. Testing the Enabled property of a control on a form whose Enabled property is False should return False. In order for this to occur, the Enabled property of the Extender object must act as a wrapper around your custom Enabled property procedures. This is accomplished by setting the Enabled property procedure to the standard Procedure ID of Enabled.

To assign the standard Enabled Procedure ID to a custom Enabled property procedure, select the control whose properties you want to set, choose Procedure Attributes from the Tools menu to display the Procedure Attributes dialog box, click Advanced to access the advanced settings, select a property procedure, and select Enabled from the Procedure ID dropdown list.

When you set the Enabled property procedure of your control to the standard Enabled Procedure ID, a container can obtain the level of control it needs to show controls as enabled while the form is not enabled. To accomplish this, the container sets the Enabled property of the Extender object of each control placed upon it to False without calling the Enabled property procedures of any of the controls. The controls, for all intents and purposes, "think" they are enabled; however, their Enabled property returns False in code.

 Owner-drawn controls must draw their own disabled interface. Your custom Enabled Property Let procedure is the best place to initiate this action. If you need to determine the enabled state of your control in other events, such as in the Paint event, test the Enabled property of the UserControl object. If you test the Enabled property of the Extender object, you might get a value of False even when your control needs to paint itself as though it were enabled.

Giving a control an About box

All commercial controls have an About box. An About box is a dialog box that displays copyright, version, and support information about a control (see Figure 5-29). Even if you don't plan to distribute a control commercially, you should still add an About box so a developer using your control has easy access to version and copyright information. About boxes of custom controls are listed in the top of the Properties window as (About), as shown in Figure 5-30. A user can display a control's About box by double-clicking the (About) property or by clicking it and then clicking the ellipsis button that displays in the property.

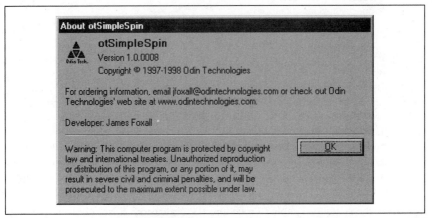

Figure 5-29: About boxes add a finishing touch to a control and can be quite useful

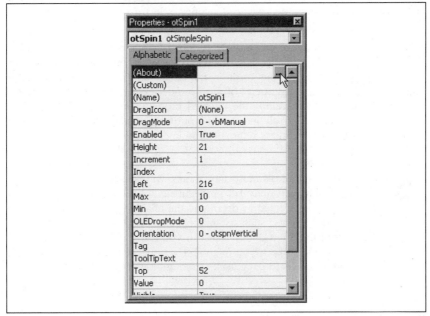

Figure 5-30: About boxes are accessed from the (About) property in the Properties window

The design of an About box form is left entirely up to you. However, there is a procedure you must follow to ensure your About box appears in the Properties window correctly.

To add an About box to your ActiveX control follow these steps:

1. Create an About box form as desired. Consider using the About box of a popular application as a model.

2. Create a method to display the About box form. You can call the procedure anything you like, and you can place whatever code you feel is necessary within the procedure. The following is a simple procedure that could be used to display an About box form:

```
Public Sub ShowAbout()

    frmAbout.Show vbModal

    Unload frmAbout
    Set frmAbout = Nothing

End Sub
```

3. Display the Procedure Attributes dialog box by choosing Procedure Attributes from the Tools menu.

4. Select the procedure used to display the About box from the Name drop-down list.

5. Click Advanced to access the advanced settings of the Procedure Attributes dialog box.

6. Select AboutBox from the Procedure ID dropdown list.

Creating a caption or Text type of property

If you add a Label control to a form and change its Caption property, you'll notice that the label changes to reflect the new Caption with each keystroke you type. This same behavior can be seen with a standard text box's Text property. As you type text into the Text property, the text box displays the current Text with each keystroke. Custom properties of controls don't ordinarily exhibit this behavior. With custom properties, the Property Let procedure isn't called until the user commits a new value by leaving the current property in the Properties window or by pressing Enter. However, you can assign this behavior to two custom properties of a control using the Procedure Attributes dialog box.

In the list of standard Procedure IDs are Caption and Text. Assigning the Procedure ID of Caption or Text to a custom property procedure forces the Property Let procedure to be called *with each keystroke entered* in the Properties window. Each time the Property Let procedure is called, an entirely new value is passed to it.

 You don't need to name your procedure's Text or Caption in order to assign them the Procedure ID of Text or Caption.

Binding a Control to a Data Source

Most standard Visual Basic controls can be bound to a field of a recordset within a database. Although not every control needs this functionality, it's rather simple to add to ActiveX controls developed in Visual Basic, and you'll encounter data-binding questions on the exams.

When an ActiveX control supports binding to a recordset, it's known as a *data consumer*. Two forms of data binding can be used to create a data consumer. The first form, *simple binding*, allows the control to be associated with a single field in a recordset. (Examples are the text box and checkbox controls.) The second form of binding, *complex binding*, allows a control to be associated with an entire row of data (an example is the data grid control). The type of binding supported by a control is determined by the UserControl's DataBindingBehavior property, which can only be set at design time. The three possible values for DataBindingBehavior are shown in Table 5-7.

Table 5-7: Possible Values for the DataBindingBehavior Property

Constant	Setting	Description
vbNone	0	(Default) The object (control) can't be bound to a data source.
vbSimpleBound	1	The object (control) can be bound to a data source using simple binding.
vbComplexBound	2	The object (control) can be bound to a data source using complex binding.

When an ActiveX control that supports binding is added to a project, it supports two basic binding properties:

* DataSource
* DataField

The DataSource property is used to link the ActiveX control to a Data control. DataSource is an Extender property and is created and maintained by Visual Basic—you don't create DataSource property procedures. To make a control data-aware, you must first identify the property or properties that you want to allow a developer to bind to a Data control. Although not commonly known, Visual Basic lets you create controls that can have more than one property bound to a field in a recordset. Once you've identified the primary bound property, you make it data-aware using the Procedure Attributes dialog box by selecting the property procedure from the Name dropdown list, then selecting the "Property is data bound" checkbox. When you select the "Property is data bound" checkbox, you enable four other checkboxes:

* This property binds to DataField
* Show in DataBindings collection at design time
* Property will call CanPropertyChange before changing
* Update Immediately

Although you can make multiple properties data-aware, you can and must designate one property as "This property binds to DataField." Once a bound field is defined, users of your control will see two new properties in the Properties window: DataSource and DataField (see Figure 5-31). The DataSource property supplies a dropdown list from which the developer can select a Data control that exists on the container of the ActiveX control. Once a DataSource is specified, the DataField property supplies a dropdown list containing all of the fields in the recordset of the selected Data control.

Figure 5-31: The DataField and DataSource properties are provided by the container; you don't create them using property procedures

Understanding the DataBindings collection

Each ActiveX control can have only one DataField property. Obviously, for Visual Basic to allow multiple bound fields, there needs to be a different mechanism for developers to assign data fields to bound properties. This functionality is exposed through the DataBindings collection. The DataBindings collection is a property of the Extender object that allows a developer to retrieve and set data fields for bound properties. For example, the following code prints a list of all of the bound properties of a control:

```
Dim intIndex As Integer

For intIndex = 0 To UserControl.DataBindings.Count - 1
    Debug.Print ControlName.DataBindings(intIndex).PropertyName
    Debug.Print ContralName.DataBindings(intIndex).DataField
Next intIndex
```

You can also access a databound property using syntax like this:

```
ControlName.DataBindings("PropertyName")
```

All bound properties are automatically added to the DataBindings collection. However, by selecting the "Show in DataBindings collection at design time" checkbox for a databound property, you expose the DataBindings collection in the Properties window at design time.

You must specifically check the "Show in DataBindings collection at design time" checkbox for each property you want exposed at design time. Even if a data-bound property does not have this item checked, it will still appear in the collection at runtime.

Once one or more data-bound properties have had their "Show in DataBindings collection at design time" checkbox selected, a new property called DataBindings appears in the Properties window (see Figure 5-32).

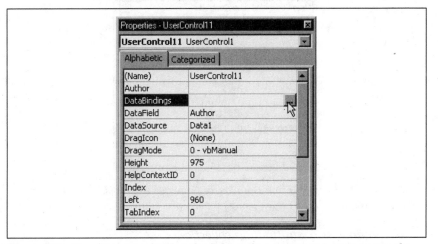

Figure 5-32: Developers can bind multiple bound properties at runtime using the DataBindings property in the Properties window

Clicking the DataBindings property displays an ellipsis button. Clicking this button or double-clicking the DataBindings property displays the DataBindings dialog box shown in Figure 5-33. Using this dialog box, a developer can select the bound properties of the control and the fields of the recordset of the DataSource property. This dialog box makes it easy for developers to assign bound properties to specific data fields at runtime.

Calling the CanPropertyChange method

You are about to study a topic that you need to understand but that currently has no relevance: the CanPropertyChange method. The reason it has no relevance is that because of a bug in Visual Basic, the property *always* returns True. This bug first cropped up in Visual Basic 5, and it hasn't yet been addressed.

The Visual Basic documentation states that you should always call the CanProperty-Change method of the UserControl before updating the value of a bound property. The CanPropertyChange function is defined as follows:

```
object.CanPropertyChange PropertyName
```

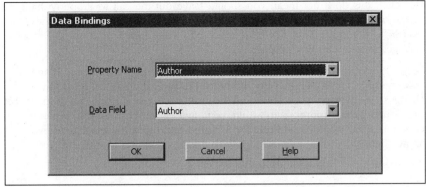

Figure 5-33: Exposing the DataBindings collection at design time simplifies the binding process for developers

In theory, the CanPropertyChange method returns True if the property can be changed, False if it cannot. For example, a property cannot be changed when the data field that the property is bound to is read-only. However, the reality is that CanPropertyChange always returns True in Visual Basic, regardless of whether or not the property can actually be changed. This is not such a problem for you as a control developer because attempting to set the value of a property bound to a read-only data field does not raise an error; the new value is simply ignored. Obviously, however, this poses problems for the developers using your controls for the same reason (they won't realize when data is not being saved because no error is raised when a new value is ignored). Even though this method is not correctly implemented in Visual Basic, you should still use it in all of your Property Let procedures to ensure future compatibility. The following Property Let procedure shows the method call in action:

```
Public Property Let Author(New_Author As String)

    If CanPropertyChange("Author") Then
        txtAuthor.Text = New_Author
    End If

    PropertyChanged("Author")

End Property
```

 In addition to calling CanPropertyChange, you should also select the "Property will call CanPropertyChange" checkbox in the Procedure Attributes dialog box.

Ensuring user updates by calling PropertyChanged

There is usually no need to add property persistence to data-bound properties; their values are saved and retrieved from a database, not from the property bag.

However, this does not mean you should leave out the call to PropertyChanged. Just as with saving properties to the property bag, Visual Basic does not know that data in a bound property needs to be saved in the data source unless Property-Changed is called for that procedure.

While PropertyChanged ensures that a property is flagged as being changed, it does nothing to ensure that the Property Let procedure is called when a user changes the data on your control. You must add code to call the Property Let procedure where appropriate within your aggregate controls. For instance, the common place to put such code for a bound text box is in its Change event, as shown here:

```
Private Sub txtAuthor_Change()

    UserControl.Author = txtAuthor

End Sub
```

 Remember that if your Property Let procedure is never called, data changed by the user will not be saved in the database.

Determining if a user has changed data of a bound property

Just as you can inform Visual Basic that a property has changed by calling the PropertyChanged method, you can also programmatically determine whether or not Visual Basic believes a property has been changed. To test if a property is currently flagged as having changed, use the DataBinding object. The following code tests a property called Author to see if its data has been changed (note that the behavior is the same as that of the DataChanged property of standard controls):

```
Print ControlName.DataBindings("Author").DataChanged
```

Creating ActiveX controls is a complex and extensive process. This chapter has covered all of the many aspects of creating professional quality controls. With all of these design aspects, you might expect testing and debugging an ActiveX control to be complicated. As you'll learn in the next section, it doesn't have to be.

Testing and Debugging ActiveX Controls

The task of testing and debugging ActiveX controls is simplified somewhat by the ability to open multiple projects in one instance of Visual Basic: you can switch between the code of a test project and the code of your control project. Obviously, the complexity of testing and debugging an ActiveX control relies heavily on many factors, including the complexity of the control itself.

To debug an ActiveX Control, follow these steps:

1. Create a project group by choosing Add Project from the File menu. The group should contain the ActiveX control project and a test project (ActiveX EXE or standard EXE), as shown in Figure 5-34.

2. Make the test project the startup project by right-clicking on it in the Project Explorer window and selecting "Set as Start Up."

3. Add a new instance of the ActiveX control to the form.

4. Test the ActiveX control by getting and settings its various properties, and otherwise attempting to use all of its functionality.

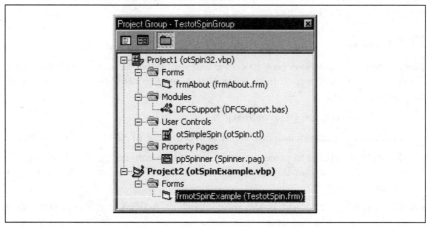

Figure 5-34: ActiveX controls are debugged using a project group

Testing ActiveX controls is similar to testing ActiveX DLLs discussed in Chapter 3. You can actually step into code of the ActiveX control while running the test project. For instance, if a runtime error is encountered in your control while changing a property, you can correct the error in the property procedure of the control without having to stop and restart the test project.

While an object in the test project is selected, the icon of the ActiveX control appears in the toolbox and you can add the control to forms just as though the control were added to the project by choosing Components from the Project menu. However, if the UserControl object is displayed in design view, the toolbox icon is disabled and the control cannot be added to the project. Furthermore, while the UserControl is in design view, all instances of the control on any forms in the test project will appear hatched (see Figure 5-35). While they are hatched, you cannot interact with the controls in design view (properties are unavailable, etc.) You must first close the UserControl object before you can interact with the control in design view in the test project.

While testing and debugging an ActiveX control using a project group, all of Visual Basic's standard debugging tools are available. (Refer to Chapter 9, *Testing and Debugging*, for information on using Visual Basic's debugging tools.)

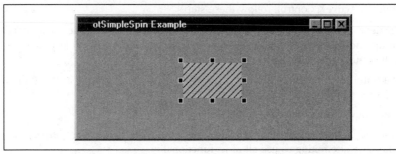

*Figure 5-35: While a UserControl is in design mode, instances of the control in the
test project are shown hatched and are unusable*

Key Facts

This chapter has discussed how to create and test ActiveX controls. The following
are key points to understand in order to pass ActiveX control–related questions on
the Visual Basic exams:

- ActiveX controls are OLE controls.

- Visual Basic 6 allows only the creation and the use of 32-bit ActiveX controls.

- Controls are added to projects using the Components dialog box. The Components dialog box can be accessed by choosing Components from the Project
menu.

- The UserControl object is the base object of ActiveX controls. UserControl
objects are similar to forms.

- UserControls can and should have unique toolbox bitmaps. Toolbox bitmaps
have the dimensions of 16 pixels wide by 15 pixels high.

- Aggregate controls, sometimes called *subclassed* controls, are custom controls
built around other controls such as the standard text box or list box. The controls contained within aggregate ActiveX controls are called constituent controls.

- Aggregate controls are designed to extend the functionality of other controls.

- Owner-draw controls are similar to blank forms in that they have no controls
on them. Their interface consists of whatever you draw on them using Visual
Basic's drawing methods or API graphics function calls.

- Owner-draw controls can be considerably more difficult to create than aggregate controls; however, they are much more flexible.

- Invisible at runtime controls are controls that aren't visible at runtime, but are
visible at design time. Examples of invisible at runtime controls are the Timer
and MAPI controls.

- Container controls are ActiveX controls that allow a user to place other controls directly on them at design time.

- The easiest and most efficient way to handle the sizing of constituent controls
is to use the Resize event of the UserControl.

- The ScaleMode property of the UserControl plays a key role in resizing constituent controls.

- The Paint method of the UserControl is the place to put code to draw a UserControl's interface. If you don't place the code to draw the interface in the Paint event, your control will not repaint itself when uncovered *unless* its AutoRedraw property is set to **True**.

- You govern the focus behavior of your UserControls by using two focus-related properties of the UserControl: CanGetFocus and ForwardFocus.

- You cannot set the CanGetFocus property of a UserControl to **False** as long is there is at least one constituent control on the UserControl that can receive the focus.

- The ForwardFocus property of the UserControl allows you to give a custom control the behavior of a label whose access key has been pressed.

- You assign access keys to your custom controls by using the AccessKeys property and the AccessKeyPress event of the UserControl.

- In order for an ActiveX custom control to be place on an MDI form, it must either be alignable or invisible at runtime.

- To make your ActiveX control a container control, set its ControlContainer property to **True**.

- To access the controls placed on a compiled UserControl by a developer, use the ContainedControls collection.

- Because container controls require additional resources, you should only set a UserControl's ContainedControls property to **True** if it is appropriate for the control.

- You cannot reference the ContainedControls collection in the Initialize event of a custom control.

- In order for contained controls to be visible, the control acting as a container must have its BackStyle set to Opaque.

- To allow a control to be edited at design time, set its EditAtDesignTime property to **True**.

- Events are not raised when a control is being edited at design time.

- You create properties of an ActiveX control using Property Let and Property Get procedures.

- To make a read-only property, create a Property Get procedure but not a Property Let procedure.

- To create object properties, use Property Set instead of Property Let.

- Property Get and Property Let procedures of the same property name must have coordinating parameter lists.

- To expose properties of a UserControl, you must delegate to them using custom Property Let and Property Get procedures.

- Because an ActiveX control is always in run mode, you cannot delegate design-time–only properties of the UserControl using custom Property Let procedures.

- Property procedures allow you to delegate properties to constituent controls and encapsulate validation routines. You can't do either by exposing constituent controls as public properties.

- To define a color property, use the OLE_COLOR datatype.

- Enums allow you to enumerate and expose named constants for a property's values.

- Enums are always Long integers.

- Using an Enum as a property datatype does *not* restrict the possible values to those declared in the Enum. You must still create data validation code to ensure that only valid property values are specified.

- Property pages allow developers to easily set complex properties of a control.

- Property pages always appear on a tabbed dialog box, even if only one property page is defined.

- Property pages always have the buttons OK, Cancel, and Apply.

- When property pages are first displayed, the property page reflects the state of the currently selected ActiveX control(s).

- Clicking Apply on a property page instantly applies any property changes made by the developer to the selected control(s).

- Switching from one tab to another on a property page instantly applies any property changes made on the page being switched *from* to the selected control(s).

- To force a property page to reflect the property values of a selected control, use the SelectionChanged event of the PropertyPage object.

- The ApplyChanges event of the PropertyPage object is where you place code to update the properties of all selected controls.

- The SelectedControls collection lets you retrieve or set properties of all selected controls from a property page.

- When writing code that uses the SelectedControls collection, always refer to element 0. Element 0 contains all of the selected controls. No other index values are currently used.

- You must set the Changed property of a PropertyPage object to True in order for changes to be applied to selected controls.

- You don't have to write validation code for property pages; the validation code of the Property Let procedures is used.

- ActiveX controls are destroyed and recreated each time the developer switches between run mode and design mode.

- Property persistence is the ability of a control to store and retrieve property data between instances.

- The Initialize event fires the first time a control instance is created, and never again.

- The ReadProperties event fires each time an instance of the control is created *after* the first time.

- The WriteProperties event occurs each time *a design-time instance* of the control is destroyed.

- Property persistence is implemented using a PropertyBag object.

- Do not put any code in the Initialize event that relies on the accuracy of property values read from the property bag, because the values haven't been read and applied to the control yet.

- Text property data is stored directly in the form, control, or document source file.

- Binary property data is stored in a support file with the same name as the parent's source file but with a different extension (FRX for forms, CTX for controls, DOX for UserDocuments, and PGX for property pages).

- To store data in the property bag, use the WriteProperty method of the PropertyBag object.

- A `Call` statement is required when using the WriteProperty method.

- To retrieve information from the property bag, use the ReadProperty method of the PropertyBag object.

- To notify Visual Basic that a property value has been changed, you must call the PropertyChanged method of the UserControl object. If you don't let Visual Basic know the property value has been changed, the change may not be written to the property bag.

- All data in the property bag is destroyed prior to writing new values in the WriteProperties event.

- Arrays can be saved to the property bag by using a `For...Next` loop and saving each array item as a property.

- Methods are added to ActiveX controls by creating Function and Sub procedures.

- The `Friend` keyword allows you to create methods and properties that are visible to all modules in your project but are hidden from all applications that use the control.

- Custom events are declared in the declarations section of the UserControl module using the `Event` statement.

- Custom events are raised using the `RaiseEvent` statement.

- When declaring custom events, you do not declare them as `Public` or `Private`. By default, they appear in the client application as private procedures, but the developer using the control can change them to public.

- The format of an event declaration's argument list is similar to a Sub or a Function declaration argument list, except events cannot have `Optional` or `ParamArray` arguments.

- To determine if events are currently frozen in a control's parent, test the EventsFrozen property of the UserControl object.

- The AmbientProperties object lets you integrate the appearance of a control with that of its container.

- No all AmbientProperties properties are supported by all containers.

- The AmbientChanged event fires each time the value of an Ambient property changes.

- The UserMode property of the AmbientProperties object tells what mode the control is in: design time or runtime. A value of `True` indicates the control is operated in runtime mode, being accessed by a user, not a developer.

- The Extender object gives you access to properties of a control supplied by its container.

- Not all Extender properties are supported by all containers.

- Avoid property collisions by not creating custom properties with the same name as a property of the Extender object. You will have to create a custom Enabled property procedure, however, in order to properly implement an Enabled property.

- The Parent property of the UserControl returns an object reference to the container on which the control is sited.

- The ParentControls property of the UserControl object returns a reference to a collection of the controls that exist on the UserControl's container (parent).

- You cannot add or remove controls through the ParentControls collection.

- The Procedure Attributes dialog box lets you control many advanced aspects of property procedures. For example, you can add descriptions to properties using the Procedure Attributes dialog box, link procedures to Help topics, hide procedures, and link a property procedure to a property page.

- You do not need to link properties declared as Type Font, `OLE_COLOR`, or Picture to property pages. Visual Basic automatically associates these types of properties with the corresponding type of property page.

- You can link more than one property to the same property page.

- You can categorize property procedures using the Procedure Attributes dialog box.

- You can, and should, designate a default event and a default property using the Procedure Attributes dialog box.

- You can obtain additional functionality for some procedures by assigning them standard Procedure IDs using the Procedure Attributes dialog box.

- To properly implement an Enabled property, you must create a custom Enabled property using a Property Get and Property Let procedure, and then assign that property to the Enabled standard Procedure ID.

- You must assign a procedure that shows an About box the AboutBox Procedure ID in order for the Properties window to properly display the (About) property.

- You can implement Text or Caption property behavior by assigning a custom property procedure the standard Text or Caption Procedure ID.

- You do not need to name your procedures Text or Caption in order to assign them the Procedure ID of Text or Caption.

- To designate a UserControl as a data consumer, set its DataBindingBehavior property to either SimpleBound or ComplexBound.

- The Procedure Attributes dialog box is used to create a bound property.

- When you create a bound property, the container hosting your control automatically creates a DataSource field.

- You can create more than one bound property for a control.

- At least one bound property must have its "This property binds to DataField" checkbox selected.

- A developer can programmatically control the bound fields of all bound properties using the DataBindings collection.

- In order for a developer to be able to access a bound property at design time, the property must have its "Show in DataBindings collection at design time" checkbox selected on the Procedure Attributes dialog box.

- You must call the PropertyChanged method in a property procedure for Visual Basic to know that a bound field's data has changed. If you don't do this, the changed data will not be saved in the database.

- To test and debug an ActiveX control, create a project group.

- While an ActiveX control in a project group is being tested and debugged, the interface of existing instances of the control, as well as the control's toolbox icon are disabled when the UserControl object is in design view.

ActiveX Controls

Applying What You've Learned

It's now time to apply what you've learned about creating ActiveX controls. Start by answering all of the questions in the Skills Assessment. If you can correctly answer all of these questions, you'll be demonstrating a solid understanding of how to create ActiveX controls. After you've answered the assessment questions, work through the hands-on exercises.

Skills Assessment

1. Visual Basic 6 allows you to create:

    a. VBX controls

    b. 16-bit ActiveX controls

    c. 32-bit ActiveX controls

    d. Both 16-bit and 32-bit controls

2. To add an ActiveX control to a project:

    a. Choose References from the Project menu and add a reference to the ActiveX control.

    b. Choose Components from the Project menu and add a reference to the ActiveX control.

    c. Choose Add Control from the Project menu.

3. The base object of an ActiveX control developed in Visual Basic is:

    a. The Form object

    b. The UserDocument object

    c. The UserControl object

    d. The CustomControl object

4. The size of toolbox bitmaps of ActiveX controls created in Visual Basic is:

    a. 16×16 pixels

    b. 16×15 pixels

    c. 32×32 pixels

    d. 10×10 pixels

5. Which type of control is built around other controls:

    a. Owner-draw

    b. Invisible

    c. Aggregate

6. To make a control that is visible at design time but invisible at runtime you should:

    a. Set the Visible property of the Extender object to **False** at runtime.

    b. Set the InvisibleAtRuntime property of the UserControl to **True**.

    c. Programmatically hide and show constituent controls.

7. An ActiveX control that allows other controls to be placed upon them at design time are called:

    a. Container controls

    b. Parent controls

    c. Holder controls

8. Synchronizing constituent control's sizes with changes of the UserControl's size should be done in what event?

    a. Initialize

    b. InitProperties

    c. ReadProperties

    d. Resize

9. If a UserControl's AutoRedraw property is set to **False**, where do you need to place code to update the Owner Draw control's interface to ensure the control is always displayed correctly?

    a. Resize event

    b. Paint event

    c. Draw event

10. You cannot set a UserControl's CanGetFocus property to **False** under which of the following conditions?

    a. When the control is an owner-draw control

    b. When the control contains constituent controls that can receive the focus

    c. When the control's TabStop property is set to **False**

11. To create a custom control with the behavior of a label whose access key has been pressed, you use which property of the UserControl?

    a. AcceleratorKeys

    b. CanGetFocus

    c. ForwardFocus

12. Which two items, when used together, let you implement access keys for an ActiveX control?

    a. AccessKeyPress event

    b. KeyPress event

    c. AccessKeys collection

    d. AccessKeys property

13. In order for an ActiveX control to be placed on an MDI form, at least one of the following must be true (select two):

    a. MDIPlaceable property must be set to **True**.

    b. Alignable property must be set to **True**.

    c. InvisibleAtRuntime property must be set to **True**.

    d. The control must be a container control.

14. To make a control a container control, you set which property to **True**?

    a. Containable

    b. CanHaveChildren

    c. Parent

    d. ControlContainer

15. To access the controls placed by a developer onto a compiled UserControl, you use which collection?

    a. Controls

    b. ContainedControls

    c. ParentControls

    d. ChildControls

16. What must be true in order for child controls to be visible on a container control?

    a. The container's BackStyle must be Opaque.

    b. The container's ChildrenVisible property must be True.

    c. The container's ContainedControlsVisible property must be True.

17. Which property of the UserControl allows the developer to activate a control at design time?

    a. DeveloperCanActivate

    b. ActivateAtDesignTime

    c. EditAtDesignTime

18. Which statement creates a read property?

    a. `Public Property Let MyProperty(New_MyProperty As String)`

    b. `Public Property Get MyProperty() As String`

    c. `Public Sub ReadMyProperty()`

    d. `Public Function MyProperty() As String`

19. Which of the following are valid Property statements? (pick two)

    a. `Public Property Let MyValue(New_Value As String)`

    b. `Public Property Set MyObject(New_Object As Object)`

    c. `Public Property Get MyObject(objTest As Object)`

    d. `Public Property Set MyValue(New_Value As String)`

20. Which Property Let statement would correspond to the following Property Get statement?

`Public Property Get MyProperty() As String`

    a. `Public Property Let MyProperty() As String`

    b. `Public Property Let MyOtherProperty(New_MyProperty _`
       `As String)`

    c. `Public Property Let MyProperty(New_MyProperty As Long)`

    d. `Public Property Let MyProperty(New_MyProperty As String)`

21. You have a text box on a user control as a constituent control. You want the text box's BackColor to change with the parent of the UserControl. What property of the UserControl do you use?

    a. Ambient

    b. Extender

    c. Appearance

22. To make a read-only property:

    a. Create a Property Let and a Property Get procedure.

    b. Create a Property Let, but not a Property Get, procedure.

    c. Create a Property Get, but not a Property Let, procedure.

    d. Create a Friend procedure.

23. Which is true about delegating custom property procedures to runtime-only properties of constituent controls?

    a. You cannot delegate to runtime-only properties of constituent controls.

    b. You can delegate Property Get procedures, but not Property Let procedures.

    c. You can delegate Property Let procedures, but not Property Get procedures.

24. What three things do you gain by exposing public properties using property procedures instead of public variables?

    a. Ability to delegate to constituent controls

    b. Less code needs to be written

    c. Ability to create read-only or write-only properties

    d. Ability to validate property values

25. Which special OLE type can you use to create a standard color property that allows a user to select colors in the Properties window?

    a. Variant

    b. OLE_COLOR

    c. COLOR

    d. OLE_PALETTE

26. Given the following Enum:

```
Public Enum eCustomEnum
    eRed = 0
End Enum
```

Which of the following could be added as a new enumeration member?

    a. eBlue = 0

    b. eBlue = "Blue"

    c. eBlue = 1

27. Complex properties of custom controls are best set using:

    a. The Properties window

    b. Visual Basic code

    c. Custom property pages

28. Which event of the PropertyPage object is used to set up the display of the property page to reflect the property values of the selected control(s)?

    a. SelectionChanged

    b. SelectedControls

    c. UpdatePropertyPage

    d. ApplyChanges

29. In which event of the PropertyPage object do you place code to update the selected control(s) with new values set on the property page?

    a. SelectionChanged

    b. ApplyChanges

    c. SelectedControls

30. Which collection do you use to access selected control(s) from the property page?

    a. SelectedControls

    b. Controls

    c. ParentControls

31. The ability of a control to store and retrieve property data between instances is called:

    a. Property persistence

    b. Data paging

    c. Data-Tier Storage

    d. Magic

32. The InitProperties event fires:

    a. Only the first time a control is instantiated on a container

    b. Each time the control is instantiated

    c. Every time except the first time a control is instantiated

33. The ReadProperties event fires:

    a. Only the first time a control is instantiated on a container

    b. Each time the control is instantiated

    c. Every time except the first time a control is instantiated

34. Which event fires each time a design-time instance of a control is destroyed and the PropertyChanged method has been called?

    a. InitProperties

    b. ReadProperties

    c. Initialize

    d. WriteProperties

35. What object is used to implement property persistence?

    a. Parent

    b. PropertyStorage

    c. PropertyBag

36. Text property values are stored:

    a. In the source file of their container

    b. In a support file of the same name as the source file of their container, but with a different extension

    c. Only in memory

37. Binary property values are stored:

    a. In the source file of their container

    b. In a support file of the same name as the source file of their container, but with a different extension

    c. Only in memory

38. Which is a valid statement that can be used to store data in the PropertyBag?

    a. `Call PropBag.WriteProperty("Min", m_Min, 0)`

    b. `PropBag.WriteProperty("Min", m_Min, 0)`

    c. `PropBag.StoreProperty("Min", m_Min, 0)`

39. Which is a valid statement that can be used to retrieve data from the PropertyBag?

    a. `m_Min = PropBag.ReadProperty("Min", 0)`

    b. `m_Min = Call PropBag.ReadProperty("Min", 0)`

    c. `m_Min = PropBag.RetrieveProperty("Min", 0)`

    d. `m_Min = Call PropBag.RetrieveProperty("Min", 0)`

40. Which statement notifies Visual Basic that the value of a property called TestProperty has changed?

    a. `PropertyChanged = "TestProperty"`

    b. `Call PropertyChanged "TestProperty"`

    c. `PropertyChanged ("TestProperty")`

41. Which two statements are true about the PropertyBag?

    a. You are required to remove the values of unused properties from the PropertyBag.

    b. All data in the PropertyBag is destroyed before new values are written in the WriteProperties event.

    c. Property values are written to the PropertyBag only if their values are not the same as the specified default value of the property.

42. Which two statements create methods in a UserControl module?

    a. `Public Method MyMethod()`

    b. `Public Sub MyMethod()`

    c. `Public Method Function MyMethod() As Long`

    d. `Public Function MyMethod() As Long`

43. Which statement declares a function that is visible to all modules within the control project, but not to those of clients using the control?

    a. `Public Friend MyFunction() As String`

    b. `Friend MyFunction() As String`

    c. `Sub Friend MyFunction()`

    d. `Friend Function MyFunction() As String`

44. Custom events must be declared:

    a. In a standard module

    b. In the Declarations section of the UserControl module

    c. Anywhere within the UserControl module

45. Which of the following is a valid statement, given the following event declaration?

`Event Change(ByVal NewText As String)`

    a. `Event.Raise Change("Some Text")`

    b. `RaiseEvent Change()`

    c. `RaiseEvent Change("Some Text")`

    d. `Event.Raise Change(Some Text)`

46. Which event fires each time an ambient property of a control's container is changed?

    a. AmbientChanged

    b. AmbientModified

    c. Changed

    d. Ambient

47. What value will the UserMode property of the AmbientProperties object return if the application containing the control is being run as a compiled executable?

    a. True

    b. False

48. Which object exposes properties of a control that are maintained by its container?

    a. AmbientProperties

    b. Parent

    c. Extender

49. Which object returns a reference to the container on which a control is sited?

    a. AmbientProperties

    b. Extender

    c. Parent

50. Which collection references the controls on a parent of a custom control?

    a. ParentControls

    b. ContainerControls

    c. Controls

51. To link a property to a PropertyPage object:

    a. Use the Procedure Attributes dialog box.

    b. Use the PropertyPage dialog box.

    c. Use the Property Manager.

52. Which statement is true about setting default property procedures?

    a. Only one procedure may be designated as a default.

    b. Only one property and one event procedure may be designated as a default.

    c. Only methods can be designated as default property procedures.

53. In order to properly implement an About box, you must:

    a. Name the method that displays the About box ShowAboutBox.

    b. Call the ShowAboutBox method of the UserControl object.

    c. Assign the Procedure ID About box to the procedure that displays the About box.

54. You can create properties that emulate Text and Caption properties by:

    a. Assigning the Procedure ID for Text or Caption to the property procedures.

    b. Naming the properties Text or Caption.

    c. This behavior is automatic; you don't have to do anything.

55. To enable a control as a data consumer that can be bound to an entire row of data, which property would you set?

    a. DataConsumer = vbRowBound

    b. DataSource = vbSimpleBound

    c. DataBindingBehavior = vbComplexBound

    d. DataConsumerBehavior = vbComplexBound

56. Which statement is true about creating a data-aware control?

    a. You must create a DataSource property.

    b. All controls have a DataSource property.

    c. Visual Basic automatically creates a DataSource property when you designate a property as being data-bound.

57. One bound property, and only one, must have which property set?

    a. DataBindings

    b. This property binds to DataField

    c. Show in DataBindings collection

58. What must be true in order for a developer to be able to access a bound property at design time?

   a. The property must have its "Show in DataBindings collection at design time" checkbox selected.

   b. The property needs only to be marked as a data-bound property.

   c. Only one databound property can be accessed at runtime.

59. If you do not call the PropertyChanged function in a bound properties Property Let procedure:

   a. Visual Basic automatically knows the data has changed and will update the database.

   b. Visual Basic does not know the data has changed and changes will be lost.

   c. An error will occur when the recordset moves to a different record.

60. To test and debug an ActiveX control:

   a. Compile the control into an executable.

   b. Open two instances of Visual Basic.

   c. Create a project group.

Answers to Skills Assessment

1. c	13. b, c	25. b	37. b	49. c
2. b	14. d	26. c	38. a	50. a
3. c	15. b	27. c	39. a	51. a
4. b	16. a	28. a	40. c	52. b
5. c	17. c	29. b	41. b, c	53. c
6. b	18. b	30. a	42. b, d	54. a
7. a	19. a, b	31. a	43. d	55. c
8. d	20. d	32. a	44. b	56. c
9. b	21. a	33. c	45. c	57. b
10. b	22. c	34. d	46. a	58. a
11. c	23. b	35. c	47. a	59. b
12. a, d	24. a, c, d	36. a	48. c	60. c

Hands-on Lab Exercises

Questions regarding the creation and testing of ActiveX controls will absolutely be on the exams. Now that you have a thorough background of creating ActiveX controls, you're going to put that knowledge to use. Complete all of these lab exercises to help solidify your understanding of ActiveX controls.

Exercise 5-1: Creating an Aggregate control

In this exercise, you'll create an ActiveX control that acts as a True/False input mechanism, applying all of these skills:

• Creating an ActiveX control

• Creating and raising a custom event

- Implementing property persistence
- Creating an Enum
- Allowing a control to be enabled and disabled
- Creating a property page
- Using the Ambient object
- Testing a control using a project group

Section 1. Creating the ActiveX controls user interface. The ActiveX control you are going to create is a simple control that displays two option buttons, one for a value of **True** and the other for a value of **False**. Setting the Value property of the control automatically selects the proper option button. To make the control more developer friendly, you'll add a property page to the control. Finally, you'll test the project by creating a project group.

1. Start Visual Basic and create a new ActiveX control.
2. Change the Name of the project to **TrueFalseControl**.
3. Change the following properties of the UserControl:

Property	Setting
Name	TrueFalse
Width	2265
Height	1140
ScaleMode	3 - Pixel

4. Add a new option button to the form and set its properties as follows:

Property	Setting
Name	optTrueFalse
Caption	True
Height	17
Left	36
Top	12
Width	81
Index	1

5. Make a copy of the option button and paste the copy on the UserControl.
6. Change the following properties of the second option button:

Property	Setting
Name	optTrueFalse
Caption	False
Left	36
Top	36

Your control should now look like the one shown in Figure 5-36.

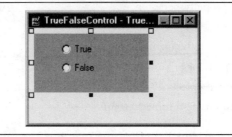

Figure 5-36: Aggregate controls use other controls for their interface

Section 2. Creating an Enum. In this part you're going to create an Enum to make it easy for the users of the control to get and set the Value property (which you'll also create):

7. In the Declarations section of the UserControl module, add the following code:

```
Public Enum tfTrueFalse
    tfTrue = -1
    tfFalse = 0
End Enum
```

Visual Basic provides internal constants for **True** and **False**; however, this example demonstrates creating an Enum in as simple a way as possible.

Section 3. Creating a public property. Now you're going to create a public Value property. This property uses the custom Enum **tfTrueFalse**.

8. Create a member variable to store the value of the Value property by adding this line of code to the Declarations section of the module:

```
Private m_Value As Boolean
```

9. Create the Property Get procedure that returns the value of the Value property by adding the following lines of code:

```
Public Property Get Value() As tfTrueFalse

    Value = m_Value

End Property
```

10. Now that the Property Get procedure is defined, you must create the Property Let procedure so that a user can change the Value property. When the property is changed, the procedure will select the appropriate option button (True or False), and let Visual Basic know that the property has changed. Add the following procedure to the UserControl module:

```
Public Property Let Value(New_Value As tfTrueFalse)

    m_Value = New_Value
```

```
optTrueFalse(m_Value * -1).Value = True

PropertyChanged ("Value")
```

```
End Property
```

Section 4. Implementing property persistence. In this section you are going to add the code to implement property persistence. You have already performed the first step of property persistence by adding the call to the PropertyChanged function in the Property Let procedure.

11. Add the following code to the WriteProperties event:

```
Call PropBag.WriteProperty("Value", m_Value, tfTrue)
```

12. Next, add the following code to the ReadProperties event:

```
Value = PropBag.ReadProperty("Value", tfTrue)
```

13. The control now has property persistence and it can restore itself based upon how the developer sets the Value property. Now you need to set up the initial behavior of the control; that is, how the control will appear when first placed on a form. In this example, the control is going to have a Value of True by default. Add the following statement to the InitProperties event:

```
Value = tfTrue
```

Section 5. Creating and raising a custom event. In this section, you're going to create an event called Change that will fire each time a user selects True or False. The Change event will pass the Value of the control as an argument so the developer can easily tell the state of the control.

14. Add the following statement to the Declarations section of the UserControl:

```
Event Change(ByVal Value As tfTrueFalse)
```

15. You need to update the value of *m_Value* when a user selects True or False. This can only occur at runtime, so you don't need to be concerned with property persistence. Add the following statements to the optTrueFalse option button click event:

```
m_Value = Index * -1
RaiseEvent Change(m_Value)
```

Section 6. Allowing the control to be enabled and disabled. In this section you'll create a custom Enabled property using Property Let and Property Get procedures. You will then assign the custom property to the Enabled Procedure ID on the Procedure Attributes dialog box:

16. Add the following Property Get and Property Let procedures to the control:

```
Public Property Get Enabled() As Boolean

    Enabled = UserControl.Enabled

End Property
```

```
Public Property Let Enabled(New_Enabled As Boolean)

    UserControl.Enabled = New_Enabled

End Property
```

17. Select Tools → Procedure Attributes . . . to display the Procedure Attributes dialog box.

18. Select the Enabled property procedure from the Name dropdown list.

19. Click the Advanced command button.

20. Select Enabled from the Procedure ID dropdown list (see Figure 5-37).

21. Click OK to save your changes and close the Procedure Attributes dialog box.

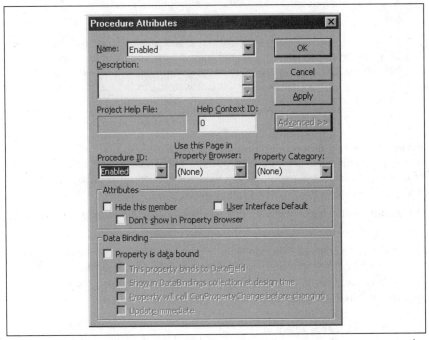

Figure 5-37: To correctly create an Enabled property for a control, you must use the standard Enabled Procedure ID

Section 7. Creating a property page. In this section you are going to add a simple property page to the control:

1. Choose Add Property Page from the Project menu.

2. Double-click the property page icon.

3. Change the name of the property page to **Value**, and the Caption property to **Value**.

The property page you're going to create will simply allow a developer to set the initial Value of the control. Since you've already used radio buttons in the control itself, you're going to use a listbox on the property page. Add a listbox to the property page and set its properties as follows:

Property	Setting
Name	lbValue
Height	645
Left	1800
Top	1560
Width	1215

Next, add a new label control to the project and set its properties as follows:

Property	Setting
Caption	Value:
Height	255
Left	1110 ˙
Top	1560
Width	555

Your property page should now look like the one in Figure 5-38.

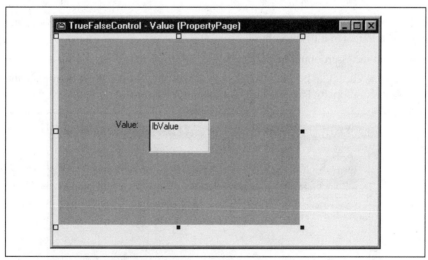

Figure 5-38: A simple property page for a simple control

25. The following code is used to reflect the current state of the selected control(s) when the property page is displayed. Add this code to the SelectionChanged event of the property page:

```
lbValue.Clear
lbValue.AddItem "True"
lbValue.AddItem "False"
```

```
If SelectedControls(0).Value Then
    lbValue.ListIndex = 0
Else
    lbValue.ListIndex = 1
End If
```

26. Your property page needs a way to apply any changes made on it to the selected control(s). To give the property page this functionality, add the following code to the ApplyChanges event of the property page:

```
If lbValue.ListIndex = 0 Then
    SelectedControls(0).Value = True
Else
    SelectedControls(0).Value = False
End If
```

27. The only step left to complete the property page is to inform the page when a user makes changes to it. You have already created code to apply changes, but changes are applied only if the property page knows that changes have been made. To inform the property page that changes have been made, you set its Changed property to True. Add the following code to the Click property of the lbValue listbox:

```
PropertyPage.Changed = True
```

Section 8. Attaching a property page. Now that your property page is complete, you need to assign it to the control:

28. Select the UserControl in design view.

29. Double-click the PropertyPages property of the UserControl to display the Connect Property Pages dialog box shown in Figure 5-39.

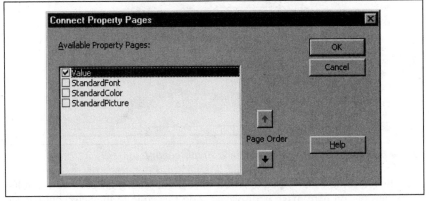

Figure 5-39: Assign the custom property page to the UserControl

30. Click the checkbox next to the Value control.

31. Click OK to accept your selection and close the Connect Property Pages dialog box.

Section 9. Testing the control using a project group. Your control, although basic, is now complete. In this section, you'll create a project group to test the design-time and runtime behavior of the control:

32. Create a project group by choosing Add Project from the File menu to add a new project to the group. The Add Project dialog box appears.

33. Usually, Standard EXE projects are used to test controls. Double-click Standard EXE on the Add Project dialog window.

34. Right-click the new project in the Project Explorer window and select Set as Startup from the Shortcut menu.

35. If any of the designers windows (UserControl, code, or property page) are open, close them. If you leave a designer window open, you may not be able to add the control to the test form.

36. Select the new form of the test project.

37. Double-click the icon for your UserControl in the Visual Basic toolbox to add a new instance of the control to the form.

38. By default, the control appears with the value of **True**. Change the value property in the Properties window and notice how the control changes immediately to reflect the new value.

39. Double-click the Custom property of the control to access its property pages (see Figure 5-40).

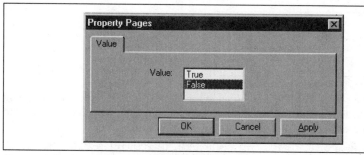

Figure 5-40: Visual Basic creates the tabbed dialog box for your property pages automatically.

40. Change the Value property by selecting **True** or **False**, using the listbox on the property page. When you want to apply the change, click the Apply button.

41. Click OK to close the property pages.

42. Finally, press F5 to run the project. Click the True and False radio buttons and notice how they are mutually exclusive.

This exercise has covered many of the principles involved in creating ActiveX controls. If you truly understand everything you've done in this exercise, you should be well on your way to performing well on the ActiveX control portion of the exams.

Exercise 5-2: Creating a data-bound control

In this exercise, you'll create a simple bound ActiveX control. This control uses a standard text box to display fields in a database. To make it more interesting, the fore color of the control will change, depending on the value of the data field to which it is bound.

Section 1. Creating the control's user interface. In this section, you're going to create the user interface of the bound control. This is an aggregate control that subclasses the standard text box:

1. Start Visual Basic and create a new ActiveX control project.

2. Change the name of the project to **BoundExample**.

3. Set the properties of the default UserControl as follows:

Property	Setting
Name	BoundTextBox
Height	525
ScaleMode	3 - Pixel
Width	1860

4. Next, add a new text box control to the UserControl and set its properties as follows:

Property	Setting
Name	txtData
Left	0
Text	Make blank
Top	0

5. You didn't set a width or height value for the text box because you are going to add code to ensure the text box always fills the entire UserControl. Add the following code to the Resize event of the UserControl:

```
txtData.Move 0, 0, UserControl.ScaleWidth, UserControl.ScaleHeight
```

Section 2. Creating the Text property. In this section, you'll add a Text property, which is the property that is bound to the database field specified by the developer:

6. The first procedure you are going to create is the Property Get procedure. This property returns the value of the text box. Add the following Property Get procedure to the UserControl's module:

```
Public Property Get Text() As String

    Text = txtData.Text

End Property
```

7. Next, you're going to create the Property Let procedure that allows the developer (and a data control) to set the text in the text box. Just to make it

interesting, you're going to make the control adjust its fore color according to the value it contains. Add the following procedure to the UserControl's module:

```
Public Property Let Text(New_Text As String)

    txtData.Text = New_Text

    Select Case Val(New_Text)
        Case Is > 2000
            txtData.ForeColor = vbRed
        Case Is > 1990
            txtData.ForeColor = vbBlue
        Case Is > 1980
            txtData.ForeColor = vbGreen
    End Select

End Property
```

Section 3. Making the Text property a bound property. In this section, you're going to make the Text property a bound property so that a developer can bind it to a data control:

8. Select Tools → Procedure Attributes . . . to display the Procedure Attributes dialog window.

9. Select the Text property in the Name dropdown list.

10. Click the Advance tab to display the advanced settings.

11. To make the property data bound, select the "Property is data bound" checkbox. When you select this checkbox, the other four data related checkboxes become enabled. Check all four of these checkboxes, as shown in Figure 5-41.

12. Click OK to save changes and close the Procedure Attributes dialog box.

Section 4. Testing the Data-Bound control. In this section, you'll create a project group to test your ActiveX control:

13. Create a project group by choosing Add Project from the File menu.

14. Double-click the Standard EXE project icon.

15. Right-click the new project in the Project Explorer window and select Set as Start Up from the Shortcut menu.

16. Make sure the UserControl designer windows is closed, and then select the default form of your test project.

17. Double-click the toolbox icon of your control in the Visual Basic toolbox to add an instance of the control to the form.

18. Add a new Data control to the form.

19. Double-click the DatabaseName property of the Data control.

20. Locate the *Biblio.mdb* database in your Visual Basic folder.

21. Change the RecordSource property of the Data control to **Titles**.

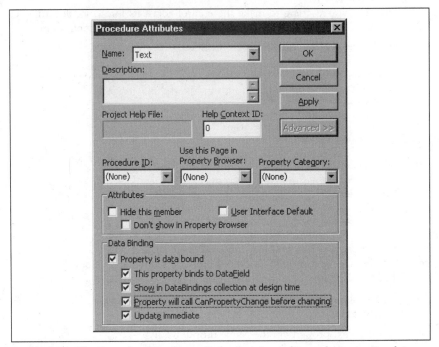

Figure 5-41: The Procedure Attributes dialog box is used to make properties data bound

22. Change the DataSource property of your custom control to **Data1**.

23. Change the DataField of your custom control to **Year Published**.

24. Press F5 to run the project.

Use the buttons on the Data control to cycle through the records. As you do so, the Year Published of the current record appears in your custom control, and the fore color changes depending on the year displayed.

Highlighter's Index

ActiveX Controls

The UserControl object
Aggregate controls use constituent controls
Invisible controls
Owner-draw controls
Can be active at design time
Properties, methods, and events

Property Pages

Make it easy to change properties
Appear as tabbed dialog boxes

PropertyPage object
SelectedControls collection
SelectionChanged event
Assigned using PropertyPages property

Property Persistence

Properties initialized in InitProperties event
Properties saved in WriteProperties event
Properties restored in ReadProperties event
Values stored in PropertyBag object
PropertyChanged method notifies control that changes have taken place

Ambient Properties

Used to integrate the appearance of control with its container
AmbientChanged event tells control when the parent's ambient properties
   have changed

Extender Object

Makes extended properties, such as Left, Top, Width, and Height available
   to the control
Host dependent
Must avoid property collisions

Procedure Attributes

Allow you to set Procedure IDs
Assign descriptions and help IDs to procedures
Can hide procedures
Can link a property page to a procedure
Can assign member defaults

Data-Bound Controls

Controls can be data providers or data consumers
Defined using the Procedure Attributes dialog box
DataBindings collection

ActiveX
Controls

CHAPTER 6

Creating and Using ActiveX Documents

ActiveX document technology is often misunderstood because it's not widely used. In this chapter, you'll learn everything you need to know about ActiveX documents, including how to create and how to test them. If you can answer all of the review questions at the end of the chapter, you should do well on the ActiveX document questions on the exams.

The Technologies and the Exams

As with ActiveX controls, you can expect to encounter questions about ActiveX documents on both exams, as Table 6-1 shows. Unlike ActiveX controls, however, you've probably never actually created or used an ActiveX document.

Table 6-1: Coverage of ActiveX Documents on the Exams

Topic	Covered on Exam
Similarities between ActiveX documents and ActiveX controls	Both
How ActiveX documents relate to embedded objects	Both
The UserDocument object	Both
Integrating an ActiveX document with its container	Both
Viewports	Both
Hyperlink object	Both
Multiple-document projects	Both
Persisting data	Both
Asynchronously receiving data	Both
Testing and debugging ActiveX documents	Both

Understanding ActiveX Documents

ActiveX documents are a specific type of ActiveX object that can be placed and activated within ActiveX document containers such as Microsoft Internet Explorer.

ActiveX documents are an extension of OLE compound document technology (commonly used for OLE linking and embedding), but they allow for considerably more control.

ActiveX documents are a relatively new type of ActiveX component, and although they offer many exciting possibilities, they aren't widely implemented. ActiveX documents are similar to ActiveX controls in that they require a host application; they cannot run as standalone applications. However, unlike ActiveX controls, ActiveX documents can't be embedded into forms, they can only be inserted into containers that support ActiveX documents (currently Microsoft Internet Explorer, Binder, and Visual Basic are the only applications that can host ActiveX documents). The construction of ActiveX documents is also similar to that of ActiveX controls. For instance, ActiveX documents can have properties, methods, and events—all created just as they are for ActiveX controls. In essence, an ActiveX document is an entire application exposed much like an ActiveX control. This chapter focuses on the unique features of creating and testing ActiveX documents. The similarities between ActiveX documents and ActiveX controls are covered, but the similar elements aren't discussed in detail in this chapter. Refer to Chapter 5, *Creating ActiveX Controls*, for specific technical information on the shared aspects of ActiveX documents and ActiveX controls.

Although not everyone has a reason to use such functionality, one of the greatest aspects of ActiveX documents is that they can be hosted within the Visual Basic design environment. What does this mean? Add-ins, add-ins, add-ins! The ActiveX document is the basis for many Visual Basic add-ins. ActiveX documents offer enormous flexibility and control in optimizing and extending the Visual Basic IDE.

Visual Basic ActiveX documents really haven't caught on, and it's not certain whether or not they ever will. With all of the new Internet development technologies and the acceptance and support of ActiveX controls, ActiveX documents may fall by the wayside. Since ActiveX documents aren't widely deployed, they're not very well understood. Microsoft's Visual Basic documentation says:

> For all intents and purposes, an ActiveX document is a Visual Basic application that is now accessible in a widely-used container.

The potential ramifications of this are amazing. For example, an ActiveX document can be deployed to all workstations on an intranet, rather than deploying a client-side application. When a user accesses the document on the intranet, if the document is newer than the one on the user's computer, an update is automatically downloaded and applied. ActiveX documents run on the client machine after being downloaded from a URL, so performance isn't hampered by the speed of the network or ISP connection once the control is deployed.

Of course, you can create client-side web applications using HTML (or DHTML), but programming in HTML takes practice and a little bit of luck. By creating ActiveX documents rather than complex HTML pages, you can leverage the incredible speed, power, and flexibility of Visual Basic's design environment and the Visual Basic language itself. Also, in HTML, you often write code for a visual interface in a text editor, and you then have to run and test the code. Visual Basic's graphical design environment makes it considerably easier to create a user interface. There are a number of other compelling reasons to use ActiveX documents, and these will be discussed in their respective sections throughout this chapter.

Visual Basic 6 lets you create DHTML applications, and you should study the uses of DHTML in Chapter 8, *Creating Internet-Aware Applications*, as well as the material in this chapter. By fully understanding DHTML and ActiveX documents, you'll be better prepared to decide for yourself which type of application is most suited to a given scenario.

While ActiveX documents are similar to ActiveX controls, they're also very similar to embedded objects in many ways. Understanding the similarities and differences between ActiveX documents and ActiveX controls and between ActiveX documents and embedded objects is crucial to fully understanding ActiveX documents and the opportunities they create.

Similarities Between ActiveX Documents and ActiveX Controls

Before learning about what makes an ActiveX document unique, you should have a full understanding of how an ActiveX document is similar to an ActiveX control. First, creating the user interface of an ActiveX document is identical to creating the user interface of an ActiveX control; you place controls on a UserDocument, just as you do on a UserControl object when creating a control.

You cannot place an OLE control on an ActiveX document, nor can you place embedded objects such as Word documents or Excel spreadsheets on an ActiveX document.

In addition to creating a user interface, like you do for ActiveX controls, you give your ActiveX document properties, methods, and events, just as you do with ActiveX controls. Refer to Chapter 5, *Creating ActiveX Controls*, for specifics on how to add these developer interfaces to your UserDocuments.

The following list compares characteristics of ActiveX documents and ActiveX controls:

- An ActiveX document can't exist without a container. Whereas an ActiveX control is contained in a form, UserDocument, or UserControl, an ActiveX document is contained in a container such as Internet Explorer, Binder, or the Visual Basic IDE.

- The developer of an ActiveX document cannot know which container will be used to view the ActiveX document, just as an ActiveX control developer can't know ahead of time what application may host the control.

- The UserDocument object features several events that are also found on the UserControl object. These events include Initialize, InitProperties, ReadProperties, EnterFocus, ExitFocus, WriteProperties, and Terminate.

If you think on a larger scale, an ActiveX document is like an entire Visual Basic application wrapped up as one ActiveX control.

 Procedure attributes do not apply to UserDocuments like they do UserControls. (See Chapter 5 for information on procedure attributes.)

How ActiveX Documents Relate to Embedded Objects

Although ActiveX documents share many traits with ActiveX controls, they actually behave more like embedded objects. An ActiveX document is placed upon a host such as Internet Explorer, and it exposes information and functionality much like embedded objects for applications such as Word (documents) or Excel (spreadsheets). Unlike controls, ActiveX documents always fill the container of their hosts, and they may (and should) contain custom menus that merge with the menus of the host application.

 ActiveX documents are currently limited to being hosted in Microsoft Internet Explorer or Binder, and as add-ins in the Visual Basic IDE. However, more ActiveX document hosts are expected.

You can cheat a little if you want to place an ActiveX document on a form. First, place a web browser control on the Visual Basic form, then use the browser to view the document.

Although ActiveX documents behave somewhat like embedded objects, they are considerably more functional. For instance, an ActiveX document can actually control its host in limited ways. Also, if you've ever embedded an object such as a Word document on a host, then you know that if the embedded document window is not large enough, it's very difficult to work with the document, because scrollbars are not present in the embedded object (see Figure 6-1). Also, many features of the server application, such as changing a Word document from Normal view to Page Layout view, are not available when the document is embedded. ActiveX documents let you control scrolling behavior for documents that are larger than the area being viewed, and they let you provide functionality that couldn't be exposed through an embedded object.

The web browser is quickly becoming a universally accepted navigational interface. As such, programmers are going to be faced with the demand to provide a browser interface for their applications. Of course, you could learn HTML, but programming in HTML is a kludge at best. Although HTML tools are getting better all the time, interface design with HTML often relies on trial and error, with a sprinkling of horseshoes and rabbit's feet. By creating ActiveX documents, you can easily write programs that run within the browser environment using your existing Visual Basic skills and the power and flexibility of Visual Basic. These ActiveX documents look and feel like a web page but run like a compiled application. An additional bonus is that unlike HTML (or DHTML), ActiveX documents don't expose their source code for the whole world to see.

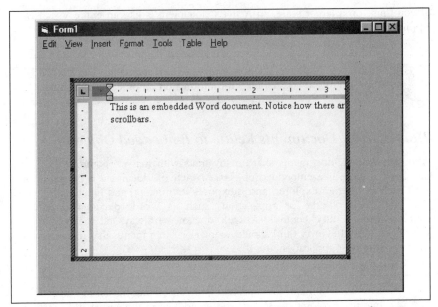

Figure 6-1: Embedded objects have no scrollbars to allow you to access the entire embedded document

Understanding how ActiveX documents are similar to other items, such as controls and embedded objects, is the first step toward truly understanding ActiveX documents themselves. The next section teaches you about working specifically with ActiveX document projects.

Working with ActiveX Document Projects

To create an ActiveX document, you create an ActiveX document project. You have the option of creating in-process (DLL) or out-of-process (EXE) ActiveX documents. You might wonder why anyone would want to create an out-of-process ActiveX document and forego the performance benefits of an in-process DLL. However, you should consider using an out-of-process EXE for the following reasons:

- Some hosts can't display nonmodal forms from a DLL. If your ActiveX document needs to display a form that is not modal, an EXE might be your only choice.

- ActiveX document EXEs share global data among instances of the server.

Fortunately, regarding the first of these two points, you can determine at runtime whether or not the host supports nonmodal forms by using the NonModal-Allowed property of the Application object, like this:

```
If App.NonModalAllowed Then
    ' Display form modally
Else
    ' Display form non-modally
End If
```

If your ActiveX Document is to be hosted in Microsoft Internet Explorer 3.x, you *must* make it an out-of-process component (EXE).

Building the Foundation: The UserDocument Object

ActiveX documents are built upon the UserDocument class. A UserDocument is very similar to a form object or a UserControl (see Figure 6-2). As with forms and UserControls, you can have as many different UserDocuments in your project as you like, but there are some special considerations that apply to projects that contain multiple UserDocuments. These considerations are discussed in the section "Creating Multiple Document Projects." If you think of the UserDocument more like a UserControl than like a form, you'll have a better understanding of how it functions. For instance, unlike with a form, you can implement property persistence in a UserDocument using the same techniques used for a UserControl.

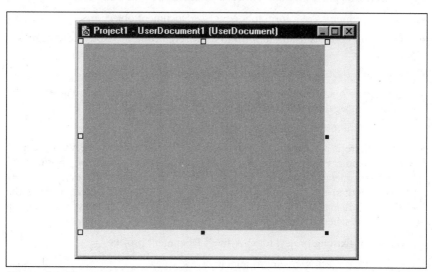

Figure 6-2: The ActiveX Document designer looks and functions like the ActiveX Control designer

Converting Projects to ActiveX Documents Using the Migration Wizard

Visual Basic includes an ActiveX Document Migration Wizard to help you convert existing applications to ActiveX documents. The ActiveX Document Migration Wizard is a Visual Basic Add-in, and it can be started from the Add-In Toolbar (see Figure 6-3).

Figure 6-3: The ActiveX Document Migration Wizard is a Visual Basic Add-In

The ActiveX Document Migration Wizard performs the following tasks:

- Copies properties of a form to a new UserDocument object.

- Copies all controls from the form to the UserDocument. (Note: Control names are retained.)

- Copies all code behind the form to the UserDocument.

- Comments out all illegal code such as **Me.Left** and **End**. (You'll learn why these are illegal later in this chapter.)

- Switches the project type to ActiveX EXE or DLL.

- When there is a corresponding event on the UserDocument, the wizard copies event handlers from the form to the UserDocument, replacing "Form" with "UserDocument." In cases where there is no counterpart, the event handlers are copied to the General section of the UserDocument object, leaving the "Form" part intact. You must then move the code to a different event or call the events where appropriate from within your ActiveX Document project.

To convert an existing project to an ActiveX Document project:

1. Open the project you want to migrate.

2. Select ActiveX Document Migration Wizard from the Add-Ins menu. If the ActiveX Document Migration Wizard command is unavailable, use the Add-In Manager to add it to the menu. When the Introduction dialog box appears, click Next to proceed.

3. On the Form Selection page, select the form that you want to convert and click Next.

4. On the Options page, select the following options, and then click Next:

    a. Comment out invalid code

    b. Remove original forms after conversion

    c. Convert to an ActiveX EXE

5. On the Finished page, click No when asked if you want to see a Summary Report after the wizard is done. Click "Save current settings as default," and then click Finish.

You should experiment with the wizard to gain an understanding of what it does. Although you probably will not be tested on the wizard itself, you will most likely encounter questions related to converting existing forms manually.

Effectively Using UserDocument Events

In Chapter 5, you learned how many different events allow you to control the appearance of your ActiveX control, how to determine the control's state (runtime or design time), how to persist properties, and much more. Most of this information is directly applicable to UserDocuments. It's important to fully understand the events of a UserDocument, including the order in which they fire, the purpose of each event, and the nuances that specifically affect ActiveX documents. Table 6-2 outlines the standard UserDocument events as they relate to the lifetime of a UserDocument.

Table 6-2: Standard UserDocument Events

Event	Description
Initialize	Occurs every time an instance of your document is created or recreated. It is always the first event in an ActiveX document's lifetime.
InitProperties	Occurs the very first time the control is placed on a container by a developer, and as long as none of the ActiveX document properties have been saved using the PropertyBag. Once a property value has been saved, this event is replaced by the ReadProperties event.
ReadProperties	Occurs every time a control is created, except for the first time. The first time the control is created, the InitProperties event is fired instead.
EnterFocus	Occurs when any object on the ActiveX document, including the ActiveX document itself, receives focus.
ExitFocus	Occurs when no object on the ActiveX document, including the document itself, has the focus any longer.
Resize	Occurs every time a container is resized.
Scroll	Occurs whenever the user clicks on the container's scrollbar or the scrolling region of the container, or if the user drags the scrollbar. Scrollbars are discussed in detail in the section "Working with Viewports," later in this chapter.
WriteProperties	Occurs immediately before the Terminate event. This event only occurs if at least one property value has changed at design time. Remember from Chapter 5 that you must notify the container that a property has changed using the Property Changed method.
Terminate	Occurs when the ActiveX document is about to be destroyed. In Internet Explorer 3.0, an ActiveX document is stored in a cache of four documents. When the user loads or navigates to a fifth document, the ActiveX document will be terminated. In later versions of Internet Explorer, documents have a different lifespan, as discussed later in this chapter. You can use the Terminate event to clean up any object references by setting all global object references to Nothing.
Show	Occurs when the ActiveX Document is displayed in a container.
Hide	Occurs when the container navigates to a different document, and the current ActiveX Document is no longer displayed.

The Form object's Load event doesn't have a direct counterpart in the UserDocument object. Instead, you can place Load event procedures in the Show event. However, you should be aware that the Show event is called *every time the user navigates to the ActiveX document* (in a web browser). To prevent Load event procedures from running every time the Show event occurs, use a module-level variable or a local static variable as a flag; if the flag has been set, don't run the code in the Show procedure.

Correctly using the events of a UserDocument is critical to having the document display and behave as expected. For more information about these events, refer to Chapter 5.

Integrating an ActiveX Document with Its Container

Just as with ActiveX controls, there are a number of things you can do to ensure your ActiveX document integrates well with its container. You can control what the user sees by creating a Viewport, you can control the behavior of the Viewport as well, and you can use the Hyperlink object to navigate to other UserDocuments or to other web sites.

Determining an ActiveX Document's Container Programmatically

Often, it's helpful to know the specific container in which a document is sited. This can be done using the VBA *TypeName* function on the UserDocument's Parent property, like this:

```
Dim strHost As String
strHost = TypeName(UserDocument.Parent)
```

At the time of this writing, there are only three possible types of containers that support UserDocuments. These are listed in Table 6-3.

Table 6-3: Possible Hosts Returned by Type Name

Host	Return String	Comments
Internet Explorer	IWebBrowserApp	
Microsoft Binder	Section	
Visual Basic IDE Window	Window	Created by the CreateToolWindow function in the Visual Basic IDE.

The following code illustrates how you can use *TypeName* to determine the container hosting a document at runtime:

```
Private Sub TestContainer()
    Dim strHost As String

    strHost = TypeName(UserDocument.Parent)
```

```
    ' Use the Select Case statement to test.
    Select Case strHost
        Case "IwebBrowserApp"
            ' Internet Explorer
        Case "Section"
            ' Microsoft Binder
        Case "Window"
            ' Visual Basic IDE
        Case Else
            ' Unknown container
    End Select
End Sub
```

 You cannot use the Initialize event to test the type of the container, because a document isn't fully sited in its host when the Initialize event occurs.

Adding a Menu to an ActiveX Document

A definite difference between ActiveX controls and ActiveX documents is the ability to add menus to ActiveX documents. ActiveX documents don't actually display their own menus as forms do; nonetheless, they do display their menus by merging them with the menus of their host container (see Figure 6-4).

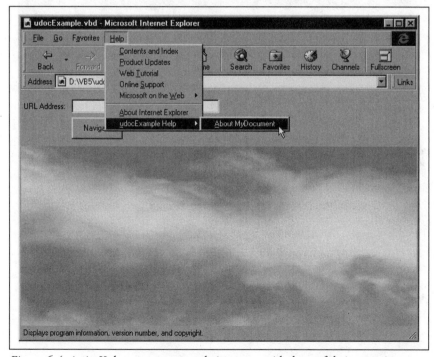

Figure 6-4: ActiveX documents merge their menus with those of their containers

ActiveX documents by their very nature can be placed on the Internet or on an intranet. When a user navigates to your UserDocument, they may have no idea of the origin of the document. Because of this, you should always provide at least a Help About . . . menu item that displays an About box for the document (see Figure 6-5).

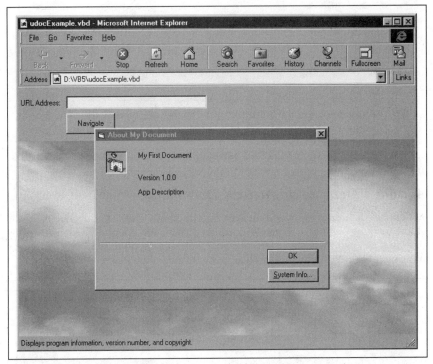

Figure 6-5: An About dialog box adds an identity to your ActiveX documents

 Some containers will not display their menus correctly unless the ActiveX document merges a Help menu with the container's Help menu. Therefore, if you plan on implementing a menu on a User-Document, you should always include a Help menu.

To add an About dialog box to a UserDocument project, follow these steps:

1. Choose Add Form from the Project menu.

2. Double-click the About Dialog icon to add a generic About form to the project.

3. Set the Caption properties of the labels on the form to include information specific to your UserDocument.

To create the Help About . . . menu, follow these steps:

1. After selecting the UserDocument, choose Menu Editor from the Tools menu to display the menu editor dialog box.

2. Type **&Help** in the Caption text box.

3. Type **mnuHelp** in the Name text box.

4. Select 3-Right from the NegotiatePosition dropdown list.

5. Click Next to create a new menu item.

6. Type **About This UserDocument** in the option text box.

7. Type **mnuAbout** in the Name text box.

8. Click the right-facing arrow button to indent the menu item.

9. Click OK.

Once you've created an About dialog box and a menu item that the user can select to display the dialog box, you need to add the following code to the mnu_About_ Click event to display the About box:

```
Private Sub mnuAbout_Click()
    frmAbout.Show vbModal
End Sub
```

By following these steps, the "About This UserDocument" menu item will appear on the Help menu whenever a user views the document (refer to Figure 6-4). Selecting the menu item displays the custom About box.

 In the unlikely event that the host container does not have a Help menu, your UserDocument will add one to the host's menus.

Working with Viewports

You'll recall from the discussion at the beginning of this chapter that one of the serious drawbacks of embedded objects is poor interactivity when the object is displayed in a window smaller than the actual document. This is not an issue with UserDocuments. As you know, UserDocuments cannot be displayed on their own. Instead, they're displayed within a client area of a container such as Internet Explorer. The container area dedicated to displaying a UserDocument is called a *Viewport* (see Figure 6-6).

Think of a Viewport as a rectangular hole cut out of a piece of cardboard. You can place this piece of cardboard over a picture such as a photograph, but you will only see what is visible through the cut-out rectangle.

As stated earlier, if a UserDocument is hosted on a container larger than the User-Document itself, the UserDocument is adjusted automatically so that it fills the entire container. Viewports allow you to handle the opposite situation—when the container is not large enough to view the entire UserDocument.

As a developer, you cannot control the size of the container on which your User-Document will be hosted. Furthermore, users can and often do adjust the size of

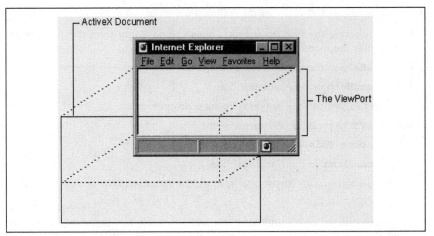

Figure 6-6: A Viewport is the visible rectangular region of an ActiveX Document when hosted in a container

the container; *you cannot control this*. What you can do is ensure that your User-Document behaves as well as possible regardless of the size of its Viewport.

Retrieving Viewport settings

The UserDocument provides four properties that allow you to easily retrieve the current Viewport settings used to display the UserDocument. These properties are:

- ViewportTop
- ViewportLeft
- ViewportHeight
- ViewportWidth

 The Viewport properties listed here always return values in the ScaleMode of the UserDocument.

Figure 6-7 shows how these properties relate to what you see within a container. Note that when scrollbars are shown, the scrollbars themselves are not computed in the width or height of the Viewport.

Knowing the size of the Viewport can be quite useful. A common example of using the Viewport settings is to make a PictureBox contained on a UserDocument resize to fill the entire Viewport. Remember, this is different from resizing the PictureBox to fill the entire UserDocument. For instance, the following procedure resizes an Image control to fill the entire area of a UserDocument:

```
Private Sub UserDocument_Resize()
    Image1.Width = UserDocument.Width
    Image1.Height = UserDocument.Height
End Sub
```

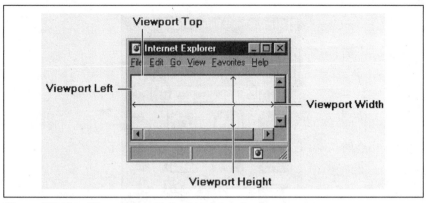

Figure 6-7: How Viewport properties are determined

If the Viewport is larger than the UserDocument, the size of the UserDocument and the Viewport size are the same so the code above works just fine (see Figure 6-8). However, if the Viewport is smaller than the UserDocument, the user will only see a small portion of the picture (see Figure 6-9). In addition, the code shown earlier does not take into consideration the left or top of the Viewport.

Figure 6-8: When a container is larger than a UserDocument, the UserDocument is adjusted to fill the container and the Viewport displays the entire document

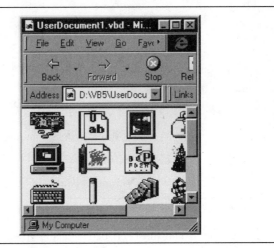

Figure 6-9: When the Viewport is smaller than the UserDocument, you see only a small portion of the document

The following code moves and resizes a PictureBox so that it always fills the Viewport:

```
Private Sub UserDocument_Resize()
    Image1.Left = UserDocument.ViewportLeft
    Image1.Top = UserDocument.ViewportTop
    Image1.Width = UserDocument.ViewportWidth
    Image1.Height = UserDocument.ViewportHeight
End Sub
```

Figure 6-10 shows what the UserDocument looks like when the previous procedure is used in place of the code that sets the image to the same size as the UserDocument.

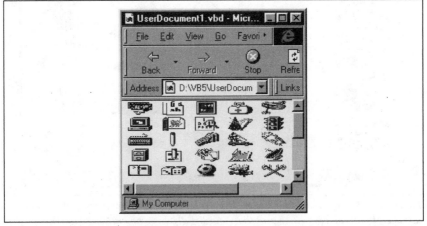

Figure 6-10: Regardless of the Viewport size, a little code makes the image fill the Viewport perfectly!

The practical applications of this particular example are questionable, but it serves to illustrate how you can use the Viewport properties.

Displaying scrollbars in a Viewport

When a Viewport is smaller than the UserDocument it contains, it's often desirable for the Viewport to display scrollbars so the user can easily scroll the Viewport to see any area of the UserDocument. Visual Basic makes it easy to implement this functionality in your UserDocuments.

The UserDocument has the following properties to let you control the scrollbar behavior of a Viewport:

- ScrollBars
- MinHeight
- MinWidth
- HScrollSmallChange
- VScrollSmallChange

Disabling scrollbars. You can prevent scrollbars from ever displaying in a Viewport by setting the UserDocument's ScrollBars property to *0 - None* (or `False`). Note, however, that *this is a design-time–only property*; you cannot change it at runtime. If the ScrollBars property is set to anything other than *0 - None*, the MinHeight and MinWidth properties discussed in the next section control the appearance of scrollbars.

The following are acceptable values of the Scrollbars property:

- 0 - None
- 1 - Horizontal
- 2 - Vertical
- 3 - Both

Just because the Scrollbars property is set to 1, 2, or 3 doesn't mean that scrollbars are displayed; it just means that the specified scrollbar *can* be displayed when the Viewport becomes the proper size, as discussed next.

Controlling the Viewport size at which scrollbars appear. Remember, you cannot control the dimensions of the Viewport. However, you can control the size at which the Viewport displays scrollbars. You do this using the MinHeight and MinWidth properties. The MinHeight property determines the minimum height of the Viewport at which a vertical scrollbar is displayed. The MinWidth property determines the minimum width of the Viewport at which a horizontal scrollbar is displayed. When a Viewport is sized smaller than the MinHeight or MinWidth property values, the appropriate scrollbar is automatically displayed. You will not see the MinHeight and MinWidth properties in the Properties window because you can't set them at design time. When a UserDocument is first displayed on a container, the MinHeight and MinWidth properties default to the Height and Width properties of the UserDocument at design time. This is acceptable the majority of the time, but you can change these properties at runtime as needed.

The MinHeight and MinWidth properties are always expressed in the ScaleMode of the UserDocument.

Setting the SmallChange values of a Viewport's scrollbars. Just as you can control the SmallChange values of standard scrollbars (the amount scrolled when the user clicks a scroll arrow), you can also control the SmallChange values of a Viewport's scrollbars. To set the small scroll amount for the vertical scrollbar of a Viewport, set the VScrollSmallChange property of the UserDocument. To set the small scroll amount for the horizontal scrollbar of a Viewport, set the HScrollSmallChange property of the UserDocument.

The VScrollSmallChange and HScrollSmallChange property values are always expressed in twips.

There are no properties that let you change the large scrolling behavior of a Viewport's scrollbars. The large change is always the Height (vertical) and Width (horizontal) of the Viewport.

Panning a Viewport programmatically

Although you can't control the size of a Viewport, you can programmatically control its *location* (see Figure 6-11). You dictate the location of the Viewport using the SetViewport method of the UserDocument object. The SetViewPort method has the following syntax:

```
UserDocument.SetViewport left, top
```

The SetViewport method is great for ensuring that objects are fully visible when they need to be. For example, you can use the SetViewport method in the GotFocus event of a text box to move the Viewport so that the text box's top and left corner align in the upper-left corner of the Viewport. The following procedure does just that:

```
Private Sub Text1_GotFocus()
    UserDocument.SetViewport Text1.Left, Text1.Top
End Sub
```

Using the HyperLink Object

A HyperLink object is an object of the UserDocument that exposes the hyperlinking functionality found in a web browser. You can use the HyperLink object to instruct the browser host of a UserDocument to go to and display a web page or another UserDocument object.

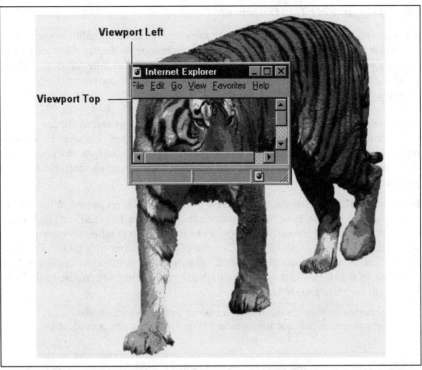

Figure 6-11: To "pan" a Viewport, use the SetViewport method and specify the top and left locations to pan to

The UserControl has a HyperLink property that references a Hyper-Link object just as UserDocuments do. Although this section discusses the HyperLink object in relation to the UserDocument, the behavior is the same with UserControls. In order to use a UserControl's Hyper-Link object, however, the UserControl must be hosted on a container that supports the HyperLink object, such as Internet Explorer.

Navigating to a web page using the HyperLink object

Use the NavigateTo method of the HyperLink object to force the browser to jump to a specific URL. The NavigateTo method has the following syntax:

```
UserDocument.HyperLink.NavigateTo URLAddress
```

The *URLAddress* can be any document type, such as an HTML, Word, or Excel document, or it may be an ActiveX document, as you'll see in the next section. For example, the following statement forces the hosting browser of a UserDocument object to navigate to the web page *http://www.tigerpawsoftware.com*:

```
UserDocument.HyperLink.NavigateTo "http:\\www.tigerpawsoftware.com"
```

Displaying another UserDocument

It was mentioned earlier that you cannot show UserDocuments in the same way as you show forms. This means that you need a technique to display UserDocuments in a project that has multiple UserDocuments. The procedure used to display another ActiveX document depends on the type of container hosting the document.

Displaying another UserDocument from within a web browser. In order to display another UserDocument from within a web browser, use the NavigateTo method of the HyperLink object. When you think of the ActiveX document *as* a document, it makes sense that you can navigate to the ActiveX document just as you can to a Word or Excel document.

In the section "Understanding an ActiveX Document's Components" at the end of this chapter, I discuss how Visual Basic creates a server file (EXE or DLL) and a document file (VBD) for each UserDocument in the project when you compile the project for distribution. All of these files are placed together in a folder on a web server, just as you would place HTML files or other documents on the server. With this in mind, you can navigate to a VBD file (a compiled Visual Basic User-Document file) using code like this:

```
' Assuming the desired ActiveX document is named MyDoc2.vbd
UserDocument.Hyperlink.NavigateTo "file://c:\ActXDocs\MyDoc2.vbd"
```

You can use the GoForward and GoBack methods of the HyperLink object to navigate the browser's history list.

Displaying another UserDocument from within the Binder. Microsoft Binder does not support hyperlinking. Instead, you must add a new section to the Binder in order to display another ActiveX document. This text is not designed to teach you how to program Binder, only to show you how to display another UserDocument from within Binder.

The following code is an example of adding another section to Binder and displaying an ActiveX document in the new section:

```
' Use the same document as before: AxDoc2.
UserDocument.Parent.Parent.Sections. Add , "c:\docs\AxDoc2.vbd"
```

If you use the NavigateTo method of the HyperLink object while your document is hosted in a container that doesn't support hyperlinks (such as Binder), then the application defined in the system registry to handle hyperlinks (such as Internet Explorer) is started and handles the request.

Dynamically constructing an Absolute Path. Using the NavigateTo method of the HyperLink object requires you to specify a full path and filename of the ActiveX document to which you want to navigate, but you can never be certain where an ActiveX document (the file with the VBD extension) will end up. In order to navigate from one ActiveX document to another, it becomes necessary to parse the path information of the location of the first object in order to use it to navigate to the second (assuming both documents are stored in the same location).

You cannot use App.Path to determine the location of the document because App. Path returns the location of the server (EXE or DLL). Servers are downloaded from a site so that they run on the client machine, but the ActiveX documents (VBD files) are left in their original location, such as on a web server.

The LocationName property of Internet Explorer returns the absolute path of the document currently being displayed. It's a simple matter of removing the filename from the absolute path and using the result to point to another ActiveX document. The following code shows one way of doing this:

```
Dim strPath As String        ' String to be parsed
Dim strAbsPath As String     ' Result of parsing
Dim intChar As Integer       ' Used to look at characters


' Return the path of the current ActiveX document.
strPath = Trim$(UserDocument.Parent.LocationName)


' Find the position of the last separator character.
For intChar = Len(strPath) To 1 Step -1
    If Mid$(StrPath, intChar, 1) = "/" Or _
        Mid$(StrPath, intChar, 1) = "\" Then Exit For
Next intChar


' Strip the name of the current VBD file.
strAbsPath = Left$(StrPath, intChar)


' Navigate to the second ActiveX document.
UserDocument.Hyperlink.NavigateTo strAbsPath & "MyDoc2.vbd"
```

Being able to navigate from one document to another, regardless of document locations, is a powerful feature of ActiveX documents. However, this ability is really not much more advanced than displaying one form from another form, and in some ways it's more limiting. In the next section, you'll learn about some of the advanced functions of the ActiveX document.

Creating Multiple Document Projects

For the most part, creating a project with multiple UserDocuments is very much like creating a project with multiple forms. The only real difference is how you display one UserDocument from another. Unlike standard Visual Basic forms, you cannot use the Show method to show ActiveX documents. This is because the container application, such as Internet Explorer, determines when to show or hide ActiveX documents. Instead of explicitly displaying the UserDocument, you tell the host to navigate from one ActiveX document to another. To navigate between the two ActiveX documents, you use the HyperLink object, as discussed previously in this chapter.

Communicating Between UserDocuments

Although it's easy to design a multiple UserDocument project, and it's relatively easy to display one UserDocument from another, it can be challenging to design your application effectively so that two different UserDocuments can communicate among themselves.

In an ordinary project, you can easily reference a form using its name; however, you can't reference a UserControl by its name. Also, in an ordinary application, you have complete control over the flow of events that occur within your application. It may take navigating three different forms in order to display a fourth. With ActiveX documents, you can never be assured of the steps taken to display a document. Since a user can navigate directly to a document using the address bar of a browser or by using their Favorites list, you can never be sure what exactly occurred before a particular document was displayed.

In order to know if a certain document has been previously displayed, and to communicate with that document, you must implement an OLE callback.

 The basic mechanics of the callback are discussed here, but you should refer to the complete explanation of callbacks in Chapter 4, *Creating and Testing ActiveX Code Components*, for more information.

The callback mechanism you create to communicate between UserDocuments makes use of a global variable. While the technique shown here uses a single global variable to communicate between two UserDocuments, you could use multiple variables or a variable array to create communications between multiple UserDocuments.

The global variable is used to hold a reference to one of the UserDocuments. For instance, say you had two UserDocuments, UserDocument1 and UserDocument2, and that UserDocument2 needed to interact with UserDocument1. The first step is to create a global variable to hold a reference to UserDocument1 in a *standard module,* like this:

```
Public g_udocFirst As UserDocument1
```

The next step would ordinarily be for UserDocument1 to place a reference to itself in the global variable. The word "ordinarily" is used because, once again, you can't be sure UserDocument1 is loaded and displayed before UserDocument2. If UserDocument1 is used to display UserDocument2 using a command button, you could use code like the following to create the global variable reference:

```
Private Sub cmdViewUserDoc2_Click()

    Set g_udocFirst = Me
    Hyperlink.NavigateTo "c:\UserDocument2"

End Sub
```

When the Show event of UserDocument2 occurs, the global variable is used to determine whether or not UserDocument1 was loaded, and to communicate with UserDocument1 if it was. For instance, say UserDocument1 has a public property called BackColor. UserDocument2 could print the BackColor property value of UserDocument1 using code like this:

```
Private Sub UserDocument2_Show()

    If Not (g_udocFirst Is Nothing) Then

        MsgBox "UserDocument1's BackColor = " & g_udocFirst.BackColor

        Set g_udocFirst = Nothing

    End If

End Sub
```

Notice how the global variable is first checked to make sure it is not Nothing. If the global variable is Nothing, UserDocument1 has not been displayed. What you would do if UserDocument1 were not displayed would depend entirely on the requirements of the task at hand.

 When UserDocument2 is finished with the object reference in the global variable, it sets the variable to Nothing to fully release the object reference. This is critical; if you don't release the object reference, the referenced UserDocument will not unload!

Persisting Data for UserDocuments

When an ActiveX document is first displayed, its InitProperties event fires much as it does for a UserControl. If a user browses to a different ActiveX document, the document being navigated *from* fires its Hide and Terminate events. If the user clicks the Back button on the browser or otherwise navigates back to the original UserDocument, the ActiveX document reinitializes itself. If you had, for instance, a number of text boxes on the UserDocument in which the user had entered information, those text boxes would be reinitialized and the user's data would be lost. Remember, the InitProperties event fires only the first time the document is displayed, but the Initialize event occurs every time the document is loaded. You can persist data of an ActiveX document just as you persist data for a UserControl so that when the user navigates back to the document, the data is not lost. Chapter 5 discusses in great detail property persistence using the PropertyBag object, so property persistence won't get much coverage here. However, this section will give you a very small illustration of how you might use property persistence to persist information entered into a text box.

When a UserDocument is first loaded, a text box on the document displays the value assigned to its Text property at design time. To ensure that data entered into the text box would persist when the user navigates to a different document or web page, you would add code similar to the following in the ActiveX document's appropriate events:

```
Private Sub UserDocument_ReadProperties(PropBag As PropertyBag)

    Text1.Text = PropBag.ReadProperty("Text", "")

End Sub


Private Sub UserDocument_WriteProperties(PropBag As PropertyBag)

    Call PropBag.WriteProperty("Text", Text1.Text, "")

End Sub
```

By using the WriteProperties and ReadProperties events in this manner, you ensure that each time your document is displayed in the browser (after the first time), changes made to the text box are restored. However, as you'll recall from the detailed discussion on property persistence in Chapter 5, Visual Basic needs to know that a property has changed or it won't fire its WriteProperties event. You can notify Visual Basic that data has changed in any number of ways, but the simplest (though not necessarily the best) way is to use the Change event of the text box, like this:

```
Private Sub Text1_Change()

    PropertyChanged ("Text")

End Sub
```

By using property persistence, as discussed in Chapter 5, you can create tremendously powerful and useful ActiveX documents that won't punish a user who chooses to navigate to another document before committing changes to the current document.

Asynchronously Receiving Data

Although UserDocuments can be hosted in Microsoft Binder, their most obvious application is within an Internet browser. You are probably well aware of some of the behaviors exhibited by web browsers that differ from those of a standard application. One such difference that is absolutely critical to the success of browsers is the ability to accept user input while resources such as bitmaps, scripts, or text are being downloaded from a site. This functionality is accomplished through *asynchronous downloading*, and you can add it to your UserDocuments.

Asynchronous downloading allows a document to partially display itself and receive user input while elements (such as large bitmaps) are still being downloaded. You are not limited to performing asynchronous downloading of bitmaps, you can also asynchronously download files and byte arrays.

Downloading data asynchronously is a two-part process. First, the UserDocument requests the data to be downloaded, and the document is then notified when the data has been fully received. It is only after the data has been fully received that the UserDocument does something with the data. Between the request and the final received notification, the UserDocument is free to execute other code, such as receiving user input and executing code procedures. The UserDocument can cancel an asynchronous download request at any time.

 You can perform asynchronous downloads using a UserControl object exactly as you do for a UserDocument. Therefore, asynchronous downloading is only discussed here using the UserDocument as an example, but the principles are the same for UserControls.

Requesting Data for Asynchronous Download

To initiate an asynchronous download, you invoke the AsyncRead method of the UserDocument. The AsyncRead method has the following format:

```
UserDocument.AsyncRead Target, AsyncType [, PropertyName]
```

Target is a string specifying the location of the data to download. This can be a normal path or a URL. For instance, to download a picture called *mypic.gif* from the web site *http://www.mywebsite.com*, you would provide the following target string:

```
"www.mywebsite.com/mypic.gif"
```

AsyncType is an integer expression that identifies how the data will be presented. The *AsyncType* parameter may be any one of the settings listed in Table 6-4 (for specific information on the different types, refer to the next section).

Table 6-4: AsyncType Parameter/Property Values

Setting	Data Is Provided In
vbAsyncTypeFile	A file that is created by Visual Basic.
VbAsyncTypeByteArray	A byte array that contains the retrieved data. (It is assumed that the control author will know how to handle the data.)
vbAsyncTypePicture	A Picture object.

The *PropertyName* parameter is a string that uniquely identifies the asynchronous download request. This can be any string you want it to be, and although it is optional, you should seriously consider always specifying a *PropertyName*. The *PropertyName* is used to cancel an asynchronous download using the CancelAsyncRead method, as well as to identify a completed download in the AsyncReadComplete event. The next section discusses the specifics of how this value is used.

Receiving Notification That an Asynchronous Download Is Complete

After an AsyncRead method is called, the download begins and the UserDocument is free to go about its business. When the download is complete, the UserDocument's AsyncReadComplete event fires. The AsyncReadComplete event has the following structure:

```
Private Sub UserDocument_AsyncReadComplete(AsyncProp As AsyncProperty)

End Sub
```

The *AsyncProp* parameter of the event contains a reference to a special type of object, an AsyncProperty object. The AsyncProperty object has the following three properties:

Value
> A Variant containing the results of the asynchronous read. This is the default property.

PropertyName
> A string containing the property name that was passed in the AsyncRead method.

AsyncType
> An integer specifying the type of the data in the Value property, as described earlier in Table 6-4.

The PropertyName property returns the string you specified as the *PropertyName* parameter when the AsyncRead method was called. This is how you can differentiate among numerous asynchronous download requests. The values for AsyncType are the same as for the AsyncType parameter you specify when the AsyncRead method is called as well. The value of AsyncType dictates the contents of the Value property, as shown earlier in Table 6-4.

The AsyncReadComplete event is best understood by looking at some examples. Bitmaps are probably the most common file type specified when asynchronously downloading data. Some bitmap files can be quite large and may take quite a bit of time to download and display on a UserDocument. Downloading the bitmaps asynchronously rather than embedding them directly on the UserDocument allows the control to accept user input and paint other parts of itself while the bitmaps are downloading.

The following line of code uses the AsyncRead method to initialize an asynchronous download of a bitmap file:

```
UserDocument.AsyncRead "c:\clouds.bmp", vbAsyncTypePicture, _
    "BackgroundBitmap"
```

Of course, this is only the first step. The next step involves receiving notification that the download is complete and then actually doing something with the downloaded data. The following event procedure assigns the downloaded picture to the Picture property of the UserDocument:

```
Private Sub UserDocument_AsyncReadComplete(AsyncProp As AsyncProperty)

    If AsyncProp.PropertyName = "BackgroundBitmap" Then
        UserDocument.Picture = AsyncProp.Value
    End If

End Sub
```

Notice how the PropertyName of the AsyncProp object variable is checked prior to assigning the value of the variable to the Picture property of the UserDocument. If your UserDocument only downloads one piece of information, you don't need to perform this check. However, by verifying the PropertyName of the data returned, you can make multiple calls to the AsyncRead method from various places in code, and then "plug-into" the AsyncReadComplete event.

Canceling an Asynchronous Download

You can cancel an asynchronous download at any time by calling the Cancel-AsyncRead method of the UserDocument object. The CancelAsyncRead method has the following syntax:

UserDocument.**CancelAsyncRead** [*PropertyName*]

PropertyName corresponds to the *PropertyName* parameter that you specified when you invoked the AsyncRead method. If you do not supply a *PropertyName* for the CancelAsyncRead method, the last asynchronous transfer initiated *without* a PropertyName is the one canceled.

ActiveX documents are a mixed bag. They exhibit behavior similar to embedded objects and ActiveX controls, and they are built much like ActiveX controls. However, as you'll find in the next section, they are tested and debugged like nothing else.

Testing and Debugging ActiveX Documents

ActiveX Documents

Testing and debugging ActiveX documents is different from testing and debugging ActiveX controls or code components. Unlike ActiveX controls and code components, ActiveX documents require a host container to run. The easiest way to test and debug an ActiveX document is to use Internet Explorer.

> If you're working with (or you plan on working with) ActiveX documents, you should consider using Internet Explorer 4 or later. Internet Explorer 4 and 5 have many improvements over Internet Explorer 3, and debugging ActiveX documents is certainly a case for which it's beneficial to be using the latest software.

If you click Run or press F5 while you're working on an ActiveX document project in the Visual Basic IDE, the UserDocument designer disappears and nothing else seems to happen. As you'll learn in the next section, something *is* happening; you just don't see it.

Understanding an ActiveX Document's Components

Before you can begin testing and debugging an ActiveX document, you must understand what happens when you compile an ActiveX document. Unlike when you compile any other type of project in Visual Basic, compiling an ActiveX document project actually creates multiple files. Compiling an ActiveX document project creates the EXE or DLL file (depending on the project type), and it creates a single document file with the extension VBD for every UserDocument object in the project.

The EXE or DLL files are called the *server* files, much as *winword.exe* is the Word server. The VBD files are the actual documents, much like Word documents with the extension DOC. In order for a user to view your ActiveX document, he must have both the server file and the document file(s).

 Chapter 13, *Packaging and Deploying an Application*, discusses how to distribute the VBD, EXE, and DLL files. This chapter focuses on the mechanics of how the files work, not how to distribute them.

The VBD file (the true document file) is actually an OLE-structured storage file, which is a file that contains data in a format supported by standard OLE interfaces. Other Microsoft applications, such as Word and Excel, save data in a similar manner. The VBD file is what you point a browser to in order to display the document. Remember, in order to test an ActiveX document, you must use a container such as Internet Explorer to host the document, and in order to host a document, you must have a VBD file. Fortunately, Visual Basic circumvents the need to compile an ActiveX document to a file just to test it by creating a temporary VBD file in the Visual Basic directory whenever an ActiveX document project is run. This VBD is given the same name as the UserDocument object.

Visual Basic 6 makes debugging ActiveX documents slightly easier through use of the new Debugging tab on the Project Properties dialog box, as shown in Figure 6-12.

Before the Debugging tab was available, you had to run your ActiveX document project by pressing F5, then start Internet Explorer, and then type in the filename of the temporary document file created in the Visual Basic folder. While not exceptionally difficult, the process was annoying. If you select "Wait for components to be created" on the Debugging tab of the Project Properties dialog box, you'll get the same behavior. However, if you select "Start component" (the default for ActiveX document projects), Visual Basic launches Internet Explorer and automatically navigates to the UserDocument specified in the text box. If you want a new instance of Internet Explorer created each time the component is put into run mode, deselect the "Use existing browser" checkbox.

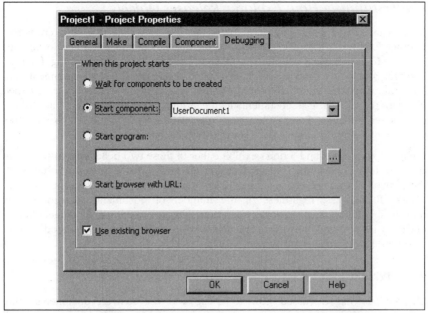

Figure 6-12: The Debugging tab of the Project Properties dialog window removes some of the tedium of debugging ActiveX documents

---

 Internet Explorer has numerous security settings designed to protect a user from unfriendly Internet components. If the security setting of Explorer is set too high, Explorer won't download the required User-Document files.

While Internet Explorer is hosting the document, you have all of Visual Basic's powerful debugging facilities at your disposal. This behavior is similar to testing ActiveX controls using a project group, only instead of using another Visual Basic project, you are running an instance of Explorer.

Stopping a Debugging Session

If you try to stop a running ActiveX document project while the control is hosted in Internet Explorer, Visual Basic warns you that stopping the project will cause an error in the application hosting the document. You should avoid doing this, since you can cause the hosting application or Windows itself to become unstable. What you should do is force Internet Explorer to release the document. The easiest way to do this is to quit Internet Explorer. While you might think you can simply navigate to a different document, you can't, for reasons that are explained in the next section.

Understanding How Explorer Releases Objects

Internet Explorer 3.x and Internet Explorer 4.x/5 release objects in different ways. Internet Explorer 3.x has a memory cache that stores the last four documents viewed. If you navigate to four web sites or other documents using Internet Explorer 3.x, the cache will no longer contain a reference to your document and you can stop the running project. There is another way to force Internet Explorer 3.x to release a document: in the Address box, type **c:** or any other drive letter and press Enter. When you instruct Internet Explorer 3.x to view the contents of a drive, you also cause it to flush its cache.

Internet Explorer 4.x and 5 don't exhibit either of these two behaviors. Instead of a cache of four documents, Internet Explorer 4.x and 5 create a hidden instance of the ActiveX document object and hold the reference to that object for approximately 10 minutes, regardless of the number of documents viewed in the meantime. Closing any version of Internet Explorer causes all document references to be released, however, and that's why it's the simplest method to use when testing documents.

Key Facts

This chapter has discussed how to create and test ActiveX documents. The following are key points to understand in order to pass ActiveX document–related questions on the Visual Basic exams.

- The creation of ActiveX documents is similar to that of ActiveX controls.

- ActiveX documents are often compared to embedded objects.

- Unlike embedded objects, ActiveX documents can actually control their host in some ways.

- You can fully control the scrolling behavior of an ActiveX document.

- Unlike HTML, ActiveX documents do not expose your source code.

- ActiveX documents must be hosted in a container. Currently, only Internet Explorer, Microsoft Binder, and the Visual Basic IDE itself can host ActiveX documents.

- ActiveX documents are essentially complete Visual Basic applications accessible in a widely used container.

- The UserDocument object is the main object of an ActiveX document project.

- You cannot place an OLE control on a UserDocument.

- You cannot place embedded objects on a UserDocument.

- Unlike ActiveX controls, UserDocuments do not have procedure attributes.

- You might consider an out-of-process ActiveX document project because some hosts can't display nonmodal forms. When the document will be hosted in Internet Explorer 3.x, or when you need to use global variables shared among documents, create an out-of-process document.

- You can determine if a host can display a nonmodal form by checking the value of the NonModalAllowed property of the Application object.

- You can use the ActiveX Document Migration Wizard to migrate forms to ActiveX documents.

- You can determine an ActiveX document's parent using the *TypeName* function on the Parent property of the UserDocument.

- ActiveX document menus are merged with the menus of the document's host.

- If you plan on implementing a menu on a UserDocument, you should always include a Help menu because some containers will not display their menus correctly unless the ActiveX document merges a Help menu with the container's Help menu.

- If a UserDocument is hosted on a container larger than the UserDocument itself, the UserDocument is adjusted automatically so that it fills the entire container.

- The container area dedicated to displaying a UserDocument is called a Viewport. Viewports allow you to handle the situation of when the container is not large enough to view the entire UserDocument.

- You cannot control the size of the container on which your UserDocument will be hosted, but you can control some aspects of the Viewport.

- Viewport properties always return values in twips, regardless of the ScaleMode of the UserDocument.

- You can dictate whether or not scrollbars appear on a UserDocument by setting the ScrollBars property.

- If Scrollbars are enabled on a document, scrollbars will appear if the Viewport becomes smaller than the MinHeight or MinWidth properties of the UserDocument.

- When a UserDocument is first displayed on a container, the MinHeight and MinWidth properties default to the Height and Width properties of the UserDocument at design time.

- MinHeight and MinWidth are always expressed in the ScaleMode of the UserDocument.

- The HScrollSmallChange and VScrollSmallChange properties control the amount scrolled, and they are always expressed in twips.

- There are no properties available to control the large scrolling behavior of a Viewport's scrollbars. The Large Change is always the Height or Width of the Viewport.

- You can programmatically control the location of the Viewport using the SetViewport method of the UserDocument.

- A HyperLink object is an object of the UserDocument that exposes hyperlinking functionality found in a web browser.

- Use the NavigateTo method of the HyperLink object to force the browser to jump to a specific URL.

- Displaying another UserDocument from within a web browser is performed using the NavigateTo method of the HyperLink object.

- To display another UserDocument from within Binder, use Sections.

ActiveX Documents

- ActiveX documents support asynchronous downloading of data.

- Asynchronous downloading allows a document to partially display itself and receive user input while elements (such as large bitmaps) are still being downloaded.

- To initiate an asynchronous download, you invoke the AsyncRead method of the UserDocument.

- The UserDocument's AsyncReadComplete event fires when an asynchronous download is complete.

- You can cancel an asynchronous download at any time by calling the CancelAsyncRead method of the UserDocument object.

- When you compile an ActiveX Document project, Visual Basic creates the EXE or DLL, and a VBD document file for each UserDocument in the project.

- ActiveX documents require a host container for testing.

- When you run an ActiveX Document project in the Visual Basic IDE, Visual Basic creates a temporary VBD file in the Visual Basic folder.

- If Internet Explorer's security settings are set too high, it will not download the necessary components to use an ActiveX document.

- You can cause problems by stopping a running ActiveX document project when the document is being hosted in a container.

- The easiest way to force a container to release a reference to an ActiveX document is to close the container application.

Applying What You've Learned

It's now time to apply what you've learned about creating ActiveX documents. First, answer all of the questions in the Skills Assessment. If you can correctly answer all of these questions, you'll be demonstrating a solid understanding of creating ActiveX documents. After you've answered the assessment questions, work through the hands-on exercises.

Skills Assessment

1. The creation of ActiveX documents is most similar to the creation of:

    a. ActiveX code components

    b. ActiveX controls

    c. Word documents

    d. Embedded objects

2. The behavior of ActiveX documents is similar to: (pick two)

    a. ActiveX code components

    b. ActiveX controls

    c. Embedded objects

    d. Forms

3. What benefits does an ActiveX document have over an embedded object? (pick two)

    a. You can control the scrolling behavior of an ActiveX document.

    b. ActiveX documents do not expose your source code.

    c. An ActiveX document can control some aspects of its container.

    d. ActiveX documents do not require a server application.

4. You can place an OLE control on an ActiveX document.

    a. True

    b. False

5. You cannot place embedded objects on an ActiveX document.

    a. True

    b. False

6. When might you want to use an out-of-process ActiveX document?

    a. When a host supports modal forms

    b. When the document will be hosted in Internet Explorer 3.x

    c. When distributing over an intranet

7. How can you determine if a host supports nonmodal forms?

    a. By checking the value of the NonModalAllowed property of the Application object.

    b. By checking the value of the ModalAllowed property of the Application object.

    c. All hosts support nonmodal forms.

    d. There is no way for a document to determine if its host supports nonmodal forms.

8. ActiveX documents are built upon which one of the following classes?

    a. UserControl class

    b. Form class

    c. UserDocument class

    d. ActiveXDocument class

9. To determine the host of an ActiveX document:

    a. Use the HostName property of the UserDocument.

    b. Use the *TypeName* function on the Parent property of the UserDocument.

    c. Use the HostType property of the parent of the UserDocument.

    d. There is no way to determine the host of an ActiveX Document.

10. Unlike ActiveX controls, ActiveX documents can have menus.

    a. True

    b. False

11. ActiveX Document menus are merged with the menus of their host.

   a. True

   b. False

12. If a UserDocument is displayed on a host larger than the UserDocument itself:

   a. The UserDocument displays at its default size.

   b. An error occurs.

   c. The host is resized to fit the UserDocument perfectly.

   d. The UserDocument is adjusted to fill the area of the host.

13. The container area of a host dedicated to displaying a UserDocument is called the:

   a. Host window

   b. Viewport

   c. View window

   d. Cut-out

14. You cannot control the size of the container on which your UserDocument will be hosted.

   a. True

   b. False

15. Viewport properties always return values in:

   a. Twips

   b. Pixels

   c. The ScaleMode of the UserDocument

   d. The ScaleMode of the host

16. You can prevent scrollbars from ever appearing for a UserDocument by setting which property?

   a. HasScrollBars

   b. ScrollBars

   c. VerticalScrollBar

   d. HorizontalScrollBar

17. The Viewport at which scrollbars are displayed is determined by which properties:

   a. ScrollHeight, ScrollWidth

   b. ScrollHSize, ScrollVSize

   c. HorizontalScroll, VerticalScroll

   d. MinHeight, MinWidth

18. The MinHeight and MinWidth properties always return values in:

   a. Twips

   b. Pixels

   c. The ScaleMode of the UserDocument

   d. The ScaleMode of the host

19. Which two properties can be used to control the amount scrolled by a scrollbar?

   a. VSmallChange, HSmallChange

   b. VScrollChange, HScrollChange

   c. VScrollSmallChange, HScrollSmallChange

   d. VScrollLargeChange, HScrollLargeChange

20. Which method programmatically sets the location of a Viewport?

   a. MoveViewport

   b. ViewportLocation

   c. ViewportXY

   d. SetViewport

21. To navigate to a URL from a UserDocument on a browser, you use which object?

   a. Browser

   b. HyperLink

   c. FTP

   d. Navigate

22. Which method of the HyperLink object navigates to a new document using the browser?

   a. NavigateTo

   b. Goto

   c. Navigate

   d. URL

23. To display a different UserDocument from a UserDocument in a browser:

   a. Use the Show method of the UserDocument.

   b. Use the NavigateTo method of the HyperLink object.

   c. Use Sections.

24. To display a different UserDocument from a UserDocument in Binder:

   a. Use the Show method of the UserDocument.

   b. Use the NavigateTo method of the HyperLink object.

   c. Use Sections.

25. What allows a document to partially display itself and receive user input while elements are still being downloaded?

    a. Bilinear transfer

    b. Synchronous downloading

    c. Asynchronous downloading

    d. ActiveX documents cannot do this

26. To start an asynchronous download, use the:

    a. AsyncRead method of the UserDocument

    b. AsyncRead method of the host

    c. AsyncInitTransfer method of the UserDocument

    d. Web browser control

27. How do you determine when an asynchronous download is complete?

    a. The AsyncReadComplete event is fired.

    b. You must poll the AsyncStatus property of the UserDocument.

    c. Code is halted while the download is in progress.

28. To cancel an asynchronous download, use the:

    a. CancelAsyncRead method of the UserDocument.

    b. CancelDownload method of the UserDocument.

    c. CancelAsyncDownload method of the UserDocument.

    d. You can't cancel a download in progress.

29. What files are created when you compile an ActiveX Document: (pick two)

    a. The EXE or DLL

    b. A DOC file for every UserDocument in the project

    c. A VBD file for every UserDocument in the project

    d. A UDC file

30. To persist data of a UserDocument when a user browses to a different document or web page:

    a. Data is persisted automatically.

    b. You cannot persist data of a UserDocument.

    c. Store the data in the registry.

    d. Use the PropertyBag object.

31. How can two UserDocuments communicate with one another?

    a. UserDocuments can reference each other just as forms do.

    b. Use a global variable to hold a reference to a UserDocument.

    c. UserDocuments cannot communicate with one another.

    d. Use the PropertyBag object.

32. To test an ActiveX document:

   a. Create a project group.

   b. Use Internet Explorer.

   c. Compile the project.

   d. Place the UserDocument on a form.

33. You attempt to access an ActiveX document in Internet Explorer, but the document doesn't open. What may be the cause?

   a. The VBD document needs to be on a web server.

   b. The UserDocument does not have code in its Paint event.

   c. Internet Explorer's security settings are set too high.

34. The most efficient and safest way to force Internet Explorer to release a reference to an ActiveX document is to:

   a. Close Internet Explorer.

   b. Navigate to four other documents.

   c. Navigate to a different document and wait approximately 10 minutes.

Answers to Skills Assessment

1. b	8. c	15. a	22. a	29. a, c
2. b, c	9. b	16. b	23. b	30. d
3. a, c	10. a	17. d	24. c	31. b
4. b	11. a	18. c	25. c	32. b
5. a	12. d	19. c	26. a	33. c
6. b	13. b	20. d	27. a	34. a
7. a	14. a	21. b	28. a	

Hands-on Lab Exercise

Now that you have a thorough background in creating ActiveX documents, you're going to put that knowledge to use. This chapter has just one exercise, but it covers most of the topics discussed in this chapter.

Exercise 6-1: Creating and testing an ActiveX document

In this exercise you'll create an ActiveX document project. This exercise applies the following topics:

- Creating an ActiveX document
- Using the HyperLink object
- Performing an asynchronous download
- Using Viewport properties
- Merging an ActiveX document's menus with its container
- Testing an ActiveX document using Explorer

Section 1. Creating the ActiveX document's user interface. The ActiveX document you create will be a DLL that allows a user to type in a valid URL and click a button to navigate to that address. The DLL then asynchronously downloads and displays a picture, and automatically adjusts the downloaded picture to fill the lower portion of the Viewport.

1. To begin, start Visual Basic and create a new ActiveX document DLL.

2. Give the default UserDocument the name **udocExample**.

3. Create a new text box control and set its properties as follows:

Property	Value
Name	txtAddress
Height	315
Left	1200
Text	<make blank>
Top	180
Width	3495

4. Add a new label control to the form and set its properties as follows:

Property	Value
Name	lblAddress
Caption	URL Address:
Height	255
Left	60
Top	240
Width	1035

5. Add a new command button to the form and set its properties as follows:

Property	Value
Name	cmdNavigate
Caption	Navigate
Height	495
Left	1200
Top	600
Width	1215

6. Add a new image control to the form and set its properties as follows:

Property	Value
Name	imgStretch
Height	1395
Left	0
Stretch	True
Top	1260
Width	2295

7. Save the project. Save the UserDocument with the name *udoc1.dob*, and the project with the name *udoc1.vbp*. Your UserDocument should now look like Figure 6-13.

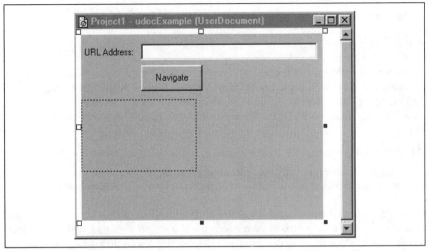

Figure 6-13: The interface of this UserDocument is simple but functional

Section 2. Adding code to navigate to a web page. In this section, you're going to add code to the command button. This code uses the NavigateTo method of the HyperLink object to navigate the browser to the URL Address specified by the user in the text box.

8. Add the following statement to the command button's Click event:

```
UserDocument.HyperLink.NavigateTo txtAddress.Text
```

Section 3. Adding code to perform an asynchronous download. When this ActiveX document first loads, it's going to perform an asynchronous download of a bitmap. The bitmap used in this example is the *Clouds.bmp* file found in the Windows folder of most computers, but any bitmap would work just as well. In this section you will add code to initiate an asynchronous download as well as code that takes the downloaded picture data and places it into the image control.

9. Place the following code statement to initiate the download in the Show event of the UserDocument:

```
UserDocument.AsyncRead "c:\Windows\clouds.bmp", _
    vbAsyncTypePicture, "BackgroundBitmap"
```

 If your Windows folder is named something other than Windows or resides on a drive other than C, adjust the foregoing statement as required. Also, if your computer does not have the *Clouds.bmp* picture in the Windows folder, substitute the filename in the code statement with a BMP picture of your choice. Just be sure the path and filename point to a BMP picture.

---

10. Initiating an asynchronous download is only half of the process; you need to do something with the data once it is received. Add the following code that places the downloaded picture into the Image control to the AsyncRead-Complete event of the UserDocument:

```
If AsyncProp.PropertyName = "BackgroundBitmap" Then
    imgStretch.Picture = AsyncProp.Value
End If
```

Section 4. Using Viewport properties. Currently, the Image control containing the downloaded *Clouds.bmp* picture is fairly small and does not adjust to the size of the Viewport. In this section, you'll add code to ensure that the Image control takes up the entire width of the Viewport, always filling the lower portion of the Viewport.

11. Add the following code to the Resize event of the UserDocument:

```
imgStretch.Width = UserDocument.ViewportWidth
imgStretch.Height = UserDocument.ViewportHeight - imgStretch.Top
```

Section 5. Creating a menu for an ActiveX document. In this section, you're going to add an About dialog box to your project and a menu item that will merge with the document's container application and display the About dialog box:

12. Click the UserDocument's designer to select it.

13. Choose Menu Editor from the Tools menu.

14. Create a menu item with the Caption **&Help** and the Name **mnuHelp**. Set the menu item's NegotiatePosition property to *3 - Right*. If you don't set this property, your menu item will not appear.

15. Create a submenu item with the Caption **&About MyDocument** and the Name **mnuAbout**. The Menu Editor should now look like Figure 6-14.

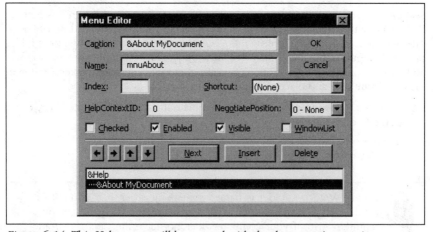

Figure 6-14: This Help menu will be merged with the document's container

16. Click OK to close the Menu Editor and save your menu design.

17. Create an About dialog box for your project by choosing Add Form from the Project menu and then double-clicking the About Dialog icon.

18. In the mnuAbout_Click event of the UserDocument, add the following code. (Note that since the menu doesn't display at design time, you'll need to select the menu item control in the object dropdown list in the code editor.)

```
frmAbout.Show vbModal
```

Section 6. Testing an ActiveX document using Internet Explorer. Now that you've created the user interface and added all necessary code, all that remains is to test the project. The easiest way to test an ActiveX document project is to use Internet Explorer, which happens to be the default testing mechanism in Visual Basic 6.

19. Choose Project Properties from the Project menu and click the Debugging tab. Select the Start Component checkbox if it is not already selected.

20. Close the Project Properties dialog box.

21. Run the project by pressing F5 or by clicking the Run button on the toolbar.

Internet Explorer loads and displays your document. Notice how the clouds bitmap is always sized to fit the lower two-thirds of the document, regardless of the size of Explorer (see Figure 6-15).

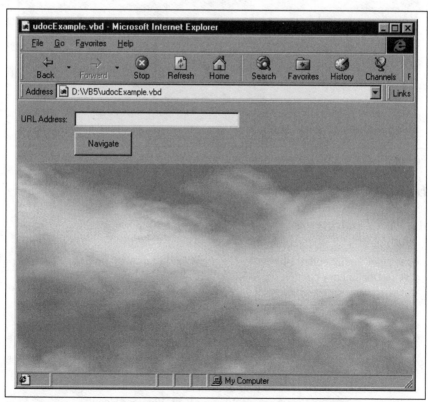

Figure 6-15: ActiveX documents look just like an advanced HTML page

22. In the Address text box of your document, enter **http://www.tigerpawsoftware.com** and click the Navigate button. When you click the button, Internet Explorer navigates to the web site using the NavigateTo method of the HyperLink object.

23. Finally, open the Help menu and see that your About MyDocument menu item is visible (see Figure 6-16).

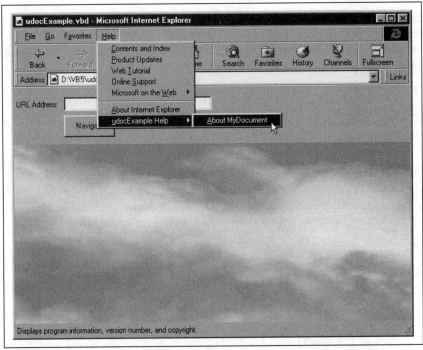

Figure 6-16: ActiveX documents' menus merge with the menus of their containers

Highlighter's Index

ActiveX Documents

Similar to ActiveX controls
Related to embedded objects
UserDocument object
Forms can be converted to ActiveX documents using the Migration Wizard
Can determine a container programmatically
Can integrate menus with the parent
Can persist data

Viewports

Viewable, scrollable area of user document
Properties include ViewportTop, ViewportLeft, ViewportHeight, ViewportWidth

Can disable scrollbars
Pan programmatically with SetViewport method

HyperLink Object

Used to navigate to a URL
Used to navigate to other UserDocuments

Asynchronously Retrieving Data

Request data with the AsyncRead method
Notification that a download is complete happens with the
    AsyncReadComplete event
Cancel an asynchronous download using CancelAsyncRead

Debugging ActiveX Documents

Debugging in a host such as Internet Explorer
Hosts release ActiveX documents in different ways

CHAPTER 7

Working with Data

One of the biggest changes in Visual Basic 6 is the way in which you access data (or the way in which Microsoft wants you to access data). Microsoft is making a conscious effort to create a paradigm in which data is accessed through a common interface, regardless of the data's underlying format. In the past, developers often used a number of data access techniques, including the two common data access object models, data access objects (DAOs) and remote data objects (RDOs), as well as directly using APIs such as the ODBC API. Usually, code used to access data with one method is incompatible with code that accesses data using another method, which creates a number of drawbacks. For instance, scaling a database (such as migrating from a Jet database to a SQL database) often means rewriting the majority of data access code. In theory, if the mechanism used to communicate with different data sources remained consistent, using different back-end data sources would require little or no code modifications.

The Technologies and the Exams

Although ActiveX Data Objects (ADO) is covered on both exams, the Desktop exam only covers ADO at a superficial level, focusing mostly on the ADO Data control. The Distributed exam, however, takes off the kid gloves and delves into more hard-core subject matter. If you are taking only the Desktop exam, use Table 7-1 as a guideline to which material to focus on.

Table 7-1: Coverage of Data Access Topics on the Exams

Topic	Covered on Exam
Universal data access	Both
OLE DB	Both
ActiveX data objects (ADO)	Both
Comparison of ADO, RDO, and DAO	Both
ADO connection object	Both

Table 7-1: Coverage of Data Access Topics on the Exams (continued)

Topic	Covered on Exam
ADO command object	Both
ADO recordsets	Both
Cursor locations and types	Distributed
Recordset locking	Distributed
The Execute method	Distributed
Recordset.Open	Both
Navigating records	Both
Managing transactions	Distributed
The ADO error object	Distributed
The ADO Data control	Both
The Data Environment Designer	Both

Universal Data Access

OLE DB is a low-level interface that introduces Microsoft's strategy of universal data access, or UDA. OLE DB is designed to be a high-performance mechanism for accessing data. Unlike previous technologies, OLE DB is not restricted to accessing Jet or ISAM databases, nor is it even restricted to accessing relational databases. Instead, OLE DB is capable of accessing data that resides in text files, mail servers, spreadsheets, and nonrelational data, in addition to the standard relational database formats. OLE DB makes this possible by way of *OLE DB providers*. An OLE DB provider is a component that exposes data through an OLE DB interface. The mechanics of how the data is retrieved, as well as the underlying format of the data, are of no consequence to OLE DB or to components accessing the data through OLE DB, as long as the provider makes the data available by way of the expected OLE DB interface.

Microsoft's UDA strategy creates an extended, layered approach to data access. At the lowest level, the OLE DB provider is designed to access some form of data and expose that data through a standard OLE DB interface. Using this interface, OLE DB itself is able to make requests and execute commands on the data. Just as OLE DB doesn't communicate directly with data (it communicates through one or more providers), client applications don't communicate directly with OLE DB. Instead, client applications use ADO to manipulate data. ADO provides a common application interface that simplifies the process of communicating with OLE DB. Figure 7-1 shows the layers of this architecture and how they communicate.

 Visual Basic is capable of creating OLE DB providers. Creating OLE DB providers is beyond the scope of the exams and therefore of this book as well.

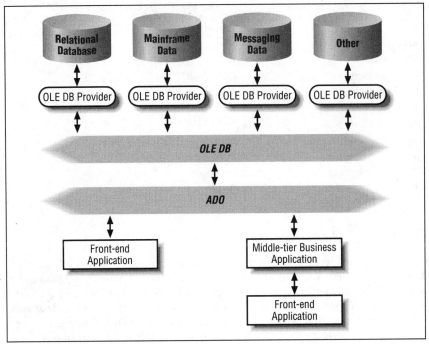

Figure 7-1: OLE DB is part of Microsoft's Universal Data Access strategy, which allows the same code to be used to access different data sources

Manipulating Data Using ActiveX Data Objects

ADO is a set of objects that act as a client interface to OLE DB. Table 7-2 lists the two primary data access methods that ADO is designed to replace: DAO and RDO. In theory, ADO takes the best of both of these data access methods and makes them better. There are differing opinions on how successful Microsoft has been in this endeavor, but one thing is for sure: ADO will replace DAO and RDO—it's only a matter of time.

Table 7-2: Data Access Object Models

Method	Purpose	Comments
DAO	Used to access Jet databases natively and ODCB and ISAM databases via Jet. DAO is best suited for single-user applications or small, local deployments.	DAO is the oldest of the three data object models. DAO is extremely well-established, and it is the fastest way to access Jet databases.
RDO	Used to access databases via ODBC. RDO can't access Jet or ISAM databases very well, and it can only access relational databases via ODBC. RDO is used to access SQL Server, Oracle, and other large relational databases.	RDO is a set of objects that act as a wrapper around the ODCB API, alleviating the need for developers to make ODBC API calls directly.

Table 7-2: Data Access Object Models (continued)

Method	Purpose	Comments
ADO	Used to access many types of data through OLE DB. ADO is the successor to DAO and RDO.	ADO is designed to minimize network traffic and impose minimal layers between the front-end application and the data source.

Microsoft wants everyone one to believe, unequivocally, that ADO is superior to all previous data access methods. In many ways, this is true. The following lists some of the reasons you might choose ADO over DAO or RDO:

- ADO can access many types of data in addition to relational and nonrelational databases.

- ADO has a smaller footprint than the other methods of data access.

- ADO has a simplified, or "flattened," object model.

- ADO is the standard data access object model in Visual Studio.

- ADO offers improved performance in most situations.

- Microsoft is phasing out DAO and RDO.

 Although Microsoft would like you to believe that DAO and RDO are dead, in reality, there are times when a data access method other than ADO makes sense. For example, DAO is *significantly faster* at accessing native Jet databases, and ADO doesn't yet support the complete feature set of DAO when interfacing with Jet. DAO and RDO may be dying, but they're far from dead. Remember, however, that Microsoft is pushing ADO *hard*. If you encounter a question about which data access method would best fit a given situation, and ADO is one of the options, chances are that it's the "correct" choice.

In order to use ADO in a Visual Basic project, the Microsoft ActiveX Data Objects Library must be referenced, using the References dialog box accessed by choosing References from the Tools menu. Once ADO is referenced, its object model is made available to the project.

One of the benefits of ADO over DAO and RDO is that it supports a simplified (flattened) object model. This means that ADO uses fewer objects, yet more properties, methods, and events than other data access methods. If you're new to programming databases, this may make it easier to learn. However, if you're one of the many experienced developers using other data access methods such as DAO (which has a rather large object model), using ADO necessitates some rethinking. In particular, if you're a DAO developer, it may be more difficult to transition to ADO than it would be for an RDO developer, because ADO is more similar to RDO than to DAO. Figure 7-2 shows the ADO object model, while Table 7-3 explains each component of the ADO hierarchy.

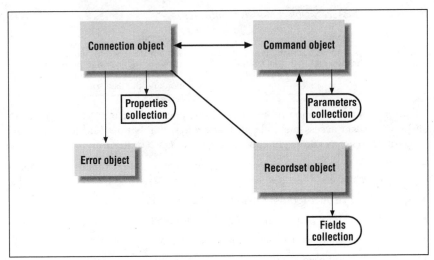

Figure 7-2: ADO has a flattened object model

Table 7-3: ADO Object Hierarchy

Object	Description
Connection	Used to establish and maintain a connection to an OLE DB data source. The Connection object allows you to specify information such as a username and password string.
Command	Defines a specific command to execute against the data source, such as a SQL statement. A Connection object isn't required in order to use a Command object; the Command object is capable of establishing a connection.
Parameter	Represents a single parameter for a command. The data placed into a Parameter object depends upon the command being executed. Command objects each have one Parameters collection that may contain zero or more parameter objects.
Recordset	Represents a set of records from a table, Command object, or SQL query result. Recordset objects can be used to select, navigate, add, edit, or delete data. Recordsets can be created without your explicitly creating an underlying Connection object.
Field	Holds information about a single column of data in a recordset. Information (i.e., properties) includes items such as name, size, type, and value. Recordset objects have a Fields collection.
Error	Contains details about data access errors such as error number, error description, and the object that created the error. The Error object is refreshed each time an error occurs.

Each of the ADO objects is described in the following sections.

The ADO Connection Object

In order to access data using ADO, a *connection to the data source* must be established. Connections can be established *explicitly* by creating a Connection object, or *implicitly* by supplying a connection to a Command object. Although an explicit connection isn't required in order to access a data source, you should create an explicit connection if you plan on referencing multiple recordsets or executing multiple commands against a single data source. Creating an explicit connection using a Connection object in cases such as this results in faster data access performance and lower overhead.

Establishing a connection using the Connection object

The first step to establishing a connection to a data source using a Connection object is to create an object variable and use it to instantiate a new connection object. The following code shows how you might do this:

```
Dim cnADOConnection As Connection
Set cnADOConnection = New Connection
```

Connections are established using the Open method of the Connection object. The Open method has the following syntax:

```
ConnectionObject.Open ConnectionString As String, UserID As String, _
                      Password As String, Options As Long
```

The parameters for the Open method of the Connection object are explained in Table 7-4. The arguments for the ADO ConnectionString are explained in Table 7-5.

Table 7-4: Parameters of the Connection Object's Open Method

Argument	Description
ConnectionString	An optional string used to specify connection information, including the name of the provider, the user and password, and the data file. Table 7-5 lists the most common arguments for ConnectionString.
UserID	An optional string containing the name of the user when connecting to the data source.
Password	An optional string containing the password for the user specified in the UserID argument.
Options	A value that determines whether the Connection object should return before the connection is established (asynchronously), or after the connection is established (synchronously). Use the enumerated value adConnectUnspecified or adAsyncConnect.

Table 7-5: ADO ConnectionString Arguments

Argument	Description
Provider=	The name of the OLE DB provider to use.
Data Source=	The name of the data source to connect to.
UID=	A valid user to use when connecting to the data source.
PWD=	A password to use when connecting to the data source.
DRIVER=	The name of the database driver to use. This isn't required if a Data Source Name (DSN) is specified.
SERVER=	The network name of the data source server.

The following example shows how you might establish a connection with the Access database named *Biblio.mdb* that ships with Visual Basic:

```
Dim cnADOConnection  As Connection
Set cnADOConnection = New Connection
```

```
cnADOConnection.Open "Provider=Microsoft.Jet.OLEDB.4.0;" & _
                     "Data Source=c:\temp\biblio.mdb"
```

If security was enabled in *Biblio.mdb*, you could use code such as this:

```
Dim cnADOConnection  As Connection
Set cnADOConnection = New Connection

cnADOConnection.Open "Provider=Microsoft.Jet.OLEDB.4.0;" & _
                     "Data Source=c:\temp\biblio.mdb", "James", _
                     "MyPassword"
```

or this:

```
Dim cnADOConnection  As Connection
Set cnADOConnection = New Connection

cnADOConnection.Open "Provider=Microsoft.Jet.OLEDB.4.0;" & _
                     "Data Source=c:\temp\biblio.mdb;UID=James;" & _
                     "PWD=MyPassword"
```

Disconnecting from a data source

Closing a connection is simpler than establishing one: use the Close method of the Connection object. For instance, to close the connection used in the previous example, you might use a statement such as **cnADOConnection.Close**. When the Close method is invoked, all pending transactions are rolled back, and any server-side resources used by the connection are released. Be sure to invoke the Close method explicitly on all connections when you are finished with them.

 Retrieving and manipulating data using the Connection object is discussed in the section "Manipulating Data."

The ADO Command Object

The Command object represents a command to execute against a database. Command objects are often used to create recordsets from a data source, execute action queries, or manipulate the structure of a data source. For example, a Command is often a SQL statement or a stored procedure. Table 7-6 lists the commonly used properties, methods, and collections of the Command object.

Table 7-6: Commonly Used Properties and Methods of the Command Object

Member	Description
ActiveConnection property	Specifies an open connection for the command to use.
CommandText property	Defines the executable text of the command (such as a SQL statement).

Table 7-6: Commonly Used Properties and Methods of the Command
Object (continued)

Member	Description
Execute method	Executes the command in CommandText and to return a Recordset object.
Prepared property	Specifies whether or not the provider saves a prepared (or compiled) version of the command prior to execution.
CommandType Property	Defines the type of command to execute; that is, it defines the type of command represented by the CommandText property.
CommandTime-out property	Sets the number of seconds a provider will wait for a command to execute.
Parameters collection	Used to define parameterized queries or stored-procedure arguments.

The way a Command object uses a connection is defined by its ActiveConnection property. A Command object can use an existing connection, or it can establish a new connection. To use an existing connection, pass an open connection object to the ActiveConnection property, like this:

```
Dim cnADOConnection  As Connection
Dim comADOCommand    As Command

Set cnADOConnection = New Connection
Set comADOCommand = New Command

cnADOConnection.Open "Provider=Microsoft.Jet.OLEDB.4.0;" & _
                "Data Source=c:\temp\biblio.mdb"

Set comADOCommand.ActiveConnection = cnADOConnection

cnADOConnection.Close
```

To have the Command object create a new connection, pass a connection string to the ActiveConnection property, like this:

```
Dim comADOCommand    As Command

Set comADOCommand = New Command

comADOCommand.ActiveConnection = _
    "Provider=Microsoft.Jet.OLEDB.4.0;" & _
    "Data Source=c:\temp\biblio.mdb"
```

Setting the ActiveConnection property to Nothing disassociates the Command object from its connection. If you close the Connection object with which a Command object is associated, the Command object's ActiveConnection property is automatically set to Nothing.

 Retrieving and manipulating data using the Command object is discussed in the following section.

Manipulating Data

Using ADO, you can manipulate data sources in many ways. You can create Recordset objects that contain a result set of a query or a stored procedure, and you can add, edit, and delete records in the data source. Both the Connection and the Command objects can be used to manipulate data. Rather than discuss data manipulation separately for each of these objects earlier in this chapter, the information is consolidated in the following sections.

ADO Recordsets

As with other data access methods such as DAO and RDO, records are manipulated by Recordset objects. However, unlike with previous data access methods, an active connection to a data source is not required to use a Recordset object. If an active connection doesn't exist when creating a recordset, one is created behind the scenes. Using a Recordset object, you can retrieve, edit, update, and delete records. There are three ways to open a Recordset object using ADO:

1. Use the Connection.Execute method.

2. Use the Command.Execute method.

3. Open the Recordset object without a Connection object or Command object by passing a valid Connect string to the second argument of the Open method of the Recordset object.

Recordset cursors

When you create a recordset, you're given the opportunity to specify a *cursor type*. The type of cursor specified determines what you can and cannot do with records returned in a recordset. Table 7-7 lists the ADO cursor types, along with a description of each.

 If you don't explicitly set the cursor type, a read-only, forward-only cursor type recordset is created. Since you can't specify a cursor type for recordsets created with the Execute method of the Connection or Command objects, such recordsets are always read-only, forward-only recordsets.

Table 7-7: ADO Cursor Types

Cursor Type	Description
Static	The recordset is a static copy of the data in the data source, similar to the Snapshot recordset type of DAO. Once a static cursor recordset is created, no changes made by other users propagate to the recordset; the recordset never changes.
Forward-only cursor	(Default) Forward-only cursors are identical to static cursors, since they create static snapshots of data. Records that use a forward-only cursor can only be scrolled from beginning to end. For instance, you can use MoveNext to move forward in the recordset, but you cannot use Move-Previous to move backward. Forward-only cursors offer optimal performance in exchange for feature limitations.

Table 7-7: ADO Cursor Types (continued)

Cursor Type	Description
Dynamic cursor	The recordset is "live," meaning that any and all additions, changes, and deletions made by other users affect the recordset. Dynamic-cursor recordsets support all types of navigation, including bookmarks (if bookmarks are supported by the provider). Dynamic cursors offer the most features of any cursor type, but at the expense of increased overhead.
Keyset cursor	Keyset cursors are like dynamic cursors, except additions made by other users are not visible in the recordset. The recordset is affected by changes and deletions, however.

Cursor location

The cursor location determines where ADO stores the cursor (the temporary rows of a recordset). You have the option of creating server-side or client-side cursors, and there are benefits and drawbacks to each. Client-side cursors, for instance, often support more features than server-side cursors, but they can take a long time to build because the data must be pulled to the client to build the cursor. However, once a client-side cursor is built, traversing the cursor's data is often very fast. One drawback to client-side cursors is that they only support static cursors; use a server-side cursor when creating nonstatic cursors.

To specify a cursor location, you set the CursorLocation property of the Connection object. Table 7-8 lists the possible values and their meanings.

Table 7-8: Cursor Location Constants and Descriptions

Value	Description
adUseServer	(Default) Cursors are created on the server by the data provider (driver-supplied). Server-side cursors allow for additional sensitivity to changes made by others, but they often support fewer features than client-side cursors.
adUseClient	Cursors are created on the client machine. Client-side cursor engines often support more features than server-side (driver-supplied) cursors.

Client-side cursors must be used for batch updating; server-side cursors don't support batch updating.

Recordset locking

The type of record locking ADO uses on a recordset is determined by the Lock-Type property of the recordset when it's created. Different applications have different locking needs, and the locking method you employ on a given recordset will need to be determined by the circumstances of the situation. Table 7-9 lists the ADO locking methods, along with the associated LockType constant.

Table 7-9: The ADO Recordset Locking Options

LockType	Locking Method	Description
adLockReadOnly	Read-only	(Default) Records can be read, but data cannot be added, changed, or deleted. This is the locking method used with static cursors and forward-only cursors.
adLockPessimistic	Pessimistic	The provider does what is necessary to ensure successful editing of records, usually by locking records at the data source immediately upon editing.
adLockOptimistic	Optimistic	The provider locks records only when you call the Update method, not when you start editing.
adLockBatchOptimistic	Optimistic Batch	Records are locked in batch update mode, as opposed to immediate update mode. This option is required for client-side cursors.

 When you create a recordset using the Execute method of the Connection or Command object, you cannot specify a locking method; all recordsets created in this manner are forward-only, read-only recordsets. If you need to specify a different type of locking method or cursor type, use the Open method of the Recordset object to create the recordset.

Creating a recordset using the Connection.Execute method

Recordset objects can be created directly from Connection objects by using the Execute method of the Connection object. The Execute method can be used to return a Recordset object, or it can be used to execute an action query (discussed later in this chapter).

The Execute method of the Connection object has the following syntax:

```
ConnectionObject.Execute(CommandText As String, _
                         RecordsAffected As Long, _
                         Options As Long) As Recordset
```

The *CommandText* parameter is the text containing a data definition or data manipulation command, such as a SQL SELECT or DELETE statement, or a table name.

RecordsAffected is an optional parameter to which the provider returns the number of records affected by the Execute method.

The *Options* parameter determines how the provider should handle the *CommandText* parameter, and can be one of the constants listed in Table 7-10. (Note that it is possible to OR either of the last two constants with one of the other constants.)

Table 7-10: Possible Values for the Options Parameter of the Connection.Execute Method

Constant	Description
adCmdText	Indicates that the provider should evaluate CommandText as a textual definition of a command.
adCmdTable	Indicates that the provider should evaluate CommandText as a table name.
adCmdStoredProc	Indicates that the provider should evaluate CommandText as a stored procedure.
adCmdUnknown	Indicates that the type of command in the CommandText argument is not known and that the provider should attempt to interpret it. Typically, this results in poor performance.
adExecuteAsync	Indicates that the command should execute asynchronously
adFetchAsync	Indicates that the remaining rows after the initial quantity specified in the CacheSize property should be fetched asynchronously.

For example, to create a recordset containing all of the authors in the *Biblio.mdb* Jet database, you could use code such as this:

```
Dim cnADOConnection  As Connection
Dim rstAuthors       As ADODB.Recordset

Set cnADOConnection = New Connection

cnADOConnection.Open "Provider=Microsoft.Jet.OLEDB.4.0;" & _
                     "Data Source=c:\temp\biblio.mdb"

Set rstAuthors = cnADOConnection.Execute("Authors", adcmdTable)

cnADOConnection.Close
```

 The recordset returned by the Execute method of the Connection object always uses a read-only, forward-only cursor. If you need to create a recordset that uses a different cursor type, use the Open method of the Recordset object, as discussed shortly.

Creating a recordset using the Command.Execute method

Creating recordsets using the Execute method of the Command object is similar to creating recordsets using Connection.Execute. However, instead of specifying *CommandText* as an argument of the Execute method, you set the CommandText property of the Command object. In addition, the Execute method of the Command object has an optional variant parameter named *Parameters*, that lets you pass parameter values to a SQL statement.

Attempting to invoke the Execute method on a Command object before setting the ActiveConnection property to an open Connection object or a valid connection string results in an error.

The Execute method of the Command object has the following syntax:

```
CommandObject.Execute(RecordsAffected As Long, _
                      Parameters() As Variant, Options As Long) _
                      As Recordset
```

RecordsAffected is an optional parameter to which the provider returns the number of records affected by the Execute method.

The *Parameters* parameter is a variant array used to specify initial parameter values.

The *Options* parameter determines how the provider should handle the Command-Text property and can be one of the values listed earlier in Table 7-10.

For example, to create a recordset containing all of the authors in the *Biblio.mdb* Jet database using a Command object, you could use code such as this:

```
Dim comADOCommand    As Command
Dim rstAuthors       As ADODB.Recordset

Set comADOCommand = New Command

comADOCommand.ActiveConnection = "Provider=Microsoft.Jet.OLEDB.4.0;" & _
                                 "Data Source=c:\temp\biblio.mdb"

comADOCommand.CommandText = "Authors"
Set rstAuthors = comADOCommand.Execute(, , adCmdTable)
```

Creating a recordset using the Recordset.Open method

In addition to using the Execute methods of the Connection and Command objects, recordsets can be established directly using the Recordset object; neither a Command object nor a Connection object is required to create a recordset. As a matter of fact, you must use a Recordset object to create anything other than a static, forward-only recordset. Records are returned to a Recordset object by invoking the Open method of the Recordset object. The Open method has the following syntax:

```
RecordsetObject.Open(Source, ActiveConnection, CursorType, LockType, _
                     Options)
```

The *Source* parameter is an optional variant that evaluates to a valid Command object, a SQL statement, a table name, a stored procedure call, or the filename of a persisted recordset.

The *ActiveConnection* parameter is an optional variant that evaluates to a valid Connection object variable name, or a string containing connection string parameters.

 For more information on the *ActiveConnection* argument, refer to the previous discussion of the ActiveConnection property of the Command object.

The *CursorType* parameter is an optional value that determines the type of cursor that the provider should use when opening the recordset. The possible values for *CursorType* are listed in Table 7-11.

Table 7-11: Possible Values for CursorType

Value	Description
adOpenForwardOnly	(Default) Used to open a forward-only cursor
adOpenKeyset	Used to open a keyset cursor
adOpenDynamic	Used to open a dynamic cursor
adOpenStatic	Used to open a static cursor

The *LockType* parameter is optional, and it's used to specify the type of locking the provider should use when opening the recordset. *LockType* can be any of the values listed in Table 7-9.

The *Options* parameter is an optional Long that indicates how the Source should be evaluated. The possible values for *Options* are the same as the values for the *Options* parameter of the Execute method of both Connection and Command objects. Refer to Table 7-10 for the possible values.

Recordsets can be created using an *explicit* or an *implicit* connection. When an existing connection is used to create a recordset (an open Connection object is specified as the *ActiveConnection* argument), the recordset is created using an explicit connection. When a connection string is specified as the *Active-Connection* argument, the recordset is created using an implicit connection. When an implicit connection is used, a Connection object is created behind the scenes; you cannot access the Connection object, and it's automatically closed when the recordset is closed.

The following code opens a recordset by calling the Open method of the Recordset object and specifying an *explicit* connection:

```
Dim cnADOConnection  As Connection
Dim rstAuthors       As adodb.Recordset

Set cnADOConnection = New Connection
Set rstAuthors = New adodb.Recordset

cnADOConnection.Open "Provider=Microsoft.Jet.OLEDB.4.0;" & _
                     "Data Source=c:\temp\biblio.mdb"
```

```
rstAuthors.Open "Authors", cnADOConnection, , , adCmdTable
```

```
rstAuthors.Close
cnADOConnection.Close
```

The following code opens a recordset by calling the Open method of the Recordset object and specifying an *implicit* connection:

```
Dim rstAuthors          As adodb.Recordset

Set rstAuthors = New adodb.Recordset

rstAuthors.Open "Authors", "Provider=Microsoft.Jet.OLEDB.4.0;" & _
                "Data Source=c:\temp\biblio.mdb", , , adCmdTable

rstAuthors.Close
```

 Creating recordsets that use implicit connections requires less coding than creating recordsets that use explicit connections. However, whenever possible, you should use explicit connections. When you share a connection by using it as an explicit connection for multiple Recordset objects, fewer connections are made on the data source and fewer resources are consumed.

Navigating records using the Recordset object

If you've used DAO or RDO, you'll find that ADO recordsets support a number of the properties and methods with which you're already familiar. In particular, all of the common navigation methods are supported (depending, of course, on the type of cursor used when the recordset was opened). Table 7-12 lists the supported navigation methods.

Table 7-12: Navigation Methods of the ADO Recordset Object

Method	Description
Move	Moves to the next record in the recordset
MoveFirst	Moves to the first record in the recordset
MoveLast	Moves to the last record in the recordset
MoveNext	Moves to the next record in the recordset
MovePrevious	Moves to the previous record in the recordset

When navigating recordsets, it's important to watch for the beginning of the file (BOF) and the end of the file (EOF) in order to prevent a runtime error. The BOF occurs when the record pointer of a recordset is positioned immediately before the first record in the recordset, while the EOF occurs when the record pointer is positioned immediately after the last record in the recordset. You can determine if a recordset's pointer is at beginning-of-file or end-of-file by evaluating the Recordset object's BOF and EOF properties, respectively. If RecordsetObject.BOF is True, the recordset pointer is at beginning-of-file. If RecordsetObject.EOF is **True**, the recordset pointer is at end-of-file. If a recordset is empty, both BOF and EOF will return **True**.

The following code illustrates how you can use EOF to check for an end-of-file condition, removing the chance that the code will attempt to retrieve data when there is no current record:

```
Dim rstAuthors As adodb.Recordset

Set rstAuthors = New adodb.Recordset

rstAuthors.Open "Authors", "Provider=Microsoft.Jet.OLEDB.4.0;" & _
            "Data Source=c:\temp\biblio.mdb", , , adCmdTable

Do While Not (rstAuthors.EOF)
    Debug.Print "Author's Name is " & rstAuthors![Author]
    rstAuthors.MoveNext
Loop

rstAuthors.Close
```

 When using DAO, only forward-only recordsets automatically position the pointer at the first record; other types of recordsets position the pointer at BOF. In ADO, the pointer is always at the first record, regardless of the cursor type, if at least one record exists in the recordset.

Accessing data in a recordset

Once a recordset is created and the recordset pointer is pointing to a record, you can access the data in the current record in one of two ways:

- Use the Fields collection of the Recordset object.

- Use the bang operator (!) followed by the name of the field.

If you don't know the name of a field, but you do know its ordinal number, use the Fields collection to access the field. For instance, the following code prints the names of all fields in the Recordset object along with the field value of the current record to the Immediate window (assuming that the recordset is a valid Recordset object):

```
Dim lngIndex      As Long

For lngIndex = 0 To rstAuthors.Fields.Count - 1
    Debug.Print rstAuthors.Fields(lngIndex).Name & ": " & _
    rstAuthors.Fields(lngIndex).Value
Next lngIndex

RstAuthors.Close
```

The Fields collection makes it easy to access the properties of any field, but it's not the only way to access the value of a field. Instead, if you know the field name, reference the Recordset object, followed by the bang symbol (!), then reference the field name as shown here:

```
Debug.Print "Author's Name is " & rstAuthors![Author]
Debug.Print "Author was born in " & rstAuthors![Year Born]
```

 You are not required to surround the field name in brackets unless the field name contains a space. To maintain good programming practices, however, you should always surround a field name with brackets, regardless of whether or not the field name contains spaces. This makes it much easier to search and replace field names in the future, should you need to do so.

Finding records using a Recordset object

Although it's usually best to create a well-defined SQL statement to locate a specific record, there are times when it's necessary to search for a record within a recordset. In DAO, you could use the FindFirst, FindLast, FindNext, and Find-Previous methods to search for particular records in a recordset. In ADO, you have just one method that replaces these four: the Find method.

The ADO Recordset.Find method has the following syntax:

```
RecordsetObject.Find Criteria As String, [SkipRecords as Long], _
               [SearchDirection As SearchDirectionEnum = _
               adSearchForward], [Start As Variant])
```

The *Criteria* argument is used to identify the records to look for. In DAO, *Criteria* could be any valid SQL WHERE clause, but ADO's Find method is more restrictive (it does accept the =, >, >=, <, <=, and LIKE operators, however). Actually, ADO's Find method has a number of limitations, including:

- ADO's Find method only allows searching a single field.

- ADO's Find method does not allow quotes in text literals.

- ADO's Find method does not allow searching on expressions.

Of course, these are huge limitations in comparison with DAO. There are workarounds for many of the limitations, but they are beyond the scope of the exam and of this book.

The *SkipRecords* parameter is used to emulate the DAO methods FindNext and FindPrevious. The *SearchDirection* argument determines in which direction the search is performed, and can be either adSearchForward or adSearchBackward. The *Start* argument is used for specifying where in the recordset to start, and may be either adBookmarkLast or adBookmarkCurrent. Table 7-13 shows how these arguments affect Find by comparing them to the DAO methods that Find is designed to replace.

Table 7-13: How the ADO Find Method's Arguments Affect a Search

DAO Find Method	SkipRecords	SearchDirection	Start
FindFirst	0	adSearchForward	adBookmarkLast
FindLast	0	adSearchBackward	adBookmarkLast
FindNext	1	adSearchForward	adBookmarkCurrent
FindPrevious	1	adSearchBackward	adBookmarkCurrent

The following example shows how you could use ADO's Find method to find the first author's name that begins with "f," then locate the next author's name that begins with "f:"

```
Dim cnADOConnection  As Connection
Dim rstAuthors       As ADODB.Recordset

Set cnADOConnection = New Connection
Set rstAuthors = New ADODB.Recordset

cnADOConnection.Open "Provider=Microsoft.Jet.OLEDB.4.0;" & _
                "Data Source=c:\temp\biblio.mdb"

rstAuthors.Open "SELECT * FROM [Authors] ORDER BY [Author]", _
            cnADOConnection, adOpenDynamic, adLockOptimistic, _
adCmdText

'* Locate the first author whose name starts with f.
rstAuthors.Find "[Author] LIKE 'f*'", 0, adSearchForward

'* Locate the next author whose name starts with f.
rstAuthors.Find "[Author] LIKE 'f*'", 1, adSearchForward, _
adBookmarkCurrent

rstAuthors.Close
```

 ADO does not support the NoMatch property that many DAO developers rely on when using the DAO Find... methods. If the ADO Find method is unsuccessful, the record pointer is positioned at the end of the recordset.

Adding records using a Recordset object

To add records to a Recordset object, the cursor type of the recordset discussed earlier in this chapter must support adding data, and the recordset pointer must first be positioned to a record. To add records to a recordset, call the AddNew method of the recordset. The recordset pointer is then positioned on a new record, and you are free to set the values of the fields as you see fit. To save the new record, invoke the Update method of the recordset. The following code illustrates adding a record to the Authors table in *Biblio.mdb*:

```
Dim rstAuthors As adodb.Recordset

Set rstAuthors = New adodb.Recordset

rstAuthors.Open "Authors", "Provider=Microsoft.Jet.OLEDB.4.0;" & _
                "Data Source=c:\temp\biblio.mdb", adOpenDynamic, _
                adLockOptimistic, adCmdTable

rstAuthors.AddNew
    rstAuthors![Author] = "Foxall"
    rstAuthors![Year Born] = 1969
rstAuthors.Update

rstAuthors.Close
```

If, after invoking the AddNew method, you decide not to save the new record, call the CancelUpdate method in place of the Update method, like this:

```
...
rstAuthors.AddNew
    rstAuthors![Author] = "Foxall"
    rstAuthors![Year Born] = 1969
rstAuthors.CancelUpdate
...
```

Editing records using a Recordset object

One of the changes from DAO to ADO that may take some getting used to is editing data in a recordset. In DAO, you explicitly placed the recordset in edit mode by calling the Edit method of the recordset. In ADO, you're not required to put the recordset in edit mode. As long as the cursor type of the recordset supports modifying data, you can freely make changes to the values in a record. As with the AddNew method, you commit changes by calling the Update method, and you cancel them by calling the CancelUpdate method. The following illustrates editing a record using the Edit method:

```
Dim rstAuthors As adodb.Recordset

Set rstAuthors = New adodb.Recordset

rstAuthors.Open "Authors", "Provider=Microsoft.Jet.OLEDB.4.0;" & _
                "Data Source=c:\temp\biblio.mdb", adOpenDynamic, _
                adLockOptimistic, adCmdTable

rstAuthors.MoveFirst

'* Start editing.
rstAuthors![Author] = "Foxall"
rstAuthors.Update

rstAuthors.Close
```

Deleting records using a Recordset object

To delete a record from a recordset, first position the record pointer so that the record you want to delete is the current record, then call the Delete method of the Recordset object. For instance, to delete the first record in a recordset, you might use code such as this:

```
Dim rstAuthors As adodb.Recordset

Set rstAuthors = New adodb.Recordset

rstAuthors.Open "Authors", "Provider=Microsoft.Jet.OLEDB.4.0;" & _
                "Data Source=c:\temp\biblio.mdb", adOpenDynamic, _
                adLockOptimistic, adCmdTable

rstAuthors.MoveFirst

rstAuthors.Delete

rstAuthors.Close
```

Processing SQL Statements Using the Execute Method

It's possible to execute SQL statements against a data source by using the Execute method of the Connection object or the Command object. If the SQL statement will be executed only once, use the Execute method of the Connection object. If you intend on executing the same SQL statement more than once during the user's session, or if you are calling a stored procedure, use the Execute method of a Command object. When used more than once, a Command object can create an optimized temporary stored procedure, making successive Execute method calls faster.

The Execute method has the following syntax:

```
ConnectionObject.Execute CommandText As String, RecordsAffected, Options
```

The Execute method in ADO is similar to the Execute method of the Database object in DAO. For instance, to change the value of a Status field of a record using a SQL statement, you could use code such as the following (this code assumes a valid Connection object):

```
strSQL = "UPDATE tblQuotes SET [WorkOrderStatus] = 'Open' WHERE " & _
         "[QuoteNumber] = " & m_lngQuoteNumber

cnADOConnection.Execute strSQL
```

In addition to performing action queries, the Execute method can perform data-definition commands (such as `Create Table`) or data-manipulation commands (such as `SELECT` statements). The Execute method can also return a recordset. For example, the following code uses Execute to create a recordset:

```
Dim cnADOConnection  As Connection
Dim rstAuthors       As adodb.Recordset
```

```
cnADOConnection.Open "Provider=Microsoft.Jet.OLEDB.4.0;" & _
                     "Data Source=c:\temp\biblio.mdb"

Set rstAuthors = cnADOConnection.Execute("SELECT [Author] FROM
tblAuthors")

cnADOConnection.Close
```

Managing Transactions

A transaction is defined by MSDN as "a unit of work that is done as an atomic operation—that is, the operation succeeds or fails as a whole." In other words, a transaction is a unit of change in a data source. Consider banking, for example. When money is moved from one account to another, one account is debited and the other credited. These two actions together define a single transaction; if one part fails, both parts must fail. If only one part of the transaction were to succeed, balances would be incorrect and money would appear to either disappear or grow.

In order for a transaction to be considered valid, it must pass the ACID test. The following list explains each of the ACID properties:

Atomicity
> A transaction must be an atomic unit of work; the transaction either commits or aborts.

Consistency
> The changes that result from completing the transaction must leave the data in a consistent state, without violating any business rules of the data source.

Isolation
> Modifications to data made by one user's transactions must not directly affect another user's transactions. Another user's transaction accesses data in the state it was in either before the transaction was started or after it was completed; another user's transaction must never use transitional data.

Durability
> Transactions must fully commit, and once a transaction is committed, its effects must persist in the data source even if there are system failures.

ADO allows you to begin and commit individual transactions explicitly (if transactions are supported by the provider). If you don't explicitly define a transaction, ADO runs in *auto-commit* mode, meaning each change to the database is treated as a single transaction. For instance, updating records using a SQL statement is considered a single transaction, as is deleting a record using the Delete method of the Recordset object.

To define and commit a transaction explicitly, you use the BeginTrans and CommitTrans methods of the Connection object. The behavior of these methods is similar to that of the Workspace object's methods of the same name in DAO. The following code initiates a transaction using the BeginTrans method, executes two distinct SQL statements, and finally commits the changes as a single transaction:

```
Private Sub TransferFunds(curAmount as Currency)
    Dim cnADOConnection   As Connection
    Dim strSQL            As String

    Set cnADOConnection = New Connection

    cnADOConnection.Open "Provider=Microsoft.Jet.OLEDB.4.0;" & _
                         "Data Source=c:\temp\biblio.mdb"

    cnADOConnection.BeginTrans
        strSQL = "UPDATE tblSavings SET [Funds] = [Funds] - " & curAmount
        cnADOConnection.Execute strSQL

        strSQL = "UPDATE tblChecking SET [Funds] = [Funds] + " & curAmount
        cnADOConnection.Execute strSQL

    cnADOConnection.CommitTrans

    cnADOConnection.Close

End Sub
```

If part of a transaction fails, the entire transaction is *rolled back* and no changes are made to the data source. To cancel a transaction explicitly, use the RollBack-Trans method of the Connection object. When you create explicit transactions, commit them or roll them back as soon as possible, because ADO imposes locks on the data source the entire time the transaction is processing.

 It's possible to nest transactions. When creating nested transactions, no database changes are committed until the final, top-level transaction commits; if the top-level transaction fails, none of the nested transactions modify the database.

The ADO Error Object

Any operation performed on an ADO data source may generate one or more errors from the data provider. To help manage these errors, the Connection object contains an Errors collection. Each time an ADO operation causes a provider error, the Errors collection is cleared, and the new error or errors are added to the Errors collection. The Errors collection supports the typical Clear, Item, and Count members found with most collections. For instance, to determine the number of errors in the Errors collection, you could use code such as this:

```
Debug.Print cnADOConnection.Errors.Count
```

Each object in the Errors collection corresponds to an individual error encountered during a *single operation*; remember, each time an operation generates an error, it clears the Errors collection before adding its errors as unique error objects. Table 7-14 lists the properties of the ADO Error object.

Table 7-14: Properties of the ADO Error Object

Property	Description
Description	Contains a textual description of the error. This text is usually provider specific, and it may contain the source of the error.
HelpContext	Contains the context ID identifying the help topic to be displayed if requested by the user.
HelpFile	Contains the help file associated with the current error.
NativeError	Contains the provider-specific error code (Long).
Number	Contains the Long integer value of the error constant.
Source	Contains text that identifies the object that raised the error.
SQLState	Contains a five-character string that follows the ANSI-SQL standard error codes.

The ADO Errors collection is completely separate from the VBA Error object. The ADO Errors collection contains only errors returned by providers, never errors encountered in your Visual Basic code. Also, ADO has an Errors collection, whereas Visual Basic keeps track of only one error at a time.

The Errors collection allows you to test and evaluate errors that may occur during an operation on a data source. Exactly how you handle a given error, however, is determined by the situation in which the error occurs.

Using the ADO Data Control

If you've read all of the information on ADO up to this point, the discussion of the ADO Data control will be anticlimactic. Essentially, the ADO Data control is the ADO version of the standard Data control, allowing you to access ADO data sources. In most situations, you're better off writing Visual Basic code to work with recordsets, rather than using the ADO control. This is because ADO Data controls can't share connections, and the ADO Data control is simply a wrapper around ADO that supports only limited functionality of ADO itself. However, there may be times when you wish to use the ADO Data control, and you may encounter questions about it on the exam, so it's mentioned here.

In order to use the ADO Data control, it must first be referenced in a project. To reference the ADO Data control in a project, choose Components from the Project menu and then select Microsoft ADO Data Control 6.0 (OLE DB). Once the control is referenced within the project, you can add it to a form just as you do a standard control. The ADO Data control has a number of properties and methods, and for the most part, they correspond to ADO objects and properties, so there's no need to discuss them here as well. The properties that you will want to set to create a recordset are:

ConnectionString
Set to a valid connection string

UserName
Set to a valid user of the database

Recordsource
Use the property pages to define a command

Once an ADO Data control contains a valid recordset, you can manipulate the data in the recordset using the Recordset property of the control, much as you manipulate Recordset objects in code. For instance, to move to the first record in a recordset of an ADO Data control, you could use a statement such as this:

```
adodc1.Recordset.MoveFirst
```

To bind a control to an ADO Data control:

1. Set the control's DataSource property to the ADO Data control.

2. Set the control's DataField property to a field in the ADO Data control's recordset.

The Data Environment Designer

Visual Basic 6 includes a new designer that may make creating database applications in Visual Basic easier: the Data Environment designer. The Data Environment designer allows you to create Connection and Command objects interactively at runtime. Although many developers prefer to write code to perform these functions rather than use yet another development component, the Data Environment designer allows you to easily create bound forms, something that you can't do using Visual Basic code alone.

 The Data Environment designer effectively replaces the ActiveX User-Connection designer available in previous releases of Visual Basic.

To use the Data Environment, you must add a Data Environment designer to the project, much as you would add a form to a project. To do this, choose Data Environment from the Project menu. The new Data Environment designer then appears in the Project Explorer window (see Figure 7-3).

 If you have many ActiveX designers installed on your computer, you may have a More ActiveX Designers submenu on the Project menu, and you may have to choose Data Environment from this submenu.

Working with Data

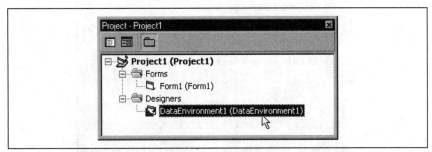

Figure 7-3: Data Environment designers appear in the Designers folder of the Project Explorer window

The Data Environment designer consists primarily of a tree view control and a toolbar (see Figure 7-4). The tree view displays all of the defined objects (Connections and Commands), and it can display them by object type or by connection. The toolbar is used to add and delete items such as connections, commands, and stored procedures, as well as to access properties for each item.

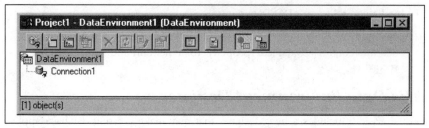

Figure 7-4: The Data Environment's main interface is a tree view of defined objects

 The general process of using the Data Environment designer is discussed in this section. For more specifics, complete Exercise 7.2 at the end of this chapter.

Generally, the first step you'll perform is to define one or more connections. By default, the first connection is made for you and it's named Connection1, though you can rename it. To edit the connection's properties, choose Properties from its Shortcut menu or select the item and click the properties button on the toolbar; either way, you're shown the Data Link Properties dialog box shown in Figure 7-5.

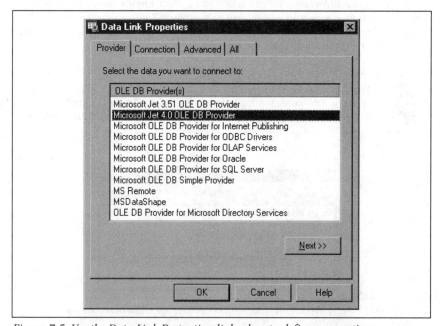

Figure 7-5: Use the Data Link Properties dialog box to define connections

Using the Data Link Properties dialog box, you can choose a provider, select a data source file, and supply a username and password—essentially the same things you can do with a Connection object in Visual Basic code.

Once a connection is defined, you can add commands. To create a command, click the Add Command button on the toolbar. Once the command appears in the list, you can rename it and edit its properties using the Command Properties dialog box shown in Figure 7-6. To aid you in building SQL commands, you can click the SQL Builder button on the Command Properties dialog box to display the SQL Builder window (see Figure 7-7).

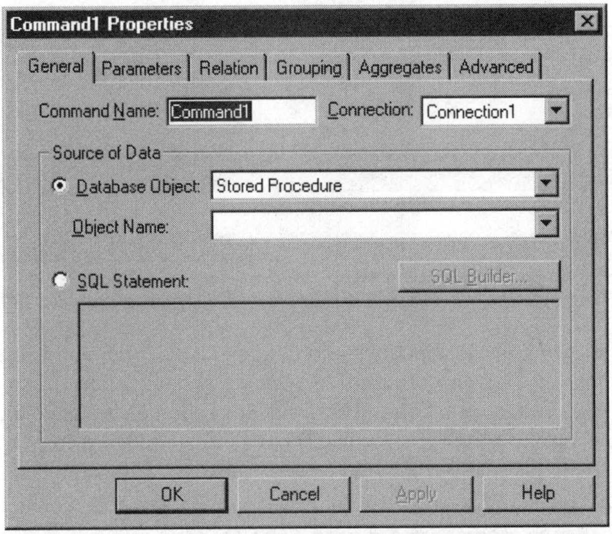

Figure 7-6: Creating commands in the Data Environment designer is similar to creating Command objects in code, with some additional functionality

Once you've created your connections and commands, you can use them in code or use them to easily build bound forms. To manipulate a connection defined in the Data Environment designer, you use the Connections collection of the Data Environment designer, and to use a command you use its Commands collection. For example, to use a connection named BiblioConnection and manipulate a recordset created with a command named AllAuthors, you could use code such as this:

```
DataEnvironment1.Connections("BiblioConnection").Open

With DataEnvironment1.Recordsets("AllAuthors")
    .Open
    .MoveFirst
    Debug.Print ![Author]
    .Close
End With

DataEnvironment1.Connections("BiblioConnection").Close
```

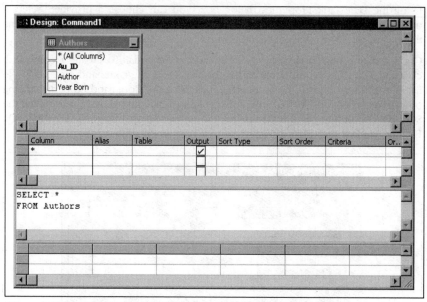

Figure 7-7: The SQL Builder helps with the task of designing complex SQL statements

In addition to using the connections and commands in code, you can easily create a bound form for a given command. To create a bound form, drag the desired command and drop it on a form. The Data Environment designer then creates a label and a control on the form for each data field (see Figure 7-8), and automatically binds the fields to the command—pretty slick.

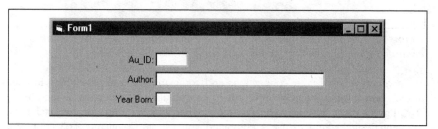

Figure 7-8: The simple act of dragging and dropping a command creates a bound form

When a control is bound to a Data Environment designer connection or command, the DataSource property of the control is set to the name of the Data Environment designer, and the DataField property is set to the name of a field in the recordset generated by a command; this is all similar to binding a control to the ADO Data control. However, controls bound to a Data Environment designer also have a Command object specified in their DataMember property, because Data Environment designers can contain multiple commands.

Key Facts

- Universal data access (UDA) is Microsoft's strategy for creating a universal interface for accessing relational and nonrelational data sources.

- OLE DB is the low-level interface of Microsoft's UDA strategy.

- OLE DB is not restricted to accessing relational data, but rather can access information in text files, spreadsheets, and mail servers—any type of information for which a provider has been created.

- OLE DB communicates with data sources through OLE DB providers. All OLE DB providers support a common OLE DB interface.

- ActiveX data object (ADO) is an application interface to OLE DB.

- ADO is designed to replace DAO and RDO.

- ADO is most similar to RDO.

- ADO has a smaller footprint than other data access methods.

- ADO has a simplified, "flattened" object model.

- ADO is the standard data access object model in Visual Studio.

- ADO offers improved performance in most situations.

- ADO does not fully support the same feature set as DAO when accessing Jet databases.

- ADO must be referenced in a project before it can be used.

- ADO Connection objects are used to establish and maintain a connection to an OLE DB data source.

- ADO Parameter objects belong to the Parameters collection of the Command object. Parameter objects are used to define parameters for a command.

- Explicit connections occur when a Connection object is used, while implicit connections occur when a connection string is passed to a Command or Recordset object.

- Shared explicit connections result in decreased overhead, faster data access performance, and fewer connections to a data source.

- Connections are established with a Connection object by passing a valid connection string as an argument of the Open method.

- Connection strings contain information necessary to connect to a data source, such as the name of the provider, data file, and username and password.

- When establishing a connection using a Connection object, the connection can be established asynchronously or synchronously by passing `adConnect-Unspecified` or `adAsyncConnect` as the `Options` argument of the Open method.

- To disconnect from a data source, use the Close method of the Connection object.

- ADO Command objects are used to define and execute commands (such as SQL commands or stored procedures) against the data source.

- A Connection object isn't required to create and use a Command object; the Command object is capable of establishing its own connection.

- To use an existing connection when creating a Command object, set the Command object's ActiveConnection property equal to an open Connection object.

- To open an implicit connection for a Command object, set the Command object's ActiveConnection property to a valid connection string.

- Closing a Connection object that is associated with a Command object sets the Command object's ActiveConnection property to Nothing.

- ADO Recordset objects represent a set of records from a table, command object, or SQL query result.

- Recordset objects do not require a Connection object; they can create their own connections.

- Recordsets can be created by using the Connection.Execute method, the Command.Execute method, or the Recordset.Open method.

- Each recordset has a cursor type.

- Static cursors create recordsets that are a static copy of the data, similar to a snapshot in DAO. Changes made by other users do not appear in the recordset.

- Forward-only cursors create static recordsets that can only be traversed from the first record to the last. Forward-only cursors are fast, but they are limited in functionality.

- Dynamic cursors create "live" recordsets. All additions, changes, and deletes made by other users affect the recordset. Dynamic cursors support many features, but require more overhead than other cursor types.

- Keyset cursors are similar to dynamic cursors, except that additions made by other users aren't reflected in the recordset.

- The locking used with a recordset is determined by the LockType property of the Recordset object.

- Read-only locking creates recordsets that cannot be modified in any way.

- Pessimistic locking creates recordsets that can be modified. The provider does what is necessary to ensure that data changes are successful, usually by locking the record when an edit is initiated.

- Optimistic locking creates recordsets that can be edited and that create minimal record locks; records are usually locked only when an update occurs.

- If a cursor type isn't specified, a forward-only recordset is created.

- Since the Execute methods of the Connection and Command objects don't let you specify a cursor type or lock type, they always create read-only, forward-only recordsets.

- To create a recordset using a Connection object, use the Execute method of the Connection object, passing the command text to execute as the *CommandText* argument, and telling the provider how to treat the command by passing a constant as the *Options* argument.

- To create a recordset using a Command object, supply the command text to the CommandText property, use the *Options* argument to specify how the command text should be treated, then invoke the Execute method.

- To create a recordset using the Recordset object, use the Open method. The Recordset.Open method accepts a valid Command object or command text, an open Connection object or a connection string, a cursor type, and a lock type.

- The Recordset.Open method is the most flexible way to create recordsets.

- If you supply a connection string rather than a Connection object to Recordset.Open, an implicit connection is created.

- ADO recordsets support the navigation methods Move, MoveFirst, MoveLast, MoveNext, and MovePrevious.

- To reference a data field in a record, use code such as `Debug.Print rstAuthors![Author]`.

- To locate records in an ADO recordset, you can use the Find method.

- The ADO Find method replaces the FindFirst, FindLast, FindNext, and FindPrevious methods of DAO, but it has many limitations: Find can search on only a single field, does not allow quotes in text literals, and does not allow searching on expressions.

- To add a record to a recordset, create a new blank record by calling the AddNew method of the Recordset object, and commit the new data using the Update method.

- To edit a record, position the record in the data source and make changes to the fields. To commit the changes, call the Update method of the Recordset object.

- You can cancel adding or editing a record by calling the CancelUpdate method of the Recordset object.

- To delete a record from a recordset, call the Delete method of the Recordset object.

- To execute a SQL statement against a data source, use the Execute method of the Connection object.

- A transaction is an atomic operation—a unit of change in a data source. To be considered valid, the transaction must pass the ACID test.

- If you don't explicitly create a transaction, ADO uses auto-commit mode, which treats every action against the database as a single transaction.

- To begin a transaction explicitly, use the BeginTrans method of the Connection object.

- To commit a transaction, use the CommitTrans method of the Connection object.

- To cancel or roll back a transaction, use the RollBackTrans method of the Connection object.

- ADO Error objects contain details about data access errors. ADO Error objects are part of the Errors collection of the Connection object.

- The Connection Errors collection is cleared when an error is encountered on a new data operation; the Errors collection always contains errors for a single operation.

- The ADO Data control is an ADO version of the standard data control. It allows you to access ADO data sources and bind controls on a form to a data source.

- The Data Environment designer can be used to build connections and commands interactively and to create bound forms.

- The Data Environment designer replaces the ActiveX UserConnection object of earlier versions of Visual Basic.

- Data Environment designers are added to a project by choosing Add Data Environment from the Project menu.

- You can create multiple connections in the Data Environment designer.

- The connections and commands defined in a Data Environment designer can be accessed in code using the Connections and Commands collections of the Data Environment designer object.

- To create a bound form using a Data Environment designer, drag a command to a form.

- A control bound to a Data Environment designer has the name of the command in the designer to which it is bound, specified in the control's DataMember property.

Applying What You've Learned

It's now time to apply what you've learned about creating ActiveX controls. Start by answering all of the questions in the Skills Assessment. If you can correctly answer all of these questions, you'll be demonstrating a solid understanding of creating ActiveX controls. After you've answered the assessment questions, work through the hands-on exercises.

Skills Assessment

1. What is the name of Microsoft's strategy to create a universal interface for accessing relational and nonrelational data sources?

    a. ADO

    b. OLE DB

    c. Universal Data Access

    d. Universal Data Interface

2. OLE DB is Microsoft's latest data access technology. OLE DB is capable of accessing what type of data?

    a. Relational databases

    b. Nonrelational databases

    c. Text files and graphics

    d. All of the above

3. The object that acts as a layer between OLE DB and a data source is called:

   a. An OLE DB Provider.

   b. ADO.

   c. ODBC.

   d. OLE DB communicates directly with data sources; no extra layer is involved.

4. What is the name of the application interface layer of OLE DB?

   a. DAO

   b. ADO

   c. RDO

   d. OLE-DO

5. Which data access method is ADO most similar to?

   a. DAO

   b. RDO

6. What are considered key features of ADO versus other data access methods? (pick two)

   a. ADO supports a flattened object model.

   b. ADO is faster at accessing native Jet databases.

   c. ADO has a smaller footprint than other data access methods.

   d. ADO has cross-platform support.

7. To establish a connection to a data source, you use which object?

   a. Connection

   b. Command

   c. Recordset

   d. All of the above

8. When a Connection object is used to process a command or create a recordset (as opposed to using a connection string), the connection is said to be:

   a. Explicit

   b. Implicit

9. Which of the following statements creates a connection using a Connection object?

   a. `cnADOConnection.Open "Provider=Microsoft.Jet.OLEDB.4.0;" _`
      `& "Data Source=c:\temp\biblio.mdb"`

   b. `cnADOConnection.Establish "Provider=Microsoft.Jet. _`
      `OLEDB.4.0;" & "Data Source=c:\temp\biblio.mdb"`

   c. `cnADOConnection.Open "Provider=Microsoft.Jet.OLEDB.4.0"`

   d. `cnADOConnection.Establish "Provider=Microsoft.Jet. _`
      `OLEDB.4.0"`

10. Which method is used to disconnect an open Connection object?

    a. Disconnect

    b. Close

    c. Terminate

    d. End

11. A Connection object is required in order to use a Command object.

    a. True

    b. False

12. Which of the following statements defines a Command object as using an implicit connection?

    a. `Set comADOCommand.ActiveConnection = conADOConnection`

    b. `comADOCommand.ActiveConnection = _`
       `"Provider=Microsoft.Jet.OLEDB.4.0;" & _`
       `"Data Source=c:\temp\biblio.mdb"`

    c. `comADOCommand.ActiveConnection = _`
       `"Provider=Microsoft.Jet.OLEDB.4.0"`

    d. `Set comADOCommand.ImplicitConnection = conADOConnection`

13. Which of the following is a valid way to execute a SQL statement?

    a. `comADOCommand.Execute("SELECT * FROM Authors", , _`
       `adCmdTable)`

    b. `comADOCommand.Execute("SELECT * FROM Authors", , _`
       `adCmdText)`

    c. `cnADOConnection.Execute("Authors", , adCmdText)`

    d. `cnADOConnection.Execute("Authors", , adCmdTable)`

14. Which method provides the most flexibility when creating a recordset?

    a. Connection.Execute

    b. Command.Execute

    c. Recordset.Open

    d. Connection.CreateRecordset

15. You want to create a recordset that reflects changes and deletes made by other users, but not additions to the recordset. Which statement would you use?

    a. `rstAuthors.Open "Authors", cnADOConnection, _`
       `adOpenKeyset, , adCmdTable`

    b. `rstAuthors.Open "Authors", cnADOConnection, _`
       `adOpenDynamic, , adCmdTable`

    c. `Set rstAuthors = cnADOConnection.Execute("Authors", , _`
       `adCmdTable)`

    d. `Set rstAuthors = comADOCommand.Execute(, , adCmdText)`

16. When optimistic locking is used, record locks are created:

    a. When the record is edited

    b. When the Edit method is called

    c. When the Update method is called

    d. When the recordset is created

17. Which cursor type creates read-only recordset that allows full navigation, and is most similar to DAO's snapshot recordset type?

    a. Keyset

    b. Dynamic

    c. Static

    d. Forward-only

18. Which cursor type offers the fastest performance, and is also the default cursor type?

    a. Keyset

    b. Dynamic

    c. Static

    d. Forward-only

19. You want to create a recordset that ensures updates to underlying records always complete successfully. Which statement would you use?

    a. `Set rstAuthors = cnADOConnection.Execute("Authors", _`
       `adLockPessimistic, adCmdTable)`

    b. `rstAuthors.Open "Authors", cnADOConnection, _`
       `adOpenStatic, adLockPessimistic, adCmdTable`

    c. `rstAuthors.Open "Authors", cnADOConnection, _`
       `adOpenKeyset, adLockOptimistic, adCmdTable`

    d. `rstAuthors.Open "Authors", cnADOConnection, _`
       `adOpenKeyset, adLockPessimistic, adCmdTable`

20. In order to execute a SQL statement using a Command object:

    a. Supply the command text as an argument in the Execute method.

    b. Supply the command text to the CommandText property of the Command object.

    c. Supply a valid CommandText object as an argument of the Execute method.

    d. Command objects cannot be used to execute SQL statements.

21. How do you instruct a Command object to treat its command text?

    a. Specify a constant in the *Options* argument of the Execute method.

    b. Specify a constant in the *CommandType* argument of the Execute method.

    c. Specify a constant in the Options property of the Command object.

    d. Specify a constant in the CommandType property of the Command object.

22. To find the first record in an Authors table where the author's last name begins with "f," you would use which statement?

    a. `rstAuthors.Find "[Author] LIKE 'f*'", 1, adSearchBackward`

    b. `rstAuthors.Find "[Author] LIKE 'f*'", 0, adSearchDefault`

    c. `rstAuthors.Find "[Author] LIKE 'f*'", 0, adSearchForward`

    d. `rstAuthors.Find "[Author] LIKE 'f*'", 1, adSearchForward`

23. Which method is used to add records to a recordset?

    a. Add

    b. AddNew

    c. Create

    d. New

24. When editing a record in a recordset, you must explicitly initiate the edit by calling the Edit method.

    a. True

    b. False

25. An atomic operation (a unit of change in a data source) is called a:

    a. UOC

    b. OOP

    c. Atom

    d. Transaction

26. A transaction has been initiated using CommitTrans, but things have occurred that necessitate the need to stop the transaction. Which method would you use?

    a. RollBack

    b. RollBackTrans

    c. CancelTrans

    d. StopTrans

27. An error has occurred while attempting to make a connection to a data source. Which of the following could be used to obtain the error number of the first error?

    a. `cnADOConnection.Errors(0).Number`

    b. `cnADOConnection.Error(1).Number`

    c. `cnADOConnection.ErrorNumber`

    d. `cnADOConnection.Error(0).Source`

28. Which user-interface element can be used to create ADO recordsets for bound controls?

    a. Data control

    b. ADO Data control

    c. Data Environment designer

    d. ADO Connection designer

29. You can only define one connection per Data Environment designer.

    a. True

    b. False

30. When binding controls to a Data Environment designer, which property of the bound control must be set that isn't set when binding to an ADO Data control?

    a. DataSource

    b. DataField

    c. DataMember

    d. DataEnvironment

Answers to Skills Assessment

1. c	7. d	13. d	19. d	25. d
2. d	8. a	14. c	20. b	26. b
3. a	9. a	15. a	21. a	27. a
4. b	10. b	16. c	22. c	28. b
5. b	11. b	17. c	23. b	29. b
6. a, c	12. b	18. d	24. b	30. c

Hands-on Exercises

Exercise 7-1: Establish a connection with a data source, and use a Command object to generate a recordset

In this exercise, you'll use the following skills:

- Use a Connection object to establish a connection with a data source.
- Use a Command object to return a recordset to a Recordset object.
- Print the contents of a field in the recordset.
- Close the recordset and close the connection.

Section 1. Establishing a connection. In this section, you'll establish a connection to the *Biblio.mdb* database that ships with Visual Basic. Since you'll have to type in the path, you may want to move the database to the root folder or perhaps a folder just off the root.

1. Start a new Standard EXE Visual Basic project.

2. Add a reference to ADO by choosing References from the Project menu, and then selecting Microsoft ActiveX Data Objects 2.x Library. (The exact version you select will depend on what is installed on your computer.)

3. Add a new command button to the form and set its properties as follows:

Property	Value
Name	cmdConnect
Caption	Connect

4. Add the following code to the command button's Click event:

```
Dim cnADOConnection  As New Connection
Dim rstAuthors       As ADODB.Recordset
Dim comADOCommand    As New Command
```

5. Add the following statement, which actually establishes a connection using the Jet OLE DB provider (change the path as necessary):

```
cnADOConnection.Open "Provider=Microsoft.Jet.OLEDB.4.0;" & _
                     "Data Source=c:\temp\biblio.mdb"
```

Section 2. Creating a recordset using a Command object. In this section, you'll use a Command object to define a SQL statement to return data, and then use the Command object's Open method to create a recordset:

6. Add the following code to the procedure:

```
Set comADOCommand.ActiveConnection = cnADOConnection
comADOCommand.CommandText = "Authors"
Set rstAuthors = comADOCommand.Execute(, , adCmdTable)
```

Section 3. Print the contents of a field in the recordset. In this section, you're going to add a line of code to display the contents of a field in the recordset:

7. Add the following statement to the Click procedure:

```
MsgBox "First Author = " & rstAuthors![Author],vbOKOnly
```

Section 4. Close the recordset and the connection. In this section, you're going to clean-up open objects the proper way, rather than letting them go out of scope:

8. Add the following statements to the end of the Click procedure:

```
rstAuthors.Close
cnADOConnection.Close
```

The Click event should now look like this:

```
Private Sub cmdConnect_Click()

    Dim cnADOConnection  As New Connection
    Dim rstAuthors       As ADODB.Recordset
    Dim comADOCommand    As New Command

    cnADOConnection.Open "Provider=Microsoft.Jet.OLEDB.4.0;" & _
                         "Data Source=c:\temp\biblio.mdb"


    Set comADOCommand.ActiveConnection = cnADOConnection

    comADOCommand.CommandText = "Authors"

    Set rstAuthors = comADOCommand.Execute(, , adCmdTable)

    MsgBox "First Author = " & rstAuthors![Author], vbOKOnly
```

```
      rstAuthors.Close
      cnADOConnection.Close

   End Sub
```

9. Run the project and click the button. The message box shown in Figure 7-9 should display (possibly with a different author name, if you've modified your database). If it does not, you may not have the Jet provider installed on your computer.

Figure 7-9: Creating the connection, command, and recordset in this exercise culminates in obtaining a value from the recordset and displaying it in this message box

Exercise 7-2: Using the Data Environment designer to create a bound form

In this exercise, you'll create a Data Environment designer containing a single Connection and Command object, and then create a bound form based on the Command object:

You'll use the following skills in this exercise:

* Add a Data Environment designer to a project.

* Define a connection object in the Data Environment designer.

* Define a command object in the Data Environment designer.

* Use the SQL builder of the Data Environment designer.

* Create a bound form based on a command object in the Data Environment designer.

Section 1. Adding the Data Environment designer to a project. In this section, you'll reference the Data Environment designer (if it's not already referenced), and add a new Data Environment designer to a project:

1. Start a new Standard EXE project in Visual Basic.

2. Ensure that the Data Environment designer is installed and referenced in the project by choosing Components from the Project menu, clicking the Designers tab, and selecting Data Environment.

3. Choose Add Data Environment from the Project menu.

Section 2. Defining a connection in the Data Environment designer. In this section, you'll define a connection to the *Biblio.mdb* Jet database that ships with Visual Basic:

4. Double-click the Data Environment designer in the Project Explorer window to display the designer.

5. Right-click Connection1 in the designer and choose Properties from the Shortcut menu.

6. Select the Microsoft Jet 3.51 OLE DB Provider, if installed on your computer (see Figure 7-10), and click Next.

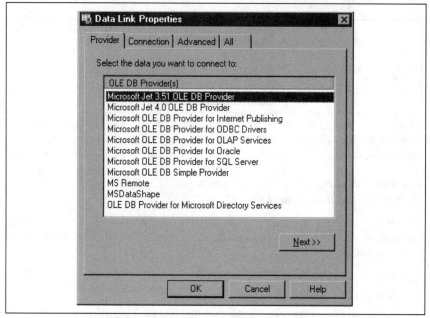

Figure 7-10: The first step to defining a connection is choosing a provider

7. Click the Browse button to the right of the Database Name field, and locate and select the *Biblio.mdb* database.

8. To test the connection, click Test Connection. If the connection you've defined is valid, you'll see the message box shown in Figure 7-11.

Figure 7-11: The Data Link Properties dialog box can test a connection for you

9. Click OK to save the connection definition.

Section 3. Defining a command in the Data Environment designer. In this section, you'll create a Command object, and you'll use the Data Environment designer's SQL builder to define the command text for the command:

10. Click the Add Command button on the toolbar to create a new command.

11. Right-click the command and choose properties from the Shortcut menu to display the Command Properties dialog box.

12. Change the Command Name to **Authors**.

13. In the Source of Data frame, select SQL Statement.

14. Get the SQL Builder started by entering the following text in the white central text box portion of the window:

    SELECT * FROM Authors

15. Click the SQL Builder button. Your screen should now look like Figure 7-12.

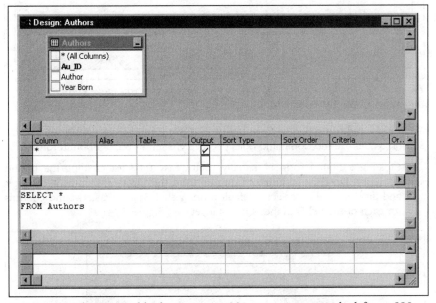

Figure 7-12: The SQL Builder lets you enter SQL text or interactively define a SQL statement

16. For this exercise, you're going to sort the recordset on the Author field. Drag the Author field from the Authors table list, and drop it in the row underneath the row with the asterisk.

17. Since the Authors field is already being returned (as part of the asterisk selection), deselect the Output checkbox for the Author row.

18. Click the Sort Type column of the Author row and select Ascending. Your window should now look like Figure 7-13.

19. Click the Close button of the SQL Builder form, and choose Yes to save changes.

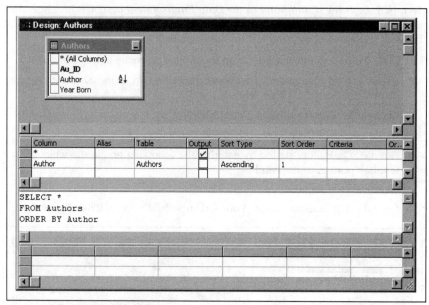

Figure 7-13: The text for the SQL statement is updated as you make changes to the definition of the SQL statement

Section 4. Creating a bound form using the Data Environment designer. In this section, you'll use the Command object you've created to build a bound form:

20. Creating a bound form is actually pretty easy (at least creating the bound fields is). Drag the command Authors from the Data Environment designer and drop it on the project's default form. Visual Basic creates bound controls for each of the fields in the SQL result set (see Figure 7-14).

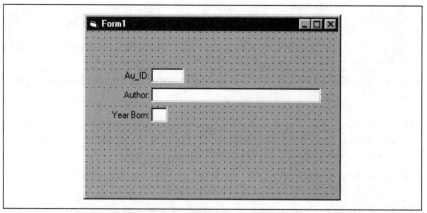

Figure 7-14: The Data Environment designer removes a lot of manual steps that are ordinarily required to create bound forms

21. Move the group of controls on the form until they're roughly in the location shown in Figure 7-14.

22. Add a new command button to the form. Change its Name to **cmdMove-Forward** and its Caption to **Move Forward**.

23. Double-click the command button to access its Click event, and add the following code:

```
DataEnvironment1.Recordsets("Authors").MoveNext
```

24. Run the project by pressing F5 and notice how the fields populate with the first record in the database. Click the command button to cycle forward through the recordset.

 This code doesn't check for end-of-file, but it serves to show how a recordset in a Data Environment designer is accessed. If you wanted to add a Move Previous button, you'd have to change the cursor type of the Command object in the Data Environment designer.

Highlighter's Index

Universal Data Access (UDA)

OLE DB is a high-performance mechanism for accessing data
OLE DB providers communicate with data sources and OLE DB

ActiveX Data Objects (ADO)

Set of objects that act as a client to OLE DB
Designed to replace DAO and RDO

Connection Objects

Are used to connect to an OLE DB data source
Uses connection strings

Command Objects

Are used to execute commands
Can execute stored procedures

Recordsets

Represent records from a table or query
Can be created using Recordset object, Connection object, or Command object
Can have client-side or server-side cursors
Can employ different locking schemes

Working with Data

Transactions

ACID (atomicity, consistency, isolation, and durability)
Auto-commit mode
Started with BeginTrans
Committed with CommitTrans

ADO Error Object

Part of an Errors collection
Error object corresponds to an error encountered in a single operation

ADO Data Control

Similar to the standard data control but used to access ADO data sources
Exposes limited ADO functionality
Controls can be bound to ADO Data control

Data Environment Designer

Makes creating database applications easier
Replaces the ActiveX UserConnection designer of Visual Basic 5

CHAPTER 8

Creating Internet-Aware Applications

Unless you've been living under a rock the last few years or so, you're probably familiar with the Internet. Paralleling the trend of everyone wanting to get onto the Internet is the growth of everyone wanting to write Internet-aware applications. As a matter of fact, Internet programmability features have been a focus of the latest Visual Basic exams.

In previous chapters, you learned how to create ActiveX controls and documents that could be embedded on a web page. Although ActiveX components open up endless possibilities, these components are actually extensions of Internet connectivity rather than core elements. The core elements of Internet connectivity really come down to web browsing and file transfers; everything else builds on these basics.

This chapter discusses:

- Adding web-browsing functionality to an application, using the WebBrowser control. Using the WebBrowser control within an application, users can navigate to and view pages on the World Wide Web or an intranet, as well as folders on their local computer.

- Automating Internet Explorer. Internet Explorer is an automation server, and you can write code to make Explorer extend the interactivity between your applications and the Internet.

- Downloading files from a site that supports the HTTP or FTP protocols, using the Internet Transfer control. File transfers across the Internet are extremely common. Using the Internet Transfer control, you can automate the process of sending and retrieving files from FTP and HTTP sites.

- Connecting to a remote computer to exchange data over the Internet, using the Winsock control. The Winsock control lets you create multiple applications that can communicate over the Internet or an intranet. The most common type of application that uses the Winsock control is an Internet chat application, but this only scratches the surface of what you can do with the Winsock control.

- Creating dynamic web pages using DHTML.

The Technologies and the Exams

Internet development has received a lot of attention in the media, from tool developers, and from development houses everywhere. It goes without saying that Microsoft has invested a lot of resources in creating Internet development tools, and you should expect to encounter Internet development questions on both exams, as shown in Table 8-1.

Table 8-1: Internet-Related Topics on the Exams

Topic	Covered on Exam
Adding browser capabilities using the WebBrowser control	Both
Automating Internet Explorer	Both
Retrieving data using the Internet Transfer control	Both
Creating Internet applications using the Winsock control	Both
Creating dynamic web pages using DHTML	Both

Adding Browser Capabilities to a Program Using the WebBrowser Control

One of the easiest ways to make an application Internet-aware is to add web-browsing capabilities. Obviously, not every application needs internal web-browsing functionality. For most purposes, having a dedicated browsing application such as Internet Explorer on the machine is the best solution, and you can use Automation to control Internet Explorer, as discussed later in this chapter. However, there are times when it's desirable to integrate browsing capabilities directly within an application. For instance, you may want to expose online help manuals as web documents. Or perhaps you're a network administrator and you'd like to create a browser that keeps a log file of every page a user visits. In either of these cases, you might prefer to create a simple browsing application that gives you the control you desire, rather than having users work with the full Internet Explorer product. The Internet Explorer automation object, discussed later in this chapter, gives you control of Internet Explorer but doesn't allow you to embed a web browser in an application.

Manually coding an application to decipher HTML documents and display them visually is a huge undertaking. Fortunately, Microsoft has done the work for you and has exposed the functionality by way of the ActiveX WebBrowser control.

The WebBrowser control isn't limited to displaying simple HTML files. It's also capable of hosting:

- Standard HTML and HTML enhancements, such as floating frames and cascading stylesheets

- Other ActiveX controls

- Most Netscape plug-ins

- Scripting, such as Microsoft Visual Basic Scripting Edition (VBScript) or JavaScript

- Java™ applets

- Multimedia content, such as video and audio playback

- Three-dimensional virtual worlds created with Virtual Reality Modeling Language (VRML)

- ActiveX documents

- Microsoft Excel spreadsheets, Microsoft Word documents, and Microsoft PowerPoint presentations (Note: If Office isn't installed, the runtime viewers of each of these documents must be installed in order to view the document in the browser control.)

In addition to viewing web-related documents, the WebBrowser control can be used to browse folders on a local hard disk or on a local area network (see Figure 8-1). The WebBrowser control even maintains a history list that can be used to navigate and view previously browsed sites, folders, and documents.

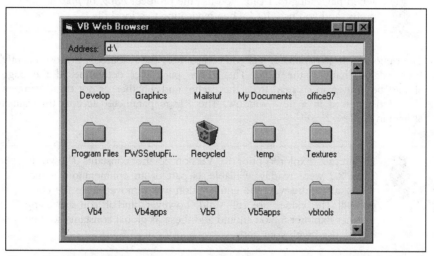

Figure 8-1: The WebBrowser control can be used to browse local and network hard disk drives

The WebBrowser control is part of an ActiveX component called Microsoft Internet Controls. To add the WebBrowser control to a project, use the Components dialog box to add the Microsoft Internet Controls component to the project.

Navigating Web Pages and Documents

The WebBrowser control has a number of methods to facilitate navigating web pages and documents. Using these methods, you can navigate:

- To a specific page or document

- Forward and backward through previously browsed pages

- To the designated home page

- To the designated search page

Browsing a specific page or document using the Navigate method

The most commonly used navigation method is, not surprisingly, the Navigate method. The Navigate method lets you browse to a specific page or document using the following syntax:

```
BrowserControl.Navigate URL, [Flags], [TargetFrameName], [PostData], _
                        [Headers]
```

The only required parameter of the Navigate method is *URL*. The universal resource locator (URL) is the address and document name to navigate to. For example, to view an HTML document, you could use a statement such as this:

```
WebBrowser1.Navigate "http://www.tigerpawsoftware.com"
```

When navigating to a URL, you use the protocol *http://* or *ftp://* as the prefix, and you use *file://* when navigating to a local file.

The optional *Flags* parameter lets you control how the resource list (most recently browsed list) handles the page. The *Flags* parameter determines if the page should be written to or read from the cache, and whether or not the document should be viewed in a new window. The *Flags* parameter accepts the values shown in Table 8-2.

In Internet Explorer prior to Version 5, the constants shown in Table 8-2 were readily available as part of an enumeration. Somewhere along the way, the enumeration was removed from the component! The values are still valid, however, and if you are using Internet Explorer 5, you should add these as global constants so they can be used with your code.

Table 8-2: Possible Values for the Flag's Parameter of the Navigate Method

Constant	Value	Description
navOpenInNewWindow	1	Open the resource or file in a new window.
navNoHistory	2	Do not add the resource or file to the history list. The new page replaces the current page in the list.
navNoReadFromCache	4	Do not read from the disk cache for this navigation.
navNoWriteToCache	8	Do not write the results of this navigation to the disk cache.

By default, whenever you navigate from one page to another, Internet Explorer adds the page you are navigating away from to the history list. If you don't want the page added to the history list, use the navNoHistory constant in the *Flags* parameter like this:

```
WebBrowser1.Navigate "http://www.tigerpawsoftware.com", navNoHistory
```

Web pages are often large and complex, and even with fast modems, downloading lots of text, graphics, and audio can take some time. To help minimize the amount of time required to display a page or document, Internet Explorer stores the components of recently viewed web sites in its cache. If a page that is navigated to is stored in the cache with its elements (graphics and so forth), the data from the cache is used to display the document very quickly. Although this feature can greatly reduce the amount of time needed to display a page or document, there are times when this behavior is undesirable. For instance, some web pages (such as those used to display current stock quotes) are built dynamically. If Internet Explorer were to display these dynamic pages from information stored in its cache, it would run the risk of displaying outdated information to the user.

You can tell Internet Explorer to not use information stored in its cache when displaying a page or document by specifying the navNoReadFromCache constant in the *Flags* parameter like this:

```
WebBrowser1.Navigate "http://www.tigerpawsoftware.com", _
    navNoReadFromCache
```

The *navNoReadFromCache* argument works great, but for sensitive pages where the user must always see the most accurate information, it's not always enough. For instance, say you're using Automation to control Explorer (as discussed later in this chapter), and you display a page using the navNoReadFromCache setting. You then decide to navigate to a different page directly, using Internet Explorer's address bar. Finally, click the Back button to redisplay the page you originally specified. Since you're not programmatically displaying the page, you can't control the cache behavior, and Internet Explorer may attempt to display the page using information in its cache. For such sensitive pages and documents, you should use the navNoWriteToCache constant when displaying the URL. This prevents Internet Explorer from *storing* the page's information in its cache, forcing it to load the page from the original site the next time the page is viewed.

It's possible to combine multiple *Flag* values using the OR operator. For example, to display Microsoft's home page while forcing Internet Explorer to load the page from Microsoft's site and not from its cache, and at the same time preventing Internet Explorer from storing the site's information in its cache, you could use a statement like this:

```
WebBrowser1.Navigate _
    "http://microsoft.com/train_cert/Internet_Explorer0.htm", _
    navNoReadFromCache Or navNoWriteToCache
```

Although it may seem odd to prevent Internet Explorer from reading from the cache, *and* from writing the page to the cache as well, there is a very good reason for it. If the user clicks the Back button or otherwise navigates back to this page through some means other than your Navigate method, Internet Explorer will attempt to read from the cache. By preventing the page from being written to the cache to begin with, you avoid this potential problem.

Although frames were once a fringe feature of web sites and could only be displayed by the most current browsers, frames are now an integral part of most web sites. Using frames, a web site can display many different HTML documents at one time. A common use of frames by a web site is to use one frame to display a site navigation document while another frame displays a document selected by the visitor. If you want to display a web site in a specific frame, rather than displaying it in the entire browser window, specify the desired frame's name in the *TargetFrameName* parameter.

 The *PostData* and *Headers* parameters require knowledge of HTML. Although you don't need to fully understand the specifics, you should have a general understanding of these parameters.

The *PostData* parameter is used to specify data to send to the server during the HTTP POST request. The POST transaction is usually employed to send data gathered by an HTML form in the body of the HTTP request. This parameter isn't often used because web pages themselves can post data as necessary. If this parameter doesn't specify any post data, the Navigate method issues an HTTP GET request. This parameter is ignored if *URL* is not an HTTP URL.

The *Headers* parameter is used to enter a value that specifies additional HTTP headers to send to the server. These headers are added to the default Internet Explorer headers, and they can specify such things as the action required of the server, the type of data being passed to the server, or a status code. This parameter is ignored if the *URL* is not an HTTP URL. Like the *PostData* parameter, the *Headers* parameter is an advanced HTML technique not often used when adding simple browsing capabilities to an application.

Navigating the history list

As you browse pages using the WebBrowser control, a history list is maintained just as it is in Internet Explorer. You can implement the functionality of the Go Back and Go Forward buttons of Internet Explorer using the GoBack and GoForward methods of the WebBrowser control.

To navigate back one page or document in the history list, use the GoBack method like this:

```
WebBrowser1.GoBack
```

To navigate one page or document forward in the history list, use the GoForward method like this:

```
WebBrowser1.GoForward
```

 If there is no page to go to in the history list (e.g., you call GoBack and you're already at the first page stored in the history list), a trappable error occurs.

Navigating to the user's home page or search page

In addition to navigating to specific locations and moving back and forward through the history list, it's common for a user to navigate to their home page (sometimes referred to as Start page). The user's home page is specified on their Internet Explorer Options dialog box. This functionality is exposed in Internet Explorer in the form of the Home button.

You can force the WebBrowser control to navigate to the user's home or start page just as if the user clicked the Home button in Internet Explorer by using the GoHome method like this:

```
WebBrowser1.GoHome
```

Navigating to Internet Explorer's search page in Explorer is done using the Search button on Explorer's toolbar. You can perform the same function as a user clicking the Search button in Explorer by using the GoSearch method of the WebBrowser control like this:

```
WebBrowser1.GoSearch
```

Using the Properties of the WebBrowser Control

The WebBrowser control has a number of properties that you can use to gather information about the currently viewed web page or document. These are more easily understood through an example. Suppose there is a WebBrowser named WebBrowser1 on a form. This control is currently displaying an ActiveX document called *udNav.vbd* located on *D:*. The document was displayed using the following call to the Navigate method:

```
WebBrowser1.Navigate "D:\udnav.vbd"
```

The following sections discuss various properties of the WebBrowser control and show the values the properties would return given this scenario.

The location and type of a browsed document

Internet Explorer is all about viewing documents. The various navigation methods give you control over displaying specific documents, but they don't give you any information about a document already displayed in the browser. You can gather specific information about the location and type of the currently displayed document using the properties listed Table 8-3.

Table 8-3: Navigation Properties of the WebBrowser Control

Property	Description
LocationName	Returns a string containing the name of the resource (page or document) that the WebBrowser control is currently displaying. If the resource is an HTML page on the World Wide Web, the name is the title of that page.
LocationURL	Returns a string containing the URL of the resource that the WebBrowser control or Internet Explorer is currently displaying. If the resource is a folder or file on the network or local computer, the name is the UNC or full path of the folder or file.

Table 8-3: Navigation Properties of the WebBrowser Control (continued)

Property	Description
Type	Returns a string expression specifying the type name of the contained document. Note: If the WebBrowser control hasn't finished displaying the page, you'll get an automation error when you attempt to reference the Type property, so be sure to use error trapping when reading the Type property.

With our sample WebBrowser control as outlined in the first paragraph of this section (displaying the ActiveX document *D:\udNav.vbd*), polling the properties would return the values shown in the following table:

Property	Value Returned
LocationName	udNav.vbd
LocationURL	file:///D:/udNav.vbd
Type	Project1.udNav

Retrieving information about the host application

In addition to gathering information about the browsed document, you can also retrieve information about the application hosting the WebBrowser control. This is not so important when working with WebBrowser controls within your own application, however, because you can always check the properties of the Application object of your application. In any case, the two properties you need to be familiar with that tell information about the host of the WebBrowser control are the FullName and Path properties, as shown in the following table:

Property	Description
FullName	Returns a string that evaluates to the fully qualified path of the executable file containing the WebBrowser control
Path	Returns a string that evaluates to the full path of the host application

Determining if the WebBrowser control is busy

As you probably know, navigating to and displaying a web page or document can take some time. There are many reasons for this, including busy servers, large bitmaps that need to be downloaded, slow connection speed, and so on. Fortunately, the WebBrowser control runs in an asynchronous mode, meaning that it actually divides and allocates its processing time to displaying all of the elements of a page or document and to accepting user input. If the WebBrowser didn't perform these tasks asynchronously, it wouldn't be able to respond to any user input until all elements of a page or document had been downloaded and displayed.

The WebBrowser control includes a property that you can evaluate to determine whether or not the WebBrowser control is engaged in a navigation or downloading operation: the Busy property. To determine if the WebBrowser is busy, check the Busy property using code such as this:

```
If WebBrowser1.Busy Then
    . . .
```

```
Else
    ...
End If
```

 Several properties that appear in the Properties window are only available when manipulating an Automation instance of Internet Explorer. The WebBrowser control is a wrapper around the Internet Explorer automation object, but it doesn't expose all of the functionality of the automation object. The properties that you can see but not use include, but aren't limited to, AddressBar, StatusBar, TheaterMode, and ToolBar. Some methods (such as Quit) may only be used with an automation object of Internet Explorer as well.

Understanding WebBrowser Events

The WebBrowser control has a number of events to keep you informed and in control of what is happening as a user browses and downloads files and documents. The basic events are listed in Table 8-4.

Table 8-4: Events of the WebBrowser Control

Event	Description
BeforeNavigate2	Occurs when the WebBrowser control is about to navigate to a new URL.
CommandStateChange	Occurs when the enabled state of a toolbar button changes.
DocumentComplete	Occurs when the document that is being navigated to is finished loading. For a document without frames, this event fires once when the document is finished loading. For a document with frames, this event fires once for each frame.
DownloadBegin	Occurs when a navigation operation is beginning, shortly after the BeforeNavigate2 event.
DownloadComplete	Occurs when a navigation operation finishes, is halted, or fails. Unlike NavigateComplete2, this event always fires after a navigation starts.
NavigateComplete2	Occurs after the browser has successfully navigated to a new URL. The document may still be downloading when this event fires, however.
NewWindow2	Occurs when a new window is to be created for displaying a resource.
OnFullScreen	Occurs when the FullScreen property changes.
OnMenuBar	Occurs when the MenuBar property changes.
OnStatusBar	Occurs when the StatusBar property changes.
OnQuit	Occurs before Internet Explorer quits.
OnTheaterMode	Occurs when the TheaterMode property changes.
OnToolbar	Occurs when the ToolBar property changes.
OnVisible	Occurs when the Visible property changes.
ProgressChange	Occurs when the progress of a download is updated.
TitleChange	Occurs when the title of a document in the WebBrowser control becomes available or changes.

As Microsoft releases updates to the WebBrowser control, they continue to add new events. Often, these new events parallel existing events but have added functionality. Since it's against the basic principles of COM to change the interface of a property, method, or event, these new events must be given new names, and consequentially, these enhanced events have been given the names of the events upon which they are based, followed by the number 2. For instance, the WebBrowser has an enhanced BeforeNavigate event called BeforeNavigate2. In cases such as this, you'll have to consult the latest documentation to find out what has been changed, but you shouldn't need to know these specifics to pass the exams.

The On . . . events fire when the state related to the On . . . event changes. The important thing to note is that while you can take action within the event, you cannot cancel any of the state changes or stop them from occurring; when any of the On . . . events other than OnQuit occur, the state change has already taken place. Although most of the On . . . events are simple and rather intuitive, others require some explanation and are therefore explored in detail in the following sections.

The BeforeNavigate2 event

The BeforeNavigate2 event occurs when the WebBrowser control is about to navigate to a different document or resource. All of the data related to navigating to the resource (frame, URL, and so on) is passed into the event. If you want to stop the WebBrowser control from navigating to this new page or document, set the Cancel parameter of the event to True. The BeforeNavigate2 event has a number of parameters that are worth mentioning (see the following code for the declaration of the event); these are shown in Table 8-5.

Table 8-5: Parameters Passed to the BeforeNavigate2 Event

Parameter	Description
pDisp	A reference to the top-level or frame WebBrowser object in which the navigation is occurring.
URL	A string expression containing the URL to which the browser is navigating.
Flags	Reserved for future use.
TargetFrameName	A string expression that indicates the name of the frame in which the resource will be displayed, or NULL if no named frame is targeted for the resource.
PostData	Data to send to the server if the HTTP POST transaction is being used.
Headers	A value that specifies the additional HTTP headers to send to the server (for HTTP URLs only). The headers can specify things like the action required of the server, the type of data being passed to the server, or a status code.
Cancel	A Boolean value that the container can set to True to cancel the navigation operation or to False (the default value) to allow it to proceed.

The following code sample shows a simple child protection filter implemented using the BeforeNavigate2 event. It assumes that a URL with *XXX* in it is an adult site, and prevents the browser from displaying the specified URL.

```
Private Sub WebBrowser1_BeforeNavigate2(ByVal pDisp As Object, _
    URL As Variant, Flags As Variant, TargetFrameName As _
    Variant,  PostData As Variant, Headers As Variant, Cancel _
    As Boolean)

    If (InStr(1, URL, "xxx") > 0) Then
        MsgBox "Access denied to URL: " & URL, vbOKOnly
        Cancel = True
    End If

End Sub
```

The CommandStateChange event

The CommandStateChange event occurs when the enabled state of a command changes (commands are the functions associated with the buttons on Internet Explorer's toolbar). The declaration of the CommandStateChange event is:

```
Private Sub WebBrowser1_CommandStateChange(ByVal Command as Long, _
    ByVal Enable As Boolean)
```

The possible values of *Command* in the CommandStateChange event are listed in Table 8-6.

Table 8-6: Possible Values of Command

Constant	Value	Meaning
CSC_UPDATECOMMANDS	−1	The enabled state of a toolbar button may have changed. The Enable parameter should be ignored.
CSC_NAVIGATEFORWARD	1	The enabled state of the Forward button has changed.
CSC_NAVIGATEBACK	2	The enabled state of the Back button has changed.

You can use the CommandStateChange event to enable and disable command buttons in your application used to perform these functions. The event's *Enable* parameter indicates the state to which a button is changing. For instance, if you've created a custom browser by embedding a WebBrowser control on a form, you will need to enable and disable the Forward and Back buttons appropriately as the user browses web sites. The following code illustrates using this event:

```
Private Sub WebBrowser1_CommandStateChange(ByVal Command As Long, _
    ByVal Enable As Boolean)

    Select Case Command
        Case CSC_NAVIGATEFORWARD
            cmdForward.Enabled = Enable

        Case CSC_NAVIGATEBACK
```

```
            cmdBack.Enabled = Enable

        End Select

    End Sub
```

The DownloadBegin event

The DownloadBegin event occurs when a download operation is beginning. This event is fired shortly after the BeforeNavigate2 event, unless the navigation is canceled. The DownloadBegin event is a good place to put any animation or a "busy" indicator to show the user that a download is in progress. All Download-Begin events have a corresponding DownloadComplete event, as discussed in the next section.

The DownloadComplete event

The DownloadComplete event occurs when a download operation has finished, was halted, or failed. Unlike NavigateComplete2, which is fired only when a URL is successfully navigated to, this event is always fired after a navigation starts. You can use this event to update any status information or animation that you initialized in the DownloadBegin event.

The NavigateComplete2 event

The NavigateComplete2 event occurs after the WebBrowser has successfully navigated to a new location.

 The new document may still be downloading (e.g., large bitmaps in an HTML document) when the NavigateComplete2 event fires. You can only rely on this event to inform you when at least part of the document has been received.

The NewWindow2 event

The NewWindow2 event occurs when a new window is created to display a document, rather than the document replacing the one currently being viewed.

A new window is created under these circumstances:

- A user shift-clicks a link
- A user right-clicks a link and selects "Open in New Window"
- A navigation is targeted to a frame name that doesn't exist

The ProgressChange event

The ProgressChange event occurs when the progress of a download operation is updated. Use the ProgressChange event to place code to display the status of an operation. The ProgressChange event has two parameters: *Progress* and

---

ProgressMax. You can use these parameters to display bytes transferred, a status bar, or whatever else you desire. The *Progress* parameter is –1 when the progress is fully complete.

For example, if a user downloads a file from the web site, the ProgressChange event fires periodically as the file is downloaded. However, the value of the *Progress* parameter changes to reflect the number of bytes downloaded. The total number of bytes to be transferred is indicated by the *ProgressMax* parameter. The following code uses the *Progress* and *ProgressMax* parameters to compute a percentage of the operation that is complete, and displays this percent in a label's caption:

```
Private Sub WebBrowser1 ProgressChange(ByVal Progress As Long, _
    ByVal ProgressMax as Long)

    Label1.Caption = (Progress * 100) / ProgressMax
    ' Force the label to update.
    Label1.Refresh

End Sub
```

The TitleChange event

The TitleChange event fires when the title of a document changes. Although not immediately apparent, titles of web pages almost always change as you download them. For instance, while downloading an HTML web page, the title of the page is set to the URL of the page. After the real title is parsed from the HTML document (sometimes while downloading the page), the title is changed to reflect the actual title and the TitleChange event fires.

 The WebBrowser control lets you easily add robust web-browsing capabilities to an application. Be aware, however, that you can't fully distribute the WebBrowser control to other users. In order for the WebBrowser control to be used within your application, users of the application must have the full version of Internet Explorer installed on their computer.

Using Automation with Internet Explorer

You don't have to add a WebBrowser control to your application to support browsing functionality. Internet Explorer exposes an automation object. Using Automation, you control an instance of Internet Explorer. When automating Explorer, you get additional functionality (properties, methods, and events) that you don't get when using the WebBrowser control.

In the earlier section discussing the WebBrowser control, it was mentioned that the WebBrowser has a number of properties that can't actually be used, most relating to the user interface of the browser. When you use Automation to control Explorer, you can use these additional properties. These properties are listed in Table 8-7.

Table 8-7: Internet Explorer's Automation Properties

Property	Description
AddressBar	Determines whether Internet Explorer's URL address bar is visible or hidden.
FullName	Specifies the fully qualified path of the executable file that contains the Internet Explorer application.
FullScreen	Indicates whether Internet Explorer is in full-screen or normal window mode. When Internet Explorer is in full screen mode, the title bar, borders, status bar, shortcut bar, and address bar of Internet Explorer are all hidden to dedicate as much space as possible to displaying the current page or document.
MenuBar	Determines whether the Internet Explorer menu bar is visible or hidden.
Name	Always returns the name `Microsoft Internet Explorer`.
OffLine	Indicates whether or not Internet Explorer is currently operating in offline mode. In offline mode, Internet Explorer is forced to read HTML pages from the local cache, rather than from the source document.
StatusBar	Determines whether the Internet Explorer status bar is visible or hidden.
StatusText	Sets or returns the text for the status bar.
TheaterMode	Performs the same functionality as the FullScreen property.
Toolbar	Determines whether the Internet Explorer toolbar is visible or hidden.

 The StatusText property is completely unavailable for the Web-Browser control. Attempting to reference the StatusText property of the WebBrowser control will generate a runtime error.

Adding the Internet Explorer Automation Library to a Project

The Internet Explorer automation object is found in the file *Shdocvw.dll*, which also contains the WebBrowser control. For best performance, you should early bind to the automation object.

To add a reference to the Internet Explorer automation object, select Microsoft Internet Controls in the References dialog box.

Creating an Automation Object Variable Reference

Once the Internet Explorer library is referenced in a project, you need only create an object variable to manipulate Internet Explorer. In order to utilize Explorer fully, you need to take advantage of its events. Therefore, you must early bind the object variable, using code such as:

```
Dim WithEvents objExplorer As InternetExplorer
Set objExplorer = New InternetExplorer
```

For information on how to use events with Automation servers, refer to Chapter 4, *Creating and Testing ActiveX Code Components.*

Once an Internet Explorer object is instantiated, you can manipulate the object in much the same way you manipulate the WebBrowser control. In fact, most of the properties, methods, and events are the same. However, more functionality is available to you when manipulating an automation object of Internet Explorer than when manipulating a WebBrowser control, which is essentially a wrapper around the basic Internet Explorer functionality (see the previous table for a listing of the additional properties that are available).

 Because most of the functionality of the Internet Explorer automation object is the same as that of the WebBrowser control, only the differences are discussed in this section. Be sure to read the section on the WebBrowser control earlier in this chapter so you'll be prepared to answer questions related to automating Internet Explorer.

Hiding and Showing Internet Explorer

When you first create a new instance of the Internet Explorer automation object, a new instance of Internet Explorer is started, but it's not visible. There may be times when you want to automate Internet Explorer in this fashion. However, it makes debugging somewhat more difficult, in that Explorer's user-interface messages are not displayed when Explorer isn't visible.

For instance, if you attempt to navigate to an invalid URL using the Navigate method, Explorer will display the message shown in Figure 8-2 if Internet Explorer is visible. If Internet Explorer isn't visible, this message is not displayed.

Figure 8-2: Informative message boxes such as the one shown here aren't displayed when Internet Explorer isn't visible

To have Internet Explorer display itself, set the Visible property of the Automation object to **True** like this:

```
objExplorer.Visible = True
```

Internet
Applications

Navigating Documents Using an Internet Explorer Automation Object

Navigation is performed in automation in the same way as when using the WebBrowser control: by using the Navigate2 (or Navigate) method. For example, the following statement could be used to navigate to a web site:

```
objExplorer.Navigate "http://www.tigerpawsoftware.com"
```

Shutting Down Internet Explorer

When a client application using objects from an automation server is shut down, the objects created by that client are released and destroyed, usually causing the server application to close. This is not the case with Internet Explorer. Any and all open windows of Internet Explorer created through automation remain open after the client application terminates. In order for a client to close Internet Explorer and all of its windows, it must invoke the Quit method of the Internet Explorer automation object, like this:

```
objExplorer.Quit
```

Using the Internet Transfer Control

The Internet Transfer control is an ActiveX control that transmits files via one of two popular protocols: hypertext transfer protocol (HTTP) and file transfer protocol (FTP). Using the Internet Transfer control, you can connect to any server supporting one of these protocols and download files. This opens many possibilities, including creating an FTP browser or creating an application that automatically downloads files from an FTP site.

Adding the Internet Transfer control to a project is similar to adding the WebBrowser control; simply select the Microsoft Internet Transfer control in the Components dialog box.

When added to a form, the Internet Transfer control appears at design time as an icon of a computer in front of a globe, and it is invisible at runtime.

The procedure used to retrieve a file using the Internet Transfer control depends upon the type of server (HTTP or FTP) from which you are retrieving information. However, the mechanics of both procedures are very similar. To retrieve files using either protocol, do the following:

1. Set the AccessType property of the Internet Transfer control.

2. Retrieve data using the OpenURL or Execute method.

3. Use the GetChunk method to retrieve data from the buffer when downloading files using the Execute method.

Setting the AccessType Property

The AccessType property of the Internet Transfer control dictates the type of connection made between the control and the server hosting the file to be retrieved. You can set the AccessType property to any of the values shown in Table 8-8.

Table 8-8: Possible Values for the AccessType Property of the Internet Transfer Control

Constant	Value	Description
icUseDefault	0	(Default) The control uses default settings found in the registry to access the Internet. In many cases, this is adequate.
icDirect	1	The control has a direct connection to the Internet.
icNamedProxy	2	This instructs the control to use the proxy server specified in the Proxy property.

Generally, the default setting of `icUseDefault` works fine. However, you may need to change the AccessType depending upon the machine's configuration. If you have a direct connection to the Internet, or use a dial-up connection such as Windows 98's Dialup Adapter, you can set the AccessType property to `icDirect`. However, if you plan on distributing your application, it may not be a good idea to use `icDirect`, since you can't be sure how the end user's computer is connected to the Internet.

If the application is running on an intranet that is connected to the Internet, additional work is required to ensure the Internet Transfer control connects properly to the Internet. In situations such as this, the computer is probably connected to the Internet via a *proxy server*. A proxy server is an intermediary between the computer and the Internet. The proxy server is managed by the intranet and acts as a firewall between the intranet and the Internet. This firewall protects the intranet from antagonistic actions coming from the Internet side of the connection.

To determine the proxy server on a computer connected to an intranet and the Internet, follow these steps:

1. From the Control Panel window, double-click the Internet Options icon.

2. Click the Connections tab to display the connections information.

3. Click LAN Settings to display the proxy server information (see Figure 8-3).

4. If a proxy server is being used, the "Use a proxy server" checkbox will be selected.

To use the default proxy server, leave the AccessType property set to `icUseDefault`. If you want to use a proxy server other than the default, you must set the Proxy property to the name of the proxy server to use, and then set the AccessType property to `icNamedProxy`. For example, the following code instructs the Internet Transfer control to use the named proxy MyProxyServer:

```
Inet1.Proxy = "MyProxyServer"
Inet1.AccessType = icNamedProxy
```

Retrieving Data Using the Internet Transfer Control

There are two techniques available for retrieving data using the Internet Transfer control: the OpenURL method and the Execute method. The OpenURL method is a *synchronous transfer*, meaning all code in the calling application is halted until the entire file is retrieved. The Execute method is an *asynchronous transfer*, meaning that the application can continue to execute code and otherwise go

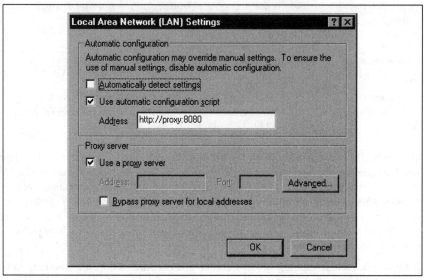

Figure 8-3: If a computer is connected to the Internet via a proxy server, the server is shown on the LAN Settings dialog box from the Internet Options dialog box

about its business while the transfer is in progress. Where the OpenURL method requires a single statement to retrieve an entire file, the Execute method requires numerous statements and an event. What you gain from the additional work when using the Execute method is more control over the download and the ability of the application or component to continue functioning while waiting for the download to complete.

Retrieving data using the OpenURL method

Using the OpenURL method is amazingly simple: specify the URL of a file you want to retrieve, and the Internet Transfer control goes out and retrieves the file. The OpenURL method returns the contents of the file as a text string by default, but it can also be used to return a binary file (as you'll see shortly). The OpenURL method has the following syntax:

```
object.OpenURL url [,datatype]
```

The *url* parameter is a valid address of a URL to retrieve. The *datatype* parameter is an optional Integer value. The possible values for *datatype* are:

Constant	Value	Description
icString	0	(Default) Retrieves data as a string
icByteArray	1	Retrieves data as a byte array

For instance, the following statement retrieves the raw HTML file from a web site and displays it in a text box:

```
Text1.Text = Inet1.OpenURL("www.tigerpawsoftware.com")
```

This works well for downloading most text files. For instance, you could download a text file from an FTP server and display its contents in a text box using a statement such as this:

```
Text1.Text = Inet1.OpenURL("ftp://ftp.microsoft.com/disclaimer.txt")
```

 You don't need to specify a protocol (HTTP or FTP) when using OpenURL, but you do when using Execute. The Internet Transfer control determines the protocol to use with OpenURL, based on the URL specified in the OpenURL method. This is just one reason why the OpenURL method is the simplest way to retrieve data using the Internet Transfer control.

You can specify any URL string that would be valid to enter into the address bar of Internet Explorer. For instance, the following statement returns the results of a search performed on Infoseek:

```
Text1.Text =  Inet1.OpenURL("http://www.infoseek.com/Titles?qt=" & _
              "ActiveX&col=WW%2Ccat_RES&sv=M6&lk=noframes&nh=10&ud4=1")
```

You can retrieve and store binary files using OpenURL by writing a little bit of code that makes use of Visual Basic's intrinsic file operations (namely Open, Put, and Close), as shown here:

```
Dim strURL     As String
Dim abytData() As Byte
Dim intFile    As Integer

strURL = "ftp://ftp.oreilly.com/pub/freebooks/mh/anacap.htm"

intFile = FreeFile()

' The result of the OpenURL method goes into the Byte
' array, and the Byte array is then saved to disk.
abytData() = Inet1.OpenURL(strURL, icByteArray)

Open "C:\anacap.htm" For Binary Access Write As #intFile

Put #intFile, , abytData()

Close #intFile
```

If the file being retrieved is a text file rather than a binary file, less code is required to save the file to disk. The following code can be used to save a retrieved text file to the local hard disk:

```
Dim strURL   As String
Dim intFile  As Integer

intFile = FreeFile()
strURL = "http://www.tigerpawsoftware.com"

Open "c:\tigerpawsource.txt" For Output As #intFile
```

Internet
Applications

```
Write #intFile, Inet1.OpenURL(strURL)

Close #intFile
```

Retrieving data from an FTP server using the Execute method

Although simple to use, the OpenURL doesn't give you much control over a download, and it processes synchronously. For more control over a download, or to download a file asynchronously, use the Execute method. For instance, FTP servers offer more functionality than simply downloading files, and the Execute method can be used to exploit this additional functionality.

There are a number of errors in the rather sparse documentation on the Internet Transfer control. First, the constant `icResolvingHost` discussed shortly is incorrectly documented as `icHostResolving-Host`. Although this is a minor annoyance, there is an even larger inaccuracy. The documentation incorrectly states that you must use the GetChunk method to retrieve data from a file on an FTP server initiated using the Execute method. This is wrong. However, you do have to use GetChunk when downloading data from an HTTP server. This text will attempt to show you how Microsoft says the Execute method works, as well as how it really works.

Logging on to FTP servers. In order to access an FTP server and retrieve information using the Execute method, you must log onto the FTP server; all FTP servers expect a username and password. There are basically two types of FTP servers: public and private. *Private servers* expect a user to be a legitimate, registered user of the server, and as such they expect a registered username and corresponding password. *Public servers*, on the other hand, can be logged onto by anyone.

It's customary to log on to a public server with the username "anonymous," supplying your email address as a password. Fortunately, the Internet Transfer control simplifies things by automatically supplying this information when you log onto a public server. When logging onto a private server, however, you must supply a valid username and password, using the UserName and Password properties of the Internet Transfer control, like this:

```
With Inet1
     .URL = "ftp://ftp.anFTPSite.com"
     .UserName = "Your Name"
     .Password = "Your Password"
End With
```

The order in which you set the properties is important; changing the URL clears the UserName and Password properties.

You can set these properties (if you so desire) when logging onto a public server by using code similar to this:

```
With Inet1
    .URL = "ftp://ftp.anFTPSite.com"
    .UserName = "anonymous"
    .Password = "myaddres@somewhere.com"
End With
```

Once you connect to an FTP site by setting the URL property or by using the Execute method (discussed shortly), the Internet Transfer control remains connected to that site until you set the URL property to a different address, invoke the OpenURL method, or invoke the Execute method with the CLOSE operation.

Downloading data using the Execute method. The versatile Execute method has the following syntax:

```
ITCObject.Execute [url], [operation], [data], [requestHeaders]
```

All of the parameters of the Execute method are officially optional, but, in fact, at least one of the parameters is always required when invoking the method. Furthermore, FTP operations use only *url* and *operation*. You'll use the *data* and *requestHeaders* parameters only when accessing HTTP servers. Table 8-9 explains the syntax of the Execute method.

Table 8-9: Parameters of the Execute Method

Parameters	Description
url	Optional. String specifying the URL to which the control should connect. If no URL is specified, the URL designated in the URL property is used.
operation	Optional. String specifying the type of operation to occur. The possible settings for operation are GET, HEAD, POST, and PUT. These are discussed later in this chapter.
data	Optional. String specifying the data for operation.
requestHeaders	Optional. String specifying additional headers to be sent from the remote server. The format for these are: header name: header value vbCrLf.

To download a file from an FTP server using the Execute method, you use the GET operation. The GET operation has the following format:

```
GET file1 file2
```

The *file1* parameter is the file to download from the FTP server, and *file2* is the name and path of the file to save on the local machine. For example, the following statement downloads a file called *disclaim.txt* from the FTP server *ftp://ftp.microsoft.com* and saves it as *d:\disclaim.txt*:

```
Inet1.Execute "ftp://ftp.microsoft.com/", _
    "GET disclaim.txt D:\disclaim.txt"
```

The URL can be specified as an argument or designated in the URL property. For example, you could perform the same operation with this code:

```
Inet1.URL = "ftp://ftp.microsoft.com/"
Inet1.Execute , "GET disclaim.txt D:\disclaim.txt"
```

Direct FTP connections using the Execute method are disallowed when using CERN proxy servers. In such a case, use the OpenURL method to retrieve a file from the server.

Navigating FTP servers using the Execute method. The FTP protocol was primarily designed for use with Unix machines and has been around for some time. Before there were web browsers and FTP browsers, you had to type all of your commands at a prompt similar to a DOS prompt. The Execute method lets you use a command set similar to the one you would use if you were navigating the FTP site using a command prompt. Table 8-10 lists the available Execute operations.

Table 8-10: FTP Server Execute Operations

Operation	Description
`CD file1`	Change Directory. Changes to the directory specified in *file1*. For example: `Inet1.Execute , "CD apps\graphics"`
`CDUP`	Change to Parent. Same as "CD .." For example: `Inet1.Execute , "CDUP"`
`CLOSE`	Closes the current FTP connection. For example: `Inet1.Execute , "CLOSE"`
`DELETE file1`	Deletes the file specified in *file1*. For example: `Inet1.Execute , "DELETE Oldfile.txt"`
`DIR [file1]`	Searches the directory specified in *file1*. If *file1* isn't supplied, the current working directory is searched. Use the GetChunk method to return the data. For example: `Inet1.Execute , "DIR /docs"`

`GET file1 file2`	Retrieves the remote file specified in *file1*, and creates a new local file specified in *file2*. For example:
	`Inet1.Execute , "GET getfile.txt _`
	`C:\savefile.txt"`

`LS file1`	List. Searches the directory specified in *file1*.
`MKDIR file1`	Creates a directory as specified in *file1*. Success is dependent on user privileges on the remote host. For example: `Inet1.Execute , "MKDIR /myDir"`
`PUT file1 file2`	Copies a local file specified in *file1* to the remote host specified in *file2*. For example: `Inet1.Execute , "PUT C:\local.txt /server.txt"`
`PWD`	Print Working Directory. Returns the current directory name. Use the GetChunk method to return the data. For example: `Inet1.Execute , "PWD"`
`QUIT`	Terminate the current connection. For example: `Inet1.Execute , "QUIT"`
`RECV file1 file2`	Same as GET. For example: `Inet1.Execute , "RECV getme.txt C:\gotme.txt"`
`RENAME file1 file2`	Renames a file. Success is dependent on user privileges on the remote host. For example: `Inet1.Execute , "RENAME old.txt new.txt"`
`RMDIR file1`	Remove directory. Success is dependent on user privileges on the remote host. For example: `Inet1.Execute , "RMDIR oldDir"`

Table 8-10: FTP Server Execute Operations (continued)

Operation	Description
SEND file1	Copies a file to the FTP site (same as PUT). `Inet1.Execute , "SEND C:\putme.txt /putme.txt"`
SIZE file1	Returns the size of the file specified in *file1*. For example: `Inet1.Execute "SIZE /largefile.txt"`

Retrieving data from an HTTP server using the Execute method

Downloading data from an HTTP server using the Execute method of the Internet Transfer is a little more complex than downloading from an FTP server. When downloading from an HTTP server, the Internet Transfer control doesn't do all of the work of saving the file to your local drive like it does when downloading files from an FTP server. Instead, you must use the StateChanged event of the Internet Transfer control in conjunction with the GetChunk method to retrieve the file from the server, and then save the file using Visual Basic's standard file statements.

The GET operation is used to initiate a download from an HTTP server. The GET operator has the following syntax:

```
Inet1.Execute url, "GET"
```

Unlike the GET operation used with FTP servers, *url* must actually point to the data file you want to retrieve. Furthermore, you don't specify any file parameters after the GET operation.

For example, to download a file from an HTTP server using the Execute method, you could use the GET operation, like this:

```
Inet1.Execute "http://www.tigerpawsoftware.com/tps.htm", "GET"
```

As stated previously, downloading files using the Execute method occurs asynchronously; that is, a request is made of the server to prepare to send the data, and then your application continues code execution. When the request is processed, the Internet Transfer control receives a response from the server and fires its StateChanged event. The StateChanged event is where you place code to retrieve the data and write it to a local file.

Actually, the StateChanged event is fired any time the state of the Internet Transfer control changes. The StateChanged event includes a *State* parameter that informs you of the new state of the control. Table 8-11 lists the *State* parameter values and their associated constants.

Table 8-11: Constants for the State Parameter of the StateChanged Event

Constant	Value	Description
icNone	0	No state to report.
icResolvingHost	1	The control is looking up the IP address of the specified host computer.
icHostResolved	2	The control successfully found the IP address of the specified host computer.
icConnecting	3	The control is connecting to the host computer.

Table 8-11: Constants for the State Parameter of the StateChanged Event (continued)

Constant	Value	Description
icConnected	4	The control successfully connected to the host computer.
icRequesting	5	The control is sending a request to the host computer.
icRequestSent	6	The control successfully sent the request.
icReceivingResponse	7	The control is receiving a response from the host computer.
icResponseReceived	8	The control successfully received a response from the host computer.
icDisconnecting	9	The control is disconnecting from the host computer.
icDisconnected	10	The control successfully disconnected from the host computer.
icError	11	An error occurred in communicating with the host computer.
icResponseCompleted	12	The request has completed and all data has been received.

 The Visual Basic documentation incorrectly lists the `icResolving-Host` constant as `icHostResolvingHost`. If you attempt to use this incorrect constant, you will receive a compile error.

A typical file transfer request using the line of code:

```
Inet1.Execute "http://www.tigerpawsoftware.com/tps.htm", "GET"
```

results in the following sequence of StateChanged events:

Value	Constant Name
1	icResolvingHost
2	icHostResolved
3	icConnecting
4	icConnected
5	icRequesting
6	icRequestSent
7	icReceivingResponse
8	icResponseReceived
11	icError
12	icResponseCompleted

Requesting data from an HTTP server is not the same as receiving it, and therefore the *State* that you're interested in when downloading files is icResponseCompleted (12). When an HTTP server receives a request for a data transfer, it prepares the data and then informs the Internet Transfer control that the data is ready to be sent via the `icResponseCompleted` state change. It's here that you receive the data and write it to the local disk. Once the `icResponse-Completed` state is achieved, you retrieve the data in pieces using the GetChunk method.

 The `icResponseReceived` state can occur when the control has completed an operation that hasn't resulted in any data in the buffer. For example, when connecting to an FTP site, the control will perform a "handshake" with the site that doesn't result in any data transfer, yet the `icResponseReceived` state will occur.

The GetChunk method has the following syntax:

```
InetControl.GetChunk( size [,datatype] )
```

The *size* parameter determines the number of bytes to retrieve at a time. (The *datatype* parameter is discussed earlier, in the section "Retrieving Data Using the OpenURL Method.") The value 1,024 is usually sufficient, but if you have a slow or unreliable connection you may want to use a smaller number. Likewise, if you have an extremely fast connection, you may want to increase the size.

You'll need to invoke the GetChunk method several times to download most files. When GetChunk doesn't return any data, it's finished receiving the file. Use GetChunk in conjunction with a loop to retrieve all of the data, and as you retrieve the data, write it to a binary file using the Put statement. The following procedure shows an example of combining all of these elements to retrieve a text file and save it on the local machine:

```
Private Sub Inet1_StateChanged(ByVal State As Integer)
    Dim varData As Variant
    Dim intFile As Integer

    If State = icResponseCompleted Then
        ' Open a file to write to.

        intFile = FreeFile()
        Open "D:\sb.htm" For Binary Access Write As #intFile

        varData = Inet1.GetChunk(1024, icString)

        Do While LenB(varData) > 0
            Put #intFile, , varData
            ' Get next chunk.
            varData = Inet1.GetChunk(1024, icString)
        Loop

        Put #intFile, , varData

        Close #intFile

    End If

End Sub
```

This code uses the constant icString to instruct the GetChunk method to retrieve the data as a string. To download binary files, use the constant icByteArray instead.

The GET operation isn't the only operation supported by HTTP servers. Table 8-12 lists the available operations for use with the Execute method on HTTP servers.

 In the examples shown in Table 8-12, all operations other than GET assume a URL has already been specified using the URL property of the Internet Transfer control.

Table 8-12: Execute Operations for Working with HTTP Servers

Operation	Description

GET	Retrieves the file named in *url*. For example:
	`Inet1.Execute _`
	`"http://www.microsoft.com/default.htm", "GET"`

HEAD	Retrieves only the headers of the file named in the URL property. For example: `Inet1.Execute , "HEAD"`
POST	Provides additional data to support a request to the remote host. For example: `Inet1.Execute , "POST", strFormData`
PUT	Replaces data at the specified URL. For example: `Inet1.Execute , "PUT", "replace.htm"`

Setting the RequestTimeout property

The Internet Transfer control includes the RequestTimeout property, which you can set to determine how long the control will wait to receive a response from a server after making a request using OpenURL or Execute. The value of this property is the number of seconds to wait. For example, the default value is 60 seconds. If you were to use the OpenURL method with this default setting, the Internet Transfer control will wait 60 seconds before it stops trying. If you have latency issues (e.g., you receive a lot of timeout errors), you may need to increase this value in order to successfully access a server. If the OpenURL method times out, a runtime error occurs. If the Execute method times out, the StateChanged event fires with an error code (icError).

Determining errors encountered using the Execute method

When the Execute method results in an error, no Visual Basic runtime error occurs because the Internet Transfer control handles the error. However, you are notified of the error in the StateChanged event by the return value icError. When this happens, you can obtain information about the error by using the ResponseCode and ResponseInfo properties of the Internet Transfer control. The ResponseCode property gives you the actual error code returned by the server you attempted to access, while the ResponseInfo property gives you the actual text of the error message.

Not every application needs integrated file transfer capability. With a little imagination, you might find a number of possible uses for the control, including enabling an application to automatically retrieve software updates from your web site, or polling a site for stock quotes. If you elect to add such functionality to your applications, the Internet Transfer control greatly simplifies the process.

Using the Winsock Control

The Winsock control is yet another ActiveX control provided with Visual Basic that allows you to easily add Internet functionality to your applications. Using the Winsock control, it's possible to write client and server applications that communicate back and forth over the Internet using the TCP or UDP protocols. Fortunately, you don't have to understand the details of the protocols; the Winsock control handles the mechanics for you.

To add the Winsock control to a project, select the Microsoft Winsock Control component on the Components dialog box.

Once you've added the Winsock control component to the project, you can place an instance of the control on any form. The Winsock control is invisible at runtime and appears as an icon at design time.

The Winsock control allows applications to communicate via *sockets*. You don't have to understand the technical details of sockets, but you should know the following three features of a socket:

- A socket has an interface to which it is bound. This is specified by an IP address.

- A socket has a port number or ID to which the socket will send data, or from which it will receive data.

- A socket has a specific type that determines the protocol of the control, and can be either *stream* or *datagram*. These are discussed in the following sections.

Selecting a Protocol for Data Transfer Using the Winsock Control

Although you don't need to understand much about the internals of the following protocols, you do need to have some basic knowledge of them.

Understanding the basics of TCP

Transfer control protocol (TCP) is used to create and maintain connections between computers. Once a TCP connection is established, both computers can transmit data to each other (called *streaming*). In order to establish a TCP connection, the client application must know:

- The IP address of the server

- The port on which that server will be listening

The IP address is set using the Winsock control's RemoteHost property, while the port is set using the RemotePort property. Once these two properties have been set, the Connect method is used to initiate a connection.

On the server side:

1. The server application listens for connection requests on a port. The port that the Winsock control listens on is designated by the LocalPort property of the Winsock control.

2. Once the LocalPort property is set, the server is placed into listen mode by invoking the Listen method.

3. Incoming requests for a connection on the designated port cause the Winsock's ConnectionRequest event to fire.

4. The request is accepted and the connection completed by invoking the Accept method of the Winsock control in the ConnectionRequest event.

Once a connection is established, a combination of two methods and one event are used to send and receive data between the applications. To transmit data, an application uses the SendData method. When the application on the other end of the connection receives notice of the data transfer, the Winsock control at the receiving side fires its DataArrival event. Within this event, the GetData method is called to retrieve the data.

Understanding the basics of UDP

User datagram protocol (UDP) is a connectionless protocol used to allow two applications to communicate, with either application being able to act as client or server. Unlike TCP, the UDP connection does not establish and maintain a connection between two computers.

In practice, the use of UDP is similar to that of TCP. First, one application sets the LocalPort property of the Winsock control to the port through which communication is to occur. The other application sets the RemoteHost property of its Winsock control to the Internet address of the first computer, and then sets the RemotePort property of its Winsock control to the same value as the LocalPort property of the first computer.

Values match up as follows:

Computer #1	Computer #2
(IP Address)	RemoteHost
LocalPort	RemotePort
RemoteHost	(IP Address)
RemotePort	LocalPort

After the LocalPort and RemoteHost properties are set, the SendData and GetData methods are used, in conjunction with the DataArrival event, just as they are with TCP to transmit data.

Microsoft's Visual Basic documentation gives the following information to help clarify the difference between the two protocols:

- TCP is a connection-based protocol, and is analogous to a telephone in that the user must establish a connection before proceeding.

- UDP is a connectionless protocol, and is analogous to passing a note: a message is sent from one computer to another, but there is no explicit connection between the two. The maximum data size of individual messages is determined by the network.

The following are guidelines for determining which protocol is most suited for an application:

- If the application requires acknowledgment from the server or client that data has been sent or received, TCP may be a better choice because it requires an explicit connection before sending or receiving data.

- If the data is extremely large (such as image or sound files), TCP may be the best choice because it maintains a connection and ensures the integrity of the data. This connection, however, uses more computing resources than the UDP does.

- If the data will be sent intermittently, rather than in one session, UDP may be the better choice because a connection is not maintained. In addition, UDP is more suited to sending small amounts of data.

Setting the protocol of the Winsock control: TCP or UDP

Setting the Winsock control connection is performed by setting the Protocol property to either sckTCPProtocol or sckUDPProtocol, using the following code:

```
Winsock1.Protocol = sckTCPProtocol
```

Specifying a RemoteHost Property

The RemoteHost property is used to designate either the IP address or the "friendly name" of the remote computer with which you want an application to communicate. The IP address of a computer appears as a series of three-digit numbers separated by periods, like this:

```
###.###.###.###
```

It's much easier to remember the friendly name of a computer, so that's the setting most often used.

To determine the friendly name of a computer, follow these steps:

1. On the Taskbar of the computer, click Start.
2. Choose Control Panel from the Settings menu.
3. Double-click the Network icon.
4. Click the Identification tab.
5. The name of the computer is found in the "Computer name" field (see Figure 8-4).

Figure 8-4: The Identification tab of the Network dialog box contains the computer's name

 There are two types of IP addresses: static and dynamic. *Dynamic addresses* are IP addresses assigned to a computer when it connects to the Internet. Each time a computer using a dynamic IP address connects to the Internet, it's assigned a different IP address. *Static IP addresses* are registered and assigned to one specific computer; each time that computer connects to the Internet, it always has the same IP address. The only way to use a computer's name, rather than its IP address, is if the computer has a registered, static IP address.

To use this information to connect to a remote computer, supply the computer's name in the RemoteHost property.

Creating a Winsock Application Using TCP

When creating applications that communicate using the TCP protocol, one application must be written as a client, the other as a server. Client applications initiate connections, while server applications listen on a designated port for a client to request a connection. Once the connection between client and server is complete, both applications can send and receive data.

The basic sequence of a TCP connection is:

1. The client application requests a connection with the server.

2. The server receives the connection request and accepts it (or rejects it).

3. Each application sends data to the other as necessary.

Requesting a TCP connection

To request a TCP connection, a client must follow these three steps:

1. Set the RemoteHost property to the name of the host with which the client will communicate.

2. Set the RemotePort property to the port on the host through which the client will communicate with the host.

3. Invoke the Connect method to initiate a connection between the client and the host.

The following code illustrates this sequence:

```
With tcpClient
    .RemoteHost = "RemoteComputerName"
    .RemotePort = 1001
    .Connect
End With
```

Accepting a TCP connection request

When the server application receives the connection request, its Connection-Request event is fired. The ConnectionRequest event passes as a parameter a *requestID*. To accept the request and complete the connection, the server application need only invoke the Accept method of the Winsock control, passing it the *requestID* (sample code appears later in this chapter).

Since the Winsock control may already be connected to a client, it's advisable to check the state of the control and terminate any existing connection before accepting the new request. If there is an existing connection, the State property returns a value other than sckClosed. (Handling multiple connections is covered later in the chapter.)

To clarify, all points discussed previously are outlined here in the order in which they occur:

1. The Protocol property is set to the protocol that the server will use when communicating with clients.

2. The LocalPort property is set to the port that the server will use when communicating with clients.

3. The Listen method is invoked to place the control in "listen" mode.

4. The ConnectionRequest event occurs when a connection request is received. The application can accept or reject the request in this event. The following procedure shows how a server might cancel a previous connection and accept an incoming connection request:

```
Private Sub tcpServer_ConnectionRequest(ByVal requestID As Long)

    If tcpServer.State <> sckClosed Then
        tcpServer.Close
    End If

    tcpServer.Accept requestID

End Sub
```

If the server doesn't accept the request in the ConnectionRequest event, the Winsock control in the client application fires its Close event. The client may then decide to attempt a connection again, notify the user that the connection attempt failed, or take any other course of action it deems necessary.

Sending and receiving data using a TCP connection

Once the TCP connection is established, either side (the client or server) may send data at any time. Data is sent via the SendData method of the Winsock control. The SendData method has the following syntax:

```
WinsockControl.SendData data
```

The *data* parameter is the actual data to send.

 Use a byte array when sending binary data.

When an application is notified that data has been sent to it, the DataArrival event of the Winsock control occurs. Within the DataArrival event, the GetData method is used to retrieve the data.

The GetData method has the following syntax:

```
WinsockControl.GetData data, [type,] [maxLen]
```

The *data* parameter defines where the retrieved data is to be stored. The *type* parameter is an optional parameter that lets you indicate a specific type of data to retrieve. The possible values for *type* are:

Description	Constant
Byte	vbByte
Integer	vbInteger
Long	vbLong
Single	vbSingle
Double	vbDouble
Currency	vbCurrency
Date	vbDate
Boolean	vbBoolean
SCODE	vbError
String	vbString
Byte array	vbArray + vbByte

The *maxLen* parameter is used to specify the desired size when receiving a byte array or a string. If this parameter is missing for a *type* of byte array or string, all available data is retrieved. This parameter is ignored when retrieving data other than a byte array or string.

If you specify a *maxLen* that is less than the *bytesTotal* value that is passed to the DataArrival event procedure as an argument, you'll get a warning indicating that the remaining bytes will be lost.

The following example illustrates using the DataArrival event:

```
Private Sub Winsock1_DataArrival(ByVal bytesTotal As Long)
    Dim strData As String

    Winsock1.GetData strData

End Sub
```

The application that initially sent the data can keep tabs on the transmission process, using two events: the SendProgress event and the SendComplete event. The SendProgress event occurs when data is being sent, and it has the following syntax:

```
Winsock1_SendProgress(bytesSent As Long, bytesRemaining As Long)
```

The SendComplete event occurs when a send operation is finished. The SendComplete event has the following syntax:

```
Winsock1_SendComplete()
```

Accepting multiple connection requests

An application can accept multiple connection requests by creating a Winsock control array. When using a Winsock control array, you don't need to close any previous connection. Instead, if a previous connection is in place, create a new instance of the Winsock control (add one instance to the control array) and invoke the Accept method on the new instance.

Consider the following example:

1. One Winsock control has been added to a form and its index has been set to 0 to make it part of a control array.

2. A variable called *intLastControl* is created and initialized to 0, the index of the first Winsock control.

3. The LocalPort property is set for the Winsock control, and the Listen method is invoked.

4. The first Winsock control is always used as the listening control. When a connection request is received, the following occurs:

    a. The *intLastControl* variable is increased by 1.

    b. The listening control loads a new Winsock control in the control array.

    c. The LocalPort property of the new Winsock control is set to 0, so it will not receive connection requests.

    d. The Accept method of the new control is triggered so that the new control handles the new request.

The Index property is always checked in the ConnectionRequest method so that only requests to the original port (Winsock control with index 0) are handled. This is accomplished using code such as this:

```
Private intLastControl As Integer

Private Sub Form_Load()
    ' Initialize Winsock Array
    intLastControl = 0

    With Winsock1(0)
        .LocalPort = 1001
        .Listen
    End With
End Sub

Private Sub Winsock1_ConnectionRequest (Index As Integer, ByVal requestID
As Long)

    If Index = 0 Then
            intLastControl = intLastControl + 1

            Load Winsock1(intLastControl)

            Winsock1(intLastControl).LocalPort = 0
            Winsock1(intLastControl).Accept requestID
    End If

End Sub
```

Creating a Winsock Application Using UDP

Although creating a TCP connection isn't very difficult, creating a UDP application is even easier. With TCP communications, one application must be written as a server and must continuously "listen" for connection requests. The other application, the client application, must be written differently so that it makes requests for a connection.

Applications communicating using UDP do not use a continuous connection, and often the same application is used on both sides of the communication. Instead, sending data between applications using the UDP protocol requires that the following three steps be performed on both computers:

1. The RemoteHost property of the Winsock control must be set to the name or IP address of the other computer.

2. The RemotePort property must be set to the LocalPort property of the other computer.

3. The Bind method must be invoked, specifying which LocalPort is to be used. The Bind method is discussed later in this section.

UDP applications are not client/server applications; they are peer-to-peer applications. Each peer is created much like the other. The most common application of the UDP protocol is the construction of chat applications. Both sides of a peer-to-peer chat application are usually identical; there is no client or server.

The Bind method is used to set the LocalPort of the Winsock control; for this, you need to use the Bind method instead of setting the LocalPort property. This ensures that the proper port is used on systems with multiple network adapters. The Bind method has the following syntax:

```
WinsockControl.Bind LocalPort, [LocalIP]
```

The *LocalPort* parameter is self-explanatory. The optional *LocalIP* argument allows you to specify a specific network adapter on computers with more than one adapter present. When omitted, the Winsock control uses the first network adapter listed in the Network Control Panel dialog box.

 Only when using UDP can you freely switch the RemoteHost and RemotePort properties while remaining bound to the same LocalPort. When using TCP, you must close the connection prior to changing these properties.

The following steps illustrate how two fictitious applications could communicate using UDP. Assume that there's a central application on a server that reports stock information that needs to notify an application residing on a user's computer when a stock's value changes by a specified amount. Since a stock's value may change many times throughout the day, a connection-based protocol such as TCP is undesirable. Instead, UDP is used so that the central application can "broadcast" a notification of the change in the stock's price.

1. The central application monitors the stock's price.

2. When the price reaches a designated point, the application running on the stock server must notify the application residing on a different computer. First, the central application must set its Winsock control's RemoteHost property to the IP address of the user's computer.

3. Once the RemoteHost property is set, the central application must set its RemotePort property to the value of the LocalPort property of the user's application.

4. The central server then binds to its local port by invoking the Bind method of the Winsock control.

5. Once the Bind method is invoked, the central application can send the stock update at any time by using the SendData method.

6. In order for the user's application to receive notifications, it must have its LocalPort property set and be in Listen mode.

7. When the user's application receives a notification, its DataArrival event occurs.

8. The user's application could be designed to send data back to the central application. To do this, the RemoteHost and RemotePort properties of the user's application would need to be set to the IP address and LocalPort properties of the central application, and the central application would also need to be placed in listen mode.

This section on the Winsock control concludes the discussion on the ways you can integrate Internet functionality directly into your applications using pre-built components. The next section discusses using the new development features of Visual Basic 6 to create web components.

Creating Dynamic Web Pages Using DHTML

When creating Internet applications, a number of options are available to you. You can create custom applications using the Internet controls, but this requires a lot of special coding. Perhaps the biggest disadvantage of creating custom applications is that they don't run in a browser or browser control. You could create ActiveX controls or documents for embedding on a web page, but there are drawbacks to these types of components. You could use hypertext markup language (HTML) to create web pages, but HTML isn't as advanced as most of today's languages. As a result, there have been a number of developments in Internet languages, such as VBScript and Java.

HTML itself is evolving, and as a result we now have Dynamic HTML, or DHTML, and Visual Basic 6 allows you to create DHTML applications. Microsoft defines DHTML as:

> A set of innovative additions to HTML that allows page authors and developers to dynamically change the style and attributes of elements on an HTML page, as well as insert, delete, or modify elements and their text after a page has been loaded. Included as part of Internet Explorer 4.x.

If we were talking about a Visual Basic form here, I'm sure the response would be "Big deal." However, for a web page, this is powerful stuff. Creating DHTML applications, as opposed to other types of Internet applications, has the following advantages:

- The ability to leverage your Visual Basic skills to harness the power of DHTML.

- The amount of server resources used are reduced because not all actions and requests need to be routed through the server.

- The browser is able to create web pages by processing data, making changes to a page's appearance, and process code. Since the server doesn't have to provide all of this functionality, web pages refresh faster.

- Web pages are dynamic, capable of processing code and user input to alter their appearances.

- DHTML pages can be used from the browser's cache, making offline interaction possible.

- DHTML applications are compiled applications, and therefore DHTML code that you write isn't visible in the web page as it is when the page is created with a scripting language.

DHTML is primarily designed for intranets and requires that the browser used to access the DHTML pages be Internet Explorer 4.0 or later.

 Web browsers are multithreaded clients, and DHTML applications must be multithreaded as well. Refer to Chapter 4 for information on threading.

Planning a DHTML Web Page

Your DHTML application should follow accepted guidelines for web pages, as opposed to guidelines for applications, and you may want to put down your copy of *The Windows Interface Guidelines for Software Design* in favor of an HTML style reference. Although you might be a fantastic GUI designer of Windows applications, the rules are different for DHTML pages. For instance, connection speeds can vary drastically for different users. If you've got a cable modem, you probably enjoy visually exciting pages. However, if you're still connecting using a 14.4 modem, the same types of pages may cause you endless frustration. Some users choose to turn off pictures completely to avoid the painful load times of visual web pages. Your DHTML pages need to be able to handle this. If your only navigation mechanism is the use of pictures, you'll alienate some users.

 You can't always know the final destination of a DHTML page. Hard-coding URL paths in your application can cause devastating results. When you hard code a path such as *C:\MyPages\MyFile.txt*, you risk the code failing when the designated file or path doesn't exist at run-time. By using relative paths, you make your application distribution friendly. Remember, the location where a DHTML application is planned to be hosted tomorrow may not be where it's hosted a month from now. Save yourself future headaches and use relative paths.

Recall from earlier in this chapter that when a file downloads synchronously, everything halts while the file is being downloaded. When a file is downloaded asynchronously, however, code continues to execute while the file is being downloaded. You can have DHTML pages download asynchronously, but this has the effect adding a certain randomness to the way a page is loaded and displayed. You can never be completely sure in what order components such as images and controls will download and display. It's very possible that some interface elements that rely on other elements existing will become available to a user, even before those elements have been downloaded and displayed. For instance, you may have code in the Click event of a control that attempts to retrieve the text of a text box. If the text box isn't loaded, the code will fail.

There are some things you can do to reduce these potential problems. First, every DHTML page has a property named AsyncLoad. Setting this property to False (the default) forces the browser to wait until all elements and code are downloaded and displayed *before* executing any of the page's code. When AsyncLoad is set to True, code starts executing as soon as all code is downloaded, regardless of the state of other elements of the page. The AsyncLoad property is a property of the HTML designer (discussed in the next section). To change the property, select the designer in the Project window and display its properties.

 If you want or need to use asynchronous loading of a DHTML page, be sure to use error trapping when referencing objects in code.

Creating a DHTML Application

A DHTML project is a project type, just like a standard EXE or ActiveX control is a project type. To create a new DHTML project, start Visual Basic and double-click the DHTML Application icon on the New Project dialog box.

Understanding the DHTML Page Designer

When a DHTML project is first created, a default DHTML Page Designer is added to the project as well as a modDHTML module. The modDHTML module is a template for creating code to use *cookies* from within your application. A cookie is a small package of data used to store persistent information on a user's computer. Using a cookie, you could store user identification and preferences on the user's computer, and retrieve the information using the cookie each time the user revisits your DHTML page. (Creating cookies is beyond the scope of the exams and this book.) The DHTML Page Designer, on the other hand, represents an individual web page; to add additional pages to a project, open the Project dropdown menu and select Add DHTML Page.

Saving web pages and DHTML designers

When you save a form in Visual Basic, a physical text file is created with the extension FRM. If the form has binary information, such as a picture placed in a picture box at design time, a binary file is created with the same name as the text file but with the extension FRX. The DHTML designer is used to create HTML web pages, which are documents external to Visual Basic itself. Since this situation is different from ordinary project files, the methods of working with designer files is different as well. You can save your HTML pages defined by a designer as a single file or set of files, or as a separate HTML file. Designer files are stored as text files with the extension DSR, and binary information is stored in a file with the same name but with the extension DSX.

The benefit of storing the HTML with the designer is that this behavior is very much like saving a form; if you need to move the project to another machine, you must move all of the project files for things to work smoothly. You can, however, elect to save the pages created by designers to HTML files on the hard disk. When you elect to save the HTML files rather than storing the pages with the designer, the following applies:

- The paths to the HTML files are stored as absolute paths. If you move the project to another computer, the paths to the HTML files may no longer be valid and will have to be changed.

- You can use an external HTML editor to manipulate the pages. When the pages are stored with the designer, you cannot use outside editors to modify them.

When you elect to save a page as a separate HTML file, you must specify either a path and filename for an existing HTML page, or designate a path and filename for a new HTML file. Specifying the method of saving an HTML page is done using the DHTML designer's properties.

Accessing the properties of the designer isn't an immediately intuitive process because they don't appear in the Properties window. To access the properties of a designer, open the designer and click the Properties button on the designer's toolbar.

The property that dictates the behavior of storing a page as an external file is SourceFile. When you set the SourceFile property to an existing HTML file (using the full path and filename), the source file is loaded into the DHTML designer for editing. If modifications are made directly to the HTML file using an external editor, those changes appear in the DHTML designer the next time the source file is loaded into the designer. Another way to access the SourceFile property is to click the Properties button on the designer's toolbar, which displays the property page shown in Figure 8-5. The benefit of using the property page is that when you click New or Open, a file dialog box is displayed, making it easier to locate an existing file. When using the Properties window, you must type in the full path and filename manually.

Visual Basic's DHTML designer is a powerful tool, but it may not do everything you need it to or do it in the way you'd like it to. There are a number of third-party HTML editing tools available. Some people even prefer to use Notepad to edit the HTML manually (masochists, I think). When a page is stored as an external HTML file, the DHTML designer can launch an external editor for you. Changes made to the HTML page in the external editor are reflected in the designer when the external editor saves the page. To launch an external editor, click the Launch Editor button on the designer's toolbar.

Placing controls on a DHTML document

Just as you can use controls to build an interface on a form, you can also use them to build an interface on an HTML page. However, the controls you can place on an HTML page are not the same set of controls you use with forms. Although

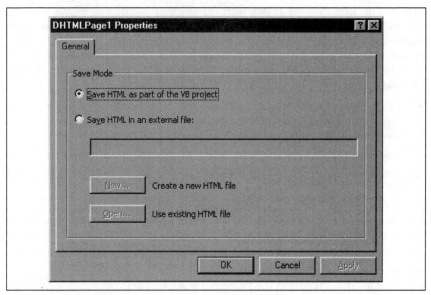

Figure 8-5: The DHTML designer's Properties dialog box makes it easy to save the page as an external HTML file

many of the HTML controls mimic the functionality of the standard controls, they aren't the same. Figure 8-6 shows the HTML toolbox, and Table 8-13 lists the available DHTML elements (controls).

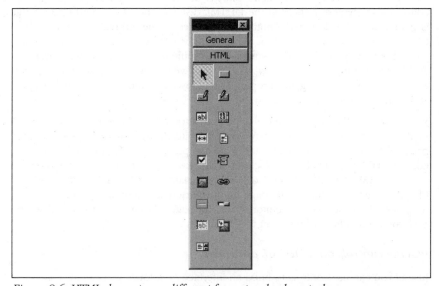

Figure 8-6: HTML elements are different from standard controls

Controls on an HTML page are referred to as HTML *elements*. Although they are not the same as the standard Visual Basic controls you place on a form, you can add ActiveX controls to a DHTML page just as you can to a form.

Table 8-13: DHTML Elements

Control	Description
Button	Similar to Visual Basic's command button.
Submit Button	Creates a button to be used to send commands to the server.
Reset Button	Creates a button to be used to clear the contents of a data entry form.
Text Field	Creates a single line text box.
Text Area	Creates a multi-line text box.
Password Field	Creates a text box with a password mask.
Option Button	Similar to Visual Basic's option button.
Checkbox	Similar to Visual Basic's checkbox.
Select	Similar to Visual Basic's combo box.
List	Similar to Visual Basic's list box.
Image	Similar to Visual Basic's image control.
Hyperlink	Creates hyperlink text on the page.
Horizontal Rule	Similar to Visual Basic's line control, but can only be used to create horizontal lines.
File Upload	Creates a text box and a button to be used to specify a file and upload that file to the server.
Hidden Field	Creates a hidden text box.
Input Image	Creates an image used for hotspot navigating. The image returns the coordinates of where the user clicks the image, which can be used to determine what page to browse to.

To make option buttons on a form mutually exclusive, you place them on the same container. To make HTML option buttons mutually exclusive, set their Name properties to the same value. When you assign the same name to multiple option buttons, you must assign a unique ID to each option button. (IDs are discussed in the next section.)

To add an element to an HTML designer, use the same techniques that you use to add controls to a form: either double-click the element's icon in the toolbox, or click once to select it and then draw the element on the designer. If you add an element that is invisible at runtime, such as the Common Dialog control, you cannot select it and move it on the page once it has been placed. To move such an element, select it in the tree view on the left of the designer, and edit its position properties or delete it altogether.

As you add elements, they are listed in the left pane of the designer in a tree view, while the page is displayed in the right pane. You can interact with the right pane, or you can select an element directly from the left pane.

Assigning element IDs

Each control on an ordinary form is assigned a unique name (except in the case of control arrays). With HTML elements, the ID property serves the same function. In order to add code behind an HTML element or to program an element from any procedure, the element must have an ID assigned to it. This is very different from how standard controls behave; the events behind a standard control are always available, but an HTML element can't respond to events unless it has a unique ID.

 Although Visual Basic requires that each element have a unique ID, DHTML outside of Visual Basic doesn't have the same restriction. If you import an HTML file from another source (by specifying a page in the SourceFile property of the designer) and there are multiple elements with the same ID, Visual Basic automatically appends a number to each duplicate ID so that each element ID is unique.

Creating element events

To add code to an element's events, double-click the element in the DHTML designer just as you would double-click a control on a form. If you haven't speci-fied a unique ID for the element you double-click, the code window won't display.

Changing element properties using code

Elements are referenced differently than standard controls. For instance, to retrieve the user input of a standard text box, you reference the text box's Text property. However, to reference the user input of an HTML text field element, you refer-ence the Value property. For example, to display the contents of a text field element with the ID *tfUserName*, you could use a code statement like this:

```
MsgBox(Me.tfUserName.Value)
```

 As with forms, using the keyword Me references the top-level parent of all of the elements. When used in code behind a form, Me refers to the form itself. When used in code behind an HTML element, Me refers to the HTML page. Me is not required, but you can use it if you wish.

Using this convention, you can manipulate HTML elements much as you do stan-dard controls. However, many HTML elements have formatting (styles) not found in standard controls.

Dynamically changing the content and style of a text element. Visual Basic makes it easy to change displayed text (both content and style) by exposing properties. For instance, to change the text displayed in a text box, you alter the text box's Text property. To change the text in a label, you alter the label's Caption property. For both the text box and the label, changing the style of the text is handled by changing the Font property, the ForeColor property, or both.

With HTML pages, it's not so simple. Although you use elements to create text on a page, and elements are similar to controls, they are very different when it comes to how they're processed in the final output. For instance, although you can't change the color of pieces of paragraph text using the page designer in Visual Basic, you can easily do this using an external HTML editor.

An HTML source document is more a stream of information than a collection of objects. The browser takes the stream of information (the source HTML) and creates a set of objects that are displayed to the viewer. In some ways, paragraph text in an HTML page is similar to text in an RTF (Rich Text Format) document in that many different pieces of the same paragraph can be formatted in many different ways. Obviously, if you want to change specific words or alter the style of a piece of paragraph text, simply setting a property is not an option.

When you change the text within an HTML page, the following options are available:

- You can exchange a portion of text with new text that is straight text, with no formatting information.

- You can exchange a portion of text with new text that contains formatting information.

In addition to replacing text, you can elect to keep or replace existing formatting information.

The format of HTML information is dictated by the *tags* within the HTML text. In order to program an element (i.e., change its attributes at runtime), the element must have a unique ID. Elements that have an ID assigned to them are denoted in the HTML with a tag containing the ID.

Internet Applications

The following is a simple example of a line of HTML code. The tags are shown in bold:

`<p id="parAlbumTitle">`Atom Heart Mother**`</p>`**

Tags are enclosed in darts (<>); the darts are considered part of the tag. The tag <p> is used to denote a paragraph. The start of the paragraph is the first appearance of the <p>, while the </p> tag denotes the end of the paragraph. The id is the ID assigned to the paragraph object. Since the object has a unique ID, it can be manipulated using Visual Basic code.

To alter the contents of an element's text, you use the InnerText and InnerHTML properties. InnerText allows you to change text in an element without adding additional formatting. Anything you provide as the replacement text will be taken as literal text. InnerHTML is used to replace text with additional HTML formatting tags. Since tags have to appear in the HTML text in a particular order, Visual Basic has to parse the original HTML and the newly supplied formatted text and replace the formatting in the HTML document as appropriate. This merging of tags occurs automatically when you use InnerHTML. Table 8-14 and Table 8-15 describe the use of InnerText and InnerHTML, and the effect each has on the same HTML element.

Table 8-14: The Effects of InnerText on an HTML Element

Description	Effects of InnerText
Original HTML	`<p id="parAlbumTitle">Atom Heart Mother</p>`
InnerText Statement	`parAlbumTitle.InnerText= _` `"Dark Side of the Moon"`
New HTML Result	`<p id="parAlbumTitle"> _` `Dark Side of the Moon</p>`
Element Appears as	`Dark Side of the Moon`

Table 8-15: The Effects of InnerHTML on an HTML Element

Description	Effects of InnerHTML
Original HTML	`<p id="parAlbumTitle">Atom Heart Mother</p>`
InnerHTML Statement	`parAlbumTitle.InnerHTML=" _` `<b>Dark Side of the Moon</b>"`
New HTML Result	`<p id="parAlbumTitle"><b> _` `Dark Side of the Moon</b></p>`
Element Appears as	`Dark Side of the Moon`

InnerText and InnerHTML let you replace text between two tags with either straight text or formatted text. If you want to replace text *and the tags surrounding the text*, use OuterText and OuterHTML. OuterText replaces the text *and* the tags of the specified element with straight text. OuterHTML replaces the text *and* the tags of an element with new text and formatting tags. Table 8-16 and Table 8-17 illustrate OuterText and OuterHTML.

Table 8-16: The Effects of OuterText on an HTML Element

Description	Effects of OuterText
Original HTML	`<p id="parAlbumTitle"><b> _` `Atom Heart Mother</b></p>`
OuterText Statement	`parAlbumTitle.OuterText= "Dark Side of the Moon"`
New HTML Result	`Dark Side of the Moon`
Element Appears as	`Dark Side of the Moon` ·

Table 8-17: The Effects of OuterHTML on an HTML Element

Description	Effects of OuterHTML
Original HTML	`<p id="parAlbumTitle"><b> _` `Atom Heart Mother</b></p>`
OuterHTML Statement	`parAlbumTitle.OuterHTML= _` `"<i>Dark Side of the Moon</i>"` ·
New HTML Result	`<i>Dark Side of the Moon</i>`
Element Appears as	`Dark Side of the Moon`

Table 8-18 helps further clarify how Visual Basic handles InnerText versus InnerHTML and OuterText versus OuterHTML.

Table 8-18: InnerText versus InnerHTML

Description	HTML and Final Appearance
Original HTML	`<p id="parAlbumTitle">Atom Heart Mother</p>`
InnerText Statement	`parAlbumTitle.InnerText= _` `"<i>Dark Side of the Moon</i>"`
Element Appears as	`<i>Dark Side of the Moon</i>`

In Table 8-18, the element text appears with the <i> and </i> tags as literal text characters because InnertText was used rather than InnertHTML. If InnerHTML had been used, the HTML tags would have been parsed and added to the existing tags of the element. The final result would have been:

`Dark Side of the Moon`

Bubbling events

Event bubbling is definitely a feature new to most Visual Basic programmers. In standard Visual Basic projects, every object has its own event handler. Although it's possible to create control arrays to share events among a set of objects, you can't share events among different types of objects. In DHTML applications, events are passed from the object firing the event all the way up the hierarchy of the page until it finds a defined event handler to handle it or until it reaches the topmost object, the Document object. This event processing is known as *event bubbling* and is illustrated in Figure 8-7.

Event bubbling allows you to write applications requiring less code. For example, you may want to perform some action whenever the user clicks on any object. In an ordinary application, you would have to write code in the Click event of every

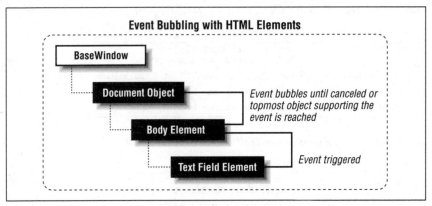

Figure 8-7: Events bubble until the topmost object supporting the event is reached or the bubbling is canceled

object in order to accomplish this. In DHTML, you could let the OnClick events bubble up to the BaseWindow object and handle them there using one event procedure.

 Not all events bubble all the way to the BaseWindow (the topmost object in the DHTML hierarchy). For instance, the BaseWindow object doesn't have an OnMouseDown event, so the OnMouse-Down event won't bubble to the BaseWindow object.

Just because an event handler is found to handle an event doesn't mean the event stops bubbling. In order to stop the event from bubbling, the cancelBubble property of the Event object must be set to **True**. The Event object is an object property of the BaseWindow object. The BaseWindow object represents an instance of the browser and is the topmost object in the DHTML hierarchy. For example, to cancel the bubbling of the OnClick event of a button element, you could use code such as the following:

```
Private Function Button1_onclick() As Boolean

    BaseWindow.event.cancelBubble = True

End Function
```

Setting cancelBubble to **True** stops only the current event, not subsequent events, from bubbling. Event bubbling is the default behavior, so you'll need to cancel the bubbling of events at the levels you choose.

Working with dynamic styles

If you changed an element's style in ordinary HTML, it was often necessary to refresh the entire page in order to see the changes, and many style attributes weren't even editable. With DHTML, element styles are programmable. In addition, when you change an attribute, Internet Explorer automatically refreshes the element. Internet Explorer is even smart enough to adjust the appearance of other elements affected by your changes. One of the key uses of dynamic styles, and one you will most likely encounter on the exams, is to adjust the position of an element on a page.

HTML elements don't have Top, Left, Width, or Height properties like ordinary controls do. However, they have equivalent properties available through their Style property. The Style property of an element is an object property that exposes a number of different of style-related properties used to modify the appearance of an element. Table 8-19 lists the positioning properties of standard controls and the corresponding Style object properties.

Table 8-19: Standard Control Properties and Their DHTML Element Counterparts

Standard Control	Style Object
Left	posLeft
Top	posTop
Height	posHeight
Width	posWidth

For example, to shift a text field 20 pixels to the right, you could use code such as this:

```
TextField1.Style.posLeft = TextField1.Style.posLeft + 20
```

There are many more properties of the Style object that can be used to further tailor the appearance of an element. For instance, you can set the text of an element to Courier by setting the FontFamily property like this:

```
parOpeningParagraph.Style.fontFamily = "Courier"
```

Or, change the background of a text field to orange using code like this:

```
TextField1.Style.backgroundColor = &HFF8000
```

Among other things, the Style object property lets you change the position of an element, the various colors of an element, the decorations of an element's text such as underline, overline, strikethrough, font, and padding. Take the time to experiment with these properties and you'll be able to build very *dynamic* HTML pages.

 Although you won't be tested on all of the various properties of the Style object, you should familiarize yourself with them. There are quite a number of them, and discussing all of them is outside the scope of this book. However, being able to manipulate the dynamic styles of elements is one of the exciting things about DHTML.

Compiling a DHTML Project

To compile a DHTML project for distribution, choose Make from the File menu (just as you do for all other project types). However, where most project types generate only a single file (EXE, OCX, DLL, and so on), compiled DHTML projects consist of a number of files. A DLL file is created, as well as an HTML file for each designer in the project. The HTML files created are determined by the BuildFile property of the designer. When you designate an HTML page for the SourceFile property, the BuildFile property defaults to the same page. Most often this is fine. If you want the final compiled HTML file to be a file other than the source file, however, specify a different file for the BuildFile property.

Deploying a DHTML Application

The most efficient way to deploy a DHTML application is to use the Package and Deployment Wizard, as discussed in Chapter 13, *Packaging and Deploying an Application.*

When you deploy a DHTML application, you must distribute the following files:

- The compiled project DLL.

- All DSR and DSX files for all designers in the project.

- All HTML pages associated with the project. This includes the HTML files created from each designer, as well as additional HTML pages your application uses.

- All files referenced by your application and its HTML pages, including images.

- The Visual Basic runtime DLL.

The Package and Deployment Wizard automatically packages the project's DLL, DSR, and DSX files into a CAB file (CAB files are discussed in Chapter 13). The Package and Deployment Wizard doesn't add the HTML files in the CAB file, but it does copy them to the web site you specify in the wizard. You will have to manually select all additional files such as images to be included in the CAB file. The Package and Deployment Wizard won't automatically detect these files.

Key Facts

This chapter has discussed how to make Internet-aware applications using the WebBrowser control, the Internet Transfer control, and the Winsock Control, as well as by automating Internet Explorer. You have also learned how to create web applications with DHTML. The following are key facts to understand in order to answer related questions on the Visual Basic exams:

- Visual Basic includes three controls that allow you to add Internet functionality to your applications: the WebBrowser control, Internet Transfer control, and the Winsock control.

- The WebBrowser control lets you add web-browsing capabilities to your application.

- To navigate to a specific document using the WebBrowser control, use the Navigate method.

- To navigate the history list using the WebBrowser control, use the GoBack and GoForward methods.

- To navigate to a user's home or start page using the WebBrowser control, use the GoHome method.

- To navigate to a user's search page using the WebBrowser control, use the GoSearch method.

- The LocationName property of the WebBrowser control returns the name of the page or document that the control is currently displaying.

- The LocationURL property of the WebBrowser control returns the URL of the page or document the control is currently displaying.

- To determine if the WebBrowser control is busy processing, check its Busy property.

- The BeforeNavigate2 event of the WebBrowser control occurs when the WebBrowser control is about to navigate to a new URL.

- The CommandStateChange event of the WebBrowser control occurs when the enabled state of a command, such as GoForward or GoBack, changes.

- The DownloadComplete event of the WebBrowser control occurs when the document that is being navigated to is finished loading.

- The DownloadBegin event of the WebBrowser control occurs when a navigation operation is beginning, shortly after the BeforeNavigate event.

- The NavigateComplete2 event of the WebBrowser control occurs after the browser has successfully navigated to a new URL.

- The NewWindow2 event of the WebBrowser control occurs when a new window is to be created for displaying a resource.

- The ProgressChange event of the WebBrowser control occurs when the progress of a download is updated.

- The TitleChange event of the WebBrowser control occurs when the title of a document in the WebBrowser control becomes available or changes.

- Internet Explorer supports automation. Automating Internet Explorer gives you the functionality available with the WebBrowser control, and much more.

- To hide or show Internet Explorer using automation, set the object variable's Visible property.

- To close an instance of Internet Explorer created through automation, invoke the Quit method of the Internet Explorer object variable.

- To control the visibility of Internet Explorer's user-interface elements using automation, set the FullScreen, MenuBar, StatusBar, and ToolBar properties.

- The Internet Transfer control lets you transfer files across the Internet.

- The Internet Transfer control supports the FTP and HTTP protocols.

- FTP stands for File Transfer Protocol.

- HTTP stands for Hyper Text Transfer Protocol.

- The basic steps for retrieving data using the Internet Transfer control are:

  a. Set the AccessType property to a valid proxy server.

  b. Retrieve data using the OpenURL or Execute method.

  c. Use the GetChunk method to retrieve data from the buffer when downloading files using the Execute method.

- The AccessType property of the Internet Transfer control dictates the type of connection made between the control and the server of the file to be retrieved.

- In order for the Internet Transfer control to use a proxy server other than the default proxy server of the computer, the AccessType property must be set to icNamedProxy, and the Proxy property must be set to the name of the proxy server.

- You don't need to specify a protocol when downloading files using OpenURL.

- To save data downloaded using OpenURL, you must use Visual Basic's file statements (Open, Put, Close, and so on).

- When logging onto secured FTP servers, you must specify a valid user name and password in the UserName and Password properties of the Internet Transfer control.

- When logging onto public FTP servers, use the UserName "anonymous" and supply your email address as your password. If you don't explicitly do this, the Internet Transfer control does it for you.

- When downloading data from an FTP server using the Execute method, the Execute method automatically saves the data to a local file that you specify.

- In addition to downloading files from an FTP server using the Execute method, you can also perform most DOS navigational functions such as changing and making directories and deleting files.

- To upload a file to an FTP server, use the PUT operation of the Execute method.

- When downloading data from an HTTP server using the Execute method of the Internet Transfer control, the control doesn't automatically save the file; you must use the GetChunk method in the StateChanged event.

- When retrieving data using the GetChunk method, use the constant icString to retrieve string data and icByteArray to retrieve binary data.

- The Winsock control lets two applications communicate with one other.

- The Winsock control can operate using TCP or UDP.

- TCP control is a connection-based protocol, and is analogous to making a telephone call: the user must establish a connection before proceeding.

- With TCP applications, one side acts as a server, the other as a client.

- UDP is a connectionless protocol. The transaction between two computers is like passing a note; a message is sent from one computer to another, but there is no explicit connection between the two. Additionally, the maximum data size of individual sends is determined by the network.

- The SendData method is used to send data from one Winsock application to another.

- When a Winsock application receives notice that data has been sent to it, it executes its DataArrival event. Data is received using the GetData method within the DataArrival event.

- An application can accept multiple Winsock connections by creating a Winsock control array.

- When using the Winsock control with the UDP protocol, the Winsock control must bind to the LocalPort by having its Bind method invoked.

- DHTML is a set of enhanced features to HTML that allows page authors and developers to dynamically change the style attributes of elements on an HTML page, as well as insert, delete, or modify elements and their text after a page has been loaded.

- In order to access a DHTML page, the user must be using Internet Explorer 4 or later.

- DHTML allows you to leverage your Visual Basic skills.

- DHTML applications run on the client, reducing server resource requirements.

- DHTML applications can be run from the user's cache.

- DHTML applications are compiled applications, thereby protecting your code.

- DHTML applications are multithreaded applications.

- DHTML applications should be built around solid web page design guidelines.

- You should avoid hard-coding paths in a DHTML application.

- To prevent code from being executed until all elements of a DHTML application are downloaded and displayed, set the AsyncLoad property of the DHTML designer to `False`.

- If you want or need to use asynchronous loading of a DHTML page, be sure to use error trapping.

- The modDHTML module created in a new DHTML project is a template for creating cookies.

- Each DHTML designer corresponds to a web page.

- DHTML designers are stored as text and binary files with the extensions DSR and DSX, respectively.

- You can store the HTML of a designer in an external HTML file by specifying the path and filename in the SourceFile property of the designer.

- In order to use an external editor to modify your HTML pages, you must store the HTML page of a designer in an external HTML file by using the SourceFile property.

- Paths of SourceFile documents are absolute paths. If the project is moved to another computer, the paths may need to be updated.

- To access a DHTML designer's properties, right-click the designer in the Project Explorer and select Properties, or click the Properties button on the designer's toolbar.

- Controls on a DHTML page are called elements, and they are not the same controls that you place on a form.

- You can place ActiveX controls on a DHTML designer page.

- To make option buttons mutually exclusive on a DHTML page, give them all the same name but assign each button a unique ID.

- In order to program an element (add code behind it or modify its other procedures), the element must have a unique ID.

- External HTML editors don't have the unique ID restriction of Visual Basic. If you import an HTML file by specifying an existing file in the SourceFile property of a DHTML designer, you may have to change the IDs. Visual Basic appends a number to all duplicate IDs.

- Elements that have similar functionality to standard controls don't necessarily have the same properties or events as their counterparts. For instance, the standard text box has a Text property, while the text field element has a Value property.

- To replace existing text with new straight text (no formatting), use the InnerText property.

- To replace existing text with new formatted text (text with tags), use the InnerHTML property.

- To replace existing text and formatting tags with new straight text (no formatting), use OuterText.

- To replace existing text and formatting tags with new formatted text (with formatting tags), use OuterHTML.

- DHTML events bubble up the chain until they encounter an event handler that stops the bubbling or they reach the topmost object in the chain that supports the type of event being bubbled.

- To cancel an event from bubbling further, use `BaseWindow.Event.cancelBubble = True`.

- To adjust the appearance or positioning of an element, alter its Style object property.

- To get or set the position of an element, use the posLeft, posTop, posWidth, and posHeight properties of the object's Style object property.

- To deploy a DHTML application, use the Package and Deployment Wizard.

- The files that must be distributed for a DHTML application are the compiled project; DLL, DSR, and DSX files; all HTML files associated with the project, all dependencies such as images; and the Visual Basic runtime library.

Applying What You've Learned

It's now time to apply what you've learned about making applications Internet-aware. First, answer all of the questions in the Skills Assessment. If you can correctly answer all of these questions, you'll be demonstrating a solid understanding of creating Internet-aware applications. After you've answered the assessment questions, work through the hands-on exercises.

Skills Assessment

1. Which control lets a user navigate to and view web pages and documents?

    a. Internet Transfer control

    b. WebBrowser

    c. Winsock

    d. ActiveX document

2. Which control allows an application to send and receive files from FTP and HTTP servers?

    a. WebBrowser

    b. Winsock

    c. Internet Transfer control

    d. File Transfer control

3. Which control allows two applications to freely communicate over the Internet?

    a. WebBrowser

    b. Winsock

    c. Internet Transfer control

    d. Internet Command Control

4. Which of the following would cause the WebBrowser control to navigate to a web page?

    a. `BrowserControl.Navigate "http://www.odintechnologies.com"`

    b. `BrowserControl.Navigate _`
    `    "URL = http://www.odintechnologies.com"`

    c. `BrowserControl.NavigateURL _`
    `    "http://www.odintechnologies.com"`

    d. `BrowserControl.GoTo "http://www.odintechnologies.com"`

5. Which two methods are used to navigate the history list of a WebBrowser control?

    a. NavigateForward, NavigateBack

    b. MoveForward, MoveBack

    c. GoForward, GoBack

    d. BackHistory, ForwardHistory

6. Which of the following are methods of the WebBrowser control? (pick two)

    a. NavigateHome

    b. GoSearch

    c. NavigateSearch

    d. GoHome

Internet
Applications

7. Which property of the WebBrowser control returns the name of the currently viewed document?

    a. CurrentDocument

    b. DocumentName

    c. LocationURL

    d. LocationName

8. Which property of the WebBrowser control returns the URL of the currently viewed document?

    a. LocationURL

    b. DocumentURL

    c. LocationName

    d. DocumentName

9. To determine if a WebBrowser control is currently processing a command, you would check which property?

    a. State

    b. Busy

    c. Command

    d. NavigationState

10. Which event of the WebBrowser control would you use to start an animation, letting the user know a navigation request is being processed?

    a. DownloadBegin

    b. DocumentComplete

    c. BeforeNavigate

    d. OnNavigate

11. When a new instance of Internet Explorer is created through Automation, it is:

    a. Invisible

    b. Visible

    c. Visible or invisible, depending on the visibility of the application creating the object

12. What protocols does the Internet Transfer control support?

    a. FTP

    b. HTML

    c. UDP

    d. HTTP

13. Which property controls the type of connection made between the Internet Transfer control and the Internet?

    a. AccessMode

    b. AccessType

c. InternetMethod

d. AccessMethod

14. Which two methods can be used to retrieve data from an FTP server?

    a. Download

    b. OpenURL

    c. Execute

    d. Retrieve

15. In order for the Internet Transfer control to use a proxy server other than the default proxy server, which two properties must be set?

    a. AccessMode

    b. AccessType

    c. Proxy

    d. ProxyName

16. You don't need to specify a protocol when downloading files using which method?

    a. Execute

    b. OpenURL

    c. Download

17. When logging onto public servers, you don't need to set the UserName and Password properties because the Internet Transfer control will do this for you.

    a. True

    b. False

18. Which download method of the Internet Transfer control saves the retrieved data automatically when downloading from an FTP server?

    a. OpenURL

    b. Execute

    c. Both

    d. Neither

19. Which protocol supports DOS-like commands on the server using the Execute method?

    a. HTTP

    b. FTP

    c. Both HTTP and FTP

    d. Neither HTTP nor FTP

20. Which operation of the Execute method sends a file to an FTP server?

    a. PUT

    b. SEND

    c. TRANSFER

    d. UPLOAD

21. When downloading a file from an HTTP server using the Internet Transfer control, you must use which method?

    a. GetData

    b. Receive

    c. GetFile

    d. GetChunk

22. The Winsock control supports which two protocols?

    a. HTTP

    b. FTP

    c. TCP

    d. UDP

23. Applications communicating via Winsock controls can act as:

    a. Peer-to-peer applications

    b. Client/server applications

    c. Either peer-to-peer or client/server applications

    d. Neither peer-to-peer nor client/server applications

24. Applications communicating via Winsock controls using TCP protocol act as:

    a. Peer-to-peer applications

    b. Client/server applications

    c. Both

    d. Neither

25. Which protocol is "connectionless?"

    a. TCP (Transfer Control Protocol)

    b. UDP (User Datagram Protocol)

    c. Both TCP and UDP

    d. Neither TCP nor UDP

26. What method is used to send data from one Winsock application to another?

    a. Transmit

    b. Upload

    c. Send

    d. SendData

27. When a Winsock control receives notification that data has been sent to it, it fires what event?

    a. DataArrival

    b. DataReceived

c. DataSent

d. SendComplete

28. What method is used to actually retrieve data sent to a Winsock control?

   a. GetChunk

   b. GetData

   c. ReceiveData

   d. ReceiveChunk

29. An application can accept multiple connections using the Winsock control by using:

   a. A control array

   b. A large block transfer request

   c. A direct connect to the Internet

   d. An application cannot accept multiple connections

30. When a Winsock control is using UDP, how must its LocalPort be set?

   a. Through the LocalPort property.

   b. Using the Bind method.

   c. The LocalPort is set automatically for UDP.

   d. The LocalPort does not need to be set for UDP.

31. DHTML applications run on:

   a. The client

   b. The server

32. In order to view DHTML pages, a user must be running:

   a. Netscape Navigator

   b. Internet Explorer 4.x or later

   c. Internet Explorer 3.x or later

   d. Either Netscape Navigator or Internet Explorer 4.x

33. Which is a true statement about DHTML applications?

   a. Users can view your code by choosing Source from the View menu in their browser.

   b. DHTML applications are compiled, so users cannot view their source.

   c. Whether or not a user can view your source depends on how you compile the application.

34. Which is true about using paths in DHTML applications?

   a. You should avoid hard coding paths.

   b. You should always hard code paths.

   c. You should always prompt a user for a path.

Internet
Applications

35. To prevent code from executing in a DHTML application until all elements are downloaded and displayed, you should:

    a. Set the AsyncLoad property of the Document object to **True**.

    b. Set the AsyncLoad property of the Document object to **False**.

    c. Set the AsyncLoad property of the DHTML designer to **True**.

    d. Set the AsyncLoad property of the DHTML designer to **False**.

36. Each DHTML designer corresponds to a single web page.

    a. True

    b. False

37. DHTML files are stored with which two extensions?

    a. DSX

    b. HTM

    c. HTX

    d. DSR

38. How do you save the HTML file of a DHTML designer to an external file?

    a. By setting the SourceFile property.

    b. By setting the Destination property.

    c. By using File → Save As . . .

    d. You cannot save the data to an external file.

39. To launch and use an external HTML editor with a DHTML page, you must:

    a. Specify the external editor in the registry.

    b. Save the HTML as an external file.

    c. You cannot use an external editor.

40. You can place ActiveX controls on a DHTML page.

    a. True

    b. False

41. To make option buttons mutually exclusive on a DHTML page, you do which of the following? (select all that apply)

    a. Give each option button the same name but a unique index.

    b. Give each option button a unique ID.

    c. Give each option button the same name.

    d. Place each option button on the same container.

42. In order to program an element, what must be true?

    a. The element must have a unique name.

    b. The element must have a unique numeric ID.

    c. The element must have a unique alphanumeric ID.

    d. All elements are inherently programmable.

43. Given the following HTML code:

```
<p id="Announce"></b>Queen takes Rook, check.</b></p>
```

What is the resultant HTML when the following statement is executed:

```
Announce.InnerText="Bishop takes Queen"
```

   a. `<p id="Announce">Bishop takes Queen</p>`

   b. `<p id="Announce"><b>Bishop takes Queen</b></p>`

   c. `<p id="Announce">Queen takes Rook, check.</p>`

   d. `<p id="Announce"><b>Bishop takes Queen, _`
      `check.Bishop takes Queen</b></p>`

44. Given the following HTML code:

```
<p id="Announce"></b>Queen takes Rook, check.</b></p>
```

What is the resultant HTML when the following statement is executed:

```
Announce.OuterText="Bishop takes Queen"
```

   a. `Bishop takes Queen`

   b. `<p id="Announce"><b>Bishop takes Queen</b></p>`

   c. `<p id="Announce"> Bishop takes Queen, _`
      `check.Bishop takes Queen</p>`

   d. `<p id="Announce">Queen takes Rook, check.</p>`

45. What code would you use to move an item 10 units to the right?

   a. `objElement.Left = objElement.Left + 10`

   b. `objElement.posLeft = objElement.posLeft + 10`

   c. `objElement.Style.Left = objElement.Style.Left + 10`

   d. `objElement.Style.posLeft = objElement.Style.posLeft + 10`

Answers to Skills Assessment

1. b	10. a	19. b	28. b	37. a, d
2. c	11. a	20. a	29. a	38. a
3. b	12. a, d	21. d	30. b	39. b
4. a	13. b	22. c, d	31. a	40. a
5. a	14. b, c	23. c	32. b	41. b, c
6. b, d	15. b, c	24. b	33. b	42. c
7. d	16. b	25. b	34. a	43. a
8. a	17. a	26. d	35. d	44. a
9. b	18. b	27. a	36. a	45. d

Hands-on Exercises

Now you're going to put the knowledge you've gained in this chapter to use. This chapter has three exercises. In Exercise 8.1, you'll create a custom web browser application. In Exercise 8.2, you'll create an FTP browser, and in Exercise 8.3 you'll build a simple DHTML application.

Exercise 8-1. Creating a web browser

In this exercise you'll create a web browser in Visual Basic. This exercise applies the following topics:

- Adding the WebBrowser control to a project
- Navigating to web pages using the Navigate method
- Navigating the history list with GoForward and GoBack
- Navigating to the home or Start page using GoHome
- Navigating to the search page using GoSearch

The web browser application you create will:

- Allow a user to enter an HTTP address and press Enter to browse to the site
- Allow a user to click a button to go backward through the history list
- Allow a user to click a button to go forward through the history list
- Allow a user to click a button to go to the home page
- Allow a user to click a button to go to the search page

Section 1. Adding the WebBrowser control to a project. In this section, you'll add the WebBrowser control to a project by doing the following:

1. Start Visual Basic and create a new standard EXE project.

2. Use the Components dialog box to add the Microsoft Internet Controls to the project.

Section 2. Creating the user interface. In this section, you'll create a basic web browsing interface:

3. Set the following properties of the default form by doing the following:

Property	Value
Name	frmBrowser
Caption	Visual Basic Web Browser
Height	4680
Width	6645

4. Add a new WebBrowser control to the form.

5. Set the properties of the WebBrowser control as follows:

Property	Value
Height	3315
Left	120
Top	900
Width	6645

6. Add a new text box to the form and set its properties as follows:

Property	Value
Name	txtAddress
Height	315
Left	960
Text	(make blank)
Top	480
Width	5475

7. Add a new label control to the form and set its properties as follows:

Property	Value
AutoSize	True
Caption	Address:
Height	195
Left	120
Top	540
Width	615

8. Add a new command button control to the form and set its properties as follows:

Property	Value
Name	cmdGoBack
Caption	Go Back
Height	375
Left	900
Top	60
Width	1095

9. Add a second Command Button control to the form and set its properties as follows:

Property	Value
Name	cmdGoForward
Caption	Go Forward
Height	375
Left	2100
Top	60
Width	1095

Internet
Applications

10. Add a third Command Button control to the form and set its properties as follows:

Property	Value
Name	cmdGoHome
Caption	Go Home
Height	375
Left	3300
Top	60
Width	1095

11. Add a fourth Command Button control to the form and set its properties as follows:

Property	Value
Name	cmdGoSearch
Caption	Go Search
Height	375
Left	4500
Top	60
Width	1095

Your form should now look like the one in Figure 8-8.

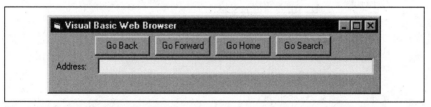

Figure 8-8: The interface for this browser isn't fancy, but it gets the job done

Section 3. Navigating to web pages using the Navigate method. Your web browser is going to let a user enter a URL in the txtAddress text box and press Enter to view the page in the WebBrowser control.

12. Add the following code to the KeyPress event of the txtAddress text box:

```
If KeyAscii = 13 Then
    WebBrowser1.Navigate txtAddress.Text
End If
```

Section 4. Navigating the history list with Go Forward and Go Back. Now, add the Go Forward and Go Back functionality to traverse the history list:

13. Double-click the Go Back command button to access its Click event.

14. Add the following code to the Click event:

```
WebBrowser1.GoBack
```

15. Double-click the Go Forward command button to access its Click event.

16. Add the following code to the Click event:

```
WebBrowser1.GoForward
```

Section 5. Navigating to the home or start page using Go Home. In this section, add the code to allow the user to click a command button to go to her home or Start page:

17. Double-click the Go Home command button to access its click event.

18. Add the following code to the Click event:

```
WebBrowser1.GoHome
```

Section 6. Navigating to the search page using Go Search. Finally, add the code to allow a user to click a button and go to his search page:

19. Double-click the Go Home command button to access its click event.

20. Add the following code to the Click event:

```
WebBrowser1.GoSearch
```

Section 7. Testing the Visual Basic web browser project. To test the web browser project, follow these steps:

21. Connect to the Internet.

22. Run the project by pressing F5.

23. In the address text box, type **www.tigerpawsoftware.com** and press Enter. Tigerpaw Software's web page appears in the browser (see Figure 8-9).

Figure 8-9: Navigating to web sites is simple with the Visual Basic Web Browser project

24. In the address text box, type **www.microsoft.com** and press Enter to navigate to Microsoft's web site.

25. Press the Go Back button and Tigerpaw Software's web site is once again displayed.

26. Press the Go Forward button and Microsoft's web site is once again displayed.

27. Press the Go Home button to navigate to the home or start page you've designated in Internet Explorer's Options dialog box.

28. Press the Go Search button to navigate to your search page.

Of course, this is a rudimentary web browser, but it demonstrates all the principles involved with adding browser capabilities to an application. If you were to distribute this application, you would probably want to add pictures to the command buttons, and make the WebBrowser control resize to fill the form whenever the form's size was changed.

Exercise 8-2. Creating an FTP browser

In this exercise, you'll create a program that retrieves the contents of a directory on an FTP server. The user can then double-click any file in the directory to download that file to her computer.

This exercise applies the following topics:

- Adding the Internet Transfer control to a project

- Retrieving directory contents using the Execute method and the StateChanged event

- Downloading files using the Execute method

Section 1. Adding the Internet Transfer control to a project. In order to add the Internet Transfer control, follow these steps:

1. Start Visual Basic and create a new Standard EXE project.

2. Use the Components dialog box to add the Microsoft Internet Transfer control to the project.

Section 2. Creating the user interface.

3. Set the default form's properties as follows:

Property	Value
Name	frmFTP
Caption	FTP Browser
Height	3480
Width	6585

4. Add a new Internet Transfer control to the default form.

5. Set the Internet Transfer control's properties as follows:

Property	Value
Protocol	icFTP
Left	3120
Top	1380

6. Add a new list box to the form and set its properties as follows:

Property	Value
Name	lstFiles
Height	2400
Left	120
Top	1080
Width	2595

7. Add a new text box to the form and set its properties as follows:

Property	Value
Name	txtFTPSite
Height	315
Left	120
Text	ftp://ftp.microsoft.com
Top	120
Width	2595

Your form should now look like the one in Figure 8-10.

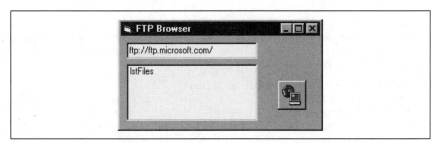

Figure 8-10: This simple form will display the contents of an FTP directory

Section 3. Adding the code. To add the code, follow these steps:

8. Add the following code to the KeyPress event of the text box. This code initiates a directory search on the FTP address entered into the text box:

```
If KeyAscii = 13 Then
    Inet1.Execute txtFTPSite.Text, "DIR"
End If
```

9. Add the following code to the StateChanged event of the Internet Transfer control. This code is used to retrieve the results of the directory search. At the end, each file and subdirectory is part of one large string. This string needs to be parsed, and the parsing is handled by the *FillDirList* procedure in step 11:

```
Dim vData As Variant
Dim strDir As String

If State = icResponseCompleted Then

    vData = Inet1.GetChunk(1024, icString)

    strDir = vData

    Do While LenB(vData) > 0
        strDir = strDir & vData
        vData = Inet1.GetChunk(1024, icString)
    Loop

    strDir = strDir & vData

    Call FillDirList(strDir)

End If
```

10. Add the following code to the DblClick event of the list box. This code retrieves the file that is double-clicked in the list box and saves it in the root directory of C. The *InStr* function is used to ensure that a file, not a subdirectory, is selected:

```
' Don't attempt to retrieve directory
If InStr(1, lstFiles, "/") = 0 Then
    Inet1.Execute , "GET " & lstFiles & " c:\" & lstFiles
End If
```

11. Add the following new procedure to the form module. This code parses the results of the directory search and looks for carriage returns. Each directory and file is separated by a carriage return/line feed combination, and this routine parses them out and adds them to the list box:

```
Private Sub FillDirList(strDir As String)
Dim strTemp As String
Dim iLoc As Integer

strTemp = strDir

TestString:
iLoc = InStr(1, strTemp, Chr$(13))
If iLoc > 0 Then
    lstFiles.AddItem Left$(strTemp, iLoc - 1)
    strTemp = Mid$(strTemp, iLoc + 2)
    GoTo TestString
End If

End Sub
```

Your code for the form module should read:

```
Option Explicit

Private Sub Inet1_StateChanged(ByVal State As Integer)
Dim vData As Variant
Dim strDir As String

If State = icResponseCompleted Then

    vData = Inet1.GetChunk(1024, icString)

    strDir = vData

    Do While LenB(vData) > 0
        strDir = strDir & vData
        vData = Inet1.GetChunk(1024, icString)
    Loop

    strDir = strDir & vData

    Call FillDirList(strDir)

End If

End Sub

Private Sub lstFiles_DblClick()

' Don't attempt to retrieve directory
If InStr(1, lstFiles, "/") = 0 Then
    Inet1.Execute , "GET " & lstFiles & " c:\" & lstFiles
End If

End Sub

Private Sub txtFTPSite_KeyPress(KeyAscii As Integer)

If KeyAscii = 13 Then
    Inet1.Execute txtFTPSite.Text, "DIR"
End If

End Sub
Private Sub FillDirList(strDir As String)
Dim strTemp As String
Dim iLoc As Integer

strTemp = strDir

TestString:
iLoc = InStr(1, strTemp, Chr$(13))
If iLoc > 0 Then
    lstFiles.AddItem Left$(strTemp, iLoc - 1)
    strTemp = Mid$(strTemp, iLoc + 2)
```

```
      GoTo TestString
End If

End Sub
```

Section 4. Testing the FTP browser application. In this section, you'll run and test the browser. If you don't have a connection to the Internet, you won't be able to complete this section of the exercise.

12. Connect to the Internet.

13. Run the project by pressing F5.

14. Click in the text box to give it the focus and then press Enter. After a pause, the list box will fill with the contents of the URL in the text box (see Figure 8-11). You could, of course, add a wait indicator such as an animation or an hourglass cursor if you wanted.

Figure 8-11: The contents of the URL specified in the text box are displayed in the list box

15. Double-click a file in the list box, and the file is downloaded to your C drive. You can use Explorer to verify that the file exists.

Exercise 8-3. Creating a DHTML application

In this exercise, you'll create a simple DHTML application. This exercise applies the following topics:

- Creating a DHTML project
- Saving an HTML page to an external file
- Adding Elements to a DHTML page
- Adding code to an element's events
- Manipulating an element's position using Styles
- Replace text using InnerHTML
- Testing the application in the browser

Section 1. Creating a DHTML project. In this section, you'll begin a project by choosing the DHTML Application option in the New Project dialog box.

1. Start Visual Basic and create a new DHTML Application project.

2. Double-click the Designers folder in the Project Explorer window.

3. Double-click the DHTMLPage1 designer to display it.

4. Change the Name of the page designer to **DHTMLExample**.

5. Your project should now look like Figure 8-12.

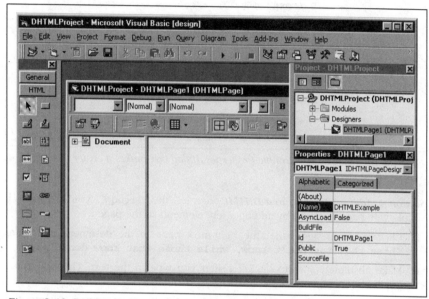

Figure 8-12: DHTML Designers have their own toolbars and interface

Section 2. Saving an HTML page to an external file. Now you're going to designate an external file to which the HTML of the page designer is to be saved. Saving pages in external files allows you to use external HTML editors to modify them.

6. Click the Properties tool button on the toolbar of the designer to display the DHTML Properties dialog box.

7. Select the Save HTML in an external file option button.

8. Click New.

9. Choose a location to save your HTML file in, enter the filename **Exercise8-03**, and click Save. Your DHTML Properties dialog box should now look like that in Figure 8-13.

10. Click OK to close the DHTML Properties dialog box and save your selections.

Notice how the path and file you selected appear in the SourceFile property in the Properties window.

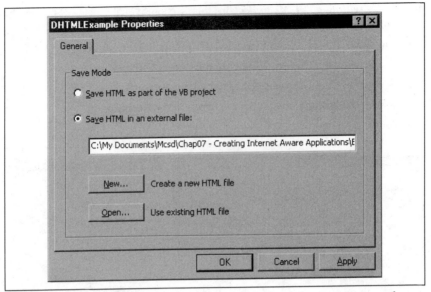

Figure 8-13: The DHTMLExample Properties dialog box makes it easier to set the SourceFile property

Section 3. Adding elements to a DHTML page. In this section, you'll create a simple web page interface by adding a few elements to the page.

11. Click in the design pane (the right-most pane in the designer), and enter **Those that say don't know, while those that know don't say.**

12. Make absolutely sure to hit Enter after you type in the text. This will make your text a paragraph object that can be manipulated.

13. Add a button to the page and move it to the lower-left corner. Change the Value of the button to **Click Me**.

   Notice how the Value property acts like the Caption property of an ordinary command button. Unlike a Caption, however, you have to commit your entry by pressing Tab or by selecting a different property before your changes take effect.

Your screen should now look similar to Figure 8-14. The Properties window and the Project Explorer have had their widths reduced to show the designer fully.

Section 4. Adding code to an element's events. The only code you're going to write is going to be placed in the Click event of the button. When you added the button to the page, it was automatically assigned the ID Button1. Remember, the ID is similar to the Name property of ordinary controls, and it's required to program an element.

14. Double-click the button to access its events.

15. Notice that the event is onclick, not Click as with ordinary command buttons. There are many subtle differences in the events of elements versus events of standard controls, and only by working with DHTML pages will you begin to remember them all.

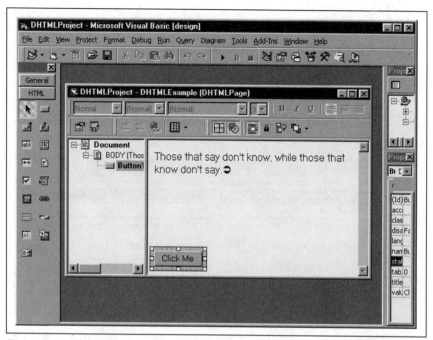

Figure 8-14: The right pane of the DHTML designer is where you build the page's interface

Section 5. Manipulating an element's position using Styles. As a simple example, you'll write code to move the position of the button to the right a small amount each time the button is clicked.

16. Add the following statement to the **onclick** event of the button:

```
Button1.Style.posLeft = Button1.Style.posLeft + 5
```

Section 6. Replace text using InnerHTML. Replacing text in an element is a common necessity, and you'll probably encounter a question about it on the exam. In this section, you'll write code that uses InnerHTML to replace text in the main paragraph of your page. InnerHTML replaces text with formatted text, so the text you'll be inserting will have formatting tags (in this case, bold tags). Before you can program the body text, you must assign an ID to the element.

17. Double-click the designer in the Project Explorer window to display it once again.

18. Click in the middle of the text you entered. In the left pane, you should see a paragraph object selected, not the BODY of the page. If a paragraph object is not visible, you didn't press Enter after typing the text into the web page.

19. Notice that the element does not have an ID assigned. Enter **MainParagraph** in the ID property in the Properties window.

20. Double-click the button once again to display its default event.

21. Add the following statement to the **onclick** event of the button after the existing statement:

```
MainParagraph.innerHTML = "<b>Advice is often worth what you " & _
    pay for it.</b>"
```

Your screen should now look similar to Figure 8-15.

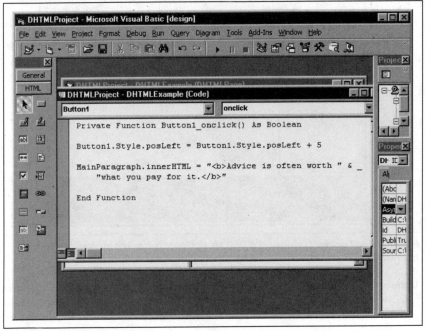

Figure 8-15: DHTML applications are written using VBA code

*Section 7. **Testing the application in the browser.*** All that's left to do is to test the application.

22. Click the Run button on the toolbar. Since this is the first time you've run the project, Visual Basic wants to know how you want to debug the application. On the Project Properties box that displays, accept the default of **Start component** and click OK (see Figure 8-16).

23. Once you click OK, Internet Explorer starts and displays your new HTML page as shown in Figure 8-17.

24. Click the button once. Notice that the initial text has not only been replaced, but the new text appears in bold. Also, the button moved to the right a bit (see Figure 8-18).

25. Continue clicking the button as many times as you like. The text won't change, but the button will continue to move across the screen.

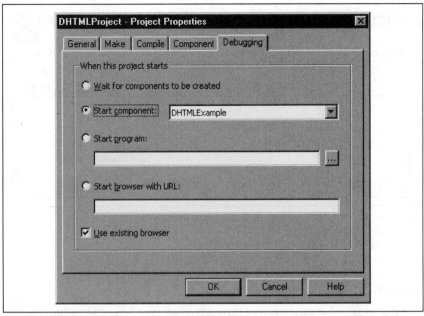

Figure 8-16: Visual Basic makes it easy to debug HTML applications by launching Internet Explorer

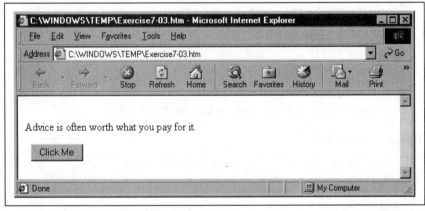

Figure 8-17: Internet Explorer displays your page exactly as your users would see it

Highlighter's Index

The WebBrowser Control

Used to add web browsing to an application

Part of Microsoft Internet Controls

You cannot distribute Microsoft Internet Controls (end users must have Internet Explorer)

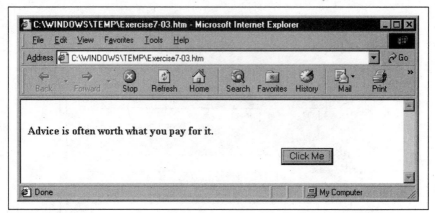

Figure 8-18: Creating dynamic web pages is what DHTML is all about

Navigate to URLs using Navigate method
Supports numerous events to control browsing

Automating Explorer

Allows you to control Internet Explorer, rather than adding browsing
    capabilities directly to your application
Automation object found in the file *shdocvw.dll*

Internet Transfer Control

Used to transmit files over the Internet
Uses HTTP or FTP
Can access secured servers
Can retrieve data synchronously (OpenURL) or asynchronously (Execute)
Can navigate FTP servers
GetChunk is used to get data retrieved asynchronously

Winsock Control

Allows you to create client/server Internet applications
Communicates via *sockets*
Sockets are bound to IP addresses
Sockets use port IDs
Can use TCP or UDP protocols
Applications can listen on ports or initiate conversations

DHTML

Extension of HTML
Creates dynamic web pages that can be used from the browser's cache
Pages designed with DHTML Page Designer
Primarily for intranets
Can dynamically change element content and style
Events bubble

CHAPTER 9

Testing and Debugging

No one writes perfect code. This is simply a fact of life for professional programmers. Of course, the "holy grail" of software development is the distribution of flawless code (although some might argue that it's money). Visual Basic lets you create amazing applications and components without the necessity of outside tools. When you add third-party components and Windows API calls to this already incredibly powerful tool, the myriad development possibilities are staggering.

Unfortunately, power and flexibility have their disadvantages. The number of ways in which errors can be introduced into code grows exponentially with the complexity of the application and the tools used to create the application. Fortunately, there are several things you can do to limit the number of problems your users may experience with your programs.

Along with power and flexibility, Visual Basic offers you a comprehensive array of tools to help you track down and eliminate errors in your code. In addition, Visual Basic allows you to write complex error handlers to shield users from the consequences of unexpected errors that find their way into your production applications.

On the Exams

Creating trouble-free code is important, and Microsoft has definitely put an emphasis on this topic on the Visual Basic exams. You must fully comprehend the topics discussed in this chapter in order to pass the testing and debugging section of the Visual Basic exams.

The Technologies and the Exams

In order to harness the power of Visual Basic to create robust applications, you must have a thorough grasp of Visual Basic's debugging capabilities. Expect to find debugging questions on both exams, as Table 9-1 shows.

Table 9-1: Testing- and Debugging-Related Topics on the Exams

Topic	Covered on Exam
Implementing different types of error handlers	Both
Determining error characteristics using the Err object	Both
Setting the behavior of errors in the IDE	Both
Setting breakpoints	Both
Using bookmarks	Both
Using the Immediate window	Both
Monitoring data using Watch expressions	Both
Using the Locals window	Both
Defining Assertions	Both
Using conditional compilation	Both

Implementing Error Handling

There are basically two different types of errors that can occur in code: *compile errors* and *runtime errors*. A compile error prevents Visual Basic from compiling the project. Visual Basic won't execute a procedure that has a compile error in it, so it's impossible to distribute a runtime version of an application with a compile error.

For example, attempting to call a procedure defined as follows:

```
Public Sub MyProcedure(MyVariable As Integer)
```

with this statement:

```
Call MyProcedure(Variable1, Variable2)
```

would generate a compile error.

Runtime errors are errors that don't occur at compile time, but rather occur while the project or program is running. Most compile errors are a result of erroneous syntax, while runtime errors are usually a result of attempting to perform an invalid operation on a variable.

For example, the following code does not generate a compile error; it's syntactically correct (assuming *MyVariable* is a declared variable):

```
Print 10/MyVariable
```

Under most circumstances, this code won't even generate a runtime error. However, what happens if the value of MyVariable is zero? Ten can't be divided by zero, so Visual Basic returns a runtime error. In design view, an error causes code execution to stop at the offending line and Visual Basic displays an error message. In a compiled application, an unhandled error is fatal and causes the entire application to crash. You can prevent code execution from stopping at encountered errors by writing error handler routines.

Compiling on Demand and Background Compilation

There are two Visual Basic settings that greatly affect your ability to create consistently solid code. These are the Compile on Demand and Background Compile options found on the General tab of the Options dialog box (see Figure 9-1).

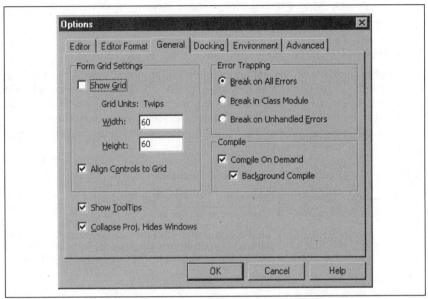

Figure 9-1: The Compile on Demand and Background Compile options affect the ability to catch compile errors while developing

When Compile on Demand is selected, Visual Basic won't fully compile a project when you click the Run button or press F5. Instead, modules are compiled only as they're referenced. This results in faster start times for larger projects or projects on slower computers, but it may cause compile errors to go unnoticed. Pressing Ctrl+F5 or choosing Start with Full Compile from the Run menu causes the project to fully compile, regardless of the Compile on Demand system setting. You won't be able to compile a project to a distributable file such as an EXE or DLL until all compile errors are fixed, so setting the Compile on Demand option won't enable you to distribute code with compile errors. However, setting Compile on Demand *can* allow compile errors to build up over time and force you to make many code corrections when you finally attempt to fully compile the project. In addition, correcting some types of compile errors forces your application out of run mode. Having to restart a project and set the program up for testing each time you're knocked out by fixing a compile error can become tedious. If your development machine can fully compile a project's code in a reasonable amount of time, you may want to disable Compile on Demand. As an alternative, leave Compile on Demand enabled, but get in the habit of periodically running your project by pressing Ctrl+F5.

When you enable Compile on Demand, the Background Compile option becomes available. If you select Background Compile, a project will compile as modules are referenced, as explained previously. But, in addition, Visual Basic uses idle time to compile modules that haven't yet been referenced. Over time, the project will fully compile. Using background compile allows you to enjoy faster start times when running a project, while keeping your compile errors to a minimum by alerting you to compile errors in modules not currently referenced.

Defining Error Handlers

Since this book assumes you are an experienced developer, there's no reason to go into the tedium of discussing elementary topics such as the Err object and all of the various types of error handlers. Instead, the two types of error handlers are presented in Table 9-2. I then discuss more advanced topics, such as how errors affect the call stack and how to use Visual Basic's tools to test and debug an application or component thoroughly.

Table 9-2: The Two Types of Visual Basic Error Handlers

Error Handler	Description
On Error Resume Next	When an error occurs, execution proceeds to the line of code following the error. This statement can be used for inline error handling. But often, using this error handler is worse than not using any error handler because errors may occur, but the user is never alerted to the fact. Data may be corrupted and the application's runtime environment may progressively worsen.
On Error Goto *label*	When an error occurs, code execution jumps to the statement following the specified code label. Execution may resume at the same line that caused the error with a Resume statement, or at the line immediately following the statement with the error by using the Resume Next statement.

 When using On Error Goto *label*, you can only divert code execution to a line that exists in the same procedure as the On Error Goto *label* statement itself. That is, the definition of the error handler and the error handling code must both reside in the same procedure.

These two error handling statements shown in Table 9-2 correspond to Visual Basic's two methods of trapping errors:

- Divert code execution when an error is encountered by using the On Error Goto statement. Execution can then resume with the statement causing the error (assuming that the error condition has been removed), with the statement following the error, or with code within the error handler itself (an error dialog box, for instance). For example:

```
Private Sub Main()

    On Error Goto ErrHandler

    ' code

    Exit Sub

    ErrHandler:

        ' code
        ' possible Resume statement
End Sub
```

Note that, since an error handler is a segment of code that ordinarily never executes unless an error is generated, the error handler is usually preceded by an **Exit Sub**, **Exit Function**, or **Exit Property** statement.

* Handle errors inline (or even completely ignore the error) without interrupting or diverting code execution by using the **On Error Resume Next** statement. For example:

```
Private Sub Main()

    On Error Resume Next

    ' code
    If Err.Number <> 0 Then
        ' code
    End If

    ' code
End Sub
```

The **On Error Resume Next** construct is generally preferable to the other **On Error** constructs when handling errors encountered while accessing external objects. Checking the Err object after each interaction with an object allows you to know, with certainty, which object caused the error (the object specified in Err.Source). Using this technique, however, can require a considerable amount of code.

Generally, you'll want to write at least one error handler for each procedure in your project, and it's usually a good idea to define the error handler in the first line of a procedure (after procedure comments). You can create as many error handlers within one procedure as you like, but only one error handler is active at a time. Visual Basic treats the most recent **On Error** statement as defining the active error handler.

Controlling Program Flow from an Error Handler

When an error does occur, assuming that an active error handler has been defined using On Error Goto *Label*, program flow branches to the error handler. Within the error handler, you can control the flow of program execution as follows:

- Allow program flow to exit the procedure and return to the calling routine.

- Use an **Exit Sub**, **Exit Function**, or **Exit Property** statement to force code execution to leave the procedure before all code in the error handler has executed.

- Use a **Resume Next** statement to force execution to continue with the line immediately following the statement that generated the error.

- Use a **Resume** statement to force execution to return to and continue with the line that generated the error. Usually, this makes sense only if the error handler has fixed the error or informed the user how to fix the error.

- Use a **Resume** *line* statement to redirect code to a specific statement.

The Error Object

Visual Basic's error object (Err) is a runtime object containing information about a specific error, making that information available to your code through a number of properties. The properties of the Err object are populated whenever an error is encountered at runtime, or when you deliberately raise an error using the Raise method discussed later in this chapter.

The properties of the Err object are reinitialized (strings are set to a zero-length value, longs are set to 0, and so forth) whenever a statement declaring an error handler is encountered, or after a procedure is exited via **Exit Sub**, **Exit Function**, or **Exit Property**. To clear the Err object explicitly, you can invoke its Clear method. (It's typically a good idea to call the Clear method in an error handler after you've finished handling the error.) Table 9-3 lists the properties of the Err object.

Table 9-3: Properties of the Visual Basic's Err Object

Property	Value
Number	The unique number that identifies the error.
Source	Name of the current Visual Basic project.
Description	A descriptive error message. If no such string exists for an error, Description contains "Application-defined or object-defined error."
HelpFile	The fully qualified drive, path, and filename of the Visual Basic Help file related to this error.
HelpContext	The Help file's context ID for the error corresponding to the Number property.
LastDLLError	On 32-bit Microsoft Windows operating systems only, contains the system error code for the last call to a dynamic-link library (DLL). The LastDLLError property is read-only.

When an error is raised, the Err object's properties are set to the appropriate values. If you need to use any of these values, you should act on them immediately or store them in variables before taking any other action because the Err object's property values may be reset. Also, the property values in the Err object reflect only the most recent error; the Err object does not maintain an error history list.

How the Call Stack Affects Error Handlers

Understanding how the call stack affects error handlers is critical to your success in effectively implementing error trapping. First of all, once an error handler becomes active, it remains active through the call stack until another error handler becomes active or the procedure containing the error handler goes out of scope. Since an error handler is no longer active when the procedure containing the error handler goes out of scope, the error handler that was last active becomes active once more when an error handler goes out of scope.

Consider the following two procedures:

```
Private Sub Command1_Click()

    On Error Resume Next

    Call TestSub

End Sub


Private Sub TestSub()

    On Error Goto TestSubErr
    ...
    Exit Sub


TestSubErr:

    Resume

End Sub
```

When the command button is clicked, the On Error Resume Next statement enables an error handler. When the *TestSub* procedure is called, its error handler becomes active; any errors encountered within the *TestSub* procedure are handled by the TestSubErr error handler. When the *TestSub* procedure is complete and code execution returns to the Click event of the command button, that event's error handler becomes active once more.

Now, consider these two procedures:

```
Private Sub Command1_Click()

    On Error Resume Next

    Call TestSub

End Sub


Private Sub TestSub()

    ...

End Sub
```

When the command button is clicked, the **On Error Resume Next** statement within the Click event enables an error hander. When the *TestSub* procedure is called, any error handlers created within that procedure become active. Since the *TestSub* procedure does not contain an error handler, the error handler made active in the Click event remains active throughout the *TestSub* procedure.

What happens when an error handler is active but an error is encountered within a procedure that does not contain the active error handler? The following two procedures illustrate this situation:

```
Private Sub Command1_Click()

    On Error Resume Next

    Call MakeError

    MsgBox "Statement in first procedure"

End Sub


Private Sub MakeError()

    Debug.Print 10 / 0

    MsgBox "Statement after error"

End Sub
```

When the Click event is fired, an active error handler is created with the **On Error Resume Next** statement. When execution transfers to the *MakeError* procedure, the error handler remains active because no error handler is activated within the *MakeError* procedure. When the division by zero error occurs, what is printed? Since there is no error handler defined in the *MakeError* procedure, the active error handler is found in the Command1_Click procedure. Since the error handler is a **Resume Next** statement, you might think that the statement immediately following the error would be the next to be executed. *It isn't*. Instead, the statement immediately following the call to the *MakeError* procedure becomes the next statement and the text "Statement in first procedure" appears in a message box.

This concept is true for multiple nested procedures. If an error is encountered within a procedure that does not have an error handler, the procedure that called the procedure containing the error is checked for an active error handler. This continues until an active error handler is found or the top of the call stack is reached. If the top of the call stack is reached, the error is treated (rightly so) as an untrapped error. If an error handler is encountered, execution continues at the statement in the procedure of the error handler designated by the On Error statement.

Disabling Error Handlers at Runtime

There may be times when you need to disable an active error handler at runtime. This is done by using the On Error Goto 0 statement. Consider this procedure:

```
Private Sub Command1_Click()

    On Error Resume Next

    On Error GoTo 0

    Debug.Print 10 / 0

End Sub
```

The first statement in this procedure creates an active error handler that essentially ignores errors. However, the On Error Goto 0 statement turns off the active error handler. Consequently, the division by zero error is not handled and the error is raised to the user.

 On Error Goto 0 only disables the active error handler in the current procedure. If an error is encountered after an On Error Goto 0 statement, the error is passed up the call tree as though there were no error handler in the procedure whatsoever.

Enabling and Disabling Error Handlers in Debug Mode

Although you don't want untrapped errors raised at runtime, it can be useful to let Visual Basic halt code execution when it encounters an error at design time. When code is halted, you receive a relevant error message and are shown the offending line of code; this greatly aids the debugging process. The approach Visual Basic takes to handling errors encountered at design time is determined by the Error Trapping property of the Visual Basic IDE. This property is set from the General tab of the Options dialog box (see Figure 9-2).

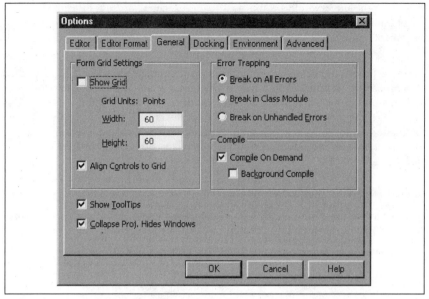

Figure 9-2: Visual Basic's IDE Error Trapping property is found on the General tab of the Options dialog box

Error Trapping is a property of the Visual Basic environment, not of a specific project. Until you explicitly change this on the Options form, each project you work with—even after having shut down and restarted Visual Basic—uses this setting. To set the error trapping option for the current session of Visual Basic only, without changing the default for future sessions, open the Toggle submenu on a Code window's Shortcut menu.

The Error Trapping property can be set to one of the following values:

- Break on All Errors
- Break in Class Module
- Break on Unhandled Errors

Break on All Errors

Break on All Errors essentially disables all of your error handlers. When an error is encountered, regardless of whether or not an error handler is active, the code enters break mode at the offending statement and an error message is displayed. This allows you to deal with unexpected errors while testing within the IDE.

Break in Class Module

The Break in Class Module setting is generally used when testing ActiveX components. Ordinarily, an error handler within a procedure that calls a method of an ActiveX component handles any unhandled errors within the ActiveX component's procedure. The Break in Class Module setting causes unhandled errors within class modules to cause *their* project to enter break mode at the line of code that caused the error, preventing unhandled errors from being passed up the call stack to the procedure in the client application. This makes debugging ActiveX components considerably easier.

Break on Unhandled Errors

This setting closely models how errors are treated in compiled applications. Errors trapped by active error handlers are dealt with by those error handlers, and only unhandled errors cause the code to enter break mode.

Raising Errors from an ActiveX Server

Most of the time you'll be trapping errors in procedures. However, there are times when you'll actually want to raise them. When creating ActiveX components, it's usually considered inappropriate for a component to display error messages to the user. Often, the user isn't even aware that a certain component is in use.

For example, an ActiveX control being used within an application wouldn't want to raise an error to the user when an invalid parameter is passed into one of its methods. The user understands they're running an application, but they couldn't care less what components the application uses. They fully expect the application to deal with its various pieces, shielding them from problems. In cases such as this, instead of displaying an error message to the user, the component should raise an error using the Raise method of the Err object. Raised errors are then handled by the active error handler in the core application.

Raising errors, rather than trapping them, is discussed in Chapter 4, *Creating and Testing ActiveX Code Components*.

Visual Basic gives you a number of ways to implement error handling within your applications, and you should use them. Every procedure of code in your application should be protected with an error handler, and On Error Resume Next should be used *only when absolutely necessary*, since it allows errors to go by unnoticed and uncorrected. Because error handlers are so vitally important, you should expect to encounter error handling questions on the exams.

Using Visual Basic's Debugging Tools

Visual Basic includes an impressive array of powerful tools to help you track down and eliminate errors in your code. Using the proper tool for the job gets a particular emphasis on the exams, so be sure to study this section to understand how all the tools work.

Working with Breakpoints

Just as a runtime error halts execution of a procedure, you can deliberately halt code execution at a specific code statement by creating a *breakpoint*. Breakpoints allow you to query or change the value of variables or properties at a specific instance in time, and they even let you step through code execution one line at a time.

Breakpoints behave as though a Stop statement is placed within a procedure.

Setting, moving, and removing breakpoints

To add a breakpoint, click in the gray area to the left of the statement at which you want to halt code execution. Visual Basic displays a red circle where you click and highlight the entire statement in red (see Figure 9-3). To clear a breakpoint, click on the red circle of the breakpoint to remove.

If you find using the keyboard preferable to using the mouse, you can use F9 to set and clear breakpoints.

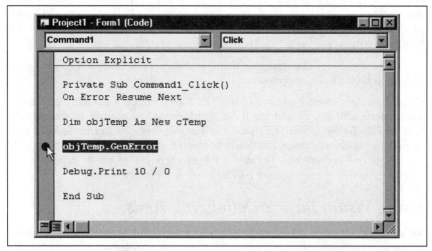

Figure 9-3: Breakpoints let you halt code execution at strategic locations in code

When Visual Basic encounters a breakpoint while executing code, execution is halted at the break statement, the statement is shown highlighted in yellow, and a small yellow arrow appears over the breakpoint's circle (see Figure 9-4). The break statement is not executed.

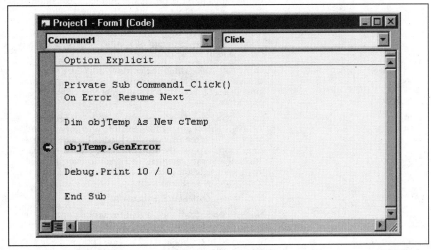

```
Project1 - Form1 (Code)                              _ □ ✕
Command1                     ▼   Click                        ▼

    Option Explicit

    Private Sub Command1_Click()
    On Error Resume Next

    Dim objTemp As New cTemp

⊙   objTemp.GenError

    Debug.Print 10 / 0

    End Sub
```

Figure 9-4: When code execution encounters a breakpoint, the execution is halted and you can use any of Visual Basic's debugging features

 To clear all breakpoints within a project, choose Clear All Breakpoints from the Debug menu.

When a project is opened in Visual Basic, it has no breakpoints; breakpoints are not saved with the project. You must reset any break statements you wish to use each time you open the project.

Taking action at a breakpoint

Breakpoints let you halt execution at a specific place within a procedure. How useful this is to you depends upon what you do once the code is stopped. You can use any of Visual Basic's debugging tools that are discussed later in this chapter. In addition, you have the options listed in Table 9-4 available to you from the Debug menu.

Table 9-4: Commands Available in Break Mode

Command	Keyboard	Action taken
Step Into	F8	Executes the code statement at the breakpoint, then halts code execution at the next statement as though it had a breakpoint as well. If the statement being executed is a procedure call, the first statement within the called procedure is the statement at which code is halted; hence, the procedure is *stepped into*.

Table 9-4: Commands Available in Break Mode (continued)

Command	Keyboard	Action taken
Step Over	Shift+F8	Similar to Step Into except for when the statement to execute is a procedure call. Unlike Step Into, which simply steps into the procedure and halts execution at the first statement it encounters, Step Over fully executes the procedure and then halts code at the statement immediately following the procedure call. When using Step Over, program execution halts only at statements within the same procedure.
Step Out	Ctrl+Shift+F8	Causes all code within the current procedure to execute, then halts code execution at the statement immediately following the statement that called the procedure.
Run to Cursor	Ctrl+F8	Lets you continue code execution up to a specified location. This is almost like creating a temporary breakpoint and is often used to skip blocks of code such as large loops. To use the Run to Cursor command, place the cursor at the statement you want to execute code up to, then select the Run to Cursor command from the code window's context menu.
Continue	F5	Continues normal code execution.
Set Next Statement	Ctrl+F9	Skips all code from the current breakpoint and sets the selected statement as the next statement to be executed.
Show Next Statement		When you're testing and debugging code while in break mode, it's not uncommon to lose your place. Selecting Show Next Statement displays the next line of code to be executed.

Working with Bookmarks

Bookmarks let you mark a statement in code that you want to easily return to later. Adding and removing bookmarks is similar to setting and removing breakpoints. However, code does not stop at bookmarked statements. Unfortunately, bookmarks share the same restrictive aspect of breakpoints in that they aren't saved with the project.

To flag a statement with a bookmark, place the cursor at the statement and choose Bookmarks → Toggle Bookmark from the Edit menu. Bookmarked statements appear with a light blue rounded-rectangle next to them (see Figure 9-5).

To remove a bookmark, perform the same procedure used to add one. Place the cursor on the statement with the bookmark and choose Bookmarks → Toggle Bookmark from the Edit menu.

In addition to toggling bookmarks, you can navigate to the next or previous bookmark within the project, and you can remove all bookmarks from the project. All bookmark functionality is accessed from the Bookmarks submenu of the Edit menu. There are no keyboard shortcuts.

Quickly Viewing the Contents of a Variable Using ValueTips

One of the great debugging features of Visual Basic, ValueTips, can't even be found in the Help text. ValueTips are essentially tooltips that display data. Before

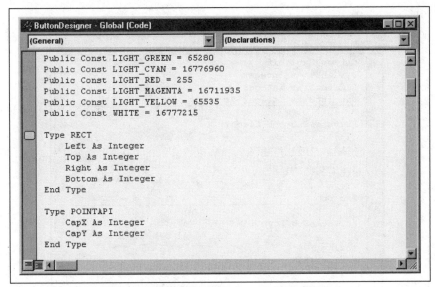

```
ButtonDesigner - Global (Code)                              _ □ ×
(General)                        ▼   (Declarations)                   ▼
    Public Const LIGHT_GREEN = 65280                               ▲
    Public Const LIGHT_CYAN = 16776960
    Public Const LIGHT_RED = 255
    Public Const LIGHT_MAGENTA = 16711935
    Public Const LIGHT_YELLOW = 65535
    Public Const WHITE = 16777215

    Type RECT
        Left As Integer
        Top As Integer
        Right As Integer
        Bottom As Integer
    End Type

    Type POINTAPI
        CapX As Integer
        CapY As Integer
    End Type                                                       ▼
 ≣ ◄                                                          ► //
```

Figure 9-5: Bookmarks are used to easily locate a section of code

ValueTips, you had to use the techniques discussed in the next section to print the contents of variables to the Immediate window in order to view them at runtime. This generally meant a lot of typing over the course of a project's development.

To use ValueTips, simply position the mouse pointer over a variable in break mode and pause for a moment. A ValueTip appears displaying the value of the variable, as shown in Figure 9-6.

Using the Immediate Window

The Immediate window is perhaps the most commonly used debugging tool of Visual Basic. The Immediate window lets you get and set variable and property values as well as call functions, all while the project is in break mode. The Immediate window can be stretched to any size, and it can even be docked in the IDE.

When in break mode, you can display the Immediate window by choosing Immediate Window from the View menu or by pressing Ctrl+G.

Getting and setting values using the Immediate window

You can print data directly to the Immediate window from within a procedure by using the Print method of the Debug object. For example, to print the contents of a variable to the Immediate window, you could use a statement like the following:

```
Debug.Print MyVariable
```

To print the contents of a variable or property from within the Immediate window itself, simply leave off the Debug qualifier like this:

```
Print MyVariable
```

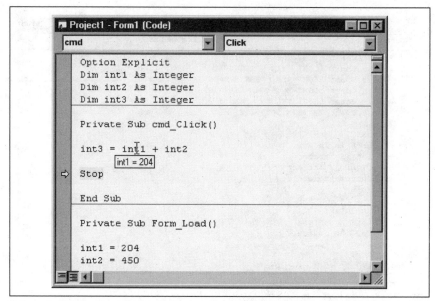

```
Project1 - Form1 [Code]                    _ □ X
cmd                           ▼    Click                      ▼
    Option Explicit
    Dim int1 As Integer
    Dim int2 As Integer
    Dim int3 As Integer

    Private Sub cmd_Click()

    int3 = int1 + int2
              int1 = 204
⇨  Stop

    End Sub

    Private Sub Form_Load()

    int1 = 204
    int2 = 450
```

Figure 9-6: ValueTips are simple in concept, yet they're an invaluable debugging tool

An old programmer's shortcut that has been around since the early days of BASIC is the ability to substitute the question mark (?) for the word `Print`. The Immediate window supports this shortcut, and it can save you many keystrokes when debugging complex projects. For example, the following statement can be used within the Immediate window to print the contents of a variable:

```
? MyVariable
```

Just as ValueTips can be used in the Code Editor, they are also available in the Immediate window while in break mode. They're not quite as useful here, since you have to type in the name of the variable or property whose value you wish to know anyway.

 While in break mode, all variables, properties, and functions are referenced in the context of the current scope. For instance, if you type `Print variablename`, *variablename* must be a local variable or a variable with module-level or global-level scope, the same as if the Print method had occurred in the procedure executing when the program was halted.

Setting the value of a property or variable is as easy as printing a value. Enter a statement just like you would in the code window. For example, to change the Text property of a text box from within the Immediate window, you could use a statement such as this:

```
Text1.Text = "My Text"
```

Executing functions from the Immediate window

Setting and retrieving values is not all you can do within the Immediate window; you can also call functions. These functions may be procedures defined within your project, built-in Visual Basic functions, declared API functions, or any combination of these three. When calling functions from within the Immediate window, the current scope applies.

Functions are called from within the Immediate window using the same statement format you would use to call them from within the code window. For example, to call one of your custom procedures from within the Immediate window, you could use code like this:

```
Call MyFunction
```

You can even direct the output of a procedure to the Immediate window. For example, if you forgot the ASCII value of the space character, you could use the following statement to print the value (32, in case you're wondering) to the Immediate window:

```
? asc(" ")
```

When you call a function from the Immediate window, you don't affect break mode; the code remains halted at the same statement that caused the IDE to go into break mode, but the entire function that you call is executed.

Monitoring Data Using Watch Expressions

Within most applications, data is constantly being manipulated at many different levels, and it's not uncommon for complex calculations to produce unexpected results during development. In a complex application, it can be quite difficult to find out just what went wrong. Often, these problems can be traced to a specific code statement setting a variable or property to an incorrect value. However, it's not always easy to find the troublesome statement.

Visual Basic allows you to set *watch expressions* to track down such problems. Once you create a watch expression, Visual Basic monitors the expression while the project is running. To view the value of a watch expression, you need only enter break mode.

If this were the only way to view the value of a watch expression, it could still take hours to step through complex loops to determine just when a data element goes bad. Fortunately, you have the ability to tell Visual Basic to automatically enter break mode when a watch expression evaluates to a condition you supply. This is extremely useful. For instance, you may want to know exactly when a flag within a loop has its value changed (see Figure 9-7).

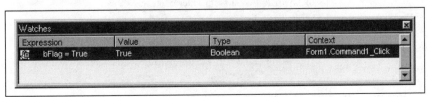

Figure 9-7: Watch expressions let you easily track the status of data

Adding watch expressions

You can add watch expressions at design time or while in break mode. Watch expressions are created using the Add Watch dialog box (see Figure 9-8). To access the Add Watch dialog box, choose Add Watch from the Debug menu.

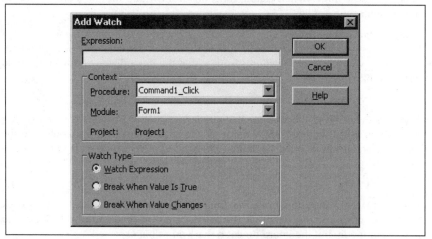

Figure 9-8: The Add Watch dialog box lets you create precision watch expressions

 You can also add an expression by dragging and dropping a selection of code from the Code Editor to the Watches window.

The components listed in Table 9-5 define a watch expression.

Table 9-5: Watch Expression Parameters

Component	Description
Expression box	The expression to be evaluated. The expression can be a variable, a property, a function call, or any other valid expression, such as `MyVariable = True`.
Context option group	Sets the scope of variables watched in the expression. Use this if you have variables of the same name with different scope. You can also restrict the scope of variables in watch expressions to a specific procedure or to a specific form or module, or you can have it apply to the entire application by selecting All Procedures and All Modules. Note: Visual Basic can evaluate variables in a narrow context more quickly than those in a broader context.
Watch type option group	Determines how Visual Basic responds to the watch expression. Visual Basic can watch the expression and display its value in the Watches window when the application enters break mode, or you can have the application enter break mode automatically when the expression evaluates to a `True` (nonzero) statement, or each time the value of the expression changes.

Editing and deleting watch expressions

To edit or delete a watch expression, select the watch you want to edit or delete in the Watches window. Once selected, you can perform one of the following:

- Right-click the item and select Edit Watch or Delete Watch from the Shortcut menu.

- Choose Edit Watch from the Debug menu.

- Press the Del key to delete the watch from the Watches window.

- Change parameters of the watch directly in the Watches window.

When you edit a watch expression, the Edit Watch dialog box is shown (see Figure 9-9). This dialog box is identical to the Add Watch dialog box, with the notable exception of the addition of a delete button.

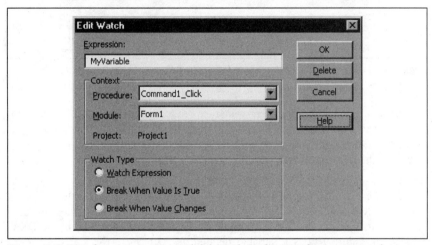

Figure 9-9: Watch expressions are edited much in the way they are created

Identify watch types using the Watches window

The Watches window clearly displays the Expression, Value, expression Type, and Context settings in columns. The small icon on the left of the watch expression denotes the type, or action, of the watch expression. Figure 9-10 illustrates the three different icons.

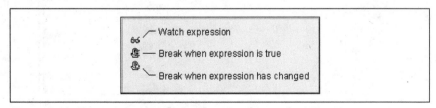

Figure 9-10: Icons are used to denote the type of a watch expression

Using the Quick Watch feature

Visual Basic includes a feature called Quick Watch, which lets you easily view watch information for which no watch expression has been explicitly created. To use this feature, place the cursor anywhere within a variable or highlight an entire expression that you want to perform a Quick Watch on, and then choose Quick Watch from the Debug menu (or press Shift+F9); the Quick Watch dialog box will appear (see Figure 9-11).

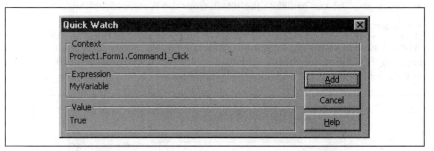

Figure 9-11: The Quick Watch feature lets you easily create temporary watch expressions

If you want to create a permanent watch expression from the Quick Watch dialog box, click Add. Otherwise, click Cancel to close the Quick Watch dialog box.

Using the Locals Window

The Locals window is an often overlooked debugging tool that shows the value of any and all variables within the scope of the current procedure in break mode. The Locals window even lets you collapse and expand object properties and user-defined datatype members. For example, the *OldXY* variable shown in the Locals window in Figure 9-12 is a variable defined as POINTAPI. The *CapX* and *CapY* variables are members of the *OldXY* variable.

Expression	Value	Type
☐ OldXY		POINTAPI
├ CapX	17	Long
└ CapY	12	Long
⊞ Me		clsCanvas/clsCanvas
Button	1	Integer
Shift	0	Integer
X	17	Single
Y	12	Single

Locals — ButtonDesigner.clsCanvas.ActionUpdate

Figure 9-12: The Locals window is a powerful tool that lets you view the values of all variables within the scope of a procedure

Unfortunately, there is no keyboard shortcut to display the Locals window. To display the Locals window, you must choose Locals Window from the View menu. You might consider displaying the Debug toolbar or otherwise customizing your toolbars so that you can display the Locals window by clicking a custom tool button.

The Locals window is an excellent tool for determining the contents of object variables. If an object variable does not contain a valid object reference, the word Nothing appears in its Value column. If an object variable does contain a valid object reference, the word Nothing does *not* appear in the Value column, and the Type column changes to reflect the instance of the class (see Figure 9-13).

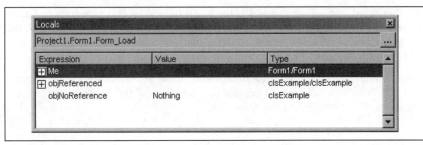

Figure 9-13: Objects that don't contain a valid reference have the word Nothing in their Value column

---

On the Exams

The Locals window and the Watches window provide the easiest ways to determine the contents of an object variable. You will probably be asked about this on the exams.

Defining Assertions

Assertions are fairly new to Visual Basic, and they're an easy way to test for conditions that should exist at specific locations in your code. For instance, you may fully expect a variable to contain a value between 1 and 10 within a particular procedure. Because you expect this to always be so, you may not want to write exception code to deal with values that fall out of range; such code could add complexity and reduce the efficiency of the procedure. However, when debugging the application, you want to be notified of any exceptions to your assumption. The raising of such exceptions is known as *assertions*. To create assertions in your code, you use the Assert method of the Debug object. The Assert method has the following syntax:

```
Debug.Assert (boolean_expression)
```

Not everyone fully understands how Debug.Assert works, because its behavior is actually counterintuitive. For example, consider the following statement:

```
Debug.Assert x <> 1
```

Logical assumption would lead you to believe that an assertion occurs whenever x is not equal to 1: in other words, when *boolean_expression* is True. In English, you might think this statement equates to:

```
Assert when x is not equal to 1
```

Since most Boolean-based functions operate based upon an evaluation of an expression to True, this isn't an unfounded assumption. However, in the case of Debug.Assert, this assumption is wholly incorrect.

In actuality, the Debug.Assert method behaves like this:

```
Debug.Assert when this assumption is not true: x <> 1
```

In other words, an assertion takes place when the expression evaluates to False. Essentially, you are specifying an expression based upon the way things should be. If, for whatever reason, reality deviates from the assumption, an assertion takes place to let you know.

For example, say you have a variable whose value should always be between 1 and 100. You can cause an assertion to take place if the value is not what is expected, using a statement like this:

```
Debug.Assert 1 <= x And x <= 100
```

When an assertion occurs, the code enters break mode at the Assert statement raising the assertion. Debug.Assert statements aren't compiled into a distributable application (compiled with the Make menu item), so you can use them freely throughout your code without worrying about removing them or commenting them before final distribution.

You've now learned about the powerful debugging tools that Visual Basic has to offer. Learning the best tool for any given situation is valuable skill gained mostly through experience. As you use these tools, you will learn to identify situations that let you take advantage of specific tools to create efficient and stable applications.

Using Conditional Compilation

Conditional compilation first appeared in Visual Basic 4.0. It's the process of writing code that may or may not be compiled into the application, depending upon conditions set at compile time. Its primary purpose was to allow a single code base for a project that could be compiled into a 16-bit or 32-bit application. This was necessary because 16-bit and 32-bit API calls required different declaration statements and often returned values of different datatypes.

Essentially, programmers need a way to perform this operation:

```
If compiling for 16bit, include this code
   ...
Else if compiling for 32bit, include this code
   ...
End If
```

In addition to being used to compile code for different operating systems, conditional compilation is often used to selectively compile debug code. For instance, debugging multithreaded components requires that you run the component as a compiled application. Say you wanted to write complex debug code that riddles the program with error checking, essentially dumping any and all pertinent information to a log file. Of course, you wouldn't want this code in the final product for many reasons. Wrapping the debug code in conditional compilation blocks allows you to easily compile either a debug version or a production version, without needing to manually comment out all of the debug code.

Writing Conditionally Compiled Code

Conditional compilation code blocks are defined with `#If...Then` and `#End If` statements. These statements behave just as the `If...Then` and `End If` statements in a normal procedure do. The difference is that conditional compilation statements are evaluated at compile time, not runtime, and the expressions they evaluate are based upon conditional compiler constants. To define a conditional compiler constant, use the `#Const` statement like this:

```
#Const CompileIn = -1
```

As you can see, declaring a compiler constant is the same as declaring a typical code constant, except you prefix the `Const` keyword with the `#`.

 Conditional compilation constants can only be of type Integer. So you can't declare a constant with the statement `#Const szLanguage = 'English'` or with the statement `#Const bEnglish = True`.

Compilation constants cannot be referenced in ordinary code statements; they can only be used in evaluating `#If...Then` statements.

As an illustration, the following code evaluates the `m_intCompileIn` compiler constant and compiles code accordingly:

```
Private Sub Form_Load()

    #If m_intCompileIn Then
        MsgBox "Code A is compiled!"
    #Else
        MsgBox "Code B is compiled!"
    #End If

End Sub
```

If the constant `m_intCompileIn` equals `True` (–1), the *MsgBox* statement "Code A is compiled!" is compiled into the program, and when the form loads the message is displayed. If the constant is set to 0 (`False`), the second *MsgBox* statement (the one that says "Code B is Compiled!") is compiled. Although there is only one statement for each condition shown in the previous example, you can place as many statements in each block as you need.

Understanding the Scope of Conditional Compilation Constants

To effectively use conditional compilation, you must understand how scope works for compiler constants. While you can define a compiler constant using #Const (which has scope limitations), this is not the only way; you can also create global compiler constants using the Project Properties dialog box and the command line.

Table 9-6 lists the scope of a compiler constants based upon the method used to declare them.

Table 9-6: Compiler Constants and Their Scope

How Set	Scope
Project Properties dialog box	Public to all modules in the project
Command line	Public to all modules in the project
#Const statement in code	Private to the module in which the constant is declared

Creating global conditional compilation constants using the Project Properties dialog box

To create global compilation constants using the Project Properties dialog box, follow these steps:

1. Choose Project Properties from the Project menu to display the Project Properties dialog box.

2. Click the Make tab to display the Conditional Compilation Arguments.

3. Enter the compiler constants and their values in the text box (see Figure 9-14).

Figure 9-14 shows the declaration of a compiler constant called m_intEnglish. This constant has its value set to –1 (all non-zero values are treated as True in Boolean arithmetic). A conditional compilation constant such as this can be used to selectively compile sections of code that are language dependent.

You can define more than one conditional compilation constant on the Project Properties dialog box by separating each constant with a colon like this:

```
g_intEnglish = -1:g_intRegistered = -1
```

Creating global conditional compilation constants using the command line

With applications that can be distributed in many different "flavors," it's not uncommon to find yourself frequently changing the values of conditional compilation constants using the Project Properties dialog box. Because of this, Visual Basic lets you specify conditional compilation constants using the command line. Using this technique, you can create separate desktop shortcuts for each flavor of your application that you need to compile.

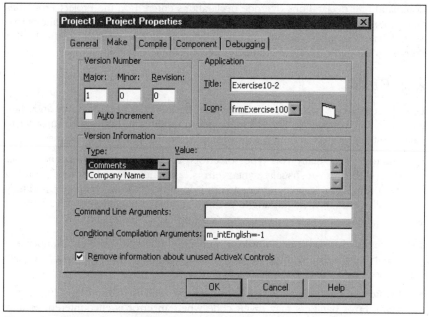

Figure 9-14: Compiler constants declared in the Project Properties dialog box are public to all modules in the project

 Command-line conditional compilation constants *cannot* be declared in the Command Line Arguments text box on the Make tab of the Project Properties dialog; they must be declared on an actual command line, as explained subsequently. Any and all conditional compilation constants you declare in the Command Line Arguments field will be ignored.

To define conditional compilation constants on the command line, use the /d switch. Enter any conditional compilation constant declarations after the /d switch just as you would enter them on the Project Properties dialog box. The following is an example of a command line that launches Visual Basic and compiles a specified project using conditional compilation constants:

```
vb.exe /make MyProj.vbp /d g_intEnglish=-1:g_intRegistered=-1
```

 No space is required between the /d and the first constant name, but you can provide one as shown here. However, you mustn't place any spaces in the constant declarations themselves (such as on either side of the equal sign).

Testing and
Debugging

Command line declarations override declarations entered on the Project Properties dialog box, but they do not remove or erase them. Subsequent compilations that do not have command line arguments specified use the settings on the Project Properties dialog box for compilation.

Key Facts

This chapter has discussed how to use Visual Basic's tools to track down and eliminate errors in your code. The following are key points to understand in order to pass questions related to testing and debugging on the Visual Basic exams:

- There are essentially two types of errors: *compile errors* and *runtime errors*. Compile errors are usually syntax errors, and they always prevent a project from compiling. Runtime errors do not stop a project from compiling, and they usually result from attempting to perform an invalid operation on a variable.

- The Err object is used to retrieve information about an error.

- If you need to work with an error number, you should store the number in a variable immediately after the error is encountered because the Err object may be reset by another code statement.

- Create *error handlers* to trap errors and prevent them from crashing a program. Error handlers may divert code when an error is encountered, or they may cause errors to be ignored completely.

- To create an error handler that skips statements that produce errors, effectively ignoring errors, use the On Error Resume Next statement.

- To divert execution to an error-handling block of code when an error is encountered, use the On Error Goto *line* statement.

- When using the On Error Goto *line* statement, *line* may be a line number or line label. If it's a number, you must explicitly create a line number for the statement to which you want code execution diverted.

- You can only divert code execution to a line that exists in the same procedure in which the error occurs.

- You can force code execution to exit the procedure from an error handler by using Exit Sub, Exit Function, or Exit Property.

- You can direct code execution to the line following the statement that generated an error from within an error handler using the Resume Next statement.

- You can direct code execution to a specific line of code from within an error handler using the Resume *line* statement.

- You can direct code execution back to the statement that caused an error from within an error handler using the Resume statement.

- When an error is encountered, the active error hander of the procedure in which the error occurred handles the error. If there is no active error handler within the procedure, the error is passed up the call stack until an error handler is found or the top of the stack is reached. If the top of the stack is reached, the error is treated as an unhandled error and is raised to the user.

- To disable an active error handler at runtime, use On Error Goto 0.

- You control how the Visual Basic IDE treats errors by setting the Error Trapping property on the Options dialog box to Break on All Errors, Break in Class Module, or Break on Unhandled Errors.

- When debugging ActiveX components, you should set the Error Trapping property to Break in Class Modules, so that all errors are raised at their source, not at the statement that referred to the object in which the error occurred.

- To halt execution at a specific statement in code, set a breakpoint. To set a breakpoint, click in the gray area next to a statement of code, or place the cursor within a statement and press F9.

- While in break mode, you can continue code execution by pressing F5 or by clicking the Run button on the toolbar.

- While in break mode, you can execute the next line of code by pressing F8 or selecting Step Into from the Debug menu. If the statement is a function call, code halts at the first statement in the function being called. If the statement is not a function call, code halts at the next statement.

- While in break mode, you can execute the next statement of code by pressing Shift+F8 or by selecting Step Over from the Debug menu. If the statement is a function call, the entire function is executed and code halts at the line immediately following the function call.

- While in break mode, you can execute all statements between the current breakpoint and any statement you desire by placing the cursor on the line you want code to execute to, and pressing Ctrl+F8 or selecting Run to Cursor on the Debug menu.

- To mark a section of code that you want to easily return to later, create a bookmark.

- While in debug mode, position the pointer over a variable or property and pause for a moment to display a ValueTip, a tool tip containing the value of the variable or property.

- Use the Immediate window to execute functions and to get values and set values in break mode.

- To monitor data in a project, create a watch expression and use the Watches window.

- You can create watch expressions to track any valid expression.

- You can define the context (scope) of a watch expression.

- You can force code to automatically enter break mode when an expression's value changes or becomes True.

- You can quickly evaluate an expression that is not defined in a watch expression by using the Quick Watch feature.

- To easily view the contents of all variables within the current procedure, use the Locals window.

- The Locals window lets you drill-down into object properties and user-defined datatype members.

- The Locals window and the Watches window are excellent tools for determining if an object variable holds a reference to a valid object.

- To be notified when a variable contains an unexpected value, create an assertion.

- To create an assertion, use the Assert method of the Debug object.

- An assertion is raised when the expression supplied for the assertion evaluates to False.

- When you compile a component to a distributable file, all Debug.Assert statements are ignored and therefore do not appear in the compiled version.

- The technique of creating code that only is compiled under certain circumstances is called *conditional compilation.*

- Use the #If...Then and #End If statements to create conditional compilation code blocks.

- The #If...Then and #End If statements only work with compiler constants.

- Compiler constants declared using #Const within a module have module-level scope.

- Compiler constants declared in the Conditional Compilation Arguments text box on the Project Properties tab have global scope.

- Compiler constants declared on a command line have global scope.

Applying What You've Learned

It's now time to apply what you've learned about testing and debugging your applications. First, answer all of the questions in the Skills Assessment. If you can correctly answer all of these questions, you'll be demonstrating a solid understanding of testing and debugging. After you've answered the assessment questions, work through the hands-on exercises.

Skills Assessment

1. A syntactical error in code produces which type of error?

    a. Runtime

    b. Compile

    c. Neither a runtime nor a compile error

    d. Both a runtime and a compile error

2. What is the most common cause of runtime errors?

    a. Misspelling a reserved word

    b. A variable going out of scope

    c. Calling a function with an incorrect number of parameters

    d. Attempting to perform an illegal operation on a variable

3. Which object is used to retrieve information about a runtime error?

    a. Err

    b. Debug

    c. Error

    d. ErrorInfo

4. Unhandled errors cause a compiled program to:

    a. Display an error message and continue running

    b. Exit the procedure that contains the error

    c. Display an error message and terminate

    d. Do nothing because untrapped errors are ignored

5. Given the code shown below, what is printed to the Immediate window?

```
Private Sub Command1_Click()
    On Error Resume Next

    Debug.Print 10 / 0     ' Causes an Error.
    Debug.Print "Checkpoint 1"

    Exit Sub

ErrorHandler:
    Debug.Print "Checkpoint 2"
    Exit Sub

End Sub
```

    a. Checkpoint 1

    b. Checkpoint 2

    c. Nothing

    d. First Checkpoint 2, then Checkpoint 1

6. Given the following code, what is printed to the Immediate window?

```
Private Sub Command1_Click()
    On Error GoTo 3

    Debug.Print 10 / 0     ' Causes an error.
    Debug.Print "Checkpoint 1"
    Debug.Print "Checkpoint 3"

    Exit Sub

ErrorHandler:
    Debug.Print "Checkpoint 2"
    Exit Sub

End Sub
```

a. Checkpoint 1

b. Checkpoint 2

c. Checkpoint 3

d. Nothing; a compile error occurs

7. Given the following code, what is printed to the Immediate window?

```
Private Sub Command1_Click()
    On Error GoTo 3

    Debug.Print 10 / 0     ' Causes an error.
    3 Debug.Print "Checkpoint 1"
    Debug.Print "Checkpoint 3"

    Exit Sub

ErrorHandler:
    Debug.Print "Checkpoint 2"
    Exit Sub

End Sub
```

a. Checkpoint 2

b. Checkpoint 2, then Checkpoint 1, then Checkpoint 3

c. Checkpoint 2, then Checkpoint 3

d. Checkpoint 1, then Checkpoint 3

8. Given the following code, what is printed?

```
Private Sub Command1_Click()
    On Error GoTo ErrorHandler

    Debug.Print 10 / 0     ' Causes an error.
    3 Debug.Print "Checkpoint 1"
    Debug.Print "Checkpoint 3"

    Exit Sub

ErrorHandler:
    Debug.Print "Checkpoint 2"
    Resume Next

End Sub
```

a. Checkpoint 2

b. Checkpoint 2, then Checkpoint 3

c. Checkpoint 1, then Checkpoint 3

d. Checkpoint 2, then Checkpoint 1, then Checkpoint 3

9. Given the following code, what is printed?

```
Private Sub Command1_Click()
    On Error GoTo ErrorHandler
```

```
      3 Debug.Print 10 / 0      ' Causes an error.
        Debug.Print "Checkpoint 1"
        Debug.Print "Checkpoint 2"

        Exit Sub

    ErrorHandler:
        Resume 3

    End Sub
```

a. Checkpoint 1, then Checkpoint 2.

b. Checkpoint 2.

c. Checkpoint 2, then Checkpoint 1.

d. Nothing is printed and the code repeats an endless loop.

10. Given the following code, what is printed?

```
    Private Sub Command1_Click()
        On Error GoTo ErrorHandler

        Debug.Print 10 / 0    ' Causes an error.
        Debug.Print "Checkpoint 1"
      3 Debug.Print "Checkpoint 2"

        Exit Sub

    ErrorHandler:
        Resume 3

    End Sub
```

a. Checkpoint 2.

b. Checkpoint 1, then Checkpoint 2.

c. Checkpoint 2, prints twice.

d. Nothing is printed.

11. Given the following two procedures, what is printed when the Command1 button is clicked?

```
    Private Sub Command1_Click()
        On Error Resume Next

        Call GenError

        Debug.Print "Checkpoint 1"

    End Sub


    Private Sub GenError()
```

```
Debug.Print 10 / 0     ' Causes an error.
Debug.Print "Checkpoint 2"

End Sub
```

a. Checkpoint 2, then Checkpoint 1.

b. Checkpoint 1.

c. Checkpoint 2.

d. Nothing is printed.

12. Given the following two procedures, what is printed when the Command1 button is clicked?

```
Private Sub Command1_Click()
   On Error Resume Next

   Call GenError
   Debug.Print "Checkpoint 1"

End Sub


Private Sub GenError()
   On Error Resume Next

   Debug.Print 10 / 0    ' Causes an error.
   Debug.Print "Checkpoint 2"

End Sub
```

a. Checkpoint 1.

b. Checkpoint 2.

c. Checkpoint 2, then Checkpoint 1.

d. Nothing is printed.

13. Given the following two procedures, what is printed when the Command1 button is clicked?

```
Private Sub Command1_Click()
   On Error Resume Next

   Call GenError
   Debug.Print "Checkpoint 1"

End Sub


Private Sub GenError()
   On Error GoTo 0

   Debug.Print 10 / 0     ' Causes an error.
   Debug.Print "Checkpoint 2"

End Sub
```

a. Checkpoint 1.

b. Checkpoint 2, then Checkpoint 1.

c. Checkpoint 2.

d. The error is unhandled and therefore raised to the user.

14. When debugging ActiveX components, which form of IDE error trapping should you use?

a. Break on All Errors

b. Break in Class Module

c. Break on Unhandled Errors

15. Which IDE error-trapping mode most closely resembles the error-trapping behavior in a compiled application?

a. Break on All Errors

b. Break in Class Module

c. Break on Unhandled Errors

16. To halt code execution at a specific statement, use:

a. A bookmark

b. A breakpoint

c. The Immediate window

d. The Break window

17. To mark a section of code you want to easily return to later, use:

a. A breakpoint

b. A bookmark

c. The Immediate window

d. The Watches window

18. Which statement is true?

a. Breakpoints are saved with the project, bookmarks are not.

b. Bookmarks are saved with the project, breakpoints are not.

c. Both bookmarks and breakpoints are saved with the project.

d. Neither bookmarks nor breakpoints are saved with the project.

19. Without typing, the quickest way to determine a variable's value in break mode is to use:

a. The Immediate window.

b. Save the value to a file.

c. ValueTips.

d. Create a watch expression.

20. To get values, set values, or call functions in break mode, use which tool?

   a. The Immediate window

   b. The Watches window

   c. The Locals window

   d. Quick Watch

21. To monitor a specific variable for a change in value, use which tool?

   a. The Immediate window

   b. The Watches window

   c. The Locals window

   d. Quick Watch

22. Which two tools are best for determining if an object variable has a reference to a valid object?

   a. The Immediate window

   b. The Watches window

   c. The Locals window

   d. Bookmarks

23. Which of the following statements is true about the Watches window?

   a. The Watches window only shows variables within the current scope.

   b. You define the scope in which you want to monitor a variable.

   c. Visual Basic automatically detects the scope of an expression.

   d. Visual Basic can't use a watch expression to halt code execution.

24. To quickly evaluate an expression that is not defined in a watch expression, use:

   a. ValueTips

   b. Quick Watch

   c. The Locals window

   d. None of the above

25. To easily view the value of all variables in the current procedure, use:

   a. The Immediate window

   b. The Watches window

   c. The Locals window

   d. The Quick Watch

26. To be notified when a variable contains an unexpected value while debugging:

   a. Create an assertion using Debug.Assert.

   b. Set a breakpoint.

c. Create a bookmark.

d. Use the Locals window.

27. Which technique can be used to create a single code-base for multiple platforms?

    a. Assertions

    b. Creating a project group

    c. Recursive procedures

    d. Conditional compilation

28. Conditional compilation constants declared using #Const have what scope?

    a. Procedure level

    b. Module level

    c. Global

    d. None of the above

29. Compiler constants declared in the Conditional Compilation Arguments text box on the Project Properties dialog box have what scope?

    a. Procedure level

    b. Module level

    c. Global

    d. None of the above

30. Compiler constants declared on the command line have what scope?

    a. Procedure level

    b. Module level

    c. Global

    d. None of the above

Answers to Skills Assessment

1. b	7. d	13. a	19. c	25. c
2. d	8. d	14. b	20. a	26. a
3. a	9. d	15. c	21. b	27. d
4. c	10. a	16. b	22. b, c	28. b
5. a	11. b	17. b	23. b	29. c
6. d	12. c	18. d	24. b	30. c

Hands-on Exercises

Now that you have a thorough background of testing and debugging a Visual Basic project, you're going to reinforce that knowledge by completing several small exercises.

Exercise 9-1: Experiencing the difference between compile and runtime errors

In this exercise, you'll create a compile error and a runtime error, and you'll use the Err object to retrieve error information.

In this exercise, you'll apply these debugging elements:

- The Immediate window
- Debug.Assert
- ValueTips

Section 1. Creating the user interface. In this section, you'll create the user interface of the project. This project uses a simple form with one text box and one command button. When the command button is clicked, it divides 100 by the value entered into the text box, and displays the result in a message box.

1. To begin, create a new standard EXE project.

2. Display the Options dialog by choosing Options on the Tools menu.

3. Deselect the Compile on Demand checkbox.

4. Select the Break on All Errors radio button.

5. Set the default form's properties as follows:

Property	Value
Name	frmExercise901
Caption	Exercise 9-01
Height	4935
Width	6705

6. Add a text box to the form and set its properties as follows:

Property	Value
Height	375
Left	2700
Text	(make blank)
Top	1500
Width	1215

7. Add a new command button to the form and set its properties as follows:

Property	Value
Caption	Divide into 100
Height	495
Left	2700
Top	2040
Width	1215

Your form should now look like the one in Figure 9-15.

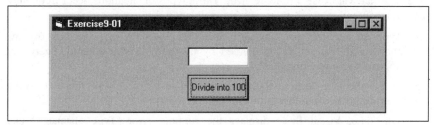

Figure 9-15: This simple interface is used to demonstrate error types

Section 2. Generating a compile error. In this section, you'll deliberately misspell a function name. This will cause an error when you attempt to compile the project.

8. Add the following code to the button's Click event (enter it *exactly* as shown here).

```
MsrBox "Decimal equals: " & 100 / Text1.Text
```

9. Press F5 to run the project. Visual Basic displays the compile error "Sub or Function Not Defined" (see Figure 9-16) and highlights the code it doesn't understand. In this example, the function *MsgBox* is spelled incorrectly, and therefore Visual Basic cannot compile the project because it doesn't know what to do with the code.

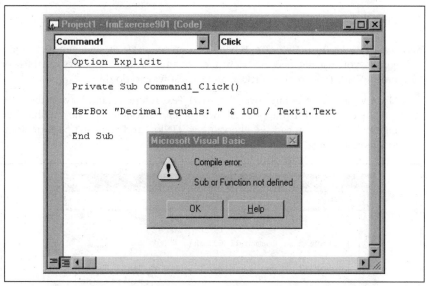

Figure 9-16: Compile errors prevent a project from running

10. Change **MsrBox** to **MsgBox** and press F5 to continue code execution. Visual Basic can now resolve the *MsgBox* statement, so the code is compiled.

Section 3. Generating a runtime error. In this section, you'll enter text into the text box that will cause a runtime error. These types of situations occur frequently, and much attention needs to be given to validating data entry.

11. Type **50** into the text box and click the button. A message box displays showing the value of 100 divided by the number you entered. Everything appears to be working fine.

12. Delete the text **50** from the text box, and in its place type the text **Hello**, then click the command button.

13. This time, Visual Basic displays the runtime error "Type Mismatch" (see Figure 9-17), indicating that you attempted to perform an operation on a variable that is incorrect for the variable's type.

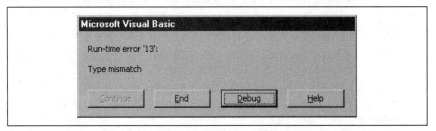

Figure 9-17: Runtime errors are usually a result of attempting an operation on a variable that is inappropriate for its datatype or value

14. Click Debug to view the offending line of code.

Section 4. Displaying a ValueTip. When a runtime error is encountered while debugging, you usually need to view the contents of one or more variables or properties. ValueTips are the quickest and easiest way to do this:

15. Move your mouse pointer over the Text1.Text reference and leave it there for a moment. A ValueTip appears showing you the contents of the variable (see Figure 9-18). As you can see, the value is "Hello," and you can't perform arithmetic on a string.

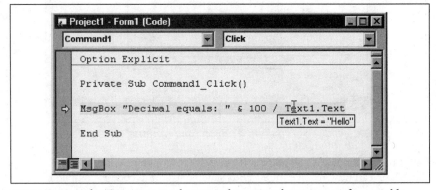

Figure 9-18: ValueTips are a quick way to determine the contents of a variable

Section 5. Changing a property value using the Immediate window. For the purposes of debugging, it's often desirable to change the value of a variable or property while the project is running. However, you don't always want to stop a program to make each change. For instance, you may want to see how a procedure works with correct data, and then address the problem of where the incorrect data came from.

16. You are now going to change the value of the text box using the Immediate window. Press Ctrl+G to display the Immediate window.

17. Type the following statement directly in the Immediate window and press the Enter key:

    ```
    Text1.Text = 25
    ```

18. Once again, move your pointer over the Text1.Text expression in the code window and leave it there for a moment. A ValueTip appears, but now it displays the value *25*. You have changed the value of the Text property of the text box, and you should be able to see the change right on the form.

19. Press F5 to continue code execution. Since the value is acceptable, the function completes without further errors.

20. Click the Stop button on the toolbar.

Section 6. Creating an assertion. You are now going to add an assertion to the procedure so that you can be notified when a non-numeric value is placed into the Text property of the text box:

21. Add the following statement to the Click procedure above the MsgBox statement. Although you might think you can leave off the equal sign and the word True, you must leave them in or the expression won't be correctly evaluated:

    ```
    IsNumeric(Text1.Text) = True
    ```

22. Press F5 to run the project.

23. Type **Hello** in the text box.

24. Click the button.

Code halts once again, but this time no error is raised. The Debug.Assert statement is highlighted so you know that it is the statement that caused the code to enter break mode, and therefore it must have created an assertion.

This exercise only touches the basics of using these techniques, but it should give you a general understanding of how they work.

Exercise 9-2: Creating an error handler

In this exercise, you'll create a small procedure with an error handler. You'll then manipulate the Error Trapping setting of the IDE to see the effects it has on your error handler.

Section 1. Creating the user interface. In this section, you'll create the user interface of the project. The only element you'll add to the default form is a command button.

1. Create a new Standard EXE project.

2. Display the Options dialog box by choosing Options from the Tools menu.

3. Deselect the Compile on Demand checkbox.

4. Set the form's properties as follows:

Property	Value
Caption	Exercise 9-02
Height	4425
Left	2400
Top	2010
Width	7175

5. Add a new command button to the form and set its properties as follows:

Property	Value
Caption	Get Object
Height	495
Left	2880
Top	1800
Width	1215

Your form should now look like the one in Figure 9-19.

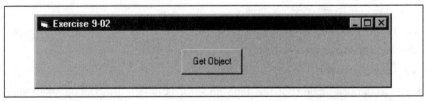

Figure 9-19: This form is not much to look at; all the action is under the hood

Section 2. Writing the code. In this section, you'll create a simple procedure that attempts to obtain an object reference to a fictitious object. You're going to include an error handler to trap the error raised when the GetObject function fails:

6. Add the following code to the Click event of the command button:

```
Dim obj As Object

On Error GoTo ErrorHandler
    ' Try to start a non-existent application
    obj = GetObject("FakeName.FakeClass")

Exit Sub
```

```
ErrorHandler:
    If Err.Number = 440 Or Err.Number = 432 Then
        MsgBox "Error: " & Err.Description
    End If
```

Section 3. Testing the code using different error-trapping settings. In this section, you'll run the project in two of the three different error-trapping modes: Break on All Errors and Break on Unhandled Errors. You won't use Break in Class Module because you are not debugging a class module.

7. Right-click the Code window and choose Break on Unhandled Errors from the Toggle submenu on the Code window's Context menu.

8. Press F5 to run the project.

9. Click the Get Object button. When the `GetObject` statement in the procedure produces an error, it's trapped by the active error handler, which then displays a message containing the error description (see Figure 9-20).

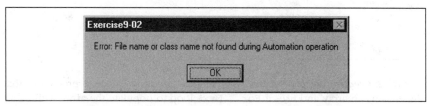

Figure 9-20: Although displaying an error message like this is similar to letting Visual Basic display an error message, using an error handler to do it does not terminate your application as Visual Basic would

10. Click OK and then click the Stop button on the toolbar.

11. Right-click the Code window and choose Break on All Errors from the Toggle submenu.

12. Press F5 to run the project.

13. Click the button. This time, Visual Basic raises an error even though you have an active error handler. To see how your error handler actually handles the error, click Debug and place the cursor on the statement immediately following `ErrorHandler`.

14. Press Ctrl+F9 to make the selected statement the next statement (the yellow highlight moves to the selected statement).

15. Press F8 to execute the current statement. The yellow highlight moves to the `MsgBox` statement because the `If...Then` statement evaluates to `True`.

16. Press F5 to continue running the procedure normally.

Exercise 9-3: Using breakpoints, and the Watches and Locals windows

In this exercise, you'll explore the Watches and Locals windows and set a breakpoint.

Section 1. Creating the user interface. In this section, you'll create the project's user interface by adding a command button to the default form.

1. Create a new Standard EXE project.

2. Set the form's properties as follows:

Property	Value
Caption	Exercise 9-03
Height	4935
Width	6705

3. Add a new command button to the form and set its properties as follows:

Property	Value
Caption	Run Code
Height	495
Left	2880
Top	1800
Width	1215

Section 2. Creating the procedure. You are now going to create a procedure that dimensions an array and uses a `For...Next` loop to populate the array with data.

4. Add the following code to the command button's Click event:

```
Dim MyArray(10)
Dim intCounter As Integer

For intCounter = 0 To 9
    MyArray(intCounter + 1) = MyArray(intCounter) + 1
Next intCounter

MsgBox "Done!", vbOKOnly
```

Section 3. Setting a breakpoint. In order to use the Locals window to view the values of the current procedure's variables, code must be in break mode. You are now going to place a breakpoint on the `MsgBox` statement so that code will enter break mode before the procedure ends.

5. Click in the gray area next to the `MsgBox` statement. A red circle will appear denoting that the statement has a breakpoint (see Figure 9-21).

6. Press F5 to run the procedure.

7. Click the command button. The `For...Next` loop is executed, and then execution enters break mode at the `MsgBox` statement.

Section 4. Using the Locals window. In this section, you'll use the Locals window to view the values of all of the procedure's variables, including the array:

8. Choose Locals window from the View menu to display the Locals window.

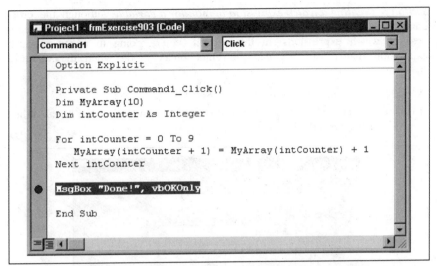

Figure 9-21: This breakpoint will halt code execution before the procedure has a chance to end

9. When the Locals window first appears, you'll see a reference to the form (Me), as well as the array and counter variables. Notice the plus sign next to the form reference and the array variable. Click the plus sign next to the *MyArray* variable and the Locals window displays the contents of each index in the array (see Figure 9-22). This would take a lot of typing if you used another means of viewing the data, such as the Immediate window.

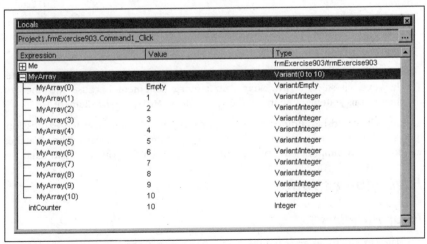

Figure 9-22: The Locals window makes viewing the contents of an array a snap

10. Press F5 to continue code execution, then click the Stop button on the toolbar.

11. Remove the breakpoint by clicking on the red circle.

Section 5. Creating a watch expression to monitor a variable. Although the procedure used in this exercise is small, it serves the purpose of illustrating the usefulness of watch expressions. In this section, you're going to create a watch expression that causes the code to enter break mode when the value of *MyArray(8)* changes:

12. Choose Add Watch from the Debug toolbar.

13. Enter **MyArray(8)** in the Expression text box, and select the Break When Value Changes radio button (see Figure 9-23).

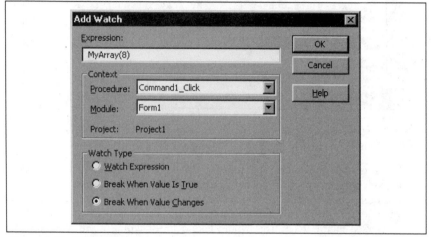

Figure 9-23: You can easily keep tabs on an array's element using the Watches window

14. Click OK to create the watch expression.

15. Press F5 to run the project.

16. Click the OK button. Once again, the code enters break mode. This time, however, it stops at the Next intCounter statement because the line just before this statement changed the value of the *MyArray(8)* element.

Although it would be fairly easy to monitor this code without a watch expression, this same technique can be applied to very complex projects. The Watches window greatly simplifies the process of tracking down the source of bad data.

Highlighter's Index

Error Handlers

Direct code to an error handler using On Error Goto
Ignore errors using On Error Resume Next
Disable the active error handler with On Error Goto 0
Return to the offending line with Resume
Return to line following the error with Resume Next

Err Object

Is reset each time an **On Error...** statement is invoked

Used to determine the characteristics of an error

Debugging in the IDE

You can break on all errors or break on unhandled errors

Use breakpoints to stop code execution at specific statements

Use bookmarks to easily return to code sections

Use the Immediate window to run commands and test values and expressions

Use the Watches window to monitor data and break under specific conditions

Use the Locals window to quickly see the value of all variables and objects within the current module

Use assertions to break (only in the IDE) when expressions aren't as expected

Conditional Compilation

Use to selectively compile or ignore debug code

Create conditional constants using **#Const**

Use **#If...#Then** to create conditional code blocks

CHAPTER 10

Implementing Help

Creating a comprehensive and useful Help system for any Windows application is a skill unto itself. Help systems are more than just online documentation. A Help system needs to explain the how-to of your application in bits and pieces, and the user needs to be able to access a specific bit or piece of information related to the task at hand with minimal effort. In addition, these bits and pieces—called *topics*— need to be linked in a comprehensive web that enables a user to travel from one related topic to another with ease. This chapter discusses the current format of Help, how to incorporate help within a Visual Basic project, and how to distribute Help with a program.

 Creating the Help files themselves is beyond the scope of the exam and therefore isn't covered in this book.

The Technologies and the Exams

Regardless of how intuitive an application is, users will always need help. Visual Basic makes it easy to integrate Help with an application, and you will be asked how to integrate Help on both exams, as Table 10-1 shows.

Table 10-1: Help-Related Topics on the Visual Basic Exams

Topic	Covered on Exams
Assigning Help files to a project	Both
Linking forms and controls to help topics	Both
Implementing What's This Help	Both
Displaying Help using the Common Dialog control	Both
Dialog control	Both
Distributing Help with an application	Both

A Brief History of Help

Visual Basic 6 is the first version to incorporate HTML help; prior versions used the traditional Windows Help system (WinHelp). WinHelp was similar to a web page; you viewed a page of information which could include any combination of text, graphics, and sound. Most help pages also had hyperlinks that let you quickly jump to a related page of information, and an incorporated search engine was available to locate specific pieces of information.

The traditional Help system consisted primarily of a compiler and a runtime engine. To create a Help file, you had to create rich text format (RTF) files using very specific formatting. The Help compiler was then used to interpret the RTF file and create a new file (HLP) that could be run with the Help runtime program. HTML rose meteorically alongside the Internet as the format of choice for creating hypertext documents. While the traditional Help system exhibited behavior similar to that of an HTML document in a browser, it had a number of drawbacks, including:

- RTF files were cumbersome to create. Many users opted to use third-party tools such as Doc-to-Help or Robohelp to create RTF files. However, this was still more cumbersome than creating HTML files.

- The traditional Help system was a proprietary system that required its own maintenance. To add a new feature in traditional Help, the feature had to be created by someone at Microsoft solely for the purpose of using it in Help.

- RTF is not a programming language. Creating an RTF file for compilation into traditional Help required a unique skill set; programmers could not leverage existing knowledge to create RTF files.

By extracting the Help system from the traditional WinHelp system to the HTML format, Microsoft and the development community have realized a number of benefits. First, there no longer needs to be a dedicated team at Microsoft working on Help. Now, anyone and everyone who writes add-ins or plug-ins to HTML is creating new features for Help. Second, since the Internet is so pervasive, more and more people know how to code in HTML, and many new and improved tools have been created to allow a novice to easily create powerful HTML documents, often without having to write a single line of HTML code! By developing your Help in HTML, you can even publish your Help documents on a web site.

HTML supplies the following additional features over WinHelp:

- The ability to display HTML documents
- Supports ActiveX, Java, and various scripting languages
- Displays HTML-supported graphics formats such as JPG, GIF, and PNG
- Allows a user to jump from a topic in the Help file to a web page on the Internet or on an intranet
- Allows the developer (and the user) to view the HTML source code for a topic.

Visual Basic 6 lets you integrate traditional Help files or HTML files. Although the act of creating these two types of files differs greatly, the process of integrating them into an application is the same.

Assigning a Help File to a Project

Regardless of the format chosen for an application's Help, the Help file must be linked to the application. Once a Help file is assigned to a project, specific topics within the Help file can be accessed by the user or through Visual Basic code. Assigning a Help file to a project is accomplished by setting the HelpFile property. As a matter of fact, most of the process of integrating Help within an application consists of assigning values to properties. To assign a Help file to a project using the Project Properties dialog box:

1. Choose Project Properties from the Project menu to display the Project Properties dialog box (see Figure 10-1).

2. Type in the full path and filename of a valid Help file in the Help File Name text box, or click the Build button next to the Help File Name text box, and use the Help File dialog box to locate and select a Help file.

Figure 10-1: The HelpFile text box on the Project Properties dialog box is used to assign a Help file to a project

 Help files created as RTF files and compiled using the traditional Help engine have the extension HLP, while HTML files created for use with the new Help format have the extension CHM.

It's not necessary to assign a Help file at design time; the HelpFile property may also be set at runtime using Visual Basic code. There are a number of situations in which this is preferable to assigning a Help file at design time. For instance, you may not know where the user will choose to install your program, and therefore you can't risk hard-coding an incorrect path. To assign a Help file at runtime, set the HelpFile property of the Application object like this:

```
Private Sub Form_Load()
    App.HelpFile = App.Path & "\Help\MyHelp.chm"
End Sub
```

 In the preceding code, it's assumed that the Help file exists in the same folder as the application executable.

Once you've assigned a Help file to a project, you can begin to link the Help file topics to objects within the project.

Understanding Help Context IDs

When you create a Help system, the tool you use will allow you to assign numeric IDs to each and every topic in your Help file. Each Topic ID must be unique in the Help file. By assigning a unique Topic ID to each topic, you gain the ability to display any topic at any given time. Also, you gain the ability to create applications with context-sensitive help, as discussed in the next section.

Since each Topic ID must be unique in a Help system, it's common for a Help developer to assign IDs in increments, and to assign ranges for specific features. For instance, in a paint program, it might make sense to use a structure similar to the following:

Range	Topic
0–500	Loading Images
501–1000	Using Editing Tools
1001–1500	Saving Images

You may then decide to number IDs in increments of 10, like so:

ID	Topic
10	Using the Open File dialog box
20	Browsing for files
30	Selecting a File Type

When you assign groups of topics a range of Topic IDs, you can logically group related topics. By incrementing IDs by a factor of 10, you allow room to add topics within the range at some point in the future.

Linking Help Topics to Objects

A user can access the Help system of an application in a number of different ways. The most common is to give a control or form in question the focus and press F1. When F1 is pressed, the application's HelpFile property is checked to verify that a valid Help file has been specified. If the Help file is found, the current control's HelpContextID property is checked. If the value of the HelpContextID property is 0, the HelpContextID of the control's container is checked. This occurs until a value other than 0 is found for a HelpContextID or until there are no further container objects in the hierarchy (a form is the last object checked). If a value other than 0 is found, the help topic with the Topic ID specified in the Help-ContextID property is displayed. In the event that no Topic ID with a value other than 0 is found, the Contents topic of the Help file is shown.

Any object that has a visual interface has (or should have) a HelpContextID property. Primarily, you will set the HelpContextID property of the following objects:

- Forms
- Standard controls
- ActiveX controls
- Menu items

Help context IDs can be used as many times as necessary, and the same ID can be assigned to controls on different forms. Remember, since Visual Basic looks at the container's HelpContextID property when the active control's HelpContextID's property value is 0, it's not necessary to assign an ID to every control on a form. You can create a single help topic with various links of interest and then assign it to the HelpContextID of the form. Then, assign a unique Topic ID only to controls that need specific topics.

Assigning a Help Topic to a Control or Form

Forms and controls are the most common objects that have associated Help topics. Although a form doesn't usually receive the focus, it's always a good idea to assign a Topic ID to each form. That way, regardless of the control that has the focus on a form, a topic related to the form will always appear when the user presses F1.

To assign a value to the HelpContextID property of a form or control at design time:

1. Select the form or control and display its properties in the Properties window.

2. Enter a value in the HelpContextID property (see Figure 10-2).

Like the HelpFile property, you can also set the HelpContextID property of any form or control at runtime using code similar to this:

```
Command1.HelpContextID = 7004
```

 The HelpContextID property is a Long Integer.

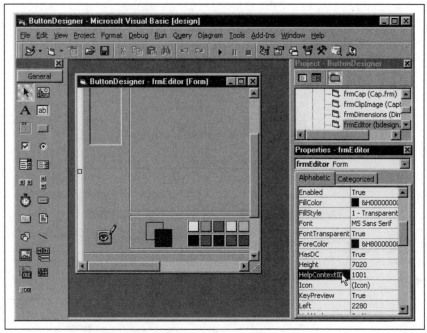

Figure 10-2: Attach a specific Help topic to an object by setting the object's HelpContextID property

Assigning a Help Topic to a Menu Item

Assigning Help topics to menu items is often overlooked. Many developers don't even realize that you can assign Help topics to individual menu items. However, users are often reluctant to select a menu item to discover its purpose (particularly menu items that call functions that modify the user's data), so providing users with Help topics linked to menu items is a good idea.

To assign a Help topic to a menu item:

1. Choose Menu Editor from the Tools menu to display the Menu Editor for the current form.

2. Click the menu item whose HelpContextID property you want to change.

3. Enter a valid Topic ID in the HelpContextID property (see Figure 10-3).

Adding What's This Help to a Form

As of Windows 95, Windows applications can now incorporate What's This Help. When a form is enabled for What's This Help, a small button with a question mark appears in the upper-right corner of the form's title bar, as shown in Figure 10-4. When the user clicks the What's This button, the cursor changes to an arrow with a question mark. The next object or form clicked on causes a small Help window to display with a relevant help topic.

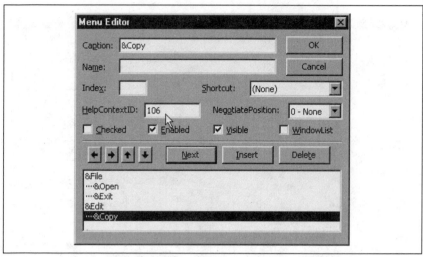

Figure 10-3: You can assign a specific Help topic to each menu item in your application using the Menu Editor

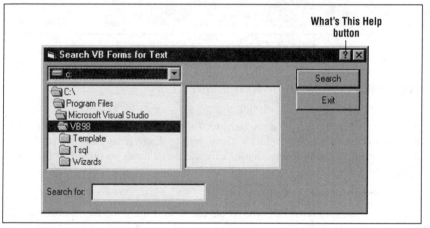

Figure 10-4: The What's This Help button used to access help for a visual element on a form appears in the title bar, near the Close button

 Although the What's This Help concept is a great idea, few applications fully implement this type of help. Microsoft is guilty of providing incomplete or non-existent What's This Help in many of its applications. Nevertheless, you'll be expected to demonstrate an understanding of implementing What's This Help on the exams.

Enabling What's This Help on a Form

To enable the What's This Help button on a form, a number of things must occur. First, you must set the form's WhatsThisHelp property to True. When WhatsThis-Help is set to True, What's This Help is shown when the user presses F1, rather than a traditional help topic window. This overrides the standard help for the form.

The next step is to set the form's WhatsThisButton property to True. However, this isn't all that's required. The form's BorderStyle must be set to *1 – Fixed Single* or *2 – Sizable*. In addition, the form *cannot have a visible Min button or Max button* (the MinButton and MaxButton properties of the form must be False). If you set the WhatsThisButton property of a form to True and there is no What's This Help button, check the BorderStyle, Min, and Max properties of the form.

 In order to implement What's This Help in an HTML Help file, you must include all of the What's This Help topics in a *Cshelp.txt* file and compile it into the CHM Help file. You won't be asked how to do this on the exam. For more information, consult your HTML authoring tool.

Assigning What's This Help Topics to Controls

Once you've enabled What's This Help on a form, you need to link the various controls on the form to specific Help topics within the Help file. It's important to note that the HelpContextID property isn't used to attach a Help topic to the What's This Help of a control. Instead, each control has a WhatsThisHelpID property. When you click the What's This button on a form and then click a control, the topic with the context ID found in the control's WhatsThisHelpID is displayed.

 If you enable What's This Help for a form, the standard HelpCon-textID property is not used. A form may have either standard Help enabled or What's This Help enabled, but not both.

Activating What's This Help Using Visual Basic Code

Just as a user can activate What's This Help by clicking the What's This Help button on the title bar of a form, you can activate it at runtime using Visual Basic code. You may want to do this, for instance, to create a custom toolbar with a What's This Help button. To activate What's This Help in code, invoke the Whats-ThisMode method of the form like this:

```
Me.WhatsThisMode
```

When you call the WhatsThisMode method of a form, it's just as though the user clicked the What's This Help button on the title bar of the form; the cursor changes to an arrow and question mark, and help is displayed for the next control clicked.

You will be asked on the exams how to activate WhatsThisMode using code. To activate WhatsThisMode in Visual Basic code, invoke a form's WhatsThisMode method.

Displaying Help Using the Common Dialog Control

Although Visual Basic's context-sensitive Help features make it easy to integrate Help into an application, they're not very flexible. (Actually, they can be downright limiting.) For instance, you're certainly familiar with the Help menu of most applications, including Visual Basic itself. Such Help menus usually have at least one menu item that is used as an entry point to the Help system. The Contents topic is the most frequently accessed topic from Help menus, but it's also common to show search results for a partial string match, or even to show Help on using Help. You can't do this very easily using the built-in features of Visual Basic, but you can do all of this and more using the Common Dialog control.

The Common Dialog control has a property called HelpContext rather than HelpContextID. This property has had this name since the early versions of Visual Basic, and it has been left as HelpContext to maintain backward compatibility with earlier versions. However, it works like the HelpContextID of forms and other controls.

The Common Dialog control is only capable of working with HLP files compiled with WinHelp's compiler, not CHM files created for HTML help.

Use the Components dialog box to add the Microsoft Common Dialog Control 6.0 to the project.

Designating a Help File for the Common Dialog Control

Before the Common Dialog control can be used to display the topic of a Help file, you must tell it the Help file to use; the control has no intrinsic knowledge of what Help file has been designated for the project. However, the Common Dialog control has a HelpFile property just like the application object does. To designate a Help file, supply the full path and filename of the Help file using code like this:

```
CommonDialog1.HelpFile = App.Path & "\MyApplication.hlp"
```

If you're using a combination of the Common Dialog control and Visual Basic's help features, you may set the HelpFile property of the Common Dialog control to the HelpFile property of the project by using a statement such as this:

```
CommonDialog1.HelpFile = App.HelpFile
```

Using the HelpCommand Property
of the Common Dialog Control

Regardless of what topic you choose to show in a Help file, you'll always use the same method of the Common Dialog control: the ShowHelp method. What determines the topic displayed is the value passed to the HelpCommand property of the Common Dialog control.

The possible values for HelpCommand are shown in Table 10-2.

 It's possible to combine some values shown in Table 10-2 using the Or operator. Examples of this are shown later in this chapter.

Table 10-2: Possible Values for the HelpCommand Property of the Common Dialog Control

Constant	Value	Description
cdlHelpCommand	&H102&	Executes a Help macro.
cdlHelpContents	&H3&	Displays the Help contents topic as defined in the Help file.
cdlHelpContext	&H1&	Displays Help for a particular Help topic. When using this setting, you must also specify a context ID (Topic ID) in the HelpContext property of the Common Dialog control.
cdlHelpContextPopup	&H8&	Displays a particular Help topic in a pop-up window. When using this setting, you must also specify a context ID in the HelpContext property.
cdlHelpForceFile	&H9&	Ensures that WinHelp displays the correct Help file. If the correct Help file is currently displayed, no action occurs. However, if an incorrect Help file is displayed, WinHelp opens the correct file.
cdlHelpHelpOnHelp	&H4&	Displays Help for using the Help application itself.
cdlHelpIndex	&H3&	Displays the index of the specified Help file. Use this value only when dealing with a Help file containing a single index.
cdlHelpKey	&H101&	Displays Help for a particular keyword. When using this setting, you must also specify a keyword using the HelpKey property of the Common Dialog control.
cdlHelpPartialKey	&H105&	Displays the topic found in the keyword list that matches the keyword passed in the *dwData* parameter if there is only one exact match. If there are multiple matches, the Search dialog box appears showing the topics found. If no match is found, the Search dialog box is displayed.
cdlHelpQuit	&H2&	Notifies the Help application that the specified Help file is no longer in use.
cdlHelpSetContents	&H5&	Determines which contents topic is displayed when the user presses the F1 key.

Table 10-2: Possible Values for the HelpCommand Property of the Common Dialog Control (continued)

Constant	Value	Description
cdlHelpSetIndex	&H5&	Sets the context specified by the HelpContext property as the current index for the Help file specified by the HelpFile property. This value is used only for Help files with more than one index.

 The constant **cdlHelpContents** doesn't work for Help files created with Microsoft Help Workshop Version 4.0x. To get the same effect, use the value **&HB**.

Displaying the Help Contents Topic

To display the Contents topic defined in a Help file, you ordinarily specify the **cdlHelpSetContents** value for the HelpCommand property. Since this doesn't work with Help files created with Microsoft Help Workshop 4.0x, you should **Or** it with **&HB** to ensure the contents are displayed regardless of the version of Microsoft Help Workshop used to create the help file. Since **&HB** does not have a symbolic constant, you can use the literal value or create a constant for it. The following code shows a Click event that shows the Contents topic of the specified Help file (see Figure 10-5):

```
Private Sub cmdShowContents_Click()

    Const HelpCNT = &HB

    With CommonDialog1
        .HelpFile = "c:\vsswork\tpssuite.hlp"
        .HelpCommand = HelpCNT Or cdlHelpSetContents
        .ShowHelp
    End With

End Sub
```

Displaying the Help Topic for a Specific Context ID

It's fairly common to have a Help button on a custom dialog box. Obviously, the Help button should display a Help topic related to the dialog box. To display a specific Help topic, supply its Topic ID as the value of the HelpContext property, then set the HelpCommand property to **cdlHelpContext**. The following Click procedures illustrates how you might do this:

```
Private Sub cmdSpecifiedTopic_Click()

    With CommonDialog1
        .HelpFile = "c:\vsswork\tpssuite.hlp"
        .HelpContext = 10
        .HelpCommand = cdlHelpContext
```

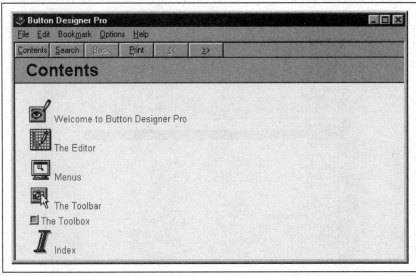

Figure 10-5: The Contents topic is a great place for users to start when they're not sure where they're going

```
        .ShowHelp
    End With

End Sub
```

Displaying the Index of Help Topics

To display the Index of Help topics in a Help file (see Figure 10-6), specify the value cdlHelpKey in the HelpCommand property. If you want to show the index without any specific index item selected, specify a zero-length string for the HelpKey property. To show the index with a specific index selected, specify the search text to be used to select an index in the HelpKey property. The following code shows how you might display the index of a Help file, with the first occurrence of a topic beginning with the word Create selected:

```
Private Sub cmdShowIndex_Click()

    With CommonDialog1
        .HelpFile = "c:\vsswork\tpssuite.hlp"
        .HelpKey = "create"
        .HelpCommand = cdlHelpKey
        .ShowHelp
    End With

End Sub
```

Displaying Help on Help

Using a Help system is not always intuitive to new users. Fortunately, you don't have to write your own text on how to use Help. Instead, you can tell the Help

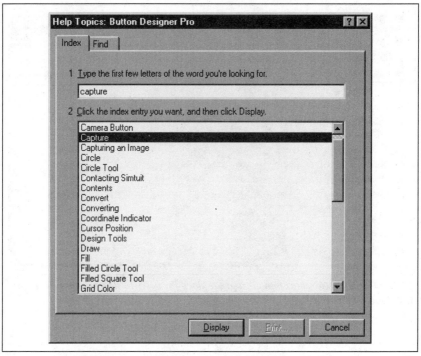

Figure 10-6: Displaying a specific index entry lets users start drilling into your Help file from a predetermined location

engine to display its Help on using Help (see Figure 10-7). To display Help on Help, specify the `cdlHelpHelponHelp` constant for the HelpCommand property. The following procedure demonstrates how you might display Help on Help to a user:

```
Private Sub cmdHelponHelp_Click()

    With CommonDialog1
        .HelpCommand = cdlHelpHelpOnHelp
        .ShowHelp
    End With

End Sub
```

 You don't need to specify a Help file in the HelpFile property to display Help on Help.

The Common Dialog control lets you easily add robust Help features to an application. Remember, however, that you cannot integrate HTML help using the Common Dialog control.

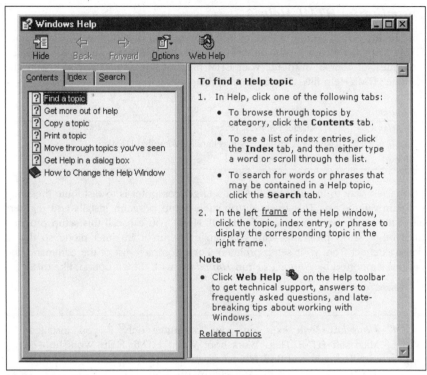

Figure 10-7: Help systems can display their own Help

Distributing Help with Your Application

When you integrate Help within a program, you must properly distribute the Help runtime and Help files with the application. Distributing WinHelp Help files differs slightly from distributing HTML Help files.

Distributing Help Created with the WinHelp Engine

One of the nice things about the WinHelp engine is that all Windows systems already have the engine installed. The only file you need to distribute is the HLP file itself. When you specify a Help file in a project on the Project Properties dialog box, the Package and Deployment Wizard can detect the reference and will automatically add the file to any setup package you create. Although you can install a Help file in the default *Windows\Help* folder used by many other applications, you may decide to install it in the application folder instead. Doing this makes it a little more tidy when a user elects not to use your uninstall program and instead deletes the application folder from his or her hard drive.

 If you use the Common Dialog control to access Help features, you will need to include it in your setup program.

Distributing HTML Help

Distributing HTML help is a little more complex than distributing WinHelp. Since HTML help is relatively new, you can't assume that it exists on a target computer. You must, of course, distribute your CHM file, but you should also distribute the runtime HTML Help files. These files include:

Filename	Description
Hhctrl.ocx	HTML Help ActiveX control
Itss.dll	Dynamic link library that handles compiled HTML
Hh.exe	HTML Help viewer

The easiest way to install these files on a target computer is to distribute the setup program *Hhupd.exe*. This freely distributable setup program installs and registers all of the necessary components for HTML Help. You can call this setup program from other setup programs, and you can even run it in quiet mode so that it doesn't detract from your setup program. For a complete list of the command-line options supported by *Hhupd.exe*, run *Hhupd.exe* with the /? option, like this:

```
Hhupd.exe /?
```

 Hhupd.exe will exist on your computer only if you installed Microsoft HTML Help Workshop. When HTML Help Workshop is installed, you will find *Hhupd.exe* in the *\Redist* folder in the folder in which you installed HTML Help Workshop.

Regardless of the installation method used to install HTML Help, HTML Help will operate only if Internet Explorer or the Internet Explorer runtime engine is installed on the computer.

Key Facts

This chapter has discussed integrating Help into an application. Although you won't be tested on creating a Help system, you will need to show competency on integrating a Help system with a Visual Basic project. The following are key facts that you should understand in order to answer questions on Help integration topics on the Visual Basic exams:

- Help systems consists of topics. Each topic covers a specific topic or feature.

- When creating Help for Visual Basic 6 applications, you can create Help systems that use the WinHelp engine or Help systems that use the new HTML Help engine.

- To create a Help file for a WinHelp system, you must compile Rich Text Documents using the WinHelp compiler.

- WinHelp help is created with Microsoft Help Workshop.

- HTML Help is created using Microsoft HTML Help Workshop. Microsoft HTML Help Workshop is included with Visual Studio.

- You can use HTML Help Workshop to create HTML help from older WinHelp projects.

- Most commercial developers use third-party tools to create Help systems.

- To assign a Help file to a project, set the project's HelpFile property to the desired Help file. You can set the HelpFile property at design time using the Project Properties dialog box or at runtime by setting the HelpFile property of the Application object.

- RTF files compiled using WinHelp have the file extension HLP.

- HTML Help files created with the new HTML Help Workshop have the file extension CHM.

- A Help topic is linked to a form or control by setting the form's or control's Context ID property.

- When the user presses F1, the HelpContextID property of the active control is considered. If the value is 0, the HelpContextID property of the form is looked at. If a valid HelpContextID is found, the corresponding topic is displayed. If the value is 0, the Help system's Contents topic is displayed.

- You can assign a value to a HelpContextID property at design time or runtime.

- You can assign Context IDs to menu items using the Menu Editor.

- What's This Help puts a ? button in the upper-right of a form's title bar. Clicking this button turns the cursor into a question mark. Clicking any control with the question mark cursor shows the What's This Help for the clicked control.

- In order to enable What's This Help on a form, the form's WhatsThisHelp property must be set to True, the form's WhatsThisButton property must be set to True, the form's BorderStyle must be set to *1 – Fixed Single* or *2 – Sizable*, and the form cannot have a visible Min button or Max button.

- To assign What's This Help to a control, set the control's WhatsThisHelpID property to a topic's Context ID.

- In order to implement What's This Help in an HTML Help file, you must include all of the What's This Help topics in a *Cshelp.txt* file and compile it into the CHM Help file.

- You can activate What's This Help mode in Visual Basic code by invoking the WhatsThisMode method of a form.

- Either standard Help or What's This Help (but not both) can be enabled for a form.

- You can invoke various Help functions when standard Help is in use by using the Common Dialog control.

- The Common Dialog control has a HelpContext property, as opposed to the HelpContextID property of forms and controls.

- The Common Dialog control only works with HLP files created with Win-Help, not CHM files created for HTML help.

- To link a Common Dialog control to a help file, set the Common Dialog control's HelpFile property.

- To invoke a Help function of the Common Dialog control, you first set the control's HelpCommand property to a valid command, then invoke the ShowHelp method of the control.

- To display Help contents using the Common Dialog control, set the Help-Command property to `cdlHelpContents`.

- To display a specific Help topic using the Common Dialog control, set the ContextID property to a Topic ID, set the HelpCommand property to `cdlHelpContext`, and invoke the ShowHelp method.

- To display the Help contents of a Help file created with Help Workshop 4.0x, you set the HelpCommand property to `&HB`.

- To display a Help file's Index of topics, set the HelpCommand property of the Common Dialog control to `cdlHelpKey`, specify optional search text for the HelpKey property, and invoke the ShowHelp method.

- To display Help on Help, set the Common Dialog control's HelpCommand property to `cdlHelpHelponHelp` and invoke the ShowHelp method.

- To distribute a Help file created with WinHelp, you need only to distribute the Help file itself; the WinHelp engine is pre-installed on all Windows operating systems.

- If you use the Common Dialog control to access Help features, you must distribute it with your application.

- You can freely distribute the file *Hhupd.exe*. This setup program installs the HTML help engine on a user's computer.

- The *Hhupd.exe* file can be run in silent mode.

- HTML Help will only operate if Internet Explorer or the Internet Explorer run-time engine is installed.

Applying What You've Learned

It's now time to apply what you've learned about integrating Help with an application. First, answer all of the questions in the Skills Assessment. If you can correctly answer all of these questions, you'll be demonstrating a solid understanding of integrating Help. After you've answered the assessment questions, work through the hands-on exercises.

Skills Assessment

1. An individual piece of information in a Help system that can be linked to a form of control is called a:

   a. Segment

   b. Piece

c. Theme

d. Topic

2. The older, yet still standard, format of Help uses which Help engine?

    a. HTML

    b. WinHelp

    c. On-Line

    d. MCSD

3. Which type of document is compiled to create a WinHelp Help system?

    a. RTF

    b. HTML

    c. DOC

    d. TXT

4. What program is used to create WinHelp Help systems?

    a. Microsoft HTML Help Workshop

    b. Microsoft Help Workshop

5. Microsoft HTML Help Workshop can be used to create HTML Help from older WinHelp projects.

    a. True

    b. False

6. To assign a Help file to a Visual Basic project, you: (pick two)

    a. Set the HelpFile property on the Project Properties dialog box.

    b. Set the HelpFile property of each form.

    c. Set the HelpFile property of the Application object.

    d. Set the LinkHelpFile property of the project.

7. Rich Text Format files compiled with WinHelp have what extension?

    a. VBH

    b. WHP

    c. HLP

    d. CHM

8. HTML files compiled for HTML Help have what extension?

    a. VBH

    b. WHP

    c. CHM

    d. HLP

9. To assign a Help topic to a form or control, you set which property of the form or control?

    a. ContextID

    b. HelpContextID

    c. HelpID

    d. HelpTopicID

10. What occurs when the user presses F1 and the active control has its Help-ContextID property set to 0?

    a. The HelpContextID of the form is considered.

    b. The Contents topic is displayed.

    c. An error occurs.

    d. Nothing happens.

11. What occurs when the user presses F1, the active control has its Help-ContextID property set to 0, and its form has its HelpContextID set to 0?

    a. The HelpContextID property of the project is checked.

    b. The Contents topic is displayed.

    c. An error occurs.

    d. Nothing happens.

12. You can set the HelpContextID property of a form or control:

    a. Only at design time.

    b. Only at runtime.

    c. At either design time or runtime.

    d. At runtime if it hasn't been set at design time.

13. A Help topic can be assigned to a menu item.

    a. True

    b. False

14. What's This Help is generally activated by: (pick two)

    a. Clicking a button on the form's title bar.

    b. What's This Help cannot be used in Visual Basic.

    c. By pressing F1 while a control has the focus.

    d. Invoking the WhatsThisMode of a form.

15. Which of the following must occur to enable What's This Help on a form?

    a. The form's WhatsThisHelp property must be set to True.

    b. The form's WhatsThisButton property must be set to True.

    c. The form's BorderStyle property must be set to *1 – Fixed Single* or *2 – Sizable*.

    d. The form cannot have a Maximize or Minimize button.

16. When a user invokes What's This Help, which property of the active control is used to display a Help topic?

    a. HelpContextID

    b. WhatsThisHelpID

    c. WhatsThisMode

    d. HelpTopicID

17. In order to implement What's This Help in an HTML Help file, you must include all of the What's This Help topics in a text file and compile it into the CHM file. What is the name of this text file?

    a. *Wth.txt*

    b. *Wthelp.txt*

    c. *Cshelp.txt*

    d. *Htmlh.txt*

18. A form may have a mixture of controls with standard Help topics linked to their HelpContextID properties and controls with What's This Help.

    a. True

    b. False

19. Which control can be used to access Help functions?

    a. System control

    b. WinHelp control

    c. Text box control

    d. Common Dialog control

20. To link a Help file to a Common Dialog control:

    a. Set the HelpFile property of the control.

    b. Set the HelpFile property of the application.

    c. Set the HelpFileLocation property of the control.

    d. Help files are linked automatically.

21. To call a Help function using the Common Dialog control:

    a. Invoke the HelpCommand method.

    b. Set the ShowHelp property.

    c. Set the control's HelpCommand property, then invoke the ShowHelp method.

    d. Set the control's ShowHelp property and invoke the HelpCommand method.

22. To display the Index of topics using the Common Dialog control:

    a. Invoke the HelpKey method.

    b. Invoke the HelpIndex method.

c. Set the HelpIndex property of the control and invoke the ShowHelp method.

d. Set the HelpKey property of the control and invoke the ShowHelp method.

23. To distribute a Help system compile with WinHelp, what files must be distributed?

    a. The compiled HLP file

    b. The RTF file

    c. The WinHelp engine

    d. Help Workshop

24. What is the name of the freely distributable installation program that installs HTML Help on a user's computer?

    a. *Hhelp.exe*

    b. *IExplorer.exe*

    c. *HTML.exe*

    d. *Hhupd.exe*

25. In addition to installing the HTML Help engine and distributing a compiled Help file, what must also be true in order for HTML help to work?

    a. The user must have an Internet connection.

    b. The user must have Internet Explorer or the Internet Explorer runtime engine installed.

    c. The user must have Visual Studio installed.

    d. The user must have Visual Basic installed.

Answers to Skills Assessment

1. d	6. a, c	11. b	16. b	21. c
2. b	7. c	12. c	17. c	22. d
3. a	8. c	13. a	18. b	23. a
4. b	9. b	14. a, d	19. d	24. d
5. a	10. a	15. a, b, c, d	20. a	25. b

Hands-on Lab Exercises

Now that you have a thorough background in integrating Help with an application, you're going to put that knowledge to use. Complete the hands-on exercises to help solidify your understanding of integrating Help with an application.

Exercise 10-1: Integrating a Help file with an application

In this exercise you'll add Help functionality to a simple project. The Help file is titled *bdpro.hlp* and can be downloaded from *http://vb.oreilly.com*. This is a small

Help file for the first commercial Visual Basic project I ever wrote (it sure isn't recent!). You'll need to copy the HLP file to the folder in which you create this exercise project in order for the exercise to work.

This exercise applies the following topics:

- Linking a Help file to a project by setting the HelpFile property of a project.
- Linking a Help file to a Common Dialog control.
- Using a Common Dialog control to display the Help contents.
- Using a Common Dialog control to display Help on Help.
- Using a Common Dialog control to display Help for a specified Index entry.
- Using a Common Dialog control to display a specific Help topic.

Section 1. Linking a Help file to a project. In this section, you'll create a link between the Help file and the application:

1. Start Visual Basic and create a new ActiveX EXE.

2. Set the following properties of the form:

Property	Value
Name	frmExercise1001
Caption	Exercise10-1
Height	4935
ScaleMode	3 – Pixel
StartUpPosition	2 – Center Screen
Width	3720

3. Double-click the form to access its Load event.

4. Enter the following code:

```
App.HelpFile = App.Path & "\bdpro.hlp"
```

5. To test that the Help file is properly linked, press F5 to start the project. Then press F1 to display the Help file (see Figure 10-8).

6. Stop the project.

Section 2. Linking a Help file to a Common Dialog control. To harness the power of Help, you need to use the Common Dialog control. Without the Common Dialog control, you'd have to write complex API calls to duplicate the features exposed by the control's properties and methods. In this section, you're going to add a Common Dialog control to the project and link it to the Help file:

7. Right-click the Toolbox and choose Components from the Shortcut menu.

8. On the Components dialog box, locate and select the Microsoft Common Dialog Control components.

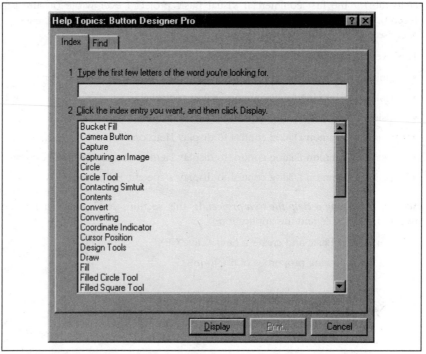

Figure 10-8: Pressing F1 automatically displays the linked Help file

9. Click OK to add the Common Dialog control to the project.

10. Add a Common Dialog control to the form and set its properties as follows:

Property	Value
Name	cmdlgHelp
Left	204
Top	132

11. Double-click the form once more to access its Load event.

12. Add the following statement to the form's Load event:

```
cmdlgHelp.HelpFile = App.Path & "\bdpro.hlp"
```

Section 3. Using the Common Dialog control to display Help contents. Once you've assigned a Help file to the Common Dialog control, you can set the control's properties and use its ShowHelp method to access Help functions. In this section, you're going to use the HelpCommand property and the ShowHelp method of the Common Dialog control to display the Contents topic of the Help file:

13. Add a new command button to the form and set its properties as follows:

Property	Value
Name	cmdContents
Caption	Show Contents
Left	68
Height	33
Top	28
Width	97

14. Double-click the cmdContents command button to access its Click event and add the following code:

```
Const HelpCNT = &HB

With cmdlgHelp
    .HelpCommand = HelpCNT Or cdlHelpSetContents
    .ShowHelp
End With
```

Section 4. Using the Common Dialog control to display Help on Help. Help is very powerful and, if used correctly, can add immense value to an application. However, Help's features are sometimes confusing to new users. In this section, you'll create a command button that displays Windows' Help on using Help when clicked:

15. Add a new command button to the form and set its properties as follows:

Property	Value
Name	cmdHelpOnHelp
Caption	Help on Help
Left	68
Height	33
Top	77
Width	97

16. Double-click the cmdHelpOnHelp command button to access its Click event and add the following code:

```
With cmdlgHelp
    .HelpCommand = cdlHelpHelpOnHelp
    .ShowHelp
End With
```

Section 5. Using the Common Dialog control to display Help for an index entry. At times, you might have a good idea of what topic the user needs Help on. For instance, you may create a Help button on a custom dialog box. When the user clicks the button, you know he wants help related to the dialog box. In situations like this, it's common to display the topic linked to the form. However, you may prefer to display the Help's list of index entries, with a specific entry highlighted. That way, the user can browse similar indexes before choosing a topic to view. You can use the Common Dialog control to accomplish this by using the cdlHelpKey constant with the HelpCommand property. If you specify an index match, and the index text is not found, the Help Index displays the index item that most closely matches the text you specify. You are now going to add this functionality to your project by creating one command button that locates and displays a topic based on its index, and one command button that attempts to display a topic based on a nonexistent index:

17. Add a new command button to the form and set its properties as follows:

Property	Value
Name	cmdHelpIndex
Caption	Index (Found)
Left	68
Height	33
Top	126
Width	97

18. Double-click the cmdHelpIndex command button to access its Click event and add the following code:

```
With cmdlgHelp
    .HelpKey = "fill"
    .HelpCommand = cdlHelpKey
    .ShowHelp
End With
```

19. Add a new command button to the form and set its properties as follows:

Property	Value
Name	cmdHelpIndexNoMatch
Caption	Index (No Match)
Left	68
Height	33
Top	175
Width	97

20. Double-click the cmdHelpIndexNoMatch command button to access its Click event and add the following code:

```
With cmdlgHelp
    '* Attempt to display topic with specified ID.
    .HelpKey = "Design"
    .HelpCommand = cdlHelpKey
    .ShowHelp
End With
```

Section 6. Using a Common Dialog control to display a specific Help topic. Often, you'll want to display a specific Help topic based on its Context ID. For example, if you were to put a Help button on a custom dialog box, you could show the form's help topic when the button is clicked. In this section, you're going to create a command button that displays the Help topic with the ID of 1000:

21. Add a new command button to the form and set its properties as follows:

Property	Value
Name	cmdHelpShowTopic
Caption	Show Topic
Left	68
Height	33
Top	224
Width	97

Your form should now look like the one in Figure 10-9.

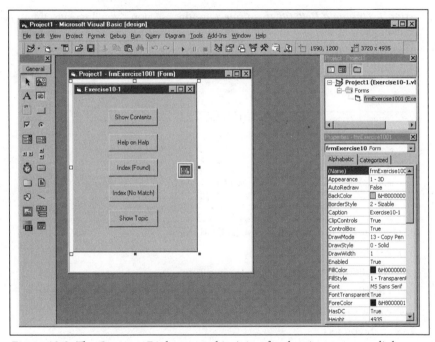

Figure 10-9: The Common Dialog control isn't just for showing common dialog boxes

22. Double-click the cmdHelpShowTopic command button to access its Click event and add the following code:

```
With cmdlgHelp
    .HelpContext = 1000
    .HelpCommand = cdlHelpContext
    .ShowHelp
End With
```

Section 7. Testing your project. The project is now complete. Run the project by pressing F5; then click the command buttons and observe the behavior exhibited by each. The code required to access the Help functions is not complex. However, this does not diminish the importance of the functions. Make sure you understand the concepts presented in this exercise for the exams, and use these techniques in your own applications.

Exercise 10-2: Implementing What's This Help

In this exercise, you'll implement What's This Help on a form. You'll not only enable the What's This Help button on the form's title bar, you'll also activate What's This Help using a command button and a single line of code. As in Exercise 10.1, the Help file is titled *bdpro.hlp* and is downloadable from *http://vb. oreilly.com*. You'll need to copy the HLP file to the folder in which you create this exercise project or the project won't work.

Section 1. Linking a Help file to a project. In this section, you'll create the link between the Help file and the application:

1. Start Visual Basic and create a new ActiveX EXE.

2. Set the following properties of the form:

Property	Value
Name	frmExercise1002
Caption	Exercise10-2
Height	3600
ScaleMode	3 – Pixel
StartUpPosition	2 – Center Screen
Width	4800

3. Double-click the form to access its Load event.

4. Enter the following code:

```
App.HelpFile = App.Path & "\bdpro.hlp"
```

5. To test that the Help file is properly linked, press F5 to start the project.

6. Press F1 to display the Help file.

7. Stop the project.

Section 2. Enabling What's This Help. In this section, you'll enable What's This Help for the form:

8. Set the form's BorderStyle to *3 – Fixed Dialog*.

9. Set the form's WhatsThisButton property to True. This will cause the WhatsThisHelp property to automatically change to True, and a What's This Help button will appear on the form.

Section 3. Linking What's This Help to a control. Linking What's This Help to controls is similar to linking standard Help topics to controls. In this section, you'll add a text box to the form and link a What's This Help topic to it:

10. Add a new command button to the center of the form by double-clicking the text box icon in the toolbox, and set its properties as follows:

Property	Value
Name	txt
Text	*Set to empty*
WhatsThisHelpID	1000

Section 4. Putting a form in What's This Help mode using code. If you create custom toolbars, you'll need a way to activate a form's What's This Help mode when a user clicks a button. In this section, you'll create a command button and add code to do just this:

11. Add a new command button to the form and set its properties as follows:

Property	Value
Name	cmdWhatsThis
Caption	What's This
Height	33
Left	116
Top	140
Width	81

Your form should now look like that shown in Figure 10-10.

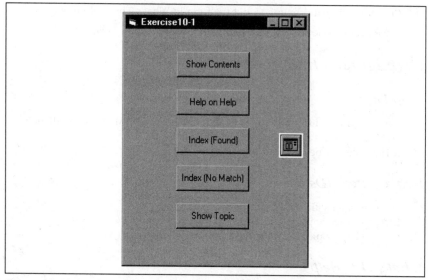

Figure 10-10: You can put a form in What's This Help mode using code

12. Double-click the command button to access its Click event and add the following statement:

```
Me.WhatsThisMode
```

Section 5. Testing the project. All that's left to do is to test the project:

13. Press F5 to put the project in run mode.

14. Click the button on the right of the title bar to put the form in What's This Help mode. The cursor will turn into an arrow with a question mark, as shown in Figure 10-11.

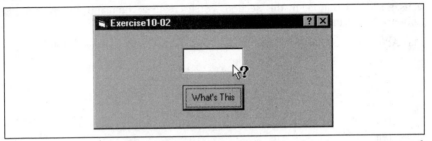

Figure 10-11: When in What's This Help mode, the cursor changes to an arrow and a question mark

15. Click the text box to display its What's This Help topic.

16. Click anywhere on the form to close the What's This Help topic.

17. Click the command button to put the form in What's This Help mode.

18. Once again, click the text box to display its What's This Help.

Highlighter's Index

Help Files

Can be compiled from RTF files (standard Help) or HTML files (HTML help)
HTML help is the newer, more advanced, help
A Help file can be assigned to a project

Help Context IDs

Refers to a specific help topic
Linked to the HelpContext IDs of objects
Used to help topics to controls, forms, and menus

What's This Help

Context-sensitive pop-up help
Cannot have a visible Min or Max button on a form that supports
What's This Help

Topics assigned to WhatsThisHelpID property
Topics must be included in a CHM file
Can be triggered by calling WhatsThisMode

Common Dialog Control

Can be used to display help topics
Only supports standard Help files (not HTML)
Can show the Help topics
Can display Help index
Can display Help on Help

CHAPTER 11

Optimizing an Application for Distribution

As of Version 5, Visual Basic allows you to compile your code to native machine code in addition to the *p-code* (or pseudo-code) format it has supported for so many years. Visual Basic's native code compiler has myriad optimization settings to let you squeeze the greatest performance possible from each and every component you deploy. In this chapter, you'll learn how these optimizations affect a compiled component, and how to choose which compilation method is best in a given situation.

The Technologies and the Exams

Although native code compilation isn't always the best choice (as discussed in the chapter text), Microsoft has put an emphasis on understanding the optimization switches, and you'll encounter such questions on both exams, as Table 11-1 shows.

Table 11-1: Optimizing Applications for Distribution on the Exams

Topic	Covered on Exams
Setting compiler optimizations for native code components	Both

Setting Compiler Optimizations

Before Version 5 of Visual Basic, you could only compile projects into p-code applications. P-code is essentially an intermediary between the high-level instructions you write as Visual Basic code, and the low-level code (called *native* code) that the computer's processor actually understands and executes. In order for the computer processor to be able to execute p-code, it must be run through an *interpreter* that translates the p-code for the low-level code. This interpretation process can reduce the efficiency of a compiled application, but this happens less frequently than one might think.

Visual Basic's native code compiler uses the same optimizing back-end compiler technology as Microsoft Visual C++, and the ability of Visual Basic 5.0 to compile applications to native code was perhaps one of the most highly anticipated features ever implemented in Visual Basic. The fact is that, for many applications, natively compiled code doesn't offer much of an increase in performance; in some circumstances, it may actually decrease the efficiency of your program.

Regardless of the method used to compile an application (p-code or native code), you *must* distribute the *Msvbvm60.dll* file in order for the application to run. Among the services provided by this DLL are startup and shutdown code for your application, functionality for forms and intrinsic controls, and runtime functions like *Format* and *CLng*. This runtime library is used by all Visual Basic programs regardless of their compilation method.

When deciding on what method of compilation to use for any given application, you should consider the following:

- If the application performs frequent direct calls to the Windows API or makes many COM method calls, compiling to p-code will give performance similar to compiling to native code. However, p-code compiled applications are considerably smaller than native code applications, and therefore consume less memory when loaded.

- If the application performs frequent string manipulations, p-code compilation will again give similar performance to native code compilation. Also, once again, p-code applications are considerably smaller than native code applications.

- If the application consists primarily of calling Visual Basic functions, such as displaying forms, then the program won't benefit much from native code compilation because the Visual Basic runtime library is already highly optimized.

- If the application performs financial or mathematical processes requiring intensive computations or manipulation of local data structures (UDTs), compiling to native code may offer substantial performance improvements.

- If the application makes a large number of calls to inline procedures (subs or functions), it may not benefit much from native code compilation. In order to make such calls, Visual Basic has to set up stack frames, initialize variables, and perform clean-up operations when the functions end. The performance of these tasks is the same between p-code and native code applications.

The native code compiler feature is only available in the Professional and Enterprise editions of Visual Basic.

Optimizing Applications

In real-world tests, Microsoft found that typically only 5% of an application's total execution time is spent executing p-code (or native code); the rest of the time is spent inside forms, data objects, Windows DLLs (APIs), and the Visual Basic for Applications runtime. Therefore, if native code could execute instantaneously, an application would only see a maximum of 5% performance increase. If much of this code is used to place calls to objects, DLLs (the Windows API or others), or Visual Basic for Applications run-time functions, the performance benefits further decrease because the method of compilation of an application does not affect the performance of these objects or DLLs.

Generally, native code compilation is designed to allow programmers to create highly optimized routines, such as computationally intensive algorithms, that are just too slow to be used in a p-code application. An application will benefit most if you can isolate the routines that gain the most from native code compilation from the rest of the application, possibly accessing them via a native code–compiled ActiveX DLL.

One advantage that native code compilation has over p-code compilation is that it allows you to squeeze performance out of specific areas by exploiting a number of compilation optimization options (called *switches*). Before you can set optimization switches, you must designate native code compilation as the compilation method of a project; optimization switches don't apply to, and therefore cannot be specified when, compiling to p-code.

The compiler options are located on the Compile tab of the Project Properties dialog box (see Figure 11-1), and they are saved with the project; each project has its own compiler options.

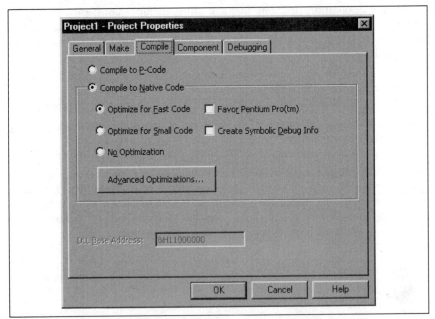

Figure 11-1: Visual Basic's compiler has many features, and they're all accessed from the Compile tab of the Project Properties dialog box

When Compile to P-Code is selected, all of the optimization techniques are disabled. When you select the Compile to Native Code option, the default, all of Visual Basic's advanced compiler options become enabled.

Setting Basic Optimization Switches

The switches that appear on the Compile tab of the Project Properties dialog box are basic optimization switches. Ordinarily, you can't cause a problem by using any of the basic optimization switches. When you get into selecting advanced settings, as discussed shortly, then a misstep can wreak havoc on a compiled component.

Setting the general optimization switch

The switch you'll always want to set first is represented by three option buttons:

- Optimize for Fast Code
- Optimize for Small Code
- No Optimization

When the compiler translates Visual Basic code statements to native code, there are often a number of different sequences of commands that can correctly perform the construct of the statements. When you select the Optimize for Fast Code option button (the default), the compiler favors faster constructs over smaller constructs. This usually results in a larger compiled file, but also a faster one.

When you select the Optimize for Small Code option button, the compiler favors smaller code constructs over faster ones. This often results in a slower compiled component, but also a smaller one. This optimization can be extremely desirable when distributing your applications over the Internet.

One time that you may want to use the No Optimization setting is when compiling an application with symbolic debug information (discussed later in this chapter). Applications compiled with this setting are larger and slower than those compiled with a method of optimization.

Favoring the Pentium Pro

Just as development tools keep improving, so does hardware. The Intel Pentium Pro, for instance, allows for a number of different coding strategies that can greatly improve the efficiency of a component. However, a component compiled with these strategies does not perform as well on earlier processors, including the standard Pentium processor. If you're deploying a component that you *know* will be run primarily on Pentium Pros, you can select the Favor Pentium Pro™ checkbox to include these optimizations in the compiled code.

Creating symbolic debug info

When you select the Create Symbolic Debug Info checkbox, the Visual Basic compiler produces a compiled file containing information that allows comprehensive debugging to be performed using Microsoft Visual C++ or a compatible debugger. Using such a debugger is beyond the scope of this book and the exams. However, you may encounter a question on how to include debugging information in a compiled program, and this is the setting that lets you do it.

Specifying a DLL base address

When the operating system first attempts to load an ActiveX DLL, it tries to load it at the memory address specified in the DLL Base Address text box. If there is insufficient space at the specified location, as happens when another DLL or application is loaded at the same address space, the operating system must relocate the DLL. Relocating the DLL takes time and resources.

You can specify any address between &H10000000 and &H80000000 within a 64k boundary, meaning that the last four digits of the address must always be 0000. The default base address is &H11000000.

 There will always be a large number of developers who never bother to read the documentation on the DLL Base Address setting, and consequently, there will always be a very large number of ActiveX DLLs out there loading at the default base address of &H11000000. You should *always* specify a different address for each DLL you compile.

Setting Advanced Optimization Switches

The basic optimization switches are essentially fool-proof; you really can't cause any harm regardless of the settings you choose. Visual Basic's compiler also has a number of advanced optimization switches that can further increase the performance of a component. Be warned, however, that improper use of these options can cause your component to become unstable, crash, and/or produce incorrect results. The fact that these switches can enhance the performance of a component, combined with the necessity to use them correctly, appears to have prompted Microsoft to dedicate a number of questions to these switches on the exams.

To access the advanced optimization switches (see Figure 11-2), click the Advanced Optimizations button on the Compile tab of the Project Properties dialog box. Table 11-2 summarizes these advanced optimization switches.

Table 11-2: Native Code Compilation Advanced Optimization Switches

Option	Description
Assume No Aliasing	Tells the compiler that your program does not use aliasing (does not pass variables by reference). Selecting this optimization allows the compiler to apply optimizations to areas such as storing variables in registers and performing loop optimizations.
Remove Array Bounds Checks	Disables Visual Basic's array bounds checking.
Remove Integer Overflow Checks	Disables Visual Basic's integer overflow checking.
Remove Floating Point Error Checks	Disables Visual Basic's floating point error checking.

Table 11-2: Native Code Compilation Advanced Optimization Switches (continued)

Option	Description
Allow Unrounded Floating Point Operations	Allows the compiler to use floating point registers more efficiently by avoiding loads and stores from memory. In addition, floating point comparisons are performed more efficiently.
Remove Safe Pentium™ FDIV Checks	Disables checking for safe Pentium processor floating point division.

The Allow Unrounded Floating Point Operations and Remove Safe Pentium™ FDIV Checks are considered by some to provide an inadequate performance increase when weighted against the potential problems they can cause.

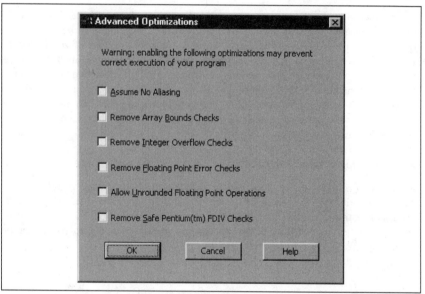

Figure 11-2: You can really fine-tune the performance of your applications by correctly setting the advanced compiler switches

Assume No Aliasing

Although few large projects can take advantage of this option, Assume No Aliasing can increase the performance of a component and should be used when possible. *Aliasing* occurs when you pass a variable by reference as opposed to by value (`ByRef` versus `ByVal`). When you pass a variable by reference, you end up with two variables that reference the same piece of data in memory: the original variable passed to a procedure, and the variable that accepts the value as a parameter of the procedure. The original reference is *aliased*. To explicitly pass a variable by reference, you use the `ByRef` keyword like this:

```
Public Sub MyFunction(ByRef X as Single)
```

In order to pass a parameter by value rather than by reference, you *must* provide the ByVal keyword like this:

```
Public Sub MyFunction(ByVal X as Single)
```

It's extremely important to remember that Visual Basic's default method of passing variables is ByRef (using aliasing). Therefore, if you don't explicitly provide the ByVal keyword to pass a variable by value, a parameter is accepted by reference (ByRef). For instance, this procedure declaration accepts a parameter by reference:

```
Public Sub MyFunction(X as Single)
```

When your application doesn't use aliasing, the compiler can apply certain optimizations such as storing variables in registers and performing loop optimizations that it could not use when aliasing occurs. Do not select this optimization if your application uses aliasing.

Remove Array Bounds Checks

Every time an access to an array occurs, a check is performed by default to verify that the specified index is within the range of the array. If the index is not valid (falls outside the bounds of the array), a trappable error is raised. If you know that your code is written so that no attempt to access an array with an invalid index will occur, you can turn this feature off by selecting the Remove Array Bounds Checks optimization switch. Although this may increase the performance of your application, it opens up the possibility that an attempt to access an incorrect index of an array will occur, causing memory corruption and the possibility of the component crashing.

Remove Integer Overflow Checks

Visual Basic checks every integer-style calculation (byte, integer, and long) by default to verify that the results of the operation won't overflow the datatype being used. For example, an Integer can hold a maximum value of 32,767. The following code generates an overflow error because an attempt is made to put a number larger than 32,767 into an Integer variable.

```
Dim i As Integer

i = 32767 + 1
```

If you select the Remove Integer Overflow Checks optimization switch, Visual Basic won't perform this error checking, and some integer type calculations may execute faster. However, if data does overflow an integer variable, incorrect results *will* occur.

Remove Floating Point Error Checks

The Remove Floating Point Error Checks optimization switch is similar to the Remove Integer Overflow Checks option except that this switch controls whether or not Visual Basic monitors floating point data calculations (Single and Double). If you select this optimization switch, Visual Basic won't check for overflow errors, nor will it check for invalid operations such as divide-by-zero errors. The net result is that some floating point division operations will execute faster. However, if an undesirable situations arises, such as an overflow error, incorrect results will occur.

Allow Unrounded Floating Point Operations

Ordinarily, Visual Basic compares floating point variables with floating point expressions at the same degree of precision. If an expression evaluates to a higher degree of precision than the datatype it's being compared to, it's rounded prior to the comparison taking place. If you select the Allow Unrounded Floating Point Operations optimization switch, the compiler won't perform this rounding operation prior to performing a compare. While this allows the compiler to perform some floating point operations faster, it can also result in incorrect expression evaluations.

For example, under ordinary circumstances, you would expect the following code to print the word True:

```
Dim X As Single

X = <floating-point computation>
  ...
If X = <floating-point computation> then
   Debug.Print "True"
Else
   Debug.Print "False"
End If
```

In an application compiled with the Allow Unrounded Floating Point Operations switch turned on, it's very possible that the word False might be printed. This happens when the expression being computed results in a number of higher precision than a Single. Because the number is rounded in order to be stored in the Single variable, the expression would be slightly different from the actual result stored in the variable. If you don't enable this optimization switch, the compiler knows to round the expression to the proper precision before performing a compare.

Removing Safe Pentium FDIV Checks

You probably remember the commotion over the Pentium floating point division (FDIV) bug that made it into many production Pentium chips. Visual Basic has the ability to automatically include extra code in a compiled application that works around this bug to ensure that mathematical operations always come out accurately. If you don't believe your application performs the type of calculations that may be affected by this bug, you can select the Remove Safe Pentium FDIV Checks switch. Selecting this optimization instructs the compiler to eliminate the extra code, resulting in a smaller and faster component, but also a component that may be susceptible to errors in floating point division.

Fully understanding the optimization switches is not only important to passing the exam, it's important for distribution of optimized components. Take the time to fully understand the ramifications of these various optimizations. Your applications and your exam scores will benefit from the effort.

Key Facts

This chapter has discussed the various optimization features of Visual Basic's compiler and how to determine what is the most desirable compilation method for a given situation. The following are key facts to understand in order to answer related questions on the Visual Basic exams:

- Visual Basic lets you compile applications to p-code or native code (low-level machine code).

- Regardless of the compilation method used to create a Visual Basic component, Visual Basic's runtime library file, *Msvbvm60.dll*, is always used and must be distributed with the component.

- The native code compiler feature is available only in the Professional and Enterprise editions of Visual Basic.

- P-code must be interpreted to lower-level machine language in order for a processor to understand and execute its statements.

- Native code isn't always the best choice for compiling applications.

- Most applications don't realize much performance benefit from being compiled to native code.

- Native code compilation produces larger component files than p-code compilation.

- Code that does a lot of primitive operations on hard-typed, nonstring variables will execute with maximum performance when compiled to native code as opposed to p-code. Complex financial calculations or fractal generation algorithms, for instance, would benefit from native code.

- Computationally intensive programs, or programs that shuffle a lot of bits and bytes around within local data structures, will show noticeable performance improvements when compiled to native code.

- For many programs, especially those doing a lot of Windows API calls, COM method calls, or string manipulations, native code won't be much faster than p-code. However, you can always count on a natively compiled executable to be larger than its p-code counterpart.

- Applications that consist primarily of functions from the Visual Basic for Applications runtime library aren't going to see much (if any) improvement when compiled to native code, because the code in the Visual Basic for Applications runtime library is already highly optimized.

- Code that involves a lot of subroutine calls relative to inline procedures is unlikely to appear much faster with native code. This is because all the work of setting up stack frames, initializing variables, and cleaning up on exit takes the same time with both the p-code engine and generated native code.

- Typically, only 5% of an application's total execution time is spent executing p-code (or native code).

- One advantage that native code compilation has over p-code compilation is that it allows you to squeeze performance out of specific areas of compilation by exploiting a number of optimization options (called switches).

- You cannot select optimizations when you compile an application to p-code.

- The Optimize for Fast Code optimization switch favors faster constructs over smaller ones. This produces faster applications, but larger application files.

- The Optimize for Small Code optimization switch favors smaller constructs over faster ones. This produces smaller application files, but slower applications. This switch is useful when creating Internet components.

- If you are deploying an application that you know will be run primarily on Pentium Pro computers, you can select the Favor Pentium Pro™ checkbox to include optimizations in your compiled code that will run faster on Pentium Pros. However, the same code will execute slower on other processors, including the standard Pentium.

- You can compile symbolic debug information for use with comprehensive debugging tools, such as the one included with Microsoft's Visual C++, by selecting the Create Symbolic Debug Info optimization switch.

- You can specify a DLL base address as a default location in which to load an ActiveX DLL. If the location is being used, the operating system must relocate the DLL.

- You should always specify a unique DLL base address for each of your ActiveX DLLs.

- Incorrectly using advanced compiler optimization switches can lead to unstable applications. These applications may produce incorrect results, and they may even crash.

- Aliasing occurs when you pass variables between procedures by reference.

- Turning off Array Bounds Checking within a compiled application may speed up statements that work with arrays. However, if the application attempts to access an invalid array index, it may cause memory corruption and it risks the possibility of crashing.

- Removing Integer Overflow Checks in a compiled application may speed up some integer computations, but if an attempt is made to place too large a value into an integer-type variable (byte, integer, or long), incorrect results may occur.

- Removing Floating Point Error Checks in a compiled application may speed up some floating-point computations. If an attempt is made to overflow a floating-type variable or perform an invalid operation, such as divide-by-zero, the application will receive incorrect results.

- Selecting the Allow Unrounded Floating Point Operations compiler optimization switch may speed up some floating point operations, but it can also cause expressions to be evaluated incorrectly.

- By default, Visual Basic includes extra code in a compiled application that ensures you always get correct results from arithmetic calculations, even on Pentium chips with the FDIV bug. This behavior can be turned off by setting the Remove Safe Pentium FDIV Checks compiler optimization switch.

Applying What You've Learned

It's now time to apply what you've learned about optimizing applications for distribution. There are no exercises for this chapter. Every application or component you create will have its own requirements for compilation. Make sure you fully understand the concepts presented in this chapter and answer all of the Skills Assessment questions. You will encounter optimization questions on the Visual Basic exams.

Skills Assessment

1. Which form of compilation is new as of Visual Basic 5?

    a. P-code

    b. Native code

    c. Both p-code and native code

    d. Neither p-code nor native code

2. When you compile a project to a native code compilation, you don't need to distribute *Msvbvm60.dll*.

    a. True

    b. False

3. P-code stands for:

    a. Protected code

    b. Pre-code

    c. Post-code

    d. Pseudo-code

4. In order for a processor to use p-code, it must be run through:

    a. A call stack

    b. An interpreter

    c. A compiler

    d. A system debugger

5. Native code is always the best choice for compiling components:

    a. True

    b. False

6. Which of the following would likely benefit most from native compilation?

    a. A program that makes lots of API calls

    b. A program that uses lots of COM objects

    c. A program that performs lots of string manipulations

    d. A program that computes financial data

7. Which form of compilation allows you to set custom optimization options?

    a. P-code

    b. Native code

    c. Both p-code and native code

    d. Neither p-code nor native code

8. Code compiled with symbolic debug information can be debugged using:

    a. Microsoft's Visual C++ debugger.

    b. Visual Basic's compiler.

    c. A text editor.

    d. A compiled application cannot be debugged.

9. Which of the following statements is true?

    a. You should always specify a unique DLL base address for all of your ActiveX DLLs.

    b. A DLL compiled with the default DLL base address will not run.

    c. DLL base addresses are specified in increments of 32 K.

10. Aliasing occurs when:

    a. You rename a variable.

    b. A variable is passed by reference.

    c. A variable is passed by value.

    d. Visual Basic is not capable of supporting aliasing.

11. Which optimization switch will remove the safety division-by-zero check?

    a. Allow Unrounded Floating Point Operations

    b. Floating Point Error Checks

    c. Remove Safe Pentium FDIV Checks

    d. None of the above

12. Your application relies on arguments that are passed by reference. Which two native code compilation options should you select to optimize the performance of numeric processing?

    a. Assume no Aliasing

    b. Optimize for Small Code

    c. Remove Floating Point Error Checks

    d. Remove Safe for Pentium FDIV Checks

13. You are creating an application that is intended to run on only Pentium Pro–based processors. You want to maximize the performance of this application. Which compiler option should you use?

    a. Assuming no Aliasing

    b. Optimize for Small Code

c. Create Symbolic Debug Info

　　d. Remove Safe for Pentium FDIV Checks

Answers to Skills Assessment

1. b	4. b	7. b	10. b	13. d
2. b	5. b	8. a	11. b	
3. d	6. d	9. a	12. c, d	

Highlighter's Index

Compiler Optimizations

Can be used only when creating native code executables

Setting optimization switches "turns off" safety catches, and applications may experience problems

Code can be optimized for speed or size, or a combination of both

CHAPTER 12

Creating Microsoft Transaction Server Components

Chances are that Microsoft Transaction Server (MTS) is the subject with which you have the least experience. If you're only taking the desktop exam, you're in luck and you won't have to demonstrate an understanding of MTS. If, however, you are going to take the Distributing exam, you will have to demonstrate an understanding of MTS. If you're already familiar with MTS, then you'll be in really good shape for the exam.

The Technologies and the Exams

If you haven't used MTS before, you'll need to study this chapter well in order to pass the MTS questions on the Distributing exam. Table 12-1 shows the MTS-related topics covered on this exam.

Table 12-1: MTS-Related Topics on the Visual Basic Exams

Topic	Covered on Exams
Understanding how MTS and DCOM relate	Distributing
Creating and distributing MTS packages	Distributing
Understanding declarative and programmatic security in MTS components	Distributing
Configuring security roles in MTS	Distributing
How to install and configure MTS	Distributing
Creating MTS components in Visual Basic	Distributing

What Is MTS?

Unless you actually use MTS, you may not know exactly what it is. MTS is difficult to describe in any brief sort of way. Microsoft Transaction Server is an application service for Windows NT that is used to develop and distribute *n*-tier component-based solutions. MTS, which extends COM, simplifies the development of middle-tier components, as well as the deployment and management of such components.

MTS provides the underlying architecture for running and managing components in an optimized and secure fashion. Designing components for use with MTS ultimately means writing less code, with the added benefit of a gain in performance, functionality, and scalability. It would be difficult (if not impossible) to design robust, scaleable components with the same capabilities provided inherently by MTS—even with a generous amount of development time.

 MTS manages in-process COM components. Therefore, only ActiveX DLLs can be used with MTS; ActiveX EXE files cannot be used with MTS.

MTS manages the middle-tier components of an *n*-tier solution. The presentation layer running on various client machines access components managed by MTS, and therefore many MTS components are used to encapsulate and enforce business rules.

MTS includes a very impressive feature set for executing and managing components (see Table 12-2)—so impressive, in fact, that it's impossible to imagine attempting to design these capabilities into your components with just Visual Basic code.

Table 12-2: Component Management Features of MTS

Feature	Description
Just-in-time Activation	MTS can cache objects when they're not used, so they don't consume server resources. When a component is needed again, MTS reacquires resources for the component so a client can use it.
Process Isolation	Processes are isolated so that a fault in one component doesn't crash components in other processes.
Database Connection Pooling	MTS provides a pool of connections to a data source which expedites database access requests by reusing existing connections.
Thread Pooling	MTS provides and manages a pool of threads on which components are created and used, resulting in components that respond much more quickly to client requests.
Role-Based Security	MTS allows components to use a high-level security implementation. The security is provided by MTS, however, rather than programmed into a component.
Automatic Transaction Support	Provides transactional functionality at the component level.

MTS and DCOM

Distributed COM (DCOM) is the mechanism used to broker communications between clients and MTS components. Therefore, DCOM must be installed in order to use MTS; if DCOM is not successfully installed, MTS won't function. (DCOM is discussed in greater detail in Chapter 13, *Packaging and Deploying an Application*.)

DCOM is automatically installed on all Windows 98 computers, and on computers running Windows NT 4.0 with Service Pack 3 or higher. For client machines running Windows 95, DCOM is automatically installed with Internet Explorer 4.x. The latest version of DCOM (as well as a DCOM installation for Windows 95 computers) can be found at *http://www.microsoft.com/com/resources/downloads.asp.*

Packages

MTS manages components by way of *packages;* a package is a set of components that perform related application functions. Packages contain component files and their associated type libraries, as well as information about the package, such as component properties and security information. In order for a component to run within MTS, it *must* be part of a package. Although a single computer can run multiple packages at a time, a component may be part of only one package on a given machine.

 When a package is added to MTS, the proper registry values are created, much like when you register an ActiveX component manually. When you remove a package, the registry is automatically updated appropriately as well.

All files within a package run in the same process space. However, whether the files run in the process space of the client or of the server is determined by the activation type of the package. Each package is either a *Library package* or a *Server package.* A Library package runs in the same process as the client, whereas a Server package runs in its own dedicated process on its machine. Although this behavior sounds much like that of DLLs versus EXEs, remember that all MTS components must be DLLs. In the case of a Server package, MTS ensures that the DLL runs in its own process space on the machine that contains the package.

Server package

When a package is run as a Server package, all of the components in the package run in the same dedicated process space on the machine on which the package resides—completely isolated from all other components in all other packages. This behavior is called *fault isolation,* and it makes for a very stable environment because a component that faults only crashes components from its package with it, never components from other packages.

When a client makes a request to a Server package component for the first time, a considerable delay may result because MTS doesn't just load the referenced component, it loads all of the components in the package. This causes performance to suffer slightly the first time a component in a Server package is referenced, but also speeds up the instantiation and referencing process when another client references a component in the package.

Library package

Components that are part of a Library package run in the process space of the client. This behavior is pretty much like that of a typical ActiveX DLL. A Library package must be installed (with MTS) on the same machine as a client that needs to access a component within the package. If the component faults, it can take out the client application as well.

 Components in one or more Server packages can use a component from a Library package. When this occurs, the component in the Library package runs in the same process space as the component in the Server package.

By creating packages, deployment and management is simplified. Later in this chapter, you'll learn how to create and manage packages within MTS.

Security

 Security is supported only for components running on a Windows NT machine, not for components running on a Windows 9x machine.

MTS allows you to implement a high level of security with little or no code. MTS's security is based upon *roles*, which in many ways is an extension of the Windows NT's security model. Roles are similar to NT groups in that you can assign multiple users to roles, but you can also assign groups to roles as well. In practice, it's recommended that you assign only groups to roles. That way, assigning a new user to a role can be accomplished by simply adding the user to a user group. If you assign users to roles directly, you'd have to modify all roles that either need the user added or need the user removed.

 This section discusses how roles are used to create secure components. Later in this chapter, you'll learn how to create and manage roles using MTS Explorer.

Roles are used to secure a component in different ways, depending on the type of security in place. The two types of security supported by MTS are:

- Declarative
- Programmatic

Declarative-level security

Declarative- (or package-) level security is used to simply allow or deny access to a component. If the user belongs to a role of the package (or is a member of a group that belongs to a role of the package), he or she is allowed full access to the components within the package. If the user is not a member of a role, he or she is denied access to the components within the package. To enable Package security, right-click a Package in the MTS Explorer (discussed later in this chapter), choose Properties, click the Security tab, then select the "Enable authorization checking" checkbox (see Figure 12-1).

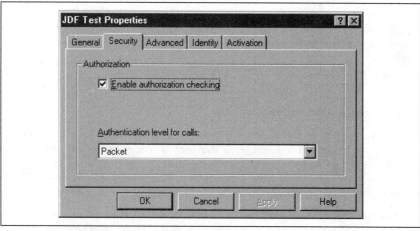

Figure 12-1: Use the Security tab of the Properties dialog box of a component to enable Package level security

When you enable authorization checking, the "Authentication level for calls" drop-down list becomes enabled. This list is used to specify the level of Package security. Table 12-3 lists the values and their meanings.

 As you can see from the table, each level of security incurs more overhead, and the highest levels of security can severely degrade performance.

Table 12-3: Authentication Levels and Their Meanings

Value	Description
None	Overrides and disables the "Enable authorization checking" checkbox.
Connect	Causes authentication to occur only when the client first accesses the package.
Call	Causes authentication to occur each time a client makes a request to access a package.

Table 12-3: Authentication Levels and Their Meanings (continued)

Value	Description
Packet	(Default) Causes authentication to occur on every packet transmitted by the server to the client. Identity information is encrypted, and therefore one user cannot impersonate another.
Packet Integrity	Similar to Packet, except that the caller's identity and digital signature are encrypted with each packet so that the integrity of each packet can be verified.
Packet Privacy	Similar to Packet Integrity, except that *all* packet information is encrypted, in addition to the caller's information.

 After changing the security level for a package, you must shut down and restart the server package before your changes take effect.

Programmatic level security

Declarative security is useful only for controlling which users have the ability to access a component in a package; if the user is a member of any role of the package, they can access components in the package. In distributed applications, this is rarely enough. When you create MTS components, you have the ability to enforce security programmatically. Roles are still used, but in a different way.

In order to implement programmatic security (and other programmatic MTS features as well), you must add a reference to the Microsoft Transaction Server Type Library to your project. If you haven't installed MTS's development components on your development machine (discussed later in this chapter), chances are you won't have the necessary type library. If you are unable to locate the type library using Visual Basic's References dialog box, install MTS, making sure to install the developer components.

The parent object used to perform most MTS programmatic functions is the ObjectContext object. Each component has an object context, and when one component creates an instance of another component, the second component inherits the object context of the first. You create an instance of this object much as you would any other object. Instead of creating a new object, however, you use GetObjectContext to return an existing object context. The following code creates an ObjectContext object:

```
Dim objObjectContext As ObjectContext
Set objObjectContext = GetObjectContext()
```

Programmatic security is performed using two methods of the MTS ObjectContext object. The first method, IsSecurityEnabled, is used to determine whether or not MTS security is enabled. Server packages always run in a protected MTS process, and therefore they are always secure. However, since Library packages run in the process space of clients, and clients don't run in an MTS process (they usually run on a local machine), security *may* not be enabled. I use the word "may" because it's possible for a Library package to run in an MTS-protected process. This occurs when a Server package accesses a component in a Library package. Because a Server package always runs in a protected process, any Library packages referenced by the Server package also run in the same protected process. Since security may not always be enabled in a component that is part of a Library package, it's best to check whether or not security is enforced before attempting to programmatically control security in the component.

To use IsSecurityEnabled, simply call the method as part of the ObjectContext object. If security is enabled, the method returns **True**, and if the component is being run as part of a Server package, it will always return **True**. If the component is being run as part of a Library package, and the client is not a Server package, then IsSecurityEnabled returns **False**. The following code shows how you might prevent a method from executing in an unsecured environment:

```
Public Sub DeleteEmployee(lngEmployeeID As Long)

    Dim objObjectContext As ObjectContext
    Set objObjectContext = GetObjectContext()

    If Not(objObjectContext.IsSecurityEnabled) Then Exit Sub

    ...

End Sub
```

The IsSecurityEnabled method certainly affords some programmatic security control, but using it is only a small step. A more powerful method of the ObjectContext object is IsCallerInRole. The IsCallerInRole method lets you specify the name of a role, and if the user running the component is a member of the role, the method returns **True** otherwise it returns **False**. This method is extremely useful. For instance, say you have a component that accesses personal records. You may want a clerk to be able to view nonsensitive information, but you want a manager to have full access to employee data. With declarative security, roles are used only to determine who has full access and who has no access. Using programmatic security (in particular, the IsCallerInRole method), you can extend the functionality of roles. The following procedure shows how you might use IsCallerInRole to limit who has access to delete an employee record:

```
Public Sub DeleteEmploye(lngEmployeeID As Long)

    Dim objObjectContext As ObjectContext
    Set objObjectContext = GetObjectContext()

    If objObjectContext.IsCallerInRole("Manager") Then
        ' Caller is a Manager, go ahead and delete employee.
        ...
    Else
        ' Caller is not a Manager, so do NOT allow them to delete
        ' the employee.
        ...
    End If

End Sub
```

If IsCallerInRole is called from within a Library package not running in a secured MTS process (i.e., not called from a Server package), the method always returns True.

Installing MTS

MTS can be found on, and installed from, the Windows NT 4 Option Pack. The installation of MTS is performed using a typical Setup Wizard. Some certification books walk you step by painstaking step through the installation, but I'm assuming you're smart enough to select components and click a Next button. Therefore, here's an abridged process of installing MTS:

1. Run the *Setup.exe* program on the Windows NT 4 Option Pack CD-ROM.

2. Select the Transaction Server component on the Select Components page of the wizard (see Figure 12-2).

3. Select any other desired components and complete the wizard (easy, no?).

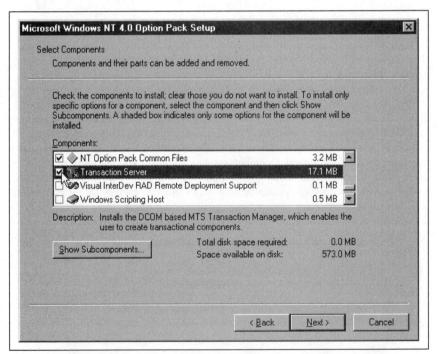

Figure 12-2: Microsoft Transaction Server is an installable component of the Windows NT 4 Option Pack

When installing MTS on a development machine, you'll need to install the MTS developer files, which include the Microsoft Transaction Server Type Library, which is needed to perform programmatic security as well as programmatic transactions.

To install the developer component, select the Transaction Server component as shown in Figure 12-2, click Show Subcomponents, then select the Transaction Server Development component on the dialog box shown in Figure 12-3.

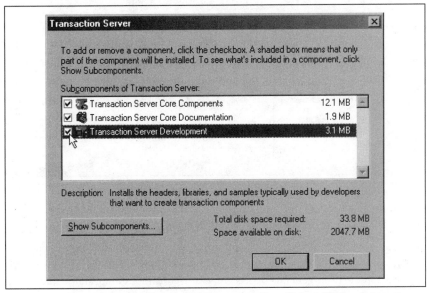

Figure 12-3: In order to develop for MTS, you must install the MTS development components on your development machine

Configuring MTS

Once MTS is installed, it must be configured. Initial configuration of MTS consists primarily of creating packages and defining roles. All of MTS configuration is performed using MTS Explorer, an application that allows you to manage MTS using an interface similar to Explorer (see Figure 12-4). MTS Explorer is used to create and manage packages, define security, and manage transaction behavior. As with Windows Explorer, selecting an item in the left TreeView control displays the contents of the selected item in the right pane.

 Many of the functions that you can perform using MTS Explorer are discussed in their respective sections throughout this chapter.

Securing MTS Using the System Package

Like most applications, MTS is first installed without any security enforced—anyone can access and use MTS Explorer. For obvious reasons, enabling security is one of the first things you'll want to do when you set up MTS. MTS includes a System package, which is used for internal operations and cannot be modified.

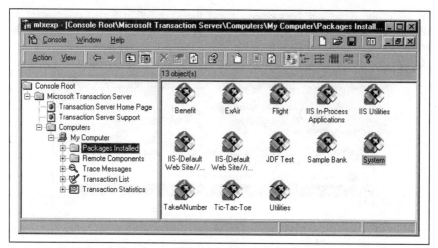

Figure 12-4: MTS Explorer is used to manage MTS

When MTS is first installed, the System package has an Administrator role, but no user is mapped to the role. This has the effect of having no security on the System package. The System package roles determine who can view and who can modify packages within MTS, and the first step to administering MTS is to secure MTS Explorer (and MTS in general) by assigning a user to the Administrator role of the System package.

As is pretty standard for Windows, the computer on which MTS resides is called My Computer, and it appears in MTS Explorer under the Computers folder. Selecting the My Computer item in MTS Explorer displays the MTS contents of the computer, including installed packages. Double-clicking the Packages Installed icon displays the packages installed on the computer, including the System package (refer to Figure 12-4).

Double-clicking the System package icon displays a folder for Components and a folder for Roles. Double-clicking the Roles folder icon displays the Administrator and Reader roles. A user assigned to the Reader role can view information in MTS but cannot make any changes. (For example, a user in the Reader role cannot change, install, or remove components.) To secure MTS, drill-down the Administrator Role until you come to the Users folder. Then select the Users folder and choose New → User from the Action menu (see Figure 12-5).

Once you've selected New → User, you're shown the Add Users and Groups to Roles dialog box, as shown in Figure 12-6. Use this dialog box to select the users and groups that are to be part of the currently selected role. To select a user or group, double-click it in the list or click once to select it and then click Add. Once you're finished, click OK to save your selections. Once a user or group is added to the Administrator role of the system package, security is enforced and only designated users will be able to make changes to MTS.

Although the System package is a unique type of package, assigning users and groups to roles is performed the same way for all types of packages.

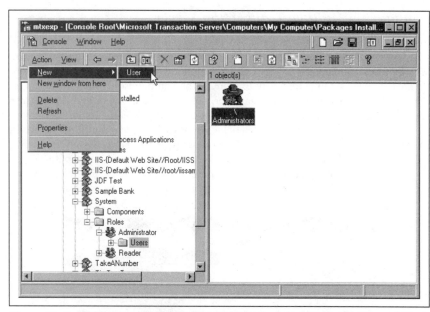

Figure 12-5: Adding users (or groups) to a role is done by selecting the Users folder of a role and then using the Action menu

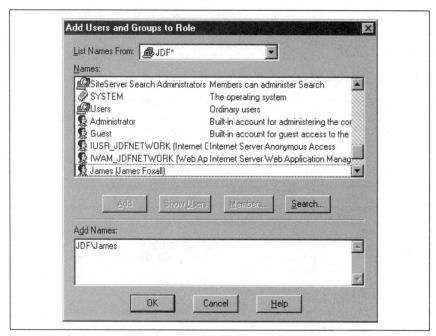

Figure 12-6: You can assign any number of users and groups to a role

Configuring Multiple Transaction Servers

In addition to serving components on the computer on which MTS is running, components can also be served by other computers running MTS, and you can use MTS Explorer to manage packages and components that exist on other machines. By default, MTS is configured only to manage the computer on which it is installed (My Computer). To add a new computer, select the Computers item in the tree view, and then choose New Computer from the Action menu. You're then given the opportunity to enter a computer name, or click a Browse button to display a list of available computers. Clicking Browse displays the Select Computer dialog box shown in Figure 12-7, which is the easiest way to specify a computer. Once you've entered a computer name, the computer shows up in the list of computers, and selecting it displays all of the packages found on the remote computer.

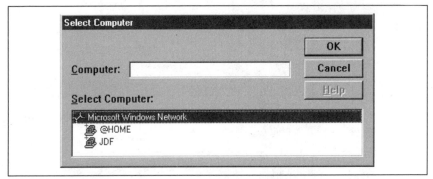

Figure 12-7: Use the Select computer dialog box to easily add computers to MTS

Creating Packages

Creating packages is a straightforward process. First, you define a package using the Package Wizard. Then, you add components and define roles. The following steps outline creating a package and adding a component to a package:

1. Select the computer on which you want to create the package in the tree view of MTS Explorer, then select Packages Installed for that computer.

2. Choose New Package from the Action menu to start the Package Wizard.

3. Click Create an Empty Package. You'll then be prompted to enter a name for the package. Enter the name and click Next.

4. On the Set Package Identity page (see Figure 12-8), choose to have the package use the identity of the user accessing the component, or have it always use a prespecified identity.

5. Click Finish to save the package.

Once the package is created, you can add components to the package and define roles.

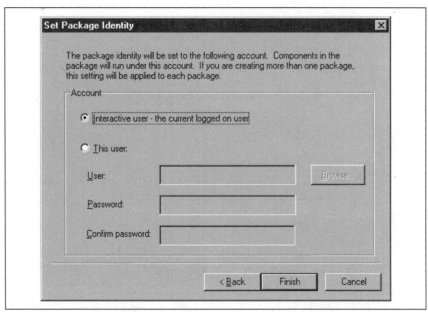

Figure 12-8: You can create packages that always run as a certain identity, rather than use the identity of the client

To add components to a package:

1. Double-click the Packages Installed folder for the computer on which you want to add new components.

2. Double-click the package to which you want to add the component(s).

3. Right-click the Components folder in the tree view, and choose New Component; or, click the Components folder once to select it, then choose New Component from the Action menu. (Note: neither of these two actions work with the Component folder displayed in the right pane.)

4. Click Install New Components to display the Install Components dialog box (see Figure 12-9).

5. Click Add Files and then browse and select the component(s) to add.

6. Click Finish to add the component(s) to the package.

All of the data that makes up the MTS environment (roles, packages, components, and so on) is stored in the MTS *catalog*. Once you add a component to a package (and hence, to the MTS catalog), you should put the component's project in binary compatibility mode to ensure that Class IDs and Prog IDs remain the same. Assuming that you maintain backward compatibility when you compile a new version of a component, you have only to have MTS perform a refresh so that the registry entries on the MTS machine are changed as necessary after each new compile.

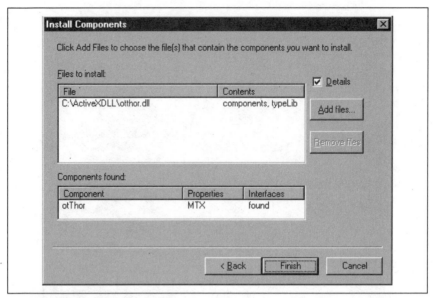

Figure 12-9: Use the Install Components dialog box to select components to include in a package

 If you don't maintain backward compatibility, you will have to manually remove the old version of a component and then add the new version to a package.

There are a few ways that you can refresh packages to deal with new versions of components. You can use MTS Explorer or you can use the MTS add-in for Visual Basic in the following ways:

Using MTS Explorer:

- To refresh the components of a single package, right-click the Components folder of the desired package and choose Refresh from the Shortcut menu.

- To refresh all components on a computer, right-click the computer and select Refresh All Components from the Shortcut menu.

Using the MTS Visual Basic Add-In (access the MTS features by choosing MS Transaction Server from the Add-Ins menu):

- Choose "AutoRefresh after compile of active project" to have Visual Basic automatically refresh the information for the component in the MTS catalog after each new build.

- Choose "Refresh all components now" to force a refresh of all components on the development machine.

Creating MTS Components Using Visual Basic

For the most part, creating an MTS component is very much like creating a traditional ActiveX DLL (recall that MTS can only manage DLLs, not EXEs). The differences between a traditional ActiveX DLL and an MTS component include using the Microsoft Transaction Server Type Library to program security (discussed earlier in this chapter in the "Security" section) and setting an MTS-specific property.

MTS Component Design Considerations

Since MTS components are ActiveX DLLs, you start by creating an ActiveX DLL project. Visual Basic allows you to create components in many different ways, however, and there are some issues you need to consider when creating a component for MTS:

- When developing an MTS component in Visual Basic, create a multithreaded component whenever possible (refer to Chapter 4, *Creating and Testing ActiveX Code Components*).

- Multithreaded MTS components should be designed for unattended execution whenever possible (this is also discussed in Chapter 4).

- Each time you recompile an MTS component for distribution, you must use binary compatibility, or you will break all clients that use the component. Refer to Chapter 13 for more information on component compatibility.

Stateless Components

Traditional component objects have a very finite lifetime: they exist while a client holds a reference to the component. The local data within the component (global- and module-level data) persists for the lifetime of the component. This is known as *maintaining state*. When creating MTS components, the goal is to create a *stateless* object; that is, an object whose local data does not persist between member calls, and therefore the success or failure of a member call does not rely on the values persisted from previous member calls.

Stateless components are often process-oriented components, consisting mostly of methods rather than properties, with no methods relying on persisted data. This is so important because when an object is deactivated (which can occur when the object calls SetComplete or SetAbort, as discussed later in this chapter), it loses all state (the persisted data is lost). If a method that is called relies on persisted data, it will fail when called after MTS exercises Just-in-Time Activation to activate the object.

Configuring a Component for Transaction Processing

In Chapter 7, *Working with Data*, you learned about using transactions in database operations, and you learned about what makes a transaction (the ACID test). MTS allows you to create components that perform transactions at the component level. This allows operations across objects to act as an autonomous unit, and allows operations to be performed against several different types of resources within one transaction. For instance, an object that has a transaction could modify data in a SQL database and create another object that modifies data in a mainframe database, and the mainframe modifications could take place as part of the client's transaction. MTS's transaction capabilities are some of its most compelling features.

Enabling and controlling transactions

The transactional behavior of a class is determined by the MTSTransactionMode property of the component class whose Instancing property has been set to MultiUse. This property is available in the properties sheet of all class modules, but if you don't use MTS, you probably haven't noticed this property before. Table 12-4 lists the possible values for MTSTransactionMode and their descriptions.

The MTSTransactionMode property is used only if the component is running as an MTS component.

Table 12-4: MTSTransactionMode Properties and Their Effects

Value	Effect
NotAnMTSObject	(Default) The component doesn't support Microsoft Transaction Server.
NoTransactions	The component does not support transactions. When a new object is created, its object context is created without a transaction, regardless of whether the client has a transaction.
RequiresTransaction	The component's objects must execute within the scope of a transaction. When a new object is created, it inherits the transaction from the client. If the client doesn't have a transaction, a new transaction is created for the object.
UsesTransaction	The component's objects can execute within the scope of their client's transactions—if the client has a transaction. If the client does not have a transaction, the new object will be created without a transaction.
RequiresNewTransaction	The component's objects must execute within their own transactions. When a new object is created, MTS creates a new transaction for the object, regardless of whether or not the client has a transaction.

The object that creates a new transaction is called the *root* of the transaction.

Simply assigning a transaction behavior using the MTSTransactionMode property does not fully implement component transactions. Since a transaction fails if any part of the transaction fails, each object involved in a transaction must "cast a vote" to determine whether the transaction commits or fails. When all objects vote to commit a transaction, MTS commits the transaction. If even one object votes to abort (roll back) the transaction, MTS aborts the transaction.

Objects vote by calling one of two methods of the ObjectContext object. However, in order for this to work, each object must be calling a method of the same ObjectContext object, which is why you can't use New to create a new Object-Context. To create an object reference to the shared ObjectContext containing the operating transaction, use GetObjectContext, as shown here:

```
Dim objMTS As ObjectContext
Set objMTS = GetObjectContext()
```

Once an object has a reference to the ObjectContext, it can vote on the outcome of the transaction. Table 12-5 lists the two methods that an object can call to cast a vote, along with a description of each method.

Table 12-5: Transactional Voting Methods of the ObjectContext Object

Method	Description
SetComplete	Notifies MTS that the object has completed its processes successfully, that the object can now be destroyed, and that, in the eyes of the object, MTS is free to commit the transaction.
SetAbort	Notifies MTS that the object was not able to complete its processes successfully. Calling SetAbort causes MTS to abort the entire transaction.

Programmatically creating transactions

In addition to defining transaction behavior at the component level, you can also explicitly create a transaction in code using the ObjectContext object.

 Explicitly creating transactions in code using the ObjectContext object is not recommended, and whenever possible, you should let MTS control transactions for you.

To create a new transaction explicitly, you first create a variable that holds the current object context, as discussed earlier in this chapter. To create objects that run within the explicitly created transaction, you use the CreateInstance method of the ObjectContext object much as you would use the *CreateObject* function, supplying the object's programmatic identifier (which usually includes the application or project name and class). For instance, to start a transaction and create an object that runs within the context of the transaction, you could use code such as this:

```
Dim objMTS       As ObjectContext
Dim objMarketing As Object

Set objMTS = GetObjectContext()

Set objMarketing = objMTS.CreateInstance("Marketing.CreateGroup")
```

In order to use programmed transactions, the objects being created within the context of the transaction must have their MTSTransactionMode set to UsesTransactions or RequiresTransactions. When creating objects that don't run within the explicit transaction, use the VBA *CreateObject* function rather than CreateInstance.

Referencing the object context during initialization and termination

The object context is not available in the Initialize or Terminate events of a class, yet there may be times when you need to use the object context at precisely these times. You can do this by implementing the ObjectControl interface. (Recall that when you implement an interface, the interface becomes available in the object dropdown list of the Code window, and selecting the interface allows you to select from its events in the Event dropdown list of the code window.) MTS uses this interface to notify your component when certain stages in its lifetime occurs. Table 12-6 lists the three events made available by the ObjectControl interface.

Table 12-6: Events of the ObjectControl Interface

Event	Description
Activate	MTS triggers this event as soon as an object context is created for the object, and just before calling any other methods.
Deactivate	MTS triggers this event just before the object is deactivated and its object context destroyed.
CanBePooled	MTS triggers this method when the object is deactivated (but not yet destroyed) in order to let the object return True if it supports pooling, and False if not. In theory, MTS won't destroy an object if it supports pooling. In reality, neither MTS 2.0 nor MTS 2.1 support object pooling, so the value returned by an object is ignored.

To use these events, implement the ObjectControl interface by adding Implements ObjectControl to the declarations section of the class module, select the ObjectControl interface from the Object dropdown list in the Code window, select an event for the ObjectControl in the Event dropdown list, then add any necessary code.

Microsoft Transaction Server is a powerful service that simplifies deployment and transactional operations and provides a robust environment for scalable and secure components. Not everyone can take advantage of MTS, but if you get the opportunity to do so, you'll be prepared to take advantage of its capabilities.

Key Facts

- Microsoft Transaction Server (MTS) is an application service for Windows NT, used to develop and distribute *n*-tier component-based solutions.

- MTS is designed to simplify the development of the middle tier.

- Designing components for use with MTS ultimately means writing less code, with the added benefit of a gain in performance, functionality, and scalability.

- All MTS components must be ActiveX DLLs.

- MTS provides Just-in-time (JIT) activation of components; components are cached when not in use so they use very little resources. When a client needs the component, MTS reactivates the component and reallocates necessary resources.

- MTS provides process isolation, which creates a more stable environment.

- MTS provides connection pooling. A pool of connections is used to access a data source, which expedites database access requests and requires less server resources.

- MTS provides thread pooling, resulting in components that respond much more quickly to client requests.

- MTS utilizes role-based security, which allows components to be secured without the need for complex programming. However, you can create programmatic security when you need more control.

- MTS provides automatic transactional functionality at the component level.

- MTS is installed from the Windows NT 4 Option Pack.

- To develop components for MTS, you must install the MTS developer components in addition to the standard MTS components on the development machine.

- DCOM is the mechanism used to broker communications between a client and an MTS component.

- DCOM is automatically installed on all Windows 98 machines, and all Windows NT 4 machines running service pack 3 or higher. DCOM must be installed on Windows 95 machines.

- A package is a set of components that perform related application functions. A package can contain component files and their type libraries, as well as information—such as security information—about the package.

- When a package is added to MTS, the proper registry values are created automatically. When a package is removed from MTS, the registry is again updated automatically.

- All components within the same package run in the same process space.

- A Library package is a package that runs in the process space of the client.

- A Server package is a package that runs in its on MTS process.

- When a Server package uses a component in a library package, the library package components run in the process space of the Server package.

- When a component is referenced in a server package, MTS loads all components in the server package. This results in some slowdown during the initial load, but subsequent calls to components in the package are much faster.

- MTS security is supported only on Windows NT machines.

- MTS packages can be secured in one of many different levels, from no security to Packet Privacy.

- MTS's role-based security is similar to NT's groups, except you can assign groups to roles in addition to assigning users to roles.

- Declarative security is enabled by assigning users and groups to roles. If a user who tries to access a component belongs to a role of the component, he or she is granted full access to that component. If the user is not a member of one of the component's roles, the user is denied access.

- Programmatic security allows you to verify that the current user is a member of a specific role and to take action based on that information.

- To perform programmatic security, you must create a reference to the current object context. To create a reference to the object context, you create a variable of type ObjectContext and use GetObjectContext to get a reference.

- Use the IsSecurityEnabled method of the ObjectContext object to determine whether or not security is enabled. Security is not enabled in Library packages running on a client machine.

- Use the IsCallerInRole method of the ObjectContext object to determine whether or not the current user belongs to a specified role.

- Calling IsCallerInRole from within a Library package not running in a secured MTS process always returns True.

- MTS configuration and management is performed using MTS Explorer.

- To secure MTS, you must add a user to the Administrator role of the System package.

- You can administer packages that exist on other computers running MTS, using MTS Explorer from one machine. In order to do this, each machine that you wish to manage must be added to MTS Explorer.

- To create a package, choose New Package from the Action menu after selecting Packages Installed in the tree view.

- To add components to a package, right-click the components folder for the package to which you want to add the component, and select New Component.

- All of the information that makes up the MTS environment (roles, packages, components, and so on) is stored in the MTS catalog.

- When you create a new version of a component and have successfully used binary compatibility, you can have MTS refresh its catalog information by using the MTS Explorer or the MTS Visual Basic add-in.

- When you create a new version of a component that is not fully compatible with the previous version, you have to manually remove the component from packages that use it, and add the new component to those packages.

- When developing an MTS component in Visual Basic, create a multithreaded, unattended execution component whenever possible.

- A component's transaction behavior is determined at design time by the MTSTransactionMode property of components whose instancing property is set to MultiUse. The possible values for MTSTransactionMode are NotAnMTS-Object, NoTransactions, RequiresTransaction, UsesTransaction, and Requires-NewTransaction.

- The object that creates a new transaction is called the *root* of the transaction.

- Objects that participate in transactions must cast a vote as to whether or not a transaction is committed.

- When an object has successfully completed its tasks, it invokes the SetComplete method of the ObjectContext object. Once all objects have invoked SetComplete, MTS commits the transaction.

- If an object is unable to successfully complete its tasks, it calls the SetAbort method of the ObjectContext object. If even a single object calls SetAbort, the entire transaction is aborted.

- Although it's not recommended, you can explicitly create transactions in code by using the CreateInstance method of the ObjectContext object.

- In order to reference the object context when a component is created or destroyed, the class must implement the ObjectControl interface.

- The Activate event of the ObjectControl interface is called when MTS first activates the component and creates the object context, and just prior to calling any methods of the component.

- The Deactivate event of the ObjectControl interface is called when MTS is about to deactivate the object and destroy its object context.

Applying What You've Learned

It's now time to apply what you've learned about optimizing applications for distribution. There are no exercises for this chapter; the complexity of installation and configuration of an MTS environment makes it impractical to create a working example in only a few pages. Make sure you fully understand the concepts presented in this chapter and work through all of the questions. You will encounter questions about creating MTS components on the Visual Basic exams.

Skills Assessment

1. Which tier is MTS designed to simplify and support?

    a. Presentation

    b. Middle tier

    c. Data Services

2. Which type of component can be used as an MTS component?

    a. ActiveX DLL

    b. ActiveX EXE

    c. Both ActiveX DLLs and ActiveX EXEs

    d. Neither ActiveX DLLs nor ActiveX EXEs

3. Which of the following is not supported by MTS?

    a. Just-in-time activation

    b. Process isolation

c. Connection pooling

d. Thread reversal

4. Which feature of MTS reduces overhead and increases performance when working with data sources?

a. Thread pooling

b. Connection pooling

c. Process isolation

d. OLE DB

5. MTS provides role-based security. Role-based security can be used at what level?

a. Declarative

b. Programmatic

c. Both declarative and programmatic

d. Neither declarative nor programmatic

6. MTS provides automatic transactional support at what level?

a. Component

b. Thread

c. Process

d. Connection

7. MTS is installed from:

a. The Windows NT 4 setup

b. The Windows 98 setup

c. The Internet Explorer 5 setup

d. The Windows NT 4 Option Pack

8. What technology is used to broker communications between a client and an MTS component?

a. COM

b. DCOM

c. Remote automation

d. Open objects

9. The entity in MTS that is used to store components, component information, and roles is called:

a. Cabinet

b. OLE DB store

c. OLE storage structure

d. Package

10. Which of the following is true?

    a. When a component is added to MTS, the proper registry values aren't updated automatically, but the registry is updated automatically when a component is removed.

    b. When a component is added to MTS, the registry is updated automatically, but the registry is not updated automatically when a component is removed.

    c. The registry is always updated automatically when a component is added or removed.

    d. The registry is never updated automatically when a component is added or removed.

11. Components within the same package always run:

    a. In the same process space.

    b. In the process space of the client.

    c. Some components run in the process space of the client, while others run in a unique process space.

    d. Each component runs in a different process space.

12. Which package runs in the process space of the client?

    a. Server

    b. Library

13. When a server package uses a component from a Library package, the Library package runs in:

    a. The process space of the client that called the Server package

    b. A unique process space

    c. The process space of the Server package

14. When the first component in a server package is called:

    a. All components in the package are loaded.

    b. Only the component being called is loaded.

15. MTS security is supported on which platforms (choose all that apply):

    a. Windows NT

    b. Windows 98

    c. Windows 95

    d. Windows 3.11

16. The highest level of security that can be implemented is:

    a. Connect

    b. Packet

    c. Packet Privacy

    d. Packet Integrity

17. IsCallerInRole and IsSecurityEnabled are both methods of which object?

    a. Security

    b. ObjectControl

    c. ObjectContext

    d. Transaction

18. MTS configuration is performed using:

    a. Windows NT Explorer

    b. MTS Explorer

    c. MTS Configuration Manager

    d. MTS Console

19. To secure MTS:

    a. Add a user to the Administrator role of the Security package.

    b. Add a user to the Administrator role of the System package.

    c. Select Enable Security on the Security tab of the MTS Properties window.

    d. MTS is secured by default.

20. All of the information stored by MTS (roles, packages, and so on) is stored in:

    a. An Oracle database

    b. A Jet database

    c. The MTS catalog

    d. The registry

21. New versions of components can be refreshed in MTS's catalog as long as which is true?

    a. The component was compiled using binary compatibility.

    b. The component was compiled using project or binary compatibility.

    c. The component was compiled on an NT computer.

    d. The component is compiled with the Ensure MTS Compatibility option selected.

22. A component's transaction behavior is determined by which property?

    a. MTSTransactionType

    b. MTSTransactionMode

    c. MTSTransactionLevel

    d. MTSTransaction

23. When an object within a transaction completes its tasks, it should:

    a. Call the CommitTrans method of the object context.

    b. Call the Complete method of the object context.

    c. Call the SetComplete method of the object context.

    d. Do nothing; transactions are handled automatically by MTS.

24. To explicitly create a transaction in code, you use which method of the object context?

    a. CreateInstance

    b. GetInstance

    c. CreateObject

    d. GetObject

25. To receive events when an object context is just created and about to be destroyed, you:

    a. Use the Initialize and Terminate events of the class.

    b. Implement the ObjectControl interface.

    c. Use the Activate and Deactivate events of the class.

Answers to Skills Assessment

1. b	6. a	11. a	16. c	21. a
2. a	7. d	12. b	17. c	22. a
3. d	8. b	13. c	18. b	23. c
4. b	9. d	14. a	19. b	24. a
5. c	10. c	15. a	20. c	25. b

Highlighter's Index

Microsoft Transaction Server (MTS)

Manages middle-tier components
Runs components in an optimized and secure environment
Runs on Windows 9x and Windows NT
Just-in-time activation
Process isolation
Database connection pooling
Thread pooling
Role-based security
Automatic transaction support
DCOM is the mechanism that brokers communications between clients
    and MTS components
Components are always DLLs

Installing MTS

Install from Windows NT 4 Option Pack
Can install MTS development files as an option

Configuring MTS

Configured with MTS Explorer
System package is used to configure overall security
Can add and administer multiple computers using MTS Explorer

Packages

A set of components that perform related application functions
MTS components *must* be part of a package
All files within a package run in same process space
Library packages run in client's process space
Server packages run in a dedicated process space
Created with MTS Explorer

MTS Security

Only available on Windows NT
Role-based security
Similar to NT's security
Declarative security determines what roles can access a component
Authorization checking can occur at different levels
Programmatic security gives you more control over component security
IsSecurityEnabled property
IsCallerInRole property

Creating MTS Components with Visual Basic

Must be ActiveX DLLs
Create multithreaded components
Create for unattended execution whenever possible
Use Binary compatibility
Create stateless components when possible

Transactions

MTS supports automatic transactions
Transaction mode of component determined by its MTSTransactionMode
    property
Components vote on their ability to process transactions by using
    an ObjectContext
Components can vote with SetComplete or SetAbort
Create explicit transactions using ObjectContext.CreateInstance
Use ObjectControl for initialization and termination routines

CHAPTER 13

Packaging and Deploying
an Application

Visual Basic's ability to create powerful ActiveX components has greatly increased the complexity of distributing applications and components. Not only do you have standard EXEs and ActiveX DLLs, you also have ActiveX controls, ActiveX documents, and DHTML applications. Distributing components over the Internet requires additional skills and techniques.

The venerable Setup Wizard is gone as of Version 5, and Microsoft devotes quite a few questions to its successor, the Package and Deployment Wizard. In this chapter, you'll learn about maintaining backward compatibility with early versions of a component to ensure that upgrades don't break existing clients. You'll also learn how to use the Package and Deployment Wizard to create slick setup programs for an application or component, and how to protect your investment by requiring licensing keys to use your ActiveX controls in the design environment.

The Technologies and the Exams

Many people (myself included) have been surprised by the number of questions about packaging and deploying applications that appear on *both* exams. My initial thought was that I'd mostly see questions related to distributing an application on the Distributing exam. However, both exams have a lot of questions about packaging and deploying, as Table 13-1 shows, and you'll have to demonstrate a competency in order to pass either exam. Don't expect just a few questions, either; you're going to get a number of them.

Table 13-1: Topics Related to Packaging and Deployment on the Exams

Topic	Covered on Exams
Maintaining backward compatibility in ActiveX components	Both
Understanding file, project, and component dependencies	Both
Creating a setup program for CD-ROM, diskette, and Internet distributing using the Package and Deployment Wizard	Both

Table 13-1: Topics Related to Packaging and Deployment on the Exams (continued)

Topic	Covered on Exams
Understanding Cabinet (CAB) files	Both
Working with packaging scripts	Both
Creating an AutoRun CD-ROM	Both
Using license keys for ActiveX controls	Both
Digitally signing an ActiveX control	Both
Distributing DCOM clients and servers	Both
Registering ActiveX controls and working with the Windows registry	Distributed

Making Components Backward Compatible (or Not Breaking What Works)

If you intend to take and pass the Visual Basic certification exams, you should already understand the concept of shared components and dependencies. Windows itself is made up of hundreds of components in the form of DLLs, EXEs, objects, and more. All of the various files required for an application to run are called *dependencies*. A missing dependency file usually results in an application either not running at all or not having its full functionality.

If ensuring that a dependent component exists on a computer meant that a component would always execute as designed, the Package and Deployment Wizard discussed in the next section would solve most of your dependency problems. However, like so many other things in life, it's just not that simple.

Things start to get complicated whenever a new version of a component is distributed. This happens frequently, often a result of a developer fixing bugs, adding new features, or both. Sometimes, the changes to a component are minor and only occur within existing functions. Applications that use such components are blind to the changes and are able to use the component (usually) without any problems.

For example, say you developed a DLL and included a function in the DLL that takes two numbers, multiplies them together, and returns the result. (Yes, you can do this with a simple Visual Basic statement; this serves to illustrate a point.) Here's the procedure:

```
Public Function Multiply(intNumber1 As Integer, _
    intNumber2 As Integer) As Long

    Dim intCount As Integer
    Dim lngResult As Long


    For intCount = 1 To intNumber1
        lngResult = lngResult + intNumber2
    Next intCount

    Multiply = lngResult

End Function
```

Although this function works, it's by no means efficient. Now, say you realize that you can actually perform this functionality using the multiplication operator (*). Since this DLL is being used by dozens of clients on hundreds of computers (quite a successful component), it's not feasible to change all applicable source code, recompile each client, and redistribute all of the components to all of the users. The solution is to optimize the code in the function and redistribute the DLL, so you change the function as follows:

```
Public Function Multiply(intNumber1 As Integer, _
    intNumber2 As Integer) As Long

    Multiply = intNumber1 * intNumber2

End Function
```

Since only the internals of the function have changed, not the interface of the function (how it is called or what it returns), all of the applications using the current version of the DLL can use the new version without modifications (assuming that the Class IDs are the same, as discussed in Chapter 4, *Creating and Testing ActiveX Code Components*). The new component is said to be backward compatible with the previous version.

Some changes to components aren't so benign. For example, say you developed an ActiveX DLL that included the following method, which accepts a first and last name and saves a record in the database:

```
Public Sub AddRecord(strFirst As String, strLast _
    As String)

    ...

End Sub
```

Now, you decide you want the function to accept a phone number as well, so you change the declaration to:

```
Public Sub AddRecord(strFirst As String, strLast As _
    String, strPhone as String)

    ...

End Sub
```

You then compile the DLL and distribute it to all of your users' computers. What happens? Their applications no longer work! This is because the definition of the method has changed, making the new DLL incompatible with the older DLL. This new component is not backward compatible with the previous version of the component and could get you reprimanded, fired, or possibly lynched. In order for existing applications to be able to use the function in the new DLL, they would need to be modified, recompiled, and redistributed.

When you compile a component using Visual Basic, a version number is included in the compiled component file. This version number is used by installation programs and can be viewed using Windows Explorer, allowing you to easily determine the version of a file on a computer. The version number compiled into the program is determined by the settings on the Make tab of the Project Properties dialog box, as shown in Figure 13-1. You should always select the Auto Increment checkbox in all of your projects prior to compiling to a component file. When Auto Increment is selected, each new version of the component created using the Make option on the File menu is embedded with a unique version number.

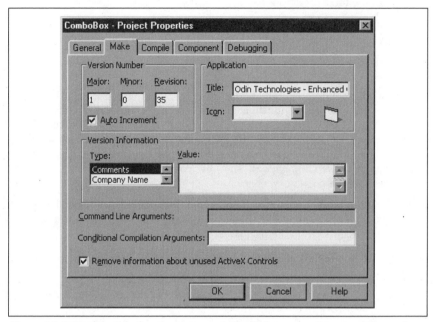

Figure 13-1: Each build of your component should have a unique version number

Ensuring Backward Compatibility

The relationship between a newer version of a component and an older one, and at what level they are interchangeable, is called *version compatibility*. Simply providing unique version numbers in each compile of an update doesn't ensure that clients using the component won't have any problems when the new version is installed. When you distribute an update to a component you should always ensure that the new component is fully *backward compatible* with previous versions of the component so that existing applications won't be broken.

In order for a component to be fully backward compatible, all of the conditions listed below must to be met.

The new version must:

Have the same class indentier (CLSID) and type library identifiers as the previous version.
  The CLSID is the GUID (Globally Unique Identifier) that uniquely identifies a component in the system registry. If a component is compiled with a CLSID that is different from that of a previous version, existing applications won't be

able to use the new component. This is discussed in more detail in the following sections and in Chapter 3, *Understanding COM.*

Support all of the properties, methods, and events of the previous version.
You can add as many new properties, methods, and events as you want in the new version of a component. However, deleting an existing property, method, or event will break applications that use the component.

Ensure that all properties, methods, and events have the same Dispatch IDs as the previous version.
Dispatch IDs are the unique identifiers of each of your component's members (properties, methods, and events). Procedure IDs (or Dispatch IDs) can be changed on the Procedure Attributes dialog box, as discussed in Chapter 5, *Creating ActiveX Controls.*

Ensure that all properties, methods, and events have the same parameters and parameter types as the previous version.
Not only do all of the existing properties, methods, and events need to be supported, but also you can't change their interfaces. Adding an additional parameter to an event, for example, causes the component to lose backward compatibility.

Exhibit the same functionality for all of the properties, methods, and events of the previous version.
Even though you can't change the interface of an existing procedure, you can change the "guts" of one as much as you like. You should not change the basic functionality, but you can change *how* the code performs its process.

Using Visual Basic's Version Compatibility Options

Visual Basic lets you control version compatibility of components at the following levels:

* No Compatibility

* Project Compatibility

* Binary Compatibility

These settings are located on the Component tab of the Project Properties dialog box, as shown in Figure 13-2.

Using the No Compatibility option

If you want to relinquish backward compatibility, you can do so by selecting No Compatibility. This is usually the least desirable option of the three. Each time a project set for No Compatibility is compiled, Visual Basic assigns a new CLSID and new procedure identifiers.

When you use No Compatibility to produce a new version of a component, you should change the Project Name property of the project and compile the project to a filename different than that of the previous version. If you do these two things, you'll create a totally unique component that won't overwrite or clash with the previously existing version of the component.

Figure 13-2: Component version compatibility is set on the Component tab of the Project Properties dialog box

Maintaining Project Compatibility

When you compile a project that uses Project Compatibility, Visual Basic maintains the same type library identifier of the previous component, but nothing more. All this does is allow you to open projects that use previous versions of the component. If the type library identifier were changed, the project couldn't load the component because the reference it had to the component would no longer be valid. You've probably seen this behavior when you open a project on a computer where a custom control used by the project is no longer available. Visual Basic doesn't know what to do, so it replaces all instances of the component with a picture box control.

When this option is selected, the text box at the bottom of the dialog box becomes enabled. In this text box, you must enter the filename and path of the component with which to maintain project compatibility; this should be a reference to the previously compiled version.

 You should always keep a copy of your compiled components somewhere safe. If you lose a compiled component, you lose the ability to create new components that are backward compatible with the lost component.

The Project Compatibility setting doesn't ensure that a project will run without modifications, only that projects will still have a valid reference to the component's library.

Maintaining Binary Compatibility

The Binary Compatibility option is the only option that truly enforces compatibility between components. When you compile a project with Binary Compatibility selected, the new component has the same CLSID and procedure identifiers as its previous version. Applications that use previous versions of the component will be able to use the new one without having to be recompiled.

 If you make any changes to the project that would prohibit backward compatibility, such as changing a Procedure ID using the Procedure Attributes dialog box, Visual Basic will warn you of this fact at compile time. If you choose to ignore the warning, you give up backward compatibility.

If you create any type of ActiveX component, you must be keenly aware of compatibility issues. You must decide what type of compatibility to use based on many factors, including prior distribution size and locations. Binary compatibility is always the best; no compatibility is always the worst. If you truly want no backward compatibility, you should create a new component, as discussed in the No Compatibility section.

Understanding File Dependencies

To properly use the Package and Deployment Wizard discussed in the next section, you need to have an understanding of *dependencies*. Dependencies are files that are necessary for a given file to run. Some components have a corresponding dependency file that is a text file with the extension DEP containing information about the runtime requirements of a component. This can include information such as where on a user's machine a component needs to be installed, and if and how the component needs to be registered. The Package and Deployment Wizard discussed in the next section allows you to take advantage of dependency files for components used by your application, and it can even generate a dependency file for your application or component. This section focuses on the composition of a dependency file.

There are two types of dependency files related to creating a setup program for your application:

- Component DEP files
- The *VB6dep.ini* (project) file

Understanding Component Dependency Files

Component dependency files contain information about the dependencies of a specific component, such as an ActiveX control or document. The first line of a dependency file contains the name of the component. Following this identifier are lines for the various pieces of information related to the component. This information may include:

- The destination folder of the installed component. The destination folder is prefixed with `Dest=`.

- The method (if any) of registering the component. Registration information is prefixed with `Register=`.

- The version number of the component. The version is in the form of *major.minor.revision.minorrevision*, and is prefixed with `Version=`.

- File dependencies. File dependencies are prefixed with `Usesx=`, where *x* is the number identifying the dependency. Each file dependency must be given a unique number.

- Cabinet file information (discussed in the "Internet Usage" section later in this chapter).

The following is an example of a dependency file:

```
[OTTOOLBX.OCX]
Register=$(DLLSelfRegister)
Dest=$(WinSysPath)
Date=1/25/1998
Time=13:02:06
Version=1.0.0.1
Uses1=MSVBVM50.dll
Uses2=StdOle2.tlb
Uses3=OleAut32.dll
Uses4=OlePro32.dll
Uses5=AsycFilt.dll
Uses6=Ctl3d32.dll
Uses7=ComCat.dll
Uses8=MsStkPrp.dll
```

 You should include a dependency file for each of the components you create and distribute. The dependency file becomes extremely useful when you include the component in a setup program for another application, because the Package and Deployment Wizard automatically adds the dependent files of the component to the setup program of the primary application. You create DEP files for Visual Basic components using the Package and Deployment Wizard.

Understanding Project Dependency Files

When you create a setup program for a component or application using the Package and Deployment Wizard, the wizard looks at the dependency file of each component used by your application and adds this information into a *Setup.lst* file. Also added to the *Setup.lst* file is information gleaned from project references and from the *VB6dep.ini* file (discussed next). This *Setup.lst* file is what your custom setup program uses to determine what files to install and where to put them.

The following is a sample *Setup.lst* file:

```
[Bootstrap]
SetupTitle=Install
SetupText=Copying Files, please stand by.
CabFile=BDPro1.CAB
Spawn=Setup1.exe
Uninstal=st6unst.exe
TmpDir=msftqws.pdw
Cabs=2
[Bootstrap Files]
File1=@VB6STKIT.DLL,$(WinSysPathSysFile),,,6/18/98 12:00:00 AM,102912,6.
0.81.69
File2=@COMCAT.DLL,$(WinSysPathSysFile),$(DLLSelfRegister),,5/31/98
12:00:00 AM,22288,4.71.1460.1
File3=@MSVCRT40.DLL,$(WinSysPathSysFile),,,5/31/98 12:00:00 AM,326656,4.
21.0.0
File4=@OLEPRO32.DLL,$(WinSysPathSysFile),$(DLLSelfRegister),,10/6/98
12:00:00 AM,164112,5.0.4265.1
File5=@STDOLE2.TLB,$(WinSysPathSysFile),$(TLBRegister),,10/6/98 12:00:00
AM,17920,2.30.4265.1
File6=@ASYCFILT.DLL,$(WinSysPathSysFile),,,10/6/98 12:00:00 AM,147728,2.
30.4265.1
File7=@OLEAUT32.DLL,$(WinSysPathSysFile),$(DLLSelfRegister),,10/6/98
12:00:00 AM,598288,2.30.4265.1
File8=@MSVBVM60.DLL,$(WinSysPathSysFile),$(DLLSelfRegister),,9/25/98
12:00:00 AM,1409024,6.0.82.68

[IconGroups]
Group0=Button Designer Pro
PrivateGroup0=True
Parent0=$(Programs)

[Button Designer Pro]
Icon1="BDPro.exe"
Title1=Button Designer Pro
StartIn1=$(AppPath)

[Setup]
Title=Button Designer Pro
DefaultDir=$(ProgramFiles)\Button Designer Pro
AppExe=BDPro.exe
AppToUninstall=BDPro.exe
```

```
[Setup1 Files]
File1=@BDPRO.HLP,$(AppPath),,,1/28/95 3:22:16 PM,59684,0.0.0.0
File2=@otSpin32.ocx,$(WinSysPath),$(DLLSelfRegister),$(Shared),11/18/97
8:34:56 PM,53760,1.0.0.2
File3=@ottoolbx.ocx,$(WinSysPath),$(DLLSelfRegister),$(Shared),1/24/99
11:45:08 AM,86016,1.0.0.9
File4=@ActBar.ocx,$(WinSysPath),$(DLLSelfRegister),$(Shared),4/13/98
9:27:46 AM,276480,1.0.3.8
File5=@PICCLP32.OCX,$(WinSysPath),$(DLLSelfRegister),$(Shared),6/24/98
12:00:00 AM,82744,6.0.81.69
File6=@MFC40.DLL,$(WinSysPathSysFile),$(DLLSelfRegister),,4/24/98
12:00:00 AM,921872,4.1.0.6038
File7=@threed32.ocx,$(WinSysPath),$(DLLSelfRegister),$(Shared),7/26/95
12:00:00 AM,200704,1.0.41.0
File8=@BDPro.exe,$(AppPath),,,1/24/99 11:51:30 AM,360448,2.5.0.12
```

The *Setup.lst* file consists of a number of sections, which are discussed next.

Using the [Bootstrap] and [Bootstrap Files] sections of the Setup.lst file

The [Bootstrap] section contains all of the files that must be loaded on the user's computer *before* your application and all of its dependency files can be loaded. These are the files that the setup program itself needs in order to run, as well as files needed to run any Visual Basic application.

The [Bootstrap] section contains the items listed in Table 13-2.

Table 13-2: [Bootstrap] Entries in Setup.lst

Item	Description
SetupTitle	The text that appears in the title bar of the dialog box displayed when the bootstrap files are being installed.
SetupText	The text that appears in the dialog box displayed when the bootstrap files are being installed.
CabFile	The name of the first cabinet file (CAB) of the install.
Spawn	The setup program to run after the bootstrap files are installed. This is the actual setup of your component; you shouldn't change this value.
TmpDir	The path you want to use for temporary files created by your setup program. You shouldn't need to change this value.
Uninstal	The name of the uninstall application to remove your component. The file *st6unst.exe* that is used as the default value is automatically installed by your setup program. You shouldn't change this value.
Cabs	The number of cabinet files in the install.

The [Bootstrap Files] section contains the specific information for each file that must be installed for the setup program and Visual Basic 6 runtime. Files are listed in the following format:

```
Filex=@file,install,path,register,shared,date,size[,version]
```

Table 13-3 lists each part of a bootstrap file declaration.

Table 13-3: Bootstrap File Definitions

Element	Description
Filex	A keyword that must appear at the beginning of each file description line. *x* is a sequence number. Each section must have a file sequence number starting at 1, and you can't skip values.
@	(Optional) Denotes that the file is to be extracted from a CAB file.
file	The name given to the file as it appears installed on the user's computer. If the file is to be extracted from a CAB file, it must be prefixed with @.
install	The name of the file that is used during installation (i.e., the name of the file as it exists on the distribution media). This can be the same as *file*.
path	An actual path or (preferably) a macro indicating a path specified by the user. This can also be a combination of a macro plus additional subdirectory names separated by backslashes. (Macros are discussed in the "Package and Deployment Wizard" section of this chapter.)
register	A key (if any) that indicates how information about the file should be stored in the system registry of the user's computer.
shared	A keyword that specifies that the file should be installed as shared and that an internal system counter should keep track of the number of applications that reference the component. A shared component is not removed from a computer during an uninstall if other applications are using the component.
date	The date the file was last modified.
size	The size of the file.
version	An optional version number of the file. This version number does not have to match the version number of the file as displayed using Windows Explorer.

The [IconGroups] section

A custom setup program can create custom program groups on the Start menu of your user's machine. The [IconGroups] section is used to define the groups that your custom Setup Wizard will create. Program group names are prefixed with the word Groupx, with *x* being a sequential number for a group. Unlike entries in the [BootStrap Files] section discussed previously, groups are numbered starting at 0, not at 1. The following is a sample [IconGroups] section from a *Setup.lst* file:

```
[IconGroups]
Group0=Button Designer Pro
Parent0=$(Programs)
```

The line beginning with Group0 designates that a new group titled "Button Designer Pro" is to be created. The line beginning with Parent0 dictates that Group 0 is to be created under the Programs folder of the Start menu. The $ and () around Programs are used to denote that Programs is a macro, and not a hard-coded string. You'll learn more about these macros later in this chapter.

The program group sections

For each program group listed in the IconGroups section of the *Setup.lst* file, there will be a custom section whose name is the name of the group. For instance, since the group in the previous section was named Button Designer Pro, there would be a corresponding Button Designer Pro section in the *Setup.lst* file that would look something like this:

```
[Button Designer Pro]
Icon1="BDPro.exe"
Title1=Button Designer Pro
StartIn1=$(AppPath)
```

These custom sections designate the icons to place within a given group. The line prefixed with `Iconx` specifies that the first icon (denoted with a 1) runs *BDPro.exe*. Icons are assigned sequential numbers just as files and groups are. For icons, the numbers begin with 1 as they do for files, not 0 as they do for groups. I don't have any idea why there isn't a standard approach for sequential numbers in the *Setup1.lst* file.

The `Title` line designates the text for the icon. Again, the number following `Title` correlates to an Icon entry. If there were to be more than one icon installed in this group, for instance, there would be `Icon2` and `Title2` entries.

The `StartIn` entry is used to specify a start folder in which to execute the program specified in `Icon1`. Once again, the value used here is a macro, and macros are discussed in the Package and Deployment section.

The [Setup] section

Once the bootstrap files are loaded on the user's computer, the custom setup program begins. The `[Setup]` section is used to specify global parameters for the custom setup program. The following is a sample Setup section:

```
[Setup]
Title=Button Designer Pro
DefaultDir=$(ProgramFiles)\Button Designer Pro
AppExe=BDPro.exe
AppToUninstall=BDPro.exe
```

Table 13-4 explains the purpose of each of the entries in the Setup section.

Table 13-4: Setup Section Entries of the Setup1.lst File

Entry	Description
Title	The name of your program as it will appear in the upper-left of the Setup window and on various dialog boxes of the setup program.
DefaultDir	The default folder in which to install your application. User's can override this folder and designate a different one if they wish.
AppExe	The name of the application's executable file.
ApptoUninstall	The name given to your program in the Add/Remove Programs utility accessed via the Control Panel.

The [Setup1 Files] section

The `[Setup1 Files]` section contains all other files required by the application. Included is the main application file (EXE, OCX, and so on), and all dependent files, such as DLLs and other OCXs—any files added by you or by the Package and Deployment Wizard. File entries follow the same format as the entries in the `[Bootstrap Files]` section.

The VB6dep.ini file

When you install Visual Basic, a master dependency list is installed with the rest of the Package and Deployment files. This dependency file is named *VB6dep.ini* and is placed in the *Wizards**PDWizard* folder under the main Visual Basic folder. The *VB6dep.ini* file contains dependency information about commonly installed components, such as the Jet engine shown here:

```
[DAO350.dll]
Dest=$(MSDAOPath)
Uses1=MSJtEr35.dll
Uses2=MSJInt35.dll
Register=$(DLLSelfRegister)
CABFileName=MSDAO350.cab
CABINFFile=MSDAO350.inf
```

The Package and Deployment Wizard uses the *VB6dep.ini* file to determine dependencies of components used by your application or component. When creating a setup program, the Package and Deployment Wizard attempts to locate a DEP file for a specific component, or to find the dependency information in the *VB6dep.ini* file. If it can't locate the dependency information in either a component-specific DEP file or in the *VB6dep.ini* file, the wizard notifies you of the missing dependency files and gives you the option of ignoring the dependencies or backing out and correcting the problem.

When you elect to ignore the fact that dependency information is missing for a component, the component may not work properly after it's installed on a user's computer. Not all files have dependencies, and some dependencies may already exist on the target computer. It's up to you to research components with missing dependencies to ensure that you create a setup program that will successfully install your application or component on all target computers.

To correct a missing dependency problem, you have the following three options:

- If you developed the component with Visual Basic, you can use the Package and Deployment Wizard to generate a dependency file for the component.

- You can manually create a dependency entry for the component in the *VB6dep.ini* file.

- If the component is not one you created, and you are unsure of the dependency information of the component, you can contact the component's manufacturer for a dependency file.

Until Version 5 of Visual Basic, the file *Swdepend.ini* served the purpose of *VB6dep.ini*. In Visual Basic 5, the *VB5dep.ini* file was born and replaced the *Swdepend.ini* file. Now, the *VB6dep.ini* file is the main dependency file.

It's very important that you understand dependencies and how they relate to installing components. If you ever use the Package and Deployment Wizard to create a custom setup program for an application or component, you'll be faced with dependency issues. Just as important, you need to understand all of the sections of the *Setup1.lst* file. While you may never need to edit a *Setup1.list* file directly, a thorough understanding of the file is necessary to understand what occurs when an application or component is installed, and to pass the Visual Basic exams.

Creating a Setup Program Using the Package and Deployment Wizard

Distributing applications has always been a trying process. In today's world, where applications make use of many shared components, distribution is no longer a simple issue of shipping one or two files to a customer. Instead, often dozens of files are involved. Not only do you have more files to distribute, but also there are many special cases in which simply placing a file on a user's machine is not sufficient or may even be counterproductive. ActiveX components, for example, need to be registered in the system registry. Fortunately, Visual Basic includes a powerful component, the Package and Deployment Wizard, which automates this process for you.

 The Package and Deployment Wizard has replaced the Setup Wizard of earlier versions of Visual Basic.

The Package and Deployment Wizard is not perfect, and tweaking is sometimes required to get your installation to do exactly what you want it to. This section discusses using the Package and Deployment Wizard and how to customize a setup program.

The Package and Deployment Wizard performs the following functions:

- Copies the necessary files for your custom setup program to the user's computer
- Installs all of the files for your application or component
- Registers appropriate components in the system registry
- Creates program manager groups and icons for your application

In addition to using the Package and Deployment Wizard to package your application or component, you can customize the Setup Toolkit project that ships with Visual Basic to create custom setup programs. Generally, if you need this level of customization, you should consider purchasing a third-party installation tool such as WISE or InstallShield.

Starting the Package and Deployment Wizard and Selecting a Project

The Package and Deployment Wizard is not part of Visual Basic itself. When you install Visual Basic, a shortcut for the Package and Deployment Wizard is created in a folder titled *Microsoft Visual Studio 6.0 Tools* under the *Microsoft Visual Studio 6.0* folder. The Package and Deployment Wizard allows you to create standard packages (installations performed by a *Setup.exe* program), Internet packages (applications downloaded from a web site), and dependency files (discussed earlier in this chapter).

Unlike its predecessor, the Setup Wizard, the Package and Deployment Wizard compresses all files into cabinet files (CAB). Cabinet files are similar to the common ZIP files in that a CAB file is a single file containing compressed versions of one or more different files. Cabinet files are discussed in detail later in this chapter.

When you launch the Package and Deployment Wizard, the window in Figure 13-3 appears. The first page of the Package and Deployment Wizard is used to designate the project for which to create a setup program, and to select what you want to do with the Package and Deployment Wizard. If you are creating a new setup program, you designate the project name in the Select Project text box and click the Package button. If you've previously created a package and want to distribute the package to diskettes, a local or network drive, or to the Internet, click the Deploy button.

Once you create a package, the information used to generate the package, such as files to install and register, are saved as packaging and deployment *scripts*. Later in this chapter, you'll learn how to manage these scripts.

The flow of the following sections follows that of creating a new package. After the details of creating a package are thoroughly discussed, the deployment features of the Package and Deployment Wizard are covered.

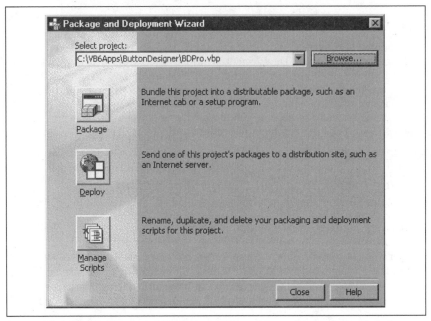

Figure 13-3: The Package and Deployment Wizard is used to create and deploy packages

Choosing an Existing Packaging Script

Once you've elected to create a package, you may be asked to select a packaging script (see Figure 13-4). If you haven't previously created and saved a packaging script, this dialog box may not display. To create a new package not based on an existing script, select (None) from the Packaging Script dropdown list.

Figure 13-4: Once a script is created and saved, you can use it or modify it at any time

Choosing a Package Type

After designating a project and optionally selecting an existing packaging script, you are asked to designate the type of package to create (see Figure 13-5). You can generate either a standard setup package or a dependency file.

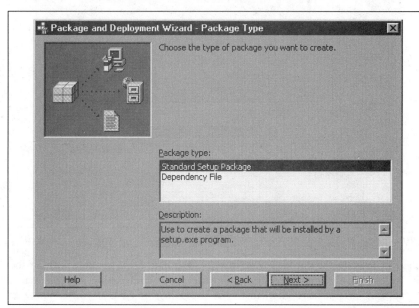

Figure 13-5: You can create standard setup packages or generate dependency files with the Package and Deployment Wizard

Choosing a Package Folder

If you elect to create a standard setup package, you'll next be asked where you want the Package and Deployment Wizard to store all of the package files (see Figure 13-6). The Package and Deployment Wizard will generate the files necessary for distribution of your package in this folder. The Package and Deployment Wizard may create subfolders within this folder, so having full access rights to the folder is a must.

By default, the Package and Deployment Wizard chooses a folder under the selected project's folder. You can change this folder. Regardless, if the specified folder doesn't exist, the Package and Deployment Wizard will ask you if you'd like it to create the folder, and it will create it if you so choose. Once you're satisfied with the package folder, click Next to continue.

Dealing with Missing Files

The Package and Deployment Wizard begins by analyzing the source files of the designated project. The first thing it looks for is missing files. If files are required by your project, but they cannot be located by the Package and Deployment Wizard, a dialog box like the one shown in Figure 13-7 is displayed. You have the

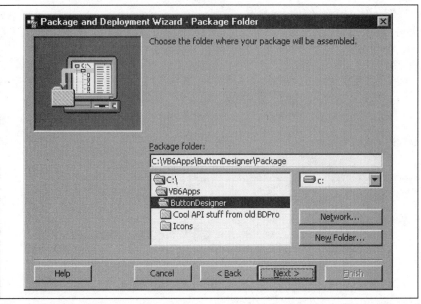

Figure 13-6: Use this page of the wizard to designate where package files are created

option of looking for the files using the Browse button, proceeding without the files by clicking OK, or canceling the wizard. If files are missing and this dialog box appears, chances are good that your program won't run if you continue to generate a package.

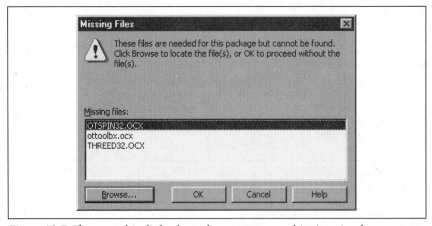

Figure 13-7: If you get this dialog box, chances are something's seriously wrong

Recompiling a Project

When the Package and Deployment Wizard analyzes the source files composing the project, it compares the dates and times of the source files to those of the compiled component file (EXE, DLL, and so on) and alerts you if there are any source files that are newer than the component. If newer files are found, you're given the option to have the Package and Deployment Wizard recompile the component.

 In theory, the analysis of the dates and times of the source files is to safeguard you from distributing a compiled component file that isn't current. However, you'll almost always receive this message if you perform the solid practice of having Visual Basic automatically increment version numbers of your components. In order to increment a version number, Visual Basic must store the new version number after a build in the project file. Obviously, since this change is made after the build, the project file will always have a time and/or date that is later than that of the component itself.

Dealing with Missing Dependencies

The Package and Deployment Wizard processes all of the dependency information it can find related to the selected application and all components that the application uses. If the Package and Deployment Wizard detects any missing dependency information, it displays a list of the missing dependencies, as shown in Figure 13-8.

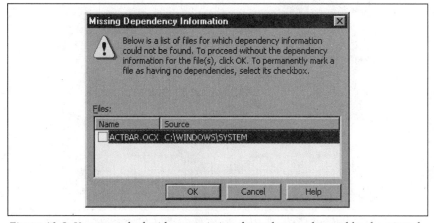

Figure 13-8: You must deal with any missing dependencies detected by the wizard

You have the following options available to you when dealing with a missing dependency:

- If you know that a listed file has dependencies, you can cancel the Package and Deployment Wizard and correct the problem by editing the *VB6dep.ini* file or by creating a dependency file.

- If you know that a listed file has no dependencies, you can select the checkbox of the component and the Package and Deployment Wizard will never again ask you the component's dependency.

- If you want to ignore the dependency for the time being, click Next to continue with the packaging. If you ignore a missing dependency, your application may not work correctly, and you will be asked about the dependency the next time the Package and Deployment Wizard encounters this component.

- Contact the component's manufacturer for information on the dependencies of the component.

You may find that you have a reference to a component that is no longer used by your application. If this is the case, you should consider removing the reference from the project, recompiling the application, and running the Package and Deployment Wizard again.

Visual Basic can remove all unused references from a project automatically. To enable this feature for a particular project, display the Project Properties dialog box and select the "Remove information about unused ActiveX controls" checkbox on the Make tab (see Figure 13-9).

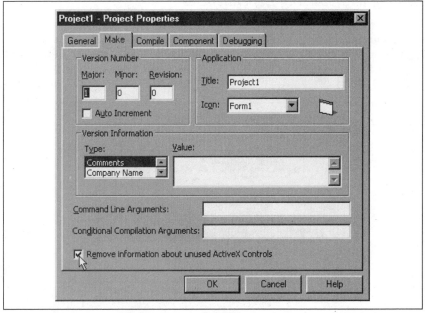

Figure 13-9: Visual Basic will clean up unused dependencies in a project when loading if this option is selected

Including Files for Distribution

The Package and Deployment Wizard compiles and displays a list of all of the files it has determined are required by your application or component, as shown in Figure 13-10. The Package and Deployment Wizard is fairly intelligent, and it can determine which files are needed by your application by analyzing the source code and dependency information. Although the list it compiles is fairly comprehensive, it's often necessary to manually add files to the package. For instance, if your application accesses an Access (Jet) database, you may need to add a custom *System.mdw* file or a *readme.txt* file to the package.

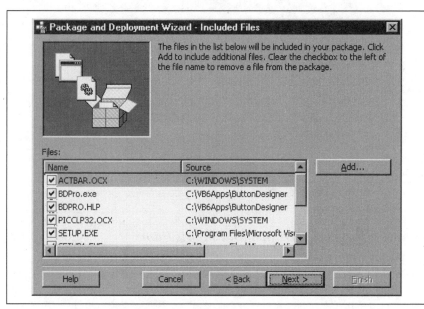

Figure 13-10: Although the Package and Deployment Wizard is fairly intelligent, you'll often need to add files to a package manually

To add additional files to the package, click Add. The Package and Deployment Wizard then displays an Add File dialog box, which you can use to locate and select files. Once you're satisfied with all of the listed files, click Next to continue.

Creating Multiple CAB Files

The Package and Deployment Wizard compresses all files for your setup program into cabinet (CAB) files (CAB files are discussed in detail later in this chapter). You have the option of generating a single CAB file or multiple CAB files. If your application is to be distributed over a network, a single CAB file might make sense. If you need to distribute your application on floppy disks, you'll need to split up the setup files into multiple CAB files. If you elect to create multiple CAB files, you must specify their maximum size. The default is 1.44 MB, the size of a floppy disk.

Specifying an Installation Title

Perhaps the simplest page of the Package and Deployment Wizard, the Installation Title page, is used to assign a title to your custom setup program (see Figure 13-11). The text you enter here is displayed on appropriate dialog boxes and in the upper-left corner of your setup program's window. This text is stored in the *Setup1.lst* file.

Figure 13-11: The Installation Title page is used to customize the appearance of a custom setup program

Creating Program Groups and Menu Items

The Package and Deployment Wizard lets you create program groups and items (see Figure 13-12). You can create groups or items underneath the Programs folder (the default), or directly underneath the Start menu (at the same level as the Programs group). To create a new group or item, click the tree in the left where you would like the group or item created, then click New Group or New Item. To remove a group or item, click it to select it and then click Remove. Clicking Properties displays properties of the group or item (see Figure 13-13 and Figure 13-14).

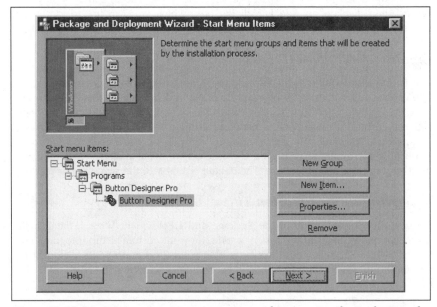

Figure 13-12: It's easy to create program groups and icons using the Package and Deployment Wizard

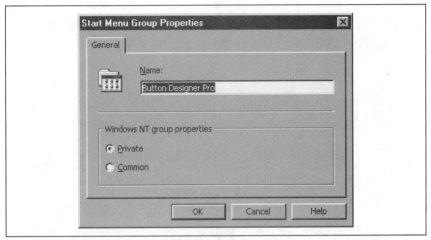

Figure 13-13: Refine program groups using the Start Menu Group Properties dialog box

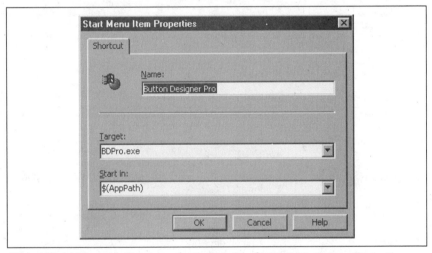

Figure 13-14: You can fine-tune shortcuts using the Start Menu Item Properties dialog box

Specifying File Installation Locations

The Package and Deployment Wizard does a fair job of estimating where you will want the files of your application installed. It displays these guesses to you, as shown in Figure 13-15. Clicking in the Install Location column of the grid displays a dropdown arrow. The dropdown arrow gives you access to a dropdown list of available installation locations. These locations are represented by *macros*. Table 13-5 lists the possible installation macro choices and their meanings.

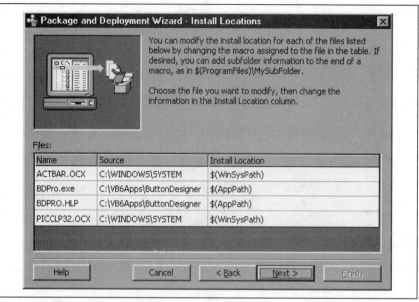

Figure 13-15: You have complete control over the locations in which application files are installed

Table 13-5: Setup Wizard Path Macros

Macro	Description
$(WinSysPath)	Installs a file in the \Windows\System (Windows 98) or \winnt\System32 (Windows NT) folder.
$(WinSysPathSysFile)	Installs a file in the \Windows\System (Windows 98) or \winnt\System32 (Windows NT) folder as a shared file. The file is not deleted when the application is uninstalled.
$(WinPath)	Installs a file in the \Windows (Windows 98) or the \winnt (Windows NT) folder.
$(AppPath)	Installs a file in the application folder specified by the user, or the DefaultDir value specified in the [Setup] section of the Setup.lst file.
$(CommonFiles)	The common directory to which shared application files are installed. For Windows 98, this is usually C:\Program Files\ Common Files\.
$(CommonFilesSys)	The same as $(CommonFiles) \System under Windows 98 and Windows NT 4, or the same as $(WinSysDir) under Windows NT 3.51.
$(ProgramFiles)	The default root directory to which applications are installed. For Windows 98 and Windows NT 4, it is C:\Program Files.
$(MSDAOPath)	The location that is stored in the registry for Data access objects (DAO) components. You should not use this for your files, only for Microsoft's DAO files.
$(Font)	The location in which fonts are stored on the user's computer.

Marking Files as Shared

Many files, such as OCX and DLL files, are meant to be shared between multiple applications. If Windows doesn't know that a particular file is a shared file, it deletes the file when the application that installed the file is uninstalled. You can mark a file as a shared file, and Windows will prevent the file from being deleted *as long as there is at least one program still installed that uses the file.*

Not all files can be marked as shared. The Package and Deployment Wizard determines which files can be shared by looking at the installation macros assigned to each file (see the previous section). Essentially, any file that is not installed as a system file (not installed into $(WinSysPathSysFile)) can be marked as shared. When the Package and Deployment Wizard displays the files that are capable of being shared, it highlights the project file by default (see Figure 13-16). To mark a file as shared, select the checkbox next to it.

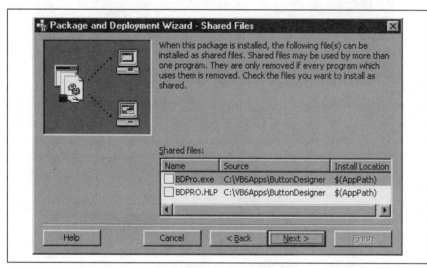

Figure 13-16: Shared files won't be deleted during an uninstall if other applications still need it

Naming and Saving the Packaging Script

The Package and Deployment Wizard has the ability to save all of the settings you have specified for each page of the wizard. It saves this information in a packaging script. There are three reasons why you would want to save your packaging definitions in a script:

- You can easily package the project again at a later time without having to answer all of the questions again.

- Packages are referred to by their script name. When you first create a package, you are asked to select a script.

- A script's name is required to create packages in silent mode.

To save the current script, simply enter a name in the Script Name text box (see Figure 13-17).

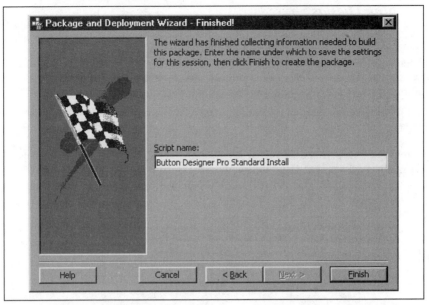

Figure 13-17: To save the current script, enter a script name and click Finish

Viewing the Packaging Report

Once the Package and Deployment Wizard has created your package, it displays a Packaging Report like that shown in Figure 13-18. When you're finished reading the report, click Close. To save the report to a text file, click Save Report.

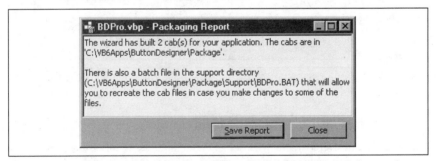

Figure 13-18: The Packaging Report contains useful information, and it can be saved to a text file

Deploying a Package Using the Package and Deployment Wizard

Creating a package is only the first step to distributing your application or component. Once a package is created, you must deploy it. Clicking the Deploy button on the Package and Deployment Wizard starts the deployment part of the wizard. The first step to deployment is to specify the package script to deploy (see Figure 13-19).

Only packages for the project selected on the main form of the Package and Deployment Wizard are shown. If the package you want to deploy belongs to another project, you'll need to cancel the Deployment Wizard and select the project. Once the correct project is specified, you can click the Deployment button to start again. Once you've selected the appropriate script, click Next to continue.

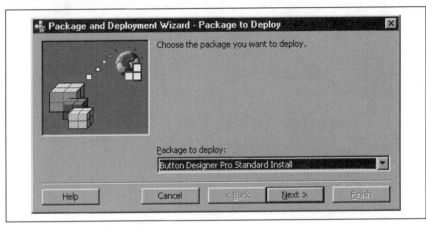

Figure 13-19: Deployment begins with selecting a package script

In the old days, floppy disk installations were the norm. Now, CD-ROM is the standard for distributing an application. However, the Internet is quickly gaining ground as the distribution method of choice. In a corporate environment, creating an install in a single shared network folder that can be accessed by the appropriate users may be the way to go. The following table lists the ways the Package and Deployment Wizard allows you to deploy your application:

Option	Description
Floppy Disks	Deploys the package to floppy disks. (This option is not available if the package consists of a single CAB file.)
Folder	Deploys the package to a folder you specify on a local or network drive.
Web Publishing	Deploys the package to a web server you specify via web publishing technology.

Deploying a Package to Floppy Disks

If you elect to deploy a package to floppy disks, you're asked to designate the floppy drive to be used to create the setup diskette set. To have the Package and Deployment Wizard automatically format each diskette prior to writing files to it, select the "Format before copying" checkbox.

The last step to deploying a package to floppy disks is to name the deployment package script (see Figure 13-20). By saving the deployment script, you can easily deploy the package at a later time or perform a silent deployment, as discussed later in this chapter. After naming the script, click Finish and the Package and Deployment Wizard will deploy the package.

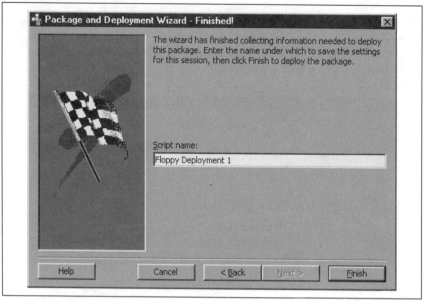

Figure 13-20: By saving scripts, it's easy to redeploy packages

Deploying a Package to a Folder

If you plan on deploying a package within an organization to users on a network, or perhaps from a CD-ROM, deploying the package to a single folder may be your best choice. After specifying Folder as the deployment method and clicking Next, you're asked to specify the folder in which to deploy the package (see Figure 13-21). You can deploy to a local drive or to a network drive. If the folder to which you would like to deploy doesn't exist, select the folder in which you'd like to create the deployment folder and click New Folder. You'll then be asked to name the new folder.

Once you've specified a folder, you'll be asked to name your deployment script. After naming the script, click Finish and the Package and Deployment Wizard will deploy the package.

Deploying a Package to a Web Server

The Package and Deployment Wizard has the ability to deploy a package directly to a web server. To distribute a package to a web server, select Web Publish as the deployment method and click Next.

You'll then be asked to select the files you want to deploy (see Figure 13-22). The files generated by the current packaging script appear selected by default. To omit one of the displayed files, deselect its checkbox.

Once you've verified the deployment files, click Next. You'll then be asked to specify any additional items to deploy (see Figure 13-23). You may want to deploy files such as folders or graphics. To include a file or folder, select its checkbox. When you're satisfied with the selected files, click Next to continue.

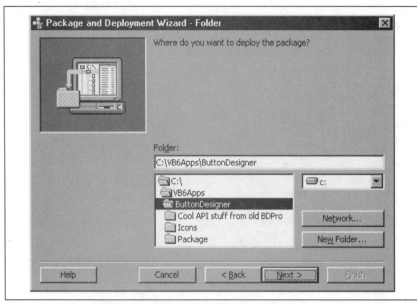

Figure 13-21: You can deploy to a local drive or network drive

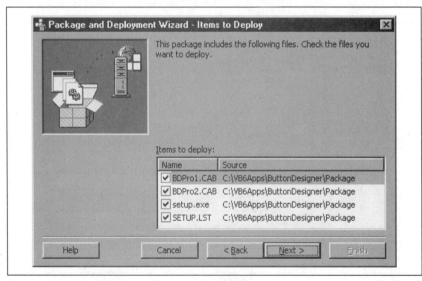

Figure 13-22: Prior to the deployment of a web server, you are asked to verify that the correct files are being deployed

Once you've designated all of the files to deploy, you need to specify the URL of the web site to which you want to deploy the package (see Figure 13-24). In addition to the URL, you must designate the publishing method (HTTP Post or FTP).

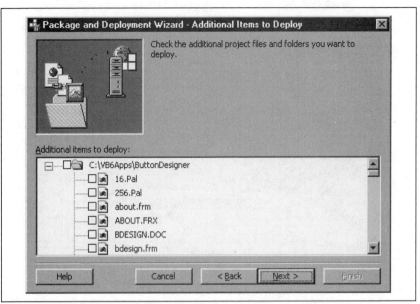

Figure 13-23: You are allowed to specify additional files to be deployed to a web server

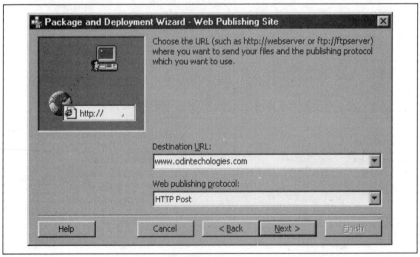

Figure 13-24: A URL and protocol must be designated in order to distribute to a web server

Once you've specified a URL and a publishing method, you'll be asked if you want to save the URL and protocol in the registry as a Web Publishing site. If you do elect to save the site, you'll be asked to name it. When you save a site, the

Package and Deployment Wizard verifies that the site information is valid and saves appropriate information in the registry, making subsequent deployments easier.

The last step to deploying a package to a web server is to name the script. Once you've named the script, click Finish to deploy the package to the web server.

Managing Packaging Scripts

The Package and Deployment Wizard makes it easy to manage packaging and deployment scripts. On the main window of the Package and Deployment Wizard, click Manage Scripts to display the Manage Scripts dialog box shown in Figure 13-25. Using the Managing Scripts dialog box, you can rename, duplicate, and delete packaging and deployment scripts.

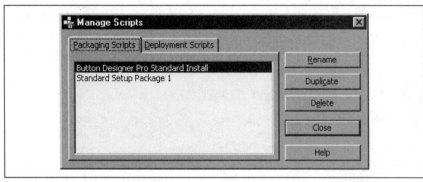

Figure 13-25: Use the Managing Scripts dialog box to rename, duplicate, and delete scripts

Creating and Deploying Packages in Silent Mode

By saving package and deployment scripts, you gain the ability to process those scripts in silent mode. In silent mode, the Package and Deployment Wizard processes your scripts with no user interaction by using the settings saved within the scripts. Silent mode can be extremely useful. For instance, if you wanted to deploy a package to an intranet late in the evening when the developers are finished for the day, and no users are accessing the site, you could create a batch process to run the script in silent mode.

To process a package and deployment script in silent mode, follow these steps:

1. At an MS-DOS prompt, type the name of the Package and Deployment Wizard executable (*Pdcmdln.exe*), followed by the path and filename of your Visual Basic project.

2. Following the path and filename of your project, add the /p and /d switches, as specified in Table 13-6.

3. Press Enter to start the Package and Deployment Wizard in silent mode.

You must specify both the /p *and* /d switches in order to fully package and deploy in silent mode.

Table 13-6: Package and Deployment Wizard Command Line Switches

Argument	Description
/p packagingscript	Specifies the packaging script to execute silently
/d deploymentscript	Specifies the deployment script to execute silently
/l	Designates the path and name of a log file in which to store all errors and success reports

Any packaging scripts that contain spaces should be enclosed in quotation marks, as shown in this example:

```
pdcmdln.exe C:\vb6apps\bdpro.vbp /p "Standard Package" /d
    Deployment1 /l "C:\Windows\Temp\SilentMode.log"
```

Creating an AutoRun CD-ROM

You may encounter a question on one of the exams about how to create an AutoRun CD using the Package and Deployment Wizard. The short answer is: you can't. What actually makes a CD an AutoRun CD is the presence of a special text file on the CD. To create an AutoRun CD, create a text file and name it *Autorun.inf.* This text file is essentially an INI file containing a single section titled [autorun]. The two entries under the section are OPEN and ICON. The following is a sample:

```
[autorun]
OPEN=Setup.exe
ICON=Setup.ico
```

The OPEN item refers to the executable file you want to automatically run when the user inserts the CD into the CD-ROM drive. Since the Package and Deployment Wizard creates a *Setup.exe* file, it makes the most sense to run this as the executable. The optional ICON setting is the icon to display for the executable.

 To create an AutoRun CD-ROM, create a text file named *Autorun.inf* that specifies which file is to be automatically executed when the CD-ROM is inserted in the drive. The Package and Deployment Wizard itself doesn't create AutoRun CDs.

Using License Keys for ActiveX Controls

If you've ever tried a shareware ActiveX control prior to purchasing it, you have experience with a licensed control. Most of the shareware controls exhibit a behavior different from their registered counterparts. Often, a nag screen appears whenever the control is added to a form or displayed in a running project. Visual Basic's ActiveX control licensing scheme is less flexible than this, but it affords you a much higher degree of protection from people distributing your control as part of their own work.

 The issue of creating licensed ActiveX controls could have been placed in Chapter 5. However, licensing a control really is a distribution issue: if you don't plan on distributing your control, you don't need to worry about protecting it with a licensing scheme. Accordingly, the material is presented here instead of in the ActiveX control chapter.

Understanding Visual Basic's Control Licensing Scheme

When you protect an ActiveX control by requiring a license key (discussed in the next section), the control checks the registry to verify that the appropriate licensing information is present whenever a user attempts to place that control on a form. If the licensing information cannot be found in the registry, the control won't be created. If the license information is found, the control is created as though the control doesn't even use licensing.

How licensed controls work in a compiled application

It follows then, that your control is completely protected from other developers using it in a project unless the control has been installed on their machine with the appropriate license key. Although a license key is required for the control to be added to a form at design time, no such restrictions are placed on the control at runtime. Say you have a valid license key for your control and have written an application that uses the control. When you compile the application, Visual Basic automatically compiles the license key into the application. When a user attempts to run your application on another computer, Visual Basic tells the control to display itself as appropriate, but it passes the license key to the control so that the control does not check the registry. In a sense, it thinks the control is licensed even though it isn't. Because of this, you can distribute applications that use a licensed control, but you don't have to give every person who receives a copy of the control the ability to develop with it.

How control licensing affects the distribution of encapsulated (constituent) controls

The licensing concept carries forth into the distribution of ActiveX aggregate–type controls. An aggregate control is an ActiveX control based upon one or more constituent controls; the aggregate control acts as a "wrapper" around the constituent controls. Say you give a developer the right to use your licensed control in design mode by providing him with an install of the control that saves the proper licensing information in the registry of his computer. This developer then builds an aggregate control that acts as a wrapper around your control, and he wants to distribute this new control to other developers. You might think you're out of luck as far as controlling licensing is concerned. However, thanks to Visual Basic, you're not.

When a developer builds a new ActiveX control and includes your control within it, the license key for your component is compiled into the control just as though it were an application. However, when an end user of the new aggregate control places an instance of the control on a form, the control looks in the registry for its license key before creating the instance. Then, the aggregate control requests that all constituent controls (including your protected control) create an instance of themselves as well using their registry keys. *The aggregate control does not pass license keys to its constituent controls.* Since your control won't be able to find its license key in the registry, it won't load. This happens because, in order for the Package and Deployment Wizard to be able to install a license key for a control, it must have access to the control's licensing file. However, the licensing file doesn't have to be distributed with the control. Therefore, you can enable developers to use your control in the design environment, but prevent them from redistributing your control with the same design-time functionality.

If a developer wants to distribute an aggregate control that includes an instance of your control, the users of the aggregate control will have to purchase the developer version of your control (the license file), or the developer will have to work out a special licensing arrangement with you. Your investment remains protected.

How licensed controls behave in user documents

When desktop applications such as Microsoft Word and Microsoft Excel create an instance of a control on a document or user form, they tell the control to create an instance of itself using the licensing key found in the registry. (The same holds true for ActiveX documents.) Accordingly, for a user to work with a document containing a licensed control, they must have a licensed version of the control. Microsoft therefore suggests that corporate developers creating ActiveX controls for use by end users within their companies may want to consider omitting licensing support from their controls. This makes it considerably more convenient for an end user to distribute a document containing the controls.

Creating and Distributing a Licensed Control

Creating and distributing a licensed control is a two-step process:

1. Create a licensing key for the ActiveX control.
2. Tell the Package and Deployment Wizard to install the ActiveX control with the licensing key.

Creating a licensing key for an ActiveX control

Making an ActiveX control require a valid license key to be present in the registry in order for the control to be used at design time is simple. On the General tab of the Project Properties dialog box is a checkbox titled Require License Key (see

Figure 13-26). Selecting this option prior to compiling the control, using the Build item on the File menu, instructs the compiler to create a control that requires a valid license key for design-time use.

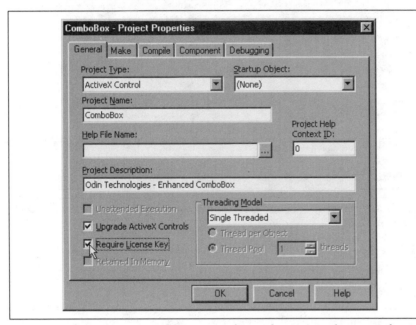

Figure 13-26: Forcing a control to require a license key is a simple matter of setting a project property

When you compile (build) an ActiveX control that has its Require License Key option selected, Visual Basic creates a file of the same name as the OCX control file but with the extension VBL (Visual Basic License). The VBL file is a text file containing the information needed by the Package and Deployment Wizard to add the correct licensing information to the registry of a user's computer.

Distributing a licensed control using the Package and Deployment Wizard

When creating a custom setup program, the Package and Deployment Wizard won't automatically include the VBL file in the set of packaged files. If you want the license information installed on the user's computer, you'll have to add the file to the package manually using the techniques discussed earlier in this chapter. If you add a VBL file to a package, you'll see an additional page of the wizard, as shown in Figure 13-27.

Associated VBL files are created in the same folder as their compiled OCX counterparts.

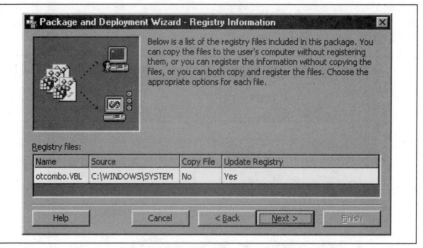

Figure 13-27: The Package and Deployment Wizard gives you implicit control over your license keys

You have three options available to you when you elect to distribute a VBL file:

- You can copy the license file to the user's computer without registering the file. The user will not be able to use the control at design time.

- You can register the license information without copying the VBL file to the user's computer. This allows the user to develop with the control, but prevents them from distributing your license file.

- You can register the license information *and* copy the VBL file to the user's computer. This allows the user to develop with the control and to distribute your license information to other users.

The option you choose depends upon your requirements. Most often, it's desirable to register the licensing information in the registry but not install the VBL file on the user's computer. This allows users to develop with your control and distribute it as part of a compiled application, but it doesn't allow them to distribute an aggregate control that uses your control as a constituent control.

Using licensed controls on web pages requires special considerations, and these are discussed in the next section.

Distributing a Component over the Internet

The Package and Deployment Wizard makes it easy to deploy a component to a web server. However, ActiveX components have the added ability of being embedded on, and therefore distributed via, a web page. This special form of distribution has its own methodology and considerations. Fortunately, the Package and Deployment Wizard can perform most of the necessary work for you. However, to pass the Internet distribution–related questions on the exam, you'll need to have a grasp of what's going on "under the hood."

Understanding How the Internet
Component Download Works

When an ActiveX component such as an ActiveX control is hosted on a web page, the component and its dependencies reside on a web server. They may be in the same location as the HTML documents containing the controls, or they may reside at another location. When a user accesses a web page containing a control, the following steps occur. The component is:

1. Downloaded in the form of a CAB file

2. Verified for safety

3. Decompressed

4. Registered in the Windows registry of the user browsing the page

5. Installed

6. Activated

The key to Internet distribution is what is known as a cabinet file (CAB). A CAB file is used to encapsulate all of the file dependencies and other information needed by your component to function. This CAB file is what a web page references in order to use your control.

Taking advantage of secondary CAB files

If you elect to deploy an ActiveX control to a web server, the Package and Deployment Wizard displays an additional page (see Figure 13-28). Just as you can package your component in a CAB file, you can include CAB files from other components as well. These additional CAB files are called secondary CAB files. Secondary CAB files can make the process of distributing your component considerably easier.

For example, all Visual Basic controls require runtime components such as *Msvbvm60.dll*. Because the need to distribute these files is so common, Microsoft has created CAB files with all of the necessary information for downloading and installing them on a user's machine. The Package and Deployment Wizard even lets you designate that secondary CAB files are to reference components on Microsoft's site, instead of from a site of your choosing.

In general, its best to have the files downloaded directly from Microsoft's site. This ensures that the most current versions of the shared components are always installed, and it frees you from having to devote valuable hard drive space on your web server for the files. There are some special situations where you might want to include the files on your own server, such as when you are distributing the component over an intranet. Placing secondary CAB files on your intranet eliminates the need for the user to be connected to the Internet, and the files will download faster.

You could add all of the necessary files for an installation into a single CAB file, but secondary CAB files offer the following benefits:

- You don't need to distribute all of the CAB files required by your application. The only file you need to distribute is the primary CAB file.

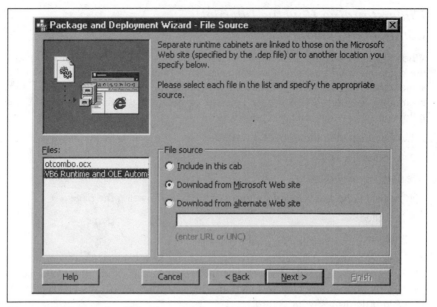

Figure 13-28: You should let the secondary CAB files install components from Microsoft's site whenever possible

- The INF file within the primary CAB file points to the Microsoft web site and downloads the necessary CAB files based on the needs of the end user.

- CAB files provide an efficient means of delivering updates to your product.

Marking a component safe

Components hosted on a web page present a unique situation. You essentially have a component written by one individual, that can be "programmed" by another individual via the HTML tags that enable the component on a web page. These components may be used by yet another individual who may not even be aware such a component is running on the computer. This poses a number of security issues for all involved. As a component developer, you need to be very concerned with producing components that can't inadvertently cause harm on an unsuspecting user's computer because of malicious scripting of the component.

In order for an ActiveX component to be hosted on a web site, an HTML document uses a scripting language, such as VBScript, to interact with the properties, methods, and events of the component, much as a developer might write Visual Basic code for an application to use a component. This opens up interesting, and terrifying, security issues. Say you exposed a method that deletes a file or files specified by the script calling the procedure. Imagine the havoc wreaked upon an unsuspecting user's machine when that user accesses a web site that sends the filename C:*.* to the Delete method!

Properties, methods, and events are not the only place a malicious directive can cause irreparable harm. When a component such as a control is first initialized, its state is set from the <PARAM> tag's <NAME> attribute that accompanies the <OBJECT>

tag in the HTML page containing the control. Malicious data placed in these tags poses a threat much like that found with malicious scripts.

In answer to these concerns, ActiveX controls have the ability to be marked as Safe for Scripting and Safe for Initialization. By default, Internet Explorer displays a warning and will not download a component that has not been marked safe for scripting *and* initialization. Beyond the defaults, Internet Explorer lets users tailor the behavior of Internet Explorer when it encounters components not marked as safe for scripting and initializing. If a user can't download your component from a web site, chances are good that the user's Internet Explorer security settings are too high. Conversely, if the user's Internet Explorer security settings are set too low, the user can download just about anything.

You can mark components as Safe for Scripting and/or Safe for Initializing using the Package and Deployment Wizard, but you should do so only if the component meets the following requirements:

- The component will not forsake security when initialized using *any* data, especially malicious data (required for Safe for Initialization).

- The component will not forsake security when scripted, especially with malicious scripts (required for Safe for Scripting).

- For components whose users don't expect information to be collected about themselves or their PCs, the component should not make such information available to a script. For instance, the component should not read and provide data from the registry.

- Scripts shouldn't be able to use controls marked Safe for Scripting to create, change, or delete arbitrary files (even temporary ones), or to change system settings.

If you're distributing an ActiveX component to a web server, the additional Package and Deployment Wizard page shown in Figure 13-29 is displayed. To mark a component as Safe for Scripting or Safe for Initialization, select the component in the list and change the value in the appropriate column.

Other than the items discussed in this section, creating an Internet download setup using the Package and Deployment Wizard is identical to creating a standard installation. However, once the Package and Deployment Wizard is complete, you'll find that in addition to the CAB file, the Package and Deployment Wizard actually creates an HTML document that includes the code necessary to package your component on a web page.

Rebuilding a CAB file

In addition to the CAB file and web file created for an Internet download setup, the Package and Deployment Wizard also creates a folder directly below the one containing the CAB and HTML files, called *Support*. This folder contains the files necessary to rebuild the CAB file, including:

- The component (OCX, and so on)

- A DDF file used by the compression program to compress the needed files into the CAB file

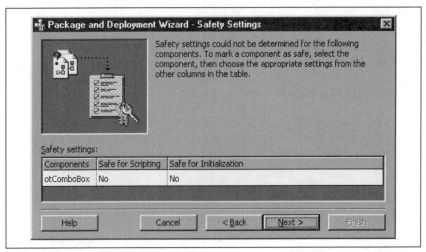

Figure 13-29: Careful consideration must be given when marking controls as safe

- An INF text file that contains all of the dependency, version, setup, and safety information for the component
- A BAT file you can use to rebuild the CAB file

In the event that you want to make changes manually to the INF file, you can create a new CAB file without the aid of the Package and Deployment Wizard by using Microsoft's *Makecab.exe* tool. This executable is located in the *wizards*\\ *pdwizard* folder under your main Visual Basic folder. To create a CAB file using the information from the *Support* folder, you run the *Makecab.exe* program, specifying the /f switch and then the name of the DDF file, like this:

```
Makecab.exe /f <filename>.ddf
```

Fortunately, the Package and Deployment Wizard creates a BAT file in the *Support* folder that calls the *Makecab.exe* file and passes it the /f switch and the DDF file as its argument, simplifying the process.

Deploying a Component to an HTML Page Using a CAB File

In an HTML document, tags such as <BODY> or <TITLE> represent instances of a web page's data. When ActiveX components and other controls are a part of the web page's data, they are linked to the web page by using the <OBJECT> tag. The <OBJECT> tag contains a number of attributes that define the object, its location, and its presentation on a web page. When a browser opens a web page that contains an ActiveX control specified using the <OBJECT> tag, it uses all the information specified in the tag to successfully install and execute the control on the user's computer. Table 13-7 lists the attributes used in the <OBJECT> tag.

Table 13-7: <OBJECT> Tag Attributes Used in HTML Documents

Attribute	Description
CLASSID	The unique identifier of the component as stored in the system registry
CODEBASE	A URL that points to the location where the cabinet (CAB) file is located
ID	The object name to use in scripting the component

The Package and Deployment Wizard creates a sample HTML document that contains the tags necessary to add your component to a web page. You can build upon this HTML document if you wish, or you can copy the object information it contains and paste it into an HTML document of your choice.

The example below shows HTML document text with an ActiveX control embedded upon it in the form of a CAB file:

```
<HTML>
<HEAD>
<TITLE>ottoolbx.CAB</TITLE>
</HEAD>
<BODY>

<OBJECT CLASSID="clsid:5220cb13-c88d-11cf-b347-00aa00a28331">

</OBJECT>

<OBJECT ID="otToolbox" WIDTH=68 HEIGHT=240
CLASSID="CLSID:8CD322B9-95C8-11D1-BB5C-D01A07C15A07"
CODEBASE="ottoolbx.CAB#version=1,0,0,4">
</OBJECT>
</BODY>
</HTML>
```

The important attribute to note in this listing is CODEBASE. The CODEBASE attribute is used to tell the browser the name of the CAB file that contains the object, as well as the version of the object. If the user's computer has a control with the same CLSID installed which is the current version or a newer version, then that component is used instead in place of downloading the one in the CAB file.

In addition to placing the necessary tags in an HTML document, you must also place the CAB file on the web server along with the document (using the Package and Deployment Wizard to deploy a component to a web server is discussed earlier in this chapter). Because the CAB files contain everything necessary for the download, you don't need to place other files on the server. The component itself, for instance, is compressed in the CAB file.

Understanding How Licensed Controls Work over the Internet

If you've created an ActiveX control that requires a license key, and you plan on deploying that control on a web page, some additional work is necessary. HTML documents aren't able to store a license key and pass it to a control when the control is asked to instantiate itself. When such a control is asked to instantiate itself, it checks the registry for a valid license key. Obviously, you don't want to distribute your license key to every single person who accesses your control through a web page; that would defeat the whole purpose of using a licensing key.

Browsers that support ActiveX controls provide a mechanism to handle licensed controls by use of a license package file, or LPK. Neither Visual Basic nor the Package and Deployment Wizard have an intrinsic capability to create an LPK file. Instead, Microsoft provides a program called *lpk_tool.exe* on your Visual Basic CD-ROM. This program acts as a compiler of sorts, letting you combine all of the licensing keys for all of the controls on a web page into a single LPK file. You must create a single LPK file containing all of the licensing keys for every control on a page that requires a licensing key. The licensing information stored in the LPK file is not written to the user's registry; it's only used to instantiate the control on the web page.

 Be warned: a user could theoretically view the contents of an LPK file and use this knowledge to fully register the component on his or her computer.

Using *lpk_tool.exe* is straightforward. When you launch the program, you are shown a list of all of the available controls on your computer (see Figure 13-30). Simply select the controls that have licensing files and that appear on the web page, click Save & Exit, then provide a name for the LPK file.

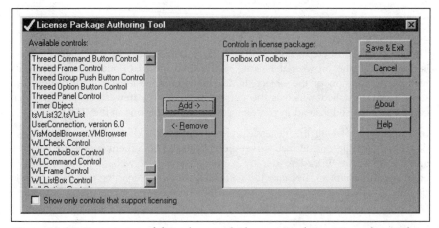

Figure 13-30: You must use lpk_tool.exe to deploy a control requiring a license key to a web page

Once the LPK file is created, you must place it on the web server and add code to the HTML document on which your control or controls are hosted. In order to access the LPK file, you must add the License Manager object to the HTML code of your web page. The necessary <OBJECT> tag is added to the sample HTML page created by the Package and Deployment Wizard and is shown in the following code listing. Within the <OBJECT> tag of the License Manager, you use the <PARAM> tag to reference an LPK file:

```
<HTML>
<HEAD>
<TITLE>ottoolbx.CAB</TITLE>
</HEAD>
<BODY>

<OBJECT CLASSID="clsid:5220cb13-c88d-11cf-b347-00aa00a28331">
    <PARAM NAME="http:\\mysite.com" VALUE="mylpkfile.LPK">
</OBJECT>

<OBJECT ID="otToolbox" WIDTH=68 HEIGHT=240
CLASSID="CLSID:8CD322B9-95C8-11D1-BB5C-D01A07C15A07"
CODEBASE="ottoolbx.CAB#version=1,0,0,4">
</OBJECT>
</BODY>
</HTML>
```

Digitally Signing an ActiveX Component

When you go to a local software store to purchase an application, you know who developed the product by looking at the packaging. In addition, you know that there is someone (the software dealer) who will stand behind the product if you have any problems. When you access an Internet site, you have no way of knowing who created a component, and there is nothing to indicate that you should trust the developer anyway. Even controls marked as safe may not be safe; anyone can mark a control as safe even if it's not.

In all actuality, you don't know that a product you buy in a store is safe, but you have added assurance because you know for a fact who developed the product. The chances of a company putting their name on a malicious product is small. There is simply no way to absolutely guarantee that a product has no malicious intent, but you can give users of your control some reassurance by *digitally signing* your controls.

In order to digitally sign a control, you must apply for a digital certificate from a certificate authority (CA), such as VeriSign. The certificate authority is responsible for verifying your identity. Once the CA has verified your identity, they issue you a unique digital certificate that, when added to your controls, tells a user accessing your control that you are the developer of the control. This doesn't ensure your control is safe, it only lets the user know without a doubt who developed the control. This knowledge goes a long way in gaining a user's trust.

The process of obtaining a certificate and signing a component or CAB file is beyond the scope of the exams; you don't need to know the specifics, but you need to have a general understanding of the principles.

To sign a component or CAB file, follow these steps:

1. Obtain a digital certificate from a certificate authority such as VeriSign.

2. Use the *Signcode.exe* program (available from Microsoft) to sign your component or CAB file.

Signcode.exe is included with Microsoft's ActiveX Developer Kit, which is available on Microsoft's web site. *Signcode.exe* lets you select a file to sign (such as a CAB file), lets you give the certificate a title, and lets you select from various encryption algorithms.

When a user attempts to access a signed component, a digital certificate like the one in Figure 13-31 is shown. The user then has the option of accepting or rejecting the signed component. Users can even instruct their browsers to always accept signed certificates so that they won't be bothered with dialog boxes each time a signed component is accessed.

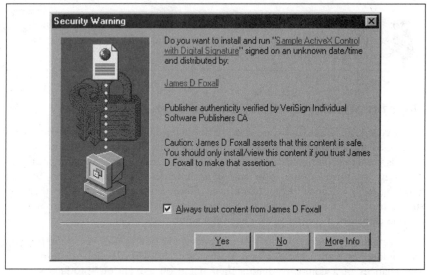

Figure 13-31: When users see a digital certificate such as this one, they can rest assured that the source shown in the certificate is the true source of the component

Remember, just because a component is digitally signed doesn't mean that it's safe. *Digital signing does nothing more than assure a user of who developed the component*. A user is always assured of the source of a digitally signed component because if a signed component is tampered with in any way, the certificate will invalidate itself. When this happens, the certificate won't display when a user accesses the component. Instead, a user is shown a dialog box similar to that in Figure 13-32.

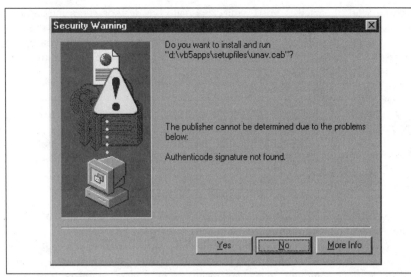

Figure 13-32: If a signed file has been tampered with in any way, a digital certificate won't display

 The ActiveX Developer's Kit includes a file called *Chktrust.exe*. You can use *Chktrust.exe* to verify that a signed component hasn't been tampered with. If the component hasn't been tampered with, a digital certificate similar to the one in Figure 13-31 will display. If the file has been tampered with, you'll see a dialog box similar to that in Figure 13-32.

Deploying ActiveX components, particularly licensed components, on a web page can be a rather complex task. Make sure you thoroughly understand the material here, and that you can answer the Internet deployment–related questions at the end of this chapter. You will be tested on this material.

Distributing DCOM Servers

Chapter 3 discussed the component object model and how ActiveX components can be accessed as servers and run in the process space of the client (DLLs) or in a separate process space (EXEs). In addition to COM, Microsoft Windows 98 and NT also support DCOM. DCOM stands for Distributed Component Object Model, an extension of COM that lets clients communicate with COM servers across machines on an LAN, intranet, or across the Internet.

DCOM gives you the ability to perform some static load balancing with your applications. For instance, you can dedicate a powerful machine to run a server that performs large amounts of data crunching, freeing the client machines from having to do the work themselves. Also, you can isolate business practices into remote servers (the second tier in three-tier applications). For example, you could create a business server that serves objects encapsulating business rules. If you make changes to the rules, you need only distribute the new object to the one machine that serves it, and all clients will use the new business rules.

 DCOM components can be EXEs or DLLs. There is additional over-head when accessing objects on a different computer because the operating system must marshal data between the machines, much like it has to marshal data between processes with out-of-process components.

All COM objects, whether local or remote, are registered with the Windows registry. When a client application attempts to use objects of a server, the class ID of the server is used to look up information about the server in the registry. In order for components to work with DCOM, the server files must be registered correctly on their computer, and client machines must also have a registry entry for the server. However, the registry entry for the client is different than it is for the server, since the former contains information pointing the client (and the operating system) to the server on the remote machine. Fortunately, the Package and Deployment Wizard can handle the registration of DCOM servers and clients for you.

Configuring DCOM

DCOM must be configured on a computer before it can be used. DCOM is configured using a utility titled *dcomcnfg.exe*, which is provided with Windows 98 and Windows NT 4.0. Using this utility (usually found in the *System* folder), you can configure a machine as a server, a client, or both (see Figure 13-33). You use *dcomcnfg.exe* to specify where components run, as well as to define security, including setting up user accounts to determine who can launch, access, and configure DCOM components.

Using DCOM on a Windows 95 or Windows 98 computer requires that the computer be set up for user-level security. If you attempt to run *dcomcnfg.exe* without configuring Windows 9x for user-level security, you'll receive an error message telling you to change the security level. To access the security level of a Windows 9x machine, double-click the Network icon in Control Panel, then click the Access Control tab.

 Configuring DCOM to run multiple components can take some fina-gling. Fully exploring the configuration of DCOM is beyond the scope of the exams and of this book. Here, you'll learn the basics for configuring DCOM.

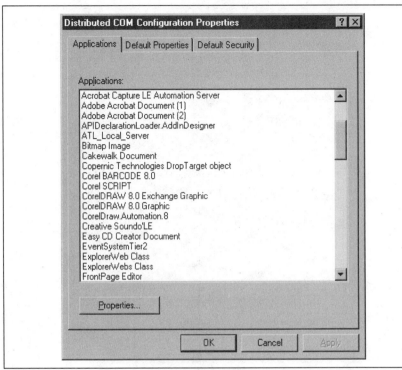

Figure 13-33: DCOM is configured with the utility dcomcnfg.exe

The primary steps for configuring DCOM are:

1. Select "Enable Distributed COM on this computer" on the Default Properties tab (see Figure 13-34).

2. Select "Enable remote connection" on the Default Security tab (see Figure 13-35).

3. Define the users that can access the server components.

 The default behavior for DCOM is to allow only administrators to access remote servers. To customize this, you must edit the allowed users by clicking the Edit Default button on the Default Security tab, or by using the Security tab of the server Document Properties dialog box discussed next.

You can customize settings for each server that appears in the Applications list. To modify the settings, select the server and click Properties to display the Document Properties dialog box shown in Figure 13-36. The General tab shows basic information that you cannot modify. The Location tab can be used to specify the location from which to run the server, though "Run application on this computer"

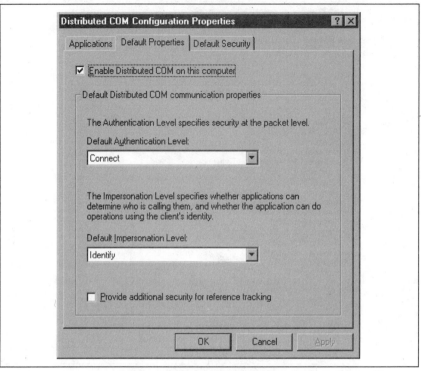

Figure 13-34: A computer must have DCOM enabled in order to support remote server access

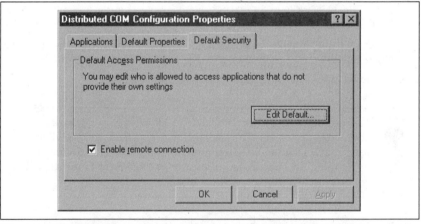

Figure 13-35: If you don't select "Enable remote connection," the computer won't be able to support remote servers

is used most frequently (see Figure 13-37). To customize the users that can access the component, click the Security tab (see Figure 13-38), select "Use custom access permissions," and click Edit to designate which users can access the component.

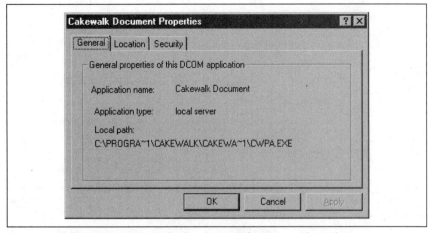

Figure 13-36: The General tab displays basic information about the component

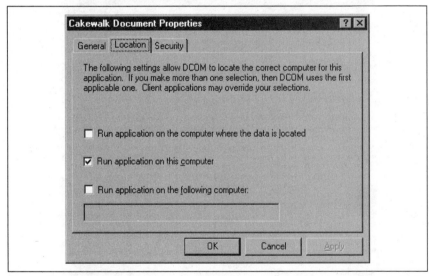

Figure 13-37: Most remote servers are configured to run on the computer on which they reside

Deploying a DCOM Server Component

In order to package and deploy a server component as a DCOM remote server, you must set select the Remote Server Files option on the Project Properties dialog box, as shown in Figure 13-39. When this option is selected and you compile the component to a file by choosing Make from the file menu, Visual Basic creates two files in addition to the component: a TLB file and a VBR file. The TLB file is a type library for the component, and the VBR file contains information needed by the Windows registry to run a COM (ActiveX) server on a remote computer.

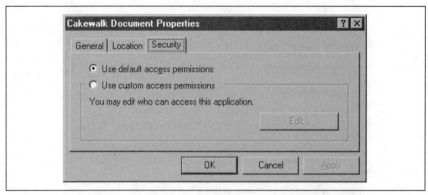

Figure 13-38: A component can be configured to use the default access permissions, or to allow access to specific users

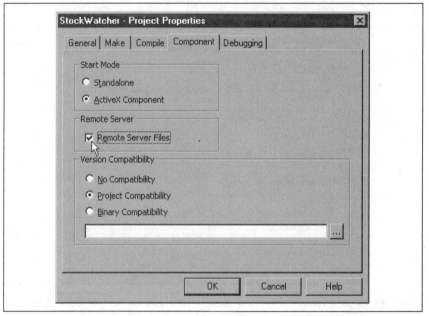

Figure 13-39: Selecting the Remote Server Files option causes Visual Basic to create two files in addition to the compiled component file

 You can only create remote servers with the Enterprise Edition of Visual Basic.

When you use the Package and Deployment Wizard to create a setup program for the server, you will receive the message shown in Figure 13-40. When you answer Yes, the Package and Deployment Wizard will add necessary files and structure the setup program so that the server can be properly registered on the computer on which it is installed, without any intervention from you.

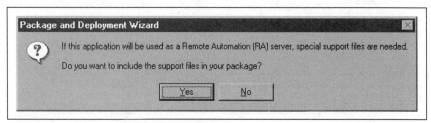

Figure 13-40: This dialog box is the only deviation you'll see when packing a remote server

Deploying a DCOM Client Application

Although you must set a project option in order to create a remote server, you don't have to do anything special to create clients that use remote servers. However, you do have to take steps in the Package and Deployment Wizard to ensure that the client is able to use a remote server. When the Package and Deployment Wizard creates a package for an ActiveX client, it will add all files that it believes are required in order for the client to run, and this includes all servers used by the client. However, you don't want to distribute a remote server file because the server file will be deployed to a computer using its own setup program. This is where the VBR file created by Visual Basic when you build a server component comes into play.

The Package and Deployment Wizard doesn't necessarily know that you want to use a server as a remote server, and therefore you must take steps to modify the package script to distribute a remote client. These steps include:

1. Manually remove the compiled server component (EXE or DLL) from the Included Files page of the Package and Deployment Wizard (refer to Figure 13-10).

2. Manually add the VBR file of the remote server using the Included Files dialog box.

When you add one or more VBR files using the Included Files page of the wizard and click Next to continue, an additional page titled Remote Servers appears (see Figure 13-41). The Remote Servers page is used to specify information required for the client to access the server on a remote computer. If any information is missing or incorrect, the user will have to supply the information when the component is installed, so you should provide information for each remote server that is as accurate as possible. Table 13-8 lists the settings and their meanings for each remote server.

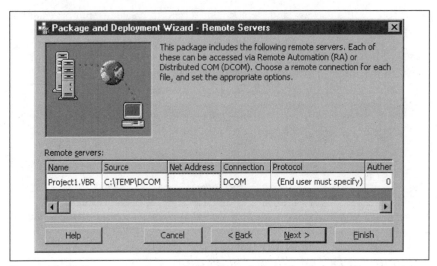

Figure 13-41: Remote servers must be configured correctly when creating a script using the Package and Deployment Wizard

Table 13-8: Parameters Required in order to Distribute Clients that Use Remote Servers

Parameter	Description
Net Address	Used to specify the net address of the computer where the remote server component will be installed. If you do not know this address when creating a package, leave the parameter blank and the user will be asked for this information when installing the client.
Connection	Used to specify whether or not to use Remote Automation or DCOM. Remote Automation is used when distributing to operating systems (such as Windows 3.x) where DCOM is not supported.
Protocol	If you choose Remote Automation as the Connection method, you must specify a network protocol for accessing the remote server.
Authentication	Used only when Remote Automation is specified as the Connection method.

Once the client is installed on a machine and the server is installed a machine, the client will be able to access and use the remote server.

Managing the Windows System Registry

You'll have to demonstrate how to register an ActiveX component and how to manipulate the Windows registry using Visual Basic commands. Although this material could have been put in any ActiveX chapter, you usually have to modify the registry when you distribute an application or component, and therefore the material is included here.

Under Windows 3.1, applications stored information in private INI files (and, at times, in the *Win.ini* file). Under Windows 95, Windows 98, and Windows NT, this information is now stored in the system registry. Visual Basic includes functions that let you manipulate registry entries; however, they don't enable you to work with all entries in the registry. Instead, Visual Basic provides a standard registry location for storing information specific to programs created in Visual Basic. This key is:

```
HKEY_CURRENT_USER\Software\Visual Basic and VBA Program Settings\appname\
section\key
```

 It should be noted that the terminology used for the Visual Basic commands for manipulating the registry (primarily the *appname* and *section* parameters) are throwbacks to the earlier days of using INI files. In reality, the registry is composed of keys and subkeys, and each subkey may contain one or more subkeys (think of the directory structure as seen in Explorer). The terms *appname* and *section* are used here in order to stay consistent with the Microsoft documentation, which is the terminology you're most likely to encounter on the exams.

The registry functions provided by Visual Basic (shown in Table 13-9) only let you manipulate string values stored under this key. However, you have control over the *appname*, *section*, and *key* values shown in italics above.

Table 13-9: Visual Basic Registry Function

Function or Statement	Description
GetSetting function	Retrieves registry settings
SaveSetting statement	Saves or creates registry settings
GetAllSettings function	Returns an array containing multiple registry settings
DeleteSetting statement	Deletes registry settings

Creating and Saving Registry Settings

To create a new registry entry or save changes to an existing registry entry, use the SaveSetting statement. The SaveSetting statement has the following syntax:

SaveSetting *appname, section, key, value*

The following code illustrates using the SaveSetting statement to store color preferences in a ColorPref section (or registry key) of an application called QuickPaint:

```
SaveSetting "QuickPaint", "ColorPref", "ForeColor", vbBlack
SaveSetting "QuickPaint", "ColorPref", "BackColor", vbWhite
SaveSetting "QuickPaint", "ColorPref", "DrawColor", vbRed
```

The SaveSetting statement exhibits the following behavior:

- If an entry for the program specified in the *appname* parameter doesn't exist, a new entry is created.

- If the section name specified in the *section* parameter doesn't exist, a new entry is created.

- If the value entry specified in the *key* parameter doesn't exist, a new entry is created.

Packaging Applications

Retrieving Registry Settings

Visual Basic provides two ways to retrieve registry settings: one setting at a time, or all settings for an application.

Retrieving registry settings one value at a time

To retrieve a single registry setting, use the *GetSetting* function. The *GetSetting* function has the following syntax:

GetSetting(*appname, section, key, [,default]*)

The *GetSetting* function always returns a string.

The **appname**, **section**, and **key** parameters refer to their counterparts in the **SaveSetting** statement. The parameter **default** is optional. If you don't specify a value for **default** and *GetSetting* attempts to retrieve a value for an entry that doesn't exist, the function returns a zero-length string (**""**). If you specify a string for the default parameter, that string is returned as the value if the specified entry doesn't exist.

Retrieving multiple settings from the registry

The *GetAllSettings* function is used to return a complete list of all registry keys (actually of all registry value entries) in a specified section for a specified program. The *GetAllSettings* function has the following syntax:

GetAllSettings(*appname, section*)

GetAllSettings returns a two-dimensional array, and therefore you should use an array (or variant) to accept the results. The first dimension of the array holds the value name, while the second holds the value.

For example, the following code retrieves all of the value entries in a section called `ColorPref` for the application called `QuickDraw`:

```
Dim avntSettings As Variant
Dim intX As Integer

avntSettings = GetAllSettings("QuickDraw", "ColorPref")

If avntSettings = Empty Then Exit Sub

For intX = 0 To UBound(avntSettings, 1)
    Debug.Print avntSettings(intX, 0), avntSettings(intX, 1)
Next intX
```

If there are no keys in the specified *section* of the specified program, the array variable will be empty. You should always check for this condition before attempting to access values within the array, or your code may generate an error.

Deleting Registry Settings

You can delete a registry key, section, or an application's entire registry location with the `DeleteSetting` statement. `DeleteSetting` has the following syntax:

```
DeleteSetting(appname, section, key)
```

Just how much the `DeleteSetting` statement deletes depends on how you use it. For example, the following statement deletes the value named `BackColor` from the section named `Colors` for the application called `QuickDraw`:

```
DeleteSetting "QuickDraw", "Colors", "BackColor"
```

If you want to delete all of the keys under a specific section, you provide the *appname* and *section* arguments, but omit the *key* parameter, like this:

```
DeleteSetting "QuickDraw", "Colors"
```

If you want to delete the entire registry location of an application, provide the *appname* argument only. For example, the following statement deletes the entire registry location for `QuickDraw`:

```
DeleteSetting "QuickDraw"
```

Registering Components Using Regsvr32.exe

In order for an in-process server (an ActiveX control or DLL) to be used on a computer, the component must be registered in the system registry. If the component isn't registered, it won't show up in lists such as the one on the References dialog box in Visual Basic. In addition, compiled applications won't be able to use the component.

Visual Basic's Package and Deployment Wizard automatically registers ActiveX components when it installs them on a user's computer. However, there are times when you'll need to register or unregister a component manually. Visual Basic includes a utility called *Regsvr32.exe* to register and unregister ActiveX components manually.

To register a component using *Regsvr32.exe*, run the program, passing it the name of the component to register, like this:

```
C:\WIN95\regsvr32.exe d:\VBTools\cooltool.ocx
```

To unregister a component using *Regsvr32.exe*, use the same syntax as when registering a component but place the /u switch before the component name, like this:

```
C:\WIN95\regsvr32.exe /u d:\VBTools\cooltool.ocx
```

By default, *Regsvr32.exe* will display a confirmation message after registering or unregistering a component. If you don't want a message displayed, you can run *Regsvr32.exe* in silent mode by specifying the /s switch like this:

```
C:\WIN95\regsvr32.exe /s d:\mailstuf\knob.ocx
```

Key Facts

This chapter has discussed the many aspects involved in compiling and distributing a Visual Basic application or component, including the issues involved with Internet deployment, control licensing, and working with the system registry. All of these topics are important and are covered on the exams to some extent. The following are key facts to understand in order to pass related questions on the Visual Basic exams:

- All of the various files that are required for an application to run are called dependencies.

- The relationship between a newer version of a component and an older one, and at what level they are interchangeable, is called version compatibility. When you distribute an update to a component, you should always ensure that the new component is fully backward compatible with previous versions of the component so that existing applications won't be broken.

- In order for a component to be fully backward compatible, it must:

  – Have the same CLSID and type library identifiers as the previous version

  – Expose all of the members (properties, methods, and events) of the previous version

  – Not modify the declarations of the previous component

  – Retain all of the procedure IDs of the previous component

  – Exhibit the same functionality for all of the members of the previous version of the component

- Visual Basic lets you control version compatibility of components at the following levels: No Compatibility, Project Compatibility, and Binary Compatibility

- When a project is compiled with the No Compatibility option selected, Visual Basic assigns a new CLSID as well as new procedure identifiers.

- When you use the No Compatibility option to produce a new version of a component, you should change the Project Name property of the project and compile the project to a filename different than that of the previous version.

- When you compile a project that uses the Project Compatibility setting, Visual Basic maintains the same type library identifier of the previous component— nothing more. All this does is allows you to open projects that use previous versions of the component.

- The Binary Compatibility option is the only option that truly enforces compatibility between components. When you compile a project with the Maintain Binary Compatibility option selected, the new component will have the same CLSID and procedure identifiers as its previous version. Applications that use previous versions of the component will be able to use the new one without having to be recompiled.

- A dependency file is a text file with the extension DEP that contains information about the runtime requirements of a component.

- There are three types of dependency files related to creating a setup program for your application: Component DEP files, Project DEP files, and the *VB6dep.ini* file.

- You should distribute a dependency file for each of your components that you create in Visual Basic.

- The Setup Wizard generates a *Setup.lst* file. This file contains all of the information necessary to install an application on a user's machine.

- The [Bootstrap] section of the *Setup.lst* file contains all of the files that must be loaded on the user's computer *before* your application and all of its dependency files can be loaded.

- The [Files] Section of the *Setup.lst* contains all other files required by your application.

- The *VB6dep.ini* file is a master dependency file that is installed on your computer with Visual Basic itself. It contains dependency information about commonly installed components such as the Jet engine.

- The Setup Wizard is a tool that creates custom setup programs for your Visual Basic developed components, and it can rebuild applications prior to creating custom setup programs for them.

- For standard distribution-type setup programs, you can create a floppy disk, single directory, or disk directories installation.

- When you instruct the Setup Wizard that an application is a shared file, that file is installed into the *Windows\System* folder. If it is installed as a stand-alone file, it is placed in the folder specified by the user.

- The Setup Wizard supports a number of macros that let you specify folders, without knowing exactly where those folders will reside on the user's computer.

- Setup Wizard definitions can be saved in the form of templates. Setup Wizard templates have the extension SWT.

- You can protect your controls from being used in building applications by requiring them to have a valid license key installed on a user's computer.

- Compiled applications can use a licensed control without the license key installed in the registry. The license key is compiled into the application, and is passed to the control when the control needs to create itself.

- Even if a developer has a license key for your control so that they can use it to build a program, they cannot distribute the license key to other users.

- Encapsulated (aggregate) custom controls that contain a licensed control will not function unless each machine using the aggregate control also has a valid license key in the registry for each licensed constituent control it contains.

- User documents do not have the ability to store license keys; a user must obtain a licensed control from the control's manufacturer in order to view a document containing the licensed control.

- Controls are distributed through web pages by use of cabinet (CAB) files.

- Your CAB file can make use of secondary CAB files that install files from other locations.

- Secondary CAB files allow for more flexible installations, because if the files of a particular CAB file already reside on the user's computer, the CAB file does not need to be downloaded.

- If your component cannot be scripted to cause harm to a user's computer, you can mark the control Safe for Scripting.

- If your component won't accept initialization data that will harm a user's computer, you can mark the control Safe for Initialization.

- Controls are marked as Safe for Scripting or Safe for Initialization, using the Setup Wizard.

- When the Setup Wizard creates an Internet setup, it creates a *Support* folder containing the component, an INF file, and a DDF file. You can use the utility *Makecab.exe* to rebuild the CAB file from these files.

- You use the `CODEBASE` attribute in HTML to specify a CAB file for an object.

- In order to use licensed controls on a web page, you must create a license package file (LPK). You create LPK files using the utility *lpk_tool.exe*. An LPK file is a text file that contains all of the license keys for all of the licensed controls on a web page.

- License keys contained in an LPK file are not stored in the registry of a user's machine. Instead, they are simply used to initialize licensed controls.

- You reference LPK files using the `NAME` attribute of the `<PARAM>` tag in HTML.

- Digitally signing a control assures a user of the source of a component, but does not ensure that a control will not cause harm on a user's computer.

- Digital signatures must be obtained through third-party certificate authorities, and are added to a component using the *Signcode.exe* utility.

- You can verify a digital signature using the *Chktrust.exe* utility.

- Visual Basic's registry commands allow you to read and write values under the `HKEY_CURRENT_USER\Software\Visual Basic and VBA Program Settings` key.

- To save a value in the registry, use the `SaveSetting` statement.

- To retrieve a single value from the registry, use the *GetSetting* function.

- To retrieve all of the keys for a specified section in the registry, use the *GetAllSettings* function.

- To delete one or more registry entries, use the `DeleteSetting` statement.

- DCOM is an extension of COM that lets applications use components located on remote computers.

- DCOM works on Windows 9x and Windows NT 4.

- DCOM allows you to perform static load balancing.

- In order for a computer running Win 9x to use DCOM, it must be set for user-level security.

- DCOM is configured on a computer using the utility *dcomcncfg.exe*. Using this utility, you can enable a computer for remote access using DCOM, and configure the security used for accessing objects.

- The default behavior of DCOM is to allow only administrators to access remote objects.

- To deploy a component for use as a remote server, the Remove Server Files option must be selected when the component is built. Selecting this option causes two additional files to be created when the component is compiled, a TLB file and a VBR file.

- The TLB file is a type library for the component.

- The VBR file contains information required by the registry to enable access to a remote server.

- To distribute remote servers and clients, use the Package and Deployment Wizard.

- To distribute clients that use remote servers, use the Package and Deployment Wizard to create a package, remove the server file from the package, and add the server's VBR file to the package.

Applying What You've Learned

It's now time to apply what you've learned about optimizing and distributing applications. Answer all of the questions in the Skills Assessment. If you can correctly answer all of these questions, you'll be demonstrating a solid understanding of the topics covered in this chapter.

Skills Assessment

1. The relationship between a newer version of a component and an older one, and at what level they are interchangeable, is called:

    a. Version compatibility

    b. Module compatibility

    c. Version control

    d. Control compatibility

2. Which of the following must be true for a component to be backward compatible?

    a. Properties in the earlier component must be renamed.

    b. The CLSID and type library identifiers must be the same.

    c. Components are always backward compatible.

    d. Visual Basic cannot maintain backward compatibility.

3. Which of the following is not a backward compatibility option supported by Visual Basic?

    a. No Compatibility

    b. Project Compatibility

    c. Binary Compatibility

    d. Previous Compatibility

4. What should you do when compiling a project with No Compatibility? (pick two)

    a. Change the Project Name

    b. Compile into a filename different than the previous version

    c. Delete the old component from the computer

    d. Overwrite the old component

5. Which of the Visual Basic compatibility options ensures backward compatibility?

    a. No Compatibility

    b. Binary Compatibility

    c. Project Compatibility

    d. System Compatibility

6. What type of files contains information about the runtime requirements of a component?

    a. The component itself

    b. Related Files (RFS)

    c. License Package (LPK)

    d. Dependency (DEP)

7. Which file is generated by the Setup Wizard and contains everything needed to know in order to install an application?

    a. *Setup.cab*

    b. *Setup.lst*

    c. *Setup.dep*

    d. *Setup.lpk*

8. Which section of the *Setup.lst* file contains all of the files that must be loaded on the user's computer *before* your application and all of its dependency files can be loaded?

    a. [Files]

    b. [Bootstrap]

    c. [User]

    d. [Setup]

9. Which file is installed by Visual Basic and contains dependency information for commonly installed components?

    a. *VB6dep.ini*

    b. *VB6dep.dep*

    c. *Common.dep*

    d. *Comdep.ini*

10. Which tool is used to create a custom setup program for an application?

    a. Visual Basic itself

    b. Installer

    c. Setup Wizard

    d. None of the above

11. When you instruct the Setup Wizard to install an application as a shared component, where is the file installed?

    a. In the folder specified by the user

    b. In the *Windows* folder

    c. In the *Windows\System* folder

    d. In the folder specified by the user's *Windows.ini* file

12. To save a Setup Wizard definition for later use, store the information in a:

    a. SWT template file

    b. DEP dependency file

    c. CAB cabinet file

    d. VBP project file

13. Licensed control requires what, in order to be used in design time?

    a. The licensing file to be installed on the computer

    b. The licensing key to be installed in the registry

    c. The source code for the control to be installed on the computer

    d. Visual Basic cannot create licensed controls

14. A developer can use a licensed control with its license key registered on their computer to create and distribute an aggregate control.

    a. True

    b. False

15. In order for compiled applications to use licensed controls, the controls must have their license keys registered on the user's computer.

    a. True

    b. False

16. Which of the following can store a license key so that a control can create itself at runtime?

    a. A user document

    b. A user control

    c. A compiled application

    d. None of the above

17. Which type of file is used to distribute an application on a web page?

    a. DEP (dependency) file

    b. CAB (cabinet) file

    c. LPK (license package) file

    d. IIS (Internet install) file

18. Which of the following is a benefit of secondary CAB files? (pick two)

    a. They may speed installations where a user already has some of the components.

    b. They require the user to have access to the Internet.

    c. They provide licensing information to a web page.

    d. Frees server space because components can be downloaded from other sites.

19. What disqualifies an object as for Safe for Scripting? (pick two)

    a. Modifies the registry

    b. Reads from the registry

    c. Deletes a file

    d. Reads a directory

20. License package files (LPK) are referenced in HTML using what tag?

    a. <PARAM>

    b. <LPKNAME>

    c. <OBJECT>

    d. <LICENSE>

21. Digitally signing a control does what? (pick two)

    a. Assures a user that the control is safe

    b. Prevents your component from being distributed

    c. Notifies the user, with certainty, who created the control

    d. Allows a browser to access the component without displaying a prompt

22. Which utility is used to digitally sign a component?

    a. *Chktrust.exe*

    b. *Signcode.exe*

    c. The Setup Wizard

    d. *Digisign.exe*

23. What type of file can you register with *Regsvr32.exe*? (pick two)

    a. DLL

    b. VBP

    c. REG

    d. OCX

24. What is the easiest way to ensure that your ActiveX control is registered correctly on a user's machine?

   a. Manually edit the registry

   b. Use *Regsvr32.exe*

   c. Use the Setup Wizard

   d. Use a third-party tool

25. How do you create a license package file containing the licensing information for all controls on a web page?

   a. With the Visual Basic License Manager

   b. With the CODEBASE attribute of an HTML page's <OBJECT> tag

   c. With the Visual Basic Application Wizard

   d. With a utility from the *LPK_TOOL* directory on the Visual Basic CD-ROM

26. What is the purpose of the ID attribute in an HTML <OBJECT> tag?

   a. It specifies a URL that points to a file containing an implementation of an object.

   b. It specifies the object's unique class identifier stored in the system registry.

   c. It specifies a URL that points to the name of the object.

   d. It specifies the object name.

27. What technology is best for running remote ActiveX servers on Windows 9x and Windows NT 4 machines?

   a. Remote Automation

   b. Remote Server Architecture

   c. Isolated Services

   d. DCOM

28. What type of load balancing can be accomplished using DCOM?

   a. Static

   b. Dynamic

   c. Both static and dynamic

   d. Neither static nor dynamic

29. Which security model must be in effect on Windows 9x machines to use DCOM?

   a. Share-level

   b. User-level

   c. Either share-level or user-level

   d. Neither share-level nor user-level

30. To configure DCOM on a computer, you:

    a. Run the utility *dcomcncfg.exe*.

    b. Run the utility *regdcom.exe*.

    c. Do nothing; installing a remote component configures DCOM automatically.

    d. Do nothing; DCOM is automatically configured when the operating system is installed.

31. In order to create a remote component, you:

    a. Set the Remote Component property of the project

    b. Set the DCOM Component property of the project

    c. Set the Remote Server Files property of the project

    d. Set the Allow Remote Connection property of the project

32. To distribute remote servers, use:

    a. The Setup Wizard

    b. The DCOM Distribution Wizard

    c. The Remote Automation Wizard

    d. The Package and Deployment Wizard

33. To distribute clients that use remote servers, you must include what file in the package?

    a. The compiled component file of the remote server

    b. The TLB file of the remote server

    c. The VBR of the remote server

    d. The license file of the remote server

Answers to Skills Assessment

1. a	8. b	15. b	22. b	29. b
2. c	9. a	16. c	23. a, d	30. a
3. d	10. c	17. b	24. b	31. c
4. a, b	11. c	18. a, d	25. d	32. d
5. b	12. a	19. a, c	26. d	33. c
6. d	13. b	20. a	27. d	
7. b	14. b	21. c, d	28. a	

Highlighter's Index

Backward Compatibility

Components must retain their CLSID and type library identifiers
Must support all properties, methods, and events of previous version
Members must have same Dispatch IDs as previous version

All members must have same parameters as previous version
Components can have No Compatibility, Project Compatibility,
or Binary Compatibility

File Dependencies

Are files necessary to run a component or other file
Dependency files are text files with a DEP extension
Visual Basic has a *VB6dep.ini* dependency file

Package and Deployment Wizard

Creates distributable installation programs
Distributes applications diskette, folder (CD-ROM), and Internet
Install files
Registers components
Creates program groups and icons
Replaces the Setup Wizard of earlier versions of Visual Basic
Compresses files into one or more cabinet CAB files
Saves packaging and deploying setups as scripts
Can recompile a project
Shows you missing dependencies
Can create and deploy packages in silent mode
Does *not* create an AutoRun CD-ROM

ActiveX Control License Keys

License keys (when required) will allow a developer to use a control
in design view only when the key is present
Not required to distribute runtime applications that use a control
Have the extension VBL
Package and Deployment Wizard can distribute a control with or without its
license key

Internet Usage

Components downloaded in the form of a CAB file, verified for safety,
decompressed, registered in the local Windows registry, installed,
then activated
Can use secondary CAB files
Control licenses must be stored in a LPK license file for a web page
Use *lpk_tool.exe* to create LPK files for licensed controls
Must reference LPK file in HTML

Digitally Signing a Component

Obtain a signature from VeriSign
Digital signing does nothing more than assure a user of who developed
the component
Use *Signcode.exe* to sign a component or CAB file
If a signed file is tampered with, the certificate will not display

DCOM Components

Configure DCOM with *dcomcnfg.exe*

Windows 9x machines must be set up for user-level security

Define users that can access the server components

Distribute a VBR file for remote servers

Installation details of DCOM components are handled by the Package and Deployment Wizard

VBR files have to be added to a packaging script manually

Managing the Windows Registry

Can only manipulate specific keys using Visual Basic commands

Use SaveSetting to create and save registry entries

Use GetSetting and GetAllSettings to retrieve registry entries

Use DeleteSetting to delete registry entries

Register components using *Regsvr32.exe*

CHAPTER 14

Visual SourceSafe and the Visual Component Manager

If you are a lone developer working on a small application, project management might not consume much of your attention. However, as a project grows in scope, and as more and more developers are added to the mix, managing source code and shared components becomes an increasingly important and challenging task. The Enterprise Edition of Visual Basic includes some tools to help with this logistics headache: Microsoft Visual SourceSafe and the Visual Component Manager. Microsoft Visual SourceSafe is a tool for managing source code, while the Visual Component manager makes it easier to manage and distribute shared components such as ActiveX controls, forms, modules, and even full projects. If you're developing in an environment where more than one developer is involved, you may already be using one or both of these tools. If not, you'll need to study this chapter because the exams test your knowledge of these tools.

The Technologies and the Exams

Although you won't encounter many questions regarding Visual SourceSafe or the Visual Component Manager, you will encounter a few questions on each exam, as Table 14-1 shows. Chances are, you won't be able to guess the correct answer if you don't know it, so study this chapter well to pass the questions on the exams.

Table 14-1: Visual SourceSafe and the Visual Component Manager on the Exams

Topic	Covered on Exam
Understanding and implementing Visual SourceSafe	Both
Using the Visual Component Manager	Both

Microsoft Visual SourceSafe

Visual SourceSafe is a solution for managing projects that are worked on by more than one developer. Visual SourceSafe addresses the multideveloper challenges of centralizing project files, making sure that multiple developers don't modify the same code and objects at the same time, preventing developers from overwriting the works of others, and tracking revisions to code and objects.

Visual SourceSafe allows you to:

- Manage all sorts of source files, including text, graphics, resource files, and sounds

- Control who has access to source code files

- Know who is working on what source code files

- Make sure only one person at a time can modify a source file

- Revert to previous versions of source files or merge current changes with earlier revisions

- Maintain a current version as well as revisions in a centralized location

Setting up Visual SourceSafe is a challenge in itself, and before you can successfully implement Visual SourceSafe in a given environment, you must understand the basic principles involved. The first thing to understand is that Visual SourceSafe isn't a single program, but rather consists of the components listed in Table 14-2. These components work in harmony; some tasks can be handled by multiple components, while others require that you use a specific component. It may seem at times that Visual SourceSafe can't accomplish a specific task, but often it's just a matter of figuring out which component performs the task and how to access a function within the component.

Table 14-2: The Visual SourceSafe Components

Component	Description
Visual SourceSafe Administrator	Used to manage tasks such as setting up source code control and creating user accounts
Visual SourceSafe Explorer	A user's program that allows each developer to manage project files
An Add-in to Visual Basic	Provides an integrated solution for managing Visual Basic project files under source code control

When a project is under source code control, no developer ever makes changes directly to the master copy of the project. Instead, each developer works with his or her own copy of the source code files. Developers check out files when they need to change them, much as you would check out a library book. When a developer has finished making changes, he or she checks in the file or files. Throughout the entire process, a complete copy of the project is kept in the user's working folder (explained later in this chapter). Except for the master project file, while you have a file checked out, no other user is allowed to check it out. Although you have access (read permissions) to all files in the project, you can alter only those files that you have checked out.

 Visual SourceSafe prevents you from making changes to files that you don't have checked out by making them read-only. When you check out a file, the read-only flag is removed and modifications can be made.

Creating and Opening a Visual SourceSafe Database

To implement source code control, you first create a Visual SourceSafe database. Once you've created a Visual SourceSafe database, you can add a Visual Basic project. Creating a SourceSafe database is done using the Visual SourceSafe Administrator, shown in Figure 14-1. To start Visual SourceSafe Administrator, choose Programs from the Start menu, select the Microsoft Visual Studio 6.0 menu option, then choose Microsoft Visual SourceSafe 6.0 Admin from the submenus.

 This chapter assumes that you have installed Visual SourceSafe.

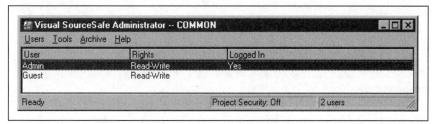

Figure 14-1: Configuring Visual SourceSafe is performed using the Visual SourceSafe Administrator

Visual SourceSafe is installed with a default source code database named Common. However, it's best to always start by creating your own source code database. You don't actually specify a name for a source code database; rather, you specify a folder in which the database is to be created. To create a source code database, choose Create Database from the Tools menu, enter the name of the folder in which you want to create the source code database, and click OK to save your folder selection.

 The folder in which you want to create a source code database should be a new, empty folder placed on the network where all developers can access it.

Unlike with other applications such as Microsoft Word or Microsoft Access, creating a new source code database doesn't immediately open the database. Instead, you must explicitly open the source code database using the Visual SourceSafe Administrator before you can make changes such as adding users. To open a Visual SourceSafe database, choose Open SourceSafe Database from the Users menu to display the Open SourceSafe dialog box as shown in Figure 14-2.

When you first display the Open SourceSafe dialog box, the database you've just created doesn't appear in the list. Click the Browse button to locate and select the Visual SourceSafe database you've created to add it to the list of databases.

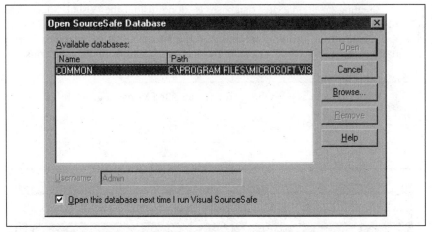

Figure 14-2: Visual SourceSafe doesn't remember the database it just created; you must locate the database manually

Managing Users in a Visual SourceSafe Database

When you create a new Visual SourceSafe database, the database includes an Admin user and a Guest user by default. You'll need to add a user account for each developer who will be given access to the protected source code; each developer must log on to Visual SourceSafe as a valid user, or she won't be able to modify the source files. If security is important to you, you can assign a unique password to each user account. If you decide to use passwords, don't forget to add a password to the Admin account, or security will be effectively disabled.

Adding new users to a SourceSafe database is easy. Choose Add User from the Users menu in the SourceSafe Administrator to display the Add User dialog box shown in Figure 14-3, then enter the name of the user and a password (if desired). To grant the user read-only access to the files under source code control, select the Read only checkbox. When finished, click OK to save the new user account. The new user will then appear in the list of users, as shown in Figure 14-4.

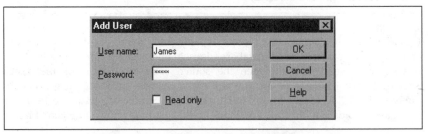

Figure 14-3: Each developer who will access files under source code control should be set up as a unique user

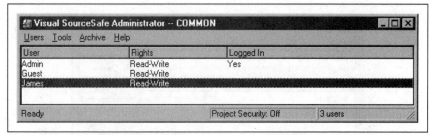

Figure 14-4: All users of a SourceSafe database appear in the user list, along with
their rights and whether or not they're logged on to the database

 Even if you decide not to assign passwords to every SourceSafe user,
you should still consider adding a password to the Admin account to
prevent users from running Visual SourceSafe Administrator and
modifying your configuration. To add a password to a user, select the
user in the list and choose Change Password from the Users menu.

Placing a Visual Basic Project
Under SourceSafe Control

In order to place a Visual Basic project under source code control, the project and
all of its files must be added to a SourceSafe database. Although adding each file
in a project to a SourceSafe database can be done manually, it's a tedious process
and there's a much easier way. To add a Visual Basic project to a SourceSafe database, open the project in Visual Basic and open the SourceSafe submenu found on
Visual Basic's Tools menu, then choose "Add Project to SourceSafe."

After choosing to add the project to source code control, you're asked to log on to
the Visual SourceSafe database, as shown in Figure 14-5. Make sure that the
correct Visual SourceSafe database is specified in the Database text box, then enter
your user name and password (if applicable), and click OK to log in to the Source-
Safe database. The Add to SourceSafe Project dialog box then displays (see
Figure 14-6). The defaults on the Add to SourceSafe Project dialog box are usually
acceptable, but you can change values if you like.

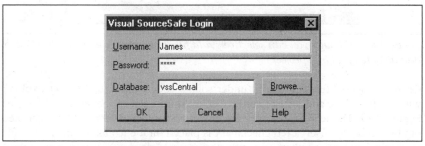

Figure 14-5: You are required to log on to the SourceSafe database as a valid user
before accessing source code control features

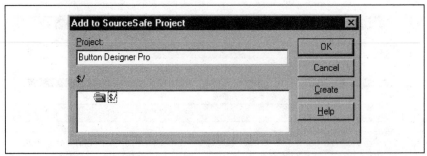

Figure 14-6: This dialog box is used to name a SourceSafe project and to specify its location in the SourceSafe database structure

After making any desired changes on the Add to SourceSafe Project dialog box and clicking OK, you're shown the Add Files to SourceSafe dialog box, where you designate which files are to be placed under source code control (see Figure 14-7). Most of the time, you'll want to add all of the files in a project to source code control (though you can selectively add files if you want). By default, all files are selected and you can just click OK to place all files under source code control.

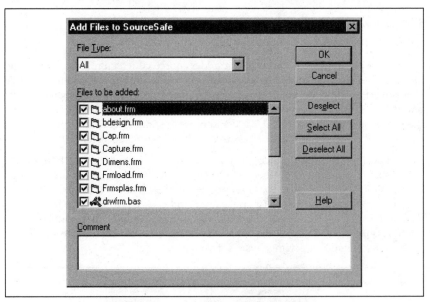

Figure 14-7: Although you can selectively add files to source code control, it's best to add all of the files in a project

Once all selected files are placed under source code control, the Project Explorer window refreshes, and a new icon is displayed for each of the selected files (see Figure 14-8). The icon is that of a document and a lock. When a file is checked out by the current user, a red checkmark is placed on the icon's document. If a file is checked out by another user, the document is displayed using gray outline, rather than a black one (this can be difficult to see on high-resolution displays).

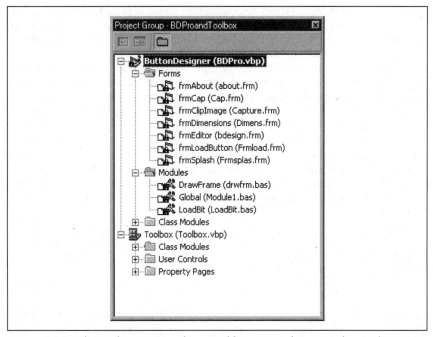

Figure 14-8: Files under source code control have special icons to denote their status

Visual Basic Projects and Visual SourceSafe

For the most part, developing a Visual Basic project under source code control is similar to working on an ordinary project. The primary difference is that you must check out files to modify them. When you check out a file, you may make changes to it, but no other person can make changes to it until you check it back in and that person checks it out. All developers have read-only access to every file in the project, however. This is necessary because you can't edit and debug a form, for example, without having access to the entire project in which the form resides.

 When you check out a file in the Visual Basic IDE that has a corresponding binary file (such as the FRX file that corresponds to a form's FRM file), the binary file is automatically checked out as well.

Designating a working folder

In order for a developer to work with a project under source code control, some setup must be performed on the developer's machine (this is in addition to adding the developer as a user of the SourceSafe database). No user ever opens a "master" project. Instead, each developer works with a copy of the project in a local folder called the *working folder*. Each developer *must* have a unique working folder that is not shared with any other developer.

When you use the "Add Project to SourceSafe" menu item in Visual Basic to add the current project to a Visual SourceSafe database, the project is treated as the working project and the folder in which it resides is automatically designated as the current user's working folder. Once the project is under source code control, there is no master project that can be opened using Visual Basic. Instead, the source files are stored in a complex file structure located in the folder in which the active Visual SourceSafe database resides. You cannot open these master files because Visual SourceSafe stores them in a complex format completely unrelated to their original format. This is why it's necessary for each user to have a working folder that contains a local copy of the files in their original format (projects, forms, modules, and so on). When a user checks a file out or obtains the current version of a file, a usable copy of the source file is placed in the user's working folder. When the user checks a file back in, Visual SourceSafe stores a copy of the file in its own special format within the Visual SourceSafe database.

It's absolutely critical that you regularly back up the entire contents of the Visual SourceSafe database folder, including all subfolders.

Working folders are created and selected using Visual SourceSafe Explorer (see Figure 14-9). Visual SourceSafe Explorer is run by choosing Microsoft Visual SourceSafe 6.0 from the Microsoft Visual SourceSafe folder off the Microsoft Visual Studio 6.0 submenu, which in turn is located off your Start menu. The current working folder is displayed in the right pane just below the toolbar. If the current user has no current working folder, this fact is displayed.

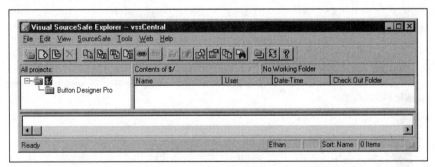

Figure 14-9: Each developer manages his or her development using Visual SourceSafe Explorer

To create or change the current working folder of a user, log on to Visual Source-Safe as the user whose folder you'd like to change using the computer on which the developer will work, choose Set Working Folder from the File menu to display the Set Working Folder dialog box shown in Figure 14-10, enter the path and folder name of the user's working folder, and click OK to save your changes. To create a new folder to be used as the working folder, enter the name and path in the text box *first*, then click Create Folder; clicking Create Folder before entering a folder name results in an error.

Although the master Visual SourceSafe database must reside on a shared drive, each and every user must have a unique working folder; the working folders don't have to be created on a shared drive.

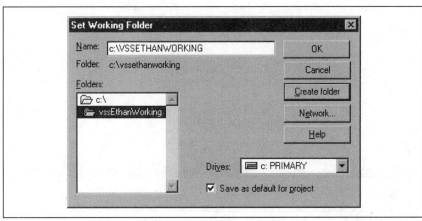

Figure 14-10: Use the Set Working Folder dialog box to create or change a user's working folder

Creating a working copy of the project

As stated earlier, each developer using a Visual Basic project under source code control works with a copy of the project in their working folder. After designating a working folder for a user, it's necessary to create a working copy of the Visual Basic project. To create a working copy of the project, select the project name in the left pane of Visual SourceSafe Explorer (the right pane will then display all of the files in the project under source code control, as shown in Figure 14-11), choose Get Latest Version from the SourceSafe menu, and confirm your intentions on the dialog box that displays. Visual SourceSafe then creates a copy of all of the current files under source code control in the working folder.

 If not all files within the project have been placed under source code control, it may be necessary to copy them to the working folder manually.

Checking out files using Visual SourceSafe Explorer and the Visual Basic IDE

Most of the time, you'll check out files using the Visual Basic IDE. However, it's possible to check out files using Visual SourceSafe Explorer, and you may choose to use Visual SourceSafe Explorer because of its additional functionality. For

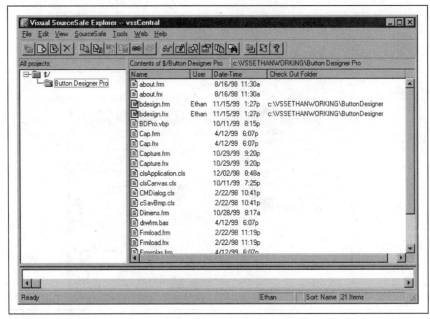

Figure 14-11: Selecting a project in Visual SourceSafe displays all of the files within the project under source code control

instance, you can't tell who has a file checked out from within the Visual Basic IDE. To check out a file using Visual SourceSafe Explorer, select the file or files in the list, right-click the selected files, and choose Check Out from the Shortcut menu. As an alternative, you can also choose Check Out from the SourceSafe menu. When a file is checked out, its icon denotes the fact and the name of the user that has the file checked out appears in the list. Visual SourceSafe Explorer even shows the working folder containing the editable copy of the file (refer to Figure 14-11).

Generally, it's a much better idea to check out files using the Visual Basic IDE. One reason is that some Visual Basic objects consist of more than one file. For example, a form file may have binary information stored in an FRX file, in addition to the text information stored in the FRM file. When you check out files as objects from within Visual Basic, Visual SourceSafe knows to check out all necessary files. When you check out files using Visual SourceSafe Explorer, you are required to select and check out all necessary files yourself. To check out a file from within Visual Basic, right-click the object (form, module, and so on) and choose Check Out from the Shortcut menu.

Once you have the associated files of an object checked out, you can make changes to them as you see fit. If you attempt to make changes to a file that you don't have checked out, you'll receive an error message similar to that shown in Figure 14-12.

Figure 14-12: Attempting to edit a file that you don't have checked out results in this error

 The only file that can be checked out by more than one developer at a time is the main project file (VBP). Whether a given developer should check out the project file depends on what the developer is doing. For instance, to add a new form to a project, you must have rights to modify the VBP file because information on all forms in a project is maintained within the VBP file; if you don't have the project's VBP file checked out, you cannot add new forms to the project. Also, if you use the Increment Version option when compiling distributable components, Visual Basic needs to be able to write the new version information to the VBP file, so once again you'll have to have the project file checked out to do this.

Checking in files

The best way to check in files is using the Visual Basic IDE. To check in one or more files, right-click any file that you want to check in in the Project Explorer window and select Check In from the Shortcut menu. Visual SourceSafe then displays the Check In Files to SourceSafe dialog box shown in Figure 14-13. This dialog box shows all of the files that you currently have checked out, with the file or files that you right-clicked selected by default. You can select additional files if you want to, then click OK to check in all selected files. When you check in a file, Visual SourceSafe updates the master Visual SourceSafe database. *This is the only way that a developer can make changes to the master project.*

Undoing a check out of a file

At times, you might make changes to a file that you have checked out and then change your mind about the changes. To undo a file check out, right-click the object in the Project Explorer window and choose Undo Check Out from the Shortcut menu.

Adding new files to a project under source code control

As you work with a project under source code control, you'll eventually have to add new files, such as a form or module, to the project. When you need to do this, add the file as you normally would. However, when you attempt to save the

Figure 14-13: This dialog box allows you to easily check in one or more files

file, Visual SourceSafe will intervene, asking you if you'd like to add the file (or files) to source code control (see Figure 14-14). When you save the file, be sure to save it in your working folder; Visual SourceSafe will make a copy of the file or files in the master Visual SourceSafe database. Users will then need to get the latest version of the project in order to see the new object files (this is discussed in the next section). Once you add a new file to Visual SourceSafe, you must explicitly check the file out to yourself in order to make further changes.

You cannot add new files to source code control if you don't have the master Visual Basic Project file checked out.

Getting the latest version of files

When a developer checks in changes to a file, other developers don't immediately see those changes. Likewise, if you add a new file to source code control, developers don't see the new file right away. To get copies of newly created files or copies of files changed by other users, you must explicitly obtain the latest version of the project files. When you retrieve the latest version of a file under source code control, the newest checked in version of the file is retrieved from the Visual SourceSafe database and a usable copy of the file is placed in your working folder.

Getting the latest version of a file can be done using Visual SourceSafe Explorer or from within the Visual Basic IDE. You can even have Visual SourceSafe obtain the

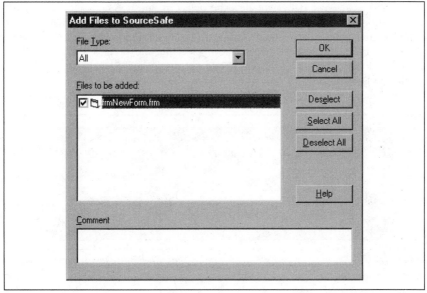

Figure 14-14: Visual SourceSafe asks you if you want to add new files to source code control

latest version of all files under source code control automatically when you open a project (or prompt you when you open a project). To have Visual SourceSafe automatically obtain the new version of files when you open a project, or to have it prompt you to obtain new versions of the project files, use the Source Code Control Options dialog box shown in Figure 14-15. To access the Source Code Control Options dialog box, open the SourceSafe submenu on Visual Basic's Tools menu, then choose Options.

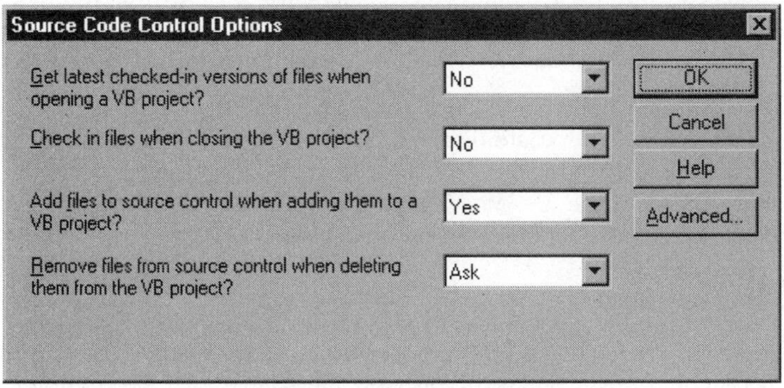

Visual SourceSafe

Figure 14-15: The Source Code Control Options dialog box is used to enhance the interaction between Visual Basic and Visual SourceSafe

In addition to having Visual SourceSafe obtain the latest version of files for you, you can also get the latest versions of files manually. To get the latest version of a file in the Visual Basic IDE, right-click the object in question and select Get Latest Version from the Shortcut menu. This is useful when you know that another developer has made changes to a particular file. To get the latest version of one or more files in Visual SourceSafe Explorer, select the file or files and choose Get Latest Version from the Tools menu. When you use Visual SourceSafe Explorer to obtain the latest version of one or more files, Visual SourceSafe displays a dialog box like that shown in Figure 14-16.

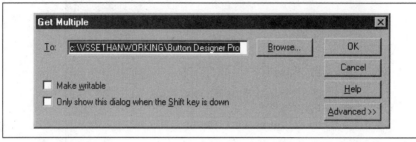

Figure 14-16: Visual SourceSafe Explorer offers more flexibility when getting the latest version of a file

 Whenever you check out a file from within Visual Basic, Visual SourceSafe always obtains the latest version of the file for you.

One setting of particular importance is the Make writable checkbox. Ordinarily, Visual SourceSafe sets the read-only flag of files that you do not have checked out, preventing you from making changes to these files. Select the Make writable checkbox if you want the ability to modify files you do not have checked out. Visual SourceSafe will then create copies of the latest files in your working folder, but it won't set the read-only flag. *This essentially removes the file or files from Visual SourceSafe control, and you might encounter problems if you alter the files.*

If you have chosen to obtain the latest version of a file that you have checked out and modified, Visual SourceSafe displays the dialog box shown in Figure 14-17. If you choose to replace the file, you'll overwrite your changes with the latest checked in version of the file. Most of the time, selecting the "Apply to all items" checkbox and then clicking Leave is your safest bet.

Comparing revisions

Visual SourceSafe maintains a full history of all revisions made to every file under source code control. Not only can you view the source of a file from any of the revisions, you can also compare the contents of any two revisions using a very slick feature of Visual SourceSafe. To view the history of a file, select the file Visual SourceSafe Explorer and choose Show History from the Tools menu to display the

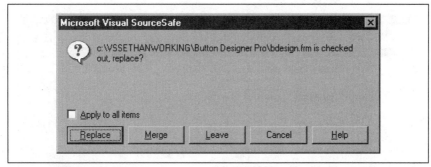

Figure 14-17: If you encounter this dialog box, stop and consider your actions carefully before proceeding

History Options dialog box (see Figure 14-18). You can use the History Options dialog box to tailor the history list, but usually the default options work well.

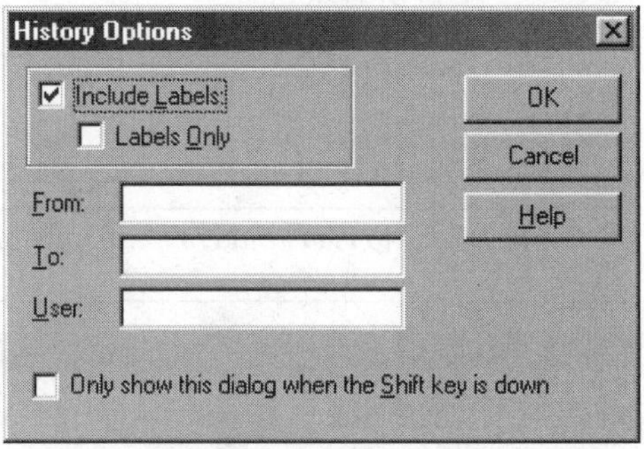

Figure 14-18: The History Options dialog box can be used to tailor the history list; often, the default settings work just fine

Clicking OK in the History Options dialog box commits your selections and displays the History dialog box (see Figure 14-19). The History dialog box displays all revisions of the file, including when the revision was checked in and by whom.

Using the History dialog box, it's possible to compare any two revisions of the file to see what changes occurred between the revisions. To view the differences between two revisions, select the two revisions by clicking the first and then Ctrl+clicking the second, then click the Diff button to display the Difference Options dialog box shown in Figure 14-20.

At times, you may need to compare a file in your working folder to a revision in the history list. For instance, you may want to compare a file that you have checked out and modified to the last revision in the Visual SourceSafe database to see what changes you have made. To do this, use the Browse button to locate and select the file in your working folder for either the Compare or the To text box. When you are satisfied with your settings, click OK to view the differences in the selected files.

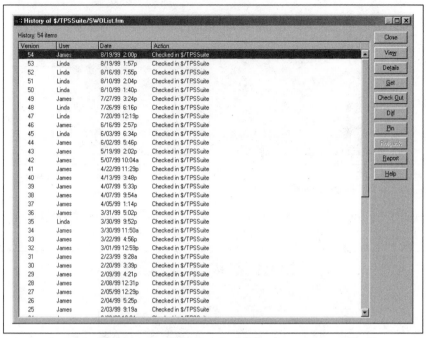

Figure 14-19: Use the History Dialog to view and compare revisions of a file

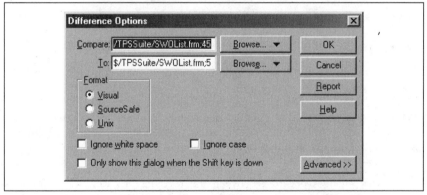

Figure 14-20: Use the Difference Options dialog box to tailor the way files are compared

 If you select only one file in the History dialog box and click Diff, the file is automatically compared to the version in your working folder.

File differences are shown in the Differences Between window shown in Figure 14-21. The Differences Between window is divided into two panes, each pane containing the source of a file. Differences between the two files are color-coded. Lines that have been changed appear red, deleted lines are blue, and new lines are green. The Differences Between window is display-only; you can't make changes to either of the files. However, you can copy text from either file to the clipboard by selecting the text to be copied and pressing Ctrl+C to copy the selection to the clipboard.

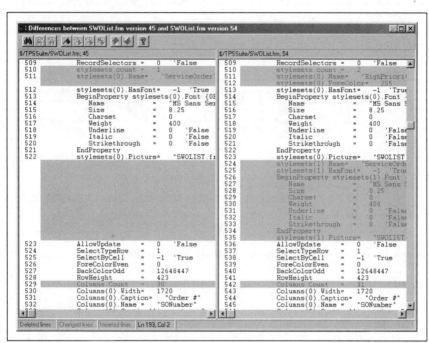

Figure 14-21: All differences between the two files are clearly displayed in an appropriate color

Visual SourceSafe is a powerful, yet somewhat convoluted, tool. Properly implementing Visual SourceSafe in a multideveloper environment can yield tremendous benefits. Attempting to manually accomplish some of the operations performed automatically by Visual SourceSafe would take a lot of effort, and some things (such as preventing multiple developers from working on the same file) are difficult or almost impossible to accomplish without using such a tool.

The Visual Component Manager

The Visual Component Manager is a repository for storing and retrieving components to be used in development projects. The Visual Component Manager provides centralized storage and a structured retrieval system that makes it easy for developers to share components of different types. It's designed to address the following three areas: publishing, finding, and using items.

The Visual Component Manager can store just about anything that can be added to a project, such as forms, ActiveX controls, COM servers, and even entire projects and templates. Storing individual components is only part of the Visual Component Manager's capabilities. The Visual Component Manager is also capable of storing related, or dependent, components so that when one component is added to a project, all related components are added as well.

The Visual Component Manager is an add-in to Visual Basic. When installed, the Visual Component Manager appears as an icon on the Visual Basic toolbar. Clicking the Visual Component Manager button on the toolbar launches the Visual Component Manager (see Figure 14-22). The Visual Component Manager's interface consists of a toolbar, a TreeView control, a ListView control, and an information pane in the lower-right corner.

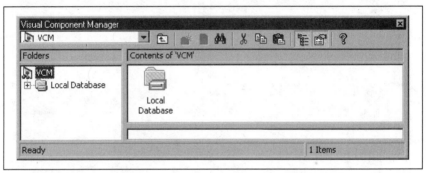

Figure 14-22: The Visual Component Manager has one rather simple interface

Navigating the Visual Component Manager

When you first run the Visual Component Manager, the interface will look pretty much like that in Figure 14-23. Visual Component Manager stores all of its information in a database. By default, this is an Access database located on the local drive, but it can use a SQL database as well. The tree view on the left shows the default database, as does the upper-right pane. Selecting the database in the tree view or double-clicking it in the upper-right pane displays the contents of the database as folders (see Figure 14-23).

To view the contents of a given folder, again select it in the left pane or double-click it in the upper-right pane. Each folder may contain components, additional folders, or a combination of both. When a folder or component is selected, information about the folder or component appears in the lower-right pane.

 Using a SQL database instead of the default Access database is beyond the scope of the exams and therefore of this book.

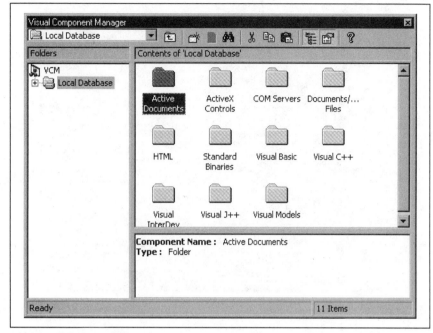

Figure 14-23: Visual Component Manager databases can hold many types of components

Publishing Items to the Visual Component Manager

Components are stored in the Visual Component Manager by *publishing* them. When you publish a component, you not only add the component to the Visual Component Manager repository, you also supply additional information so that developers can search for, learn about, and use the component. To publish a Visual Basic object, right-click the object in the Project Explorer window and choose Publish Component from the Shortcut menu. Alternatively, you can click the object once to select it and then choose Source Files from the Publish submenu on the Tools menu. To publish the compiled version of a component, rather than the source files, choose Build Outputs from the Publish submenu on the Tools menu.

After choosing to publish a component, the Visual Component Manager Publish Wizard displays (see Figure 14-24). The first page of the wizard is an introductory page and can be skipped in the future by selecting "Skip this screen in the future." Click Next to proceed with the wizard.

The next page of the wizard is used to specify where in the Visual Component Manager database the component will be placed, and what it will be called (see Figure 14-25). Using this page of the wizard, you can navigate the current Visual Component Manager database, add new folders in the database, and even open a different database. When you are satisfied with your selections, click Next to continue.

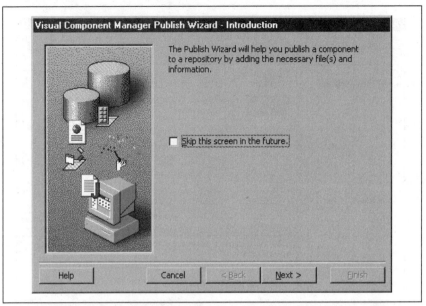

Figure 14-24: The first page of the wizard doesn't offer you much

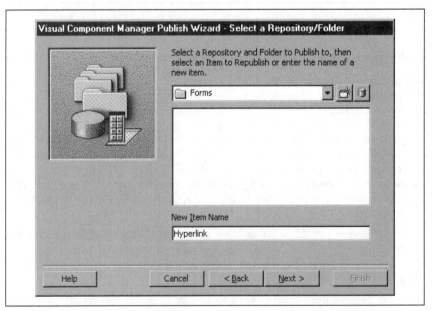

Figure 14-25: Use this page of the wizard to name the component and determine where in the database it will be saved

The Title and Properties page of the wizard is used to enter information about the component (see Figure 14-26). It's always to your advantage to enter as much accurate information as possible. When satisfied with your entries, click Next to continue.

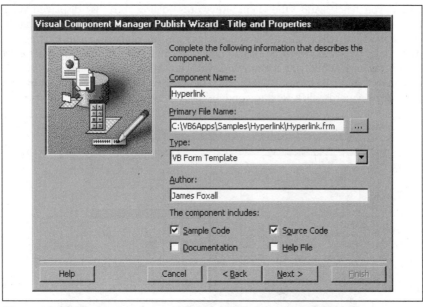

Figure 14-26: Enter as much accurate information as you can for each component

The More Properties page of the wizard is used to enter textual information about the component as well as to assign keywords (see Figure 14-27). First, enter as accurate a description as possible into the Description text box. Then, click Add to assign keywords to the component.

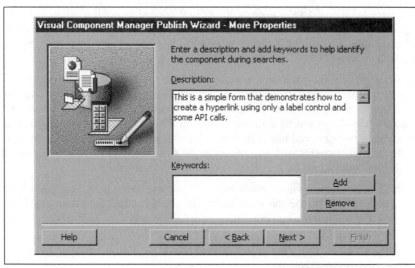

Figure 14-27: In order for developers to get the most benefit from your component, enter as accurate a description as possible

When you click Add, the Item Keywords dialog box is displayed (see Figure 14-28). On the left side of the Item Keywords dialog box is a list of available keywords, while selected keywords are on the right. You can change the database in which keywords are listed, and you can add keywords that don't exist in the database. When you are satisfied with your keyword assignments, click OK to commit your selections. When you are finished entering a description and assigning keywords, click Next to continue with the wizard.

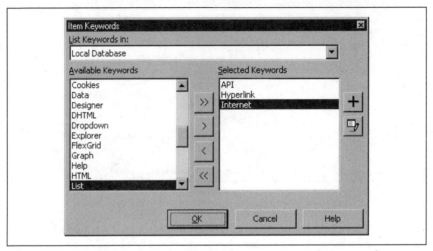

Figure 14-28: Concise and accurate keyword assignments make it easier for a developer to locate a component

The Select Additional File(s) page of the wizard is used to publish additional files as part of the component (see Figure 14-29). When you are finished designating additional files, you can click Finish to end the wizard, or click Next to continue with advanced options.

The COM registration page of the wizard is used to designate components that must be registered with the operating system (see Figure 14-30). This page is useful, for example, if you're publishing an ActiveX control. When a developer adds the ActiveX control to a project using the Visual Component Manager, the control must be registered first. The Visual Component Manager will automatically register any components that you designate on this page. When you are finished designating components for registration, click Next to continue.

The final page of the wizard serves no other purpose than to let you know that you're done. You can use the Back button to change entries on other pages, or click Finish to publish the component.

Finding and Using Items in the Visual Component Manager

Publishing items to the Visual Component Manager is only part of the process. Once components are published, users can easily locate the components and add them to a project. The first step to using a component in the Visual Component

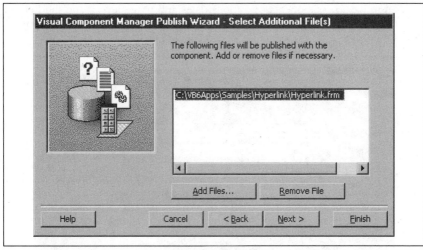

Figure 14-29: You can create Visual Component Manager components made up of multiple files

Figure 14-30: The Visual Component Manager can automatically register components on a machine when a component is added to a project

Manager is to open the Visual Basic project in which you want to add a component, and then start the Visual Component Manager. If the developer knows the exact location within the Visual Component Manager database in which the component is stored, he could navigate the folders within the database as discussed earlier. However, more often a developer is unsure of where the component resides, and possibly even which component that she is looking for.

To search for a component in the Visual Component Manager, click the Find button on the toolbar to display the Find Items in Visual Component Manager dialog box (see Figure 14-31). Using this dialog box, you can locate a published component in many different ways. You can search by name or type, and you can even search for specific text. If you click the Build button next to the Containing text box, you can select from a list of predefined keywords. The History tab can be used to locate components by various dates and usage levels, and the Related Files tab can be used to locate components by what type of data a component includes (sample code, source code, documentation, help files, and more).

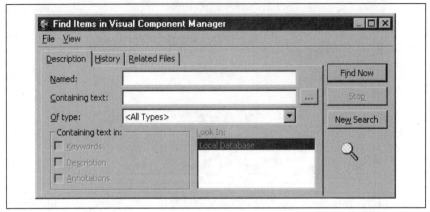

Figure 14-31: The Find Items in Visual Component Manager dialog box offers you a plethora of searching methods for locating specific components

Once you've entered your search criteria and clicked Find Now, the Find Items in Visual Component Manager dialog box displays all matches, if any are found (see Figure 14-32). To add the component to the current project, simply double-click the component in the list.

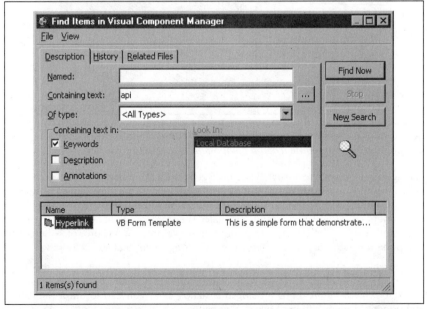

Figure 14-32: The Find Items in Visual Component Manager dialog box displays all matching components at the bottom of the window

Sometimes, it's not quite clear if a found component is the one you need. To view more information about a found component, select it in the list and choose Open Containing Folder from the File menu. The Visual Component Manager will then show the component's folder, with the component selected and all of its information displayed in the lower-right pane, as shown in Figure 14-33. To add a component to the current project from the main Visual Component Manager window, double-click the component in the upper-right pane.

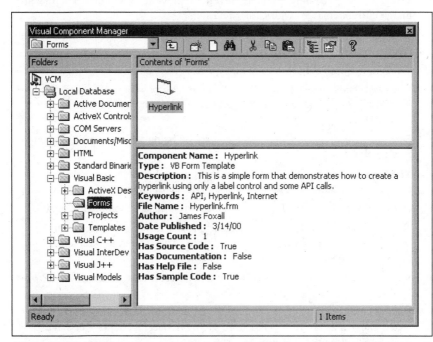

Figure 14-33: Viewing a component on the main window of the Visual Component Manager displays all of the information about it

The Visual Component Manager is a powerful repository that greatly simplifies the process of sharing components of all types between developers and across projects. If you work on only one project within your organization, you might not realize many benefits from using the Visual Component Manager. However, if you or a team of developers work on a number of projects that often require reusing components of different types, the benefits gained from using the Visual Component Manager can be great.

Key Facts

- Microsoft Visual SourceSafe is a tool for managing source code in a multi-developer environment.

- Visual SourceSafe addresses the challenges of centralizing project files, making sure that multiple developers don't modify the same code and objects at the same time, preventing developers from overwriting the works of others, and tracking revisions to code and objects.

- Visual SourceSafe allows you to manage all sorts of files, including text, graphics, resource files, and sound files.

- Visual SourceSafe gives you control over who has access to source code files.

- Visual SourceSafe lets you know who is working on what files.

- Visual SourceSafe ensures that only one developer is changing a file at a time.

- Visual SourceSafe allows you to revert to previous revisions of a file and merge current changes with earlier revisions.

- Visual SourceSafe maintains a current version of the source code files, as well as revisions, in a centralized location.

- Visual SourceSafe ships with the Enterprise edition of Visual Basic.

- Visual SourceSafe is composed of three components: Visual SourceSafe Administrator, Visual SourceSafe Explorer, and an add-in component for Visual Basic.

- Files are placed under source code control by being added to a Visual Source-Safe database.

- You don't actually specify a name for a new Visual SourceSafe database; rather, you designate a folder in which to create the database.

- Once a Visual SourceSafe database is created, it must be explicitly opened.

- The easiest way to add a Visual Basic project to source code control is to open the project in Visual Basic and choose "Add Project to SourceSafe" from the SourceSafe submenu on the Tools menu.

- When a file is under source code control, its icon reflects this in the Project Explorer.

- Each developer who will access the Visual SourceSafe database (and the pro-tected files) must have a valid user account. User accounts can have pass-words, but this is not required.

- Each developer has a full copy of the project under source code control. This copy is located in the user's working folder.

- A copy of the project is created in the working folder by running Visual SourceSafe Explorer and getting the latest version of the project file.

- Developers never make changes to the master copy of a file under source code control. Instead, they check out copies of the files. When a file is checked in, the changes are made by Visual SourceSafe to the master documents.

- Visual SourceSafe prevents users from changing files that they don't have checked out by flagging them as read-only files.

- Files can be checked out using Visual SourceSafe Explorer or directly from within the Visual Basic IDE.

- The main project file (VBP) is the only file that can be checked out by multiple developers. You must have the project file checked out in order to add and save new objects in the project.

- In addition to checking files in and out and getting the latest version of a file, you can also undo a check out.

- Visual SourceSafe maintains a revision history of each file under source code control. Any two revisions can be compared (including an edited copy in the current user's working folder).

- The Visual Component Manager is a tool for managing and sharing components such as forms, controls, COM components, modules, and more among developers.

- The Visual Component Manager is a hierarchical structure of folders and components.

- The Visual Component Manager creates a local Access database by default, but you can use a SQL database instead.

- Publishing a component is the act of placing it in the Visual Component Manager database.

- When you publish a component to the Visual Component Manager, use the Visual Component Manager Publish Wizard, which allows you to specify all sorts of information about the component.

- Developers can perform complex searches to locate components in the Visual Component Manager.

- Once a component is selected in the Visual Component Manager, it can be easily added to the current project.

- The Visual Component Manager can add multiple files to a project, and it can even register COM components on the user's computer.

Applying What You've Learned

It's now time to apply what you've learned about Visual SourceSafe and the Visual Component Manager. First, answer all of the questions in the Skills Assessment. If you can correctly answer all of these questions, you'll be demonstrating a solid understanding of these topics. After you've answered the assessment questions, work through the hands-on exercise.

Skills Assessment

1. Which tool would you use to manage source code in a multideveloper environment?

    a. Visual SourceSafe

    b. Visual Component Manager

    c. Source Code Control Panel

    d. Developer Manager

2. Visual SourceSafe allows you to manage almost any type of file.

    a. True

    b. False

3. Which of the following statements are true about Visual SourceSafe?

    a. It lets you control who has access to source code files.

    b. It lets you easily publish and retrieve compiled components.

    c. It can tell you who has a file checked out.

    d. It ensures that only one developer is working on a source file at a time.

4. If you find that a new bug has been introduced into a file under source code control, what can you do using Visual SourceSafe?

    a. Revert to a previous revision.

    b. Nothing; once a version is checked in, it can't be altered.

    c. Send an email to the previous developer requesting the original source code.

    d. View a previous revision, but nothing more.

5. Visual SourceSafe is part of which version of Visual Basic?

    a. Standard

    b. Professional

    c. Enterprise

    d. None of the above (Visual SourceSafe must be purchased separately)

6. Which of the following is not a component of Visual SourceSafe?

    a. Visual SourceSafe Explorer

    b. Visual SourceSafe Manager

    c. Visual SourceSafe Administrator

    d. The Visual Basic add-in component

7. Before you can place files under source code control, you must:

    a. Set the read-only flags on the files

    b. Open the files within Visual Basic

    c. Create a Visual SourceSafe database

    d. Create a working folder

8. The easiest way to place a Visual Basic project under source code control is to:

    a. Use the Visual SourceSafe Explorer

    b. Use the Visual SourceSafe Administrator

    c. Use the Visual SourceSafe Manager

    d. Use the SourceSafe menu from within Visual Basic

9. Each developer works with a copy of the project files. The files exist where?

    a. In the user's Temp folder.

    b. In the user's SourceSafe folder.

    c. In the user's designated working folder.

    d. The developer works from the master files, not a copy.

10. How is a copy of a Visual Basic project protected by Visual SourceSafe created?

    a. By choosing Create Local Copy from the File menu in Visual SourceSafe Explorer

    b. By choosing Create Local Copy from the File menu in Visual SourceSafe Administrator

    c. By manually copying files from the central Visual SourceSafe database

    d. By running Visual SourceSafe Explorer and getting the latest version of the project file

11. In order for a developer to modify a file, he must:

    a. Open the file using Visual Basic

    b. Check out the file

    c. Check in the file

    d. Request rights from the Visual SourceSafe Administrator

12. Master project files are updated:

    a. Whenever a user changes a file.

    b. Whenever a user gets the latest version of a file.

    c. Whenever a user checks in a file.

    d. Changes are made to the master project files in real-time.

13. Which statement is true about Visual Basic project files?

    a. Any file can be checked out by multiple developers.

    b. The only file that can be checked out by multiple developers is the project file.

    c. No files can be checked out by multiple developers.

    d. The security settings in Visual SourceSafe Administrator determine which files can be checked out by multiple developers.

14. If you needed to compare changes you've made to a file to the last checked-in version of the file, you would:

    a. Open the last checked-in source file using a second instance of Visual Basic.

    b. Open the master project file using a text editor.

    c. View the History list of revisions for the file, select the older revision, and then view the differences.

    d. Right-click the file in the Project Explorer and select Compare to Last Revision.

15. Which tool would you use to share components by publishing and retrieving them?

    a. Visual SourceSafe

    b. Visual Component Manager

c. Source Code Control Panel

d. Developer Manager

16. The act of adding a component to Visual Component Manager is called:

    a. Inserting

    b. Publishing

    c. Notation

    d. Depositing

17. Which of the following is not an advantage of publishing a component to the Visual Component Manager?

    a. Developers can use complex searches to locate the component.

    b. Developers can drag the components and drop them in a project.

    c. COM components are automatically registered when added to a project.

    d. You can publish complex components, such as file dependencies and full projects.

Answers to Skills Assessment

1. a	5. c	9. c	13. b	17. b
2. a	6. b	10. d	14. c	
3. a, c, d	7. c	11. b	15. b	
4. a	8. d	12. c	16. b	

Hands-on Exercise

The complexity of installation and configuration of Visual SourceSafe makes it almost impossible to create a concise exercise; you'll have to use it "for real" to really get a feel for how it works. Since publishing a component to the Visual Component Manager is covered fairly thoroughly in the text, this exercise will focus on adding a published component to a Visual Basic project.

Exercise 14-1: Adding a published component to a project

In this exercise, you'll use the Visual Component Manager to locate a published component and add it to a project. The component you will use is a standard component that ships with the Visual Component Manager.

Step 1. Accessing the Visual Component Manager. Since the Visual Component Manager is a Visual Basic add-in, it's accessed from within the Visual Basic IDE by doing the following:

1. Create a new Standard EXE project in Visual Basic.

2. Click the Visual Component Manager button on the toolbar to launch the Visual Component Manager.

3. You are going to use the Visual Component Manager to add a Visual Basic project template. This template demonstrates dynamic control creation. To locate the component, start by clicking Find on the toolbar.

4. In the Containing Text box, enter **ActiveX Controls**, select the Keywords checkbox, and click Find Now. The component CtlsAdd will appear in the list.

5. To view more information on the component, select it in the list and choose Open Containing Folder from the File menu. The folder in which the component is stored will open, with the component selected. You can then view all of the information about the component in the bottom-right pane.

6. To add the component to the project, double-click its icon. You will then be asked to select a destination folder (see Figure 14-34). You can use the defaults and specify a different folder, or you can even create new folders using this dialog box. When you are satisfied with your selection, click OK and the component (and all of its files) is added to the project.

Figure 14-34: When you add a component to a project, you must specify where the component file will be created

Highlighter's Index

Microsoft Visual SourceSafe

Can manage project files, resource files, text files, graphics, and sounds
You can control who has access to source files
Tells you who is working on what files
Prevents multiple people from working on the same file
Can be used to revert to a previous version of a file
Stores files in a central location
A working version of a project is saved in the user's working folder
Each developer must have a unique working folder

Visual SourceSafe Administrator

Used to create and open Visual SourceSafe databases
Used to set up users

Visual SourceSafe Explorer

Used to place projects and files under source code control
Used to check files in and out
Tells you who is working on what files
Used to compare revisions of files
Used to create a working copy of a project
Can be used to get the latest version of files

Visual SourceSafe Add-in for Visual Basic

Used to easily add a Visual Basic project to source code control
Can be used to check files in and out

Visual Component Manager

A repository for storing and retrieving components used
     in development projects
Is an add-in to Visual Basic
Components are published to the Visual Component Manager
Components can be searched
Registers components automatically when they are added to a project

Index

Symbols

@, Bootstrap File, 499
= equal sign, 27

A

About box, 181–183, 226
About Dialog icon, 255
absolute path, dynamically
        constructing, 235
abstract classes, 81
Accept method, 328, 333
Access Control tab, 534
Access Key combination, 130
AccessKeyPress event, 131
AccessKeys property, 131
ACID test, 278, 477
Action property, 28
Activate event, ObjectControl
        interface, 480
Active Data Objects (see ADO)
active documents, 3, 5
ActiveCell object, 58
ActiveConnection argument, 271
ActiveX clients, 23, 56
ActiveX Component setting,
        StartMode, 102
ActiveX components, 23
    digitally signing, 531
    exam topics, 63

Highlighter's Index, 120
Key Facts, 107–109
Skills Assessment, 109–111
ActiveX controls, xiii, 3, 10, 23, 30
    adding properties to, 136
    alignment, 132
    code components, compared to, 122
    container control, 132
    creating, 124
    custom events, 163
    exam topics, 121
    heavyweight controls, 132
    HelpContextID property, 424
    Highlighter's Index, 214
    ImageList, 14
    in-process versus out-of-process
        components, 47
    instancing, 66
    Key Facts, 190–195
    license keys, 520
    lifetime, 155
    ListView, 13
    methods, creating, 162
    Skills Assessment, 195–204
    StatusBar, 17
    TabStrip, 18
    testing and debugging, 188
    Toolbar, 16
    TreeView, 11
    types of, 124

ActiveX controls (*continued*)
  user interface, 126, 205
  UserControl objects, 123
  VBX controls, 122
ActiveX Data Objects Library, 261
ActiveX designers, 96, 105
ActiveX DLL, xiii, 29, 47, 66
  creating, 112
  invisible runtime control, compared
    to, 135
  testing and debugging, 99
ActiveX Document DLL, 47
ActiveX Document EXE, 47
ActiveX Document Migration
    Wizard, 221
ActiveX document projects
  in-process ActiveX documents, 220
  out-of-process ActiveX
    documents, 220
  UserDocument class, 221
ActiveX documents, 23, 30
  ActiveX controls, compared to, 218
  add-ins, 217
  applications, converting to, 221
  components, 242
  containers, integrating with, 224
  creating, 251
  embedded objects, compared to, 219
  exam topics, 216
  Highlighter's Index, 256
  menus, adding, 225
  Skills Assessment, 246–251
  testing, 241–244, 255
ActiveX EXE, xiii, 47, 66
  compared to ActiveX DLL, 66
  component testing, 117
  creating, 115
  testing and debugging, 101–104
ActiveX objects
  Automation descriptions, 35
  creating, 31
  lifetime, 43
  priority, 35
  referenced versus embedded, 29
  releasing, 45
  types of, 23
ActiveX Server, creating, 114
ActiveX servers, xiii, 30, 385

ActiveX UserControls (CTX) files, binary
    property information, 157
ActiveX WebBrowser control, 302
Add Command button, 283
Add Files to SourceSafe dialog
    box, 560
Add method, 11, 13
Add Project dialog box, 99
Add User dialog box, 558
Add Users and Groups to Roles dialog
    box, 472
Add Watch dialog box, 392
Add-In Toolbar, 221
add-ins, 217
AddItem method, 28
AddNew method, 275
AddRef function, IUnknown
    interface, 29
Address text box, 256
AddressBar property, 309, 314
AddressOf, 63
  function pointers, risk of using, 93
  restrictions, 93
  subclassing, 93
  syntax, 90
Administrator role, 472
ADO (ActiveX Data Objects), xiv
  DAO, 260
  data control limitations, 280
  exam topics, 258
  object hierarchy, 261
  RDO, 260
  reasons to use, 260
  referencing, 261
ADO Command object, 264
ADO Connection object, 262
ADO Error object, 279
ADO Errors collection, 4
ADO Recordset object, 266
  accessing data, 273
  Command.Execute method, 269
  Connection.Execute method, 268
  cursors, 266
  deleting records, 277
  editing records, 276
  Find method, 274
  locking, 267
  Recordset.Open method, 270

Advanced Optimizations button, 454
aggregate controls, 124, 129, 140, 190,
    522
aliasing, 455
Align property, 132
Alignable property, 27
Allow Unrounded Floating Point
    Operations optimization
    switch, 457
Alt key, 10, 131
Ambient property, 166
AmbientChanged event, 168, 170, 173
apartment model threading, 96, 98
App object, 105, 423
appearance
    controlling, 168
    controls and containers, 166
    design-time, 170
    runtime, 170
Application icon, 338
application logic, 50
Application object, 84
    Instancing property, 84
    naming, 84
applications
    database, 49
    packaging and deploying, xii
    web-enabled, xiv
Apply button, 150, 152
ApplyChanges event, 152
App.Path, 235
$(AppPath), Setup Wizard path
    macros, 512
architecture
    object-oriented, 25
    three-tiered, 49
argumentlist, 78
arguments
    passing by reference, 78
    passing by value, 78
arrays, 157
    cells, 74
    constant elements, 161
    saving, 161
As keyword, 35
As New keyword, 43
As Object declaration, 76, 142

ASP Application object, 99
Assert method, 395
assertions, 395, 413
Assume No Aliasing option, 455
asynchronous downloading, 253
    cancelling, 241
    completion notification, 240
    requesting data, 239
AsyncLoad property, 338
AsyncRead method, 239
AsyncReadComplete event, 239, 254
atomicity, 278
Authentication level for calls dropdown
    list, 467
authentication levels, 467
Author, 188
authoring time, 133
Authors table, 276
Auto Increment, 492
auto-commit mode, 278
autolist members dropdown list, 144
Automatic Transaction Support feature,
    MTS, 464
Automation, xiv, 30, 35
Automation object
    navigation, 316
    properties, 313
    variable references, 314
automation object
    early binding, 314
Automation servers, 38, 66
AutoRedraw property, 129
AutoRun CD, creating, 520
Autorun.inf, 520

B

BackColor property, 27, 126, 139, 157,
    167
Background Compile, 377
BackStyle property, 134
backward compatibility, 492–495
bang operator (!), accessing current
    record, 273
base address, 454
BaseWindow object, 346
BAT file, 528

batch optimistic locking, 4
BDPro.exe, 500
BDPRO.HLP, 440
BeforeUpdate event, 78
beginning-of-file (BOF), 272
BeginTrans method, 278
Biblio.mdb, 263, 269, 276, 295
binary compatibility mode, 475
Binary Compatibility option, 495
binary information
    file extensions, 157
    single-value, 157
binary properties, saving and
        retrieving, 160
Bind method, 334
Binder, 30, 217, 234
binding, 31, 184
    DispID binding, 38
    early binding, 34, 38
    late binding, 34
    vtable binding, 38
bitmaps, 123, 157, 160, 190, 238, 253
bln prefix, Boolean datatype, 20
BOF (beginning-of-file), 272
bookmarks
    adding, 388
    removing, 388
Boolean datatype, 20
Bootstrap Files section, 500
Bootstrap section, 498
bound form, 298
bound property, 213
brackets, surrounding field names
        with, 274
Break in Class Module, 385, 415
break mode, 93
Break on All Errors, 384, 415
Break on Unhandled Errors, 385, 415
break points, 386–388, 415
Break When Value Changes, 418
bubbling events, 345
BuildFile property, 348
business rules, xi, 3, 49
Busy property, WebBrowser
        control, 308
Button Designer Pro, 499
Button, DHTML element, 341

ButtonClick event, 17
Buttons collection, 16
ByRef keyword, 78, 94, 164, 455
ByVal keyword, 20, 78, 94, 164, 455

C

C++, COM programming, xiii
C language, ActiveX control
        development, 30
C libraries, 90
CA (certificate authority), 531
CAB (cabinet) files
    creating multiple, 509
    digitally signing, 532
    Internet distribution, 525
    Package and Deployment
        Wizard, 503
    rebuilding, 527
    secondary, 525
CAB file extension, 348
CabFile, Setup.lst, 498
Cabs, Setup.lst, 498
cache, Internet Explorer, 305
call stack, 383
Call statement, 158
callback function, 93
callback procedures, 3
CallBackObject method, 89
CanBePooled event, ObjectControl
        interface, 480
Cancel argument, 78, 165
Cancel button, 150
Cancel parameter, 78
Cancel property, 171
CancelAsyncRead method, 239
CanGetFocus, 130
CanPropertyChange method, 186
Caption property, 150, 183
categories, property, 179
Categorized tab, 179
CD, FTP server Execute operation, 322
CD-ROMs, xv
CDUP, FTP server Execute
        operation, 322
cells, worksheet, 58
CERN proxy servers, 322
certificate authority (CA), 531

chat applications, 335
checkbox, 153
Checkbox, DHTML element, 341
child class, 117
child forms, 98
Chktrust.exe, 533
CHM file extension, 422, 428
class identifier (see CLSID)
class modules, 3, 24, 39, 67, 415
classes
    importance of understanding, 24
    working with, 24
Classes list box, 46
clean-up operations, 451
Clear method, 28
Click event, 17, 20, 89, 134, 382
Click procedure, 294
client interface, 50
clients, notifying, 76
client/server data provider, 50
client/server development, xi
clipping, 132
CLng function, 451
CLOSE, FTP server Execute
        operation, 322
Close method, 264
Clouds.bmp, 253
CLSID (class identifier), 492, 529
cmdCloseWorkbook, 59
cmdMoveForward, 299
cmdTriggerCallback, 118
cmdTriggerError, 119
cmdUseDLL, 113
Code Editor, 390
CODEBASE, 529
code-only timer, 91
collections
    1-based versus 0-based, 12
    Buttons, 16
    ColumnHeaders, 13
    ContainedControls, 133
    DataBindings, 185
    Errors, 279
    Fields, 273
    Forms, 8
    ParentControls, 175
    SelectedControls, 151
    Tabs, 18
collisions, property, 174

color properties, 143
columnar lists, 13
ColumnCount property, 147
ColumnHeaders collection, 13
columns, 13, 134
COM (Component Object Model), xi,
        23
    client, 3
    exam topics, 22
    Highlighter's Index, 60
    Key Facts, 52
    object oriented programming, 25
    Skills Assessment, 54
COM components, xv, 3
COM interfaces, 24, 26, 29
COM objects, 24
    characteristics, 25
    maintainability, 26
combo box, 125
command button control, 361
Command Line Arguments field, 399
command line conditional compilation
        constants, 399
command line declarations, 400
Command object
    ActiveConnection property, 264
    CommandText property, 264
    CommandTime-out property, 265
    CommandType Property, 265
    Execute method, 265
    Parameters collection, 265
    Prepared property, 265
Command objects, 277
    ADO, 262
    connections, 265
Command Properties dialog box, 283,
        297
Commands collection, 283
commands, defining in Data
        Environment designer, 297
CommandStateChange event,
        WebBrowser control, 311
CommitTrans method, 278
Common Dialog control, xv, 30, 432
    display Help contents, 442
    displaying Help on Help, 443
    HelpFile property, 428
    index entry Help, 443
    invisible elements, 341

Common Dialog control (*continued*)
  linking Help file to, 441
  ShowHelp method, 429
  specific Help topics, displaying, 444
$(CommonFiles), Setup Wizard path
    macros, 512
$(CommonFilesSys), Setup Wizard path
    macros, 512
compact disc, deployment, 4
compilation
  exam topics, 450
  methods, choosing best, xv
  optimization options, 452
compile errors, 142, 376, 410
Compile on Demand, 377
Compile tab, 452
Compile to Native Code option, 453
Compile to P-Code option, 453
compiled component file, 506
compiler, error checking, 34
compiler options, 4
complex binding, 184
Complex properties, 157
component interface
  custom, 29
  events, 27
  exposing, 26
  methods, 26
  properties, 26
Component Object Model (see COM)
Component tab, 69, 101
components
  distributing over the Internet, 524
  registering, 543
  updating, 491
Components dialog box, 122, 135
Components folder, 472
components, MTS
  design considerations, 477
  stateless, 477
  transaction processing, 477
composite controls, 124
Computer name field, 329
conditional compile, 396–400
Connect PropertyPages dialog box, 154
Connection object, 262, 277
connection-based protocol, 329
connectionless protocol, 328

ConnectionRequest event, 328, 331
ConnectionRequest method, 334
connections
  closing, 264
  creating, 265
  establishing, 263
Connections collection, 283
ConnectionString parameter, Open
    method, 263
ConnectionString property, ADO data
    control, 280
consistency, 278
#Const statement, 397
constants, conditional compilation, 398
constituent controls, 124, 128
  delegating properties to, 140
  licensing and, 521
  maintaining authority, 142
  mapping a property to multiple, 141
  owner-draw controls and, 129
ContainedControls collection, 133
container controls, 126
  controls placed on, 133
  creating, 132
Container property, 172
containers
  AcitveX documents, 218
  appearance, 166
Contents collection, 99
Contents topic, 428, 430
context ID (identifier), 86
Context option group component,
    Watch expression
    parameter, 392
Continue command, Break mode, 388
control array, 9
Control datatype, 20
control functions, invoking, 136
control notifications, 136
Control Panel, 534
ControlContainer property, 132
controls
  adjusting BackColor, 169
  appearance, 136, 166
  assigning property pages to, 154
  defaults, 180
  enabling and disabling, 180, 207
  Help, 424

invisible, 135
naming conventions, 20
What's This Help, 427
Controls collection, 133, 175
cookies, 338
Create an Empty Package, 474
Create Symbolic Debug Info
checkbox, 453
Create Table, 277
CreateInstance method, 479
CreateObject function, 41, 64, 68, 479
cross-thread marshaling, 98
cross-thread method, 95
Cshelp.txt file, 427
CTL file extension, 123, 157
ctl prefix, Control datatype, 20
Ctrl key, state of, 10
Ctrl+G (Immediate window), 389
CTX file extension, 123, 157
cur prefix, Currency datatype, 20
CursorLocation property, 267
cursors
location, 4, 267
types, 4, 266
custom error, 87
custom events
ActiveX controls, 163
creating and raising, 207
(Custom) property, 147
custom property pages, 148–149
custom setup program, 500, 502
custom sliders, 125

D

/d switch, 399
DAO (data access objects), xiv, 258
Data
Connection object, 293
Highlighter's Index, 299
Key Facts, 285–288
recordset, creating, 293
Skills Assessment, 288–293
data access objects (see DAO)
data and routines, encapsulating, 25
data binding, 3, 184
Data Bound Grid control, 134
data consumer, 184

Data Environment designer, 295
adding to projects, 281
bound forms, 281, 284
defining connections, 282
tree view, 281
data input forms, 3
data integrity, 4
Data Link Properties dialog box, 282
data maintenance, 25
data services, xi
DataArrival event, 328, 333
database applications, 49
Database Connection Pooling feature,
MTS, 464
database controls, binding to
fields, 184
Database Name field, 296
database security, 50
database transactions, 4
DataBinding object, 188
DataBindingBehavior property, 184
DataBindings collection, 185
Data-Bound control, creating, 212
data-definition commands, 277
DataField property, 184, 284
datagram, 327
data-manipulation commands, 277
DataSource property, 184, 284
datatypes, 20, 36
date, Bootstrap File, 499
DateFormat, 137
Dates, 20
dbl prefix, Double datatype, 20
DCOM (Distributed Component Object
Model), 4, 464
client applications, 539
configuring, 534
distributing, 533
remote servers, 537
DCOMCNFG.EXE, 534
DDF file, 527
Deactivate event, ObjectControl
interface, 480
Debug object, 389
Debug toolbar, 418
Debug.Assert statement, 395, 413
debugging, 4
ActiveX components, 99
ActiveX DLL, 99

debugging (*continued*)
  ActiveX EXE, 101
  Key Facts, 400–402
  multihreaded projects, 98
  multithreaded components, 104–106
  sessions, stopping, 243
  Skills Assessment, 402–409
  standalone application, 102
Debugging tab, 242
debugging tools, xiv
  assertions, 395
  bookmarks, 388
  break points, 386–388
  conditional compile, 396–400
  exam topics, 376
  Immediate window, 389
  Locals window, 394
  ValueTips, 388
  watch expressions, 391–394
declarations, command line, 400
Declarations section, 39, 71
declarative level security, 467
Declare statement, 93
default base address, 454
default event, ActiveX control, 179
default property, ActiveX control, 179
default property, Dispatch ID, 33
default, Standard Extender
    property, 171
DefaultValue, 157
delegation, 83, 140
DELETE, FTP server Execute
    operation, 322
Delete function, 26
Delete method, 277
DELETE statement, SQL, 268
Delete Watch, 393
DeleteSetting statement, Registry, 541
deleting records, Recordset object, 277
dependencies, 490
dependency files
  component, 496
  project, 497
  types, 495
deploying DHTML applications, 348
Description field, 176
Description property, ADO Error
    object, 280
Description property, Err object, 380

design mode, 133
design-time appearance, 170
design-time instance, 156
Desktop exam, 2
destination folder, 496
destroy, ActiveX objects, 45
development interface, 136
DHTML application, 348, 368
DHTML (dynamic hypertext markup
    language), xiv, 30, 217
  advantages, 336
  controls, 339
  default page designer, 338
  element events, 342
  element IDs, 342
  element styles, 346
  elements, 341
  saving web pages, 338
  web page design, 337
DHTML page, adding elements, 370
DHTML Page Designer, 3
DHTML project, compiling, 347
dialog boxes, 3
dialog boxes, tabbed, 18, 126, 147
Difference Options dialog box, 569
Differences Between window, 571
digital certificates, 532
Dim statement, 35, 38, 79
dimensioning, objects and, 39
DIR, FTP server Execute operation, 322
DISPID (Dispatch ID), 32, 38, 180, 493
DisplayAsDefault property, 167
DisplayName property, 167
Distributed Component Object Model
    (see DCOM)
Distributing exam, 2
distributing presentation services, xi
division by zero error, 382
DLL Base Address text box, 454
DLL file extension, 23, 35
DLL, testing, 114
Do loop, 7
DOB file extension, 157
DOC file extension, 42, 242
Document Properties dialog box, 535
DoEvents statement, 95
Don't Show in Property Browser
    checkbox, 177
Double datatype, 20

DownloadBegin event, WebBrowser
    control, 312
DownloadComplete event,
    WebBrowser control, 312
downloading, asynchronous, 238
downloading speed, web pages, 305
DOX file extension, 157
Drag method, 173
DragDrop event, 173
DragIcon property, 172
DragMode property, 172
DragOver event, 173
dropdown menu, 10
dropdowns, 16
DSR file extension, 338
DSX file extension, 338
dual interfaces, 38
durability, 278
Dynamic cursor, 267
dynamic hypertext markup language
    (see DHTML)
dynamic IP addresses, 330

E
early binding
    approaches to, 38
    binding methods, 31
    creating a new Word object with, 41
    Excel's Application object and, 56
    OLE callbacks with, 88
    reasons to use, 34
Edit menu, 10
Edit Watch, 393
EditAtDesignTime property,
    UserControl, 134
editing, enabling at design time, 134
editing records, Recordset object, 276
EditProperty event, 179
elements, changing position of, 347
ellipsis button, 179, 186
Enabled property, 158, 172, 180
Enabled property procedure, 181
encapsulation, 25
encryption algorithms, 532
End Function, 72
#End If statement, 397
End Property, 72

End Sub, 72
end-of-file (EOF), 272
EnterFocus event, 218, 223
enumerations (enums), 144–146, 206
EOF (end-of-file), 272
equal (=) sign, in property
    references, 27
Err object, 85, 378, 380, 385
err prefix, ErrObject datatype, 20
ErrObject, 20
error handlers, xiv, 3, 133, 378
    creating, 413
    debug mode, 383
    disabling at runtime, 383
    Hightligher's Index, 418
Error object, ADO, 262
Error Trapping property, 383
ErrorHandler, 415
errors, 5
    compiler versus runtime, 410
    messages, 87, 105
    trapping, 378
    types, 376
Errors collection, 279
errors, raising, 83, 119
    ActiveX components and, 84
    Err object, 85
    Raise method, 85
    retrieving number, 88
    runtime, 88
    standard versus custom, 86
    trapped, 85
error-trapping settings, 415
event bubbling, 345
Event declaration, 164
event handler, 77
event source, 38, 79
events
    component interface, 27
    creating, 76
    custom, 76
    declaration, 77
    frozen, 166
EventsFrozen property, 166
Exam 70-175, xi, 2
Exam 70-176, xi, 2
Excel Application object, 56
Excel client, creating in Visual Basic, 56

Excel object, releasing, 59
EXE file extension, 23, 35
Execute Direct model, 3
Execute method, 268, 277, 317
    downloading data with, 321
    errors, 326
    logging onto FTP servers, 320
    navigating FTP servers, 322
Execute method (*continued*)
    retrieving data from FTP servers, 320
    retrieving data from HTTP
        servers, 323–326
execution, threads of, 94
Exit Function statement, 380
Exit Property statement, 380
Exit Sub statement, 380
ExitFocus event, 218, 223
explicit connections, 262, 271
Explorer folder navigation, 11
Expression box component, Watch
        expression parameter, 392
Extender object, 180
    accessing, 173
    additional events, 173
    additional extender properties, 172
    additional methods, 173
    late bound properties, 174
    standard extender properties, 171

F

F1 key, viewing help text, 177
fault isolation, 465
FavoriteColor, 144
Favorites list, 236
Field object, ADO, 262
Fields collection, 273
file, Bootstrap File, 499
file server data provider, 50
File Transfer Protocol (FTP), xiv
File Upload, DHTML element, 341
files
    checking in, 565
    shared, 513
Filex, Bootstrap File, 499
Find Items in Visual Component
        Manager dialog box, 577

Find method, 274
FindFirst, 274
FindLast, 274
FindNext, 274
FindPrevious, 274
firewall, 317
floppy disks, xv, 4
focus, 129
folders, deploying packages to, 516
Font property, 126, 139, 167
$(Font), Setup Wizard path macros, 512
fonts, 157
ForeColor property, 167, 343
form module, 39
Form object, Load event, 224
Format function, 451
forms, 5, 96, 105, 122
    binary elements, 123
    dragging and dropping between, 99
    Help, 424
    HelpContextIP property, 424
    referencing, 8
    unloading, 8
    What's This Help, 427
Forms collection, xiii, 8
forms (FRM) files, 157
forms (FRX) files, binary property
        information, 157
For...Next loop, 161
forward-only cursor, 4, 266
frames, 126, 306
Friend keyword, 75
Friend methods, compared to Public
        methods, 75
Friend procedures, 137, 163
Friend properties, 99
FRM file extension, 157, 338, 564
frozen events, 166
FRX file extension, 123, 157, 338, 564
FTP browser, 364
FTP (File Transfer Protocol), xiv
FTP servers
    Execute method, 321
    Execute operations, 322
    logging on to, 320
    retrieving data from, 320
    types of, 320

FullName property, 314
FullScreen property, 314
Function keyword, 75
function pointers, 91
Function procedure, 137
functions
    exposing as methods, 75
    publicly exposed, 26

G

general optimization switch, 453
general protection fault (see GPF)
General tab, 69
GET operation, 321, 323
    FTP server, 322
    HTTP servers, 326
GetAllSettings function, Registry, 541
GetChunk method, 325
GetData method, 328
GetIDsOfNames, IDispatch
    interface, 33
GetObject function, 41, 414
GetObjectContext, 468, 479
GetSetting function, Registry, 541
GetTypeInfo, IDispatch interface, 33
GetTypeInfoCount function, IDispatch
    interface, 33
global conditional compilation
    constant, 398
global data, 96, 220
global parameters, 500
global variables, 67, 236
Globally Unique Identifier (GUID), 492
GlobalMultiUse setting, Instancing
    property, 66
GlobalSingleUse setting, Instancing
    property, 65
GoBack method, 234, 306, 362
GoForward method, 234, 306, 362
GoHome, 363
GoSearch, 363
GotFocus event, 173, 232
GPF (general protection fault), 91, 94
graphical design environment, 217
grid controls, 147
GUID (Globally Unique Identifier), 492

H

Handle datatype, 20
HEAD execute operation, HTTP
    servers, 326
heavyweight controls, 132
Height property, 128, 142, 172
Help
    Common Dialog control, 428–432
    controls, assigning to, 424
    exam topics, 420
    forms, assigning to, 424
    history, 421
    Key Facts, 434–436
    linking to objects, 424
    menu items, 425
    on Help, 431
    projects, assigning to, 422
    Skills Assessment, 436–440
    Topic ID, 423
    What's This Help, 425–427
Help About menu, 226
Help file
    linking to a project, 441
    linking to Common Dialog
        control, 441
Help File dialog box, 422
Help File Name text box, 422
Help on Help, displaying, 443
help topics, 35, 177
HelpCommand
    propertycdlHelpContents, 429
HelpContext property, 280, 380, 428
HelpContextID property, 172, 424, 427
HelpFile property, 280, 380, 422–424
Hidden Field, DHTML element, 341
Hide event, 223
Hide this Member checkbox, 178
hiding menu items, 9
hierarchical lists, 11
history list, 306, 362
History Options dialog box, 569
HitTest method, 13
HLP file extension, 421, 428
Home button, 307
home page, 307
horizontal mouse coordinate, 10
Horizontal Rule, DHTML element, 341

host application, retrieving information about, 308
HScrollSmallChange property, 231
HTML authoring tool, 427
HTML (hypertext markup language), 219, 336
  editing tools, 339
  elements, 341, 343
  formatting tags, 344
  Help files, 421
HTML (hypertext markup language) (*continued*)
  source document, 343
  tags, 344
  toolbox, 340
HTTP (Hypertext Transfer Protocol), xiv
HTTP servers
  GetChunk method, 325
  operations, Execute method, 326
  retrieving data from, 323
  StateChanged event, 323
hwnd prefix, Handle datatype, 20
HyperLink object, 224, 232, 235, 253, 256
Hypertext Markup Language (see HTML)
Hyptertext Transfer Protocol (HTTP), xiv

I
IconGroups section, 499
icons, display modes, 15
Icons property, 15
ID property, HTML elements, 342
IDE, 94, 99
IDispatch interface, 24, 33
#If...Then statement, 397
If...Then statement, 168
Image, DHTML element, 341
image list, associating with toolbars, 16
ImageList control, 14, 17
ImageList property, 14
images
  display size, 15
  referencing by key, 15

Immediate window, 4, 28, 273, 389, 413
Implements statement, 80
ImplementsObjectControl, 480
implicit connections, 262, 271
Increment property, spin button, 150
index entry, Help, 443
Index of Help topics, 431
Index property, 172, 334
indexes, 14
INF text file, 528
Infoseek, 319
Initialize event, 133, 155, 218, 223
InitProperties event, 155, 169, 218, 223, 237
InnerHTML property, 344, 371
InnerText property, 344
in-place activation, OLE control, 31
in-process COM components, 464
in-process servers, 47
Input Image, DHTML element, 341
install, Bootstrap File, 499
Install Location column, 511
installation locations, 511
Installation Title page, 509
InstallShield, 502
Instancing property, 62, 103, 478
instantiation, 28
int prefix, Integer datatype, 20
Integer datatype, 20
integers, 32
Intel Pentium Pro, 453
IntelliSense dropdown lists, 34, 144
interface calls, 32
interfaces
  exposing, 26
  implementing, 70
  sharing common, 81
  tabular, 18
  type of, 26
internal reference counter, 29
Internet, ActiveX documents, 226
Internet component download, 525
Internet Explorer, xiv, 219, 224, 233, 301
  Automation properties, 313–316
  creating new instances of, 242

debugging ActiveX documents, 241
Quit method, 316
releasing objects, 244
security settings, 243
visible versus invisible, 315
Internet Explorer 3, 221
Internet Explorer 5, 304
Internet Explorer automation
    object, 302, 309
Internet languages, 336
Internet publishing, xv
Internet Transfer control, xiv, 301, 364
    AccessType property, 316
    Execute method, 317
    FTP, Execute method, 320–323
    OpenURL method, 317–319
    Request Timeout property, 326
    retrieving files, 316
Internet-aware applications
    exam topics, 302
    Highlighter's Index, 373
    Key Facts, 348–352
    Skills Assessment, 352–359
interpreter, 450
intranet, 301
invisible controls, 125, 135
InvisibleAtRuntime property, 135, 174
Invoke function, IDispatch interface, 34
Invoke, IDispatch interface, 33
Invoke method, 38
IP addresses, 327–330
ISAM databases, xiv, 259
IsCallerInRole method, 469
isolation, 278
IsSecurityEnabled method, 468
Item Keywords dialog box, 576
IUnknown interface, 24, 29, 33

J

Java, 336
Jet, xiv, 50, 258, 269, 296, 509
Just-in-time Activation feature,
    MTS, 464

K

keys, 14
Keyset cursor, 4, 267

L

Label control, 13
labels, 131
large images, 15
LargeIcon property, 16
LastDLLError property, Err object, 380
late binding, 31, 34, 41, 89
Launch Editor button, 339
Left property, 27, 128, 142, 172
library files, standalone type, 35
library name, 68
Library package, 465
license key, 529
licensed controls, 521
lifetime
    ActiveX controls, 155
    test project, 43
limit-to-list functionality, 124
LineStyle property, TreeView
    control, 12
list box, 124, 129
List, DHTML element, 341
list view, 10
ListBox control, 13, 28
Listen method, 328, 331
ListImages collection, 14
ListItems, 13
lists, adding items to, 13
ListView control, 11, 13
lng prefix, Long datatype, 20
load balancing, 5
Load event, 224
Load statement, 8
local data structures, 451
LocaleID property, 167
LocalPort property, 328, 331, 333
Locals window, 44, 394, 416
LocationName property, 235, 307
LocationURL property, 307
locking contentions, 50
locking methods, 267
locking strategies, 4
LockType property, 267
LogEvents method, 106
logging, automatic, 106
logical design, 2
LogMode property, 105
LogModeConstants enumeration, 106
LogPath property, 105

logText, 106
Long datatype, 20
LostFocus event, 173
LPK (license package file), 530
LPK_TOOL.EXE, 530
LS, FTP server Execute operation, 322
lvwReport value, View property, 14

M

macros, 511
mail servers, xiv, 259
Main subroutine, 68
maintainability, COM objects, 26
Make tab, 492
Makecab.exe, 528
MakeError procedure, 382
Managing Scripts dialog box, 519
MAPI controls, 125, 135
Marking feature, exam software, 6
marshaling, 48, 98
Max button property, 427
Max property, spin button, 150
MDI forms, 98, 132
member type, 27
member variable, 137
Members list box, 47
menu array, 9
Menu Editor, 9, 227, 254
menu items, 254
MenuBar property, 314
menus
   adding to forms, 7
   assigning items an Index, 9
   dropdown, 10
   dynamically creating at runtime, 9
   Help, 425
   HelpContextID property, 424
   pop-up, 9
   shortcut, 10
message boxes, 96, 105
MessageReflect property, 167
methods
   component interface, 26
   cross-thread, 95
   exposing, 28
Microsoft ActiveX Developer Kit, 532

Microsoft ADO Data Control 6.0
      (OLE DB), 280
Microsoft Binder, 224
Microsoft Data Bound Grid
      control, 134, 147
Microsoft Excel, 30, 56, 219
Microsoft Explorer, 30
Microsoft Internet Controls, 303, 314
Microsoft Internet Explorer, 216
Microsoft Package and Deployment
      Wizard, xv
Microsoft Setup Wizard, xv
Microsoft Transaction Server (see MTS)
Microsoft Transaction Server Type
      Library, 468, 470
Microsoft Visual C++, 453
Microsoft Visual Studio 6.0, 503, 562
Microsoft Windows API, 90
Microsoft Windows applications, 47
Microsoft Windows Help file, 86
Microsoft Winsock Control
      component, 327
Microsoft Word, 30, 219
   Application objects, 37, 41
   opening existing document, 42
middle-tier components, 464
Migration Wizard, 222
Min button property, 427
Min property, spin button, 150
MinHeight property, 231
MinWidth property, 231
missing dependency information, 507
missing dependency problem, 501
missing files, 505
MKDIR, FTP server Execute
      operation, 322
More ActiveX Designers submenu, 281
MouseDown event
   declaring custom events for, 164
   shortcut menus, 10
   tabs, 19
MouseDown procedure, 77
MouseUp event
   shortcut menus, 10
   tabs, 19
Move, ADO Recordset Object, 272
Move method, 128, 173
MoveFirst, ADO Recordset Object, 272

MoveLast, ADO Recordset Object, 272
MoveNext, ADO Recordset Object, 272
MovePrevious, ADO Recordset
        Object, 272
MS Transaction Server option, 476
MSChart control, 98
$(MSDAOPath), Setup Wizard path
        macros, 512
MsgBox statement, 411
Msvbvm60.dll, 451, 525
MTS components
    Highlighter's Index, 487
    Key Facts, 480–483
    Skills Assessment, 483–487
MTS Explorer, 472, 476
MTS (Microsoft Transaction Server), xv,
        49, 63
    catalog, 475
    components, 476–480
    configuration, 471–474
    exam topics, 463
    features, 463
    installation, 470
    multiple transaction servers, 474
    packages, 465, 474–476
    security, 466–469, 471
MTS Visual Basic Add-In, 476
MTSTransactionMode property, 478,
        480
    NotAnMTSObject, 478
    NoTransactions, 478
    RequiresNewTransaction, 478
    RequiresTransaction, 478
    UsesTransaction, 478
multi-developer environment, xv
multiple CAB files, 509
multiple connection requests, 333
multiplication operator (*), 491
multitasking environment, 47
multithreaded client, 95
multithreaded components, xiii, 63,
        104–106, 477
multithreaded servers, 94
multitier application, 2
multitier environment, xi
MultiUse setting, Instancing
        property, 66
My Computer, 472

N

Name dropdown list, 183
Name property, 27, 68, 150, 171, 314
Name text box, 227
naming conventions, 20
native code, xv
native code compiler, 451–453
NativeError property, ADO Error
        object, 280
Navigate method, 304, 307, 362
NavigateComplete2 event, WebBrowser
        control, 312
NavigateTo method, 233–235, 253
navigation methods, 272
navigational design, 3
navigational interfaces, 219
nested transactions, 279
New keyword, 36, 39, 43
New operator, 64
New Project dialog box, 63, 338
NewValue parameter, 78
NewWindow2 event, WebBrowser
        control, 312
No Compatibility option, 493
No Optimization setting, 453
Node, variable declaration, 11
NodeClick event, 12
nodes
    adding to tree views, 11
    code example, 12
    detecting when clicked, 11
    determining location, 11
    displaying text of clicked, 12
    text, placing under mouse in label
        control, 13
Nodes collection, 11
Nodes.Add method, 11
NoMatch property, 275
nonmodal forms, 220
non-relational data, xiv
Notepad, 339
Nothing keyword, 37, 43, 161
notification, download complete, 240
Number property, ADO Error
        object, 280
Number property, Err object, 380
numeric properties, spin button, 150

O

obj object variable, 44
obj prefix, Object datatype, 20
Object Browser, 46, 64, 68, 163, 176
object context, initialization and
    termination, 480
Object datatype, 20
object feedback, exposing as events, 28
object libraries, 46
Object Linking and Embedding
    (OLE), 23
object servers, 38
OBJECT tag, 528
object variables, 31
ObjectClass, 79
ObjectContext object, 468, 479
ObjectControl interface, 480
objects
    Automation descriptions, 35
    destroying, 42
    dimensioning, 39
    instantiating, 28
    late bound, 76
    linking Help to, 424
    priority, 35
    referencing, 29, 31, 45
    releasing, 25
    unused, 42
OCX file extension, 23, 122, 125
ODCB databases, 260
OffLine property, 314
OK button, 150
OLE 2.0, 23
OLE callbacks, 28, 76, 117, 236
    ByRef arguments, 90
    creating, 88
    late-bound servers, 90
    reasons to use, 88
OLE compound document
    technology, 217
OLE controls, 31, 122
OLE drag and drop, 99
OLE (Object Linking and
    Embedding), 23
OLE DB, xiv
    providers, 259
    universal data access, 259
OLE DB (Microsoft ADO Data Control
    6.0), 280

OLE_COLOR, 140, 143
OLEDropMode, 158
On Error Goto 0 statement, 383
On Error Goto statement, 84, 378
On Error Resume Next statement, 94,
    379, 382, 385
On Error statement, 383
OnClick event, 346
online user assistance, 3
OnMouseDown event, 346
Opaque setting, BackStyle
    property, 134
Open method, 263, 269
OpenURL method, 317–319, 326
optimistic locking, 4
optimization switches, 453
optimization, Visual Basic compiler
    Highlighter's Index, 462
    Key Facts, 458
    Skills Assessment, 460–462
Optimize for Fast Code option
    button, 453
Optimize for Small Code option
    button, 453
option button, 153
Option Button, DHTML element, 341
option group, 16
Optional arguments, 78, 164
Options form, 384
Options parameter, Open method, 263
Out of Stack Space error, 106, 140
outer object, 81, 83
OuterHTML property, 344
OuterText property, 344
out-of-process servers, 47
owner-draw controls, 125, 129

P

Package and Deployment Wizard, xv,
    4, 348, 489, 500
    AutoRun CD, 520
    file distribution, 508
    floppy disks, 515
    HTML documents, creating, 529
    license key, 522
    missing dependencies, 507
    package deployment, 514
    registry verification, 519

setup program, creating, 502
silent mode, 519
starting, 503
VBL file, 523
package folder, 505
Package security, 467
package type, 505
Package Wizard, 474
packages
  deploying to floppy disk, 515
  deploying to folders, 516
  MTS, 465
  web server deployment, 516
Packages Installed, 472, 474
packaging and deploying
  applications, 2
  exam topics, 489
  Highlighter's Index, 552–554
  Key Facts, 543–547
  Skills Assessment, 547–552
Packaging Report, 514
Packaging Script dropdown list, 504
packaging script, saving, 513
PAG file extension, 157
Paint event, 129, 156
palette, color, 143
Palette property, 167
Panel objects, 17
panels, defining with code, 18
ParamArray argument, 78, 164
Parameter object, ADO, 262
parameters, passing as arguments, 20
parameters, Property Let and Property
  Get procedures, 139
parent object, 29
Parent property, 171, 174, 224
ParentControls collection, 175
Password Field, DHTML element, 341
Password parameter, Open
  method, 263
passwords, 320, 559
path, Bootstrap File, 499
pathname, GetObject function, 42
p-code (pseudo-code) format, xv, 450
Pdcmdln.exe, 519
peer-to-peer chat application, 335
Pentium processor, 453
performance, compiler, 451
performance, middle-tier objects, 51

period (.), dropdown lists and, 34
permissions, database, 50
pessimistic locking, 4
PGX file extension, 157
phrasing, exam questions, 5
Picture object, 15
Picture property, 161
PictureBox, 228
pictures, adding to ImageList
  control, 14
placeholders, 16
POINTAPI, 394
pointers, 90
pop-up menu, 9
PopupMenu method, 10
port, 327
posHeight Style object, 347
posLeft Style object, 347
POST execute operation, HTTP
  servers, 326
POST request, HTTP, 306
posTop Style object, 347
posWidth Style object, 347
practice exam, 6
prefixes, variable, 20
prefixing, 140
Prepare/Execute model, 3
Print method, 389
priority, objects, 35
Private cmdCancel_Click( ), 164
private servers, 320
Private setting, Instancing property, 64
procedure attributes
  descriptions, 176
  help file, linking to, 177
  hiding, 177
  Tools menu, 176
  UserDocuments, 219
Procedure Attributes dialog
  box, 176–179, 183, 493
Procedure ID, 493
Procedure ID dropdown list, 181
Process Isolation feature, MTS, 464
process space, 47
ProcessComplete method, 89
processor, yielding control of, 95
Product Category dropdown list, 179
program group sections, 499
program groups, 510

$(ProgramFiles), Setup Wizard path macros, 512
programmatic ID (identifier), 85
programmatic security, 468
Programs folder, 510
Project Compatibility option, 494
Project Explorer window, 99, 296
Project Group, 211
project groups, 4
Project Options dialog box, 101
Project Properties dialog box, 67, 242, 399, 422, 452
Project Properties window, 63, 101
projects
  ActiveX project, converting to, 222
  multiple UserDocuments, 235
properties
  adding to a class, 70
  categorizing, 179
  collision, avoiding, 174
  component interface, 26
  databound, 185
  delegating, 140
  exposing, 28
  linking to property pages, 178
  referring to with equal sign, 27
Properties window, 14, 64, 147, 154, 179
property array, 74
property changes, notifying Visual Basic, 159
Property Get procedure, 71, 137, 140, 180
Property is data bound checkbox, 184
Property Let procedure, 71, 138, 140, 180, 183
property page (PAG) files, 157
property pages, 13, 16, 147
  applying changes to selected controls, 152
  assigning to controls, 154
  attaching, 210
  creating, 208
  custom, 148
  linking controls to ActiveX control properties, 150
  linking properties to, 178

property pages (PGX) files, binary property information, 157
property persistence, 155, 207, 238
property procedures, 71, 139, 141
Property Set procedure, 71, 74, 89
property settings, storing between instances, 155
property value, UserControl object, 123
Property will call CanPropertyChange checkbox, 187
PropertyBag object
  arrays, 161
  binary properties, 160
  persistence, 156
  ReadProperty method, 158
  WriteProperty method, 157
PropertyChanged statement, 138, 140, 160, 188
PropertyName parameter, 179, 239
PropertyName property, 240
PropertyPage object, 149, 152, 178
PropertyPages property, 154
Protocol property, 331
protocols, connectionless versus connection-based, 329
Provider argument, ConnectionString parameter, 263
proxy server, 317
pseudo-code (see p-code format)
Public method, 28
Public property, 28
  creating, 206
public servers, 320
public variables, 71, 138
PublicNotCreatable setting, Instancing property, 64
published component, adding to project, 584
publishing method, 518
PUT statement, 325
  FTP servers, 322
  HTTP servers, 326
PWD, FTP server Execute operation, 322

Q

QueryInterface function, IUnknown
  interface, 29
question mark (?), 390
queuing, 49
Quick Watch dialog box, 394
QUIT, FTP server Execute
  operation, 322
Quit method, 316

R

radio buttons, 126
radio knobs, 125
Raise method, 85, 380
RaiseEvent statement, 78, 134, 164
Range object, 58
RDO (remote data objects), xiv, 258
Reader role, 472
readme.txt file, 509
read-only locking, 4
read-only property, 71
ReadProperties event, 133, 156, 169,
  218, 238
ReadProperty function, 157
ReadProperty method, 157
read-write property, 71
record locking, 267
recordset, field contents, 294
Recordset object, 262
  accessing data, 273
  Command.Execute method, 269
  Connection.Execute method, 268
  cursors, 266
  deleting records, 277
  editing records, 276
  Find method, 274
  locking, 267
  opening, 266
  Recordset.Open method, 270
Recordsource property, ADO data
  control, 280
RECV, FTP server Execute
  operation, 322
ReDim command, 161
references
  COM objects, 28
  destroying, 29

incorrect, 140
  objects, 25
  passing arguments by, 20
References dialog box, 35, 100, 102,
  261
register, Bootstrap File, 499
registry, 42, 85
registry settings, retrieving, 542
Regsvr32.exe, 543, 554
Release function, IUnknown
  interface, 29
releasing objects, 25, 45, 244
relocatable code, 93
remote data objects (see RDO), 258
Remote Server setting, Component
  tab, 70
remote servers, 94
Remote Servers page, 539
RemoteHost property, 328, 331
RemotePort property, 331, 334
Remove Array Bounds Checks
  native code compilation, 454
  optimization switch, 456
Remove Floating Point Error Checks
  native code compilation, 454
  optimization switch, 456
Remove Integer Overflow Checks
  native code compilation, 454
  optimization switch, 456
Remove Safe Pentium FDIV Checks
  native code compilation, 455
  optimization switch, 457
RemoveItem method, 28
RENAME, FTP server Execute
  operation, 322
requestID, 331
RequestTimeout property, 326
Require License Key checkbox, 522
Reset Button, DHTML element, 341
Resize event, 127, 156, 223
Resume Next statement, 378, 382
Resume statement, 378
retrieving data, Internet Transfer
  control, 317
re-usable objects, 25
rich text format (see RTF files)
Right property, 142
RightToLeft property, 167

RMDIR, FTP server Execute
operation, 322
Role-Based Security feature, MTS, 464
roles, 466
Roles folder, 472
RollBackTrans method, 279
root lines, Line Style property, 12
root, transaction, 478
RTF (rich text format) files, 343, 421
run mode, 133, 140
Run to Cursor command, Break
mode, 388
runtime
appearance, 170
displaying menus, 9
errors, 376, 410, 412

S

Safe for Initialization, 527
Safe for Scripting, 527
SaveSetting statement, Registry, 541
scalability, 2
ScaleHeight, 129
ScaleMode, 128, 228
ScaleUnits, 167
ScaleWidth, 128
sckClosed, 331
scope
conditional compilation
constants, 398
watch variables, 4
scripts, xv, 238, 503, 519
Scroll event, 223
scrollbars, 228
disabling, 231
displaying, 231
SmallChange values, 232
ScrollBars property, 231
Search button, Internet Explorer, 307
searching, Object Browser, 46
searching, recordsets, 274
secondary CAB files, 525
secondary columns, 13
security, 2
ActiveX components, 526
Internet Explorer, 243
MTS, 466, 471

Select Case construct, 168
Select Computer dialog box, 474
Select, DHTML element, 341
SELECT statement, SQL, 268, 277
SelectedControls collection, 151
SelectedItem property, 19
SelectionChanged event, 151
SEND, FTP server Execute
operation, 323
SendData method, 328
separators, 16
serialization, 95
server application, 65
server files, 242
Server package, 465
servers
apartment-threaded, 98
Automation, 35
in-process versus out-of-process, 47
notifying clients, 88
running in a separate process
space, 67
unattended execution, 105
Set Next Statement command, Break
mode, 388
Set Package Identity page, 474
Set statement, 31, 39, 57
Dim statement, compared to, 36
late binding, 34
New keyword, 43
object references, assigning to
variables, 31
SetFocus method, 173
SetTimer API function, 91
Setup section, 500
Setup Toolkit project, 502
Setup Wizard, xv, 470
Setup1 Files section, 500
Setup1.list file, 502
Setup.exe program, 503
Setup.lst file, 497, 499
SetupText, Setup.lst, 498
SetupTitle, Setup.lst, 498
SetViewPort method, 232
shared, Bootstrap File, 499
shared files, 513
Shdocvw.dll, 314
Shift key, state of, 10

Shift parameter, 10
shortcut menus, 10
Show event, 223, 253
Show in DataBindings collection at
    design time checkbox, 185
Show method, 8, 235
Show Next Statement command, Break
    mode, 388
Show procedure, 224
ShowGrabHandles property, 167
ShowHatching property, 167
ShowWhatsThis method, 173
Signcode.exe, 532
silent mode, deploying packages, 519
simple binding, 184
Single datatype, 20
single-threaded ActiveX server, 94
SingleUse setting, Instancing
    property, 65
Single-value binary information, 157
Single-value text information, 157
size, Bootstrap File, 499
SIZE, FTP server Execute
    operation, 323
skills, measured by each exam, 2
sliders, 125
small images, 15
SmallChange values, 232
SmallIcons property, 15
sng prefix, Single datatype, 20
sockets, 327
source code control, 556, 562
Source Code Control Options dialog
    box, 567
source code database, 557
source code value, UserControl
    object, 123
source code version control, 2
Source property, ADO Error object, 280
Source property, Err object, 380
SourceFile property, 339, 348
space character, 69
Spawn, Setup.lst, 498
special exception code, 151
speed, early binding, 34
spin button, 150
spreadsheets, 219, 259
SQL (Structured Query Language), 4

SQL Builder button, 283
SQL Server, 50
SQL statements, executing, 277
SQL WHERE clause, 274
SQLState property, ADO Error
    object, 280
stack frames, 451
standard combo box, 124
Standard Controls, HelpContextID
    property, 424
Standard EXE, 62, 66
Standard EXE test project, 113
standard interfaces, 25
standard module, 236
standard procedure ID (see DISPID)
standard text box, 124
StandardColor property page, 154
StandardFont property page, 154
StandardPicture property page, 154
StandardSize property, 149
Start Mode setting, Component tab, 69
Start page, 307
StartIn entry, 500
StartLogging method, 106
StartMode property, 101
StartTimer procedure, 91
startup form, 68
state, maintaining, 477
StateChanged event, 323
stateless object, 477
Static cursor type, 266
static IP addresses, 330
StatusBar control, 17
StatusBar property, 309, 314
StatusText property, 314
Step Into command, Break mode, 387
Step Out command, Break mode, 388
Step Over command, Break mode, 388
Stop statement, 44, 386
storage files, OLE-structured, 242
stored procedure, 277
Stored Procedures model, 3
str prefix, String datatype, 20
stream, 327
String datatype, 20
strings, 32
Structured Query Language (SQL), 4
studying, recommended approach, xvi

Style property, 16, 347
Styles, 371
Sub Main procedure, 68, 96
Sub procedure, 138
subclass, 93
subclassed controls, 124, 190
SubItems collection, 13
Submit Button, DHTML element, 341
Summary Report, 223
SupportsMnemonics property, 167
Swdepend.ini, 501
switches, 452
system callback, 90
system colors, 150
system errors, logging, 106
System package icon, 472
System package, MTS, 471
system resources, freeing, 29
System.mdw file, 509

T

TabIndex property, 172
tabs
  container controls, 19
  creating at runtime, 18
Tabs collection, 18
TabStop property, 172
TabStrip control, 7, 18
Tag property, 172
Target, 239
TCP (transmission control
    protocol), 327
  accepting, 331
  data, sending and receiving, 332
  requesting, 331
Terminate event, 156, 218, 223
testing
  ActiveX components, 99
  ActiveX DLL, 99
  ActiveX EXE, 101
  multihreaded projects, 98
  multithreaded components, 104–106
  standalone application, 102
TestSub procedure, 381
Text Area, DHTML element, 341
text box, 31, 129, 142, 153
text box control, 27
Text Field, DHTML element, 341

text files, xiv
Text property, 13, 27, 140, 183, 390
text, saving, 157
TextAlign property, 167
TheaterMode property, 309, 314
"This property binds to DataField"
    checkbox, 185
Thread per Object option, 97
Thread per Object property, 98
Thread Pool option, 97
Thread Pool property, 98
Thread Pooling feature, MTS, 464
threading, xiii, 63
  ActiveX DLL, 98
  ActiveX EXE, 97
  apartment model, 96, 98
  controlling, 97
  global variables and resources, 97
  multithreaded clients, 94
  Project Properties dialog box, 97
  serialization, 95
threading model, 5
thread-safe interface elements, 97
three-tiered applications, 49
  benefits, 51
  databases, 49
  middle-tier, 50
  performance, 51
  two-tiered applications, compared
      to, 49
thunking, 93
time limits, exam, 5
Timer controls, 125, 135
TimerOccurred event, 91
timers, creating, 91
TitleChange event, WebBrowser
    control, 313
TLB file extension, 35, 537
TmpDir, Setup.lst, 498
Toggle Bookmark, 388
toggle button, 16
toggle group, 16
Toggle submenu, 384
Toolbar control, 16
Toolbar property, 309, 314
toolbars, associating images list
    with, 16
toolbox icon, 189
ToolboxBitmap property, 123, 135

Tools menu, 67, 176, 227
ToolTipText property, 172
Top property, 27, 128, 172
Topic ID, 423, 430
traditional button, 16
transactional voting methods, 479
transactions
    ACID test, 278
    controlling, 478
    creating programmatically, 479
    nested, 279
    rolling back, 279
transmission control protocol
        (TCP), 327
Transparent setting, BackStyle
        property, 134
trapping errors, 378
tree view, 10
TreeView control, 7, 11
    associating with ImageList
        control, 14
    HitTest method, 13
twips, 129, 232
two-tiered applications, 49
Type column, 44
type library, 35
type library, Excel, 56
Type Mismatch error, 412
Type property, WebBrowser
        control, 308
type-definition characters, 77
TypeName function, 224
typographic conventions, xvi

U

UDA (Universal Data Access), xiv, 259
udoc1.dob, 253
UDP (user datagram protocol), 328
UDT file extension, 451
udt prefix, User-defined type, 20
UIDead property, 168
Unattended Execution checkbox, 105
unattended execution property, 69, 96
Uninstal, Setup.lst, 498
uninstall, 4
Universal Data Access (see UDA)
universal resource locator (URL), 304
Unload statement, 8

unused references, 508
URL paths, hard-coding, 337
URL (universal resource locator), 304
URLAddress, 233
user assistance, 3
user datagram protocol (UDP), 328
user input, writing code to validate, 3
user interface, 8, 49, 212, 360, 364
user interface, ActiveX controls
    design considerations, 126
    dynamic resizing, 127–129
user updates, PropertyChanged
        statement, 188
UserControl, 96, 105, 221
    AccessKeys property, 131
    Ambient property, 166
    authoring time, 133
    background, 127
    CanGetFocus property, 130
    DataBindingBehavior property, 184
    EditAtDesignTime property, 134
    EventsFrozen property, 166
    forms, 127
    ForwardFocus property, 131
    HyperLink property, 233
    Initialize event, 133
    InvisibleAtRuntime property, 135
    objects, 123
    Paint event, 129
    Parent property, 174
    property procedures, delegating, 139
    Resize event, 127
    sizing, 128
    toolbox bitmap, 135
UserControl (CTL) file, 157
user-defined procedures, 93
User-defined type, 20
UserDocument, 96, 105
    adjusting to container size, 229
    asynchronous downloading, 238
    Binder, displaying, 234
    communicating between, 236
    displaying, 234
    HyperLink object, 232
    persistence, 237
    web browser, displaying, 234
UserDocument class, 221
UserDocument (DOB) file, 157
UserDocument events, 223

UserDocument objects, 218
  forms, compared to, 221
  procedure attributes, 219
UserDocument projects, 226
UserDocuments (DOX) files, binary
      property information, 157
UserID parameter, open method, 263
UserMode property, 167, 170
username, 320
UserName property, ADO data
      control, 280

V

validation code, 141, 154
value, passing arguments by, 20
Value property, 212
Value property, spin button, 150
ValueTips, 388, 412
variables, naming conventions, 20
Variant datatype, 20, 240
Variant variables, 32
VB6dep.ini, 497, 501
VBA Error object, 280
vbBoolean constant, 332
vbByte constant, 332
vbCurrency constant, 332
VBD file extension, 234, 242
vbDate constant, 332
vbDouble constant, 332
vbError constant, 332
vbevents.log, 105
vbInteger constant, 332
VBL (Visual Basic License) file, 523
vbLong constant, 332
vbModal, 99
vbNone, 184
vbObjectError constant, 87
VBP file, 565
VBR file, 537
VBScript, 336, 526
vbSingle constant, 332
VbSModeAutomation constant, 102
vbSModeStandalone constant, 102
vbString constant, 332
VBX controls, 28, 122
VeriSign, 531
version, Bootstrap File, 499

version compatibility, 492
Version Compatibility setting,
      Component tab, 70
version number, 491, 496
vertical mouse coordinate, 10
View property, ListView control, 14
Viewport, 224
  location, 232
  panning, 232
  PictureBox, resizing, 230
  scrollbars, 228, 231
  settings, 228
  size, 228
  SmallChange value, 232
  UserDocuments and, 227
Viewport properties, 254
ViewportHeight property, 228
ViewportLeft property, 228
ViewportTop property, 228
ViewportWidth property, 228
virtual function table (vtable), 38
Visible box, 9
Visible property, 9, 171, 174
Visual Basic, 451
  COM programming, xiii
  MTS add-in, 476
  notifying when property values
      change, 160
Visual Basic 4, 24, 122
Visual Basic 5, 30, 96, 105, 122
Visual Basic 6, 96, 105, 218, 242, 281
Visual Basic debugging tools
  assertions, 395
  bookmarks, 388
  break points, 386–388
  conditional compile, 396–400
  Immediate window, 389
  Locals window, 394
  ValueTips, 388
  watch expressions, 391–394
Visual Basic form, 31
Visual Basic Help file, 86
Visual Basic IDE, 219, 561, 563
Visual Basic License (VBL) file, 523
Visual Basic Timer control, 91
Visual Component Manager, xv, 3
  accessing, 584
  COM Registration page, 576

database, 573
exam topics, 555
features, 571
locating components, 576
navigating, 572
Publish Wizard, 573
publishing components, 573
visual elements, 105
Visual SourceSafe, xv
adding new files, 566
Administrator, 557
components, 556
database, 557
exam topics, 555
Explorer, 562
file differences, 571
folders, 557
Highlighter's Index, 585
History Options dialog box, 569
Key Facts, 579
Make Writable checkbox, 568
project copies, 563
revisions, comparing, 568
setting up, 556
Skills Assessment, 581
undoing check out, 565
updating master database, 565
users, managing, 558
versions, latest, 566
Visual Basic projects, 559, 561
working folders, 561
Visual SourceSafe Explorer, 563, 568
Visual Studio, 261
vnt prefix, Variant datatype, 20
VScrollSmallChange property, 231
vtable (virtual function table), 38

W

watch expressions, 4, 391–394, 418
Watch type option group component,
    Watch expression
    parameter, 392
watch variable, 4
Watches window, 44, 393
web browsers, 5, 219, 234, 360
web pages, 122

web server, deploying packages to, 516
Web-based deployment, 4
WebBrowser control, 301, 360
BeforeNavigate2 event, 309
CommandStateChange event, 309
DocumentComplete event, 309
DownloadBegin event, 309
DownloadComplete event, 309
events, 309–313
NavigateComplete2 event, 309
navigating web pages, 303–307
NewWindow2 event, 309
OnFullScreen event, 309
OnMenuBar event, 309
OnQuit event, 309
OnStatusBar event, 309
OnTheaterMode event, 309
OnToolbar event, 309
OnVisible event, 309
ProgressChange event, 309, 312
properties, 307
TitleChange event, 309
web-enabled applications, xiv
What's This Help, 425–427
enabling, 446
linking to control, 446
WhatsThisButton property, 427
WhatsThisHelpID property, 427
WhatsThisMode method, 427
WhatThisHelpID property, 172
WHERE clause, SQL, 274
Width property, 128, 142, 172
Window, 224
WindowProc (Windows procedure), 94
Windows 95, 425, 465
Windows 98, 94, 317, 533, 534
Windows API, 451
Windows Help system (see WinHelp)
Windows NT, 463, 465, 533
Windows NT 4 Option Pack, 470
Windows NT Application Event
    Log, 105
Windows Paint, 135
Windows procedure (WindowProc), 94
Windows registry, managing, 540
WinHelp (Windows Help system), 421,
    428

$(WinPath), Setup Wizard path
    macros, 512
Winsock applications
    TCP, 330–334
    UDP, 334–336
Winsock control, xiv, 301
    adding to projects, 327
    setting up connection, 329
    sockets, 327
    TCP, 327
    UDP, 328
$(WinSysPath), Setup Wizard path
    macros, 512
$(WinSysPathSysFile), Setup Wizard
    path macros, 512WISE, 502
WithEvents keyword, 38, 76, 79, 88

WithEvents variable declaration, 116
Word Automation server, 36
working folders, 561
worksheets, 58
Workspace object, 278
World Wide Web, 301
WriteProperties event, 156, 158, 218,
    223, 238
WriteProperty method, 157

Z

zero-length string, 106
ZIP files, 503
ZOrder, 20
Zorder method, 173

About the Author

James Foxall is a Microsoft Certified Solution Developer (MCSD) and Vice President of Tigerpaw Software, Inc. (*http://www.tigerpawsoftware.com*), a Microsoft Certified Solution Provider specializing in commercial database applications and known for the award-winning Tigerpaw Business Suite. James' experience in creating distributed, certified, Microsoft Office–compatible software has made him an authority on application interface and behavior standards of applications designed for the Microsoft Windows and Office environment.

James has personally written over 90,000 lines of commercial production Visual Basic code in both single-programmer and multiple-programmer environments.

James has written several books about both Visual Basic and Microsoft Access, including the authoritative work, *Practical Standards for Microsoft Visual Basic* (Microsoft Press). He has also written for *Access/Office/VBA Advisor* magazine and is an international speaker on Microsoft Access and Visual Basic. In addition to speaking and writing, James has taught Visual Basic at the college level and has been featured on numerous television news shows, in trade publications, and in newspaper articles for his technology expertise.

James can be reached at *jamesf@tigerpawsoftware.com*.

Colophon

Our look is the result of reader comments, our own experimentation, and feedback from distribution channels. Distinctive covers complement our distinctive approach to technical topics, breathing personality and life into potentially dry subjects.

The animal on the cover of *MSCD in a Nutshell: The Visual Basic Exams* is a purple-capped, or purple-naped, lory (*Lorius domicellus*). Lories constitute one third of all parrots, an order of birds characterized by their brilliantly colored feathers, zygodactylous feet (two toes pointing frontward, two pointing backward), and hooked beaks. Parrots dwell in tropical forests, where they feed on fruit, buds, seeds, and pollen, furthering forest propagation.

Each lory species' distinctive coloring provides its common name. The purple-capped lory sports a red body with a yellow breast, green wings, violet thighs, reddish-brown tail, orange bill, and an identifying purple streak on the back of its head. Purple-capped lories live nomadic lives—singly or in pairs—over the Indonesian Moluccan islands Seram and Ambon. Almost all parrot species are in danger of extinction due to habitat loss and trapping for trade as pets. The Convention on International Trade in Endangered Species of Wild Fauna and Flora (CITES) helps to protect parrot species, but the purple-capped lory may already be extinct on Ambon Island. Only breeding programs can save the purple-capped lory now.

Jeffrey Holcomb was the production editor for *MSCD in a Nutshell: The Visual Basic Exams*. Ann Houska was the copyeditor. Sarah Jane Shangraw proofread the text. Catherine Morris and Leanne Soylemez provided quality control. Molly Shangraw, Mary Sheehan, and Ann Schirmer provided production support. Pamela Murray wrote the index.

Edie Freedman designed the cover of this book. The cover image is a 19th-century engraving from the Dover Pictorial Archive. Emma Colby produced the cover layout with QuarkXPress 4.1 using Adobe's ITC Garamond font.

Alicia Cech and David Futato designed the interior layout based on a series design by Nancy Priest. Mike Sierra implemented the design in FrameMaker 5.5.6. The text and heading fonts are ITC Garamond Light and Garamond Book. The illustrations that appear in the book were produced by Robert Romano and Rhon Porter using Macromedia FreeHand 8 and Adobe Photoshop 5. This colophon was written by Sarah Jane Shangraw.

Whenever possible, our books use a durable and flexible lay-flat binding. If the page count exceeds this binding's limit, perfect binding is used.